Essential Readings in Health Behavior
Theory and Practice

Mark C. Edberg, PhD

Associate Professor
Department of Prevention and Community Health
School of Public Health and Health Services
Joint Appointment, Department of Anthropology
The George Washington University
Washington, DC

JONES AND BARTLETT PUBLISHERS
Sudbury, Massachusetts
BOSTON   TORONTO   LONDON   SINGAPORE

BP45

World Headquarters
Jones and Bartlett Publishers
40 Tall Pine Drive
Sudbury, MA 01776
978-443-5000
info@jbpub.com
www.jbpub.com

Jones and Bartlett Publishers
Canada
6339 Ormindale Way
Mississauga, Ontario L5V 1J2
Canada

Jones and Bartlett Publishers
International
Barb House, Barb Mews
London W6 7PA
United Kingdom

Jones and Bartlett's books and products are available through most bookstores and online booksellers. To contact Jones and Bartlett Publishers directly, call 800-832-0034, fax 978-443-8000, or visit our website, www.jbpub.com.

Substantial discounts on bulk quantities of Jones and Bartlett's publications are available to corporations, professional associations, and other qualified organizations. For details and specific discount information, contact the special sales department at Jones and Bartlett via the above contact information or send an email to specialsales@jbpub.com.

This publication is designed to provide accurate and authoritative information in regard to the Subject Matter covered. It is sold with the understanding that the publisher is not engaged in rendering legal, accounting, or other professional service. If legal advice or other expert assistance is required, the service of a competent professional person should be sought.

Production Credits
Publisher: Michael Brown
Production Director: Amy Rose
Editorial Assistant: Catie Heverling
Editorial Assistant: Teresa Reilly
Senior Production Editor: Tracey Chapman
Senior Marketing Manager: Sophie Fleck
Manufacturing and Inventory Control Supervisor: Amy Bacus
Composition: Auburn Associates, Inc.
Cover Design: Kristin E. Parker
Cover Image: © Alvaro Pantoja/ShutterStock, Inc.; © emin kuliyev/ShutterStock, Inc.;
    © Ximagination/ShutterStock, Inc.; © Photos.com
Printing and Binding: Courier Stoughton
Cover Printing: John Pow Company

Library of Congress Cataloging-in-Publication Data
Edberg, Mark Cameron, 1955-
    Essential readings in health behavior: theory and practice / Mark C. Edberg.
        p. ; cm.
    Includes bibliographical references and index.
    ISBN-13: 978-0-7637-3818-1 (pbk.)
    ISBN-10: 0-7637-3818-2 (pbk.)
    1. Health behavior. I. Title.
    [DNLM: 1. Health Behavior—Collected Works. W 85 E21ea 2009]
    RA776.9.E33 2009
    613—dc22
                                                                        2008051159

6048
Printed in the United States of America
13 12 11 10 09   10 9 8 7 6 5 4 3 2 1

10/2/09

Contents

The Essential Public Health Series

Log on to *www.essentialpublichealth.com* for the most current information on availability.

CURRENT AND FORTHCOMING TITLES IN THE *ESSENTIAL PUBLIC HEALTH SERIES*:

Essentials of Public Health Ethics—Ruth Gaare Bernheim, JD, MPH & James F. Childress, PhD

Foundations of Public Health Management and Leadership—Robert Burke, PhD & Leonard Friedman, PhD, MPH

Essentials of Public Health Preparedness—Rebecca Katz, PhD, MPH

ABOUT THE EDITOR:

Richard K. Riegelman, MD, MPH, PhD, is Professor of Epidemiology-Biostatistics, Medicine, and Health Policy, and Founding Dean of The George Washington University School of Public Health and Health Services in Washington, DC. He has taken a lead role in developing the Educated Citizen and Public Health initiative which has brought together arts and sciences and public health education associations to implement the Institute of Medicine of the National Academies recommendation that "... all undergraduates should have access to education in public health." Dr. Riegelman also led the development of George Washington's undergraduate major and minor and currently teaches "Public Health 101" and "Epidemiology 101" to undergraduates.

Acknowledgments

The editor would like to thank Kendall Adkins, Masters of Public Health candidate at The George Washington University School of Public Health and Health Services, for her truly invaluable assistance, skill, and dedication in locating articles, formatting, and obtaining permissions. This book would not have been possible without her work.

About the Editor

Mark Edberg, PhD, is an applied and academic anthropologist with almost 20 years of significant experience in social and community research, primarily in public health. Currently an Associate Professor in the Department of Prevention and Community Health, The George Washington University School of Public Health and Health Services, with a joint appointment in the Department of Anthropology, Dr. Edberg has been Principal Investigator or Co-Principal Investigator on numerous studies for the Centers for Disease Control and Prevention (CDC), National Institutes of Health, Department of Health and Human Services, and other agencies, focusing on HIV/AIDS, violence, substance abuse prevention, minority health/disparities in health, and marginalized and at-risk populations. Currently, Dr. Edberg is Principal Investigator (PI) on a four-year research effort funded by the CDC to develop and evaluate a youth violence prevention intervention targeting community-modifiable factors in a Latino community in the Washington, DC, metro area, and he is Co-PI on a new CDC RO1 to examine the etiology of gender violence in the same community. He is also Co-PI on a CDC research panel effort to investigate linkages between macroeconomic factors and youth violence, Co-PI on an effort to evaluate a sexual exploitation/trafficking prevention program,[1] as well as a consultant to UNICEF (Latin America–Caribbean) regarding adolescent/youth data collection. Recently he was lead consultant on a community assessment of HIV, STI, and hepatitis risk among Latino and African-American youth in Washington, DC. For the U.S. Office of Minority Health (OMH), he was Co-Project Director on an effort to develop an evaluation framework for efforts by states and U.S. territories to eliminate minority health disparities, and he is Science Advisor on the continuing implementation of a Uniform Data Set (evaluation) for all OMH-funded activities.

Recently, Dr. Edberg was Co-PI on an innovative quantitative/qualitative study for the National Institute on Drug Abuse (NIDA) on substance abuse and HIV risk among three Southeast Asian populations in the Washington, DC, metro area. Dr. Edberg also directed an effort to develop an evaluation data system for *all* grant programs funded by the U.S. Office of Minority Health (Department of Health and Human Services). This system is now Internet based and was the result of two previous projects for the same agency involving in-depth evaluation of agency programs. The Department of Health and Human Services gave this project a *Best Practices in Evaluation* award. Other recent research efforts include: ethnographic research in the United States–Mexico border region on the public image of narcotraffickers and the relationships between this public image to violence and other risk behaviors (this work is documented in a recent book published by the University of Texas Press); Co-PI for the Washington, DC, site under the NIDA Cooperative Agreements to Evaluate HIV/AIDS Risk Behavior Interventions with injection drug and crack users; PI for two small NIH-funded efforts to research and develop strategies for reaching out-of-treatment drug users for HIV testing and for reaching low-income Hispanic/Latino women toward the goal of increasing use of prenatal care and reducing infant mortality; field ethnographer for a NIDA study on risk behavior among runaway youth; and evaluator,

---

[1]Both of these projects are in collaboration with a private research organization, Development Services Group, Inc. (DSG).

trainer, and other positions for a range of community intervention and social marketing projects concerning substance abuse, smoking, HIV/AIDS, and violence. Dr. Edberg has also worked, under USAID contract, in Honduras and Puerto Rico as part of a democracy development project.

At the graduate level, Dr. Edberg teaches Health Behavior and Health Education (PH206) and Qualitative Research Methods (PH364); at the undergraduate level he developed and has taught two new courses in Social and Behavioral Theory for Health Education/Promotion (PH121) and the Impact of Culture on Health (PH185). He has also taught Research Methods in Sociocultural Anthropology and Psychological Anthropology for the Department of Anthropology. Dr. Edberg is the author of a text for undergraduate social/behavioral theory entitled *Essentials of Health Behavior: Social and Behavioral Theory in Public Health* (Jones and Bartlett Publishers, 2007), and he has published a number of other books and articles. Dr. Edberg is a Fulbright short-term scholar awardee and a Fellow of the Society for Applied Anthropology.

Dr. Edberg's outside interests include music; he is founder, songwriter, lead guitar, and vocals for an original modern-rock group called the Furies (www.furiesmusic.com). In addition to performing at clubs and other venues, the Furies have performed at benefit and social-issue-related events.

Preface

Essential Readings in Health Behavior: Theory and Practice is organized into parts that parallel the main text. In each chapter, a selection of readings relevant to the part topic is presented. For purposes of space, readings are primarily excerpts, not entire articles or chapters. In some cases, these readings are from key articles by or about the social/behavioral theories discussed in that part; in other cases the readings are taken from commentary on theories or examples of studies and programs in which a particular theoretical approach was used or assessed.

Because the material covered in the main text is extensive and comprehensive, no reader can adequately represent what is covered in the text. However, *Essential Readings in Health Behavior* can be viewed as a sample of material that can supplement the text and provide additional insight with respect to the thinking behind, and uses of, the range of theoretical approaches and models covered in the text and their applications to health promotion programs.

Introduction: The Links Between Health and Behavior

The two selections in Part 1 provide a general introduction to an *ecological approach* toward understanding health behavior. An ecological approach assumes that there is a kind of "behavioral ecology" where multiple factors work together to influence people's health-related behavior. The first selection, from Lawrence Green and Marshall Kreuter's *Health Promotion Planning: An Educational and Ecological Approach* (3rd Edition), is an excellent summary of the evolution of the ecological approach in public health as well as the key issues involved. The second selection, from *Healthy People 2010*, is a slightly different take on an ecological approach that sets out *determinants of health* in different domains, including access to care, policies/interventions, biology, and the physical and social environment. *Healthy People* is the major planning document for all health promotion interventions supported by the federal government.

Health Promotion Planning—An Educational and Ecological Approach

Source: Excerpt from Green, L. W., & Kreuter, M. W. (1999). *Health Promotion Planning—An Educational and Ecological Approach.* McGraw Hill: New York, pp. 20–26.

THE ECOLOGICAL APPROACH

The interaction of behavior and environment in the middle of Figure 1-1 isolates the essence of the ecological approach to health promotion. The reciprocal, virtually inseparable, relationship of behavior and its environment is what makes the combination of educational and ecological approaches a defining feature of health promotion.

Precedents for Ecological Approaches

One can find several streams of thought and action from which ecological perspectives have influenced health promotion.

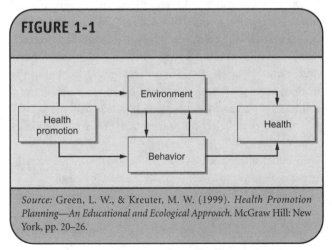

FIGURE 1-1

Environment

Health promotion

Behavior

Health

Source: Green, L. W., & Kreuter, M. W. (1999). *Health Promotion Planning—An Educational and Ecological Approach.* McGraw Hill: New York, pp. 20–26.

Before that, they influenced public health education, and public health before that. These disciplines converged with various social and behavioral sciences and other professional perspectives to form the ecological and behavioral foundations of health promotion.

Public Health. The ecological perspective has been central to public health concepts and methods from their earliest formulations and applications.[108] It was influenced by the 19th century development of biological, especially Darwinian, concepts of the "web of life" and the role of the environment and adaptation in the survival of species. Public health first sought to ensure the survival of human species by controlling the physical environment. John Snow's removal in 1854 of London's Broad Street pump handle to prevent people from using cholera-contaminated water was heralded as the first classic epidemiological study. By mapping the sources of drinking water of those who died of cholera, Snow identified the environmental source of the illness 30 years before Koch isolated the cholera organism. The host-agent-environment triad was central to the development of epidemiology, but this ecological analysis informed an effective public health intervention even before the discovery of the agent.

Epidemiology. Epidemiology remained almost exclusively preoccupied with the physical, chemical, and biological environments until the 1960s. Its host-agent-environment triad kept it tied to human ecology, but its avoidance of social science theory made it a diffident partner of social ecology. The refocusing of epidemiology on chronic diseases in the 1960s added a growing concern with behavioral determinants of health, accelerated in the 1980s with the advent of HIV and AIDS as the newest epidemic. The behavioral emphasis resulted in a narrowing of the focus and methodologies of epidemiology. This has led to a growing clamour in other sectors of public health, especially public health education, to widen the focus to include social, economic, organizational, and political environments as determinants of health and points of intervention.[109]

Sociology. In 1921, Park and Burgess introduced the term *human ecology* in an attempt to apply the basic theoretical scheme of plant and animal ecology to the study of human communities.[110] The subdiscipline of demography had risen earlier, when Malthus and others in the 19th century attempted to interpret population growth and movement in relation to environmental capacity to support the survival of populations. Borrowing a mathematical model of population growth and distribution from demography, rural sociology examined the patterns of social forces that could account for the diffusion and adoption of new farm practices and other innovations in agricultural communities or geographic areas. These ecological concepts of diffusion and adoption of innovations influenced the breadth of early thinking about mass health-education campaigns,[111] and later family planning[112] and chronic disease control in public health.[113] Medical sociology and cultural contexts in which health conditions and health behavior developed and distributed in populations.[114]

Psychology. Because of its interest in individual differences in behavior, psychology had an ecological awakening,[115] even in its most behaviorist areas of specialization, including behavior modification and analysis.[116] Psychology's focus on micro-ecologies offers as much to health promotion within settings (such as clinical settings, workplaces, and schools) as the public health and sociological analyses of wider-ranging environments (macro-ecology) offer community, state or provincial, and national health promotion planning and policy. Further, the subdisciplines of social, community, and environmental psychology have emerged to encompass ecological perspectives on individual behavior. They have influenced health education since World War II in the formulation of theories about how the mass media influence behavior through social networks.[117] They also have influenced health education's use of group dynamics in resolving social conflict and bringing social forces into play in the decision-making process.[118] These applications spilled over into early public health applications of community organization, community development, and planned change.[119]

Education. Learning theory has always given prominence to the interaction of learner and environment.[120] This has been elaborated in latter-day Social Learning Theory (more recently called Social Cognitive Theory) and its core concept of reciprocal determinism between person and environment.[121] Education formalized theories in which the role of the environment and its interdependency with the person were paramount considerations in the development of educational policies and programs.[122] These concepts extended into the development of the subspecialty of school health education and the broader field of school health, which encompassed health curriculum, school environment, school lunch programs, and school health services, among other elements in an ecological approach to the health of schoolchildren.[123] These ideas persist in the modern practice of school health promotion, in which ecological notions of school-community coordination[124] and multilevel interventions with students, faculty, school environment, school policy, and school districts have been studied.[125]

Other Disciplines and Professional Contributions. Human and medical geography have lent particular emphasis on place to the study of health and health behavior. This has blended with health promotion concepts of setting-specificity in the planning of interventions for schools, workplaces, neighborhoods, and clinical settings. Within the broader field of community health promotion, geography has provided critical analyses of the relation of environment and health.[126] Geography has teamed with social work and other professions in the development and critique of indicators of health communities.[127]

The Central Lessons of Ecology for Health Promotion

Ecological approaches in health promotion view health as a product of the interdependence of the individual and *subsystems* of the ecosystem (such as family, community, culture, and physical and social environment).[128] To promote health, this ecosystem must offer economic and social conditions conducive to health and healthful lifestyles. These environments must also provide information and life skills so individuals can make decisions to engage in behavior that maintains their health. Finally, healthful options among goods and services offered must be available.[129] In the ecological model of health promotion, all these aspects are envisioned as determinants of health. They also provide essential support in helping individuals modify their behaviors and reduce their exposure to risk factors.[130]

Ecological perspectives have insinuated themselves into the consciousness of most health practitioners working outside the clinical setting because it is what distinguishes their work most from the one-to-one patient or client relationships of the more numerous clinical health professionals. Community health and public health textbooks make ecology one of the four or five scientific foundations on which they build the community or population approach to health analysis and planning.[131] Besides the descriptive aspects of ecology, what do the lessons of ecology have to say to health promotion practitioners?

Unanticipated Effects. Ecology cautions social reformers and practitioners in the applied sciences against tampering with change in smaller systems without considering and anticipating, before the intervention, their second- and third-order consequences, "not merely to rue them afterward."[132] The unintended consequences on smaller systems may be even greater from larger systems when policy makers fail to consider cultural, geographic, and demographic variations within their scope of influence with technological and legislative changes. This has clearly also been the admonition and the contribution of cultural anthropology and applied anthropology to the field of public health.[133]

Reciprocal Determinism. The ecological or transactional view of behavior holds that the organism's functioning is mediated by behavior-environment interaction. This has two implications for behavioral and social change:

1. Environment largely controls or sets limits on the behavior that occurs in it.
2. Changing environmental variables results in the modification of behavior.

These two points lead to the recognition that health promotion can achieve its best results by exercising whatever control or influence it can over the environment. But the reciprocal side of this equation also holds that the behavior of individuals, groups, and organizations also influences their environments. This leads to the credo of health promotion that seeks to "empower" people by giving them control over the determinants of their health, whether these are behavioral or environmental. By taking greater control themselves, rather than depending on health professionals to exercise the control for them, they should be in a better position to adjust their behavior to changing environmental conditions, or to adjust their environments to changing behavioral conditions.

Environmental Specificity. The same person will behave differently when observed in different environments.[134] This principle has led to a recognition in health promotion that environment modifies or conditions the more direct attempts to predispose, enable, and reinforce individual and collective behavior through persuasive or informative communications, training, rewards, or incentives. Its implication for health promotion planning and evaluation is that there is nothing *inher-*

ently superior or inferior in any health promotion method or strategy. A method's effectiveness always depends on its appropriate fit with the people, the health issue at stake, and the environment in which it is to be applied. This gives further credence to the local or community focus of health promotion as its center of gravity, because it can be more adaptable and sensitive to particular traditions, cultural variations, and circumstances when planned at a community rather than a state, provincial, or national level.

Multilevel and Multisectoral Intervention. Because of its emphasis on the complex interdependencies of the elements making up an ecological web, an ecological approach would seem to demand interventions directed at several levels within an organizational structure or system and at multiple sectors (such as health, education, welfare, commerce, and transportation) of a social system. This is where most descriptions of ecological approaches take us and where most of them leave us. The specificity with which ecological guidelines can identify the particular levels and sectors in need of attention is inherently limited by the infinite variety of interactions that might apply in each idiosyncratic organization, community, or other social system. Following the first principle, "Do no harm," and falling back on the prior lesson on environmental specificity, one might best in some instances restrict one's interventions to selected levels and sectors of a complex system. At most, one should intervene where one can with certainty match interventions with need appropriately and where one can be accountable for side effects. The first calls for an assessment such as that offered by the Precede-Proceed model. The second requires restraint and a touch of humility.

Limitations of the Ecological View for Health Promotion

Much as it forces a broader perspective on planning and practice that might otherwise drift into a reductionist, person-centered, or victim-blaming orientation, ecological thinking has its own traps and pitfalls. Because of their complexity, ecological approaches have not been worked out in great detail. Slobodkin complains that ecology is an intractable science, immature and not very helpful.[135] Others have reproached ecologists for not producing simple testable hypotheses. But the usual conclusion of such debates is that the scientific method requires the simplification of ecosystems, making artificial what is inherently complex. Health promotion is drawn to ecology because it enlarges the spotlight from a sharper focus on behavior to include the environment. But we are forced to retreat to behavior at some level. "We will have to learn that we don't manage ecosystems, we manage our interaction with them."[136] Ecological approaches in health promotion cannot have been as thoroughly evaluated as clinical interventions, because the units of analysis lend themselves neither to random assignment to experimental and control groups nor to manipulation as independent variables, given the interdependence of persons and environments. Here follow some particular limitations that ecological approaches will face in health promotion in the near future.

Complexity Breeds Despair. If the ecological credo that everything influences everything else is carried to its logical extreme, the average health practitioner has good reason to do nothing, because the potential influence of or consequences on other parts of an ecological system lie beyond comprehension, much less control. Some specific forms of this despair include the following questions:

1. *How much is enough?* When trying to set the parameters around any given program, health planners, administrators, or practitioners must ask if they are doing enough to make a difference, but they will always be subject to the criticism that they have not gone deeply enough to the root of the problem. For example, even after public health workers had disavowed more strictly educational approaches to alcohol control, Pittman challenged the field, stating,

   > Environmental factors that impact alcohol problems are broader than such questions as alcohol availability, advertising, and the alcohol beverage industry's marketing practices . . . It is much easier to mandate warning labels . . . or propose further restrictions on alcohol advertising or alcohol availability than to address and enact legislations to reduce social inequality, racism, discrimination, and inadequate health care in the United States.[137]

2. *Is everything that takes an educational approach, or attempts to help individuals, to be regarded as trivial and misguided?* Those health practitioners and teachers whose jobs are organized around helping or education people in clinical, school, or workplace settings are made to feel by some of the academic politically correct rhetoric that their efforts are a waste of time and, worse, part of the problem. The most vituperative epitaphs for such work are "victim blaming" and "Band-Aid" treatment of the symptoms rather than the cause.

The Level of Analysis in an Ecosystem Hierarchy Is Observer-Dependent. Neither a reductionist (small number, highly controllable), nor a holistic (large number, statistically described) approach suffices to study or describe an ecosystem, because neither captures the system-subsystem relationships. One must examine both the system as a whole and the component subsystems. The frustration and inevitable criticism comes when one must acknowledge that the ecosystem within which one was examining subsystems is itself a subsystem of a larger ecosystem. The observer must decide what to include and what to omit from the analysis—that is, what slice of the hierarchy of subsystems to take for analysis.[138] This necessarily subjective decision will be invariably too narrow or too broad for the tastes (or values) of some other observers. Combine this problem with the dynamic rather than static nature of ecosystems, making the chosen slice a time-dependent set of observations, and one is left unavoidably with a case study of limited generalizability.

Planners wondering which slice of complex systems to analyze and target for intervention can do well by choosing those close enough to reach the people whose needs are to be served. Further, planners should reach as far as they can beyond that to assure support for the more immediate environmental changes needed, but not so far that the unknown needs of others might be affected adversely. Again, some restraint and humility might be blended with the courage it took to undertake an ecological approach in the first place.

ENDNOTES

108. Green, L. W., & Ottoson, J. M. (1999). *Community and population health* (8th ed.). Boston: WCB/McGraw-Hill.

Rogers, E. S. (1960). *Human ecology and health: An introduction for administrators.* New York: Macmillan.

Rosen, G. (1958). *A history of public health.* New York: MD Publications.

Sydenstricker, E. (1933). *Health and environment.* New York: McGraw-Hill.

109. Brown, E. R., & Margo, G. E. (1978). Health education: Can the reformers be reformed? *International Journal of Health Services, 8,* 3–25.

Freudenber, N. (1978). Shaping the future of health education: From behavior change to social change. *Health Education Monographs, 6,* 372–377.

Green, L. W. (1979b). National policy in the promotion of health. *International Journal of Health Education, 22,* 161–168.

Pearce, N. (1996). Traditional epidemiology, modern epidemiology, and public health. *American Journal of Public Health, 86,* 678–683.

Schwab, M., & Syme, S. L. (1997). On paradigms, community participation, and the future of public health. *American Journal of Public Health, 87,* 2049–2050.

110. Park, R. E., Burgess, E. W., & McKenzie, R. D. (Eds.). (1925). *The city.* Chicago: University of Chicago Press.

111. Griffiths, W., & Knutson, A. L. (1960). The role of mass media in public health. *American Journal of Public Health, 50,* 515–523.

Young, M. A. C. (1967). Review of research and studies related to health education communication: Methods and materials. *Health Education Monographs, 1*(25), 18–24.

112. Green, L. W. (1970a). Identifying and overcoming barriers to the diffusion of knowledge about family planning. *Advances in Fertility Control, 5,* 21–29.

Rogers, E. M. (1973). *Communication strategies for family planning.* New York: Free Press.

113. Green, L. W. (1975). Diffusion and adoption of innovations related to cardiovascular risk behavior in the public. In A. Enelow, & J. B. Henderson

(Eds.), *Applying Behavioral Sciences to Cardiovascular Risk.* New York: American Heart Association.

Green, L. W., Gottlieb, N. H., & Parcel, G. S. (1991). Diffusion theory extended and applied. In W. Ward, & F. M. Lewis (Eds.), *Advances in health education and promotion* (Vol. 3, pp. 91–117). London: Jessica Kingsley.

114. Anderson, O. W. (1957). Infant mortality and social and cultural factors: Historical trends and current patterns. In E. G. Jaco (Ed.), *Patients, physicians and illness* (pp. 10–24). Glencoe, IL: Free Press.

115. Barker, R. G. (1965). Explorations in ecological psychology. *American Psychologist, 20,* 1–14.

116. Baer, D. M. (1974). A note on the absence of a Santa Claus in any known ecosystem: A rejoinder to Willems. *Journal of Applied Behavior Analysis, 7,* 167–170.

117. Flay, B. R. (1987). Social psychological approaches to smoking prevention: Review and recommendations. In W. B. Ward, & P. D. Mullen (Eds.), *Advances in Health Education and Promotion* (Vol. 2, pp. 121–180). Greenwich, CT: JAI Press.

Hovland, C., Janis, I. L., & Kelley, H. H. (1953). *Communication and persuasion.* New Haven, CT: Yale University Press.

Worden, J. K., Flynn, B. S., Geller, B. M., et al. (1988). Development of a smoking prevention mass-media program using diagnostic and formative research. *Preventive Medicine, 17,* 531–558.

118. Lewin, K. (1943). Forces behind food habits and methods of change. *Bulletin of the National Research Council, 108,* 35–65.

Nyswander, D. (1942). *Solving school health problems.* New York: Oxford University Press.

119. Mico, P. R. (Ed.). (1982). *The heritage collection of health education monographs* (4 vols.). Oakland, CA: Third Party Associates.

Morgan, L. S., & Horning, B. G. (1940). The community health education program. *American Journal of Public health, 30,* 1323–1330.

Steuart, G. W. (1965). Health, behavior and planned change: An approach to the professional preparation of the health education specialist. *Health Education Monographs, 1*(20), 3–26.

120. Miller, N. E. (1984). Learning: Some facts and needed research relevant to maintaining health. In J. D. Matarazzo et al. (Eds.), *Behavioral health: A handbook of health enhancement and disease prevention* (pp. 199–208). New York: Wiley.

121. Bandura, A. (1977b). *Social learning theory.* Englewood Cliffs, NJ: Prentice-Hall.

Clark, N. M. (1987). Social learning theory in current health education practice. In W. B Ward, S. K. Simonds, P. D. Mullen, & M. H. Becker (Eds.), *Advances in Health Education and Promotion* (vol. 2, pp. 251–275). Greenwich, CT: JAI Press.

Parcel, G. S., & Baranowski, T. (1981). Social learning theory and health education. *Health Education, 12*(3), 14–18.

122. Dewey, J. (1946). *The public and its problems: An essay in political inquiry.* Chicago: Gateway.

123. Creswell, W., Jr., & Newman, I. M. (1997). *School health practice* (10th ed.). St. Louis: Times Mirror/Mosby.

124. Kolbe, L. J. (1986). Increasing the impact of school health promotion programs: Emerging research perspectives. *Health Education, 17*(5), 47–52.

125. Parcel, G. S., Simons-Morton, B. G., & Kolbe, L. J. (1988). Health promotion: Integration organizational change and student learning strategies. *Health Education Quarterly, 15,* 435–450.

126. Poland, B., Green, L., & Rootman, I. (Eds.). (in press). *Settings for health promotion.* Thousand Oaks, CA: Sage.

127. Hayes, M. V., & Manson Willms, S. (1990). Healthy community indicators: The perils of the search and the paucity of the find. *Health Promotion International, 5,* 161–166.

128. Macdonald, G., & Bunton, R. (1992). Health promotion, discipline or disciplines? In R. Bunton, & G. Macdonald (Eds.), *Health promotion: Disciplines and diversity* (pp. 6–19). London: Routledge.

McLeroy, K. R., Bibeau, D., Steckler, A., & Glanz, K. (1988). An ecological perspective on health promotion programs. *Health Education Quarterly, 15,* 351–377.

129. Thorogood, N. (1992). What is the relevance of sociology for health promotion? In R. Bunton, & G. MacDonald (Eds.), *Health promotion: Disciplines and diversity* (pp. 42–65). London: Routledge.

130. Green, L. W., & Raeburn, J. (1998). Health promotion: What is it? What will it become? *Health Promotion International, 3,* 151–159. Revised and reprinted as L. W. Green, & J. Raeburn (1990). Contemporary developments in health promotion: Definitions and challenges. In N. Bracht (Ed.), *Health promotion at the community level* (pp. 29–44). Newbury Park, CA: Sage.

Minkler, M. (1989). Health education, health promotion and the open society: An historical perspective. *Health Education Quarterly, 16,* 17–30.

131. Green, L. W., & Ottoson, J. M. (1999). *Community and population health* (8th ed.). Boston: WCB/McGraw-Hill.

132. Eisenberg, L. (1972). The *human* nature of human nature. *Science, 176,* 123–128.

Foster, G. M. (1962). *Traditional cultures and the impact of technological change.* New York: Harper.

Paul, B. D. (Ed.). (1955). *Health, culture and community.* New York: Russell Sage Foundation.

133. Foster, G. M. (1962). *Traditional cultures and the impact of technological change.* New York: Harper.

Paul, B. D. (Ed.). (1955). *Health, culture and community.* New York: Russell Sage Foundation.

134. Sells, S. B. (1969). Ecology and the science of psychology. In E. P. Willems, & H. L. Raush (Eds.), *Naturalistic viewpoints in psychological research* (pp. 15–30). New York: Holt, Rinehart, & Winston.

135. Slobodkin, L. B. (1988). Intellectual problems of applied ecology. *Bioscience, 38,* 337–342.

136. Kay, J. J., & Schneider, E. (1994). Embracing complexity: The challenge of the ecosystem approach. *Alternatives, 20*(3), 39.

137. Pittman, D. J. (1993). The new temperance movement in the United States: What happened to macro-structural factors in alcohol problems? *Addiction, 88,* 169.

138. King, A. W. (1993). Considerations of scale and hierarchy. In S. Woodley, J. J. Kay, & G. Francis (Eds.), *Ecological integrity and the management of ecosystems* (pp. 19–46). Delray, FL: St. Lucie Press.

Determinants of Health

Source: Excerpt from Healthy People 2010: A Systematic Approach to Health Improvement—DHHS 2000. Available at www.healthypeople.gov.

Topics covered by the objectives in Healthy People 2010 reflect the array of critical influences that determine the health of individuals and communities.

For example, individual behaviors and environmental factors are responsible for about 70 percent of all premature deaths in the United States. Developing and implementing policies and preventive interventions that effectively address these determinants of health can reduce the burden of illness, enhance quality of life, and increase longevity.

Individual *biology* and *behaviors* influence health through their interaction with each other and with the individual's *social* and *physical environments*. In addition, *policies and interventions* can improve health by targeting factors related to individuals and their environments, including *access to quality health care* (see Figure 1-2).

Biology refers to the individual's genetic makeup (those factors with which he or she is born), family history (which may suggest risk for disease), and the physical and mental health problems acquired during life. Aging, diet, physical activity, smoking, stress, alcohol or illicit drug abuse, injury or violence, or an infectious or toxic agent may result in illness or disability and can produce a "new" biology for the individual.

Behaviors are individual responses or reactions to internal stimuli and external conditions. Behaviors can have a reciprocal relationship to biology; in other words, each can react to the other. For example, smoking (behavior) can alter the cells in the lung and result in shortness of breath, emphysema,

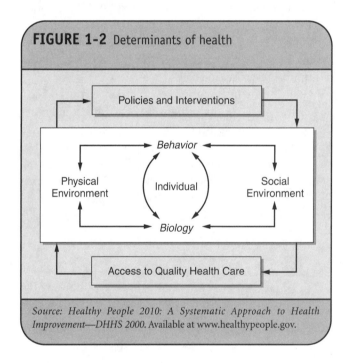

FIGURE 1-2 Determinants of health

Source: *Healthy People 2010: A Systematic Approach to Health Improvement—DHHS 2000.* Available at www.healthypeople.gov.

or cancer (biology) that then may lead an individual to stop smoking (behavior). Similarly, a family history that includes heart disease (biology) may motivate an individual to develop good eating habits, avoid tobacco, and maintain an active lifestyle (behaviors), which may prevent his or her own development of heart disease (biology).

Personal choices and the social and physical environments surrounding individuals can shape behaviors. The social and physical environments include all factors that affect the life of individuals, positively or negatively, many of which may not be under their immediate or direct control.

Social environment includes interactions with family, friends, coworkers, and others in the community. It also encompasses social institutions, such as law enforcement, the workplace, places of worship, and schools. Housing, public transportation, and the presence or absence of violence in the community are among other components of the social environment. The social environment has a profound effect on individual health, as well as on the health of the larger community, and is unique because of cultural customs; language; and personal, religious, or spiritual beliefs. At the same time, individuals and their behaviors contribute to the quality of the social environment.

Physical environment can be thought of as that which can be seen, touched, heard, smelled, and tasted. However, the physical environment also contains less tangible elements, such as radiation and ozone. The physical environment can harm individual and community health, especially when individuals and communities are exposed to toxic substances; irritants; infectious agents; and physical hazards in homes, schools, and worksites. The physical environment also can promote good health, for example, by providing clean and safe places for people to work, exercise, and play.

Policies and interventions can have a powerful and positive effect on the health of individuals and the community. Examples include health promotion campaigns to prevent smoking; policies mandating child restraints and safety belt use in automobiles; disease prevention services, such as immunization of children, adolescents, and adults; and clinical services, such as enhanced mental health care. Policies and interventions that promote individual and community health may be implemented by a variety of agencies, such as transportation, education, energy, housing, labor, justice, and other venues, or through places of worship, community-based organizations, civic groups, and businesses.

The health of individuals and communities also depends greatly on **access to quality health care**. Expanding access to quality health care is important to eliminate health disparities and to increase the quality and years of healthy life for all people living in the United States. Health care in the broadest sense not only includes services received through health care providers but also health information and services received through other venues in the community.

The determinants of health—individual biology and behavior, physical and social environments, policies and interventions, and access to quality health care—have a profound effect on the health of individuals, communities, and the Nation. An evaluation of these determinants is an important part of developing any strategy to improve health.

Our understanding of these determinants and how they relate to one another, coupled with our understanding of how individual and community health affects the health of the Nation, is perhaps the most important key to achieving our Healthy People 2010 goals of increasing the quality and years of life and of eliminating the Nation's health disparities.

REFERENCES

U.S. Department of Health and Human Services, November 2000. *Healthy People 2010.* 2nd ed. With Understanding and Improving Health and Objectives for Improving Health. Washington, DC: U.S. Government Printing Office.

PART 2

Health Issues and Behavior

Three health issues are considered in this part with respect to their links to behavior: obesity, youth violence, and HIV/AIDS. The following are selections from the research and program literature that address the behavior–health link for each of these three issues. The first selection (concerning obesity) is an excerpt from a chapter of a major report prepared by the World Health Organization (2003) that examines obesity and its behavioral/ecological determinants in the context of a worldwide increase in chronic diseases related to issues of diet and lifestyle. The second selection (Edberg, 2007), which focuses on youth violence, examines a spectrum of psychosocial theories explaining factors that contribute to violent behavior, while the third selection (Tonry & Moore, 1998) describes the influence of gun availability on violent behavior. The fourth and fifth selections (Bhattacharya, 2004; UNAIDS, 2006) address causal factors for HIV/AIDS in a global context.

Diet, Nutrition, and the Prevention of Chronic Diseases

Source: Excerpt from World Health Organization. 2003. *Diet, Nutrition, and the Prevention of Chronic Diseases: Report of a Joint WHO/FAO Expert Consultation* (Chapter 5). Geneva: World Health Organization.

5.2 RECOMMENDATIONS FOR PREVENTING EXCESS WEIGHT GAIN AND OBESITY

5.2.1 Background

Almost all countries (high-income and low-income alike) are experiencing an obesity epidemic, although with great variation between and within countries. In low-income countries, obesity is more common in middle-aged women, people of higher socioeconomic status and those living in urban communities. In more affluent countries, obesity is not only common in the middle-aged, but is becoming increasingly prevalent among younger adults and children. Furthermore, it tends to be associated with lower socioeconomic status, especially in women, and the urban–rural differences are diminished or even reversed.

It has been estimated that the direct costs of obesity accounted for 6.8% (or US$ 70 billion) of total health care costs, and physical inactivity for a further US$ 24 billion, in the United States in 1995. Although direct costs in other industrialized countries are slightly lower, they still consume a sizeable proportion of national health budgets (1). Indirect costs, which are far greater than direct costs, include workdays lost, physician visits, disability pensions and premature mortality. Intangible costs such as impaired quality of life are also enormous. Because the risks of diabetes, cardiovascular disease and hypertension rise continuously with increasing weight, there is much overlap between the prevention of obesity and the prevention of a variety of chronic diseases, especially type 2 diabetes. Population education strategies will need a solid base of policy and environment-based changes to be effective in eventually reversing these trends.

5.2.2 Trends

The increasing industrialization, urbanization and mechanization occurring in most countries around the world is associated with changes in diet and behaviour, in particular, diets are becoming richer in high-fat, high energy foods and lifestyles more sedentary. In many developing countries undergoing economic transition, rising levels of obesity often coexist in the same population (or even the same household) with chronic undernutrition. Increases in obesity over the past 30 years have been paralleled by a dramatic rise in the prevalence of diabetes (2).

5.2.3 Diet, physical activity and excess weight gain and obesity

Mortality rates increase with increasing degrees of overweight, as measured by BMI. As BMI increases, so too does the proportion of people with one or more comorbid conditions. In one study in the USA (3), over half (53%) of all deaths in women with a BMI>29 kg/m^2 could be directly attributed to their obesity. Eating behaviours that have been linked to overweight and obesity include snacking/eating frequency, binge-eating patterns, eating out, and (protectively) exclusive breastfeeding.

Nutrient factors under investigation include fat, carbohydrate type (including refined carbohydrates such as sugar), the glycaemic index of foods, and fibre. Environmental issues are clearly important, especially as many environments become increasingly "obesogenic" (obesity-promoting).

Physical activity is an important determinant of body weight. In addition, physical activity and physical fitness (which relates to the ability to perform physical activity) are important modifiers of mortality and morbidity related to overweight and obesity. There is firm evidence that moderate to high fitness levels provide a substantially reduced risk of cardiovascular disease and all-cause mortality and that these benefits apply to all BMI levels. Furthermore, high fitness protects against mortality at all BMI levels in men with diabetes. Low cardiovascular fitness is a serious and common comorbidity of obesity, and a sizeable proportion of deaths in overweight and obese populations are probably a result of low levels of cardiorespiratory fitness rather than obesity per se. Fitness is, in turn, influenced strongly by physical activity in addition to genetic

factors. These relationships emphasize the role of physical activity in the prevention of overweight and obesity, independently of the effects of physical activity on body weight. The potential etiological factors related to unhealthy weight gain are listed in Table 2-1.

5.2.4 Strength of evidence

Convincing etiological factors

Regular physical activity (protective) and sedentary lifestyles (causative). There is convincing evidence that regular physical activity is protective against unhealthy weight gain whereas sedentary lifestyles, particularly sedentary occupations and inactive recreation such as watching television, promote it. Most epidemiological studies show smaller risk of weight gain, overweight and obesity among persons who currently engage regularly in moderate to large amounts of physical activity (4). Studies measuring physical activity at baseline and randomized trials of exercise programmes show more mixed results, prob-

TABLE 2-1 Summary of strength of evidence on factors that might promote or protect against weight gain and obesity[a]

Evidence	Decreased risk	No relationship	Increased risk
Convincing	Regular physical activity High dietary intake of NSP (dietary fibre)[b]		Sedentary lifestyles High intake of energy-dense micronutrient-poor foods[c]
Probable	Home and school environment that support healthy food choices for children[d] Breastfeeding		Heavy marketing of energy-dense foods[d] and fast-food outlets[d] High intake of sugars-sweetened soft drinks and fruit juices Adverse socioeconomic conditions[d] (in developed countries, especially for women)
Possible	Low glycaemic index foods	Protein content of the diet	Large portion sizes High proportion of food prepared outside the home (developed countries) "rigid restraint/periodic disinhibition" eating patterns
Insufficient	Increased eating frequency		Alcohol

[a]Strength of evidence: The totality of the evidence was taken into account. The World Cancer Research Fund schema was taken as the starting point but was modified in the following manner: randomized control trials were given prominence as the highest ranking study design (randomized controlled trials were not a major source of cancer evidence); associated evidence and expert opinion was also taken into account in relation to environmental determinants (direct trials were usually not available).

[b]Specific amounts will depend on the analytical methodologies used to measure fibre.

[c]Energy-dense and micronutrient-poor foods tend to be processed foods that are high in fat and/or sugars. Low energy-dense (or energy-dilute) foods, such as fruit, legumes, vegetable and whole grain cereals, are high in dietary fibre and water.

[d]Associated evidence and expert opinion included.

Source: World Health Organization. 2003. Diet, Nutrition, and the Prevention of Chronic Diseases: Report of a Joint WHO/FAO Expert Consultation (Chapter 5). Geneva: World Health Organization.

ably because of the low adherence to long-term changes. Therefore, it is ongoing physical activity itself rather than previous physical activity or enrollment in an exercise programme that is protective against unhealthy weight gain. The recommendation for individuals to accumulate at least 30 minutes of moderate-intensity physical activity on most days is largely aimed at reducing cardiovascular diseases and overall mortality. The amount needed to prevent unhealthy weight gain is uncertain but is probably significantly greater than this. Preventing weight gain after substantial weight loss probably requires about 60–90 minutes per day. Two meetings recommended by consensus that about 45–60 minutes of moderate-intensity physical activity is needed on most days or every day to prevent unhealthy weight gain (5, 6). Studies aimed at reducing sedentary behaviours have focused primarily on reducing television viewing in children. Reducing viewing times by about 30 minutes a day in children in the United States appears feasible and is associated with reductions in BMI.

A high dietary intake of non-starch polysaccharides (NSP)/ dietary fibre (protective). The nomenclature and definitions of NSP (dietary fibre) have changed with time, and many of the available studies used previous definitions, such as soluble and insoluble fibre. Nevertheless, two recent reviews of randomized trials have concluded that the majority of studies show that a high intake of NSP (dietary fibre) promotes weight loss. Pereira & Ludwig (7) found that 12 out of 19 trials showed beneficial objective effects (including weight loss). In their review of 11 studies of more than 4 weeks duration, involving ad libitum eating Howarth Saltzman & Roberts (8) reported a mean weight loss of 1.9 kg over 3.8 months. There were no differences between fibre type or between fibre consumed in food or as supplements.

High intake of energy-dense micronutrient-poor foods (causative). There is convincing evidence that a high intake of energy-dense foods promotes weight gain. In high-income countries (and increasingly in low-income countries) these energy-dense foods are not only highly processed (low NSP) but also micronutrient-poor, further diminishing their nutritional value. Energy-dense foods tend to be high in fat (e.g. butter, oils, fried foods), sugars or starch, while energy-dilute foods have a high water content (e.g. fruits and vegetables). Several trials have covertly manipulated the fat content and the energy density of diets, the results of which support the view that so-called "passive over consumption" of total energy occurs when the energy density of the diet is high and that this is almost always the case in high-fat diets. A meta-analysis of 16 trials of ad libitum high-fat versus low-fat diets of at least 2 months duration suggested that a reduction in fat content by 10% corresponds to about a 1 MJ reduction in energy intake

and about 3 kg in body weight (9). At a population level, 3 kg equates to about one BMI unit or about a 5% difference in obesity prevalence. However, it is difficult to blind such studies and other non-physiological effects may influence these findings (10). While energy from fat is no more fattening than the same amount of energy from carbohydrate or protein, diets that are high in fat tend to be energy-dense. An important exception to this is diets based predominantly on energy-dilute foods (e.g. vegetables, legumes, fruits) but which have a reasonably high percentage of energy as fat from added oils.

The effectiveness over the long term of most dietary strategies for weight loss, including low-fat diets, remains uncertain unless accompanied by changes in behaviour affecting physical activity and food habits. These latter changes at a public health level require an environment supportive of healthy food choices and an active life. High quality trials to address these issues are urgently needed. A variety of popular weight-loss diets that restrict food choices may result in reduced energy intake and short-term weight loss in individuals but most do not have trial evidence of long-term effectiveness and nutritional adequacy and therefore cannot be recommended for populations.

Probable etiological factors

Home and school environments that promote healthy food and activity choices for children (protective). Despite the obvious importance of the roles that parents and home environments play on children's eating and physical activity behaviours, there is very little hard evidence available to support this view. It appears that access and exposure to a range of fruits and vegetables in the home is important for the development of preferences for these foods and that parental knowledge, attitudes and behaviours related to healthy diet and physical activity are important in creating role models (11). More data are available on the impact of the school environment on nutrition knowledge, on eating patterns and physical activity at school, and on sedentary behaviours at home. Some studies (12), but not all, have shown an effect of school-based interventions on obesity prevention. While more research is clearly needed to increase the evidence base in both these areas, supportive home and school environments were rated as a probable etiological influence on obesity.

Heavy marketing of fast-food outlets and energy-dense, micronutrient poor foods and beverages (causative). Part of the consistent, strong relationships between television viewing and obesity in children may relate to the food advertising to which they are exposed (13–15). Fast-food restaurants, and foods and beverages that are usually classified under the "eat least" category in dietary guidelines are among the most heavily marketed products, especially on television. Young children are often the target group for the advertising of these products because they have a significant influence on the foods bought by parents (16). The huge expenditure on marketing fast-foods and other "eat least" choices (US$ 11 billion in the United States alone in 1997) was considered to be a key factor in the increased consumption of food prepared outside the home in general and of energy-dense, micronutrient-poor foods in particular. Young children are unable to distinguish programme content from the persuasive intent of advertisements. The evidence that the heavy marketing of these foods and beverages to young children causes obesity is not unequivocal. Nevertheless, the Consultation considered that there is sufficient indirect evidence to warrant this practice being placed in the "probable" category and thus becoming a potential target for interventions (15–18).

A high intake of sugars-sweetened beverages (causative). Diets that are proportionally low in fat will be proportionally higher in carbohydrate (including a variable amount of sugars) and are associated with protection against unhealthy weight gain, although a high intake of free sugars in beverages probably promotes weight gain. The physiological effects of energy intake on satiation and satiety appear to be quite different for energy in solid foods as opposed to energy in fluids. Possibly because of reduced gastric distension and faster transit times, the energy contained in fluids is less well "detected" by the body and subsequent food intake is poorly adjusted to account for the energy taken in through beverages (19). This is supported by data from cross-sectional, longitudinal, and cross-over studies (20–22). The high and increasing consumption of sugars-sweetened drinks by children in many countries is of serious concern. It has been estimated that each additional can or glass of sugars-sweetened drink that they consume every day increases the risk of becoming obese by 60% (19). Most of the evidence relates to soda drinks but many fruit drinks and cordials are equally energy-dense and may promote weight gain if drunk in large quantities. Overall, the evidence implicating a high intake of sugars-sweetened drinks in promoting weight gain was considered moderately strong.

Adverse socioeconomic conditions, especially for women in high-income countries (causative). Classically the pattern of the progression of obesity through a population starts with middle-aged women in high-income groups but as the epidemic progresses, obesity becomes more common in people (especially women) in lower socioeconomic status groups. The relationship may even be bi-directional, setting up a vicious cycle (i.e. lower socioeconomic status promotes obesity, and obese people are more likely to end up in groups with low socioeconomic status). The mechanisms by which socioeconomic status influences food and activity patterns are probably multiple and

need elucidation. However, people living in circumstances of low socioeconomic status may be more at the mercy of the obesogenic environment because their eating and activity behaviours are more likely to be the "default choices" on offer. The evidence for an effect of low socioeconomic status on predisposing people to obesity is consistent (in higher income countries) across a number of cross-sectional and longitudinal studies (23), and was thus rated as a "probable" cause of increased risk of obesity.

Breastfeeding (protective). Breastfeeding as a protective factor against weight gain has been examined in at least 20 studies involving nearly 40,000 subjects. Five studies (including the two largest) found a protective effect, two found that breastfeeding predicted obesity, and the remainder found no relationships. There are probably multiple effects of confounding in these studies; however, the reduction in the risk of developing obesity observed in the two largest studies was substantial (20–37%). Promoting breastfeeding has many benefits, the prevention of childhood obesity probably being one of them.

Possible etiological factors

Several other factors were defined as "possible" protective or causative in the etiology of unhealthy weight gain. Low-glycaemic foods have been proposed as a potential protective factor against weight gain and there are some early studies that support this hypothesis. More clinical trials are, however, needed to establish the association with greater certainty.

Large portion sizes are a possible causative factor for unhealthy weight gain (24). The marketing of "supersize" portions, particularly in fast-food outlets, is now common practice in many countries. There is some evidence that people poorly estimate portion sizes and that subsequent energy compensation for a large meal is incomplete and therefore is likely to lead to overconsumption.

In many countries, there has been a steady increase in the proportion of food eaten that is prepared outside the home. In the United States, the energy, total fat, saturated fat, cholesterol and sodium content of foods prepared outside the home is significantly higher than that of home-prepared food. People in the United States who tend to eat in restaurants have a higher BMI than those who tend to eat at home (25).

Certain psychological parameters of eating patterns may influence the risk of obesity. The "flexible restraint" pattern is associated with lower risk of weight gain, whereas the "rigid restraint/periodic disinhibition" pattern is associated with a higher risk.

Several other factors were also considered but the evidence was not thought to be strong enough to warrant defining them as protective or causative. Studies have not shown consistent associations between alcohol intake and obesity despite the high energy density of the nutrient (7 kcal/g). There are probably many confounding factors that influence the association. While a high eating frequency has been shown in some studies to have a negative relationship with energy intake and weight gain, the types of foods readily available as snack foods are often high in fat and a high consumption of foods of this type might predispose people to weight gain. The evidence regarding the impact of early nutrition on subsequent obesity is also mixed, with some studies showing relationships for high and low birth weights.

5.2.5 General strategies for obesity prevention

The prevention of obesity in infants and young children should be considered of high priority. For infants and young children, the main preventive strategies are:

- the promotion of exclusive breastfeeding;
- avoiding the use of added sugars and starches when feeding formula;
- instructing mothers to accept their child's ability to regulate energy intake rather than feeding until the plate is empty;
- assuring the appropriate micronutrient intake needed to promote optimal linear growth.

For children and adolescents, prevention of obesity implies the need to:

- promote an active lifestyle;
- limit television viewing;
- promote the intake of fruits and vegetables;
- restrict the intake of energy-dense, micronutrient-poor foods (e.g. packaged snacks);
- restrict the intake of sugars-sweetened soft drinks.

Additional measures include modifying the environment to enhance physical activity in schools and communities, creating more opportunities for family interaction (e.g. eating family meals), limiting the exposure of young children to heavy marketing practices of energy dense, micronutrient-poor foods, and providing the necessary information and skills to make healthy food choices.

In developing countries, special attention should be given to avoidance of overfeeding stunted population groups. Nutrition programmes designed to control or prevent undernutrition need to assess stature in combination with weight to prevent providing excess energy to children of low weight-for-age but normal weight-for-height. In countries in economic transition, as populations become more sedentary and able to access energy-dense foods, there is a need to maintain the healthy components of traditional diets (e.g. high intake of vegetables, fruits and NSP). Education provided to mothers and low socioeconomic status communities that are food insecure should stress that overweight and obesity do not represent good health.

Low-income groups globally and populations in countries in economic transition often replace traditional micronutrient-rich foods by heavily marketed, sugars-sweetened beverages (i.e. soft drinks) and energy dense fatty, salty and sugary foods. These trends, coupled with reduced physical activity, are associated with the rising prevalence of obesity. Strategies are needed to improve the quality of diets by increasing consumption of fruits and vegetables, in addition to increasing physical activity, in order to stem the epidemic of obesity and associated diseases.

REFERENCES

1. Colditz G. Economic costs of obesity and inactivity. *Medicine and Science in Sport and Exercise*, 1999, 31(Suppl. 11):S663–S667.

2. *The world health report 2002: reducing risks, promoting healthy life.* Geneva, World Health Organization, 2002.

3. Manson JE et al. Body weight and mortality among women. *New England Journal of Medicine*, 1995, 333:677–685.

4. Fogelholm M, Kukkonen-HarjulaK. Does physical activity prevent weight gain—a systematic review. *Obesity Reviews*, 2000, 1:95–111.

5. *Weight control and physical activity.* Lyon, International Agency for Research on Cancer, 2002 (IARC Handbooks of Cancer Prevention, Vol. 6).

6. Saris WHM. Dose-response of physical activity in the treatment of obesity—How much is enough to prevent unhealthy weight gain. Outcome of the First Mike Stock Conference. *International Journal of Obesity*, 2002, 26(Suppl. 1):S108.

7. Pereira MA, Ludwig DS. Dietary fiber and body-weight regulation. Observations and mechanisms. *Pediatric Clinics of North America*, 2001, 48:969–980.

8. Howarth NC, Saltzman E, Roberts SB. Dietary fiber and weight regulation. *Nutrition Reviews*, 2001, 59:129–139.

9. Astrup A et al. The role of low-fat diets in body weight control: a meta-analysis of ad libitum dietary intervention studies. *International Journal of Obesity*, 2000, 24:1545–1552.

10. Willett WC. Dietary fat plays a major role in obesity: no. *Obesity Reviews*, 2000, 3:59–68.

11. Campbell K, Crawford D. Family food environments as determinants of preschool-aged children's eating behaviours: implications for obesity prevention policy. A review. *Australian Journal of Nutrition and Dietetics*, 2001, 58:19–25.

12. Gortmaker S et al. Reducing obesity via a school-based interdisciplinary intervention among youth: Planet Health. *Archives of Pediatrics and Adolescent Medicine*, 1999, 153:409–418.

13. Nestle M. *Food politics.* Berkeley, CA, University of California Press, 2002.

14. Nestle M. The ironic politics of obesity. *Science*, 2003, 299:781.

15. Robinson TN. Does television cause childhood obesity? *Journal of American Medical Association*, 1998, 279:959–960.

16. Borzekowski DL, Robinson TN. The 30-second effect: an experiment revealing the impact of television commercials on food preferences of preschoolers. *Journal of the American Dietetic Association*, 2001, 101:42–46.

17. Lewis MK, Hill AJ. Food advertising on British children's television: a content analysis and experimental study with nine-year olds. *International Journal of Obesity*, 1998, 22:206–214.

18. Taras HL, Gage M. Advertised foods on children's television. *Archives of Pediatrics and Adolescent Medicine*, 1995, 149:649–652.

19. Mattes RD. Dietary compensation by humans for supplemental energy provided as ethanol or carbohydrate in fluids. *Physiology and Behaviour*, 1996, 59:179–187.

20. Tordoff MG, Alleva AM. Effect of drinking soda sweetened with aspartame or high-fructose corn syrup on food intake and body weight. *American Journal of Clinical Nutrition*, 1990, 51:963–969.

21. Harnack L, Stang J, Story M. Soft drink consumption among US children and adolescents: nutritional consequences. *Journal of the American Dietetic Association*, 1999, 99:436–441.

22. Ludwig DS, Peterson KE, Gortmaker SL. Relation between consumption of sugar-sweetened drinks and childhood obesity: a prospective, observational analysis. *Lancet*, 2001, 357:505–508.

23. Peña M, Bacallao J. *Obesity and poverty: a new public health challenge.* Washington, DC, Pan American Health Organization, 2000 (Scientific Publication, No. 576).

24. Nielsen SJ, Popkin BM. Patterns and trends in food portion sizes, 1977–1998. *Journal of the American Medical Association*, 2003, 289:450–453.

25. Jeffery RW, French SA. Epidemic obesity in the United States: are fast foods and television viewing contributing? *American Journal of Public Health*, 1998, 88:277–280.

Connections Between Violence, Adolescent Identity, and Poverty

Source: Edberg, M. 2007. Connections Between Violence, Adolescent Identity and Poverty: The Limits of Current Theory in Understanding and Preventing Youth Violence. *International Journal of Interdisciplinary Social Sciences* Vol. 2, Issue 5, pp. 91–104.

CURRENT PSYCHOSOCIAL APPROACHES TO YOUTH VIOLENCE

While current theories on violence behavior include both biological (DHHS 2001) and psychosocial approaches, the focus of this paper is on the latter. Prevalent psychosocial theories of youth violence (in the U.S.) draw primarily from psychology, social psychology, and sociology. They can be categorized into risk and protective factor models, problem behavior syndrome/ behavior cluster models, self-concept models, socioecological models, and social–cognitive models (Note that these approaches often address violence as one of a number of risk behaviors, including delinquency, substance abuse, sexual risk, school dropout, and others.).

Risk and Protective Factor Models

Risk and protective factor models comprise the predominant theoretical approach guiding U.S.–based prevention programs in recent years. The overall model is epidemiological in nature, addressing correlations between the presence or absence of one or more risk factors in the lives of youth and negative behavioral outcomes, including violence. Risk factors are said to be precursors to or predictors of risky behavior, and these risk factors are organized in various domains, where exposure across multiple domains is said to be typical (see, for example, Beier et al., 2000; Lipsey & Derzon, 1998; Loeber & Hay, 1997; Yoshikawa 1994; Grizenko and Fisher 1992; Hawkins et. al. 1992; Dryfoos 1990; Tolan and Guerra 1994; Kumpfer and Turner 1990–91; Brook et al 1990; Petraitis et al 1995; Dembo et al 1989; Spatz-Widom, 1989; Bell & Jenkins, 1993; Osofsky & Fenichel, 1994). Hawkins, Catalano, and colleagues (Hawkins, Catalano & Miller, 1992; Catalano & Hawkins, 1995; Hawkins et al., 2000) synthesized the risk factor research into a widely used, comprehensive approach that has been a template for prevention program funding across multiple agencies. In brief, the model lays out an algorithm of factors that, over the youth development process, are said to increase or decrease the likelihood that a given youth will engage in problem behaviors (violence, delinquency, substance abuse, school dropout, HIV/AIDS risk behavior, or others): *Risk factors* increase the likelihood of problem behavior—for example, being a victim of child abuse, low attachment to school, high community crime levels, or family conflict. *Protective factors* buffer risk factors and reduce the likelihood of problem behavior—for example, strong family and school attachment, clear school/community values (that do not support problem behavior) or a positive relationship with an adult mentor. Under the Hawkins & Catalano model, risk factors are organized into the following domains: *individual* (e.g., biological and psychological dispositions, attitudes, values, knowledge, skills, problem behaviors); *peer* (e.g., norms, activities, attachment); *family* (e.g., function, management, bonding, abuse/violence); *school* (e.g., bonding, climate, policy, performance); *community* (e.g., bonding, norms, resources, poverty level, crime, awareness/mobilization); and sometimes, the domain of *society/environmental* (e.g., norms, policy/sanctions) as well. Protective factors under this model are not as well specified, and have been organized into a smaller set of similar domains: *individual* (e.g., gender, intelligence, temperament); *social bonding* (attachment/commitment to positive, prosocial individuals and groups); *healthy beliefs* and *clear standards for behavior* (in families, schools, communities).

However, others following the same general approach have focused more extensively on protective factors. Thus several variants of this model focus more on protective rather than risk factors, with resulting programs concentrating more on enhancing protective factors and less on mitigating risk factors (Pransky 1991; Benson, Galbraith, & Espeland, 1994; Search Institute 1998; Benard, 1996, 1991)—using the terminology *resilience* for these protective qualities (Garmezy, 1991). Behavioral outcomes are said to be determined by the degree of resiliency that exists in the face of risk factors that may be present (Benard, 1991).

A key strength of the risk and protective factors approach—its clarity and cohesiveness—also leads to an important weakness. As described above, risk and protective factor approaches seek to identify specific correlates or predictive factors that can be analytically isolated and addressed as if the risk behaviors at issue were the output of an algorithm, where the various risk factors or precursors are essentially equivalent operational units within that algorithm. Lost in this paradigm is the synthetic perspective, the idea that behavior and its antecedents have a coherence beyond any such algorithmic model. People process the conditions of their existence into ways of life that have their own meanings and justifications which then contribute to motivation for action. Exposure to risk and protective factors may *set up* such conditions, but it does not explain what happens as a consequence of that exposure, nor does it explain how people configure and act in their worlds in light of such exposure.

Moreover, there is a downside to the fact that the risk and protective factor approach offers a "well-packaged" protocol for identifying risk factors to be addressed, selecting programs that have an evidence base with respect to the selected risk factors, and then evaluating impact with measures designed to capture change in the identified risk factors. Indeed, Federal government agencies in the United States that have adopted the model for planning and funding prevention programs have spurred the development of this protocol, because it fits well with agency accountability requirements and with a range of standard scientific evaluation methodologies. At the same time, the cohesiveness of the approach, and its widely disseminated applied protocol have created a bounded world within which "best practice" and "evidence based" programs refer to programs successful vis a vis criteria specified within the model—even while youth violence itself continues apace.

Problem Behavior Syndrome and Behavioral Cluster Models

A second group of theoretical models represents some movement towards recognizing that exposure to risk factors *creates* a meaningful context for action beyond mechanistic behavioral responses to that exposure. These models have viewed risk for substance abuse, delinquency, early sexual activity and other practices together as a "problem behavior syndrome" of one form or another, where the risk factors and trajectories are similar and/or overlapping (Jessor & Jessor 1977; Donovan and Jessor 1985; Jessor et al., 1991; Donovan et al., 1988; Elliott et al., 1989), for example, in peer clusters (Oetting and Beauvais 1986, 1987). Hawkins and Catalano (1996), for example, noted that of the 19 risk factors they identified for adolescent problem behavior, 16 are common for both delinquency and substance abuse; 11 are common for violence and substance abuse; and 9 are common for all three. These approaches are different than the others described above in part because they understand risk behavior not just as discrete or specific behaviors, but as elements within a pattern that reflects a general relationship of some kind between the individuals involved in these behaviors and the "conventional world", that is, the segment of society for which the risk behaviors are viewed as negative or antisocial. (Keeping in mind that it is not just risk behavior, viewed objectively, that is at issue, for there are many risk behaviors that are conventionally viewed as acceptable, even admirable.)

Viewing risk behavior as reflective of an operative worldview draws from Hirschi (1969) and other classic social control models in their reference to the strength or weakness of bonds (or commitment) to conventional society, its values, goals, its institutions and socializing forces. Adolescents who, for a wide variety of reasons—including the frustration of aspirations due to poverty, school failure, social disorganization in the community or family, or other such factors—are said to have a low commitment to conventional society and do not endorse its values are more likely to engage in delinquent behavior and substance abuse, and are more likely to have stronger bonds to peers who are involved in the same behavior patterns (see Elliott et al., 1985, 1989; Hawkins and Weis, 1985). This certainly makes intuitive sense; however, there is little in the way of followup about what that kind of "worldview" may entail, whether or not it represents a rational response to social conditions, what the relationship is between worldview and peer bonds, and how it may interact with constructs of self and motivation for action.

Self-Concept Models

Going beyond the syndrome or cluster theories is another body of research that seeks to understand an internal dynamic behind such clusterings of behavior and risk factors (interestingly, the bulk of this research occurred in the 1980s and early 1990s and has not been pursued extensively since). A key construct in this research is *self-concept*. Markus and Wurf (1987) describe self-concept as more dynamic than simply a reflection of behavior; because it *mediates and regulates* behavior. "It interprets and organizes self-relevant actions and experiences; it has motivational consequences, providing the incentives, standards, plans, rules and scripts for behavior; and it adjusts in response to challenges from the social environment" (Ibid, 299–300). It is an interpretive structure that mediates significant intrapersonal processes (e.g., information processing, affect, motivation) as well as many interpersonal processes (e.g., social perception; choice of situation, partner, and interaction strategy; reaction to feedback).

The self-concept has been said to consist of images, schemas, prototypes, theories, goals, tasks, and other forms (Ibid and, for example, Markus & Sentis 1982, Markus 1983, Epstein 1980, Carver & Scheier 1981, Greenwald & Pratkanis 1984, Kihlstrom & Cantor 1984, and others). Whatever the form, it is viewed as a dynamic structure implicated in all social information processing. Markus and Nurius (1986) posit that an individual's array of self-representations also include *possible selves*—that is, representations about selves that could be, should be, are not desirable, and so on, or that represent past, current or future selves. These, according to Markus (1987) serve as incentives or motivation for behavior.

But where do these representations come from? The sources cited in much of the literature on this subject from psychology are limited to internal physiological and cognitive processes or indirect learning (e.g., Bandura 1977, 1986; Anderson 1984a and b), including self-assessments (Trope 1983) or specific types of social interactions and social comparisons (McGuire 1984; Suls & Miller 1977; Schoeneman 1981). This leaves wanting the question of *mechanisms* through which broader sociocultural information about possible selves is processed and incorporated.

Oyserman & Markus (1990) made the link between self-concept and delinquent behavior in adolescents, including violence, by proposing self-concept as a construct that could organize the diverse explanations for delinquency (as described in this review). The "task of adolescence", as it were, is to "try on," experiment, and move towards resolving the question of identity/social role (Erikson 1968). Thus the "possible selves" element of the self-concept is said to be highly salient. If an adolescent is able to construct satisfying possible selves in the "conventional domains" of family, friends or school, these will serve as motivational resources in a successful transition to adulthood. If not, the adolescent may seek alternative ways to define the self. A pattern of delinquency and violence is one such alternative route towards positive self-definition. "Through

rebellious activity, adolescents can define themselves as adventurous, independent, powerful, tough, or in control, and success at delinquent activity can bring with it considerable prestige among one's peers" (Ibid, 114; Hirschi, 1969; Sutherland & Cressey, 1978).

Closer to the integrative approach to violence and identity advocated in this paper, self-concept theorists have also described the process of youth identity formation within specific social contexts. In particular, Oyserman and Packer (1996) explain the way in which the sociocultural group or context serves as a semiotic mediator, assigning meanings, possibilities and values to different patterns of action and thus providing a frame for interpreting and generating action. Drawing from the theories of Ogbu (1991) and Bourdieu (1990; 1977) among others, they note that the identity-formation process is connected to the limits inherent in specific social fields as well; thus, for example, in high poverty situations where academic success, generally speaking, may not be perceived as related significantly to available life-paths, then the behavior patterns and meanings associated with academic success may not be valorized. By contrast, behaviors and meanings associated with life-paths that are viewed as salient will be more highly valorized. In a circumscribed social world where violence is connected to such life-paths, it will have a correspondingly higher social value and thus individual decisions to engage in violence are likely to be influenced accordingly. This is close to some of the work described in the next section connecting social ecology, street codes and identities (e.g., Wilkinson 2004), and to the integrative approach I discuss as well. A primary difference is that the possible selves construct has been operationalized via defined typologies of self—feared selves, expected selves, the popular self, etc., for purposes of assessing relationships between specific typologies and behavior. Although this provides a useful tool for comparative research, it may also limit the kinds of data obtained about the role and types of possible identities. [That limitation may be mitigated by a new version of the Possible Selves Questionnaire (PSQ) called the PSQ-QE, for "Qualitative Extension," in which the respondent is asked to provide an open-ended description of their most important future possible self and its meaning to them (see Kurtines et al. in press).]

Socioecological Models

The self-concept theorists, particularly in the more recent work (e.g., Oyserman & Packer 1996) move towards a connection with an important body of theory that centers on the relationship between specific risk behaviors, particularly violence and drug dealing, and social position; that is, where the nature of the involvement in violence and its causal constellation differ by the social position of particular groups, and the political-economic context that shapes marginality and alterity. In this sense, the "possible selves" aspect of self-concept (to use Oyserman & Markus' terminology) is directly influenced by socioeconomic constraints present in particular communities. For example, it has been argued that drug use/involvement is motivated more powerfully by economic factors for minority youth than for nonminority youth. Research has shown that experimental drug use among adolescents is *positively* related to socioeconomic status (Baumrind 1985; Kaplan et. al. 1986; Simcha–Fagan et. al. 1986); that is, the kind of drug use characteristic of lower SES youth is less experimental and more connected to drug trafficking. And, clearly, drug trafficking places youth at much higher risk for violence (Herrekhol et al., 2000; Blumstein 1995; Spunt et al., 1990; Goldstein, 1985). The aggregation of conditions that promote a co-occurrence of risk behaviors has been described in other contexts by Singer as a *syndemic* (Singer 1994).

These arguments also draw from theories concerning the isolated and uniformly poverty-ridden nature of inner city "underclass" communities (Wilson 1987; Sampson & Wilson 1995), where economic opportunities are so limited and there is a historical pattern of disconnection from mainstream economic activity, that drug selling and other aspects of the "street economy" become the dominant playing field for achievement and status (see also Bourgois 1996, 1989; Anderson 1999; 1992, 1990; Fagan 1992; Fagan & Wilkinson 1998; Edberg 1992), and thus have a strong role in the development and perpetuation of norms and attitudes about violence. Some of the work in this area describes "codes of the street" that govern violent or potentially violent interactions, with reference to the immediate social context of such codes.

Data on homicide patterns offer very strong support for both the socioecological models and, by extension, the issues of adolescent identity that are closely tied to them. For example, a number of studies have documented the general increase in gun use by youth following the steep rise in *juvenile* homicide from the mid-1980s to the mid-1990s (Cook & Laub 2001; Blumstein 1995 and 2001; Blumstein & Waller 2000), and the subsequent incorporation of guns as part of the norm for violent interaction even well after the decline of the crack boom and its related violence (Fagan & Wilkinson 1998). Thus the codes or culture of the street now include the use of guns as routine.

Several theorists working from a socio-ecological approach do in fact connect the structural context to identity. Messerschmidt (1993; 1997) described violence and crime as a means to achieve an appropriate performance of male gender where other routes are circumscribed. Wilkinson's rich interview data from interviews with violent offenders is an exploration of the ways in which violence—and gun violence in particular—becomes such an important tool for negotiating personal status (Wilkinson 2004).

Social-Cognitive Models

Lastly, while focusing on different, yet related aspects of violent behavior, social-cognitive models of violence focus on decision-making, reasoning and other cognitive processes surrounding acts of aggression. In what is generally called the social information processing model of aggression (e.g., Crick & Dodge 1994; Crick & Dodge 1996, also Coie & Dodge 1998), aggressive behavior is an output of an information processing sequence that includes the encoding and appraisal of social/behavioral cues followed by selection and enactment of responses—based on underlying cognitive schemata. Aggressive behavior is said to result from difficulties in coding and interpretation of social cues, or to a limited repertoire of nonaggressive behavioral response options. Interpretation of cues and selection of responses is, not surprisingly, related to normative beliefs about aggression; and in numerous studies, aggressive behavior in youth has been related to beliefs about the legitimacy of aggression (see, for example, Huesmann & Guerra, 1997; Farrington, 1995; Lochman & Dodge, 1994; Slaby & Guerra, 1988). Social-cognitive approaches also focus on relationships between emotion and cognition (Bandura et al., 2001).

Thankfully, the focus on decision making and cognitive processes is not entirely decontextualized. For example, several aspects of the environmental context, such as prevalence of violence in the community, utility of violence for achieving desired outcomes, significant others' (e.g., peers) perceptions of violence, and consequences of violence involvement, are viewed as having implications for youth beliefs about aggressive behavior and their involvement in violence (Wilkinson 2004 also addresses the event-context in this manner). Witnessing community violence has been linked with normative beliefs about aggression, aggressive fantasies, and involvement in violence (Guerra, Heusmann, & Spindler 2003), with beliefs about aggression partly mediating the association between community violence exposure and aggressive behavior (Guerra et al., 2003). Likewise, perceived neighborhood danger has been associated with positive beliefs about aggression which, in turn, have been linked with aggressive behavior (Colder, Mott, & Levy 2000).

Yet even though there are links made between cognitive processes and certain external conditions or exposures, violent behavior is often still framed as a kind of "error in process" or "error in perception," or an interpretation linked to specific attitudes or norms, as if those attitudes or norms existed as discrete information processing inputs. There is here, to use a common metaphor, an excessive focus on the trees and not the forest.

REFERENCES

Anderson E. (1999). Violence and the inner city street code. Chicago, IL: University of Chicago Press.

Anderson, E. (1992). The story of John Turner. In A.V. Harrell and G.E. Peterson (Eds.), Drugs, crime and social isolation. Washington, DC: Urban Institute Press.

Anderson, E. (1990). Streetwise: Race, class and change in an urban community. Chicago: University of Chicago Press.

Anderson, S.M. (1984a). Self-knowledge and social inference. I: The impact of cognitive/affective and behavioral data. Journal of Personality and Social Psychology 46, 2280–2293.

Anderson, S.M. (1984b). Self-knowledge and social inference. II: The diagnosticity of cognitive/affective and behavioral data. Journal of Personality and Social Psychology 46, 294–307.

Bandura, A.; G.V. Caprara; C. Barbaranelli; and C. Regalia. (2001). Social–cognitive regulatory systems governing transgressive behavior. Journal of Personality and Social Psychology 80, 125–35.

Bandura, A. (1986). Social foundations of thought and action: A social cognitive theory. Englewood Cliffs, NJ: Prentice-Hall.

Bandura, A. (1977). Social learning theory. Englewood Cliffs, NJ: Prentice-Hall.

Baumrind, D. (1985). Familial antecedents of adolescent drug use: A developmental perspective. In C.L. Jones & R.J. Battjes (Eds.), Etiology of drug abuse: implications for prevention (pp. 13–44). Rockville, MD: National Institute on Drug Abuse.

Beier, S.R., Rosenfeld, W.D., Spitalny, K.C., Zansky, S.M., & Bontemp, A.N. (2000). The potential role of an adult mentor in influencing high risk behavior in adolescents. Annals of Pediatrics and Adolescent Medicine 154(4), 327–331.

Bell, C.C. & Jenkins, E.J. (1993). Community violence and children on Chicago's Southside. Psychiatry 56, 46–54.

Benard, B. Fall (1996). Mentoring: New study shows the power of relationship to make a difference. Research Report. Berkeley, CA: Resiliency Associates.

Benard, Bonnie (1991). Fostering resiliency in kids: Protective factors in the family, school, and community. Unpublished paper.

Benson, P., Galbraith, J., & Espeland, P. (1994). What kids need to succeed. Search Institute and Free Spirit Publishing, Inc.

Blumstein, A. (2001). Why is crime falling? – Or is it? Perspectives on Crime and Justice Lecture Series. Washington, DC: National Institute of Justice.

Blumstein, A. & Walkman, J. (Eds.) (2000). The crime drop in America. New York: Cambridge University Press.

Blumstein, A. (1995). Youth violence, guns, and the illicit-drug industry. Journal of Criminal Law and Criminology, 86, 10–36.

Bourdieu, P. (1990). The logic of practice. (Trans. R. Nice.) Cambridge, England: Polity (originally published 1980).

Bourgois, P. (1996). In search of respect: Selling crack in el barrio. Cambridge: Cambridge University Press.

Bourgois, P. (1989). In search of Horatio Alger: Culture and ideology in the crack economy. Contemporary Drug Problems, 16(4), 619–50.

Brook, J.S., Brook, D.W., Gordon, A.S., Whiteman, M., & Cohen, P. (1990). The psychosocial etiology of adolescent drug abuse use: A family interactional approach. Genetic, Social, and General Psychology Monographs, 116, 111–267.

Carver, C.S. and Scheier, M.F. (1981). Attention and self-regulation: A control theory approach to human behavior. New York: Springer-Verlag.

Catalano, R.F. and Hawkins, J.D. (1995). Risk focused prevention: Using the social development strategy. Seattle, WA: Developmental Research and Programs, Inc.

Coie, J.D., and K.A. Dodge. (1998). Aggression and antisocial behavior. In W. Damon and N Eisenberg (Eds.). Handbook of child psychology: Vol.3. Social, emotional and personality development. New York: Wiley, 779–862.

Colder, C.R.; J. Mott; and S. Levy. (2000). The relation of perceived neighborhood danger to childhood aggression. American Journal of Community Psychology 28(1), 83–103.

Cook, P.J., and Laub, J.H. August (2001). After the epidemic: recent trends in youth violence in the United States. Working Paper SAN01-22, Terry Sanford Institute of Public Policy. Durham, NC: Duke University.

Crick, N.R. and Dodge, K.A. (1994). A review and reformulation of social information-processing mechanisms in children's social adjustment. Psychological Bulletin 115, 74–101.

Crick, N.R., and Dodge, K.A. (1996). Social information processing mechanisms in reactive and proactive aggression. Child Development 67, 993–1002.

Dembo, R., Williams, L., LaVoie, L., Berry, E., Getreu, A., Wish, E.D., Schmeidler, J., and Washburn, M. (1989). Physical abuse, sexual victimization, and illicit drug use: Replication of a structural analysis among a new sample of high risk youth. Violence and Victims (4), 2.

Donovan, J.E., and Jessor, R. (1985). The structure of problem behavior in adolescence and young adulthood. Journal of Consulting and Clinical Psychology 53, 890–904.

Donovan, J.E., Jessor, R., and Costa, F.M. (1988). Syndrome of problem behavior in adolescence: A replication. Journal of Consulting and Clinical Psychology 56(5), 762–765.

Dryfoos, J.G. (1990). Adolescents at risk: Prevalence and prevention. New York: Oxford University Press.

Edberg, M. (1992). AIDS risk behavior among runaway youth in the Washington, DC-Baltimore Area. In Report of multi-site runaway risk behavior study. Rockville, MD: National Institute on Drug Abuse.

Elliott, D.S., Huizinga, D., and Ageton, S. (1985). Explaining delinquency and drug abuse. Beverly Hills, CA: Sage.

Elliott, D.S., Huizinga, D., and Menard, S. (1989). Multiple problem youth: Delinquency, substance use, and mental health problems. New York: Springer-Verlag.

Epstein, S. (1980). The self-concept: A review and the proposal of an integrated theory of personality. In E. Staub (Ed.), Personality: Basic issues and current research. Englewood Cliffs, NJ: Prentice-Hall.

Erikson, E.H. (1968). Identity: Youth and crisis. New York: W.W. Norton.

Fagan, J. and D. L. Wilkinson. (1998). Guns, youth violence and social identity in inner cities. In M. Tonry and M.H. Moore (Eds.), Youth violence. Chicago: University of Chicago Press.

Fagan, J. (1992). Drug selling and licit income in distressed neighborhoods: The economic lives of street-level drug users and dealers. In A.V. Harrell and G.E. Peterson (Eds.), Drugs, crime and social isolation. Washington, DC: Urban Institute Press.

Farrington, D.P. (1995). The psychosocial milieu of the offender. In J. Gunn & P.J. Taylor (Eds.), Forensic psychiatry: Clinical, legal and ethical issues (pp. 252–285). Oxford: Butterworth-Heinemann.

Garmezy, N. (1991). Resiliency and vulnerability to adverse developmental outcomes associated with poverty. American Behavioral Scientist 34(4), 416–430.

Goldstein, P. (1985). The drugs/violence nexus: A tripartite conceptual framework. Journal of Drug Issues, 493–506.

Greenwald, A.G, and Pratkanis, A.R. (1984). The self. In R.S. Wyer and T.K. Srull (Eds.), Handbook of social cognition, Vol. 3. Hillsdale, NJ: Erlbaum.

Grizenko, N., and Fisher, C. (1992). Review of studies of risk and protective factors for psychopathology in children. Canadian Journal of Psychiatry, 37, 711–721.

Guerra, N.G., Huesmann, L.R., and Spindler, A. (2003). Community violence exposure, social cognition and aggression among urban elementary school children. Child Development 74(5), 1561–1576.

Hawkins et al. (2000). Predictors of youth violence. Juvenile Justice Bulletin. Washington, DC: Office of Juvenile Justice and Delinquency Prevention.

Hawkins, J.D., Catalano, R.F., and Miller, J.Y. (1992). Risk and protective factors for alcohol and other drug problems in adolescence and early adulthood: Implications for substance abuse prevention. Psychological Bulletin 112, 64–105.

Hawkins, J.D. and Catalano, R.F. (1992). Communities that care. San Francisco, CA: Jossey-Bass.

Hawkins, J. D. and Weis, J.G. (1985). The social development model: an integrated approach to delinquency prevention. *Journal of Primary Prevention* 6, 73–97.

Herrenkhol, T.L., Maguin, E., Hill, K.G., Hawkins, J.D., Abbott, R.D., and Catalano, R.F. (2000). Developmental risk factors for youth violence. *Journal of Adolescent Health* 26, 176–186.

Hirschi, T. (1969). Causes of delinquency. Berkeley, CA: University of California Press.

Huesmann, L.R. and Guerra, N.G. (1997). Children's normative beliefs about aggression and aggressive behavior. *Journal of Personality and Social Psychology* 72, 408–419.

Jessor, R. Donovan, J., and Costa, F.M. (1991). Beyond adolescence: Problem behavior and young adult development. New York: Cambridge University Press.

Jessor, R. and Jessor, S.L. (1977). Problem behavior and psychosocial development: A longitudinal study of youth. New York: Academic Press.

Kaplan, H. B., Martin, S. S., Johnson, R. J., and Robbins, C. (1986). Escalation of marijuana use: Application of a general theory of deviant behavior. *Journal of Health and Social Behavior,* 27, 44–61.

Kihlstrom, J.F., and Cantor, N. (1984). Mental representations of the self. *Adv. Exp. Social Psychology* 17, 1–47.

Kumpfer, K.L., & Turner, C.W. (1990–1991). The social ecology model of adolescent substance abuse: implications for prevention. *International Journal of Addictions* 25, 435–463.

Kurtines WM et al. In press. Promoting identity development in troubled youth: A developmental intervention science approach. *Identity: An international journal of theory and research.*

Lipsey, M.W., and J.H. Derzon. (1998). Predictors of serious delinquency in adolescence and early adulthood: A synthesis of longitudinal research. In R. Loeber and D.P. Farrington (Eds.), Serious and violent juvenile offenders: Risk factors and successful interventions. Thousand Oaks, CA: Sage Publications.

Lochman, J.E. and Dodge, K.A. (1994). Social-cognitive processes of severely violent, moderately aggressive and non-aggressive boys. *Journal of Consulting and Clinical Psychology* 62: 366–374.

Loeber, R. and Hay, D.F. (1997). Key issues in the development of aggression and violence from childhood to early adulthood. *Annual Review of Psychology* 48, 371–10.

Markus, H. and Wurf, E. (1987). The dynamic self-concept: A social-psychological perspective. *Annual Review of Psychology* 38, 299–337.

Markus, H., and Nurius, P. (1986). Possible selves. *American Psychologist* 41, 954–69.

Markus, H. (1983). Self-knowledge: An expanded view. *Journal of Personality* 51, 543–65.

Markus, H. and Sentis, K. (1982). The self in social information processing. In Suls J. (Ed.) Psychological perspectives on the self, Vol I. Hillsdale (pp. 41–70). New Jersey: Erlbaum.

McGuire, W.J. (1984). Search for the self: going beyond self-esteem and the reactive self. In R.A. Zucker, J Aronoff, A I Rabin (Eds.), Personality and the prediction of behavior. New York: Academic Press.

Messerschmidt JW. (1997). Crime as structured action. Thousand Oaks, CA: Sage Publications.

Messerschmidt JW. (1993). Masculinities and crime: Critique and reconceptualization of theory. Lanham, MD: Rowman & Littlefield.

Oetting, E.R. and Beauvais, F. (1987). Peer cluster theory, socialization characteristics and adolescent drug use: A path analysis. *Journal of Counseling Psychology* 34(2), 205–220.

Ogbu, J.U. (1991). Minority coping responses and school experience. *Journal of Psychohistory* 18, 433–456.

Osofsky, J.D., and Fenichel, E. (Eds). (1994). *Caring for Infants and Toddlers in Violent Environments: Hurt, Healing and Hope.* Arlington, VA: Zero to Three/National Center for Clinical Infant Programs.

Oyserman, D. and Packer, M.J. (1996). Social cognition and self-concept: A socially contextualized model of identity. In J.L. Nye and A.M. Brower (Eds.), What's social about social cognition? Research on socially shared cognition in small groups. Thousand Oaks, CA: Sage Publications.

Oyserman, D. and Markus, H. (1990). Possible selves and delinquency. *Journal of Personality and Social Psychology* 59(1), 112–125.

Petraitis, J., Flay, B.R., and Miller, T.Q. (1995). Reviewing theories of adolescent substance use: Organizing pieces in the puzzle. *Psychological Bulletin,* 117(1), 67–86.

Pransky, J. (1991). Prevention: The critical need. Springfield, MO: Burrell Foundation and Paradigm Press.

Sampson R.J., and Wilson, W.J. (1995). Race, crime and urban inequality. In J.H.R. Peterson (Ed.), Crime and inequality. Stanford, CA: Stanford University Press.

Schoeneman, T.J. (1981). Reports of the sources of self-knowledge. *Journal of Personality* 49, 284–94.

Search Institute. (1998). Developmental assets: An investment in youth. January 4, 1999. http://www.search-institute.org/assets/index.htm.

Simcha-Fagan, O., Gersten, J. C., and Langer, T. S. (1986). Early precursors and concurrent correlates of patterns of illicit drug use in adolescents. *The Journal of Drug Issues,* 16, 7–28.

Singer, M. (1994). AIDS and the health crisis of the U.S. urban poor: The perspective of critical medical anthropology. *Social Science and Medicine* 39(7), 931–948.

Slaby, R.G., and Guerra, N.G. (1988). Cognitive mediators of aggression in adolescent offenders: 1 Assessment. *Developmental Psychology* 24, 580–588.

Spatz-Widom, C. (1989). Does violence beget violence? A critical examination of the literature. *Psychological Bulletin* 106(1), 3–28.

Spunt, B.J., Goldstein, P.J., Bellucci, P.A., Miller, T. (1990). Race/ethnicity and gender differences in the drugs-violence relationship. *Journal of Psychoactive Drugs,* 22(3), 291–303.

Suls, J.M. and Miller, R.L.K. (Eds.). (1977). Social comparison processes. Washington, DC: Hemisphere.

Sutherland, E.H. and Cressey, D.R. (1978). Criminology. Philadelphia, PA: Lippincott.

Tolan, P., and Guerra, N. (1994). What works in reducing adolescent violence: An empirical review of the field. Report to the center for the study and prevention of violence, University of Illinois at Chicago.

Trope, Y. (1983). Self-assessment in achievement behavior. In J. Suls and A.G. Greenwald (Eds.), Psychological Perspectives on the Self, Vol. 2 (pp. 93–121) Hillsdale, NJ: Erlbaum.

Wilkinson D.L. (2004). Guns, violence and identity among African American and Latino youth. New York: LFB Scholarly Publishing LLC.

Wilson, W.J. (1987). The truly disadvantaged: The inner city, the underclass, and public policy. Chicago: University of Chicago Press.

Yoshikawa, H. (1994). Prevention as cumulative protection: Effects of early family support and education on chronic delinquency and its risks. *Psychological Bulletin* 115, 28–54.

Youth Violence in America

Source: Excerpt from Tonry, M., & Moore, M. (1998). "Youth Violence in America." In M. Tonry and M. Moore (Eds.), *Youth Violence.* Chicago: The University of Chicago Press. pp. 174–188.

IV. UNDERSTANDING THE EPIDEMIC OF YOUTH VIOLENCE

The crisis of youth gun violence reflects broader trends in youth violence but also significant changes in material conditions and social controls in the communities where gun violence is most common. Understanding youth gun violence requires that we also understand the dynamic contexts of these neighborhoods, the influence of these social processes on socialization, social control, and behavior, and the role of guns in shaping norms and behaviors. Youth gun violence is central to the ecological background of many neighborhoods and also to the developmental landscape that shapes behavioral expectancies and scripts.

A. Guns as Cues of Danger

The development of an ecology of danger reflects the confluence and interaction of several sources of contagion. First is the contagion of fear. Weapons serve as an environmental cue that in turn may increase aggressiveness (Slaby and Roedell 1982). Adolescents presume that their counterparts are armed and, if not, could easily become armed. They also assume that other adolescents are willing to use guns, often at a low threshold of provocation.

Second is the contagion of gun behaviors themselves. The use of guns has instrumental value that is communicated through urban "myths" and also through the incorporation of gun violence into the social discourse of everyday life among preadolescents and adolescents. Guns are widely available and frequently displayed. They are salient symbols of power and status, and strategic means of gaining status, domination, or material goods.

Third is the contagion of violent identities, and the eclipsing or devaluation of other identities in increasingly socially isolated neighborhoods. These identities reinforce the dominance hierarchy built on "toughness" and violence, and its salience devalues other identities. Those unwilling to adopt at least some dimensions of this identity are vulnerable to physical attack. Accordingly, violent identities are not simply affective styles and social choices, but strategic necessities to navigate through everyday dangers. The complexities of developing positive social and personal identities among inner-city males is both structurally and situationally determined. Our data and previous research suggests that for inner-city males, prestige is granted to those who are tough, who have gained respect by proving their toughness, and who reenact their appropriate role in public. Majors and Billson (1992) explain the structural difficulties young African American males encounter in identity development. They state: "Masculine attainment refers to the persistent quest for gender identity among all American males. Being a male means to be responsible and a good provider for self and family. For black males, this is not a straightforward achievement. Outlets for achieving masculine pride and identity, especially in political, economic, and educational systems, are more fully available to white males than to black males. . . . The black male's path toward manhood is lined with pitfalls of racism and discrimination, negative self-image, guilt, shame, and fear" (Majors and Billson 1992, p. 31).

One important development is a breakdown in the age grading of behaviors, where traditional segmentation of younger adolescents from older ones, and behavioral transitions from one developmental stage to the next, are short-circuited by the strategic presence of weapons.

The street environment provides the "classroom" for violent "schooling" and learning about manhood. Elsewhere we present a conceptual model for understanding the relationship between age and violence in this context (see Wilkinson 1997b). Mixed age interactions play an important role in this process. Older adolescents and young adults provide modeling influences as well as more direct effects. We found that they exert downward pressure on others their own age and younger through identity challenges which, in part, shape the social identities for both parties. At younger ages, boys are pushing upward for status by challenging boys a few years older.

The social meanings violent events reach a broader audience than those immediately present in a situation. Each violent event or potentially violent interaction provides a lesson for the participants, firsthand observers, vicarious observers, and others influenced by the communication of stories about the situation which may follow. Children learn from both personal experience and observing others using violence to "make" their social identity or "break" someone else's identity on the street. In addition, we have attempted to illustrate what happens when an identity challenge occurs for both primary actors in the situation. We describe three different types of performance that may be given in a violent event: poor, successful, and extraordinary performance. Again, guns define what constitutes each class of violent performance uniquely compared to a nongun performance (see Wilkinson 1997b).

Gun use may involve "crossing a line" or giving what we call an extraordinary performance that shifts one's view of oneself from a "punk" or even "cool/holding your own" to "crazy" or "wild." Guns were used by many as a resource for improving performance. We hypothesize that the abundance of guns in these neighborhoods have increased the severity for violent performances. For the majority of our sample, guns became relevant for conflict resolution around the age of fourteen.

B. The Complexities of Adolescent Identity Development

The maintenance and reinforcement of violent identities is made possible by an effective sociocultural dynamic that sets forth a code that includes both behaviors and the means of resolving violations of the code. The illustrations in this chapter show the strong influence of street code, similar to the codes identified by Anderson (1994, in this volume), over the behaviors of young children, adolescents, and young adults. Children growing up in this environment learn these codes, or behavioral-affective systems, by navigating their way through interpersonal situations which oftentimes involve violence encounters.

Delinquency research in earlier eras showed how conventional and deviant behaviors often lived side by side within groups and also within individuals (Cohen 1955; Cloward and Ohlin 1960). One effect of "danger" as a dominant ecological marker is the difficulty that adolescents face in maintaining that duality of behavior and of orientation. The street code has a functional purpose for attaining status and avoiding danger, even for adolescents who harbor conventional attitudes and goals. Negotiating safety within this context is extremely difficult, especially when much of the social activity available to young men who have left school and are "hanging out" on the inner-city street corner involves expressing dominance over others. But the opportunities for dual identities are narrow. The social isolation of areas of concentrated poverty has given rise to oppositional cultures that devalue conventional success and even interpret conventional success as a sign of weakness. For adolescents who may want to have one foot in the conventional world and the other on the street, this balancing act has become not only difficult but also dangerous. The effects are a hardening of street codes and an eclipsing of other avenues for social status and respect.

C. Research and Intervention on Adolescent Gun Violence

These perspectives suggest specific directions for research and interventions. The development of scripts, the contingencies within scripts that lead to violence, the diffusion and contagion of lethal violence, and the role of violence in both scripts themselves and the contingencies that evoke them, should be specific foci of prevention and intervention efforts. Because fun events are different from other violent events (Fagan and Wilkinson 1997; Wilkinson 1997a, 1997b), these efforts should focus on guns.

Focusing on the role of guns within scripts assumes that guns may alter scripts in several ways. For example, guns may change the contingencies and reactions to provocations or threats, and change strategic thinking about the intentions and actions of the other person in the dispute. The presence of guns in social interactions may also produce "moral" judgments that justify aggressive, proactive actions. Accordingly, the development of interventions should be specific to the contexts and contingencies of *gun* events, rather than simply interpersonal conflicts or disputes.

For example, decisions involving firearms often are effected under conditions of angry arousal (i.e., "hot cognitions") and intensified emotional states. In many cases, firearms introduce complexity in decision making introduced by the actions of third parties or the long-standing nature of disputes that erupt periodically over many months. In other cases, firearms simply trump all other logic.

Preventive interventions should address the growing reality of firearms in the ecological contexts of development of behavioral norms. Firearms present a level of danger–or strategic uncertainty–that is unequaled in events involving other weapons or in "fair fights." In other words, guns trump other decision logics in the course of a dispute. These attributes of conflict, including the presence of guns and their effects on cognition and decision making, should inform the design of preventive efforts and interventions. Contingencies in a variety of contexts should be included: schools, parties, street corner life, the workplace, and in dating situations.

Prevention and interventions should be specific to developmental stages. At early developmental stages, preventive efforts must recognize that for many youngsters with high exposure to lethal violence, the anticipation of lethal violence influences the formation of attitudes favorable to violence and scripts that explicitly incorporate lethal violence. At later developmental stages, the incorporation of strategic violence via firearms in the presentation of self can alter the course of disputes and narrow options for nonviolent behavioral choices or behavioral choices that do not include firearms or other lethal weapons.

Prevention and intervention efforts should be built on a foundation of research that also specifically addresses gun violence. This research should address several concerns. First, comparison of gun and nongun events within persons can illustrate how guns shape decision making. Second, sampling plans should generate data across both social networks and neighborhoods. If diffusion and contagion are central to the dynamics of gun violence, then research should address how these processes link across networks of adolescents and also how neighborhood contexts shape interactions within and across social networks where much violence unfolds.

The important role of age-grading also suggests longitudinal designs with both younger and older cohorts. If identity is a central focus of these dynamics, research with younger children is necessary to assess how behavioral progressions are tied to personality development and situational avoidance techniques. The interactions of adolescents across age cohorts also is an important point of diffusion of behavioral norms and identity development. The development of scripts at specific age junctures also is important.

Other methods also can help understand processes of contagion and diffusion of "violent identities" and behavioral norms surrounding the use of guns. For example, capture-recapture designs may inform us about the extent to which vi-

olence transgresses social networks, neighborhood boundaries, and age strata.

Finally, the development of prevention efforts should be based on "hot cognitions" that better typify the types of situations in which guns are used. Research on the avoidance of violence, even in the face of weapons and other strong cues and motivations, should be central to prevention theory.

D. Conclusion

While youth violence has always been with us, the modern version of it seems distinctly different: the epidemic of adolescent violence is more lethal, in large part due to the rise of gun violence by adolescents. In this essay, we provide perspective and data on the role of guns in shaping the current epidemic of youth violence. At the descriptive level, the answer is clear: Adolescents in cities are possessing and carrying guns on a large scale, guns often are at the scene of youth violence, and guns often are being used. This is historically unique in the United States, with significant impacts on an entire generation of adolescents. The impacts are most seriously felt among African American youths in the nation's inner cities.

It is logical and important to ask whether an exogenous increase in gun availability fueled the increase in youth violence. If this were true, then, regardless of its initial role in causing the epidemic, reducing the availability of guns to kids would in turn reduce the levels and seriousness of youth violence. However, we know little about changes in gun availability to adolescents; estimating supply-side effects is difficult. Ethnographic reports show a steadily increasing possession of guns by youths, but little insight into how guns were obtained.

Instead, we consider competing hypotheses that see a less central (but not insignificant) role of guns in initiating, sustaining, or elevating the epidemic of youth violence. These include the idea that the demand for guns among youth was driven up by the development of an "ecology of danger," with behavioral norms that reinforce if not call for violence, and in which popular styles of gun possession and carrying fuel beliefs that violence will be lethal. These shifts in demand, occurring in the context of widespread availability of weapons, led to increased possession, carrying, and use. Concurrently, guns became symbols of respect, power, and manhood in an emerging youth culture that sustained a continuing demand and supply side of weapons, reciprocally increasing the overall level of gun possession and the desire to use them.

This essay offers a framework to explain how the supply and demand for guns has had an impact on the overall level and seriousness of youth violence, resenting evidence both from existing literature and from original sources to help understand the complex relationship between guns and youth violence. However, the relationship is a complex one in which the effects of guns are mediated by structural factors that increase the youth demand for guns, the available supply, and culture and scripts which teach kids lethal ways to use guns. These effects appear to be large enough to justify intensive efforts to reduce availability, possession, and use of guns by American adolescents.

REFERENCES:

Anderson, Elijah. 1994. "The Code of the Streets." *Atlantic Monthly* (May), pp. 81–94.

Cloward, Richard A., and Lloyd E. Ohlin. 1960. *Delinquency and Opportunity.* Glencoe, Ill.: Free Press.

Cohen, Albert. 1955. *Delinquent Boys.* New York: Free Press.

Fagan, Jeffrey, and Deanna L. Wilkinson. 1997. "Firearms and Youth Violence." In *Handbook of Antisocial Behavior,* edited by D. Stoff, J. Belinger, and J. Maser. New York: Wiley.

Majors, R., and J. M. Billson. 1992. *Cool Pose: The Dilemmas of Black Manhood in America.* New York: Simon & Schuster.

Slaby, R.G., and W.C. Roedell. 1982. "Development and Regulation of Aggression in young Children." In *Psychological Development in the Elementary Years,* edited by J. Worrell. New York: Academic Press.

Wilkinson, Deanna L. 1997a. "Decision Making in Violent Events among Adolescent Males: A Comparison of Gun and Non-gun Events." Paper presented at the forty-ninth annual American Society of Criminology meeting, San Diego, California, November.

Wilkinson, Deanna L. 1997b. "Male Adolescent Social Identity in the Inner-City 'War Zone.' " Paper presented at the American Sociological Association annual meeting, Toronto, August.

Sociocultural and Behavioral Contexts of Condom Use in Heterosexual Married Couples in India: Challenges to the HIV Prevention Program

Source: Excerpts from Bhattacharya, G. (2004), "Sociocultural and Behavioral Contexts of Condom Use in Heterosexual Married Couples in India: Challenges to the HIV Prevention Program." *Health Education & Behavior,* Vol. 31 (1): 101–117.

HIV INFECTION AND AIDS: IMPACT IN INDIA

India has one of the highest number of HIV-infected people in the world (4). In 2001, there were an estimated 3.97 million HIV-infected people in the country, and as of September 30, 2002, a cumulative total of 40,708 AIDS cases had been reported to NACO (1,10). Cultural stigma associated with HIV testing and the public disclosure of AIDS are linked to under-reporting (2,11). It is feared that as the epidemic progresses, the number of HIV positive and AIDS patients will increase—a large population in India will be exposed to HIV infection via unprotected sex with infected partners. India has been declared the epicenter of AIDS in Asia, and interventions are urgently needed to prevent an HIV epidemic nationwide (1,2,12).

Critical Trends in HIV Prevalence Data in India

Epidemiological data highlight four critical trends for developing HIV prevention programs. First, HIV infection has shifted from the at-high-risk population, described as CSWs, truck drivers, and IDUs; to the bridge population, clients of sex workers, patients with sexually transmitted diseases (STDs), and partners of drug users; and to the general population, married women and children. As of September 2002, 88.5% of a cumulative total of 40,708 AIDS cases reported to NACO were between 15 and 44 years, and the ratio of female to male was 1:3 (1). A national behavioral surveillance survey conducted by NACO between March and August 2001 reported that 3 of every 4 participants were married—similar to data reported by the census of India in 1991 (13). For this reason, it is essential to include women and especially married women as an emerging at-high-risk group to develop any HIV infection prevention strategies in India.

Second, the prevalence of HIV-infected people throughout India shows that the virus is spreading from urban to rural areas. Because approximately 75% of India's 1 billion people live in rural areas, understanding the reasons (such as more jobs in cities, trucking, and delivery of goods) for the mobility of the population and the pathways through which HIV transmission may occur (e.g., unsafe sex with CSWs during separations from wives) is critical. For the prevention of HIV, obstacles to consistent condom use by a mobile population, mostly men, in social situations (e.g., on the roads) may be different from barriers to condom use by heterosexual married couples at home. Third, the increased number of STD patients in clinics indicates the enormity of the problem of HIV infection. One study conducted in a Delhi clinic found that 21.9% of 319 women presenting with the symptom of vaginal discharge had an STD (14). In one prenatal clinic, a 4-year prospective study found that 45% of 71 women who were 8 to 10 weeks pregnant had AIDS symptoms (15). According to a NACO report, the STD prevalence rates vary from 10% to 5% in the general population in urban communities (2). Fourth, the spread of HIV among the adult population in India varies sharply from state to state. Although overall, 1% of India is estimated to be HIV positive, in five states—Maharashtra (in the West), Tamil Nadu, Karnataka, and Andhra Pradesh (all in the South); and Manipur and Nagaland (in the Northeast)—more than 1% of the adult population is infected with HIV (2).

Unless this differential is taken into account for planning strategies, HIV prevention and treatment efforts will be inadequate in some states and inappropriate in others (16).

SOCIOCULTURAL CONTEXT

India's internal diversity of sociodemographic characteristics, traditions, and values can lead to differences in individual health behavior from region to region; create differences in sexual behavior; and thus may either heighten or reduce the vulnerability of heterosexual men and women to HIV infection. India is a linguistically and religiously diverse country. Its citizens speak 18 official languages and hundreds of dialects. According to the 1991 census, the population was 82% Hindu, 12% Muslim, 2% Christian, 2% Sikh, and 0.6% of all other religions (17). Other population characteristics, such as literacy rates and social customs (including rituals and clothing), vary from state to state.

At the same time, within that diversity, significant sociocultural commonalities are present among the entire population. These commonalities in cultural beliefs are embedded in (a) the role of women in the society and family traditions that influence differential expectations of behaviors for men and women and thus may make decisions to use condoms more community based than individualistic; (b) sociocultural contexts that influence and shape sexual practices; (c) the holistic perception of health, the role of semen in maintaining sexual health, and the possible conflict that may be attributed to condom use (18,19) and (d) myths and cultural beliefs that HIV infection is transmitted exclusively via vaginal sex, which may overlook other HIV risk behaviors of men who have sex with men (MSMs) and IDUs in addition to CSWs. These four issues are the focus of an analysis of how beliefs develop in sociocultural contexts, the ways in which these beliefs influence sexual behavior, and how they may create barriers to the use of condoms by married heterosexual couples in India.

Role of Women

The role of women as individuals and as sexual beings, the institution of marriage, and the relationship between procreation and the position of women in the family describe the very premises of the cultural norms and values prevalent in India (19,20).

Patriarchal Family Structure

The most common patriarchal family structure in Indian society has two unique characteristics: patrilineal descent, meaning that the family name, succession, and inheritance pass from father to son, and patrivirilocal residence, meaning that after marriage, a woman lives with her husband in his father's house. This family structure instills the expected sexual behaviors that

are most relevant to understanding married women's risk of HIV infection. First, although societal norms do not encourage premarital sexual activity, a double standard is in effect. Unmarried girls are expected to remain virgins in order to maintain their "purity" and to engage in sexual activities with their husbands for procreation and motherhood. Men, on the other hand, are permitted to engage in premarital sex for the sake of gaining "experience" and learning to be sexual decision makers (19, 21). Although the official marriage act in India requires a minimum age of 18 years for women and 21 for men, the law is not obeyed. Because all Indian communities value virgin brides, parents often feel pressured to arrange for their daughters' weddings before or by the attainment of puberty (22). The early onset of coital activity and repeated sexual intercourse with infected partners further increase young women's chances of contracting the virus, even when they do not express their sexuality outside traditionally defined boundaries. Second, marriage is the institution that gives women permission to initiate sexual relationships with their partners and gain societal identity as members of their husbands' families. If women enter marriage with knowledge of HIV transmission and safer-sex practices, they may be suspected of having engaged in premarital sex. Moreover, because sons are deemed necessary to continue the family lineage, women experience family pressure to procreate after they marry and especially to bear sons. Thus, sexual activity is often not a matter of choice but a duty for married women. Third, because the patriarchal family structure allows only sons to inherit property, married women often find it economically difficult to leave their husbands even in cases of domestic violence.

Law, Rights, and Women

Ideally, law can be a potent force for changing the existing social structure; for ensuring social rights for women, such as property rights; and for improving the status of women in India. These changes, in turn, could be used as a public health practice tool and to influence social norms for healthy behavior, to identify and respond to threats that can enhance health risks, and to enforce health and safety standards (23). However, the following examples reveal the gaps in the process in India. (1) A marriage is legal and valid even if the legal ages of 18 for women and 21 for men are violated. (2) Even when Indian law permits married women to share family property, women often find it difficult to fight social customs and assert their rights within the family (24). (3) Although reported cases of violence against women, including rape, domestic violence, and dowry deaths, increase every year, legal discourses resulting in convictions remain few because of lapses in investigation and medical reports (25). (4) Indian law does not even recognize that nonconsensual sex with his wife is a crime for the husband (26).

The interpretation of the law in the dominant social culture within which such justice is sought further reinforces the expected subservient role of Indian women in the society and often shapes the perception of their sexual roles. Unless the links between legal rights and social justice issues, including reproductive health rights, in the context of gender roles in India are established, law as a tool will fail to be an instrument for the empowerment of women.

Sexual Practices, Contexts, and Condom Use

Sexual acts could mean different things to those who participate in them and different things to the same individuals in different contexts and thus could influence the practice of condom use. Beliefs associated with condom use among married women and men are discussed next.

Condoms Are Identified With Contraception

Since the early 1960s, the government of India's Family Planning and Welfare Department has advocated condoms primarily for use by men and as contraceptives to space births to married couples of reproductive age. Although family planning services have emphasized condom use, this method represented only 2% of all contraceptives used in 1994–1995. The overall use of conventional contraceptive methods did increase from 1% of the total reproductive population in 1970–1971 to 3% in 1994–1995 (22). (These figures for "conventional" methods chiefly reflect the use of condoms, and although they also include such contraceptives as diaphragms, jellies/creams, and foam tablets, the rates of use were so low that they were not reported separately.)

Condom Use Conflicts With the Desire to Procreate

Precisely because condoms are identified with birth control, married heterosexual couples may be disinclined to use them for HIV prevention. Because procreation is considered the purpose of marriage, women experience societal pressure after marriage to prove their fertility and see no reason to delay childbirth and use condoms as a contraceptive. In 1992–1993, 97% of women did not use any contraceptive before their first child was born (22,27). In India, women are expected to have at least two sons who survive to adulthood (19). This expectation influences them to undergo repeated pregnancies in the hope of bearing sons. Because 30% of all child mortality occurs under the age of 5, the fear of losing a child may influence fertility-related behaviors that have an impact on family size, birth spacing, and the nonuse of condoms as a contraceptive (22,27). Women may not use condoms because of the belief that contraception will interfere with their efforts to establish their position in the family. Such beliefs make it difficult to promote condom use for the prevention of HIV infection.

Sterilization Rules Out Contraceptive Use of Condoms

The fact that in India, sterilization is a far more widely used and preferred method among women shows that the use of condoms, even as a contraceptive, is low. The ratio of men to women who resort to sterilization underwent a dramatic reversal—from 2:1 in 1970–1971 to 1:31 in 1994–1995. During that period, sterilization sharply increased, from 8% to 30.2% of all methods used (22). The median age of sterilization for women is 27 years and is dropping. Because more than 75% of the total fertility in urban and rural areas occurs between the ages of 20 and 30, this means that women undergo sterilization during their peak reproductive years (22,27). One decisive factor for wives to undergo permanent sterilization once they have completed their families might be men's reluctance to use condoms. Sterilization may also be preferred by women as a method of contraception to men using condoms. Couples in which either the husband or wife has been sterilized may not be motivated to consider using condoms.

Condom Use Is Linked With Commercial Sex Work

Indians often perceive condoms as devices to prevent conception during "illicit" sexual encounters with female CSWs (19,27). By consistently using condoms, CSWs could reduce the risk of HIV infection for themselves and their clientele and thus prevent primary HIV infection among the population. However, because condoms are associated with CSWs, married women may think that using condoms with their husbands is not compatible with female virtue. If a woman suggests or insists that her husband use condoms, he may believe that she suspects him of having an STD or being HIV positive already. At the same time, he may accuse her of having extramarital sex and thus defying the institution of marriage (as it is understood in the Indian context). In addition, because of the widespread belief that condoms are for avoiding HIV infection during "illicit" sex with female CSWs, husbands buying condoms in stores for use with their wives may be misinterpreted as seeking sex with CSWs.

Health Beliefs and Sexual Practices

The need to understand how the internalization of individual beliefs about health and illnesses may create barriers to the use of condoms in that particular sociocultural context is described next.

Condom Use Is Believed to Interrupt the Natural Flow of Body Fluids

The cultural underpinning of health beliefs about semen in India may justify and heighten the risk of not using condoms. Scientific research has not yet substantiated this possible link between the cultural health belief system and condom use behaviors. The generalizability of any such link to the entire Indian population must also be systematically explored through studies comparing and contrasting, for example, persons of different ages, educational levels, socioeconomic status, and places of residence (urban versus rural). In the meantime, it is worthwhile to gain an overview of health beliefs that are both common throughout India and possibly relevant to condom use.

In Asian cultures, health is conceptualized as a state of balance with the natural elements of earth, fire, water, air, and metal. Good health results when the individual's body, mind, and environment function in total harmony, with the universe. Thus, some Indians may prefer to prevent illness by naturally regulating their bodies and synchronizing their various bodily functions to maintain a state of balance and harmony (19) In India, semen is called *dhatu*, which literally means "metal"— one of the five elements of nature—and is considered the highest expression of virility. Because condoms block the flow of semen and collect it, they are feared to cause an unnatural rise in body heat for men and burns for women. The disposal of semen in condoms is considered a waste of bodily powers that breaks the natural law of harmony, and men fear that condom use can make them ill (18). The extent to which the characteristics and functions of semen are acknowledged may differ among individuals, and determinants of individual differences may be related to perceived susceptibility, perceived consequences of illnesses, and the availability of information on diseases. Because any open discussions on preconceptions about sex, including semen, sexuality, and sexual practices, are taboo in India, and people's reluctance to talk about their views reinforces the sensitive nature of the issue, and also indicates the need to explore lay beliefs about health and illness.

The available research has documented that married Indian women have similar beliefs to their husband's that "body heat" should be discharged only through "natural" sexual intercourse (19). When their husbands are on the road, women believe that their husbands need sexual intercourse for entertainment and the relief of work pressures and that CSWs could fulfill that need. It may be worthwhile to study if married Indian women share the same belief as do their Thai counterparts: "Prostitutes are Better Than Lovers"(28). Such beliefs that men must release body heat through "natural" sexual intercourse may also encourage women to undergo permanent sterilization and thus not to use condoms when they have completed their families. Health promotion interventions for reducing HIV-related risks should address the cultural expectations of masculinity and virility and the complementary sexual roles of women, especially in the Indian

sociocultural context, where extramarital sex by men, although not actively encouraged, is societally tolerated and accepted by their wives.

Cultural Beliefs, Myths, and HIV Transmission

Marriage Protects One From HIV/AIDS

Strong cultural beliefs in marriage as an institution and the husband as the protector of family well-being have been found to be the driving force for the belief that a married woman cannot "get" HIV from her husband (29). This belief may encourage wives not to use condoms even within the apparently contradictory societal acceptance of their husbands' extramarital sexual practices. In the prevailing social and cultural norms, women may accept the situation as "their lot," as a punishment for sins committed in a previous lifetime, or as part of their Karma or fate (22,30). Interpretation of the situation—the husband's infidelity—as resulting from one's Karma often seems to be probably the most viable approach to accepting the situation in the cultural context in India. Because women often do not face situations when they have to make a decision, generally, coping strategies include not challenging or not changing the situation but denying or avoiding the problem (30). Educating women about the HIV risks necessitates providing them family and social support and economic survival skills that will empower them to challenge the husband's risk behavior, to encourage him to go for HIV testing and treatment, and to protect herself and the family from HIV infection.

Only Vaginal Sex Transmits HIV

Because of the widespread belief in India that the sexual mode of transmission of HIV is primarily through vaginal sex, men may not use condoms during anal sex with other sex partners (19,21). Because men believe they are not involved in any risky sex, they may find no reason to use condoms even in sexual encounters with their wives. Questions about the use of condoms often do not ask about the type of sexual practices involved or the sex partner and hence may miss data on anal sex. The promotion of safe sex must communicate specific and explicit messages on HIV risks and condom use for anal, vaginal, and oral sexual practices.

MSMs

A survey on MSMs who were engaged in MSM activities in the past 6 months in five cities—Delhi, Kolkata, Mumbai, Chennai, and Bangalore—reported that overall, 42% of the respondents were between 19 and 25 years and 39% between 26 and 35 years (31). Because of the stigma associated with same-sex activity, research indicates that MSMs in India often identify themselves as heterosexuals, marry, and engage in occasional sex with their wives to produce children (32,33). Indeed, the same NACO survey reported that one in four MSMs were married and living with their wives. Moreover, the criminalization of all acts of sodomy under Indian Penal Code 377-B makes "homosexual" practices illegal (29). MSMs often engage in anal sex practices covertly in such places as secluded parks after dark to avoid police harassment. The use of condoms is rare in such situations, and thus there is a risk for HIV transmission. MSMs, often because of their unsafe sexual practices, are a bridge population between same-sex activities and heterosexual activities with their wives to HIV infection. Because of the sensitivity associated with self-identification as MSMs in the Indian sociocultural context, it is a challenge to collect data on the full extent of the MSMs in the general population. It is promising to note that two studies are being conducted in Chennai and Mumbai that will help to develop appropriate interventions or a public health surveillance programs for this group. Implementation of the condom use program in India requires addressing the sociolegal issues surrounding the risk of HIV infection for sexual practices of men who identify themselves as married heterosexuals but also engage in MSM activities.

IDUs

IDU is the method by which infection is transmitted in 3% of all AIDS patients and is regarded as an epidemic in the northeastern Indian states of Nagaland and Manipur (1,2). The mobility of high-risk groups, such as truck drivers for business and interstate migrant workers for seeking jobs, and the close links of Indian border states with other IDU epidemic countries, including Nepal, Thailand, and Myanmar, raise serious concerns about the further spread of this emerging HIV risk-transmission mode. The lack of knowledge of IDU risks for HIV transmission and the false belief that HIV can be transmitted only by unsafe sexual practices should be emphasized in health promotion strategies.

IMPLICATIONS FOR HIV INFECTION PREVENTION

This article suggests issues that have significant implications for developing HIV infection prevention programs in India. First, the ways in which the status of women, legal discourses, sexuality, and beliefs are constructed and organized in the society are not conducive to condom use among married couples in India. Men and women may thus be vulnerable to HIV risks. Changing the perception of vulnerability to HIV risks within the institutions of marriage and family settings refers to changing these social customs and practices that are often based on the interpretation of culture (34). This "inter-

pretation" influences the sexual behavior of both men and women and is an important component of lifestyle changes as described in the population-based prevention efforts mentioned in the conceptual model. The gender role constructs and the importance of societal conformation to them have been linked to both women's and men's vulnerability to HIV worldwide (34,35).

Second, as perceptions of gender roles and social relations influence various dimensions of life (e.g., parental family, husband's family, children) and interact at various levels of intensity (e.g., bearing not only children but sons, availability of support including economic and legal resources), HIV prevention strategies need to address multiple fronts to be effective. The population-based perspective focuses on the interactions between individual, community, and environmental factors for initiating any health-related behavior changes. Changes in attitude and behavior are not immediate and require sustained and continued public health education efforts. Moreover, cultural beliefs and social norms may undergo changes over time due to increased globalization (e.g., via television, movies) and can influence gender roles—and thus, social relations of married heterosexual couples—positively (e.g., increased awareness of HIV risks) or negatively (e.g., false liberal attitudes for sexual practices) and reduce or enhance sexual risk behavior for HIV. Third, accessibility of condoms is a critical issue that influences their use when needed. In a NACO survey, more than one-third (37.4%) reported that it takes more than 30 minutes to procure a condom—the accessibility is more difficult in rural areas than in urban cities (13). The respondents reported that pharmacies and government family planning centers are the most convenient places to get a condom. Social marketing initiated by the government thus needs to be more accessible to all, regardless of rural and urban locations.

Challenges to the HIV Prevention Program

The urgent need in India is to prevent the transmission of HIV from infected heterosexual men to their monogamous regular sex partners. Although the consistent use of condoms in all sexual acts is considered the immediate strategy, the government of India must focus on ensuring secondary and tertiary care—including the identification and treatment of STD symptoms, HIV testing, and AIDS treatment and care—in policy and funding decisions. It is envisioned that changes in perceptions and beliefs related to societal mores and expectations of sexual behavior require long-term efforts. However, the government needs to evaluate the fundamental barriers to developing HIV prevention programs and to conduct more research on sexuality, traditions, and HIV risks.

REFERENCES

1. National AIDS Control Organization: *HIV/AIDS Surveillance in India*, 2002. Retrieved from http://naco.nic.in/vsnaco/indianscene/overv.htm.

2. National AIDS Control Organization: *Combating HIV/AIDS in India 2000–2001*, 2001. Retrieved from http://naco.nic.in/vsnaco/indianscene/country.htm.

3. National AIDS Control Organization: *Combating HIV/AIDS in India, 1999-2000*. New Delhi, Ministry of Health and Family Welfare, Government of India, 2000.

4. World Health Organization: *HIV/AIDS in Asia and the Pacific Region*. Geneva, Office of the Publications, World Health Organization, 2001.

5. Davis KR, Weller SC: The effectiveness of condoms in reducing heterosexual transmission of HIV. *Fam Plann Perspect* 31:272–279, 1999.

6. Parker R, Barbosa RM, Aggleton P. (eds.): *Framing the Sexual Subject: The Politics of Gender, Sexuality, and Power*. Berkeley, University of California Press, 2000. Bhattacharya/Sociocultural Contexts 115

7. Diaz R: Cultural regulation, self-regulation, and sexuality: A psychocultural model of HIV risk in Latino gay men, in Parker R, Barbosa RM, Aggleton P (eds.): *Framing the Sexual Subject: The Politics of Gender, Sexuality, and Power*. Berkeley, University of California Press, 2000, pp. 191–215.

8. Novick LF: Defining public health: Historical and contemporary developments, in Novick LF, Mays GP (eds.): *Public Health Administration: Principles for Population-Based Management* (pp. 3–33). Gaithersburg, MD, Aspen, 2001.

9. Bandura A: *Social Foundation of Thought and Action: A Social Cognitive Theory*. Englewood Cliffs, NJ: Prentice Hall, 1986.

10. National AIDS Control Organization: *HIV Estimates for Year 2001*, 2001. Retrieved from http://naco.nic.in/vsnaco/indianscene/esthiv.htm.

11. United Nations on AIDS: *HIV and AIDS-Related Stigmatization, Discrimination and Denial: Forms, Contexts and Determinants, Research Studies from Uganda and India*. Geneva, Switzerland, United Nations on AIDS, 2000.

12. United Nations on AIDS: *Report on the Global HIV/AIDS Epidemic*. Geneva, Switzerland, United Nations on AIDS, 2002.

13. National AIDS Control Organization: *Executive Summary: General Population*, 2001. Retrieved from http://naco.nic.in/vsnaco/indianscene/executive.htm.

14. Vishwanath S, Talwar V, Prasad R, Coyaji K, Elias C, De Zoysa I: Syndromic management of vaginal discharge among women in a reproductive health clinic in India. *Sex Transm Infect* 76:303–306, 2000.

15. Kumar R, Singh MM, Kaur A, Kaur M: Reproductive health behavior of rural women. *J Indian Med Assoc* 93(4):129–131, 1995.

16. The World Bank Group: *India HIV/AIDS Brief*. Retrieved from http://wb1n1018.worldbank.org/SAR/sa.nsf/All.

17. Government of India: *Census of India: General Population*. New Delhi, Office of the Registrar General, 1991.

18. Nichter M, Nichter M: Modern methods of fertility regulation: When and for whom are they appropriate? In Nichter M (ed.): *Anthropology and International Health: South Asian Case Studies*. Dordrecht, the Netherlands, Kluwer, 1989, pp. 57–82.

19. Nag M: *Sexual Behavior and AIDS in India*. New Delhi, Vikas, 1996.

20. Das Gupta M, Chen LC: Overview, in Das Gupta M, Chen LC, Krishnan TN (eds.): *Women's health in India: Risk and vulnerability*. Bombay, India, Oxford University Press, 1995, pp. 1–15.

21. Mukhopadadhyay S, Nandi R, Nundy M, Sivaramayya J: *Gender Dimensions of HIV/AIDS: A Community Based Study in Delhi*. New Delhi, Institute of Social Studies Trust, 2000.

22. Gopalan S, Shiva M (eds.): *National Profile on Women, Health and Development: Country Profile—India*. New Delhi, Voluntary Health Association of India and World Health Organization, 2000.

23. Gostin LO: Public health law, in Novick LF, Mays GP (eds.): *Public Health Administration: Principles for Population-Based Management* (pp. 140–153). Gaithersburg, MD, Aspen, 2001.

24. Gandhi N, Shah N: *The issues at stake*. New Delhi, Kali for Women, 1992.

25. Agnes F: Violence against women: Review of recent enactments, in Mukhopadhyay S (ed.): *In the Name of Justice*. New Delhi, Manohar, 1998.

26. Ramaseshan G: Some reflections on women and health, in Mukhopadhyay S (ed.): *In the Name of Justice*. New Delhi, Manohar, 1998.

27. Pachauri S: *Implementing Reproductive Health Agenda in India: The Beginning*. New York: Population Council, 1999.

28. Saengtienchai C, Knodel J, Van Landingha M, Pramualratana A: Prostitutes are better than lovers: Wives' views on the extramarital sexual behavior of Thai men, in Jackson P, Cook N (eds.): *Genders and Sexualities in Modern Thailand*. Chiang Mai, Thailand, Silkworm Books, 1999, pp. 78–92.

29. Ramasubban R: HIV/AIDS in India: Gulf between rhetoric and reality, in Pachauri S (ed.): *Implementing a Reproductive Health Agenda in India: The Beginning*. New Delhi, Population Council, 1998.

30. Chandra PS, Prasadrao PSDV: Stressors in HIV infection in a developing country: The Indian experience, in Nott KH, Vedhara K (eds.): *Psychosocial and Biomedical Interactions in HIV Infection*. Singapore, Harwood, 2000, pp. 65–78.

31. National AIDS Control Organization: *Executive Summary: MSM & IDUs*, 2001. Retrieved from http://naco.nic.in/vsnaco/indianscene/executive2.htm.

32. Asthana S, Oostvogels R: The social construction of male "homosexuality" in India: Implications for HIV transmission and prevention. *Soc Sci Med* 52:707–721, 2001.

33. Khan S: Under the blanket: Bisexualities and AIDS in India, in Aggleton P (ed.): *Bisexualities and AIDS: International Perspectives*. London: Taylor & Francis, 1996, pp. 161–177.

34. Rao Gupta G: Gender, sexuality, and HIV/AIDS: The what, the why, and how. *Can HIV/AIDS Policy Law* 5(4), 2000. Retrieved from http://www.aidslaw.ca/maincontent/otherdocs/Newwsletter/5no42000/guptadurban.htm.

35. Mane P, Aggleton P (2001): Gender and HIV/AIDS: What do men have to do with it? *Curr Sociol* 49(6):23–37.

36. Indian Network for People Living with HIV/AIDS (INP+): *A Needs Assessment Study of People Living with HIV/AIDS*. Chennai, India, Indian Network for People Living with HIV/AIDS, 2000.

37. Raju S: Men as supportive partners in reproductive health: NGOs pave the way, in Pachauri S (Ed.): *Implementing Reproductive Health Agenda in India: The Beginning*. New York, Population Council, 1999, pp. 313–333.

38. Society for Education, Welfare, and Action—Rural Research Team: *Enhancing roles and responsibilities of men in women's health*. Paper presented at the workshop on Men as Supportive Partners in Reproductive and Sexual Health, organized by the Population Council, New Delhi, India, June 1998.

39. Nath LM: The epidemic in India, in Godwin P (ed.): *The Looming Epidemic: The Impact of HIV and AIDS in India*. London, Hurst, 1998, pp. 29–64.

40. Khatri GR, Friedman TR: Controlling tuberculosis in India. *N Engl J Med* 347(18):1420–1425, 2002.

Report on the Global AIDS Epidemic

Source: Excerpt from *Report on the Global AIDS Epidemic: Executive Summary*. A UNAIDS 10th Anniversary Special Edition. 2006. pp. 10–17.

THE DECLARATION OF COMMITMENT ON HIV/AIDS: PROGRESS SINCE 2001

Leadership

Overall, leadership and political action on AIDS have increased significantly since 2001.

- Internationally, in 2005 the United Nations World Summit, the G8 industrialized countries, and the African Union all endorsed the universal access goal, while the Group of 77 countries acted to prioritize enhanced South-South cooperation on HIV prevention, treatment, care and support. Increased regional collaboration has been demonstrated by the efforts of the Pan Caribbean Partnership against HIV/AIDS; the Asia Pacific Leadership Forum on HIV/AIDS and Development; the European Union and the Commonwealth of Independent States focus on increased action against AIDS in eastern Europe; and the collaborative efforts of Latin American countries to negotiate antiretroviral drug price reductions.
- Ninety per cent of reporting countries now have a national AIDS strategy; 85% have a single national body to coordinate AIDS efforts; and 50% have a national monitoring and evaluation framework and plan.
- Systems to implement these plans remain inconsistent, however, as does civil society involvement and, specifically, involvement of people living with HIV.

HIV Prevention

While some countries have significantly increased prevention coverage, prevention programmes still reach only a small minority of those in need, and a number of prevention targets are not being reached.

- Analyses consistently show that interventions to change behaviour reduce the frequency of sexual risk behaviours. Countries that have lowered HIV incidence have benefited from the emergence of new sexual behaviour patterns—fewer commercial sex transactions in Cambodia and Thailand, delayed sexual debut in Zimbabwe, increasing emphasis on monogamy in Uganda and an increase in condom use overall.
- Most countries, however, appear to have missed the Declaration target of ensuring that 90% of young people in 2005 have access to critical HIV prevention services including services to develop the life-skills needed to reduce vulnerability to HIV. In fact, none of the 18 countries in which young people were surveyed by the Demographic Health Survey/AIDS Indicator Survey between 2001 and 2005 had knowledge levels exceeding 50%.
- UNFPA, the largest public-sector purchaser of male condoms, estimates the global supply of public-sector condoms is less than 50% of that needed and that current funding for condom procurement and distribution must increase threefold.
- More than 340 million people contract a curable sexually transmitted infection each year, with women having greater vulnerability to infection than men. Despite the fact that untreated sexually transmitted infections increase

the risk of HIV transmission by several orders of magnitude, coordination of diagnosis and treatment of sexually transmitted infections and HIV remains very low.

- There are also disturbing signs that support for HIV prevention may be diminishing in some regions. This represents a tremendous lost opportunity, as scaling up available prevention strategies in 125 low- and middle-income countries would avert an estimated 28 million new HIV infections between 2005 and 2015—more than half of those that are projected to occur during this period—and would save US$ 24 billion. Unsafe injections and contaminated blood transfusions in health-care settings are still cause for concern. National HIV prevention programmes should promote adherence to sound infection control practices in health-care settings.

Care, Support and Treatment

In recent years, AIDS has helped drive a global revolution in the delivery of complex therapy in resource-limited settings. The 2001 Declaration of Commitment on HIV/AIDS embraced equitable access to care and treatment as fundamental to an effective global HIV response. Since then, the "3 by 5" initiative, the US President's Emergency Plan for AIDS Relief, the Global Fund to Fight AIDS, Tuberculosis and Malaria, and initiatives such as employer programs have definitively demonstrated the feasibility of delivering HIV treatment in resource-limited settings.

- Between 2001 and 2005, the number of people on antiretroviral therapy in low- and middle-income countries increased from 240 000 to approximately 1.3 million.
- The number of sites providing antiretroviral drugs increased from roughly 500 in 2004 to more than 5000 by the end of 2005.
- By the end of 2005, 21 countries met the "3 by 5" target of providing treatment to at least half of those who need it.
- Expanded treatment access was estimated to have averted 250 000 to 350 000 AIDS deaths between 2003 and 2005.
- Globally, however, antiretroviral drugs still reach only one in five who need them.
- Ongoing obstacles to expanding treatment access include out-of-pocket costs for patients, the concentration of treatment sites in urban areas, and inadequate efforts to address the needs of vulnerable populations, including sex workers, men who have sex with men, injecting drug users, prisoners and refugees.
- As many second-line antiretroviral drugs remain too costly for use in many countries, further price declines are likely to be needed to sustain and expand treatment access initiatives.

- Maintaining and expanding momentum in treatment scale-up towards the universal access goal will require more leadership to overcome key barriers to treatment access through efforts to:
  - increase individual knowledge of HIV status through a sharp increase in use of voluntary HIV counseling and testing services;
  - reduce HIV stigma including fear, misinformation and discrimination against people living with or perceived to be at risk of HIV, both among health providers and among the general public;
  - build human capacity to sustain treatment through training and better use of current human resources. WHO's training tools for the Integrated Management of Adolescent and Adult Illness and the Integrated Management of Childhood Illness have enabled the training of more than 15 000 providers of HIV-related services in an integrated approach to antiretroviral therapy, care and prevention;
  - improve supply management to minimize delays in procurement and disbursement of antiretroviral drugs by building capacity to gauge future demand for antiretroviral drugs and to implement reliable procurement, delivery and supply systems; and
  - integrate HIV care with other health services to increase uptake of antiretroviral therapy and deliver more comprehensive, higher-quality care, for example by linking HIV care with tuberculosis diagnosis and treatment, and with antenatal and reproductive health care.

Human Rights

Despite some improvements between 2003 and 2005, the global AIDS response in many countries is still insufficiently grounded in human rights.

- In 18 of 21 countries surveyed from sub-Saharan Africa, the Asia-Pacific region, eastern and western Europe, and north Africa, national reports cited improvement in policies, laws and regulations to promote and protect human rights.
- Although six out of every 10 countries surveyed report the existence of laws and regulations to protect people living with HIV from discrimination, many indicate that national laws have not been fully implemented or enforced, often due to lack of budget allocations.
- Half of reporting countries also acknowledge the existence of policies that interfere with the accessibility and

effectiveness of HIV prevention and care measures, such as laws criminalizing consensual sex between males, prohibiting condom and needle access for prisoners, and using residency status to restrict access to prevention and treatment services.

Reducing Vulnerability

While funding for HIV programmes has increased in recent years, many countries fail to direct financial resources towards activities that address the prevention needs of the populations at highest risk, opting instead to prioritize more general prevention efforts that are less cost-effective and less likely to have an impact on the epidemic.

- Evidence from Uganda shows that a child who drops out of school is three times more likely to be HIV-positive in his or her twenties than a child who completes basic education. Three-quarters of responding countries have established structures to coordinate ministry of education responses to the epidemic. Yet, only 59% of these ministries in all countries and 70% in high-prevalence countries have a dedicated budget.
- In sub-Saharan Africa, 21 of 25 countries reported having reduced or eliminated school fees for vulnerable children and having implemented community-based programmes to support orphans and other vulnerable children.
- Some countries are adopting more progressive approaches to reduce vulnerability for injection drug users:

- Despite a strong commitment to compulsory treatment for drug dependence and abstinence-based programmes, Malaysia recently decided to introduce harm reduction programmes.
- In 2005, a judge in the Islamic Republic of Iran ordered that individuals who use illegal drugs no longer be targets of criminal repression but instead be treated as patients by the public health system.
- In Central Asia, the Kyrgyz Government supports needle and syringe exchange programmes in three cities and in prisons in the country.
- Overall, however, fewer than 20% of people who inject drugs received HIV prevention services, with coverage of less than 10% reported in eastern Europe and central Asia, where drug use is a major driver of the rapidly expanding epidemic; counterproductive laws and policies in some countries still prohibit substitution therapy with buprenorphine or methadone, which were added in 2005 to the WHO Model List of Essential Medicines.
- Only 10 of 24 countries that reported data for sex workers achieved at least 50% coverage of prevention services for this population.
- Public health authorities are devoting fewer resources to men who have sex with men than epidemiological evidence suggests is necessary—a short-sighted policy in light of rising HIV prevalence among this population in many countries.

Social/Behavioral Theory and Its Roots

Part 3 is a relatively brief overview of the roots and assumptions underlying the kinds of social and behavioral theories, discussed throughout the book, that are used to understand health-related behavior and to develop a wide range of health promotion programs. Understanding these roots is important because, ultimately, health promotion professionals need to make informed choices about what theories or theoretical combinations are useful in explaining health-related behavior in specific communities and circumstances. Informed choice includes knowing what the various theories and approaches can and cannot offer. The readings presented here represent a small sample of the theoretical background material for social/behavioral theory in health promotion. The first selection (Thornton, 2006) is a description of the philosophy of Karl Popper that has influenced the way scientific research and the formulation of hypotheses is done in the current tradition of Western science. The second selection is a brief discussion, from the American Psychological Association (1999), of the place of behaviorist psychology among current approaches. The third reading is from Mark Nichter (2003), a prominent public health anthropologist, on the role of culture in smoking and tobacco research. Finally, the fourth reading is an excerpt from an article by psychologist Urie Bronfenbrenner (1986) that outlines his highly influential ecological model of behavior.

Karl Popper

Source: Excerpt from Thornton, S. 2006. "Karl Popper." *The Stanford Encyclopedia of Philosophy.* http://plato .stanford.edu/entries/popper.

3. THE PROBLEM OF DEMARCATION

As Popper represents it, the central problem in the philosophy of science is that of demarcation, i.e., of distinguishing between science and what he terms 'non-science', under which heading he ranks, amongst others, logic, metaphysics, psychoanalysis, and Adler's individual psychology. Popper is unusual amongst contemporary philosophers in that he *accepts* the validity of the Humean critique of induction, and indeed, goes beyond it in arguing that induction is never actually used by the scientist. However, he does not concede that this entails the scepticism which is associated with Hume, and argues that the Baconian/Newtonian insistence on the primacy of 'pure' observation, as the initial step in the formation of theories, is completely misguided: all observation is selective and theory-laden—there are no pure or theory-free observations. In this way he destabilises the traditional view that science can be distinguished from non-science on the basis of its inductive methodology; in contradistinction to this, Popper holds that there is no unique methodology specific to science. Science, like virtually every other human, and indeed organic, activity, Popper believes, consists largely of problem-solving.

Popper, then, repudiates induction, and rejects the view that it is the characteristic method of scientific investigation and inference, and substitutes *falsifiability* in its place. It is easy, he argues, to obtain evidence in favour of virtually any theory, and he consequently holds that such 'corroboration', as he terms it, should count scientifically only if it is the positive result of a genuinely 'risky' prediction, which might conceivably have been false. For Popper, a theory is scientific only if it is refutable by a conceivable event. Every genuine test of a scientific theory, then, is logically an attempt to refute or to falsify it, and one genuine counter-instance falsifies the whole theory. In a critical sense, Popper's theory of demarcation is based upon his perception of the logical asymmetry which holds between verification and falsification: it is logically impossible to conclusively verify a universal proposition by reference to experience (as Hume saw clearly), but a single counter-instance conclusively falsifies the corresponding universal law. In a word, an exception, far from 'proving' a rule, conclusively refutes it.

Every genuine scientific theory then, in Popper's view, is *prohibitive*, in the sense that it forbids, by implication, particular events or occurrences. As such it can be tested and falsified, but never logically verified. Thus Popper stresses that it should not be inferred from the fact that a theory has withstood the most rigorous testing, for however long a period of time, that it has been verified; rather we should recognise that such a theory has received a high measure of corroboration and may be provisionally retained as the best available theory until it is finally falsified (if indeed it is ever falsified), and/or is superseded by a better theory.

Popper has always drawn a clear distinction between the *logic* of falsifiability and its *applied methodology.* The logic of his theory is utterly simple: if a single ferrous metal is unaffected by a magnetic field it cannot be the case that all ferrous metals are affected by magnetic fields. Logically speaking, a scientific law is conclusively falsifiable although it is not conclusively verifiable. Methodologically, however, the situation is much more complex: no observation is free from the possibility of error—consequently we may question whether our experimental result was what it appeared to be.

Thus, while advocating falsifiability as the criterion of demarcation for science, Popper explicitly allows for the fact that in practice a single conflicting or counter-instance is never sufficient methodologically to falsify a theory, and that scientific theories are often retained even though much of the available evidence conflicts with them, or is anomalous with respect to them. Scientific theories may, and do, arise genetically in many different ways, and the manner in which a particular scientist comes to formulate a particular theory may be of biographical interest, but it is of no consequence as far as the philosophy of science is concerned. Popper stresses in particular that there is no unique way, no single method such as induction, which functions as the route to scientific theory, a view which Einstein personally endorsed with his affirmation that 'There is no logical path leading to [the highly universal laws of science]. They can only be reached by intuition, based upon something like an intellectual love of the objects of experience'. Science, in Popper's view, starts with problems rather than with observations—it is, indeed, precisely in the context of grappling with a problem that the scientist makes observations in the first instance: his observations are selectively designed to test the extent to which a given theory functions as a satisfactory solution to a given problem.

On this criterion of demarcation physics, chemistry, and (non-introspective) psychology, amongst others, are sciences, psychoanalysis is a pre-science (i.e., it undoubtedly contains useful and informative truths, but until such time as psychoanalytical theories can be formulated in such a manner as to be falsifiable, they will not attain the status of scientific theories), and astrology and phrenology are pseudo-sciences. Formally, then, Popper's theory of demarcation may be articulated as follows: where a 'basic statement' is to be understood as a particular observation-report, then we may say that a theory is scientific if and only if it divides the class of basic statements into the following two non-empty sub-classes: (a) the class of all those basic statements with which it is inconsistent, or which it prohibits—this is the class of its *potential falsifiers* (i.e., those statements which, if true, falsify the whole theory), and (b) the class of those basic statements with which it is consistent, or which it permits (i.e., those statements which, if true, corroborate it, or bear it out).

4. THE GROWTH OF HUMAN KNOWLEDGE

For Popper accordingly, the growth of human knowledge proceeds from our problems and from our attempts to solve them. These attempts involve the formulation of theories which, if they are to explain anomalies which exist with respect to earlier theories, must go beyond existing knowledge and therefore require a leap of the imagination. For this reason, Popper places special emphasis on the role played by the independent creative imagination in the formulation of theory. The centrality and priority of *problems* in Popper's account of science is paramount, and it is this which leads him to characterise scientists as 'problem-solvers'. Further, since the scientist begins with problems rather than with observations or 'bare facts', Popper argues that the only logical technique which is an integral part of scientific method is that of the deductive testing of theories which are not themselves the product of any logical operation. In this deductive procedure conclusions are inferred from a tentative hypothesis. These conclusions are then compared with one another and with other relevant statements to determine whether they falsify or corroborate the hypothesis. Such conclusions are not directly compared with the facts, Popper stresses, simply because there are no 'pure' facts available; all observation-statements are theory-laden, and are as much a function of purely subjective factors (interests, expectations, wishes, etc.) as they are a function of what is objectively real.

How then does the deductive procedure work? Popper specifies four steps:

(a) The first is *formal*, a testing of the internal consistency of the theoretical system to see if it involves any contradictions.

(b) The second step is *semi-formal*, the axiomatising of the theory to distinguish between its empirical and its logical elements. In performing this step the scientist makes the logical form of the theory explicit. Failure to do this can lead to category-mistakes—the scientist ends up asking the wrong questions, and searches for empirical data where none are available. Most scientific theories contain analytic (i.e., *a priori*) and synthetic elements, and it is necessary to axiomatise them in order to distinguish the two clearly.

(c) The third step is the comparing of the new theory with existing ones to determine whether it constitutes an advance upon them. If it does not constitute such an advance, it will not be adopted. If, on the other hand, its explanatory success matches that of the existing theories, and additionally, it explains some hitherto anomalous phenomenon, or solves some hitherto unsolvable problems, it will be deemed to constitute an advance upon the existing theories, and will be adopted. Thus science involves theoretical progress. However, Popper stresses that we ascertain whether one theory is better than another by deductively testing both theories, rather than by induction. For this reason, he argues that a theory is deemed to be better than another if (while unfalsified) it has greater empirical content, and therefore greater predictive power than its rival. The classic illustration of this in physics was the replacement of Newton's theory of universal gravitation by Einstein's theory of relativity. This elucidates the nature of science as Popper sees it: at any given time there will be a number of conflicting theories or conjectures, some of which will explain more than others. The latter will consequently be provisionally adopted. In short, for Popper any theory *X* is better than a 'rival' theory *Y* if *X* has *greater empirical content*, and hence *greater predictive power*, than Y.

(d) The fourth and final step is the testing of a theory by the empirical application of the conclusions derived from it. If such conclusions are shown to be true, the theory is corroborated (but never verified). If the conclusion is shown to be false, then this is taken as a signal that the theory cannot be completely correct (logically the theory is falsified), and the scientist begins his quest for a better theory. He does not, however, *abandon* the present theory until such time as he has a better one to substitute for it. More precisely, the method of theory-testing is as follows: certain singular propositions are deduced from the new theory—these are predictions, and of special interest are those predictions which are 'risky' (in the sense of being intuitively implausible or of being startlingly novel) and experimentally testable. From amongst the latter the scientist next selects those which are not derivable from the current or existing theory—of particular importance are those which contradict the current or existing theory. He then seeks a decision as regards these and other derived statements by comparing them with the results of practical applications and experimentation. If the new predictions are borne out, then the new theory is *corroborated* (and the old one falsified), and is adopted as a working hypothesis. If the predictions are not borne out, then they fal-

sify the theory from which they are derived. Thus Popper retains an element of empiricism: for him scientific method does involve making an appeal to experience. But unlike traditional empiricists, Popper holds that experience cannot *determine* theory (i.e., we do not argue or infer from observation to theory), it rather *delimits* it: it shows which theories are false, not which theories are true. Moreover, Popper also rejects the empiricist doctrine that empirical observations are, or can be, infallible, in view of the fact that they are themselves theory-laden.

The general picture of Popper's philosophy of science, then is this: Hume's philosophy demonstrates that there is a contradiction implicit in traditional empiricism, which holds both that all knowledge is derived from experience *and* that universal propositions (including scientific laws) are verifiable by reference to experience. The contradiction, which Hume himself saw clearly, derives from the attempt to show that, notwithstanding the open-ended nature of experience, scientific laws may be construed as empirical generalisations which are in some way finally confirmable by a 'positive' experience. Popper eliminates the contradiction by rejecting the first of these principles and removing the demand for empirical verification in favour of empirical falsification in the second. Scientific theories, for him, are not inductively inferred from experience, nor is scientific experimentation carried out with a view to verifying or finally establishing the truth of theories; rather, *all knowledge is provisional, conjectural, hypothetical*—we can never finally prove our scientific theories, we can merely (provisionally) confirm or (conclusively) refute them; hence at any given time we have to choose between the potentially infinite number of theories which will explain the set of phenomena under investigation. Faced with this choice, we can only eliminate those theories which are demonstrably false, and rationally choose between the remaining, unfalsified theories. Hence Popper's emphasis on the importance of the critical spirit to science—for him critical thinking is the very essence of rationality. For it is only by critical thought that we can eliminate false theories, and determine which of the remaining theories is the best available one, in the sense of possessing the highest level of explanatory force and predictive power. It is precisely this kind of critical thinking which is conspicuous by its absence in contemporary Marxism and in psychoanalysis.

Behaviorism: The Rise and Fall of a Discipline

Source: American Psychological Association. December 1999. "Behaviorism: The Rise and Fall of a Discipline." *APA Monitor,* Vol. 30, No. 11. Also available online at http://www.apa.org/monitor/dec99/ss6.html.

Behavior theory, while still viable, no longer holds the dominance it once did in theoretical psychology.

The 20th century has seen the rise and, if not the fall, certainly the reappraisal of behaviorism in psychology. The roots of objective psychology, of which behaviorism is a part, go back to the late 19th century and the rise of experimental physiology and the transition from anecdotal methods to scientific observation in comparative psychology. The development of experimental physiology permitted the work on digestion by Ivan Pavlov and eventually to his work on conditioning.

The study of learning by psychologists like Hermann Ebbinghaus and G.E. Müeller also demonstrated the use of objective methods in psychological research. Edward L. Thorndike had an early interest in comparative psychology. As a student at Harvard, he carried out his classic experiments on trial and error learning in animals which later led to his "connectionism."

One of the results of this early experimentation was Thorndike's "law of effect," the idea that rewarded behaviors are increased in an animal's repertoire while punished behaviors are decreased. (Thorndike later replaced punishment with nonreward in his definition.)

But the founding of behaviorism as a movement is credited to John B. Watson, who, while a doctoral student with James R. Angell at the University of Chicago, carried out animal research in maze learning. To Watson, the study of consciousness became irrelevant in predicting the behavior of animals and even humans.

In his 1913 manifesto, "Psychology as the Behaviorist Views It," Watson claimed that the introspective psychology was unscientific because it did not deal with objective states. He rejected all subjective states such as sensation, imagery and thought unless they could be observed by others. His movement, called Behaviorism, would be a stimulus-response psychology, dealing only with the reactions of muscles and glands to stimulus situations.

Behaviorism grew slowly before World War I, but use of behavior in applications of psychology during the war led to many people becoming converts afterwards.

In 1935, S. Smith Stevens at Harvard called on psychologists to think of behavior operationally: to represent concepts in psychology in terms of the ways they are objectively found. Thus, hunger became the amount of time without food. Operational definitions would become deeply embedded in behavioral psychology.

About the same time, Clark Hull, like an Isaac Newton, sought to provide lawful mathematical relationships to describe the nature of behavior. His research and that of Kenneth Spence centered on conditioning and the growth of habits and the factors that govern them.

Another strain of behavior research called "purposivistic behaviorism" was carried out in the early 1930s by Edward C. Tolman. Having been exposed to aspects of Gestalt and other nonbehavioral fields, Tolman approached the learning process with the idea that the animal or human was viewing the solution as a whole rather than as incremental elements to be learned to gain success.

It was Tolman who in 1938 introduced the concept of "intervening variables" into the psychological scene and urged study of their relationship to independent and dependent variables.

B.F. Skinner represented yet another branch of behaviorism. Skinner's research was concerned with the experimental analysis of behavior, and specifically, the effect of reinforcement on behavior. While Pavlovians used "hard-wired" reflexes as the raw material for conditioning, Skinner was able to use any overt action of the organism, from the smile of a baby to working harder for a grade.

Perhaps Skinner's most significant contribution to conditioning was his work on partial reinforcement. He worked with "schedules of reinforcement" to study and manipulate behavior.

If Skinner moved behavior theory away from the physiology of the organism for explanation, Donald Hebb brought behaviorism into the physiology of the organism itself. Hebb was influential in establishing physiological psychology as part of behavior theory. He worked widely with behavioral physiological psychologists Karl Lashley and Robert M. Yerkes, as well as with the brain surgeon Wilder Penfield.

In 1949, Hebb introduced his theory of cell-assembly: a group of neurons clustered together functionally because of a past history of being stimulated together. The cells are capable of functioning together for a time as a closed unit. Cell assemblies that are activated at the same time may become organized into "phase sequences," which become the basic elementary or functional units of behavior.

By the 1940s and 1950s, behaviorism reigned supreme in American experimental psychology, moving into virtually every sphere in psychology, applied and theoretical. With it came an environmentalist view, emphasizing learning and experience over inheritance of traits. But, around 1965, the tide began to turn with the coming of the "cognitive revolution" in experimental psychology.

Just why behavior theory declined is complicated. Perhaps the extensions of behavior theory into issues of everyday life demonstrated in ways the laboratory could not that the extant behavior theories were overly simplistic and inadequate, particularly as they applied to human beings. Psychologists sought something more to explain the complexity of human conduct.

At the turn of the new century, behavior theory, while still viable, no longer holds the dominance it once did in theoretical psychology. Applications, such as behavior modification, have remained fruitful, although even in the clinical area, more cognitively oriented therapies and approaches are gaining favor.

FURTHER READING:

Mills, J.A. (1999). Control: A history of behavioral psychology. New York: New York University Press.

Hilgard, E.R. (1989). Psychology in America: A historical survey. New York: Harcourt Brace Jovanovich.

Watson, R. I. & Evans, R. B. (1990). The great psychologists: An intellectual history (5th ed.). New York: HarperCollins.

Smoking: What's Culture Got to Do With It?

Source: Excerpt from Nichter, M. 2003. "Smoking: What's Culture Got to Do With It?" *Addiction,* 98 Suppl. 1: 139–145.

A better understanding of tobacco uptake, trajectories of use, expressions of dependence and quitting attempts requires a careful consideration of the interaction between individual and contextual factors, the way in which nested social contexts interface and influence one another and an appreciation of risk and protective factors. The study of nested contexts is challenging. A move from the study of additive to interactive factors influencing tobacco use demands both a new vision of what types of data need to be collected and new methods of data analysis. The papers in this special issue go a long way towards summarizing what we know about family, peer, neighborhood, media, economic and political economic influences on tobacco use. Rather than revisit themes already covered in the papers, I wish to raise a few additional issues related to ethnicity and 'culture' as a context influencing adolescent smoking. Ways will then be suggested in which ethnographic studies of smoking can add to our understanding of smoking behavior as a phenomenon influenced by both structural locations which bound subjective experience and cultural play which involves experimentation with self-image and identity (Pavis *et al* 1998).

Let me comment first on the role of 'culture', a factor influencing tobacco use that was raised by several of the authors. When this volume was first discussed, 'culture' was considered as a context meriting its own review. Given that a Surgeon General's Report (US Department of Health & Human Re-

sources, 1998) had recently summarized ethnic differences in rates of smoking, it appeared redundant to restate what is already known and more useful to consider how cultural norms and institutions, gender roles and aesthetics played out in each of the other contexts being addressed. I would urge future researchers investigating 'culture' and tobacco use to continue to look at the interaction between culture and social and economic contexts, and to consider 'culture' on two fronts: (a) culture as it is commonly regarded in relation to ethnic differences, and (b) popular culture as an ongoing project subject to both the identity needs of youth and the influence of an advertising industry that manipulates these needs to sell cigarettes and develop market niches.

Ethnicity and culture are terms that public health researchers need to differentiate and take seriously, especially when studying adolescence (Fergerson 1998).[1] When using the term 'ethnicity' it is important to differentiate between an ethnic identity one assumes in context and an ethnic label that is imposed by others. One's ethnic identity is an identity one chooses to assume on the basis of some sense of social and political affiliation. Far from being fixed or static, which would render ethnicity a reified construct (a 'thing'), ethnic identity may be claimed or distanced in particular contexts, at particular times, and for particular reasons. One's sense of ethnic identity is situational and changes in accord with life-style, residence, etc. At its core, ethnic identity is based on shared meanings that emerge from collective experiences and as such it is produced and reproduced in social interaction. An ethnic label, on the other hand, is a static designation assigned to a person by someone else. It is based on a set of criteria that distinguishes them from others in the eyes of whomever it is that controls the categorization scheme. The history of ethnic categorization in the United States has been politically motivated and has been influenced by a changing agenda (Edmontson & Schultze 1994).

Ethnic labeling, whether by skin color, language or region of origin, lumps people together who may have as many differences as similarities. Lumping has diverse ramifications. It can contribute to misleading and sometimes disempowering stereotypes as well as provide an opportunity for those labeled to gain critical mass and mobilize forces toward particular ends. For example, diverse groups categorized as Hispanic may mobilize as a collective based on the common experience of oppression and assume an ethnic identity as much for political as cultural reasons.

When ethnicity is employed as a category in public health, it is important to be clear about one's assumptions and how ethnic designation is going to be used in data analysis. Is an ethnic label being used to examine the possible role of biological differences? Is ethnicity a proxy for a whole bundle of social and economic factors associated with the position a group of people has been forced to assume as a result of a history of discrimination or oppression (e.g. as a marker of social inequity and structural violence)? Or is ethnicity being examined to determine whether the distinctive characteristics of an ethnic groups' 'culture' are protecting or exposing this group to particular types of risk? If the latter is the case, we must bear in mind that 'culture' is one of the most highly debated concepts in cultural anthropology (Sewell 1999).

Culture is commonly thought of as an enduring set of social norms and institutions that organize the life of members of particular ethnic groups giving them a sense of continuity and community. It is often described rather vaguely as an all-encompassing associational field in which ethnicity is experienced. Numerous anthropologists have discussed the limitations of such conceptualization of 'culture', especially in complex societies subject to the forces of modernity. When 'culture' is thought about in terms of consensus and as a template for ideal behavior, the positions of different stakeholders (defined by gender, generation, class, power relations, etc.) are forgotten and heterogeneity is ignored. A processual rendering of culture is more productive. Such an approach directs attention to cultural dimensions of social transactions and asks what is cultural about particular types of behavior in different contexts. Culture is treated more as an adjective than a noun (Appadurai 1996).

Why is a discussion of ethnicity and culture important for tobacco research? There has been mounting criticism of late about the way in which race/ethnicity has been used in public health research as a set of pigeonholes, if not black boxes. This fosters an analysis of 'difference' that focuses on individual and group traits rather than the contexts in which people live (Lillie-Blanton & LaVeist 1996). Despite warnings against reading too much into aggregate (e.g. state, national) data on smoking and ethnicity, it is easy to overlook ethnic heterogeneity and see ethnicity as a risk factor rather than a risk marker. A question often posed in debates about ethnicity and smoking is the following: are cultural factors responsible for ethnic differences in levels of smoking (at different ages by gender), or is ethnicity merely a marker for multiple social and economic factors predisposing one to smoke or abstain from smoking? Adopting an 'action is in the interaction' perspective, I would argue that there is a much better way of framing this important issue. Two questions appear more relevant to ask:

1. Is smoking behavior in particular social and economic contexts influenced by cultural norms and processes and if so, how?
2. What has smoking come to represent to those sharing an ethnic identity in an environment in which the tobacco industry often targets ethnic pride in marketing campaigns?

I would argue that it is far more productive to look for cultural differences in smoking after first accounting for other factors known to predispose an individual to smoke, including education, social class, economic insecurity, stressors (e.g. discrimination), other drug use, etc. Following an analysis which pays credence to the shortcomings of quantitative research—for example, that it often overlooks important differences between socio-economic indices (King 1997)—ethnic differences should be examined more closely. At a minimum the following three issues should be addressed by ethnographic research. What is the role that cultural institutions, values, and processes play in: (1) protecting against smoking in the general population, as well as particular patterns of smoking among males and females, (2) fostering smoking as a normative behavior within particular gender and age cohorts and (3) affecting the distribution of particular smoking trajectories (e.g. early versus late onset of smoking, smoking characterized by rapid versus slow escalation, etc.). This ethnographic analysis would serve as a complement to assessments by researchers who examine intraethnic group differences by examinations of social class, education, residence, racial segregation and acculturation.

ENDNOTE

1. For a complementary discussion of the meaning of 'race', see Freeman (1998).

REFERENCES

Appadurai, A., ed. (1996) *Modernity at Large: Cultural Dimensions of Globalization*. Minneapolis: University of Minnesota Press.

Edmontson, B. & Schultze, C., eds (1994) *Modernizing the US Census; Panel on Census Requirements in the Year 2000 and Beyond*. National Research Council. Washington, DC: National Academy Press.

Fergerson, G. (1998) Whither 'culture' in adolescent health research [Commentary]? *Journal of Adolescent Health*, 23, 150–152.

King, G. (1997) The 'race' concept in smoking: a review of the research on African Americans. *Social Science and Medicine*, 45, 1075–1087.

Lillie-Blanton, M. & LaVeist, T. (1996) Race/ethnicity, the social environment, and health. *Social Science and Medicine*, 43, 83–91.

Pavis, S., Cunningham-Burley, S. & Amos, A. (1998) Health related behavioural change in context: young people in transition. *Social Science and Medicine*, 47, 1407–1418.

Sewell, W. H. Jr (1999) The concepts of culture. In: Bonnell, V. E. & Hunt, L., eds. *Beyond the Cultural Turn: New Directions in the Study of Society and Culture*, pp. 35–61. Berkeley, CA: University of California Press.

US Department of Health and Human Resources (1998) *Tobacco Use Among U.S. Racial/Ethnic Minority Groups—African American, American Indians and Alaska Natives, Asian Americans and Pacific Islanders, and Hispanics*. A Report of the Surgeon General. Atlanta, GA: US Department of Health and Human Services, Centers for Disease Control and Prevention: National Center for Chronic Disease Prevention and Health Promotion, Office on Smoking and Health.

Ecology of the Family as Context for Human Development

Source: Excerpt from Bronfenbrenner, U. 1986. "Ecology of the Family as Context for Human Development: Research perspectives." *Developmental Psychology* 22(6): 723–742.

This review collates and examines critically a theoretically convergent but widely dispersed body of research on the influence of external environments on the functioning of families as contexts of human development. Investigations falling within this expanding domain include studies of the interaction of genetics and environment in family processes; transitions and linkages between the family and other major settings influencing development, such as hospitals, day care, peer groups, school, social networks, the world of work (both for parents and children), and neighborhoods and communities; and public policies affecting families and children. A second major focus is on the patterning of environmental events and transitions over the life course as these affect and are affected by intrafamilial processes. Special emphasis is given to critical research gaps in knowledge and priorities for future investigation.

The purpose of this article is to document and delineate promising lines of research on external influences that affect the capacity of families to foster the healthy development of their children. The focus differs from that of most studies of the family as a context of human development, because the majority have concentrated on intrafamilial processes of parent-child interaction, a fact that is reflected in Maccoby and Martin's (1983) recent authoritative review of research on family influences on development. By contrast, the focus of the present analysis can be described as "once removed." The research question becomes: How are intrafamilial processes affected by extrafamilial conditions?

PARADIGM PARAMETERS

In tracing the evolution of research models in developmental science, Bronfenbrenner and Crouter (1983) distinguished a series of progressively more sophisticated scientific paradigms for investigating the impact of environment on development. These paradigms provide a useful framework for ordering and analyzing studies bearing on the topic of this review. At the most general level, the research models vary simultaneously along two dimensions. As applied to the subject at hand, the first pertains to the structure of the external systems that affect the family and the manner in which they exert their influence. The second dimension relates to the degree of explicitness and differentiation accorded to intrafamilial processes that are influenced by the external environment.

External Systems Affecting the Family

Research paradigms can be distinguished in terms of three different environmental systems that can serve as sources of external influence on the family.

Mesosystem models. Although the family is the principal context in which human development takes place, it is but one of several settings in which developmental process can and do occur. Moreover, the processes operating in different settings are not independent of each other. To cite a common example, events at home can affect the child's progress in school, and vice versa. Despite the obviousness of this fact, it was not until relatively recently that students of development began to employ research designs that could identify the influences operating, in both directions, between the principal settings in which human development occurs. The term *mesosystem* has been used to characterize analytic models of this kind (Bronfenbrenner,

1979). The results of studies employing this type of paradigm in relation to the family are summarized below, in the section "Mesosystem Models."

Exosystem models. The psychological development of children in the family is affected not only by what happens in the other environments in which children spend their time but also by what occurs in the other settings in which their parents live their lives, especially in a place that children seldom enter—the parents' world of work. Another domain to which children tend to have limited access is the parents' circle of friends and acquaintances—their social network. Such environments "external" to the developing person are referred to as "exosystems." The findings of investigations employing exosystem designs are reviewed below, in the section "Exosystem Models."

Chronosystem models. Traditionally in developmental science, the passage of time has been treated as synonymous with chronological age; that is, as a frame of reference for studying psychological changes within individuals as they grow older. Especially during the past decade, however, research on human development has projected the factor of time along a new axis. Beginning in the mid 1970s, an increasing number of investigators have employed research designs that take into account changes over time not only within the person but also in the environment and—what is even more critical—that permit analyzing the dynamic relation between these two processes. To distinguish such investigations from more traditional longitudinal studies focusing exclusively on the individual, I have proposed the term *chronosystem* for designating a research model that makes possible examining the influence on the person's development of changes (and continuities) over time in the environments in which the person is living (Bronfenbrenner, 1986a). The simplest form of chronosystem focuses around a life transition. Two types of transition are usefully distinguished: normative (school entry, puberty, entering the labor force, marriage, retirement) and nonnormative (a death or severe illness in the family, divorce, moving, winning the sweepstakes). Such transitions occur throughout the life span and often serve as a direct impetus for developmental change. Their relevance for the present review, however, lies in the fact that they can also influence development indirectly by affecting family processes.

A more advanced form of chronosystem examines the cumulative effects of an entire sequence of developmental transition over an extended period of the person's life—what Elder (1974, 1985) has referred to as the life course. During the past decade, studies of the impact of personal and historical life events on family processes and on their developmental outcomes have received increasing attention. Several of these investigations have yielded findings of considerable substantive

and theoretical significance. These are described, along with other relevant researches employing a chronosystem design, below ("Chronosystem Models").

Family Processes in Context

With respect to explicitness and complexity, research paradigms can again be differentiated at three successive levels.

Social address model. At the first level, the family processes are not made explicit at all, because the paradigm is limited to the comparison of developmental outcomes for children or adults living in contrasting environments as defined by geography (e.g., rural vs. urban, Japan vs. the United States), or by social background (socioeconomic status, ethnicity, religion, etc.). Hence the name "social address" (Bronfenbrenner, 1979).

Given their restricted scope, social address models have a number of important limitations summarized in the following passage:

> No explicit consideration is given... to intervening structures or processes through which the environment might affect the course of development. One looks only at the social address—that is, the environmental label—with no attention to what the environment is like, what people are living there, what they are doing, or how the activities taking place could affect the child. (Bronfenbrenner & Crouter, 1983, pp. 361–362)

Despite these shortcomings, social address models remain one of the most widely used paradigms in the study of environmental influences on development. Two reasons may account for their scientific popularity. The first is their comparative simplicity, both at a conceptual and an operational level. Indeed, they can be, and sometimes have been, employed without doing very much thinking in advance, a procedure, alas, that is reflected in the product. But social address models, when appropriately applied, can also serve as a helpful scientific tool. Precisely because of their simplicity, they can be implemented easily and quickly. Hence, they may often be the strategies of choice for exploring uncharted domains. Like the surveyor's grid, they provide a useful frame for describing at least the surface of the new terrain. A case in point is their application in identifying developmental outcomes associated with what Bronfenbrenner and Crouter (1983) have called the "new demography"—single parents, day care, mothers in the labor force, remarriage, or (perhaps soon) fathers in the role of principal caregiver.

Process-context model. Paradigms at this second level explicitly provide for assessing the impact of the external environment on particular family processes. As documented in Bronfenbrenner and Crouter's analysis (1983), such paradigms represent a fairly recent scientific development, appearing in a reasonably full form only in the late 1960s and early 1970s. Because the corresponding research designs tend to be more complex than those employed in social address models, a concrete illustration may be helpful. For this purpose, I have selected one of the earliest examples of its kind, but one that still deserves to be emulated as a model for future research. In a series of researches growing out of his doctoral dissertation, Tulkin and his colleagues (Tulkin, 1973a, 1973b, 1977; Tulkin & Cohler, 1973, Tulkin & Covitz, 1975; Tulkin & Kagan, 1972) sought to go beyond the label of social class in order to discover its manifestations in family functioning. The first study focused on families with an infant under one year of age. To control for the child's sex and ordinal position, the sample was limited to firstborn girls, first studied when they were 10 months old. The initial publication (Tulkin & Kagan, 1972), based on home observations, reported that middle-class mothers engaged in more reciprocal interactions with their infants, especially in verbal behavior, and provided them with a greater variety of stimulation. The second study (Tulkin & Cohler, 1973) documented parallel differences in maternal attitudes; middle-class mothers were more likely to subscribe to statements stressing the importance of perceiving and meeting the infant's needs, the value of mother-child interaction, and the moderate control of aggressive impulses. Furthermore, the correlations between maternal behavior and attitudes were substantially greater in middle-class than in lower-class families. Next, in two experiments, Tulkin (1973a, 1973b) found that middle-class infants cried more when separated from their mothers, but were better able to discriminate the mother's voice from that of an unfamiliar female from the same social class. Finally, several years later, Tulkin and Covitz (1975) reassessed the same youngsters after they had entered school. The children's performance on tests of mental ability and language skill showed significant relationships to the prior measures of reciprocal mother-infant interaction, strength of maternal attachment, and voice recognition when the children had been 10 months old. Once again, the observed correlations were higher for middle-class families. Even more important from a developmental perspective, the relationships of maternal behavior at 10 months to the child's behavior at age 6 were considerably greater than the contemporaneous relationships between both types of variables in the first year of life. The investigators, however, were quick to reject the hypothesis of a delayed "sleeper effect." Rather, they argued that mothers who engage in adaptive reciprocal activity with their infants at early ages are likely to continue to do so as the child gets older, thus producing a cumulative trend.

Although a number of other investigators of socialization and social class have observed mother-child interaction, Tulkin's work remains unique in combining three critical features: (a) an emphasis on social class differences in *process* rather than merely in outcome; (b) demonstration of the key role played by child rearing values and the higher correspondence between parental values and behavior among middle-class than working-class families; and (c) evidence of developmental effects over time.

Person-process-context model. As its name indicates, the next and last process paradigm adds a new, third element to the system. Although the process-context model represented a significant advance over its predecessors, it was based on an unstated assumption—namely, that the impact of a particular external environment on the family was the same irrespective of the personal characteristics of individual family members, including the developing child. The results of the comparatively few studies that have employed a triadic rather than solely dyadic research paradigm call this tacit assumption into question. Research by Crockenberg (1981) illustrates both the model and its message. Working with a middle-class sample, she found that the amount of social support received by mothers from their social network when their infants were 3 months old was positively related to the strength of the child's attachment to its mother at one year of age. The beneficial impact of social support varied systematically, however, as a function of the infant's temperament. It was strongest for mothers with the most irritable infants and minimal for those whose babies were emotionally calm. In addition, the author emphasizes that "the least irritable infants appear somewhat impervious to the low support environments which disrupt the development of their more irritable peers . . . the easy babies in this study were unlikely to develop insecure attachments even when potentially unfavorable social milieus existed" (p. 862).

As documented subsequently in this review, the personal characteristics of parents, especially of fathers, are of no less—and perhaps even greater—importance than those of the child in determining the positive or negative impact of the external environment on family processes and their developmental outcomes.

Although research paradigms in the study of development-in-context have become progressively more complex over time both with respect to the analysis of family processes and of environmental systems, this does not mean that the correlation applies at the level of individual studies. Indeed, the opposite is often the case. Thus one encounters chronosystem designs that still rely primarily on social address models for analyzing data, and, conversely, person-process-context designs that give no consideration to the length of time that a family has been exposed to a particular environmental context (for example, unemployment). Moreover, seldom in either instance is there recognition of the ambiguity of interpretation produced by the failure to use a more sophisticated design. Fortunately, a number of studies, reported below, do employ paradigms that are comparatively advanced on both dimensions and, thereby, produce a correspondingly rich scientific yield.

REFERENCES

Bronfenbrenner, U. (1979). *The ecology of human development: Experiments by nature and design.* Cambridge, MA: Harvard University Press.

Bronfenbrenner, U. (1986a). Recent advances in research on the ecology of human development. In R. K. Silbereisen, K. Eyferth, & G. Rudinger (Eds.), *Development as action in context: Problem behavior and normal youth development* (pp. 287–309). Heidelberg and New York: Springer-Verlag.

Bronfenbrenner, U., & Crouter, A. C. (1983). The evolution of environmental models in developmental research. In W. Kessen (Ed.), *History, theory, and methods,* Volume 1 of P.H. Mussen (Ed.), *Handbook of child psychology* (4th ed., pp. 357–414). New York: Wiley. 357–414.

Crockenberg, S. B. (1981). Infant irritability, other responsiveness, and social support influences on the security of infant-mother attachment. *Child Development, 52,* 857–865.

Elder, G. H., Jr. (1974). *Children of the Great Depression.* Chicago: University of Chicago Press.

Elder, G. H., Jr. (Ed.) (1985). *Life course dynamics: Trajectories and transitions, 1968-1980.* Ithaca, NY: Cornell University Press.

Tulkin, S. R. (1973a). Social class differences in infants' reactions to mother's and stranger's voices. *Developmental Psychology, 8,* 137.

Tulkin, S. R. (1973b). Social class differences in attachment behaviors of ten-month-old infants. *Child Development, 44,* 171–174.

Tulkin, S. R. (1977). Social class differences in maternal and infant behavior. In P.H. Leiderman, A. Rosenfeld, & S.R. Tulkin (Eds.). *Culture and infancy* (pp. 495–557). New York: Academic Press.

Tulkin, S. R., & Cohler, B. J. (1973). Child-rearing attitudes and mother-child interaction in the first year of life. *Merrill-Palmer Quarterly, 19,* 95–106.

Tulkin, S. R., & Covitz, F. E. (1975). *Mother-infant interaction and intellectual functioning at age six.* Paper presented at the meeting of the Society of Research in Child Development, Denver.

Tulkin, S. R., & Kagan, J. (1972). Mother-child interaction in the first year of life. *Child Development, 43,* 31–41.

Individual Health Behavior Theories

Following the ecological approach, we start with theories that explain behavior at the level of the individual—that is, factors, characteristics, and processes that occur within individuals as opposed to the social or physical environment around them. The selections in Part 4 are examples of some of these theoretical approaches. The first reading (Janz & Becker, 1984) is a classic review of studies examining the utility of the Health Belief Model in early studies, in which specific constructs within the model are found to have the most predictive power. Additional constructs (e.g., self-efficacy) are also considered for their relevance to the model. The second selection (Ajzen, 1991) is an outline of the Theory of Planned Behavior and its evolution from the Theory of Reasoned Action. In the third selection, Prochaska and DiClemente (1983) explain their rationale for development of the Transtheoretical Model of behavior change (TTM).

The Health Belief Model: A Decade Later

Source: Excerpts from Janz, N.K., and Becker, M.H. 1984. "The Health Belief Model: A Decade Later." *Health Education Quarterly* 11(1): 1–47.

INTRODUCTION

In 1974, *Health Education Monographs* devoted an entire issue to "The Health Belief Model and Personal Health Behavior." This monograph summarized findings from research applying the Health Belief Model (HBM) as a conceptual formulation for understanding why individuals did or did not engage in a wide variety of health-related actions, and provided considerable support for the model. During the decade that has elapsed since the monograph's publication, the HBM has continued to be a major organizing framework for explaining and predicting acceptance of health and medical care recommendations. The present article provides a critical review of HBM investigations conducted since 1974, and subsequently combines these results with earlier findings to permit an overall assessment of the model's performance to date.

Dimensions of the Model

The HBM was developed in the early 1950s by a group of social psychologists at the U.S. Public Health Service in an attempt to understand "the widespread failure of people to accept disease preventives or screening tests for the early detection of asymptomatic disease"; it was later applied to patients' responses to symptoms, and to compliance with prescribed medical regimens. The basic components of the HBM are derived from a well-established body of psychological and behavioral theory whose various models hypothesize that behavior depends mainly upon two variables: (1) the value placed by an individual on a particular goal; and (2) the individual's estimate of the likelihood that a given action will achieve that goal. When these variables were conceptualized in the context of health-related behavior, the correspondences were: (1) the desire to avoid illness (or if ill, to get well); and (2) the belief that a specific health action will prevent (or ameliorate) illness (i.e., the individual's estimate of the threat of illness, and of the likelihood of being able, through personal action, to reduce that threat).

Specifically, the HBM consists of the following dimensions.

- *Perceived susceptibility.*—Individuals vary widely in their feelings of personal vulnerability to a condition (in the case of medically-established illness, this dimension has been reformulated to include such questions as estimates of resusceptibility, belief in the diagnosis, and susceptibility to illness in general). Thus, this dimension refers to one's subjective perception of the risk of contracting a condition.
- *Perceived severity.*—Feelings concerning the seriousness of contracting an illness (or of leaving it untreated) also vary from person to person. This dimension includes evaluations of both medical/clinical consequences (e.g., death, disability, and pain) and possible social consequences (e.g., effects of the conditions on work, family life, and social relations).

- *Perceived benefits.*—While acceptance of personal susceptibility to a condition also believed to be serious was held to produce a force leading to behavior, it did not define the particular course of action that was likely to be taken; this was hypothesized to depend upon beliefs regarding the effectiveness of the various actions available in reducing the disease threat. Thus, a "sufficiently-threatened" individual would not be expected to accept the recommended health action unless it was perceived as feasible and efficacious.
- *Perceived barriers.*—The potential negative aspects of a particular health action may act as impediments to undertaking the recommended behavior. A kind of cost benefit analysis is thought to occur wherein the individual weighs the action's effectiveness against perceptions that it may be expensive, dangerous (e.g., side effects, iatrogenic outcomes), unpleasant (e.g., painful, difficult, upsetting), inconvenient, time-consuming, and so forth.

Thus, as Rosenstock notes, "The combined levels of susceptibility and severity provided the energy or force to act and the perception of benefits (less barriers) provided a preferred path of action" (8). However, it was also felt that some stimulus was necessary to trigger the decision-making process. This so-called "cue to action" might be internal (i.e., symptoms) or external (e.g., mass media communications, interpersonal interactions, or reminder postcards from health care providers). Unfortunately, few HBM studies have attempted to assess the contribution of "cues" to predicting health actions. Finally, it was assumed that diverse demographic, sociopsychological, and structural variables might, in any given instance, affect the individual's perception and thus indirectly influence health-related behavior. The dimensions of the Health Belief Model are depicted in Figure A [not included in this excerpt].

Review Procedures

The following criteria were established for the present review: (1) only HBM-related investigations published between 1974 and 1984 were included; (2) the study had to contain at least one behavioral outcome measure; (3) only findings concerning the relationships of the four fundamental HBM dimensions to behaviors are reported; and (4) we chose to limit our literature survey to medical conditions (thus, no dental studies are reviewed), and to studies of the health beliefs and behaviors of adults (the corresponding literature for children has recently been examined (9)). Results in Table 1 [not included] have been grouped under three headings: (1) preventive health behaviors (actions taken to avoid illness or injury); (2) sick-role

behaviors (actions taken after diagnosis of a medical problem in order to restore good health or to prevent further disease progress); and (3) clinic-visits (clinic utilization for a variety of reasons). Within each medical category, studies are presented chronologically.

[The detailed review of studies is not included in this excerpt.]

DISCUSSION

HBM Studies 1974–1984

Table 4-1 provides a numerical summary of the findings reported in Table 1 [not included]. It is apparent from these data that research published during the past decade provides substantial support for the usefulness of the HBM as a framework for understanding individuals' health-related decision-making. To facilitate discussion, we have created a "significance ratio" wherein the number of positive and statistically significant findings for an HBM dimension are divided by the total number of studies which reported significance levels for that dimension. Examination of this ratio across the 29 investigations reviewed reveals that the best results are obtained by the "barriers" dimension (91%) followed (in descending order) by "benefits" (81%), "susceptibility" (77%), and "severity" (59%). This ordering among the dimensions holds for both prospective and retrospective studies. An early concern about HBM findings appearing before 1974 was that they were derived predominantly from research employing retrospective designs; thus, one often could not be confident that the positive correlations obtained indicated that these beliefs were the cause (and not the effect) of the behavior in question. However, it is apparent from Table 4-1 that the predictive results yielded by the 12 prospective studies produce higher significance ratios for each dimension category than those obtained by investigations with retrospective designs. In the three instances where significant results were obtained in a direction opposite to that predicted by the HBM, two were found in retrospective studies (where the issue of time order may account for the results); in the prospective instance, the authors argued that this unanticipated outcome was due to regimen-compliant patients reporting (logically) that they were less likely to be susceptible to the untoward consequences associated with not following instructions.

Turning to the results for preventive health behavior, we find that "susceptibility," "benefits," and "barriers" are consistently associated with outcomes (indeed, "barriers" was significantly associated with behavior in all of the 13 studies reviewed). "Susceptibility" and "benefits" yielded equivalent levels of effectiveness. However, "severity" is seen as making a relatively poor showing, producing significant results in only

TABLE 4-1 Summary of Findings from Health Belief Model Studies Published 1974–1984

Number of HBM Studies 1974–1984	Findings	Susceptibility	Severity	Benefits	Barriers
29 Total	Significant	20	16	21	21
	Nonsignificant	4	10	5	2
	Significant but opposite to HBM Prediction	2	1	—	—
	Significance not reported	—	—	1	1
	Dimension not measured	3	2	2	5
	Significance ratio:	20/26(77%)	16/27(59%)	21/26(81%)	21/23(91%)
12 Prospective (Summary)	Significant	10	8	11	10
	Nonsignificant	1	4	1	—
	Significant but opposite to HBM Prediction	1	—	—	—
	Significance not reported	—	—	—	—
	Dimension not measured	—	—	—	2
	Significance ratio:	10/12(83%)	8/12(67%)	11/12(92%)	10/10(100%)
17 Retrospective (Summary)	Significant	10	8	10	11
	Nonsignificant	3	6	4	2
	Significant but opposite to HBM Prediction	1	1	—	—
	Significance not reported	—	—	1	1
	Dimension not measured	3	2	2	3
	Significance ratio:	10/14(71%)	8/15(53%)	10/14(71%)	11/13(85%)
	PREVENTIVE HEALTH BEHAVIORS				
13 Total	Significant	10	4	9	10
	Nonsignificant	1	6	2	—
	Significant but opposite to HBM Prediction	1	1	—	—
	Significance not reported	—	—	1	1
	Dimension not measured	1	2	1	2
	Significance ratio:	10/12(83%)	4/11(36%)	9/11(82%)	10/10(100%)
3 Prospective (Summary)	Significant	3	1	3	3
	Nonsignificant	—	2	—	—
	Significant but opposite to HBM Prediction	—	—	—	—
	Significance not reported	—	—	—	—
	Dimension not measured	—	—	—	—
	Significance ratio:	3/3(100%)	1/3(100%)	3/3(100%)	3/3(100%)

continues

TABLE 4-1 (continued)

Number of HBM Studies Prior to 1974	Findings	Susceptibility	Severity	Benefits	Barriers
10 Retrospective (Summary)	Significant	7	3	6	7
	Nonsignificant	1	4	2	—
	Significant but opposite to HBM Prediction	1	1	—	—
	Significance not reported	—	—	1	1
	Dimension not measured	1	2	1	2
	Significance ratio:	7/9(78%)	3/8(38%)	6/8(75%)	7/7(100%)

SICK-ROLE BEHAVIORS

13 Total	Significant	8	11	6	10
	Nonsignificant	2	2	1	1
	Significant but opposite to HBM Prediction	1	—	—	—
	Significance not reported	—	—	—	—
	Dimension not measured	2	—	1	2
	Significance ratio:	8/11(73%)	11/13(85%)	9/12(75%)	10/11(91%)
7 Prospective (Summary)	Significant	5	6	6	6
	Nonsignificant	1	1	1	—
	Significant but opposite to HBM Prediction	1	—	—	—
	Significance not reported	—	—	—	—
	Dimension not measured	—	—	—	1
	Significance ratio:	5/7(71%)	6/7(86%)	6/7(86%)	6/6(100%)
7 Retrospective (Summary)	Significant	3	5	3	4
	Nonsignificant	1	1	2	1
	Significant but opposite to HBM Prediction	—	—	—	—
	Significance not reported	—	—	—	—
	Dimension not measured	2	—	1	1
	Significance ratio:	3/4(75%)	5/6(83%)	3/5(60%)	4/5(80%)

CLINIC UTILIZATION

3 Total	Significant	2	1	3	1
	Nonsignificant	1	2	—	1
	Significant but opposite to HBM Prediction	—	—	—	—
	Significance not reported	—	—	—	—
	Dimension not measured	—	—	—	1
	Significance ratio:	2/3(67%)	1/3(33%)	3/3(100%)	1/2(50%)

Source: Reprinted with permission from Janz, N.K., and Becker, M.H. 1984. "The Health Belief Model: A Decade Later." *Health Education Quarterly* 11(1): 1–47.

about one-third of the studies. We would speculate that these findings for "perceived severity" may be due in part to difficulties that study respondents have in conceptualizing this dimension: (1) when they are asymptomatic; (2) for health threats that are usually thought to be long term; and (3) concerning medical conditions with which they have had little or

TABLE 4-2 Summary of HBM Studies Published Prior to 1974

Number of HBM Studies Prior to 1974	Findings	Susceptibility	Severity	Benefits	Barriers
17 Total	Significant	10	8	8	4
	Nonsignificant	1	2	3	1
	Significant but opposite to HBM Prediction	—	—	—	—
	Significance not reported	3	3	3	2
	Dimension not measured	3	4	3	10
	Significance ratio:*	10/11(91%)	8/10(80%)	8/11(73%)	4/5(80%)
	PREVENTIVE HEALTH BEHAVIORS				
11 Total	Significant	8	5	5	3
	Nonsignificant	1	2	3	1
	Significant but opposite to HBM Prediction	—	—	—	—
	Significance not reported	2	2	2	1
	Dimension not measured	—	2	1	6
	Significance ratio:	8/9(89%)	5/7(71%)	5/8(62%)	3/4(75%)
	SICK-ROLE BEHAVIORS				
6 Total	Significant	2	3	3	1
	Nonsignificant	—	—	—	—
	Significant but opposite to HBM Prediction	—	—	—	—
	Significance not reported	1	1	1	1
	Dimension not measured	3	2	2	4
	Significance ratio:	2/2(100%)	3/3(100%)	3/3(100%)	1/1(100%)

*Ratio of positive statistically significant findings to all studies reporting significance levels for that dimension.
Source: Reprinted with permission from Janz, N.K., and Becker, M.H. 1984. "The Health Belief Model: A Decade Later." *Health Education Quarterly* 11(1): 1–47.

no personal experience. Also, in some cases (e.g., cancer), most subjects tend to view the condition as very serious; thus, there is little variability in the "severity" measure, and the item does not distinguish compliers from noncompliers (i.e., yields nonsignificant results).

Only three of the 13 PHB (preventive health behavior) studies were prospective; this may reflect problems that investigators encounter in trying to find relevant populations for study (i.e., it is relatively easier to examine prospectively individuals just diagnosed as ill and asked to begin a therapeutic regimen-sick-role behavior). However, given the paucity of prospective PHB-HBM research, it is worth noting that (with the exception of "severity"), the significance ratios for the prospective findings are 100%. In the case of sick-role behavior (SRB), "perceived severity" takes on greater importance, producing the second highest significance ratio (lending support to the argument that this HBM dimension is more meaningful to individuals diagnosed as ill and/or experiencing symptoms). In general, all of the HBM dimensions appear to contribute to an understanding of SRB—and, as was the case with PHB, the highest significance ratio is produced by "perceived barriers." The fact that "susceptibility" does not do quite as well with SRB as it did with PHB may result from difficulties in attempting to operationalize the concept of vulnerability in instances where diagnosis of illness has already been made.

For HBM-SRB research, we found more prospective than retrospective investigations. Similar to the results for PHB, the prospective SRB significance ratios tend (with the exception of "susceptibility") to run above those obtained in the retrospective studies. For the prospective SRB studies, the most powerful HBM dimension was "perceived barriers" (significance ratio = 100%).

The three HBM studies related to clinic utilization cannot be summarized easily. These studies covered a wide range of PHB, SRB, and overall appointment-keeping behavior. In general, perceptions of "benefits" produced the strongest findings, followed by "susceptibility," "barriers," and "severity." However, examining the results in greater detail, one finds that: (1) HBM dimensions are most productive in relation to visits to providers for treatment of illness; and (2) "severity" is important as a predictor of acute visits. (Because of the limited number of clinic utilization studies reviewed, Table X does not summarize these findings by type of study design.)

HBM Studies Prior to 1974

Results of HBM-PHB and HBM-SRB investigations published prior to 1974 were summarized in a 1977 supplement to Medical Care (51). Table 4-2 compiles these data in a manner similar to Table 4-1. Because only six of the seventeen pre-1974 studies were prospective, the data in Table 4-2 are not subclassified by type of study design. Examination of the significance-ratio orderings among the HBM dimensions reveals that the highest ratio (91%) is produced by "susceptibility" (the comparable figure in the post-1974 data was 77%); it may be that this strong showing by "susceptibility" results from the fact that most of the early HBM work examined preventive health behaviors. "Severity" and "barriers" yield identical significance ratios (80%); however, only seven of the seventeen pre-1974 studies measured the "barriers" dimension, and an additional two did not assess their measure's statistical significance. "Benefits" produced the relatively lowest significance ratio (73%).

The overall dimensions ordering remains essentially unchanged when one examines the findings of PHB research. However, although most of the six early HBM-SRB investigations failed to assess (or report the significance for) all of the major model dimensions, significant findings were obtained in every instance where the dimension was measured and significance was reported.

Summary of All HBM Studies

Table 4-3 permits an overall evaluation of the Health Belief Model by combining the pre- and post-1974 findings. In the preponderance of cases, each HBM dimension was found to be significantly associated with the health-related behaviors under study; the significance-ratio orderings (in descending order) are "barriers" (89%), "susceptibility" (81%), "benefits" (78%), and "severity" (65%).

Of the 46 studies reviewed, 18 are prospective and 28 are retrospective. As noted previously, the significance ratios for the prospective findings are at levels at or above those obtained from retrospective research, and the orderings of the significance ratios for the HBM dimensions are the same regardless of study design. It is particularly noteworthy that, in the case of the prospective studies, all of the 11 studies examining "perceived barriers" obtained positive and statistically-significant results—and that the poorest outcomes are yielded by the "perceived severity" dimension.

Slightly more than one-half (24) of the studies focused on PHB. While "barriers" was most productive, "susceptibility" was a close second. Most dramatic is the finding that only 50% of the PHB studies reporting significance levels for "severity" had obtained positive, significant results. It was suggested earlier that "perceived severity" may be a concept of relatively-low relevance in the area of PHB, but of greatest salience to individuals with diagnosed illness. The results in Table 4-3 from HBM-SRB research appear to support this contention: the significance ratio for "severity" (88%) is second highest among the four dimensions. Here, "susceptibility" yields the lowest significance ratio (first place is still held by "barriers"). Again, the relatively-poorer results produced by "susceptibility" in the instance of SRB may be due to difficulties in operationalizing this dimension of the model for cases where a diagnosis of illness has been established.

CONCLUSION

This article has summarized results from 46 studies of the Health Belief Model, 29 (63%) of which were published since 1974, and 18 (39%) of which were prospective in design. Overall, these investigations provide very substantial empirical evidence supporting HBM dimensions as important contributors to the explanation and prediction of individuals' health-related behaviors. Moreover, it is especially encouraging that findings from studies with prospective designs produced significance ratios as good or better than those derived from retrospective surveys. While there are many other extant models of health-related behaviour (52), we know of none approaching the HBM in terms of research attention or research corroboration. This support is particularly remarkable given the wide diversity of populations and settings studied, health conditions and health-related actions examined, and the multiplicity of different approaches and tools used to assess health beliefs and behavioral outcomes.

TABLE 4-3 Summary of Findings From All HBM Studies

Number of HBM Studies	Findings	Susceptibility	Severity	Benefits	Barriers
46 Total	Significant	30	24	29	25
	Nonsignificant	5	12	8	3
	Significant but opposite to HBM Prediction	2	1	—	—
	Significance not reported	3	3	4	3
	Dimension not measured	6	6	5	15
	Significance ratio:*	30/37(81%)	24/37(65%)	29/37(78%)	25/28(89%)
18 Prospective (Summary)	Significant	14	11	13	11
	Nonsignificant	2	6	3	—
	Significant but opposite to HBM Prediction	1	—	—	—
	Significance not reported	—	—	—	—
	Dimension not measured	1	1	2	7
	Significance ratio:	14/17(82%)	11/17(65%)	13/16(81%)	11/11(100%)
28 Retrospective (Summary)	Significant	16	13	16	14
	Nonsignificant	3	6	5	3
	Significant but opposite to HBM Prediction	1	1	—	—
	Significance not reported	3	3	4	3
	Dimension not measured	5	5	3	8
	Significance ratio:	16/20(80%)	13/20(65%)	16/21(76%)	14/17(82%)

PREVENTIVE HEALTH BEHAVIORS

Number of HBM Studies	Findings	Susceptibility	Severity	Benefits	Barriers
24 Total	Significant	18	9	14	13
	Nonsignificant	2	8	5	1
	Significant but opposite to HBM Prediction	1	1	—	—
	Significance not reported	2	2	3	2
	Dimension not measured	1	4	2	8
	Significance ratio:	18/21(86%)	9/18(50%)	14/19(74%)	13/14(93%)

SICK-ROLE BEHAVIORS

Number of HBM Studies	Findings	Susceptibility	Severity	Benefits	Barriers
19 Total	Significant	10	14	12	11
	Nonsignificant	2	2	3	1
	Significant but opposite to HBM Prediction	1	—	—	—
	Significance not reported	1	1	1	1
	Dimension not measured	5	2	3	6
	Significance ratio:	10/13(77%)	14/16(88%)	12/15(80%)	11/12(92%)

CLINIC UTILIZATION

continues

TABLE 4-3 (continued)

Number of HBM Studies	Findings	Susceptibility	Severity	Benefits	Barriers
3 Total	Significant	2	1	3	1
	Nonsignificant	1	2	—	1
	Significant but opposite to HBM Prediction	—	—	—	—
	Significance not reported	—	—	—	—
	Dimension not measured	—	—	—	1
	Significance ratio:	2/3(67%)	1/3(33%)	3/3(100%)	1/2(50%)

*Ratio of positive statistically significant findings to all studies reporting significance levels for that dimension.
Source: Reprinted with permission from Janz, N.K., and Becker, M.H. 1984. "The Health Belief Model: A Decade Later." *Health Education Quarterly* 11(1): 1–47.

Prior to 1974, it appeared that "perceived susceptibility" was the most powerful dimension of the HBM; however, few of these studies had attempted to measure "perceived barriers." In the post-1974 research, "barriers" consistently yielded the highest significance ratios, regardless of study design, for both PHB and SRB—and this overall finding persists when all HBM studies are summarized. In general, "susceptibility" appears somewhat more important in PHB than in SRB, and the reverse is observed for "benefits." However, the most notable difference among the HBM dimensions is the relatively lower power of "perceived severity" with the major exception of its importance to understanding SRB. In the 1974–1984 research, the significance ratio for "severity" in PHB studies was only 36%; in SRB studies, the figure is 85%.

Despite the impressive body of findings linking HBM dimensions to health actions, it is important to remember that the HBM is a psychosocial model; as such, it is limited to accounting for as much of the variance in individuals' health-related behaviors as can be explained by their attitudes and beliefs. It is clear that other forces influence health actions as well; for example: (1) some behaviors (e.g., cigarette smoking; tooth-brushing) have a substantial habitual component obviating any ongoing psychosocial decision-making process; (2) many health-related behaviors are undertaken for what are ostensibly *nonhealth* reasons (e.g., dieting to appear more attractive; stopping smoking or jogging to attain social approval); and (3) where economic and/or environmental factors prevent the individual from undertaking a preferred course of action (e.g., a worker in a hazardous environment; a resident in a city with high levels of air pollution). Furthermore, the model is predicated on the premise that "health" is a highly valued

concern or goal for most individuals, and also that "cues to action" are widely prevalent: where these conditions are not satisfied, the model is not likely to be useful in, or relevant to, explaining behavior. However, these concerns excepted, it is evident from this review that health education programs should attend to the attitude and belief dimensions of the HBM in addition to other likely influences on health-related behaviors.

Recent research has demonstrated the importance of variables which, although they fit conceptually within the HBM framework, were not developed or examined in that context. For example, in addition to more traditional HBM elements (i.e., "the person's beliefs that the behavior leads to certain outcomes and his evaluation of these outcomes"), a behavioral model developed by Ajzen and Fishbein (53) also emphasizes the importance of considering "the person's beliefs that specific individuals or groups think he should or should not perform the behavior." This normative (or "social approval") variable may be viewed as a logical refinement of the "benefits" or "barriers" dimensions of the HBM. In other words, the prospect of undertaking a socially-approved behavior (e.g., jogging) would be seen as a benefit, while having to perform a socially disapproved action (e.g., a young unmarried woman obtaining contraceptive advice/method) might be viewed as a barrier. Similarly, a person who wants to quit smoking might be inhibited by fear of experiencing the social disapproval of his/her prosmoking coworkers.

Another example comes from work begun by Bandura on the concept of "self-efficacy," which he defined as "the conviction that one can successfully execute the behavior required to produce the outcomes." There is evidence in the smoking literature that the strength of a person's belief in his/her ability to undertake and/or maintain cessation is related to behavior (55). This variable may similarly be viewed as a particular aspect of "perceived barriers"; i.e., a smoker who has repeatedly tried to quit and failed would be likely to develop feelings of low self-efficacy in this area, and would therefore interpret his previous failures as a barrier to undertaking further attempts at cessation. (It is noteworthy that both the "social approval" and "self-efficacy" examples fall within the "barriers" category, which we have found to be the most powerful dimension of the HBM.)

Given the numerous survey-research findings on the HBM now available, it is unlikely that additional work of this type will yield important new information. However, there is a paucity of experimental-design research evaluating the efficacy of different interventions in modifying HBM dimensions to achieve desired health behaviors. While the HBM specifies relevant attitude and belief dimensions, it does not dictate any particular intervention strategy for altering those elements. A few available investigations (14,31,43,56) have generated promising results; hopefully, these studies and the supportive survey findings will stimulate further experimental research.

Finally, there exists a need to refine and standardize tools used to measure HBM components. For the most part, every investigator has developed a unique approach to operationalizing each variable (it is a testament to the robustness of the model that the dimensions remain predictive despite these different measures). The variability which now exits renders interpretation of results and comparison of findings across studies problematic. Thus, although some attention has been devoted to HBM-related scale development and evaluation (44,51,51), this critical issue deserves considerable further research.

REFERENCES

1. Becker MH (ed): The health belief model and personal health behavior. *Health Educ Monogr* 2:324–508, 1974.

2. Rosenstock IM: Historical origins of the health belief model. *Health Educ Monogr* 2:328, 1974.

3. Kirscht JP: The health belief model and illness behavior. *Health Educ Monogr* 2:387–408, 1974.

4. Becker MH: The health belief model and sick role behavior. *Health Educ Monogr* 2:409–419, 1974.

5. Maiman LA, Becker MH: The health belief model: Origins and correlates in psychological theory. *Health Educ Monogr* 2:336–353, 1974.

6. Rosenstock IM: Historical origins of the health belief model. *Health Educ Monogr* 2:328–335, 1974.

7. Becker MH, Maiman LA: Strategies for enhancing patient compliance. *J Community Health* 6:113–135, 1980.

8. Rosenstock IM: Historical origins of the health belief model. *Health Educ Monogr* 2:332, 1974.

9. Gochman DS, Parcel GS (eds): Children's health beliefs and health behaviors. *Health Educ Quart* 9:104–270, 1982.

10. Aho WR: Participation of senior citizens in the Swine Flu inoculation program: An analysis of health belief model variables in preventive health behavior. *J Gerontology* 34:201–208, 1979.

11. Cummings KM, Jette AM, Brock BM, et al: Psychosocial determinants of immunization behavior in a Swine Influenza campaign. *Med Care* 17:639–649, 1979.

12. Rundall TG, Wheeler JRC: Factors associated with utilization of the Swine Flu vaccination program among senior citizens. *Med Care* 17:191–200, 1979.

13. Larson EB, Olsen E, Cole W, et al: The relationship of health beliefs and a postcard reminder to influenza vaccination. *J Fam Prac* 8:1207–1211, 1979.

14. Larson EB, Bergman J, Heidrich F, et al: Do postcard reminders improve influenza vaccination compliance? *Med Care* 20:639–648, 1982.

15. Becker MH, Kaback MM, Rosenstock IM, et al: Some influences on public participation in a genetic screening program. *J Community Health* 1:3–14, 1975.

16. Hallal JC: The relationship of health beliefs, health locus of control, and self concept to the practice of breast self-examination in adult women. *Nurs Res* 31:137–142, 1982.

17. Stillman MJ: Women's health beliefs about breast cancer and breast self-examination. *Nurs Res* 26:121–127, 1977.

18. Manfredi C, Warnecke RB, Graham S, et al: Social psychological correlates of health behavior: Knowledge of breast self-examination techniques among black women. *Soc Sci Med* 11:433–440, 1977.

19. Kelly PT: Breast self-examinations: Who does them and why. *J Behav Med* 2:31–38, 1979.

20. King JB: The impact of patients' perceptions of high blood pressure on attendance at screening. *Soc Sci Med* 16:1079–1091, 1982.

21. Langlie JK: Social networks, health beliefs, and preventive health behavior. *J Health Soc Behav* 18:244–260. 1977.

22. Aho WR: Smoking, dieting, and exercise: Age differences in attitudes and behavior relevant to selected health belief model variables. *Rhode Island Med J* 62:85–92, 1979.

23. Rundall TG, Wheeler JRC: The effect of income on use of preventive care: An evaluation of alternative explanations. *J Health Soc Behav* 20:397–406, 1979.

24. Dutton DB: Explaining the low use of health services by the poor: Costs, attitudes, or delivery systems? *Am Soc Rev* 43:348–368, 1978.

25. Tirrell BE, Hart LK: The relationship of health beliefs and knowledge to exercise compliance in patients after coronary bypass. *Heart Lung* 9:487–493, 1980.

26. Sackett DL, Becker MH, MacPherson AS, et al: *The standardized compliance questionnaire.* Hamilton, Ontario, Canada, McMaster University, 1974.

27. Beck KH: Driving while under the influence of alcohol: Relationship to attitudes and beliefs in a college population. *Am J Drug Alcohol Abuse* 8:377–388, 1981.

28. Weinberger M, Greene JY, Mamlin JJ, et al: Health beliefs and smoking behavior. *Am J Public Health* 71:1253–1255. 1981.

29. Croog SH, Richards NP: Health beliefs and smoking patterns in heart patients and their wives: A longitudinal study. *Am J Public Health* 67:921–930, 1977.

30. Aho WR: Relationship of wives' preventive health orientation to their beliefs about heart disease in husbands. *Public Health Rep* 92:65–71, 1977.

31. Inui TS, Yourtee EL, Williamson JW: Improved outcomes in hypertension after physician tutorials. *Ann Int Med* 84:646–651, 1976.

32. Kirscht JP, Rosenstock IM: Patient adherence to antihypertensive medical regimens. *J Community Health* 3:115–124, 1977.

33. Nelson EC, Stason WB, Neutra RR, et al: Impact of patient perceptions on compliance with treatment for hypertension. *Med Care* 16:893–906, 1978.

34. Taylor DW: A test of the health belief model in hypertension, in Haynes RB, Taylor DW, Sackett DL (eds): *Compliance in Health Care.* Baltimore, Johns Hopkins University Press. 1979, pp 103–109.

35. Sackett DL, Haynes RB, Gibson ES, et al: Randomized clinical trial of strategies for improving medication compliance in primary hypertension. *Lancet* May 31:1205–1207, 1975.

36. Alogna M: Perception of severity of disease and health locus of control in compliant and noncompliant diabetic patients. *Diabetes Care* 3:533–534, 1980.

37. Cerkoney KAB, Hart LK: The relationship between the health belief model and compliance of persons with diabetes mellitus. *Diabetes Care* 3:594–598, 1980.

38. Harris R, Skyler JS, Linn MW, et al: Relationship between the health belief model and compliance as a basis for intervention in diabetes mellitus, in *Psychological Aspects of Diabetes in Children and Adolescents. Pediatric Adolescent Endocrinology*, Vol. 10. Basel, Karger, 1982, pp 123–132.

39. Hartman PE, Becker MH: Non-compliance with prescribed regimen among chronic hemodialysis patients. *Dialysis & Transplantation* 7:978–985, 1978.

40. Cummings KM, Becker MH, Kirscht JP, et al: Psychosocial factors affecting adherence to medical regimens in a group of hemodialysis patients. *Med Care* 20:567–579, 1982.

41. Cummings KM, Becker MH, Kirscht JP, et al: Intervention strategies to improve compliance with medical regimens by ambulatory hemodialysis patients. *J Behav Med* 4:111–127, 1981.

42. Becker MH, Drachman RH, Kirscht JP: A new approach to explaining sick-role behavior in low income populations. *Am J Public Health* 64:205–216, 1974.

43. Becker MH, Haefner DP, Maiman LA, et al: The health belief model and prediction of dietary compliance: A field experiment. *J Health Soc Behav* 18:348–366, 1977.

44. Maiman LA, Becker MH, Kirscht JP, et al: Scales for measuring health belief model dimensions: A test of predictive value, internal consistency, and relationships among beliefs. *Health Educ Monogr* 5:215–230, 1977.

45. Becker MH, Radius SM, Rosenstock IM, et al: Compliance with a medical regimen for asthma: A test of the health belief model. *Public Health Rep* 93:268–277, 1978.

46. Berkanovic E, Telesky C, Reeder S: Structural and social psychological factors in the decision to seek medical care for symptoms. *Med Care* 19:693–709, 1981.

47. Kirscht JP, Becker MH, Eveland JP: Psychological and social factors as predictors of medical behavior. *Med Care* 14:422–431, 1976.

48. Becker MH, Nathanson CA, Drachman RH, et al: Mothers' health beliefs and children's clinic visits: A prospective study. *J Community Health* 3:125–135, 1977.

49. Leavitt F: The health belief model and utilization of ambulatory care services. *Soc Sci Med* 13A:105–112, 1979.

50. Becker MH, Drachman RH, Kirscht JP: A field experiment to evaluate various outcomes of continuity of physician care. *Am J Public Health* 64:1062–1070, 1974.

51. Becker MH, Haefner DP, Kasl SV, et al: Selected psychosocial models and correlates of individual health-related behaviors. *Med Care* 15:27–46, 1977.

52. Cummings KM, Becker MH, Maile MC: Bringing the models together: An empirical approach to combining variables used to explain health actions. *J Behav Med* 3:123–145, 1980.

53. Ajzen I, Fishbein M: *Understanding Attitudes and Predicting Social Behavior*. New Jersey, Prentice Hall, 1980.

54. Bandura A: Self-efficacy: Toward a unifying theory of behavioral change. *Psychol Rev* 84:191–215 (p 193), 1977.

55. Condiotte MM, Lichtenstein E: Self-efficacy and relapse in smoking cessation programs. *J Consult Clin Psychol* 49:648–658, 1981.

56. Haefner DP, Kirscht JP: Motivational and behavioral effects of modifying health beliefs. *Public Health Rep* 85:478–484, 1970.

57. Jette AM, Cummings KM, Brock BM, et al: The structure and reliability of health belief indices. *Health Serv Res* 16:81–98, 1981.

58. Given CW, Given BA, Gallin RS, et al: Development of scales to measure beliefs of diabetic patients. *Res Nurs Health* 6:127–141, 1983.

The Theory of Planned Behavior

Source: Excerpt from Ajzen, I. 1991. "The Theory of Planned Behavior." *Organizational Behavior and Human Decision Processes* 50: 179–211. *Predicting Behavior: Intentions and Perceived Behavioral Control*

The theory of planned behavior is an extension of the theory of reasoned action (Ajzen & Fishbein, 1980; Fishbein & Ajzen, 1975) made necessary by the original model's limitations in dealing with behaviors over which people have incomplete volitional control. Figure 4-1 depicts the theory in the form of a structural diagram. For ease of presentation, possible feedback effects of behavior on the antecedent variables are not shown.

As in the original theory of reasoned action, a central factor in the theory of planned behavior is the individual's intention to perform a given behavior. Intentions are assumed to capture the motivational factors that influence a behavior; they are indications of how hard people are willing to try, of how much of an effort they are planning to exert, in order to perform the behavior. As a general rule, the stronger the intention to engage in a behavior, the more likely should be its performance. It should be clear, however, that a behavioral intention can find expression in behavior only if the behavior in question is under volitional control, i.e., if the person can decide at will to perform or not perform the behavior. Although some behaviors may in fact meet this requirement quite well, the performance of most depends at least to some degree on such non-motivational factors as availability of requisite opportunities and resources (e.g., time, money, skills, cooperation of others; see Ajzen, 1985, for a discussion). Collectively, these factors represent people's actual control over the behavior. To the extent that a person has the required opportunities and resources, and intends to perform the behavior, he or she should succeed in doing so.[1]

The idea that behavioral achievement depends jointly on motivation (intention) and ability (behavioral control) is by no means new. It constitutes the basis for theorizing on such diverse issues as animal learning (Hull, 1943), level of aspiration (Lewin, Dembo, Festinger, & Sears, 1944), performance on psychomotor and cognitive tasks (e.g., Fleishman, 1958; Locke, 1965; Vroom, 1964), and person perception and attribution (e.g., Heider, 1944; Anderson, 1974). It has similarly been suggested that some conception of behavioral control be included in our more general models of human behavior, conceptions in the form of "facilitating factors" (Triandis, 1977), "the context of opportunity" (Sarver, 1983), "resources" (Liska, 1984), or "action control" (Kuhl, 1985). The assumption is usually made that motivation and ability interact in their effects on behavioral achievement. Thus, intentions would be expected to influence performance to the extent that the person has

---

[1]The original derivation of the theory of planned behavior (Ajzen, 1985) defined intention (and its other theoretical constructs) in terms of trying to perform a given behavior rather than in relation to actual performance. However, early work with the model showed strong correlations between measures of the model's variables that asked about trying to perform a given behavior and measures that dealt with actual performance of the behavior (Schifter & Ajzen, 1985; Ajzen & Madden, 1986). Since the latter measures are less cumbersome, they have been used in subsequent research, and the variables are now defined more simply in relation to behavioral performance. See, however, Bagozzi and Warshaw (1990, in press) for work on the concept of trying to attain a behavioral goal.

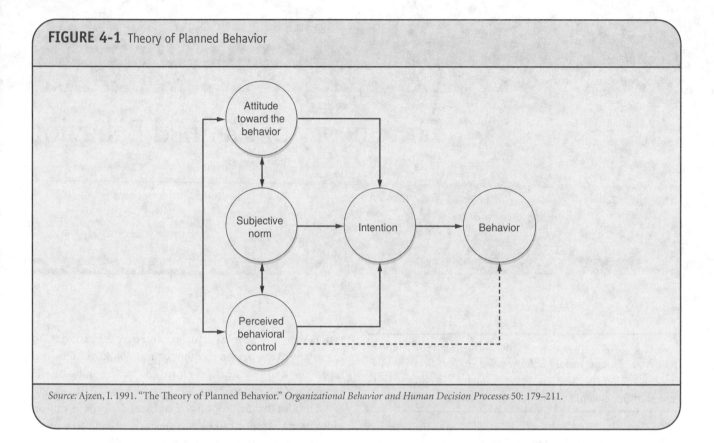

FIGURE 4-1 Theory of Planned Behavior

Source: Ajzen, I. 1991. "The Theory of Planned Behavior." *Organizational Behavior and Human Decision Processes* 50: 179–211.

behavioral control, and performance should increase with behavioral control to the extent that the person is motivated to try. Interestingly, despite its intuitive plausibility, the interaction hypothesis has received only limited empirical support (see Locke, Mento, & Katcher, 1978). We will return to this issue below.

Perceived behavioral control. The importance of actual behavioral control is self evident: The resources and opportunities available to a person must to some extent dictate the likelihood of behavioral achievement. Of greater psychological interest than actual control, however, is the perception of behavioral control and is impact on intentions and actions. Perceived behavioral control plays an important part in the theory of planned behavior. In fact, the theory of planned behavior differs from the theory of reasoned action in its addition of perceived behavioral control.

Before considering the place of perceived behavioral control in the prediction of intentions and actions, it is instructive to compare this construct to other conceptions of control. Importantly, perceived behavioral control differs greatly from Rotter's (1966) concept of perceived locus of control. Consistent with an emphasis on factors that are directly linked to a particular behavior, perceived behavioral control refers to

people's perception of the ease or difficulty of performing the behavior of interest. Whereas locus of control is a generalized expectancy that remains stable across situations and forms of action, perceived behavioral control can, and usually does, vary across situations and actions. Thus, a person may believe that, in general, her outcomes are determined by her own behavior (internal locus of control), yet at the same time she may also believe that her chances of becoming a commercial airplane pilot are very slim (low perceived behavioral control).

Another approach to perceived control can be found in Atkinson's (1964) theory of achievement motivation. An important factor in this theory is the expectancy of success, defined as the perceived probability of succeeding at a given task. Clearly, this view is quite similar to perceived behavioral control in that it refers to a specific behavioral context and not to a generalized predisposition. Somewhat paradoxically, the motive to achieve success is defined not as a motive to succeed at a given task but in terms of a general disposition "which the individual carries about him from one situation to another" (Atkinson, 1964, p. 242). This general achievement motivation was assumed to combine multiplicatively with the situational expectancy of success as well as with another situation-specific factor, the "incentive value" of success.

The present view of perceived behavioral control, however, is most compatible with Bandura's (1977, 1982) concept of perceived self-efficacy which "is concerned with judgments of how well one can execute courses of action required to deal with prospective situations" (Bandura, 1982, p. 122). Much of our knowledge about the role of perceived behavioral control comes from the systematic research program of Bandura and his associates (e.g., Bandura, Adams, & Beyer, 1977; Bandura, Adams, Hardy, & Howells, 1980). These investigations have shown that people's behavior is strongly influenced by their confidence in their ability to perform it (i.e., by perceived behavioral control). Self-efficacy beliefs can influence choice of activities, preparation for an activity, effort expended during performance, as well as thought patterns and emotional reactions (see Bandura, 1982, 1991). The theory of planned behavior places the construct of self-efficacy belief or perceived behavioral control within a more general framework of the relations among beliefs, attitudes, intentions, and behavior.

According to the theory of planned behavior, perceived behavioral control, together with behavioral intention, can be used directly to predict behavioral achievement. At least two rationales can be offered for this hypothesis. First, holding intention constant, the effort expended to bring a course of behavior to a successful conclusion is likely to increase with perceived behavioral control. For instance, even if two individuals have equally strong intentions to learn to ski, and both try to do so, the person who is confident that he can master this activity is more likely to persevere than is the person who doubts his ability.[2] The second reason for expecting a direct link between perceived behavioral control and behavioral achievement is that perceived behavioral control can often be used as a substitute for a measure of actual control. Whether a measure of perceived behavioral control can substitute for a measure of actual control depends, of course, on the accuracy of the perceptions. Perceived behavioral control may not be particularly realistic when a person has relatively little information about the behavior, when requirements or available resources have changed, or when new and unfamiliar elements have entered into the situation. Under those conditions, a measure of perceived behavioral control may add little to accuracy of behavioral prediction. However, to the extent that perceived control is realistic, it can be used to predict the probability of a successful behavioral attempt (Ajzen, 1985).

---

[2]It may appear that the individual with high perceived behavioral control should also have a stronger intention to learn skiing than the individual with low perceived control. However, as we shall see below, intentions are influenced by additional factors, and it is because of these other factors that two individuals with different perceptions of behavioral control can have equally strong intentions.

REFERENCES

Ajzen, I. (1985). From intentions to actions: A theory of planned behavior. In J. Kuhl & J. Beckmann (Eds.), *Action-control: From cognition to behavior* (pp. 11–39). Heidelberg: Springer.

Ajzen, I., & Fishbein, M. (1980). *Understanding attitudes and predicting social behavior*. Englewood Cliffs, NJ: Prentice-Hall.

Ajzen, I., & Madden, T. J. (1986). Prediction of goal-directed behavior: Attitudes, intentions, and perceived behavioral control. *Journal of Experimental Social Psychology*, 22, 453–474.

Anderson, N. H. (1974). Cognitive algebra: Integration theory applied to social attribution. In L. Berkowitz (Ed.), *Advances in experimental social psychology* (Vol. 7, pp. 1–101). New York: Academic Press.

Atkinson, J. W. (1964). *An introduction to motivation*. Princeton, NJ: Van Nostrand.

Bandura, A. (1977). Self-efficacy: Toward a unifying theory of behavioral change. *Psychological Review*, 84, 191–215.

Bandura, A. (1982). Self-efficacy mechanism in human agency. *American Psychologist*, 37, 122–147.

Bandura, A. (1991). Social-cognitive theory of self-regulation. *Organizational Behavior and Human Decision Processes*, 50.

Bandura, A., Adams, N. E., & Beyer, J. (1977). Cognitive processes mediating behavioral change. *Journal of Personality and Social Psychology*, 35, 125–139.

Bandura, A., Adams, N. E., Hardy, A. B., & Howells, G. N. (1980). Tests of the generality of self-efficacy theory. *Cognitive Therapy and Research*, 4, 39–66.

Bagozzi, R. P., & Warshaw, P. R. (1990a). *An examination of the etiology of the attitude behavior relation for goal-directed and mindless behaviors.* Unpublished manuscript, School of Business Administration, University of Michigan at Ann Arbor.

Fishbein, M., & Ajzen, I. (1975). *Belief, attitude, intention, and behavior: An introduction to theory and research.* Reading, MA: Addison-Wesley.

Fleishman, E. A. (1958). A relationship between incentive motivation and ability level in psychomotor performance. *Journal of Experimental Psychology*, 56, 78–81.

Heider, F. (1944). Social perception and phenomenal casuality. *Psychological Review*, 51, 358–374.

Hull, C. L. (1943). *Principles of behavior.* New York: Appleton-Century-Crofts.

Kuhl, J. (1985). Volitional aspect of achievement motivation and learned helplessness: Toward a comprehensive theory of action control. In B. A. Maher (Ed.), *Progress in experimental personality research* (Vol. 13, pp. 99–171). New York: Academic Press.

Lewin, K., Dembo, T., Festinger, L., & Sears, P. S. (1944). Level of aspiration. In J. McV. Hunt (Ed.), *Personality and the behavior disorder* (Vol. 1, pp 333–378). New York: Ronald Press.

Liska, A. E. (1984). A critical examination of the causal structure of the Fishbein/Ajzen attitude-behavior model. *Social Psychology Quarterly*, 47, 61–74.

Locke, E. A. (1965). Interaction of ability and motivation in performance. *Perceptual and Motor Skills*, 21, 719–725.

Locke, E. A., Mento, A. J., & Katcher, B. L. (1978). The interaction of ability and motivation in performance: An exploration of the meaning of moderators. *Personnel Psychology*, 31, 269–280.

Rotter, J. B. (1966). Generalized expectancies for internal versus external control of reinforcement. *Psychological Monographs*, 80(1, Whole No. 699).

Sarver, V. T., Jr. (1983). Ajzen and Fishbein's "theory of reasoned action": A critical assessment. *Journal for the Theory of Social Behavior*, 13, 155–163.

Schifter, D. B., & Ajzen, I. (1985). Intention, perceived control, and weight loss: An application of the theory of planned behavior. *Journal of Personality and Social Psychology*, 49, 843–851.

Triandis, H. C. (1977). *Interpersonal behavior.* Monterey, CA: Brooks/Cole.

Vroom, V. H. (1964). *Work and motivation.* New York: Wiley.

Stages and Processes of Self-Change of Smoking: Toward an Integrative Model of Change

Source: Excerpt from Prochaska, J.O., and DiClemente, C.C. 1983. "Stages and Processes of Self-Change of Smoking: Toward an Integrative Model of Change." *Journal of Consulting and Clinical Psychology* 51: 390–395.

Formalized treatment programs for smoking fail with a majority of smokers (Hunt, Barnett, & Branch, 1971). Nevertheless, 30 million Americans quit smoking in the past decade, with 70% to 80% quitting on their own (Adult Use of Tobacco, 1975). Furthermore, 70% of smokers surveyed indicated that if they were to quit, they would not attend a formal treatment program (McAlister, 1975). In spite of the preponderance of and preference for self-change approaches, research on smoking cessation has focused primarily on formalized treatments. The present study reports on the change processes that were emphasized by 872 self-changers representing five different stages of quitting smoking.

In one of the few studies on self-change, self-changers did not differ from individuals in formalized treatments on smoking habits, locus of control, and measures of the Jackson Personality Inventory (Pederson & Lefcoe, 1976). DiClemente and Prochaska (1982) also found that self-changers did not differ from subjects in two types of therapy programs in terms of smoking history variables, including history of previous attempts to quit smoking. DiClemente and Prochaska (1982) found that self-changers did differ from therapy changers in terms of the processes of change that were emphasized in recent attempts to quit smoking. More importantly, both self-changers and therapy changers reported retrospectively that they had used affective and cognitive processes more during early stages of change and emphasized behavioral processes during later stages.

Perri, Richards, and Schulteis (1977) completed retrospective interviews with 24 successful and 24 unsuccessful college students who had made attempts to quit smoking on their own. The successful self-changers reported using self-reinforcement procedures significantly more than the relapsers. Although encouraging, this study was limited by focusing on just two stages and four processes of change. Baer, Foreyt, and Wright (1977) analyzed letters describing the quitting experiences of 51 self-changers who had maintained nonsmoking for at least 2 years. While most of the self-changers used multiple techniques, the investigators were not able to discover any systematic clustering of their quitting methods.

Research to date on self-change approaches to smoking cessation has been limited by inadequate models of change and retrospective methodologies. The present research applied the transtheoretical model that has been developed both from the therapy literature (Prochaska, 1979; Prochaska & DiClemente, 1982) and from data on self-changers (DiClemente and Prochaska, 1982; Prochaska, DiClemente, Velicer, & Zwick, Note 1). The present research applied the model in a cross-sectional design to study self-changers who were in one of the following five stages of change: precontemplation, contemplation, action, maintenance, and relapse.

The transtheoretical model involves 10 processes of change receiving differential application during the five stages of change (Prochaska & DiClemente, 1982). The 10 processes of change are as follows: consciousness raising, self-liberation, social liberation, self-reevaluation, environmental reevaluation, counterconditioning, stimulus control, reinforcement management, dramatic relief, and helping relationships.

Based on the transtheoretical model (Prochaska & DiClemente, 1982) and previous research (DiClemente &

Prochaska, 1982), the following predictions were made. Because precontemplators tend to be defensive and avoid changing their thinking and behavior, they would use the change processes significantly less than subjects in other stages. Because contemplators are seriously thinking about changing their smoking behavior, they would use consciousness raising the most to gather further information about their smoking. Because self-reevaluation appears to be a process that bridges contemplation and action, self-reevaluation would be used most in the contemplation and action stages. Because subjects in the action stage are most committed to making behavioral changes, they would use self-liberation, counter-conditioning, stimulus control, and reinforcement management the most. No clear predictions had emerged from previous research on which processes would be emphasized during the maintenance and relapse stages.

METHOD

Subjects

There were 872 subjects from Rhode Island and Houston, Texas who volunteered to participate in the study in response to newspaper articles and ads. All subjects were assigned to one of the following five groups, depending on the stage of change they currently were in:

Long-term quitters (LTQs). These 247 subjects represented the maintenance stage, since they had maintained their nonsmoking for at least 6 months. The mean duration of maintenance was 5.9 years. The mean age was 44 years, and there were 133 females and 114 males. They had begun smoking at a mean age of 17.2 years.

Recent quitters (RQs). These 134 subjects represented the action stage, since they had quit smoking on their own within 6 months of entering the study. The mean duration of time since they had quit was 2.2 months. The mean age of these subjects was 35 years, and there were 80 females and 54 males. They had begun smoking at a mean age of 16.6 years.

Contemplators (Cs). These 187 subjects represented the contemplation stage, since they were smoking regularly for the past year but reported that they were seriously thinking about quitting smoking in the next year. The mean age of these subjects was 40 years, and there were 113 females and 74 males. They had begun smoking at a mean age of 17.4 years.

Immotives (I's). These 108 smokers represented the precontemplation stage, since they reported that they had no intention of quitting smoking in the next year. The mean age of this group was 38 years, and there were 74 females and 34 males. Their mean age of beginning smoking was 16.3 years.

Relapsers (RLs). An exploratory group of 196 relapsers was included to investigate how individuals use particular change processes after having failed within the past year in their attempt to quit smoking. The mean age of this group was 36 years, and there were 129 females and 67 males. Their mean age of beginning smoking was 17.3 years.

Basic demographic data on the subjects indicated that they were middle-age and middle-class adults who began smoking as teenagers ($M = 17$ years). The mean age was 40 and the median 37 years. Of the total sample 62% were married, 27% single, 16.5% divorced, and 5.8% separated or widowed. Of the total sample, 19.3% completed high school or less, 41.7% had attended some college classes, 17.8% had bachelor degrees, and 19.3% had some postgraduate education or a graduate degree. Approximately one half of the subjects had incomes of less than $15,000, and 8% had incomes of more than $30,000.

Measures

The processes of change test. This test is a 40-item questionnaire that measures 10 processes of change in a statistically well-defined and highly reliable manner (Prochaska et al., Note 1).[1] Table 4-4 presents a sample item and the alpha coefficient for each process. There are four items representing each of the 10 processes. Subjects were asked to rate on a 5-point Likert scale how frequently they employed each item in the past month ($1 = $ not at all; $5 = $ repeatedly).

Smoking-status measures. Saliva samples were taken from each subject to increase validity of self-reports via the bogus pipeline phenomenon (Jones & Sigall, 1971).

When subjects are aware that smoking status will be validated by physiological measures, the accuracy of self-reports increases. Because the laboratory in charge of analyzing thiocyanate levels was unaware of the latest techniques for extracting saliva from cotton swabs, they did not have adequate saliva for testing all subjects. There were adequate samples for 64% of the sample. Thus, thiocyanate levels were used to simply provide some group validation of self-reports. Thiocyanate data were available for 304 smokers ($M = 296.9$; $SD = 127.2$) and 250 nonsmokers ($M = 148.6$; $SD = 93.2$). A one-way analysis of variance (ANOVA) between these groups was highly significant, $F(l, 552) = 235.1$, $p < .0001$.

Self-report measures of smoking status were used in the present study for three reasons. First, the present study involved more than discriminating smokers from nonsmokers, since it also compared types of smokers (immotives, contemplators, and relapsers) and types of nonsmokers (recent and long-term quitters). Secondly, self-report measures were avail-

TABLE 4-4 Sample Items and Alpha Coefficients for the 10 Processes of Change

Processes	Alpha	Sample item
Consciousness raising	.88	I look for information related to smoking.
Self-liberation	.89	I tell myself I am able to quit smoking if I want to.
Social liberation	.81	I notice that public places have sections set aside for nonsmokers.
Self-reevaluation	.87	My depending on cigarettes makes me feel disappointed in myself.
Environmental reevaluation	.88	I stop to think that smoking is polluting the environment.
Counterconditioning	.88	I do something instead of smoking when I need to relax.
Stimulus control	.81	I remove things from my place of work that remind me of smoking.
Reinforcement management	.78	I am rewarded by others if I don't smoke.
Dramatic relief	.91	Warnings about health hazards of smoking move me emotionally.
Helping relationships	.84	I have someone who listens when I need to talk about my smoking.

Source: Prochaska, J.O., and DiClemente, C.C. 1983. "Stages and Processes of Self-Change of Smoking: Toward an Integrative Model of Change." *Journal of Consulting and Clinical Psychology* 51: 390–395.

able for all subjects. Finally, recent evidence suggests that self-reports may be more valid indicators of smoking status than are thiocyanate levels (Petitti, Friedman, & Kahn, 1981).

Procedure

When subjects called the Self Change Lab to volunteer, they were given the following information: The study would last for 2 years and they would be asked to complete a questionnaire and an interview every 6 months. In return the subjects would be paid $4 for completing the questionnaire and $4 for the interview and would be eligible for one of 10 bonus prizes ranging from $50 to $500 to be given every 6 months. The subjects were asked a series of five questions to determine which stage of change they were in. The present study reports cross-sectional data from the initial assessment. Longitudinal data will be reported in future publications.

TABLE 4-5 T Scores of the 10 Processes of Change for the Five Stages of Change Groups

	Group					
Process	I	C	RQ	LTQ	RL	F
Consciousness raising	45.3	53.1	48.5	48.6	52.2	15.64***
Self-liberation	41.3	48.2	55.9	51.3	50.8	40.82***
Social liberation	51.0	51.4	46.6	50.3	50.1	5.19**
Self-reevaluation	41.5	52.4	51.9	47.8	53.7	38.13***
Environmental reevaluation	44.3	50.8	48.9	51.4	51.4	12.22**
Counterconditioning	42.6	49.3	52.6	52.0	50.4	21.48***
Stimulus control	45.6	48.3	52.5	51.3	50.7	10.28***
Reinforcement management	45.2	49.4	53.8	49.6	51.0	12.41***
Dramatic relief	46.6	51.3	49.0	50.6	51.1	7.21***
Helping relationship	48.5	49.6	51.4	49.2	51.2	2.50*

Note. I = immotives; C = contemplators; RQ = recent quitters; LTQ = long-term quitters; RL = relapsers.
*$p < .05$. **$p < .001$. ***$p < .0001$.
Source: Prochaska, J.O., and DiClemente, C.C. 1983. "Stages and Processes of Self-Change of Smoking: Toward an Integrative Model of Change." *Journal of Consulting and Clinical Psychology* 51: 390–395.

RESULTS

Table 4-5 presents *T* scores for each of the five groups representing the stages of change on each of the 10 processes of change. A multivariate analysis of variance (MANOVA) for these data was significant, $F(l, 40) = 11.199$, $p < .001$. The first three dimensions of the MANOVA were significant. The significant MANOVA was followed up by separate ANOVAS because the 10 change processes have been found to be relatively independent (Prochaska, et al., Note 1) and because the results from the separate ANOVAS can be more clearly communicated than results from discriminant function analysis. Table 4-5 presents the *Fs* and probability levels for these one way ANOVAS. The ANOVAS indicate that there were significant differences in how frequently the groups used each of the 10 processes of change.

To determine exactly which groups differed on how frequently they used each of the change processes, Newman-Keuls comparisons were run. Each of the five groups was compared on each of the 10 processes of change. Table 4-6 presents the results of the Newman-Keuls comparisons, indicating which groups differed from each other at a $p < .05$ level or greater.

Relationships between the processes of change and the stages of change can be seen most clearly if the relapse group is temporarily bracketed. The relapse group was included as an exploratory group, with no predictions from the transtheoretical model about which processes of change would be empha-

sized by this group. More importantly, the results in Table 4-6 suggest that the relapse group behaves like a mixture of the contemplation and action groups.

Table 4-7 presents a diagram showing the stages in which particular processes of change are emphasized the most and the least. Table 4-7 indicates that, as predicted by the transtheoretical model, subjects in the precontemplation stage use 8 of the 10 processes significantly less than any other group. As predicted, consciousness raising is emphasized the most by individuals in the contemplation stage. Self-reevaluation appears to bridge contemplation and action since it is emphasized in both stages. Self liberation is emphasized when subjects take action, as are helping relationships and reinforcement management. Counterconditioning and stimulus control appear to bridge action and maintenance since these two processes are emphasized in both stages. The only relationship of social liberation to a stage is the unexpected finding that subjects in the action group emphasize this process the least.

DISCUSSION

The results of this study provide important data for enhancing our understanding of self-change of smoking and for developing a more integrative model of change. Assuming that the stages-of-change groups represent a cross-sectional analysis of quitting smoking, the following pattern emerges. As predicted from the transtheoretical model, subjects in the precontemplation stage used the processes of change the least. Specifically, the precontemplators used 8 of 10 processes of change significantly less than subjects in any other stage. This suggests that precontemplators process less information about smoking, spend less time reevaluating themselves as smokers, experience fewer emotional reactions to the negative aspects of smoking, and do little to shift their attention or their environment away from smoking.

What moves individuals into seriously contemplating change is not clear from the data. However, as predicted, once in the contemplation stage, subjects are the most likely to respond to feedback and education as sources of information about smoking. Along with this increased openness to information about smoking, contemplators report feeling and thinking more about themselves in relationship to their problem behavior. As predicted, the increased reevaluation of themselves appears to carry over into action as subjects perhaps become upset enough with themselves and their smoking to make commitments to quit. As predicted, during the action stage subjects use both counterconditioning and stimulus-control procedures for actively changing their smoking behavior and environment. They report more self- and social reinforce-

---

TABLE 4-6 Group Comparisons on Each of the Processes of Change

Process	Comparisons of stage-of-change groups
Consciousness raising	I < RQ, LTQ < RL, C
Self-liberation	I < C < RL, LTQ < RQ
Social liberation	RQ < I, C, LTQ, RL
Self reevaluation	I < LTQ < C, RQ, RL
Environmental reevaluation	I < C, RQ, LTQ, RL
Counterconditioning	I < C, RL < RQ, LTQ
Stimulus control	I < C < RQ, LTQ, RL
Reinforcement management	I < C, LTQ, RL < RQ
Helping relationship	I, C, LTQ, < RL, RQ

Note: I = immotives; C = comtemplators; RQ = recent quitters; LTQ = long-term quitters; RL = relapsers; $< = p < .05$, using Newman-Keuls tests.
Source: Prochaska, J.O., and DiClemente, C.C. 1983. "Stages and Processes of Self-Change of Smoking: Toward an Integrative Model of Change." *Journal of Consulting and Clinical Psychology* 51: 390–395.

TABLE 4-7 Processes of Change Listed Under the Stages in Which They Are Emphasized Most

Precomtemplation (I's)[a]	Contemplation (Cs)	Action (RQs)	Maintenance (LTQs)
	Consciousness raising		
		Self-reevaluation[b]	
		Self-liberation	
		Helping relationship	
		Reinforcement management	
			Counterconditioning[b]
			Stimulus control[b]

[a]Eight processes were used the least in the precontemplation stage.
[b]Processes emphasized in two stages are shown overlapping both stages.
Source: Prochaska, J.O., and DiClemente, C.C. 1983. "Stages and Processes of Self-Change of Smoking: Toward an Integrative Model of Change." *Journal of Consulting and Clinical Psychology* 51: 390–395.

ment for their changes and rely more on helping relationships for support and understanding. It is interesting that the subjects experience less reinforcement during the maintenance stage, although they continue to emphasize counterconditioning and stimulus-control processes for coping with temptations to smoke.

The results also provide a view of how individuals respond after having recently relapsed following a period of quitting smoking. The subjects report emphasizing change processes that are used most often by individuals in the contemplation and action stages. Specifically, the relapsers used consciousness raising as often as contemplaters, self-reevaluation as often as contemplaters and recent quitters, helping relationships as often as recent quitters, and stimulus control as often as subjects in the action and maintenance stages. The relapsers may be preparing themselves to quit smoking again as they engage in processes associated with contemplation. They may also be attempting to prevent complete relapse as they use action and maintenance processes to control their current levels of smoking.

These results provide support for recent modifications in the transtheoretical model of change. First of all, cathartic processes were originally thought to provide the bridge between contemplation and action (Prochaska & DiClemente, 1982). Rather than emotional experiences moving people to act, the results suggest that it is a combined cognitive/affective reevaluation process that carries over from contemplation into action. Second, the results suggest that the self-liberating process is emphasized most during the action stage. This result is consistent with earlier findings that commitments are realized once

action is taken (DiClemente & Prochaska, 1982). Finally, counterconditioning and stimulus control processes appear to bridge action and maintenance rather than being emphasized just in action. This result is consistent with the view that maintenance is indeed an active stage of change rather than an absence of change (Prochaska & DiClemente, 1982).

The model and data of self-change could be used to increase the effectiveness of smoking cessation programs and to maximize self-help approaches. Rather than assume that all smokers coming for treatment are ready for action, as is the case in most behaviorally based programs (Prochaska & DiClemente, 1982), clients would be grouped according to which stage of change they are in. Research with clients applying for therapy indicates that there are clusters of clients in each of the stages of change (McConnaughy, Prochaska, & Velicer, in press). Thus, smokers in the contemplation stage would begin with consciousness raising and self-reevaluation processes, whereas smokers ready for action could begin to apply the more behaviorally-based processes.

Smokers preferring to quit on their own report that they would take advantage of self-help manuals. The problem is that current self-help manuals for smokers are not particularly effective (Glasgow & Rosen, 1978; Glasgow, Schafer, & O'Neill, 1981). The authors are currently developing and testing self-help manuals based on self-change data and models, with the anticipation of improving the effectiveness of such materials.

The present results provide both substantial support for the transtheoretical model of change as well as suggesting important modifications in the model. What is needed are longitudinal data to determine the predictive validity of the model as individuals move from one stage of change to another. Also needed are comparative studies with other problem behaviors to determine the extent to which change processes vary in emphasis as different problem behaviors are being changed.

REFERENCE NOTE

1. Prochaska, J. O., DiClemente, C. D., Velicer, W. F., & Zwick, W. *Measuring processes of change.* Paper presented at the annual meeting of the International Council of Psychologists, Los Angeles, August, 1981.

REFERENCES

Adult Use of Tobacco, 1975 (U.S. Department of Health, Education and Welfare Publication). Washington, D.C.: U.S. Government Printing Office, 1976.

Baer, P. E., Foreyt, J. P., & Wright, S. Self directed termination of excessive cigarette use among untreated smokers. *Journal of Behavior Therapy and Experimental Psychiatry,* 1977, *5,* 71–74.

DiClemente, C. C., & Prochaska, J. O. Self change and therapy change of smoking behavior: A comparison of processes of change in cessation and maintenance. *Addictive Behavior,* 1982, *7,* 133–142.

Glasgow, R. E., & Rosen, G. M. Behavioral bibliotherapy: A review of self-help, behavior therapy manuals. *Psychological Bulletin,* 1978, *85,* 1–23.

Glasgow, R. E., Schafer, L, & O'Neill, N. K. Self-help books and amount of therapist contact in smoking cessation programs. *Journal of Consulting and Clinical Psychology,* 1981, *49,* 659–667.

Hunt, W. A., Barnett, G. W., & Branch, L. G. Relapse rates in addiction programs. *Journal of Clinical Psychology,* 1971, *27,* 455–456.

Jones, E. E., & Sigall, H. The bogus pipeline: A new paradigm for measuring affect and attitude, *Psychological Bulletin,* 1971, *76,* 349–364.

McAlister, A. Helping people quit smoking: Current progress. In A. M. Enelow & J. B. Henderson (Eds.), *Applying behavioral science to cardiovascular risk.* New York: American Heart Association, l975.

McConnaughy, E. A., Prochaska, J. O., & Velicer, W. F. Stages of change in psychotherapy: Measurement and sample profiles. *Psychotherapy: Theory, Research and Practice,* in press.

Pederson, L. L., & Lefcoe, N. M. A psychological and behavioral comparison of ex-smokers and smokers. *Journal of Chronic Diseases,* 1976, *29,* 431–434.

Perri, M. G., Richards, S. C., & Schultheis, K. R. Behavioral self control and smoking reduction: A study of self initiated attempts to reduce smoking. *Behavior Therapy,* 1977, *8,* 360–365.

Petitti, D. B., Friedman, G. D., & Kahn, W. Accuracy of information on smoking habits provided on self administered research questionnaires. *American Journal of Public Health,* 1981, *71,* 308–311.

Prochaska, J. O. *Systems of psychotherapy: A transtheoretical analysis.* Homewood, Ill.: Dorsey Press, 1979.

Prochaska, J. O., & DiClemente, C. C. Transtheoretical therapy: Toward a more integrative model of change. *Psychotherapy: theory, research and practice,* 1982, *19,* 276–288.

PART 5

Social, Cultural, and Environmental Theories, Part I

This is the first of two parts that include readings related to social/behavioral theories that move away from a focus on the individual to social, societal, and cultural influences on behavior. In this part, we begin that move by reviewing approaches that address social factors a step or two away from the individual level but not quite at the broader societal/cultural level. The first selection, from social psychologist Albert Bandura, refers to a recent discussion about one of the most important and widely referenced theoretical formulations of this kind, generally known as Social Cognitive Theory (SCT). In this selection, Dr. Bandura discusses specific aspects of SCT (human agency, efficacy), focusing on the more recent concerns within SCT as opposed to earlier emphases on learning and vicarious learning (Note: Some of the terminology in this article may be difficult for the introductory student). The second selection (Bertrand, 2004) describes the use of Diffusion of Innovations theory to develop a diabetes management program. The third selection, by Kotler and Zaltman, is a key article that proposes the behavioral change approach known as *social marketing*, which is the application of marketing techniques to influence behavior change in groups and communities.

Social Cognitive Theory: An Agentic Perspective

Source: Excerpts from Bandura, A. 2001. "Social Cognitive Theory: An Agentic Perspective." *Annual Review of Psychology* 52: 1–26. Reprinted with permission from the *Annual Review of Psychology,* Volume 52 ©2001 by Annual Reviews www.annualreviews.org

INTRODUCTION

To be an agent is to intentionally make things happen by one's actions. Agency embodies the endowments, belief systems, self-regulatory capabilities and distributed structures and functions through which personal influence exercised, rather than residing as a discrete entity in a particular place. The core features of agency enable people to play a part in their self-development, adaptation, and self-renewal with changing times. Before presenting the agentic perspective of social cognitive theory, the paradigm shifts that the field of psychology has undergone in its short history warrant a brief discussion. In these theoretical transformations, the core metaphors have changed but for the most part, the theories grant humans little, if any, agentic capabilities.

PARADIGM SHIFTS IN PSYCHOLOGICAL THEORIZING

Much of the early psychological theorizing was founded on behavioristic principles that embraced an input-output model linked by an internal conduit that makes behavior possible but exerts no influence of its own on behavior. In this view, human behavior was shaped and controlled automatically and me-chanically by environmental stimuli. This line of theorizing was eventually put out of vogue by the advent of the computer, which likened the mind to a biological calculator. This model filled the internal conduit with a lot of representational and computational operations created by smart and inventive thinkers.

If computers can perform cognitive operations that solve problems, regulative thought could no longer be denied to humans. The input-output model was supplanted by an input-linear throughput-output model. The mind as digital computer became the conceptual model for the times. Although the mindless organism became a more cognitive one, it was still devoid of consciousness and agentic capabilities. For decades, the reigning computer metaphor of human functioning was a linear computational system in which information is fed through a central processor that cranks out solutions according to preordained rules. The architecture of the linear computer at the time dictated the conceptual model of human functioning.

The linear model was, in turn, supplanted by more dynamically organized computational models that perform multiple operations simultaneously and interactively to mimic better how the human brain works. In this model, environmental input activates a multifaceted dynamic throughput that produces the output. These dynamic models include multi-level neural networks with intentional functions lodged in a subpersonal executive network operating without any consciousness via lower subsystems. Sensory organs deliver up information to a neural network acting as the mental machinery that does the constructing, planning, motivating, and regulating nonconsciously. Harré (1983) notes in his analysis of computationalism that it is not people but their componentized subpersonal parts that are orchestrating the courses of action. The personal level involves phenomenal consciousness and the purposive use of information and self-regulative means to make desired things happen.

Consciousness is the very substance of mental life that not only makes life personally manageable but worth living. A functional consciousness involves purposive accessing and deliberative processing of information for selecting, constructing, regulating, and evaluating courses of action. This is achieved through intentional mobilization and productive use of semantic and pragmatic representations of activities, goals, and other future events. In his discerning book on experienced cognition, Carlson (1997) underscores the central role that consciousness plays in the cognitive regulation of action and the flow of mental events. There have been some attempts to reduce consciousness to an epiphenomenal by-product of activities at the subpersonal level, to an executive subsystem in the information processing machinery, or to an attentional aspect of information processing. Like the legendary ponderous elephant that goes unnoticed, in these subpersonal accounts of consciousness there is no experiencing person conceiving of ends and acting purposefully to attain them. However, these reductive accounts remain conceptually problematic because they omit prime features of humanness such as subjectivity, deliberative self-guidance, and reflective self-reactiveness. For reasons to be given shortly, consciousness cannot be reduced to a nonfunctional by-product of the output of a mental process realized mechanically at nonconscious lower levels. Why would an epiphenomenal consciousness that can do nothing evolve and endure as a reigning psychic environment in people's lives? Without a phenomenal and functional consciousness people are essentially higher-level automatons undergoing actions devoid of any subjectivity or conscious control. Nor do such beings possess a meaningful phenomenal life or a continuing self-identity derived from how they live their life and reflect upon it.

Green & Vervaeke (1996) observed that originally many connectionists and computationalists regarded their conceptual models as approximations of cognitive activities. More recently, however, some have become eliminative materialists, likening cognitive factors to the phlogiston of yesteryear. In this view, people do not act on beliefs, goals, aspirations, and expectations. Rather, activation of their network structure at a subpersonal level makes them do things. In a critique of eliminativism, Greenwood (1992) notes that cognitions are contentful psychological factors whose meaning does not depend on the explanatory propositions in which they figure. Phlogiston neither had any evidential basis nor explanatory or predictive value. In contrast, cognitive factors do quite well in predicting human behavior and guiding effective interventions. To make their way successfully through a complex world full of challenges and hazards, people have to make good judgments about their capabilities, anticipate the probable effects of different events and courses of action, size up sociostructural opportunities and constraints, and regulate their behavior accordingly. These belief systems are a working model of the world that enables people to achieve desired outcomes and avoid untoward ones. Forethoughtful, generative, and reflective capabilities are, therefore, vital for survival and human progress. Agentic factors that are explanatory, predictive, and of demonstrated functional value may be translatable and modeled in another theoretical language but not eliminatable (Rot Schaefer, 1985, 1991).

PHYSICALISTIC THEORY OF HUMAN AGENCY

As has already been noted, people are not just onlooking hosts of internal mechanisms orchestrated by environmental events. They are agents of experiences rather than simply undergoers of experiences. The sensory, motor, and cerebral systems are tools people use to accomplish the tasks and goals that give meaning, direction, and satisfaction to their lives (Bandura, 1997; Harré & Gillet, 1994).

Research on brain development underscores the influential role that agentic action plays in shaping the neuronal and functional structure of the brain (Diamond, 1988; Kolb & Whishaw, 1998). It is not just exposure to stimulation, but agentic action in exploring, manipulating, and influencing the environment that counts. By regulating their motivation and activities, people produce the experiences that form the functional neurobiological substrate of symbolic, social, psychomotor, and other skills. The nature of these experiences is, of course, heavily dependent on the types of social and physical environments people select and construct. An agentic perspective fosters lines of research that provide new insights into the social construction of the functional structure of the human brain (Eisenberg, 1995). This is a realm of inquiry in which psychology can make fundamental unique contributions to the biopsychosocial understanding of human development, adaptation, and change.

Social cognitive theory subscribes to a model of emergent interactive agency (Bandura, 1986, 1999a). Thoughts are not disembodied, immaterial entities that exist apart from neural events. Cognitive processes are emergent brain activities that exert determinative influence. Emergent properties differ qualitatively from their constituent elements and therefore are not reducible to them. To use Bunge's (1977) analogy, the unique emergent properties of water, such as fluidity, viscosity, and transparency are not simply the aggregate properties of its microcomponents of oxygen and hydrogen. Through their interactive effects they are transformed into new phenomena.

One must distinguish between the physical basis of thought and its deliberative construction and functional use. The human mind is generative, creative, proactive, and reflective, not just reactive. The dignified burial of the dualistic Descartes forces us to address the formidable explanatory challenge for a physicalistic theory of human agency and a nondualistic cognitivism. How do people operate as thinkers of the thoughts that exert determinative influence on their actions? What are the functional circuitries of forethought, planful proaction, aspiration, self-appraisal, and self-reflection? Even more important, how are they intentionally recruited?

Cognitive agents regulate their actions by cognitive downward causation as well as undergo upward activation by sensory stimulation (Sperry, 1993). People can designedly conceive unique events and different novel courses of action and choose to execute one of them. Under the indefinite prompt to concoct something new, for example, one can deliberatively construct a whimsically novel scenario of a graceful hippopotamus attired in a chartreuse tuxedo hang gliding over lunar craters while singing the mad scene from the opera *Lucia di Lammermoor*. Intentionality and agency raise the fundamental question of how people bring about activities over which they command personal control that activate the subpersonal neurophysiological events for realizing particular intentions and aspirations. Thus, in acting on the well-grounded belief that exercise enhances health, individuals get themselves to perform physical activities that produce health promotive biological events without observing or knowing how the activated events work at the subpersonal level. The health outcome is the product of both agent causality and event causality, operating at different phases of the sequence.

Our psychological discipline is proceeding down two major divergent routes. One line of theorizing seeks to clarify the basic mechanisms governing human functioning. This line of inquiry centers heavily on microanalyses of the inner workings of the mind in processing, representing, retrieving, and using the coded information to manage various task demands, and locating where the brain activity for these events occurs. These cognitive processes are generally studied disembodied from interpersonal life, purposeful pursuits, and self-reflectiveness. People are sentient, purposive beings. Faced with prescribed task demands, they act mindfully to make desired things happen rather than simply undergo happenings in which situational forces activate their subpersonal structures that generate

solutions. In experimental situations, participants try to figure out what is wanted of them; they construct hypotheses and reflectively test their adequacy by evaluating the results of their actions; they set personal goals and otherwise motivate themselves to perform in ways that please or impress others or bring self-satisfaction; when they run into trouble they engage in self-enabling or self-debilitating self-talk; if they construe their failures as presenting surmountable challenges they redouble their efforts, but they drive themselves to despondency if they read their failures as indicants of personal deficiencies; if they believe they are being exploited, coerced, disrespected, or manipulated, they respond apathetically, oppositionally, or hostilely. These motivational and other self-regulative factors that govern the manner and level of personal engagement in prescribed activities are simply taken for granted in cognitive science rather than included in causal structures (Carlson, 1997).

The second line of theorizing centers on the macroanalytic workings of socially situated factors in human development, adaptation, and change. Within this theoretical framework, human functioning is analyzed as socially interdependent, richly contextualized, and conditionally orchestrated within the dynamics of various societal subsystems and their complex interplay. The mechanisms linking sociostructural factors to action in this macroanalytic approach are left largely unexplained, however. A comprehensive theory must merge the analytic dualism by integrating personal and social foci of causation within a unified causal structure. In the paths of influence, sociostructural influences operate through psychological mechanisms to produce behavioral effects. We shall return later to this issue and to the bidirectionality of influence between social structure and personal agency.

CORE FEATURES OF HUMAN AGENCY

The core features of personal agency address the issue of what it means to be human. The main agentic features are discussed in the sections that follow.

Intentionality

Agency refers to acts done intentionally. For example, a person who smashed a vase in an antique shop upon being tripped by another shopper would not be considered the agent of the event. Human transactions, of course, involve situational inducements, but they do not operate as determinate forces. Individuals can choose to behave accommodatively or, through the exercise of self-influence, to behave otherwise. An intention is a representation of a future course of action to be performed. It is not simply an expectation or prediction of future actions but a proactive commitment to bringing them about. Intentions and actions are different aspects of a functional relation separated in time. It is, therefore, meaningful to speak of intentions grounded in self-motivators affecting the likelihood of actions at a future point in time.

Planning agency can be used to produce different outcomes. Outcomes are not the characteristics of agentive acts; they are the consequences of them. As Davidson (1971) explains, actions intended to serve a certain purpose can cause quite different things to happen. He cites the example of the melancholic Hamlet, who intentionally stabbed the man behind a tapestry believing it to be the king, only to discover, much to his horror, that he had killed Polonius. The killing of the hidden person was intentional, but the wrong victim was done in. Some of the actions performed in the belief that they will bring desired outcomes actually produce outcomes that were neither intended nor wanted. For example, it is not uncommon for individuals to contribute to their own misery through intentional transgressive acts spawned by gross miscalculation of consequences. Some social policies and practices originally designed with well-meaning intent turn out bad because their harmful effects were unforeseen. In short, the power to originate actions for given purposes is the key feature of personal agency. Whether the exercise of that agency has beneficial or detrimental effects, or produces unintended consequences, is another matter.

Intentions center on plans of action. Future-directed plans are rarely specified in full detail at the outset. It would require omniscience to anticipate every situational detail. Moreover, turning visualized futurities into reality requires proximal or present-directed intentions that guide and keep one moving ahead (Bandura, 1991b). In the functionalist approach to intentional agency enunciated by Bratman (1999), initial partial intentions are filled in and adjusted, revised, refined or even reconsidered in the face of new information during execution of an intention. We shall see shortly, however, that realization of forward looking plans requires more than an intentional state because it is not causally sufficient by itself. Other self-regulatory aspects of agency enter into the successful implementation of intentions. To add a further functional dimension to intention, most human pursuits involve other participating agents. Such joint activities require commitment to a shared intention and coordination of interdependent plans of action. The challenge in collaborative activities is to meld diverse self-interests in the service of common goals and intentions collectively pursued in concert.

Forethought

The temporal extension of agency goes beyond forward-directed planning. The future time perspective manifests itself in many different ways. People set goals for themselves, antic-ipate the likely consequences of prospective actions, and select and create courses of action likely to produce desired outcomes and avoid detrimental ones (Bandura, 1991b; Feather, 1982; Locke & Latham, 1990). Through the exercise of forethought, people motivate themselves and guide their actions in anticipation of future events. When projected over a long time course on matters of value, a forethoughtful perspective provides direction, coherence, and meaning to one's life. As people progress in their life course they continue to plan ahead, reorder their priorities, and structure their lives accordingly.

Future events cannot, of course, be causes of current motivation and action because they have no actual existence. However, by being represented cognitively in the present, foreseeable future events are converted into current motivators and regulators of behavior. In this form of anticipatory self-guidance, behavior is motivated and directed by projected goals and anticipated outcomes rather than being pulled by an unrealized future state.

People construct outcome expectations from observed conditional relations between environmental events in the world around them, and the outcomes given actions produce (Bandura, 1986). The ability to bring anticipated outcomes to bear on current activities promotes foresightful behavior. It enables people to transcend the dictates of their immediate environment and to shape and regulate the present to fit a desired future. In regulating their behavior by outcome expectations, people adopt courses of action that are likely to produce positive outcomes and generally discard those that bring unrewarding or punishing outcomes. However, anticipated material and social outcomes are not the only kind of incentives that influence human behavior, as a crude functionalism would suggest. If actions were performed only on behalf of anticipated external rewards and punishments, people would behave like weather vanes, constantly shifting direction to conform to whatever influence happened to impinge upon them at the moment. In actuality, people display considerable self-direction in the face of competing influences. After they adopt personal standards, people regulate their behavior by self-evaluative outcomes, which may augment or override the influence of external outcomes.

Self-Reflectiveness

People are not only agents of action but self-examiners of their own functioning. The metacognitive capability to reflect upon oneself and the adequacy of one's thoughts and actions is another distinctly core human feature of agency. Through reflective self-consciousness, people evaluate their motivation, values, and the meaning of their life pursuits. It is at this higher level of self-reflectiveness that individuals address conflicts in motivational inducements and choose to act in favor of one over another. Verification of the soundness of one's thinking also relies heavily on self-reflective means (Bandura, 1986). In this metacognitive activity, people judge the correctness of their predictive and operative thinking against the outcomes of their actions, the effects that other people's actions produce, what others believe, deductions from established knowledge and what necessarily follows from it.

Among the mechanisms of personal agency, none is more central or pervasive than people's beliefs in their capability to exercise some measure of control over their own functioning and over environmental events (Bandura, 1997). Efficacy beliefs are the foundation of human agency. Unless people believe they can produce desired results and forestall detrimental ones by their actions, they have little incentive to act or to persevere in the face of difficulties. Whatever other factors may operate as guides and motivators, they are rooted in the core belief that one has the power to produce effects by one's actions. Meta-analyses attest to the influential role played by efficacy beliefs in human functioning (Holden, 1991; Holden et al., 1990; Multon et al., 1991; Stajkovic & Luthans, 1998).

Perceived self-efficacy occupies a pivotal role in the causal structure of social cognitive theory because efficacy beliefs affect adaptation and change not only in their own right, but through their impact on other determinants (Bandura, 1997; Maddux, 1995; Schwarzer, 1992). Such beliefs influence whether people think pessimistically or optimistically and in ways that are self-enhancing or self-hindering. Efficacy beliefs play a central role in the self-regulation of motivation through goal challenges and outcome expectations. It is partly on the basis of efficacy beliefs that people choose what challenges to undertake, how much effort to expend in the endeavor, how long to persevere in the face of obstacles and failures, and whether failures are motivating or demoralizing. The likelihood that people will act on the outcomes they expect prospective performances to produce depends on their beliefs about whether or not they can produce those performances. A strong sense of coping efficacy reduces vulnerability to stress and depression in taxing situations and strengthens resiliency to adversity.

Efficacy beliefs also play a key role in shaping the courses lives take by influencing the types of activities and environments people choose to get into. Any factor that influences choice behavior can profoundly affect the direction of personal development. This is because the social influences operating in selected environments continue to promote certain competencies, values, and interests long after the decisional determinant has rendered its inaugurating effect. Thus, by choosing and shaping their environments, people can have a hand in what they become.

The rapid pace of informational, social, and technological change is placing a premium on personal efficacy for self-development and self-renewal throughout the life course. In the past, students' educational development was largely determined by the schools to which they were assigned. Nowadays, the Internet provides vast opportunities for students to control their own learning. They now have the best libraries, museums, laboratories, and instructors at their fingertips, unrestricted by time and place. Good self-regulators expand their knowledge and cognitive competencies; poor self-regulators fall behind (Zimmerman, 1990).

Self-regulation is also becoming a key factor in occupational life. In the past, employees learned a given trade and performed it much the same way and in the same organization throughout their lifetime. With the fast pace of change, knowledge and technical skills are quickly outmoded unless they are updated to fit the new technologies. In the modern workplace, workers have to take charge of their self-development for a variety of positions and careers over the full course of their worklife. They have to cultivate multiple competencies to meet the ever-changing occupational demands and roles. Collective agentic adaptability applies at the organizational level as well as the workforce level. Organizations have to be fast learners and continuously innovative to survive and prosper under rapidly changing technologies and global marketplaces. They face the paradox of preparing for change at the height of success. Slow changers become big losers.

Health illustrates self-regulation in another important sphere of life. In recent years, there has been a major change in the conception of health from a disease model to a health model. Human health is heavily influenced by lifestyle habits and environmental conditions. This enables people to exercise some measure of control over their health status. Indeed, through self-management of health habits people reduce major health risks and live healthier and more productive lives (Bandura, 1997). If the huge health benefits of these few lifestyle habits were put into a pill, it would be declared a spectacular breakthrough in the field of medicine.

MODES OF HUMAN AGENCY

Theorizing and research on human agency has been essentially confined to personal agency exercised individually. However, this is not the only way in which people bring their influence to bear on events that affect how they live their lives. Social cognitive theory distinguishes among three different modes of human agency: personal, proxy, and collective.

The preceding analyses centered on the nature of direct personal agency and the cognitive, motivational, affective, and choice processes through which it is exercised to produce given effects. In many spheres of functioning, people do not have direct control over the social conditions and institutional practices that affect their everyday lives. Under these circumstances, they seek their well-being, security, and valued outcomes through the exercise of proxy agency. In this socially mediated mode of agency, people try by one means or another to get those who have access to resources or expertise or who wield influence and power to act at their behest to secure the outcomes they desire. No one has the time, energy, and resources to master every realm of everyday life. Successful functioning necessarily involves a blend of reliance on proxy agency in some areas of functioning to free time and effort to manage directly other aspects of one's life (Baltes, 1996; Brandtstiidter 1992). For example, children turn to parents, marital partners to spouses, and citizens to their legislative representatives to act for them. Proxy agency relies heavily on perceived social efficacy for enlisting the mediative efforts of others.

People also turn to proxy control in areas in which they can exert direct influence when they have not developed the means to do so, they believe others can do it better, or they do not want to saddle themselves with the burdensome aspects that direct control entails. Personal control is neither an inherent drive nor universally desired, as is commonly claimed. There is an onerous side to direct personal control that can dull the appetite for it. The exercise of effective control requires mastery of knowledge and skills attainable only through long hours of arduous work. Moreover, maintaining proficiency under the ever-changing conditions of life demands continued investment of time, effort, and resources in self-renewal.

In addition to the hard work of continual self-development, the exercise of personal control often carries heavy responsibilities, stressors, and risks. People are not especially eager to shoulder the burdens of responsibility. All too often, they surrender control to intermediaries in activities over which they can command direct influence. They do so to free themselves of the performance demands and onerous responsibilities that personal control entails. Proxy agency can be used in ways that promote self-development or impede the cultivation of personal competencies. In the latter case, part of the price of proxy agency is a vulnerable security that rests on the competence, power, and favors of others.

People do not live their lives in isolation. Many of the things they seek are achievable only through socially interdependent effort. Hence, they have to work in coordination with others to secure what they cannot accomplish on their own. Social cognitive theory extends the conception of human agency to collective agency (Bandura, 1997). People's shared belief in their collective power to produce desired results is a key ingredient of collective agency. Group attainments are the product not only of the shared intentions, knowledge, and skills of its members, but also of the interactive, coordinated, and synergistic dynamics of their transactions. Because the collective performance of a social system involves transactional dynamics, perceived collective efficacy is an emergent group-level property, not simply the sum of the efficacy beliefs of individual members. However, there is no emergent entity that operates independently of the beliefs and actions of the individuals who make up a social system. It is people acting conjointly on a shared belief, not a disembodied group mind that is doing the cognizing, aspiring, motivating, and regulating. Beliefs of collective efficacy serve functions similar to those of personal efficacy beliefs and operate through similar processes (Bandura, 1997).

Evidence from diverse lines of research attests to the impact of perceived collective efficacy on group functioning (Bandura, 2000). Some of these studies have assessed the effects of perceived collective efficacy instilled experimentally to differential levels. Other studies have examined the effects of naturally developed beliefs of collective efficacy on the functioning of diverse social systems, including educational systems, business organizations, athletic teams, combat teams, urban neighborhoods, and political action groups. The findings taken as a whole show that the stronger the perceived collective efficacy, the higher the groups' aspirations and motivational investment in their undertakings, the stronger their staying power in the face of impediments and setbacks, the higher their morale and resilience to stressors, and the greater their performance accomplishments.

Theorizing about human agency and collectivities is replete with contentious dualisms that social cognitive theory rejects. These dualities include personal agency versus social structure, self-centered agency versus communality, and individualism verses collectivism. The agency-sociostructural duality pits psychological theories and sociostructural theories as rival conceptions of human behavior or as representing different levels and temporal proximity of causation. Human functioning is rooted in social systems. Therefore, personal agency operates within a broad network of sociostructural influences. For the most part, social structures represent authorized systems of rules, social practices, and sanctions designed to regulate human affairs. These sociostructural functions are carried out by human beings occupying authorized roles (Giddens, 1984).

Within the rule structures of social systems, there is a lot of personal variation in their interpretation, enforcement, adoption, circumvention, and even active opposition (Burns & Dietz, 2000). These transactions do not involve a duality between a reified social structure disembodied from people and personal agency, but a dynamic interplay between individuals and those who preside over the institutionalized operations of social systems. Social cognitive theory explains human functioning in terms of triadic reciprocal causation (Bandura, 1986). In this model of reciprocal causality, internal personal factors in the form of cognitive, affective, and biological events, behavioral patterns, and environmental influences all operate as interacting determinants that influence one another bidirectionally. The environment is not a monolithic entity. Social cognitive theory distinguishes between three types of environmental structures (Bandura, 1997). They include the imposed environment, selected environment, and constructed environment. These different environmental structures represent gradations of changeability requiring the exercise of differing scope and focus of personal agency.

In social cognitive theory, sociostructural factors operate through psychological mechanisms of the self system to produce behavioral effects. Thus, for example, economic conditions, socioeconomic status, and educational and family structures affect behavior largely through their impact on people's aspirations, sense of efficacy, personal standards, affective states, and other self-regulatory influences, rather than directly (Baldwin et al., 1989; Bandura, 1993; Bandura et al., 1996a, 2000a; Elder & Ardelt, 1992). Nor can sociostructural and psychological determinants be dichotomized neatly into remote and proximate influences. Poverty, indexed as low socioeconomic status, is not a matter of multilayered or distal causation. Lacking the money to provide for the subsistence of one's family impinges pervasively on everyday life in a very proximal way. Multicausality involves codetermination of behavior by different sources of influence, not causal dependencies between levels.

The self system is not merely a conduit for sociostructural influences. Although the self is socially constituted, by exercising self-influence human agents operate generatively and proactively, not just reactively, to shape the character of their social systems. In these agentic transactions, people are producers as well as products of social systems. Personal agency and social structure operate interdependently. Social structures are created by human activity, and sociostructural practices, in turn, impose constraints and provide enabling resources and opportunity structures for personal development and functioning.

Another disputable duality inappropriately equates self-efficacy with self-centered individualism feeding selfishness, and then pits it against communal attachments and civic responsibility. A sense of efficacy does not necessarily exalt the self or spawn an individualistic lifestyle, identity, or morality that slights collective welfare. Through unwavering exercise of commanding self-efficacy, Gandhi mobilized a massive collective force that brought about major sociopolitical changes. He lived ascetically, not self-indulgently. If belief in the power to produce results is put in the service of relational goals and beneficial social purposes, it fosters a communal life rather than eroding it. Indeed, developmental studies show that a high sense of efficacy promotes a prosocial orientation characterized by cooperativeness, helpfulness, and sharing, with a vested interest in each other's welfare (Bandura et al., 1996a, 1999, 2000b).

Another dualistic antithesis inappropriately equates self-efficacy with individualism and pits it against collectivism at a cultural level (Schooler, 1990). Cultures are not static monolithic entities, as the stereotypic portrayals would lead one to believe. These global cultural classifications mask intracultural diversity as well as the many commonalities among people of different cultural backgrounds. Both individualistic and collectivistic sociocultural systems come in a variety of forms (Kim et al., 1994). There is substantial generational and socioeconomic heterogeneity in communality among individuals in different cultural systems, and even greater intraindividual variation across social relationships with family members, friends, and colleagues (Matsumoto et al., 1996). Moreover, people express their cultural orientations conditionally rather than invariantly, behaving communally under some incentive structures and individualistically under others (Yamagishi, 1988). Bicultural contrasts, in which individuals from a single collectivistic locale are compared on global indices to individuals from a single individualistic one, can spawn a lot of misleading generalizations.

If people are to pool their resources and work together successfully, the members of a group have to perform their roles and coordinated activities with a high sense of efficacy. One cannot achieve an efficacious collectivity with members who approach life consumed by nagging self-doubts about their ability to succeed and their staying power in the face of difficulties. Personal efficacy is valued, not because of reverence for individualism, but because a strong sense of efficacy is vital for successful functioning regardless of whether it is achieved individually or by group members working together. Indeed, a strong sense of personal efficacy to manage one's life circumstances and to have a hand in effecting societal changes contributes substantially to perceived collective efficacy (Fernández-Ballesteros et al., 2000).

Cross-cultural research attests to the general functional value of efficacy beliefs. Perceived personal efficacy contributes to productive functioning by members of collectivistic cultures just as it does to functioning by people raised in individualistic cultures (Earley, 1993, 1994). However, cultural embeddedness shapes the ways in which efficacy beliefs are developed, the purposes to which they are put, and the socio-structural arrangements through which they are best exercised. People from individualistic cultures feel most efficacious and perform best under an individually oriented system, whereas those from collectivistic cultures judge themselves most efficacious and work most productively under a group-oriented system. A low sense of coping efficacy is as stressful in collectivisitic cultures as in individualistic ones (Matsui & Onglatco, 1991).

There are collectivists in individualistic cultures and individualists in collectivistic cultures. Regardless of cultural background, people achieve the greatest personal efficacy and productivity when their psychological orientation is congruent with the structure of the social system (Earley, 1994). Both at the societal and individual level of analysis, a strong perceived efficacy fosters high group effort and performance attainments.

Cultures are no longer insular. Transnational interdependencies and global economic forces are weakening social and cultural normative systems, restructuring national economies and shaping the political and social life of societies (Keohane, 1993; Keohane & Nye, 1977). Social bonds and communal commitments that lack marketability are especially vulnerable to erosion by global market forces unfettered by social obligation. Because of extensive global interconnectedness, what happens economically and politically in one part of the world can affect the welfare of vast populations elsewhere. Moreover, advanced telecommunications technologies are disseminating ideas, values and styles of behavior transnationally at an unprecedented rate. The symbolic environment feeding off communication satellites is altering national cultures and homogenizing collective consciousness. With further development of the cyberworld, people will be even more heavily embedded in global symbolic environments. In addition, mass migrations of people are changing cultural landscapes. This growing ethnic diversity accords functional value to bicultural efficacy to navigate the demands of both one's ethnic subculture and that of the larger society.

These new realities call for broadening the scope of cross-cultural analyses beyond the focus on the social forces operating within the boundaries of given societies to the forces impinging upon them from abroad. With growing international embeddedness and interdependence of societies, and enmeshment in the Internet symbolic culture, the issues of interest center on how national and global forces interact to shape the nature of cultural life. As globalization reaches ever deeper into people's lives, a strong sense of collective efficacy to make transnational systems work for them becomes critical to furthering their common interests.

LITERATURE CITED

Alland A Jr . 1972. *The Human Imperative.* New York: Columbia Univ. Press

Austin JH. 1978. *Chase, Chance, and Creativity: The Lucky Art of Novelty.* New York: Columbia Univ. Press

Baldwin C, Baldwin A, Sameroff A, Seifer R. 1989. *The role of family interaction in the prediction of adolescent competence.* Presented at Bienn. Meet. Soc. Res. Child Dev., Kansas City, MO

Baltes MM. 1996. *The Many Faces of Dependency in Old Age.* New York: Cambridge Univ. Press

Bandura A. 1973. *Aggression: A Social Learning Analysis.* Englewood Cliffs, NJ: Prentice-Hall

Bandura A. 1982. The psychology of chance encounters and life paths. *Am. Psychol.* 37: 747– 55

Bandura A. 1986. *Social Foundations of Thought and Action: A Social Cognitive Theory.* Englewood Cliffs, NJ: Prentice-Hall

Bandura A. 1991a. *Social cognitive theory of moral thought and action.* In *Handbook of Moral Behavior and Development,* ed. WM Kurtines, JL Gewirtz, 1: 45–103. Hillsdale, NJ: Erlbaum

Bandura A. 1991b. *Self-regulation of motivation through anticipatory and self-reactive mechanisms.* In *Perspectives on Motivation: Nebraska Symposium on Motivation,* ed. RA Dienstbier, 38: 69– 164. Lincoln: Univ. Nebraska Press

Bandura A. 1993. Perceived self-efficacy in cognitive development and functioning. *Educ. Psychol.* 28: 117–48

Bandura A, ed. 1995. *Self-Efficacy in Changing Societies.* New York: Cambridge Univ. Press

Bandura A. 1997. *Self-Efficacy: The Exercise of Control.* New York: Freeman

Bandura A. 1998. Exploration of fortuitous determinants of life paths. *Psychol. Inq.* 9: 95–99

Bandura A. 1999a. *A social cognitive theory of personality.* In *Handbook of Personality,* ed. L Pervin, O John, pp. 154–96. New York: Guilford. 2nd ed.

Bandura A. 1999b. Moral disengagement in the perpetration of inhumanities. *Pers. Soc. Psychol. Rev.* (*Special issue on Evil and Violence*) 3: 193–209

Bandura A. 2000. Exercise of human agency through collective efficacy. *Curr. Dir. Psychol. Sci.* 9: 75–78

Bandura A, Barbaranelli C, Caprara GV, Pastorelli C. 1996a. Multifaceted impact of self-efficacy beliefs on academic functioning. *Child Dev.* 67: 1206–22

Bandura A, Barbaranelli C, Caprara GV, Pastorelli C. 1996b. Mechanisms of moral disengagement in the exercise of moral agency. *J. Pers. Soc. Psychol.* 71: 364–74

Bandura A, Barbaranelli C, Caprara GV, Pastorelli C. 2000a. Self-efficacy beliefs as shapers of children's aspirations and career trajectories. *Child Dev.* In press

Bandura A, Barbaranelli C, Caprara GV, Pastorelli C, Regalia C. 2000b. Sociocognitive Self-Regulatory Mechanisms Governing Transgressive Behavior. *J. Pers. Soc. Psychol.* In press

Bandura A, Pastorelli C, Barbaranelli C, Caprara GV. 1999. Self-efficacy pathways to childhood depression. *J. Pers. Soc. Psychol.* 76: 258–69

Brandtstädter J. 1992. *Personal control over development: implications of self-efficacy.* In *Self-Efficacy: Thought Control of Action,* ed. R Schwarzer, pp. 127–45. Washington, DC: Hemisphere

Bratman ME. 1999. *Faces of Intention: Selected Essays on Intention and Agency.* New York: Cambridge Univ. Press

Bunge M. 1977. Emergence and the mind. *Neuroscience* 2: 501–9

Burns TR, Dietz T. 2000. Human agency and evolutionary processes: institutional dynamics and social revolution. In *Agency in Social Theory,* ed. B Wittrock. Thousand Oaks, CA: Sage. In press

Buss DM, Schmitt DP. 1993. Sexual strategies theory: an evolutionary perspective on human mating. *Psychol. Rev.* 100: 204–32

Bussey K, Bandura A. 1999. Social cognitive theory of gender development and differentiation. *Psychol. Rev.* 106: 676–713

Carlson RA. 1997. *Experienced Cognition.* Mahwah, NJ: Erlbaum

Davidson D. 1971. Agency. In *Agent, Action, and Reason,* ed. R Binkley, R Bronaugh, A Marras, pp. 3–37. Univ. Toronto Press

Diamond MC. 1988. *Enriching Heredity.* New York: Free Press

Dobzhansky T. 1972. Genetics and the diversity of behavior. *Am. Psychol.* 27: 523–30

Earley PC. 1993. East meets West meets Mideast: Further explorations of collectivistic and individualistic work groups. *Acad. Manage. J.* 36: 319–48

Earley PC. 1994. Self or group? Cultural effects of training on self-efficacy and performance. *Admin. Sci. Q.* 39: 89–117

Eisenberg L. 1995. The social construction of the human brain. *Am. J. Psychiatry* 152: 1563–75

Elder GH, Ardelt M. 1992. *Families Adapting to Economic Pressure: Some Consequences for Parents and Adolescents.* Presented at Soc. Res. Adolesc., Washington, DC

Fausto-Sterling A. 1992. *Myths of Gender: Biological Theories About Women and Men.* New York: Basic Books. 2nd ed.

Feather NT, ed. 1982. *Expectations and Actions: Expectancy-Value Models in Psychology.* Hillsdale, NJ: Erlbaum

Fernández-Ballesteros R, Díez-Nicolás J, Caprara GV, Barbaranelli C, Bandura A. 2000. *Structural Relation of Perceived Personal Efficacy to Perceived Collective Efficacy.* Submitted for publication

Giddens A. 1984. *The Constitution of Society: Outline of the Theory of Structuration.* Cambridge: Polity/Berkeley: Univ. Calif. Press

Gould SJ. 1987. *An Urchin in the Storm.* New York: Norton

Green CD, Vervaeke J. 1996. *What kind of explanation, if any, is a connectionist net?* In *Problems of Theoretical Psychology,* ed. CW Tolman, F Cherry, R van Hezewijk, I Lubek, pp. 201–8. North York, Ont.: Captus

Greenwood JD. 1992. Against eliminative materialism: from folk psychology to völkerpsychologie. *Philos. Psychol.* 5: 349–67

Hamburg DA. 1992. *Today's Children: Creating a Future for a Generation in Crisis.* New York: Times Books

Harré R. 1983. *Personal Being: A Theory for Individual Psychology.* Oxford: Blackwell

Harré R, Gillet G. 1994. *The Discursive Mind.* Thousand Oaks, CA: Sage

Holden G. 1991. The relationship of self-efficacy appraisals to subsequent health-related outcomes: a meta-analysis. *Soc. Work. Health Care* 16: 53–93

Keohane RO. 1993. *Sovereignty, interdependence and international institutions.* In *Ideas and Ideals: Essays on Politics in Honor of Stanley Hoffman,* ed. L Miller, M Smith, pp. 91–107. Boulder, CO: Westview

Keohane RO, Nye JS. 1977. *Power and Interdependence: World Politics in Transition.* Boston: Little, Brown

Kim U, Triandis HC, Kâğitçibasi C, Choi S, Yoon G, eds. 1994. *Individualism and Collectivism: Theory, Method, and Applications.* Thousand Oaks, CA: Sage

Kolb B, Whishaw IQ. 1998. Brain plasticity and behavior. *Annu. Rev. Psychol.* 49: 43–64

Krantz DL. 1998. Taming chance: social science and everyday narratives. *Psychol. Inq.* 9: 87–94

Levy D. 2000. *Djerassi sees shift in reproductive roles.* Stanford Rep. 32: 1

Locke EA, Latham GP. 1990. *A Theory of Goal Setting and Task Performance.* Englewood Cliffs, NJ: Prentice-Hall

Maddux JE. 1995. *Self-efficacy, adaptation, and adjustment: Theory, research, and application.* New York: Plenum

Masten AS, Best KM, Garmezy N. 1990. Resilience and development: contributions from the study of children who overcome adversity. *Dev. Psychopathol.* 2: 425–44

Matsui T, Onglatco ML. 1991. Instrumentality, expressiveness, and self-efficacy in career activities among Japanese working women. *J. Vocat. Behav.* 41: 79–88

Matsumoto D, Kudoh T, Takeuchi S. 1996. Changing patterns of individualism and collectivism in the United States and Japan. *Cult. Psychol.* 2: 77–107

Midgley M. 1978. *Beast and Man: The Roots of Human Nature.* Ithaca, NY: Cornell Univ. Press

Moerk EL. 1995. Acquisition and transmission of pacifist mentalities in Sweden. *Peace Confl.: J. Peace Psychol.* 1: 291–307

Multon KD, Brown SD, Lent RW. 1991. Relation of self-efficacy beliefs to academic outcomes: a meta-analytic investigation. *J. Couns. Psychol.* 38: 30–38

Nagel E. 1961. *The Structure of Science.* New York: Harcourt, Brace and World

Pasteur L. 1854. *Inaugural lecture.* University of Lille, France

Rottschaefer WA. 1985. Evading conceptual self-annihilation: some implications of Albert Bandura's theory of the self-system for the status of psychology. *New Ideas Psychol.* 2: 223–30

Rottschaefer WA. 1991. Some philosophical implications of Bandura's social cognitive theory of human agency. *Am. Psychol.* 46: 153–55

Rutter M. 1990. *Psychosocial resilience and protective mechanisms.* In *Risk and Protective Factors in the Development of Psychopathology,* ed. J Rolf, AS Masten, D Cicchetti, KH Neuchterlein, S Weintraub, pp. 181–214. New York: Cambridge Univ. Press

Sanday PR. 1981. The socio-cultural context of rape: a cross-cultural study. *J. Soc. Issues* 37: 5–27

Schooler C. 1990. *Individualism and the historical and social-structural determinants of people's concerns over self-directedness and efficacy.* In *Self-Directedness: Cause and Effects Throughout the Life Course,* ed. J Rodin, C Schooler, KW Schaie, pp. 19–58. Hillsdale, NJ: Erlbaum

Schwarzer R, ed. 1992. *Self-Efficacy: Thought Control of Action.* Washington, DC: Hemisphere

Singhal A, Rogers EM. 1999. *Entertainment-Education: A Communication Strategy for Social Change.* Mahwah, NJ: Erlbaum

Sperry RW. 1993. The impact and promise of the cognitive revolution. *Am. Psychol.* 48: 878–85

Stajkovic AD, Luthans F. 1998. Self-efficacy and work-related performance: a meta-analysis. *Psychol. Bull.* 124: 240–61

Wilson EO. 1998. *Consilience: The Unity of Knowledge.* New York: Knopf

Yamagishi T. 1988. The provision of a sanctioning system in the United States and Japan. *Soc. Psychol. Q.* 51: 265–71

Zimbardo PG. 1995. The psychology of evil: a situationist perspective on recruiting good people to engage in anti-social acts. *Res. Soc. Psychol. (Japn. J.)* 11: 125–33

Zimmerman BJ. 1990. Self-regulating academic learning and achievement: the emergence of a social cognitive perspective. *Educ. Psychol. Rev.* 2: 173–201

Diffusion of Innovations and HIV/AIDS

Source: Bertrand, J. T. "Diffusion of Innovations and HIV/AIDS." *Journal of Health Communication*, Volume 9: 113–121, 2004.

As the HIV/AIDS epidemic continues its relentless spread in many parts of the world, DOI provides a useful framework for analyzing the difficulties in achieving behavior change necessary to reduce HIV rates. The DOI concepts most relevant to this question include communication channels, the innovation-decision process, homophily, the attributes of the innovation, adopter categories, and opinion leaders. The preventive measures needed to halt the transmission of HIV constitute a "preventive innovation." This article describes the attributes of this preventive innovation in terms of relative advantage, compatibility, complexity, trialability, and observability. It reviews studies that incorporated DOI into HIV/AIDS behavior change interventions, both in Western countries and in the developing world. Finally, it discusses possible reasons that the use of DOI has been fairly limited to date in HIV/AIDS prevention interventions in developing countries.

THE CHALLENGE OF HIV/AIDS

HIV/AIDS has emerged as the greatest public health challenge in contemporary times. Given the lack of a vaccine or cure, behavior change is the only means to curb the further spread of this epidemic. In the vast majority of afflicted countries, the primary route of transmission is sexual. In response, many countries have instituted prevention efforts focused on the ABCs: abstinence, being faithful, and condom use. However, transmission by injection drug use has fueled the epidemic in other parts of the world, especially in the former Soviet Union and parts of Asia, including India and China. Needle exchange programs—to avoid the reuse of infected needles—are the response of choice to reduce the rate of infection in such countries. The epidemic initially spreads within subgroups of the population with high-risk behaviors, including commercial sex workers, migrant workers, truck drivers, and injection drug users. As HIV rates increase among these groups, the epidemic slowly progresses into the general population through sexual transmission from these groups to spouses, casual partners, and others. Indeed, once the HIV prevalence rate reaches five percent in a given country, the epidemic has generalized into the larger population and becomes much more difficult to contain.

The HIV/AIDS epidemic continues to advance at a relentless pace. Over 40 million persons were infected with the HIV virus as of 2002; over 70% live in sub-Saharan Africa. Five African countries have an HIV prevalence of over 20%. The two demographic giants in Asia—China and India—have relatively low prevalence rates, but the number of persons infected runs into the millions (UNAIDS, 2002). Eastern Europe and Central Asia have the fastest growing regional epidemics, with the number skyrocketing from an estimated 5000 cases in 1990 to 1 million in 2001 (Lamptey, Wigley, Carr, Colleymore, 2002). San Francisco was one of the first communities to recognize the threat of the HIV/AIDS epidemic, and in the early 1980s members of the gay community mobilized to educate and persuade others to practice safer sex. The results were dramatic, and demonstrated the potential of political advocacy and community mobilization to halt the spread of HIV/AIDS.

In the developing world, only four countries to date have successfully reduced HIV rates or blocked the spread of the virus into the general population. Thailand and Uganda dramatically reduced levels of HIV/AIDS in the 1990s, and descriptions of these successes are frequent in the HIV/AIDS literature (Hogle et al., 2002; Singhal and Rogers, 2003; Steinfatt, 2002). Cambodia has shown more modest reductions, but appears to be following the Thai model. And Senegal, with an HIV prevalence less than 1%, has been successful in blocking the entry of HIV into the general population. However, these countries represent the exception to the rule. Despite millions of dollars that have gone into prevention programs, the majority of developing countries have not been able to curb the spread of the epidemic.

Why has HIV/AIDS been so difficult to stop? The public health community has had dramatic success in other areas of public health requiring behavior change, such as family planning, control of diarrhea through oral rehydration salts, use of Vitamin B, and immunization. However, behavior change for HIV/AIDS has proven far more problematic.

Diffusion of Innovations (DOI) Theory provides useful insight into the difficulty of achieving the behavior change necessary to curb the HIV/AIDS epidemic in developing countries. This paper uses elements of DOI to examine both the lack of success in changing behavior that has resulted in the continued spread of HIV/AIDS in much of the developing world, and in the successful programmatic initiatives that have come to be known as the San Francisco model. Finally, we address the question: why is DOI generally absent from the vast literature on HIV/AIDS prevention in developing countries, with a few notable exceptions described below.

DIFFUSION OF INNOVATIONS CONCEPTS RELEVANT TO HIV/AIDS PREVENTION

The Diffusion of Innovations is characterized by four elements: an innovation, communicated via certain channels, over a period of time, to members of a social system (Rogers, 1995). The innovation refers to an idea, practice, or object that is perceived as new to an individual. The DOI literature is replete with examples of successful innovations: hybrid corn, modern math, new prescription drugs, and family planning, to name a few. However, the changes in behavior needed to halt the HIV/AIDS epidemic constitute what Rogers has labeled a "preventive innovation," defined as "an idea that an individual adopts at one point in time in order to lower the probability that some future unwanted event may occur" (Rogers, 2003). In countries where HIV transmission occurs primarily through sexual relations, the specific behaviors include abstinence, being faithful (to an uninfected partner), or condom use—known as the "ABCs." In countries with a high level of injection drug use, the behavior change intervention includes both needle exchange for injection drug users and adherence to the ABCs. For the sake of brevity, this paper will focus on the ABCs only. Although the theory of DOI is very comprehensive, Rao and Svenkerud (1998) have identified the six DOI concepts that are most relevant to HIV/AIDS prevention:

- Communication channels are the means by which a message is transmitted from one person to another.
- The innovation-decision process is an over-time sequence through which a target audience member passes. This sequence has five stages:
  1. awareness,
  2. knowledge,
  3. persuasion,
  4. adoption, and
  5. implementation.
- Homophily is the extent to which two or more people who communicate perceive that they are similar to one another.
- An attribute is a characteristic of the innovation that may be perceived either positively or negatively; these include:
  - relative advantage
  - comparability
  - complexity
  - trialability
  - observability
- Adopter categories or classifications of individual groups on basis of relative time at which they adopted a new idea, technique, or process.
- Opinion leaders are people who are respected for their knowledge and reputation on some particular topic.

These concepts provide a useful framework for analyzing the effectiveness of programs in the handful of countries that have been successful, as well as the failure of prevention efforts to halt the epidemic in the majority of afflicted countries.

USE OF DOI AS A FRAMEWORK FOR HIV/AIDS PREVENTION

There is no single theory that informs or guides the development of HIV/AIDS prevention programs. Indeed, many different theories have emerged, both to design programs and to evaluate their effectiveness (King, 1999; McKee et al., forthcoming). King (1999) classifies these different theories in one of three categories:

1. focus on individual change,
2. social theories and models, and
3. structural and environmental.

DOI corresponds to the second category, given that it explains how a new practice can diffuse through a given social system to the point it becomes a social norm. As Rogers explained (1995), when "trend setters" in a social group begin to model a new behavior to others, they alter the perception of what is normative. Subsequently, others will begin to adopt the new behavior. Ultimately, community members, regardless of whether they have had contact with the original trendsetters, are expected to adopt the new behavior as it diffuses throughout the community's social networks. Members of the social system in question pass through the stages of the innovation-decision process (awareness, knowledge, persuasion, adoption, and implementation) at different rates, leading to the well-known categories of acceptors: from innovators to laggards.

The early experience with HIV/AIDS in the United States lends credence to this theory. DOI was central to one of the most effective HIV/AIDS prevention programs to date: STOP AIDS in San Francisco. The intervention program drew on Kurt Lewin's Small Group Communication Theory and the Diffusion of Innovation Theory (Singhal & Rogers, 2003). In the early 1980s, gay men in San Francisco took action to combat this deadly disease that had hit their community with brutal force. STOP AIDS began by conducting focus groups to learn how much gay men already knew about HIV/AIDS (Wohlfeiler, 1998) as a basis for designing effective interventions. However, the founders soon realized that the focus groups were having a strong educational effect, as men shared information about HIV prevention. STOP AIDS then employed a group of outreach workers from the gay community to conduct small group meeting in homes and apartments throughout the gay neighborhoods, which launched the diffusion process. From 1985 to 1987, STOP AIDS reached 30,000 men through its various outreach activities (Singhal & Rogers, 2003). According to DOI and as shown in San Francisco, only those early adopters, who make up a relatively small segment of the population, need to initiate a new behavior for it to spread throughout the population (Wohlfeiler, 1998). In the case of STOP AIDS, a well-respected individual who was seropositive led the session attended by other gay and bi-sexual men. He would explain how the virus spreads and encourage participants to either use condoms or seek monogamous relationships. At the end of each session, participants were asked to make a pledge to safer sex, and to volunteer to organize and lead future small group meetings with gay men. Concurrently with the small group meetings, media campaigns helped to increase awareness and knowledge of HIV/AIDS among the gay community. The rate of new infections dropped precipitously by the mid-1980s. Curiously, attendance at the STOP AIDS meetings fell off, and STOP AIDS found it difficult to recruit new volunteers. The program had reached the critical mass of early adopters of safer sex. In 1987, STOP AIDS declared victory and discontinued its local operation, only to reopen in 1990 for new cohorts of younger gay men migrating to the city (Singhal & Rogers, 2003).

Unquestionably, the San Francisco experience demonstrated the power of diffusion and the importance of DOI concepts such as homophily and opinion leaders. STOP AIDS had effectively recruited staff who were part of the community to serve as outreach workers. The opinion leaders within the gay community championed the cause, despite the fear of negative publicity it could bring to the gay community.

One cannot attribute the success of the San Francisco program exclusively to DOI. Indeed, it relied heavily on the epidemiological concept of targeting a group at high risk of spreading the disease, and it utilized other strategies such as Lewin's theories of the social psychology of individual behavior change. However, the experience of San Francisco was sufficiently compelling to lead Kelly and colleagues to study other interventions among gay men in different U.S. communities. Kelly and his colleagues adapted the San Francisco model to reach gay men in small U.S. cities through bars that served as a major congregating point for this group in these cities. The model called for identifying the natural opinion leaders in the community and enlisting them to endorse behavior change. The intervention consisted of four steps:

1. bar staff were trained to identify natural "opinion leaders" among bar patrons;
2. patrons who had been independently nominated by several bar staff were recruited into the project as opinion leaders;
3. opinion leaders were trained in basic communication skills; and
4. contracts were made with opinion leaders to have a specified number of conversations with peers following the training sessions.

Researchers surveyed bar patrons in both intervention and comparison cities, before and after the intervention. These bar-based opinion leader interventions produced community-level adoption of condom use in two-city and three-city comparison group studies (Kelly, St. Lawrence, Diaz, et al., 1991; Kelly, St. Lawrence, Stevenson, et al., 1992) and in a multi-city randomized field trial (Kelly, Winett et al., 1993). Kelly et al.'s work (1991, 1992, 1993) underscores that the nature of urban gay male bar networks provides a particularly powerful place in which diffusion might occur. It also acknowledges the important role that perceived peer norms play in influencing individuals' behavior (Miller et al., 1998).

Inspired by the Kelly et al. research and by Diffusion of Innovation Theory, Miller et al. (1998) attempted to replicate and adapt the bar-based intervention with male prostitutes and other patrons in New York City "hustler" bars. Moreover, these researchers were more systematic in establishing and testing the underlying theoretical model for the intervention. As with the Kelly et al. (1991, 1992, 1993) studies, they sought to alter peer norms to encourage safer sexual behavior by having opinion leaders endorse these behaviors with their peers. Analysis of data on a sample of 1741 male prostitutes and bar patrons indicated significant reductions in paid, unprotected sexual intercourse and oral sex following the intervention. The changes were generally small, though statistically significant. However, the study failed to demonstrate that peer norms mediated the relationship between intervention and behavior.

DOI was also used in the design and evaluation of a study among gay men in London. Elford et al. (2002) noted that the most rigorous studies to date on HIV/AIDS prevention among gay men were all U.S.-based, and they set out to replicate the work for gays in London. However, instead of bars, Elford et al. (2002) tested the design in gyms that gay men frequented. However, they were not able to replicate the significant change in behavior found in the earlier studies among gay men, possibly because the peer educators found it difficult to approach clients and discuss HIV/AIDS in the atmosphere of the gym.

If HIV/AIDS prevention proved so effective in San Francisco in the early 1980s, why then has the epidemic continued to spread so virulently in many countries around to world, infecting over a third of the population in the most extreme cases? Unquestionably, numerous factors favored the intervention in San Francisco: the gay men were highly educated, had a very cohesive sense of community, and had pre-established media channels that targeted the gay community. Moreover, they could focus high levels of energy on this one problem, in contrast to persons in developing countries who must simultaneously struggle with hunger, unemployment, inadequate housing, and other consequences of poverty.

DOI provides useful insights into the failure of prevention efforts in many developing countries worldwide, as outlined below.

WHY HAS BEHAVIOR CHANGE (THE ABCS) BEEN SO DIFFICULT IN DEVELOPING COUNTRIES?

As mentioned above, a handful of countries in the developing world have been successful in curbing the spread of HIV/AIDS: Thailand, Uganda, Senegal, and, to a lesser extent, Cambodia. Zambia appears to be making progress as well. Yet in contrast to these few nations, the vast majority of developing countries affected by HIV/AIDS have been unsuccessful in reducing their HIV rates. DOI theory provides a compelling rationale for the failure of prevention efforts throughout much of the developing world. According to DOI, the pace of diffusion relates directly to the five attributes (characteristics) of the innovation, described earlier. If we consider these five attributes in relation to the ABCs, it becomes clear why this "preventive innovation" has been slow to diffuse in the large majority of developing countries. Relative advantage is the degree to which an innovation is perceived as better than the idea it supersedes. In the case of HIV/AIDS, we are asking sexually active individuals to adopt safer sex practices or forgo sex for a period of time. To do so requires foregoing (or reducing) the pleasure associated with a fundamental biological drive. Adoption of innovations is more rapid when the innovation confers prestige, convenience, or satisfaction. Safer sex confers none of these. Indeed, for a young woman struggling to survive or feed her children, risky transactional sex (not abstinence) offers the greater advantage, at least in the short term.

Compatibility is the degree to which an innovation is perceived as being consistent with the existing values, past experiences, and needs of potential adopters. By contrast, the practice of safer sex (or no sex) often challenges the existing value structure. For example, a woman's negotiating for condom use would be taken as a direct affront to the male's position of dominance in sexual decision-making in many societies. Remaining faithful or limiting the number of partners is contrary to "past experience" in societies that condone multiple sexual partners for males, including visits to commercial sex workers, as well as for females in some societies. By contrast, in many societies it is high-risk behaviors—including multiple sexual partners, visits to commercial sex workers, dry sex, unprotected sex, and transactional sex—that fulfill the immediate needs of the population in question.

Complexity is the degree to which an innovation is perceived as difficult to understand and use. Whereas the behaviors that comprise the ABCs are not particularly complex, they are difficult to sustain over an extended period. Young, sexually active adults must maintain constant vigilance over a 30–50 year period if they are to avoid HIV infection. The burden is onerous and for many of those buying condoms, expensive. Trialability is the degree to which an innovation may be experimented with on a limited basis. Of the five attributes of an innovation, trialability is perhaps the least problematic. A person can experiment with the ABCs on a trial basis. Young people can attempt to delay sexual debut; spouses can commit to being faithful; those who are unable to abstain or remain monogamous can try to use the condom and decide whether it works for them. Thus, the ABCs do offer trialability. Yet trialability is closely linked to observability, on which the ABCs score low. Observability is the degree to which the results of an innovation are visible to others. In contrast to the early diffusion experiments with hybrid corn in rural Iowa, in which farmers could readily observe the improvements available from adopting a new type of corn, the ABCs do not produce a readily observable outcome. Indeed, the ultimate goal (avoiding HIV infection) is a non-event that is highly desired but low on immediate, tangible rewards. It is particularly difficult to convince sexually active individuals that practicing safer sex is worth the sacrifice, given that they may not get infected anyway. Moreover, the problem itself is not observable; and if they do contract HIV, the symptoms of AIDS may not surface for years to come.

In short, HIV/AIDS prevention provides a textbook example of how the attributes of the innovation can affect its rate of diffusion. The handful of success stories indicates that it is possible to overcome the obstacles outlined above, but the challenge is immense.

USE OF DOI FOR THE DESIGN AND IMPLEMENTATION OF HIV/AIDS INTERVENTIONS IN DEVELOPING COUNTRIES

Despite the utility of DOI in explaining the slow diffusion of the ABCs in developing countries, DOI Theory has played a relatively small role in prevention programs in developing countries. It is often cited as one of the theories that underscores the design or evaluation of HIV/AIDS prevention efforts (King, 1999; McKee et al., forth-coming). Yet there are surprisingly few citations to DOI in the vast literature of HIV/AIDS prevention in the developing world.

One exception is the study by Rao and Svenkerud (1998), who analyzed the extent to which relatively more effective and relatively less effective HIV/AIDS prevention programs in San Francisco and Bangkok used Diffusion of Innovations Theory and Social Marketing Theory in reaching culturally unique populations. In Bangkok, as in San Francisco, the programs recruited members of unique populations (e.g., commercial sex workers in the case of Thailand) to reach peers with lifesaving information about HIV/AIDS and condom use. With respect to DOI, the authors concluded that program administrators should use outreach workers who are either homophilous with the intended audience or are opinion leaders in the community. A second exception is the study by Celentano et al. (2000), also from Thailand, which tested the diffusion model in a different way. The researchers designed a field experiment among Royal Thai Army conscripts, including an intervention group, a "diffusion group" (men housed in barracks at the same base but who did not receive the intervention) and controls at a distant base. The intervention promoted condom use, reduced alcohol consumption and brothel patronage, and improved sexual negotiation and condom skills. Whereas the intervention reduced sexually transmitted diseases among the intervention group, it did not produce results in the diffusion group. Celentano and colleagues are currently involved in a five-country randomized trial of DOI through popular opinion leaders in China, India, Peru, Russia, and Zimbabwe (Celentano, personal communication). However, the research is ongoing, and the results are not yet available.

Given the relevance of numerous elements (e.g., homophily, channels of communication, attributes of the program, information-decision process) and mention of DOI as a key theory for HIV/AIDS prevention in several review articles, why is DOI not more prominent in the literature on HIV/AIDS in developing countries?

Several explanations seem plausible. First, DOI is largely a sociological theory that uses social roles, norms, and networks to explain behavior. It does not provide an answer to the key question "what triggers a given individual to action?" Rather, those designing programs have tended to look to the psycho-social theories for guidance on changing deeply rooted sexual mores and behaviors (e.g., the Health Belief Model, Theory of Reasoned Action, Social Learning [modeling] theory, and Prochaska's stages of change theory, to name a few).

Second, the DOI model implies a certain rationality of purpose and sequencing of behavior (i.e., awareness, knowledge, persuasion, adoption, and implementation). Adoption of safer sex diffused effectively through the highly educated, cohesive community of gay men in San Francisco. However, critics of Western-based models are quick to point out that sexual behavior is often irrational (Airhihenbuwa & Obregon, 2000; UNAIDS, 1999). Emotions and sexual arousal may overtake the best of intentions (Perloff, 1995), especially where alcohol, drugs, or fear of violence are also involved. Given that adolescents represent a major target audience for prevention programs in developing countries worldwide, this criticism is particularly relevant.

Third, structural and environmental factors strongly influence sexual behavior (Sweat & Denison, 1995). Migrant workers and truck drivers by definition live apart from their families for significant portions of time, increasing their likelihood of seeking out other partners. Poverty causes the families of young girls to sell them into prostitution, and it prompts mothers to accept transactional sex to provide the bare essentials for their children. School girls whose parents can't afford school fees are more vulnerable to the advances of "sugar daddies." As Perloff (1995) stated, "individuals simply may not be in a position to undo the circumstances that led them to the activity in the first place."

Fourth, cultural norms also dictate sexual behavior. As Singhal & Rogers (2003) explained, culture can be a barrier or a facilitator in controlling the epidemic. One aspect of culture—the role of women in a given society—is recognized as central to HIV/AIDS prevention. In many societies the inferior status of women makes them particularly vulnerable to HIV/AIDS. A faithful wife who suspects her husband of having multiple partners can not refuse to have sexual relations with him or negotiate condom use. Young women are often the victims of forced sexual relations, including by members of their own family. Indeed, there is a growing literature on sexual violence related to women's efforts to protect themselves from HIV/AIDS.

Fifth, leaders in a position to be highly influential at the local or national level may not model appropriate behavior. Such individuals lose their credibility by preaching one behavior but practicing another (e.g., the school teacher who teaches about responsible sexual behavior but then seduces his students after class). A similar problem arises when a prominent national figure engages in high-risk behavior (e.g., the King of Swaziland, who takes on a new adolescent wife every year, implicitly legitimizing the practice of multiple sexual partners).

Sixth, the innovation-decision process may derail in the face of new situations. For example, the introduction of anti-retroviral drugs has caused many young gay men to let down their guard vis-a-vis preventive behaviors. They may be highly knowledgeable about the HIV risk, but the introduction of drugs has caused them to minimize this risk. Some gay men may perceive certain benefits of being HIV positive, such as a strong sense of community with others living with HIV/AIDS and special medical treatment for those participating in clinical trials.

In sum, the preventive interventions for HIV/AIDS increasingly address the context in which behavior change must take place. This approach is highly consistent with Roger's basic definition of the elements of DOI: an innovation, communicated via certain channels, over a period of time, to members of a social system (Rogers, 1995). Certain concepts from DOI have been central to prevention initiatives in countries worldwide (e.g., homophily, communication channels, opinion leadership). One possible reason that DOI has not been more prominent in the literature on HIV/AIDS prevention in developing countries is that it recognizes context as an important factor but does not provide explicit guidance on addressing the social, cultural, and economic obstacles related to context. Another reason is the seeming preference for cognitive or psychosocial models that directly address the question: "What triggers behavior?" As the field of prevention gradually shifts from a predominant focus on individual behavior to recognition of the importance of social norms in defining sexual behavior, DOI may reemerge as a useful theory in fight against HIV/AIDS.

REFERENCES

Airhihenbuwa, C. O., & Obregon, R. (2000). A critical assessment of theories/models in health communication for HIV/AIDS. *Journal of Health Communication*, 5, 5–15.

Celentano, D. (2003, personal communication).

Celentano, D., Bond, K. C., Lyles, C. M., Eiumtrakul, S., Go, V., Beyrer, C., Chiangmai, C., Nelson, K., Kahamboonruang, C., & Vaddhanaphuti, C. (2000). Preventive intervention to reduce sexually transmitted infections. A field trial in the Royal Thai Army. *Archives of Internal Medicine*, 160, 535–540.

Elford, J., Sherr, L., Bolding, G., Serle, F., & Maguire, M. (2002). Peer-led HIV prevention among gay men in London: Process evaluation. *AIDS CARE*, 14(3), 351–360.

Hogue, Jan (ed.). (2002). Project lessons learned case study: What happened in Uganda? In *Declining HIV prevalence, behavior change, and the national response*. Washington, DC: The Synergy Project. pp. 1–13.

Kelly, J. A., St. Lawrence, J. S., Diaz, Y. E., Stevenson, L. Y., Hauth, A. C., Brasfield, T. L., Kalichman, S. C., Smith, J. C., & Andrew, M. E. (1991). HIV risk behavior reduction following intervention with key opinion leaders of population: an experimental analysis. *American Journal of Public Health*, 81, 168–171.

Kelly, J. A., St. Lawrence, J. S., Stevenson, L. Y., Hauth, A. C., Kalichman, S. C., Diaz, Y. C., Brasfield, T. L., Koob, J. J., & Morgan, M. G. (1992). Community AIDS/HIV risk reduction: The effects of endorsements by popular people in three cities. *American Journal of Public Health*, 82, 1483–1489.

Kelly, J. A., Winett, R. A., Roffman, R. A., Solomon, L. J., Sikkema, K. J., Kalichman, S. C., Stevenson, L. Y., Koob, J. J., Desiderato, L. J., Perry, M. J., Norman, A. D., Lemke, A. L., Hauth, A. C., Flynn, B. S., Yaffe, D. M., Steinder, S., & Morgan, M. G. (1993). Social diffusion models can produce population-level HIV risk behavior reduction: Field trial results and mechanisms underlying change. Paper presented at 9th International Conference on AIDS, Berlin, June.

King, R. 1999. Sexual behavior change for HIV: Where have theories taken us? Geneva: UNAIDS.

Lamptey, P., Wigley, M., Carr, D., & Collymore, Y. (2002). Facing the AIDS pandemic. *Population Bulletin*, 57(3), 3–38.

McKee, N., Bertrand, J. T., & Benton-Becker, A. (forthcoming 2004). *Strategic communication in the HIV/AIDS epidemic*. New Delhi: Sage Publications.

Miller, R. L., Klotz, D., & Eckholdt, H. M. (1998). HIV prevention with male prostitutes and patrons of hustler bars: Replication of an HIV preventive intervention. *American Journal of Community Psychology*, 26(1), 97–131.

Perloff, R. M. (2001). *Persuading people to have safer sex. Applications of social science to the AIDS crisis*. Mahwah, NJ: Lawrence Erlbaum Associates.

Rao, N., & Svenkerud, P. J. (1998). Effective HIV/AIDS prevention communication strategies to reach culturally unique populations: Lessons learned in San Francisco, U.S.A. and Bangkok, Thailand. *International Journal of Intercultural Relations*, 22(1), 85–105.

Rogers, E. M. (1995). *Diffusion of innovations* (4th ed.). New York: Free Press.

Rogers, E. M. (2003). *Diffusion of innovations* (5th ed.). New York: Free Press.

Singhal, A., & Rogers, E. (2003). *Combating AIDS: Communication strategies in action*. New Delhi: Sage Publications.

Steinfatt, T. M. (2002). *Working at the bar: Sex work and health communication in Thailand*. Westport, CT: Ablex.

Svenkerud, P. J., & Singhal, A. (1998). Enhancing the effectiveness of HIV/AIDS prevention programs targeted to unique population groups in Thailand: Lessons learned from applying concepts of diffusion of innovations and social marketing. *Journal of Health Communication*, 3, 193–216.

Sweat, M., & Dennison, J. (1995). Reducing HIV incidence in developing countries with structural and environmental interventions. AIDS 9,(suppl A), S251–S257.

UNAIDS (2002). Report on the Global HIV/AIDS epidemic. Geneva: Joint United Nations Programme on HIV/AIDS.

Wohlfeiler, D. (1998). Community organizing and community building among gay and bisexual men: The STOP AIDS Project. In M. Minkler (ed.), *Community organizing and community building for health* (pp. 230–243).

Social Marketing: An Approach to Planned Social Change

Source: Kotler, P. and Zaltman, G. 1971. "Social Marketing: An Approach to Planned Social Change." *Journal of Marketing* 35: 3–12.

In 1952, G. D. Wiebe raised the question "Why can't you sell brotherhood like you sell soap?"[1] This statement implies that sellers of commodities such as soap are generally effective, while "sellers" of social causes are generally ineffective. Wiebe examined four social campaigns to determine what conditions or characteristics accounted for their relative success or lack of success. He found that the more the conditions of the social campaign resembled those of a product campaign, the more successful the social campaign. However, because many social campaigns are conducted under quite un-market-like circumstances, Wiebe also noted clear limitations in the practice of social marketing.

A different view is implied in Joe McGinniss's best-selling book *The Selling of the President 1968*. Its theme seems to be "You can sell a presidential candidate like you sell soap." Once Nixon gave the word: "We're going to build this whole campaign around television . . . you fellows just tell me what you want me to do and I'll do it." The advertising men, public relations men, copywriters, makeup artist, photographers, and others joined together to create the image and the aura that would make this man America's favorite "brand."

These and other cases suggest that the art of selling cigarettes, soap, or steel may have some bearing on the art of selling social causes. People like McGinniss—and before him John K. Galbraith and Vance Packard—believe everything and anything can be sold by Madison Avenue, while people like Wiebe feel this is exaggerated. To the extent that Madison Avenue has

this power, some persons would be heartened because of the many good causes in need of an effective social marketing technology, and others would despair over the spectre of mass manipulation.

Unfortunately there are few careful discussions of the power and limitations of social marketing. It is the authors' view that social marketing is a promising framework for planning and implementing social change. At the same time, it is poorly understood and often viewed suspiciously by many behavioral scientists. The application of commercial ideas and methods to promote social goals will be seen by many as another example of business's lack of taste and self-restraint. Yet the application of the logic of marketing to social goals is a natural development and on the whole a promising one. The idea will not disappear by ignoring it or railing against it.

This article discusses the meaning, power, and limitations of social marketing as an approach to planned social change. First, this will require delineating the generic nature of marketing phenomena and some recent conceptual developments in the marketing field. This will be followed by a definition of social marketing and an examination of the conditions under which it may be carried out effectively. The instruments of social marketing are defined, followed by a systems view of the application of marketing logic to social objectives.

WHAT IS MARKETING?

The following statement testifies that there is no universal agreement on what marketing is.

> It has been described by one person or another as a business activity; as a group of related business activities; as a trade phenomenon; as a frame

of mind; as a coordinative, integrative function in policy making; as a sense of business purpose; as an economic process; as a structure of institutions; as the process of exchanging or transferring ownership of products; as a process of concentration, equalization, and dispersion; as the creation of time, place and possession utilities; as a process of demand and supply adjustment; and many other things.[3]

In spite of the confusing jumble of definitions, the core idea of marketing lies in *the exchange process. Marketing does not occur unless there are two or more parties, each with something to exchange, and both able to carry out communications and distribution.* Typically the subject of marketing is the exchange of goods or services for other goods or services or for money. Belshaw, in an excellent study of marketing exchange and its evolution from traditional to modern markets, shows the exchange process in marketing to be a fundamental aspect of both primitive and advanced social life.[4]

Given that the core idea of marketing lies in exchange processes, another concept can be postulated, that of marketing management, which can be defined as:

> Marketing management is the analysis, planning, implementation, and control of programs designed to bring about desired exchanges with target audiences for the purpose of personal or mutual gain. It relies heavily on the adaptation and coordination of product, price, promotion, and place for achieving effective response.[5]

Thus marketing management occurs when people become conscious of an opportunity to gain from a more careful planning of their exchange relations. Although planned social change is not often viewed from the client's point of view, it involves very much an exchange relationship between client and change agent.[6]

The practice of marketing management as applied to products and services has become increasingly sophisticated. The responsibility of launching new products on a national basis involving the investment and risk of millions of dollars and the uncertainties of consumer and competitor responses, has led to an increased reliance on formal research and planning throughout the product development and introduction cycle. Marketing management examines the wants, attitudes, and behavior of potential customers which could aid in designing a desired product and in merchandising, promoting, and distributing it successfully. Management goes through a formal process of strategy determination, tactical program-

ming, regional and national implementation, performance measurement, and feedback control.

There has been a shift from a sales to a marketing orientation in recent years. A sales orientation considers the job as one of finding customers for existing products and convincing them to buy these products. This sales concept is implicit in *The Selling of the President 1968*, since one is actually not developing a new "product" for the job, but rather trying to sell a given one with a suggestion that it is somewhat "new and improved." The marketing concept, on the other hand, calls for most of the effort to be spent on discovering the wants of a target audience and then creating the goods and services to satisfy them. This view seems privately and socially more acceptable. In private terms, the seller recognizes that it is easier to create products and services for existing wants than to try to alter wants and attitudes toward existing products. In social terms, it is held that this marketing philosophy restores consumer sovereignty in the determination of the society's product mix and the use of national resources.

In practice, since at any time there are both products in existence and new products being born, most marketing efforts are a mixture of selling and marketing: that is, a change strategy and a response strategy. In both cases, marketing management is becoming a sophisticated action technology that draws heavily on the behavioral sciences for clues to solving problems of communication and persuasion related to influencing the acceptability of commercial products and services. In the hands of its best practitioners, marketing management is applied behavioral science.

SOCIAL MARKETING

An increasing number of nonbusiness institutions have begun to examine marketing logic as a means to furthering their institutional goals and products. Marketing men have advised churches on how to increase membership, charities on how to raise money, and art museums and symphonies on how to attract more patrons. In the social sphere, the Advertising Council of America has conducted campaigns for social objectives, including "Smokey the Bear," "Keep America Beautiful," "Join the Peace Corps," "Buy Bonds," and "Go to College." In fact, social advertising has become an established phenomenon on the American scene. Sandage says:

> True, (advertising's) communication function has been confined largely to informing and persuading people in respect to products and services. On the other hand, it can be made equally available to those who wish to inform and persuade people in respect to a city bond issue

cleaning up community crime, the "logic" of atheism, the needs for better educational facilities, the abusive tactics of given law and enforcement officers, or any other sentiment held by any individual who wishes to present such sentiment to the public.[7]

Social advertising has become such a feature of American society that it is no longer a question of whether to use it, but how to use it. It has been very successful in some cases and conspicuously unsuccessful in others. At fault to a large extent is the tendency of social campaigners to assign advertising the primary, if not the exclusive, role in accomplishing their social objectives. This ignores the marketing truism that a given marketing objective requires the coordination of the promotional mix with the goods and services mix and with the distribution mix. Social marketing is a much larger idea than social advertising and even social communication. To emphasize this, the authors define social marketing in the following way:

Social marketing is the design, implementation, and control of programs calculated to influence the acceptability of social ideas and involving considerations of product planning, pricing, communication, distribution, and marketing research.

Thus, it is the explicit use of marketing skills to help translate present social action efforts into more effectively designed and communicated programs that elicit desired audience response. In other words, marketing techniques are the bridging mechanisms between the simple possession of knowledge and the socially useful implementation of what knowledge allows.

REFERENCES

1. G. D. Wiebe, "Merchandising Commodities and Citizenship on Television," *Public Opinion Quarterly,* Vol. 15 (Winter, 1951–52), pp. 679–691, at p. 679.

2. Joe McGinniss, *The Selling of the President 1968* (New York: Trident Press, 1969).

3. Marketing Staff of the Ohio State University, "A Statement of Marketing Philosophy," *Journal of Marketing,* Vol. 29 (January, 1965), p. 43.

4. Cyril S. Belshaw, *Traditional Exchange and Modem Markets* (Englewood Cliffs, N.J.: Prentice-Hall, Inc., 1965).

5. Philip Kotler, *Marketing Management: Analysis, Planning and Control,* Second Edition (Englewood Cliffs, N.J.: Prentice-Hall, Inc., 1972).

6. Arthur H. NiehofT, *A Casebook of Social Change* (Chicago: Aldine, 1966); Warren G. Bennis, Kenneth D. Benne and Robert Chin, *The Planning of Change* (New York: Holt, Rinehart & Winston, 1969).

7. C. H. Sandage, "Using Advertising to Implement the Concept of Freedom of Speech." in *The Role of Advertising,* C. H. Sandage and V. Fryburger, eds. (Homewood, Ill.: Richard D. Irwin, Inc., 1960), pp. 222–223.

PART 6

Social, Cultural, and Environmental Theories, Part II

This is the second of two parts with readings that describe social and behavioral theories that move away from a focus on the individual to social, societal, and cultural influences on behavior. In this part, we complete that move by reviewing approaches that address social factors that affect broader societal and cultural processes influencing behavior. The first reading comes from the well-known "pink book" on health communications (*Making Health Communication Programs Work*), developed by the DHHS, and discusses the process of developing health messages for communications campaigns. The second reading, by Meredith Minkler and colleagues, describes a study of the community involvement experience of nine Healthy Start sites in their efforts to reduce infant mortality (Healthy Start is a federal program sponsored by the Health Resources and Services Administration within the Department of Health and Human Services). The third selection touches on a theoretical contribution (Foster, 1976) from anthropology—the construct of the ethnomedical system—that is useful in understanding health beliefs and practices cross-culturally by understanding differences in beliefs about disease causation (etiology).

Making Health Communication Programs Work

Source: Excerpt from *Making Health Communication Programs Work*. Rockville, MD: National Cancer Institute, U.S. Department of Health and Human Services.

Message concepts are messages in rough form and represent ways of presenting the information to the intended audiences. These may include statements only or statements and visuals . . . In this step, you will learn about the components that go into developing and testing message concepts, including working with creative professionals, creating culturally appropriate communication concepts, choosing a type of appeal, and testing concepts.

To develop, pretest, and eventually produce messages and materials, assemble a team of creative professionals, market research experts, and others. See the Communication Research Methods section for tips on working with market research experts.

NCI's Cancer Research Awareness Initiative: From Message Concepts to Final Message

In 1996, the NCI's Office of Communications (OC), then the Office of Cancer Communications, launched the Cancer Research Awareness Initiative to increase the public's understanding of the process of medical discoveries and the relevance of discoveries to people's lives. OC's concept development and message testing for this initiative included the following activities.

Three values of medical research were selected for concept development:

1. Progress (e.g., we are achieving breakthroughs)
2. Benefits (e.g., prevention, detection, and treatment research are benefiting all of us)
3. Hope (e.g., we are hopeful that today's research will yield tomorrow's breakthroughs)

Based on these values, the following message concepts were developed and explored in focus groups with intended audience members:

- Research has led to real progress in the detection, diagnosis, treatment, and prevention of cancer
- Everyone benefits from cancer research in some fashion
- Cancer research is conducted in universities and medical schools across the country
- Cancer research gives hope
- At the broadest level, research priorities are determined by societal problems and concerns; at the project level, research priorities are driven primarily by past research successes and current opportunities

The following messages were crafted after listening to intended audience members' reactions and their language and ideas about the importance of medical research:

A. Cancer Research: Discovering Answers for All of Us
B. Cancer Research: Because Cancer Touches Us All
C. Cancer Research: Discovering More Answers Every Day
D. Cancer Research: Because Lives Depend on It
E. Cancer Research: Only Research Cures Cancer

Mall-intercept interviews were conducted to pretest them. Based on responses from the intended audience in these interviews, message D was selected as the program theme.

Source: Making Health Communication Programs Work. Rockville, MD: National Cancer Institute, U.S. Department of Health and Human Services.

WORKING WITH CREATIVE PROFESSIONALS

Developing a communication campaign usually involves working with creative professionals, either within your organization or on a contract basis. In either case, managing the relationship effectively is critical to getting the creative materials you want:

- Get to know and feel comfortable with the people who will be working on the project. If you are considering a contract with an advertising agency, public relations firm, or consulting firm, interview the professionals who will staff your effort (not just the agency representatives who solicit your business) and review samples of their specific work (not just the agency's). Write into the contract *who* will work on the project.
- Be a good client. Use the creative brief to lay out the communication strategy (developed in Stage 1) and make sure the team understands the brief and that it must be followed. Think about what you want before you discuss the assignment and show the creative team examples of other materials that worked well or didn't and explain why. If you say, "I don't know what I want; you're the creative one," you lose a valuable opportunity to give creative professionals the fundamental direction they want and need. This does not mean asking for a blue brochure; it means helping members of the creative staff understand the objectives and concerns and what you've learned about the intended audience so that they can use their expertise to suggest effective approaches. Discuss sensitive issues, key content points, and other aspects that you want to see conveyed in the messages and materials, based on your knowledge and expertise.
- Agree at the outset to what pretesting and approvals will be required, when they will occur, and how long they will take.
- Discuss the theoretical grounding of the communication effort and help creative professionals understand and apply health communication theory to messages and materials development. Brainstorm with them about how the theory might shape the messages and materials and evaluate works in progress with this perspective in mind.
- Involve the creative team in concept exploration and pretesting. Ask its members what questions they would like addressed and make sure they can observe (not participate in) concept exploration sessions. Listening to the intended audience can help them craft messages and materials that use language and ideas that the audience will identify with.
- Assess draft messages and materials against the creative brief and what you know about an intended audience member's point of view. If the intended audience is urban teens at high risk of pregnancy, and you are a middle-aged suburbanite, recognize that the materials most likely to be effective with the intended audience may not appeal to you at all.
- Trust the team's professional expertise, provided that the material is consistent with your program's strategy and the intended audience's culture. While you have a key role to play in ensuring the appropriateness and accuracy of substantive content and in maintaining the program's strategic focus, developing the team's insights and commitment will keep the team involved.

DEVELOPING CULTURALLY APPROPRIATE COMMUNICATIONS

Culture encompasses the values, norms, symbols, ways of living, traditions, history, and institutions shared by a group of people. Culture affects how people perceive and respond to health messages and materials, and it is intertwined in health behaviors and attitudes. Often, an individual is influenced by more than one culture; for example, teenagers are influenced by their individual family cultures as well as the norms, values, and symbols that comprise teen culture in their locale.

To develop effective health communications, you must understand key aspects of the cultures influencing the intended audience and build that understanding into the communication strategy. Messages must take into account cultural norms in terms of what is asked (e.g., don't ask people to make a behavior change that would violate cultural norms), what benefit is promised in exchange (in some cultures, community is most important; in others, individual benefit is), and what image is portrayed. The symbols, metaphors, visuals (including clothing, jewelry, and hairstyles), types of actors, language, and music used in materials all convey culture.

While it is important to acknowledge and understand the cultures within an intended audience, developing separate messages and materials for each cultural group is not always necessary or even advisable. For example, when print materials for a state program for low-income people depicted people of only one race, some intended audience members who were of that race felt singled out and said the materials suggested that only members of their racial group were poor. Careful intended audience research can help your program identify messages and images that resonate across groups or identify situations in which different messages or images are likely to work best.

According to a Center for Substance Abuse Prevention *Technical Assistance Bulletin*, culturally sensitive communications:

- Acknowledge culture as a predominant force in shaping behaviors, values, and institutions
- Understand and reflect the diversity within cultures. In designing messages that are culturally appropriate, the following dimensions are important:
  - *Primary cultural factors* linked to race, ethnicity, language, nationality, and religion
  - S*econdary cultural factors* linked to age, gender, sexual orientation, educational level, occupation, income level, and acculturation to mainstream
- Reflect and respect the attitudes and values of the intended audience; some examples of attitudes and values that are interrelated with culture include:
  - Whether the individual or the community is of primary importance
  - Accepted roles of men, women, and children
  - Preferred family structure (nuclear or extended)
  - Relative importance of folk wisdom, life experience, and value of common sense compared with formal education and advanced degrees
  - Ways that wealth is measured (material goods, personal relationships)
  - Relative value put on different age groups (youth versus elders)
  - Whether people are more comfortable with traditions or open to new ways

- Favorite and forbidden foods
- Manner of dress and adornment
- Body language, particularly whether touching or proximity is permitted in specific situations
- Are based on concepts and materials developed for and with the involvement of the intended audience. (Substituting culturally specific images, spokespeople, language, or other executional detail is not sufficient unless the messages have been tested and found to resonate with the intended audience. Formative research with audience members takes on added importance when planners and designers have different cultural backgrounds than the intended audience does.)
- Refer to cultural groups using terms that members of the group prefer (e.g., many people resent the term "minority" or "nonwhite." Preferred terms are often based on nationality, such as Japanese or Lakota.)
- Use the language of the intended audience, carefully developed and tested with the involvement of the audience.

Identifying Messages That Resonate Across Cultures

As part of an effort to design messages that are meaningful and appealing to women in different ethnic groups and to older women, NCI's Office of Communications conducted separate focus groups with African-American, American-Indian, Asian, Caucasian, and Latina women.

The groups tested 10 motivational messages about mammography. Once participants had individually selected the motivational messages they found most and least persuasive, the moderator led them in a more detailed discussion of each message's strengths and weaknesses. Throughout the discussion, the moderator probed participants' knowledge, attitudes, and behaviors concerning breast cancer and mammography, sometimes exploring underlying motivations and barriers.

Across focus groups, the following message elements were viewed most positively:

- Breast cancer can develop at any time
- All women are at risk—even those age 65 and older, or those without a family history
- Mammograms can detect breast cancer early
- Early detection can save lives

The least persuasive messages made explicit reference to issues that were considered turnoffs, fear and age. Participants were uncomfortable with messages that specified age and, in some cases, gender. Many said that cancer was a risk for all people (some pointed out that men can get breast cancer), stating that older women (i.e., over 40) should not be singled out. The notion of a mammogram being able to "save your life" was persuasive not only because it was positive but also because it did not distinguish between age groups. In general, messages that seemed to tell women what to think were deemed offensive, while messages that were phrased as explanation or encouragement were more effective.

Note. From *Multi-Ethnic Focus Groups to Test Motivational Messages on Mammography and Breast Cancer*, by National Cancer Institute, August 2000. Bethesda, MD. In the public domain.

CHOOSING THE TYPE OF APPEAL

To capture the intended audience's attention, you can scare people, tug at their hearts, make them laugh, make them feel good, or give them straight facts. What will work best? The answer generally depends on the intended audience's preferences, what your program is asking people to do, and how you plan to use the appeal in asking them to do it.

Positive emotional appeals show the benefits intended audience members will gain when they take the action portrayed in the message. Research has shown that, in general, messages that present a major benefit but do not address any drawbacks tend to be most appropriate when intended audience members are already in favor of an idea or practice. In contrast, messages that present a major benefit and directly address any major drawbacks work best when people are not favorably predisposed.

Humorous appeals can work for simple messages, especially if most competing communication is not humorous. The humor should be appropriate for the health issue and convey the main message; otherwise, people tend to remember the joke but not the message. Also, humorous messages can become irritating if repeated too frequently.

Threat (or fear) appeals have been shown to be effective with two groups. Research has shown that such appeals tend to be more effective with "copers" (people who are not anxious by nature) and "sensation seekers" (certain youth), and when exposure to the message is voluntary (picking up a brochure rather than mandatory attendance at a substance abuse prevention program). Research has also shown that, to be effective, a threat appeal should include:

- A compelling threat of physical or social harm
- Evidence that the intended audience is personally vulnerable to the threat
- Solutions that are both easy to perform (i.e., intended audience members believe they have the ability to take the action) and effective (i.e., taking the action will eliminate the threat)

In general, however, the effectiveness of threat appeals is widely debated.

The most appropriate type of appeal may differ from this general guidance, depending upon gender, age, ethnicity, severity of the problem, and the intended audience's relationship to the problem. For more information, please consult the following sources under Selected Readings at the end of this section: Backer, Rogers, and Sopory (1992); Goldberg, Fishbein, and Middlestadt (1997); Kotler and Roberto (1989); Maibach and Parrott (1995); Palmgreen et al. (1995); Siegel and Doner (1998).

Choosing Messages for Young Sensation Seekers

Research has found that some youth have a preference for novel experiences and stimuli. Called "sensation seekers," members of this group have four subcategories that represent degrees of the characteristic:

1. Thrill- and adventure-seeking (e.g., parachuting and scuba diving)
2. Experience-seeking (e.g., nonconforming lifestyle and musical tastes, drugs, unconventional friends)
3. Disinhibition (sensation through social stimulation; e.g., parties, social drinking, a variety of sex partners)
4. Boredom susceptibility (restlessness when things are the same for too long)

Some health communicators working on drug abuse prevention programs have found that focusing on sensation seekers with messages that appeal to this aspect of their personalities can be effective in promoting attention to and recall of the message and in affecting factors such as behavioral intention and attitudes.

For example, a University of Kentucky program designed for adolescents a creative high-sensation television PSA that focused on the importance of alternatives to substance use for meeting sensation needs. The PSA, titled "Common," featured heavy metal music and quick-action cuts of high-sensation activities. "Wasted," which had the highest sensation value, also had heavy metal music and displayed the words "wasted," "blasted," "stoned," and "fried." Voice-over and illustrative footage accompanied each word (e.g., "with drugs you can get fried" had footage of a monk's self-immolation). It closed with the words "without drugs you can still get high" and offered examples of high-sensation alternatives.

Note. From "Reaching At-Risk Populations in a Mass Media Drug Abuse Prevention Campaign: Sensation Seeking as a Targeting Variable," by P. Palmgreen et al. In *Drugs & Society* 8(3), pp. 29–45. 1995, Binghamton, NY: Haworth Press. Adapted with permission.

Using Community Involvement Strategies in the Fight Against Infant Mortality

Source: Excerpts from Minkler M, Thompson M, Bell J, Rose K, and Redman D. 2001. "Using Community Involvement Strategies in the Fight Against Infant Mortality: Lessons From a Multisite Study of the National Healthy Start Experience." *Health Education & Behavior* Vol. 28 (6): 783–807.

When President Clinton introduced his bold new public health initiative aimed at eliminating racial and ethnic disparities in health by the year 2010, he identified infant mortality as one of the six key problem areas that the U.S. Department of Health and Human Services (1998) had elected to target. This choice was an important one because infant mortality is an area in which many communities of color, and particularly African American communities, continue to experience serious disparities in health access and outcomes (U.S. Department of Health and Human Services, 1998). But it was important also because the tragedy of infant death is compounded by the fact that it so often could have been prevented through adequate prenatal and neonatal care (Kotch, Blakely, Brown, & Wong, 1992). As efforts are mounted to reach the goal of ending racial and ethnic disparities in infant mortality and other health problem areas, it is critical that we reexamine and lift up the experiences of earlier comprehensive community-based public health efforts. Key among these is the National Healthy Start Program (NHSP) to reduce infant mortality.

This article will present findings from a multisite study of the community involvement experience of nine Healthy Start sites (Thompson et al., 2000) highlighting lessons learned for this program and other public health initiatives designed to help eliminate health disparities. The study was conducted for and with PolicyLink, a new national policy, research, commu-

nications, and capacity-building organization concerned with advancing social and economic equity and building strong, organized communities. Consistent with PolicyLink's mission, the study used empowerment theory as a broad conceptual framework. The research involved an in-depth look at the nature and functioning of community involvement strategies at each Healthy Start site, as well as changes in the areas of program, policy, and practice that might be related in part to each site's community involvement strategies. Following a brief overview of the NHSP, the study's conceptual framework and methods briefly will be described. In Table 6-1, we summarize key features of each of the nine sites examined and sample community involvement activities. In the body of the article we then highlight themes that emerged in the cross site analysis, which in turn helped inform our understanding of and ability to document the topic of the present article—what community involvement did for Healthy Start. We examine the six key ways in which community involvement enriched the program, and discuss the implications of these findings for health promotion practice targeting the elimination of health disparities.

BACKGROUND—THE NHSP

When the NHSP commenced in 1991, the United States ranked 22nd in the world in infant mortality, and the Black infant death rate was more than twice the White rate (U.S. Department of Health and Human Services, Public Health Service, 1996; Kotch et al., 1992). The Healthy Start Initiative had as its goal reducing infant mortality by 50% during a 5-year period in 15 demonstration sites, plus an additional 80 sites added by the late 1990s. With the exception of the Northern Plains area, which had a high proportion of Native Americans, all of the original Healthy Start communities had populations composed of at least 50% African Americans, and 5 had sizable Latino populations as well (Howell et al., 1998).

Although the communities selected for participation in Healthy Start had high rates of unemployment, homelessness, and other poverty-related problems, they also had many strengths, and Healthy Start was committed to reducing infant mortality in part by building on these community assets. Administered by the Health Resources and Services Administration (HRSA) and later its Maternal and Child Health Bureau, the program indeed was "founded on the premise that communities themselves could best develop the strategies necessary to attack the causes of infant mortality and low birth weight, especially among high risk populations" (Badura, 1999, p. 263). Early guidelines for the program included the stipulation that "substantive and informed" consumer participation be a "central consideration in organizing a Healthy Start project," and that it extend from the initial conceptualization through project evaluation (HRSA, 1991, p. 4).

The heavy accent placed on community involvement included the mandated development of community consortia at each site, composed of program participants, providers, community leaders, and other stakeholders. These collaborative partnerships were to have a major role in program planning and decision making on the premise that such community-driven approaches would lead to better, more culturally relevant service delivery (Bailey, 1992; Health Resources and Services Administration, 1996; McCoy-Thompson, 1994). Healthy Start grantees (e.g., health departments, large nonprofit organizations, or other entities) were given considerable flexibility in what these consortia should look like and, as indicated in Table 6-1, considerable variation in their form and functioning could be observed.

Although the consortia constituted the primary means of facilitating community involvement in Healthy Start and were, for that reason, the main focus of our research, a range of other community involvement processes also were employed.

TABLE 6-1 Healthy Start Site Summaries and Sample Community Involvement Activities

Site	Fiscal Agent	Consortia Structure and Role in Governance	Activities and Achievements Sample Community Involvement
Boston	Boston Public Health Commission	Very strong consumer participation model with seven committees Policy decisions on type and level of services Influence on outreach strategies and marketing tools	Strong tenant leadership training program with requirement of participation in another community initiative Hiring of consultant to help 20 community-based organization (CBO) subcontractors find new funding sources
Chicago	State of Illinois, Department of Human Services	Very strong consumer participation model with three committees Policy decisions on type and level of services	Annual consumer conference on topics identified by participants in consortia subcommittee Community Mobilization Committee's catalytic role in consortia organizing on welfare reform resulting in state policy change
Cleveland	Cleveland Department of Public Health	Eight sites serving 15 neighborhoods; each site represented on Consortium Leadership Committee Executive Council and Administrative Management Group make policy decisions	Consortia involvement in organizing around community identified problems (e.g., sale of tainted meat and hospital's use of incinerator) Training and hiring of 235 residents as lay health workers
Kansas City	Heart of America United Way	Strong provider representation with three committees No involvement in governance	Consortium-sponsored conference on cultural sensitivity in relation to growing Hispanic population

TABLE 6-1 (continued)

Site	Fiscal Agent	Consortia Structure and Role in Governance	Activities and Achievements Sample Community Involvement
New Orleans	Mayor's office receives funds; passes through to Healthy Start nonprofit (Great Expectations Foundation)	10 local councils represented on Consortia Steering Committee; some input on budget and personnel decisions Council members and consumer representatives make policy decisions on nonprofit board of directors	Training for selected consortia members and subsequent inclusion on governing board Inclusive strategic planning process and follow-up allocation of minigrants by consortium
New York	Medical and Health Research Association of New York City, Inc.	Regional model; local consortia representatives on citywide consortium that makes governance-level decisions Community members trained in public speaking, board involvement, and resource development strategies	Hiring and training of 19 program participants as violence prevention peer educators, who also helped create a health education video Creation of job training center focusing on computer skills; 80% of participants subsequently found full- or part-time jobs
Pee Dee	Private, nonprofit	Separate consortia for providers and consumers, now working more closely together Additional consortia focused on males Agency's board of directors makes governance decisions	Creation of van transportation system to enable resident participation in Healthy Start and consortium activities Separate community consortium and development of nonprofit in part in response to felt community need for strong African American–led organizations
Philadelphia	Philadelphia Department of Public Health Maternal Child Health (MCH)	Very strong consumer participation model with six communities Consumers trained at community colleges for their roles in the consortium	Day-long event to build trust between consortia providers and community members Creation of Asian Advisory Committee, later integrated into health department
Philadelphia	Philadelphia Department of Public Health, maternal child health	Policy decisions on type and level of services Strong community-led consortia with minimal staff input	Day-long event to build trust between providers and community members Materials translated into several Asian languages to encourage involvement
Pittsburgh	Alleghany County Health Department; passes funds through to Healthy Start nonprofit	Regional model with one consortium in each of six target areas Policy decisions on type and level of services Input on budget and personnel decisions	Strong, active participation of county health department since inception of program encourages community involvement Very strong training for community residents hired for staff positions Extensive male involvement program

Source: Minkler M, Thompson M, Bell J, Rose K, and Redman D. 2001. "Using Community Involvement Strategies in the Fight Against Infant Mortality: Lessons From a Multisite Study of the National Healthy Start Experience." *Health Education & Behavior* Vol. 28 (6): 783-807.

Prominent among these were the hiring, training, and extensive use of indigenous lay health workers, and the holding of focus groups, town hall meetings, health fairs, and other special events and activities (Thompson et al., 2000). The community involvement component of Healthy Start has been called the "defining feature" of the program, and one that most distinguishes it from other maternal child health programs (Howell et al., 1998).

With the signing of the Children's Health Act of 2000, Healthy Start became a permanent program. With a fiscal year 2001 budget allocation of $90 million and a mandate to continue to emphasize community involvement, it offers a unique opportunity to explore the role that community involvement can play in enhancing community capacity while improving service delivery.

CONCEPTUAL FRAMEWORK

As noted above, the study was grounded in a conceptual framework of empowerment theory. An enabling process through which individuals and communities take control over their lives and their environment (Rappaport, 1984), empowerment also involves social action. For as Wallerstein (1992) noted, through this process "individuals, organizations and communities gain mastery over their lives *in the context of changing their social and political environment to improve equity and quality of life*" [italics added] (p. 198). As Zimmerman (2000) suggested, empowerment operates at multiple levels simultaneously, and three key factors—participation, control, and critical awareness—are involved on each level. The involvement of individuals in decision making and in understanding the root causes of problems, organizational effectiveness in service delivery and the policy process, and the creation of contexts enabling communities to identify and address their felt needs all are a part of empowerment process and outcomes (Zimmerman, 2000).

Fawcett et al. (1995) identified four major strategies that appear to facilitate the process of empowerment and the achievement of empowerment-related outcomes: "(a) enhancing experience and competence, (b) enhancing group structure and capacity, (c) removing social and environmental barriers, and (d) enhancing environmental support and resources" (p. 679). Below we draw on these various dimensions and strategies of empowerment to examine the contributions of community involvement to Healthy Start in nine different geographic areas.

METHOD

The research aims of this study were to examine multiple aspects of the community involvement component of the NHSP, including the nature and functioning of the community involvement component at each Healthy Start site examined;

the conditions and processes that facilitated or impeded well-functioning consortia and other community involvement efforts; and whether and how community involvement was seen by key stakeholders as resulting in changes such as new or modified programs, policies, and practices.

To address these research goals, a multisite case study design (Yin, 1994) was used that would enable us to examine the specific contexts, conditions, and processes of change at individual sites and the themes that emerged across sites in the area of community involvement. Multiple methods were used to collect data at each site, including key informant interviews, focus groups with participants and other community members, observations of consortia meetings and other relevant events, and documents review.

To create a working partnership that would foster critical discussion, planning, review, and implementation of the project's goals, a 15-member advisory committee was constituted and actively involved in study design, questionnaire construction, and other aspects of the project. The advisory group included individuals knowledgeable about Healthy Start and community involvement, researchers, policy advocates, physicians, and NHSP participants and consortia members from several of the study sites. The inclusion of local community members reflected PolicyLink's and Healthy Start's commitments to and belief in the value of community involvement. Although the full advisory committee met with the project team only twice, individual members and subgroups were consulted as needed throughout the project period and provided crucial feedback on site selection and study design, the interpretation of findings, and the development and dissemination of recommendations and study products.

[This excerpt does not include the sections which discuss methodology or design.]

RESULTS

A full discussion of the findings of this study is beyond the scope of this article (see Minkler et al., 2001; Thompson et al., 2000). Above we provide a profile of the nine participating NHSPs, the structure and functioning of their consortia, and sample community involvement activities and accomplishments at each site (see Table 6-1). We then examine below in more detail the role of community involvement strategies in the program's fight against infant mortality. Our research indicated that the community involvement component of the nine Healthy Start sites contributed to the program in six principal ways:

1. *Community involvement helped create the conditions in which individuals could change their behavior to improve health outcomes and become better parents.* A consistent

theme in our study involved the heavy accent on health education and training. At virtually every site, a strong emphasis was placed on delivering health education and life skills training to the community. Infant CPR and first aid, immunizations, English as a second language (ESL) classes, and computer training were among the ongoing classes provided at most sites. Through them, and often by taking part in their site's consortia or leadership training activities, individuals were helped to acquire skills and a sense of mastery in their own lives. A New Orleans participant described how her sense of failure at becoming pregnant while in college had shifted to an increased sense of self-esteem through her involvement with the consortium and eventual appointment as a member of the board of directors. In other instances, leadership skills developed through consortia trainings and meetings resulted in career advancement for consortia members, who progressed to become consortia leaders and coordinators. For other individuals, new skills and competencies made possible a return to school, greater civic involvement, or the attaining of employment. In the words of Chicago's consortia chair:

> When families leave Healthy Start they fare well. They know how to apply for a job, how to use community resources like the Bottomless Closet, they know where the jobs are, how to navigate the health care system, and how to advocate for themselves.

2. *Community involvement helped individuals become empowered to take action in the broader community.* A second theme identified by all three reviewers involved the attention that was paid to community-identified issues and concerns. Following the health education principle of "starting where the people are" (Nyswander, 1956), the programs, through their community consortia and other means, engaged participants around issues they identified, which ranged from problems specific to their neighborhoods to broader community issues such as domestic violence and substance abuse. In Cleveland, participants were concerned about a local store that was selling tainted meat and a hospital's use of an incinerator that was creating an environmental hazard. The consortia helped residents successfully change these situations. Philadelphia engaged in neighborhood organizing, culling issues identified by residents into action plans that included a focus on reducing infant mortality.

Healthy Start also helped develop leadership skills among participants who then could apply these skills to a broad range of community health issues. In Boston, Healthy Start provided strong tenant leadership training but required, as a condition of participation, that individuals commit to becoming actively involved in at least one other neighborhood initiative (e.g., around economic development, or crime and safety) to make their community "a better place." Outcomes of constructive community engagement frequently were felt beyond the NHSP. In Boston and Philadelphia, for example, project directors reported that community input increasingly was sought by political leaders and others. In the words of the Philadelphia project director, "Professionals will readily call the community now. The Health Commissioner now listens to our consortium chair!" Boston's project director similarly noted that "our consortium members have been in focus groups across the city for all kinds of issues. When they want consumer input they call Boston Healthy Start."

3. *Community involvement mobilized the community to work for health-related goals and objectives.* In many communities, there was a "call to action" that resulted in a real coming together in the fight against infant mortality. In Cleveland, neighborhood events in settlement houses were used by Healthy Start community organizers to link infant mortality to other issues of concern to the community, and local churches sponsored "Healthy Baby Sundays" in which part of a service was focused on increasing awareness about infant mortality. In New York City, growing critical awareness about the links between poor birth outcomes and domestic violence, and the fact that fully 80% of program participants had been in abusive situations, led to the training and hiring of 19 domestic violence peer educators. In addition to their one-on-one work, the women also helped develop a video on domestic violence that they subsequently used in group education efforts. As these examples illustrate, preexisting community organizations (e.g., settlement houses) and program participants themselves were recognized as important community assets and provided training and other assistance that facilitated their growth and contributions.

There also was real attention to addressing the race-, ethnic-, and class-based tensions that could hamper effective mobilization. Indeed, a theme identified by all three reviewers involved the presence of tensions based on race, ethnicity, and professional hierarchy, and the emphasis on addressing these tensions in a constructive manner. Kansas City's Healthy Start, for example, hosted a training conference on cultural competence in relation to a growing Hispanic population. In Boston and Philadelphia, special efforts were made to reach out to a growing Asian population, with Philadelphia creating an Asian Advisory Committee that later was integrated into the health department. In Pee Dee, two separate consortia initially had been formed, one for the predominately White service providers and a second for program participants who were disproportionately African American. To help bridge this divide, which was based in part on tensions related to race, class, and professional hierarchy, efforts later were undertaken to develop an overarching structure that could facilitate communication between the two entities.

Finally, small steps were taken at different sites to address racial/ethnic tensions and divisions. Chicago's consortium chair thus described how, at the first participant-planned Consumer Conference, all of the Hispanic and White participants sat on one side of the room and all of the African Americans on the other. By having each individual cross the room to take the hand of someone from the other side and bring that person to sit with her, the chair helped create an atmosphere in which more open communication could take place. Although race-, ethnic-, and class-based tensions remained apparent at most sites, the diverse strategies for and the commitment to addressing them head on were encouraging to witness.

4. *Community involvement contributed to community capacity building and infrastructure.* As suggested in Table 6-1, community empowerment and capacity building were central elements for many of the NHSPs and their consortia, and they were manifested in the building of local infrastructure. The very nature of program operation, for example, involved the provision of subcontracts to grassroots organizations and other local entities that in turn could expand their range of services and broaden their networks. In Boston, Healthy Start hired consultants to help 20 of its small community-based contractors find alternative sources of funding when the program's own funds were cut. New York City Healthy Start used its carry-over monies to build a state-of-the-art job-training center, and between 1997 and 2000, approximately 100 women were trained in computer skills and related areas. Eighty percent of these women later obtained full- or part-time jobs, earning up to $35,000 annually.

Many sites trained and hired community residents as outreach workers, with Cleveland hiring 235 local residents and Pittsburgh reporting that the extensive training they provided often led to staff hired from the community being "lured away" to work for other organizations. The often extensive trainings provided for community members of the consortia also had the potential for contributing to capacity building, with Philadelphia Healthy Start coordinating with local community colleges that trained community members for their roles in its consortia.

5. *Community involvement mobilized the community to help bring about changes in programs, policies, and practices.* Healthy Start and its consortia knitted together the complexity of community institutions in each site to help address infant mortality in comprehensive ways. A dynamic problem-solving process existed at most of the sites examined, including reports from outreach workers concerning realities in the field, reports from case managers concerning the realities of families being served, and identification by consortia members of other challenges in the community. These parties then worked together to design and implement solutions. When consortia members in Pee Dee identified the dearth of public transportation as a major barrier to families receiving regular medical attention, for example, they devised a supportive system of van transportation that also enabled community members to participate more actively in other aspects of the NHSP. When Cleveland outreach workers noted the displacement of pregnant women due to gentrification in the central city, they came to the consortium to devise focused new housing partnerships that could find families both emergency housing and long-term affordable places to live.

Cleveland and Chicago partnered with local correctional facilities to create programs for pregnant or parenting women who were incarcerated, whereas Pittsburgh created an extensive male involvement program in response to its consortium's emphasis on the need for more constructive involvement of fathers in the lives of children. New Orleans established one-stop shopping centers for a range of health and prenatal services but also located housing, general equivalency diploma (GED) support, career counseling, and job training in the same location.

Healthy Start consortia also built constructive links with health departments with New York City's program, for example, forming a strategic partnership with the local health department and the Children's Defense Fund to do aggressive outreach on immunizations.

Finally, several NHSPs started new nonprofits. Such organizations stood as important symbols of community commitment to institutionalizing the local NHSP. But they also served another purpose in places like rural Pee Dee, where the creation of a strong African American–led nonprofit was a source of considerable local pride. Healthy Start staff indeed appeared to heed Gutierrez and Lewis's (1997) reminder of the need to "understand and support the need women of color [and by extension, communities of color] may have for their own separate programs and organizations" (p. 220).

Evidence of actual effects of community involvement in Healthy Start on policy was more difficult to document. But on this level, too, we were able to find examples of consortia efforts that really made a difference. Chicago's consortium, for example, played a key role in a successful mobilization to stop a proposal to mandate Medicaid-managed care on a statewide basis. That site's Community Mobilization Committee also played a catalytic role in efforts by the larger consortium to lead a successful fight for exemptions to welfare reform's work requirement for mothers of special needs children (Minkler et al., 2001; Thompson et al., 2000).

6. *Community involvement helped institutionalize best practices in the community.* Elsewhere we document a wealth of new or newly institutionalized programs and practices in which the NHSP at each site played a key role (Thompson et al., 2000). Some examples include

- Kansas City's KC WAIT teen pregnancy prevention program, which Healthy Start helped expand to involve a host of new community partners;
- Boston's establishment of a health center within a public housing facility;
- Philadelphia's implementation of peer empowerment debate teams for teens;
- Pittsburgh's partnership with a local hospital and health council to establish two residential programs for clients—House of Hope, for pregnant and parenting women with substance abuse histories, and Healthy Start House, for pre- or postnatal women needing short-term residential care;
- Cleveland's partnerships with the March of Dimes and a local sorority to create the "Stork's Nest" program providing baby clothes and supplies to expectant mothers;
- New York's development of a Bronx high school–based prenatal care clinic; and
- Pee Dee's leadership role in working for the consolidation of the Medicaid application process in re-

sponse to lay health workers' concerns with the growing number of uninsured part-time workers.

It was often difficult to tease apart the role of Healthy Start from that of other programs and entities that frequently contributed to such developments (Minkler et al., 2001; Thompson et al., 2000). At the same time, our interviews, observations, focus groups, and document reviews (including, e.g., relevant newspaper articles and other media coverage) clearly indicated that community involvement through Healthy Start had played a substantial role in each of these cases.

DISCUSSION

As this article has attempted to demonstrate, community involvement contributed to the NHSP in a multitude of ways, ranging from creating the conditions in which individuals could improve their parenting skills to mobilizing communities to help change programs, policies, and practices. Each of these contributions, moreover, illustrated one or more of Fawcett et al.'s (1995) strategies for empowering processes and outcomes. The program's emphasis on health education and life skills training thus enhanced experience and competence on the individual level, with spillover effects for the consortia and other groups and communities to which these individuals belonged. The development of strong, community-based consortia, which in turn emphasized community definition of need, directly contributed to enhancing group structure and capacity by creating organizational entities that increased community competence or problem-solving ability. In rural Pee Dee, where no consortia had existed prior to Healthy Start, this contribution was particularly important in role modeling the use of a collaborative approach to problem solving that later was emulated beyond Healthy Start as community groups and organizations worked together to address other problem areas.

Healthy Start's emphasis on "starting where the people are" demonstrated how Fawcett et al.'s (1995) empowering strategies may work in tandem. Involvement through the consortia in identifying and addressing local needs thus enhanced experience and capacity at the individual and group or organizational levels. At the same time, many of the solutions devised (e.g., Pee Dee's development of a van transportation system and Cleveland's success in fighting a hospital's use of an incinerator) were illustrative of empowering outcomes involving the removal of social/environmental barriers and/or enhancing environmental supports and resources.

The role of community involvement in mobilizing the community to work for health-related goals and objectives similarly may be seen as illustrating several strategies that facilitate empowerment. Of particular importance in this regard was the emphasis placed on addressing racial- and ethnic-based tensions as integral to the achievement of more traditionally defined and distal health outcomes. For example, when the Kansas City consortia and staff recognized and acted on the need to increase cultural competence in relation to a growing Hispanic population, their hosting of a day-long conference on this topic enhanced the experience and capacity of participants in a critical domain. But by increasing the cultural competence of providers, it also may have helped weaken a critical social barrier to the receipt of services by Hispanics (Molina & Aguirre-Molina, 1994) and may have improved environmental supports and resources for the participation of this previously neglected group.

The findings of our study are consistent with those of a growing body of literature suggesting that community participation in neighborhood organizations, consortia and coalitions, and community-based health interventions can have substantial benefits for those involved (Eng, Briscoe, & Cunningham, 1990; Fawcett et al., 1995; Israel, 1985; Kreuter, Lezin, & Young, 2000; Wandersman & Florin, 2000; Zimmerman, 2000). Such involvement also may be seen as laying important groundwork for intermediate benefits and outcomes including behavioral changes, improved self-esteem, enhanced local infrastructure, and new and modified programs, practices, and policies (Fawcett et al., 1995; Zimmerman, 2000). Finally, and although the evidence base is still unfortunately in its infancy, these intermediate factors may help identify or enhance community assets that in turn may aid in building the foundation for the achievement of long-term program goals (Fawcett et al., 1997; Kreuter et al., 2000).

Elsewhere, we discuss in detail a variety of factors that appeared to facilitate community involvement in NHSP (Thompson, Minkler, Bell, Rose, & Butler, in press). Briefly, these factors include flexibility in the development of locally appropriate consortia structures, strong individual and community identification with the mission of the program, a variety of incentives for participation (including, importantly, transportation and child care), an adequate resource base including fiscal support and dedicated personnel, and broad community and institutional support. We also discuss in more detail the variety of forms that involvement took. These included resident participation in the consortia, partnerships with a host of community-based organizations, training and hiring of lay health workers, the hosting of health fairs and other community events, and subcontracting with a variety of local groups and organizations (Minkler et al., 2001; Thompson et al., 2000).

As Figure 6-1 shows, the general facilitators of community involvement and the potential for engaging a diversity of individuals and community partners through a range of mechanisms appeared to contribute to the intermediate benefits and outcomes of community involvement described in this article. These benefits in turn ideally may play a role in the achievement of Healthy Start's long-term goals of reducing infant mortality and improving health outcomes.

As Kreuter and Lezin (1998) have suggested, however, "Health status and health systems change are not only difficult to achieve but also relatively difficult to detect—at least in a form that is attributable to any particular intervention" (p. ii). Indeed, a recent national evaluation of the NHSP for HRSA (Moreno, Davaney, Chu, & Seeley, 2000), which tracked progress in the 15 original Healthy Start cities and 29 comparison sites, was able to show statistically significant declines in infant mortality that could be linked to the program in only 2 of the program sites (New Orleans and Pittsburgh). More positive findings were observed in some other areas (e.g., with Healthy Start associated with significant improvements in prenatal care utilization in 8 of the 15 sites). But the failure of the evaluation to demonstrate that the program played a more substantial role in infant mortality declines (which amounted to 21.7% nationally between 1990 and 1997; Moreno et al., 2000) was disappointing. Shifts in population composition within the Healthy Start sites and inadequate time and tools to detect the effects of this intervention program (Kreuter & Lezin, 1998) may be among the factors that could explain the lack of effect observed. Furthermore, and although an interim report by the national evaluation team did examine community involvement (Howell et al., 1998), the final evaluation did not include a recent focus on this major program component. The decision not to collect and include new (post-1996) data on the observed effects of community involvement on Healthy Start in the final evaluation makes it even more difficult to demonstrate the role of this factor in relation to those health outcome changes that were observed and those that may still be detected during the longer long term.

Based on the findings of the current study, however, we believe that community involvement should be a major goal and strategy of the new generation of community-based health initiatives aimed at eliminating health disparities. For although consortia and other community involvement approaches are time-consuming and labor intensive (Green, 2000; Howell et al., 1998; Mizrahi & Rosenthal, 1992; Plough & Olafson, 1994), they can make a real difference in developing programs that are culturally responsive and that truly "start where the people are" by linking program concerns with other community-identified issues.

The findings of our study also suggest that to help ensure meaningful, sustained community involvement, initiatives to eliminate racial and ethnic disparities in health should

- Initiate and maintain active, substantive community consortia to participate in the building of integrated

FIGURE 6-1 Community Involvement: Facilitators, Forms, and Benefits

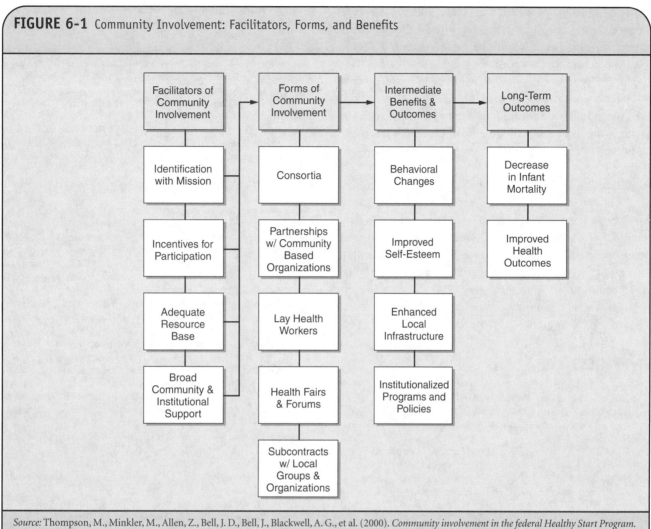

Source: Thompson, M., Minkler, M., Allen, Z., Bell, J. D., Bell, J., Blackwell, A. G., et al. (2000). *Community involvement in the federal Healthy Start Program.* Oakland, CA: PolicyLink.

health delivery systems. Roles for the consortia should include identifying community issues; strategic planning; identification and recruitment of potential community partners; and ongoing outreach, monitoring, program development, and evaluation.

- Provide substantial support for the consortia, including high-level administrative personnel; adequate financial resources; clear guidance and access to technical assistance; and ongoing membership training for members and leaders in governance, program planning, and evaluation skills and other areas.

- Focus communities on transforming programs, policies, and practices (rather than focusing solely on individual behavior change). Geographic mapping of community risk factors, analysis of mapping by diverse community stakeholders, identification of community

institutions that can address priority concerns, and community accountability for specific and realistic targets for risk factor reduction might be among the approaches used in this regard.

- Require that programs specifically analyze and develop plans to address racial and ethnic disparity in health outcomes. Plans and outcomes should address cultural competency of health care providers, ability to reach a variety of racial/ethnic groups with culturally appropriate services, specific analysis of health indicators by race and ethnic community, and the development of interventions that address specific racial and ethnic disparities. Collaboration with a variety of partners, including subcontracting with agencies that specialize in working with particular racial/ethnic groups, should be encouraged to help achieve these goals.

In his opening remarks at the "Call to Action" conference on eliminating racial and ethnic disparities in health, noted physician and public health leader, Dr. Reed Tuckson, commented that "health is the place where all the social forces converge." He went on to suggest that "the fight against infant mortality is also one against smoking, against poor nutrition, and against substance abuse . . . the fight against disparities in health is also one against the absence of hope for a meaningful future" (U.S. Department of Health and Human Services, 1998, p. 10).

As this study has suggested, the heavy accent on community involvement as the "defining feature" of the NHSP helped broaden the focus of the program from infant mortality narrowly defined to the plethora of related issues and concerns that must be addressed in the fight against health disparities. By building on community strengths and facilitating meaningful community involvement, the NHSP stands as an important example of a community health initiative grounded in some of central tenets of health education practice.

REFERENCES

Bandura, M. (1999). The Healthy Start Program: Mobilizing to reduce infant mortality and morbidity. *Journal of Pediatric Nursing, 14*(4), 263–265.

Bailey, D. (1992). Using participatory research in community consortia development and evaluation: Lessons from the beginning of a story. *American Sociologist, 23*, 71–82.

Eng, E., Briscoe, J., & Cunningham, A. (1990). Participation effect from water project on EPI. *Social Science and Medicine, 30*(12), 1349–1358.

Fawcett, S. B., Lewis, R. K., Paine-Andrews, A., Francisco, V. T., Richter, K., Lewis, R., et al. (1997). Evaluating community coalitions for prevention of substance abuse: The case of Project Freedom. *Health Education & Behavior, 24*(6), 812–828.

Fawcett, S., Paine-Andrews, A., Francisco, V., Schultz, J., Richter, K. P., Williams, E. L., et al. (1995). Using empowerment theory in collaborative partnerships for community health and development. *American Journal of Community Psychology, 23*(5), 677–697.

Green, L.W. (2000). Caveats on coalitions: In praise of partnerships. *Health Promotion Practice, 1*(1), 64–65.

Gutierrez, L. M., & Lewis, E. A. (1997). Education, participation, and capacity building in community organizing with women of color. In M. Minkler (Ed.), *Community organizing and community building for health* (pp. 216–229). New Brunswick, NJ: Rutgers University Press.

Health Resources and Services Administration. (1991). *Guidance for the Healthy Start Program.* Washington, DC: Author.

Health Resources and Services Administration. (1996). *Guidance for the Healthy Start Program.* Washington, DC: Author.

Howell, E. M., Dulvaney, B., McCormick, M., & Raykovich, K. T. (1998). Back to the future: Community involvement in the healthy start program. *Journal of Health Politics, Policy and Law, 23*(2), 291–317.

Israel, B. (1985). Social networks and social support: Implications for natural helper and community level interventions. *Health Education Quarterly, 12*(1), 66–80.

Kotch, J. B., Blakely, C. H., Brown, S. S., & Wong, F. Y. (1992). *A pound of prevention: The case for universal maternity care.* Washington, DC: American Public Health Association.

Kreuter, M., & Lezin, N. (1998, January 9). *Are consortia/collaboratives effective in changing health status and health systems?* Paper prepared for the Health Resources and Services Administration.

Kreuter, M., Lezin, N. A., & Young, L. A. (2000). Evaluating community-based collaborative mechanisms: Implications for practitioners. *Health Promotion Practice, 1*(1), 49–63.

McCoy-Thompson, M. (1994). *Consortium development: The Healthy Start initiative: A community-driven approach to infant mortality reduction* (Vol. 1). Arlington, VA: National Center for Education in Maternal and Child Health.

Miles, M. R., & Huberman, A. M. (1994). *Qualitative data analysis: An expanded sourcebook* (2nd ed.). Thousand Oaks, CA: Sage.

Minkler, M., Thompson, M., Bell, J., & Rose, K. (2001). Contributions of community involvement to organizational level empowerment: The federal Healthy Start experience. *Health Education and Behavior, 28*(6), 783–807.

Mizrahi, T., & Rosenthal, B. (1992). Managing dynamic tensions in social change coalitions. In T. Mizrahi & J. D. Morrison (Eds.), *Community organization & social administration: Advances, trends and emerging principles* (pp. 1–33). New York: Hayworth.

Molina, C., & Aguirre-Molina, M. (1994). *Latino health in the United States: A growing challenge.* Washington, DC: American Public Health Association.

Moreno, L., Davaney, B., Chu, D., & Seeley, M. (2000). *Effects of Healthy Start on infant mortality and birth outcomes* (Final Report prepared for HRSA, DHHS). Princeton, NJ: Mathematica Policy Research.

Nyswander, D. B. (1956). Education for health: Some principles and their applications. *Health Education Monographs, 14*, 65–70.

Plough, A., & Olafson, F. (1994). Implementing the Boston Healthy Start initiative: A case study of community empowerment and public health. *Health Education Quarterly, 21*(2), 221–224.

Rappaport, J. (1984). Studies in empowerment: Introduction to the issue. *Prevention in Human Services, 3*(2–3), 1–7.

Thompson, M., Minkler, M., Allen, Z., Bell, J. D., Bell, J., Blackwell, A. G., et al. (2000). *Community involvement in the federal Healthy Start Program.* Oakland, CA: PolicyLink.

Thompson, M., Minkler, M., Bell, J., Rose, K., & Butler, L. (in press). Facilitators of well functioning consortia: Lessons from the National Healthy Start Program. *Health and Social Work.*

U.S. Department of Health and Human Services. (1998). *Call to action: Eliminating racial and ethnic disparities in health.* Washington, DC: U.S. Department of Health and Human Services and Grantmakers in Health.

U.S. Department of Health and Human Services, Public Health Service. (1996, May). *Health: U.S. 1995* (DHHS Pub. No. [PHS] 96-1232). Hyattsville, MD: Author.

Wallerstein, N. (1992). Powerlessness, empowerment and health: Implications for health promotion programs. *American Journal of Health Promotion, 6*(3), 197–205.

Wandersman, A., & Florin, P. (2000). Citizen participation and community organizations. In J. Rappaport & E. Seidman (Eds.), *Handbook of community psychology* (pp. 247–272). New York: Academic/Plenum.

Yin, R. K. (1994). *Case study research design methods* (2nd ed.). Newbury Park, CA: Sage.

Zimmerman, M. A. (2000). Empowerment theory: Psychological, organizational and community levels of analysis. In J. Rappaport & E. Seidman (Eds.), *Handbook of community psychology* (pp. 43–63). New York: Academic/Plenum.

Disease Etiologies in Non-Western Medical Systems

Source: Foster, G. M. (1976). "Disease Etiologies in Non-Western Medical Systems." *American Anthropologist* 78: 773–782.

Impressive in ethnographic accounts of non-Western medicine is the tendency of authors to generalize from the particulars of the system(s) within which they have worked.

Subconsciously, at least, anthropologists filter the data of all exotic systems through the lens of belief and practice of the people they know best. Whether it be causality, diagnosis, the nature and role of the curer, or the perception of illness within the wider supernatural and social universe, general statements seem strongly influenced by the writers' personal experiences. Glick, for example, in one of the most interesting of recent general essays, notes that in many cultures religion and medical practices are almost inseparable, and he adds that "We must think about how and where 'medicine' fits into 'religion'. . . . In an ethnography of a religious system, where does the description of the medical system belong; and how does it relate to the remainder?" (Glick 1967:33).

Yet in many medical systems, as, for example, those characterizing mestizo villagers and urbanites in Latin American, medicine would have the most minimal role in an ethnography of religious beliefs and practices. Illness and curing are dealt with largely in nonreligious terms. In Tzintzuntzan, for example, in many hours of recording ideas about origins and cures of illness, not once has religion been mentioned—even though most villagers, if asked, would certainly agree that illness ultimately comes from God.

The ethnologist analyzing medical beliefs and practices in an African community can scarcely avoid dealing with witchcraft, oracles, magic, divining, and propitiation, all of which are categories of only modest concern to the student of Indian Ayurvedic medicine. In short, there has been all too little dialogue between anthropologists who have studied dramatically different non-Western medical systems. So striking is the parochialism at times that one is tempted to agree with the medical sociologist Freidson who notes the existence of a "very large body of sociological and anthropological information about popular knowledge about *particular* illnesses. Such studies are essentially catalogues, often without a classified index" (Freidson 1970:10).

Yet if we can successfully classify kinship, political and economic systems, and witchcraft and sorcery beliefs, and find the significant behavioral correlates associated with each, then certainly we can do the same with medical systems. We are, after all, dealing with limited possibilities in each of these cases. In this paper I am concerned with the cross-cultural patterning that underlies non-Western medical systems, and with identifying and explicating the primary independent variable—disease etiology—around which orbit such dependent variables as types of curers, the nature of diagnosis, the roles of religion and magic, and the like. This is, then, an essay on comparative ethnomedicine, a term Hughes aptly defines as "those beliefs and practices relating to disease which are the products of indigenous cultural development and are not explicitly derived from the conceptual framework of modern medicine" (Hughes 1968:99).

THE PROBLEMS OF TERMINOLOGY

Throughout most of anthropology's brief history ethnologists have labeled the institutions of the peoples they have studied as "primitive," "peasant," or "folk," depending on the basic societal type concerned. Until relatively recently we investigated primitive religion, primitive economics, primitive art—and, of course, primitive medicine. The seminal writings of the ethnologist-physician Ackerknecht during the 1940's display no uncertainty as to what interested him: it was "primitive medicine," a pair of words that appeared in the title of nearly every article he published (Ackerknecht 1971). Caudill, too, in the first survey of the new field of medical anthropology spoke unashamedly of "primitive medicine" (Caudill 1953).

When, following World War II, studies of peasant communities became fashionable, these peoples were described as possessing a "folk culture." Not surprisingly their medical beliefs and practices were labeled "folk medicine," a frequent source of confusion since the popular medicine of technologically complex societies also often was, and is, so described.

In recent years, however, this traditional terminology has come to embarrass us. In a rapidly changing world, where yesterday's nonliterate villagers may be today's cabinet ministers in newly independent countries, the word "primitive"—initially a polite euphemism for "savage"—is increasingly outmoded. Ackerknecht himself recognizes this change, for in the 1971 collection of his classic essays most titles have been edited to eliminate the word "primitive." "Peasant" and "folk" are less sensitive words, but they too are being replaced by "rural," "agrarian," or something of the kind. The extent to which we have been troubled by terminology is illustrated by the circumlocutions and quotation marks found in the major review articles of recent years: "popular health culture," "indigenous or fold medical roles," "nonscientific health practices," "native conceptual traditions about illness," "culture specific illness," "the vocabulary of terms," and the like (e.g., Polgar 1962; Scotch 1963; Fabrega 1972; Lieban 1973).

ETIOLOGY: THE INDEPENDENT VARIABLE

Yet the greatest shortcoming of our traditional medical terminology—at least within the profession itself—is not that it may denigrate non-Western people, but rather that, by focusing on societal types it has blinded us to the basic characteristics of the medical systems themselves. There is more than a grain of truth in Freidson's comments, for many accounts *are* "grossly descriptive," with lists of illnesses and treatments taking precedence over interpretation and synthesis. So where do we start to rectify the situation? Glick (1967:36), I believe, gives us the critical lead when he writes that "the most important fact about an illness in most medical systems is not the underlying pathological process but *the underlying cause.* This is such a central consideration that most diagnoses prove to be statements about causation, and most treatments, responses directed against particular causal agents" (emphasis added).

A casual survey of the ethnomedical literature tends to confirm Glick's statement. In account after account we find that

the kinds of curers, the mode of diagnosis, curing techniques, preventive acts, and the relationship of all these variables to the wider society of which they are a part, derive from beliefs about illness causality. It is not going too far to say that, if we are given a clear description of what a people believe to be the causes of illness, we can in broad outline fill in the other elements in that medical system. It therefore logically follows that the first task of the anthropologist concerned with medical systems is to find the simplest taxonomy for causality beliefs. Two basic principles, which I call *personalistic and naturalistic,* seem to me to account for most (but not all) of the etiologies that characterize non-Western medical systems. While the terms refer specifically to causality concepts, I believe they can conveniently be used to speak of entire systems, i.e., not only causes, but all of the associated behavior that follows from these views.

A personalistic medical system is one in which disease is explained as due to the *active, purposeful intervention* of an *agent,* who may be human (a witch or sorcerer), nonhuman (a ghost, an ancestor, an evil spirit), or supernatural (a deity or other very powerful being). The sick person literally is a victim, the object of aggression or punishment directed specifically against him, for reasons that concern him alone. Personalistic causality allows little room for accident or chance; in fact, for some peoples the statement is made by anthropologists who have studied them that *all* illness and death are believed to stem from the acts of the agent.

Personalistic etiologies are illustrated by beliefs found among the Mano of Liberia, recorded by the physician Harley, who practiced medicine among them for 15 years. "Death is unnatural," he writes, "resulting from the intrusion of an outside force," usually directed by some magical means (Harley 1941:7). Similarly, among the Abron of the Ivory Coast, "People sicken and die because some power, good or evil, has acted against them. . . . Abron disease theory contains a host of agents which may be responsible for a specific condition. . . . These agents cut across the natural and supernatural world. Ordinary people, equipped with the proper technical skills, sorcerers, various supernatural entities, such as ghosts, bush devils, and witches, or the supreme god *Nyame,* acting along or through lesser gods, all cause disease" (Alland 1964:714–715).

In contrast to personalistic systems, naturalistic systems explain illness in impersonal, systemic terms. Disease is through to stem, not from the machinations of an angry being, but rather from such *natural forces or conditions* as cold, heat, winds, dampness, and, above all, by an upset in the balance of the basic body elements. In naturalistic systems, health conforms to an *equilibrium* model: when the humors, the yin and yang, or the Ayurvedic *dosha* are in the balance appropriate to the age and condition of the individual, in his natural and social environment, health results. Causality concepts explain or account for the upsets in this balance that trigger illness.

Contemporary naturalistic systems resemble each other in an important historical sense: the bulk of their explanations and practices represent simplified and popularized legacies from the "great tradition" medicine of ancient classical civilizations, particularly those of Greece and Rome, Indian, and China. Although equilibrium is expressed in many ways in classical accounts, contemporary descriptions most frequently deal with the "hot-cold dichotomy" which explains illness as due to excessive heat or cold entering the body. Treatment, logically, attempts to restore the proper balance through "hot" and "cold" foods and herbs, and other treatments such as poultices that are thought to withdraw excess heat or cold from the body.

In suggesting that most non-Western etiologies can be described as personalistic or naturalistic I am, of course, painting with a broad brush. Every anthropologist will immediately think of examples from his research that appear not to conform to this classification. Most troublesome, at least at first glance, are those illnesses believed caused by emotional disturbances such as fright, jealousy, envy, shame, anger, or grief. Fright, or *susto*, widespread in Latin America, can be caused by a ghost, a spirit, or an encounter with the devil; if the agent *intended* harm to the victim, the etiology is certainly personalistic. But often accounts of such encounters suggest chance or accident rather than purposive action. And, when an individual slips beside a stream, and fears he is about to fall into the water and drown, the etiology is certainly naturalistic.

The Latin American *muina*, an indisposition resulting from anger, may reflect a disagreeable interpersonal episode, but it is unlikely that the event was staged by an evil doer to bring illness to a victim. In Mexico and Central America the knee child's envy and resentment of its new sibling-to-be, still in the mother's womb, gives rise to *chipil*, the symptoms of which are apathy, whining, and a desire to cling to the mother's skirt. The foetus can be said, in a narrow sense, to be the cause of the illness, but it is certainly not an active agent, nor is it blamed for the result. Since in a majority of emotionally explained illnesses it is hard to identify purposive action on the part of an agent intent upon causing sickness, I am inclined to view emotional etiologies as more nearly conforming to the naturalistic than to the personalistic principle. Obviously, a dual taxonomy for phenomena as complex as worldwide beliefs about causes of illness leaves many loose ends. But it must be remembered that a taxonomy is not an end in itself, something to be polished and admired; its value lies rather in the understanding of relationships between apparently diverse phenomena that it makes possible. I hope that the following pages will illustrate how the personalistic-naturalistic classifi-

cation, for all its loose ends, throw into sharp perspective correlations in health institutions and health behavior that tend to be overlooked in descriptive accounts.

Before proceeding, a word of caution is necessary: *the two etiologies are rarely if ever mutually exclusive* as far as their presence or absence in a particular society is concerned. Peoples who invoke personalistic causes to explain most illness usually recognize some natural, or chance, causes. And peoples for whom naturalistic causes predominate almost invariably explain some illness as due to witchcraft or the evil eye. But in spite of obvious overlapping, the literature suggests that many, if not most, peoples are committed to one or the other of these explanatory principles to account for a majority of illness. When, for example, we read that in the Venezuelan peasant village of El Morro 89% of a sample of reported illnesses are "natural" in origin, whereas only 11% are attributed to magical or supernatural causes (Suarez 1974), it seems reasonable to say that the indigenous causation system of this group is naturalistic and not personalistic. And, in contrast, when we read of the Melanesian Dobuans that all illness and disease are attributed to envy, and that "Death is caused by witchcraft, sorcery, poisoning, suicide, or actual assault" (Fortune 1932:135, 150), it is clear that personalistic causality predominates.

Although in the present context I am not concerned with problems of evolution, I believe the personalistic etiology is the more ancient of the two. At the dawn of human history it seems highly likely that *all* illness, as well as other forms of misfortune, was explained in personalistic terms. I see man's ability to depersonalize causality, in all spheres of thought, including illness, as a major step forward in the evolution of culture.

REFERENCES

Ackerknecht, Erwin H. 1971. Medicine and Ethnology: Selected Essays. Baltimore: Johns Hopkins Press.

Alland, Alexander, Jr. 1964. Native Therapists and Western Medical Practitioners among the Abron of the Ivory Coast. Transactions of the New York Academy of Sciences. Vol. 26 Pp. 714–725.

Caudill, William. 1953. Applied Anthropology in Medicine. *In* Anthropology Today. A.L. Kroeber, ed. Pp. 771–806. Chicago: University of Chicago Press.

Fabrega, Horacio, Jr. 1972. Medical Anthropology. *In* Biennial Review of Anthropology: 1971. Bernard J. Siegel, ed. Pp. 167–229. Stanford: Stanford University Press.

Fortune, Reo F. 1932. Sorcerers of Dobu: the Social Anthropological of the Dobu Islanders of the Western Pacific. London: George Routledge.

Freidson, Eliot. 1970. Professional Dominance: The Social Structure of Medical Care. New York: Atherton.

Glick, Leonard B. 1967. Medicine as an Ethnographic Category: The Gimi of the New Guinea Highlands. Ethnology 6:31–56.

Harley, George Way. 1941. Native African Medicine: With Special Reference to Its Practice in the Mano Tribe of Liberia. Cambridge: Harvard University Press.

Hughes, Robin. 1967. African Traditional Thought and Western Science. Africa 37:50–71, 155–187.

Lieban, Richard W. 1973. Medical Anthropology. *In* Handbook of Social and Cultural Anthropology. John J. Honigmann, ed. Pp. 1031–1072. Chicago: Rand McNally.

Polgar, Steven. 1962. Health and Human Behavior: Areas of Interest Common to the Social and Medical Sciences. Current Anthropology 3:159–205.

Scotch, Norman A. 1963. Medical Anthropology. *In* Biennial Review of Anthropology. Bernard J. Siegel, ed. Pp. 30–68. Stanford: Stanford University Press.

PART 7

Doing Something About It: The Ecological Perspective and the Move from Theory to Practice

In this part we present excerpts from two readings describing widely used, multifactor, or ecological program planning models that include the basic steps present in any such model: (1) assessment; (2) intervention development and implementation (based on the assessment); and (3) evaluation. The first selection, from Green and Kreuter (1999), describes one of the most comprehensive planning models for health promotion, called PRECEDE-PROCEED. The second selection, taken from the Surgeon General's Report on Youth Violence (2002), describes the risk and protective factors planning model used so often in youth risk behavior prevention programming.

Health Promotion Planning—An Educational and Ecological Approach

Source: Excerpt from Green, L. W. & Kreuter, M. W. (1999). *Health Promotion Planning—An Educational and Ecological Approach*. McGraw Hill: New York, pp. 32–36.

THE PRECEDE-PROCEED MODEL

The ideas of **intervention** and support are important for understanding the fore-going definitions of health education and health promotion. Organized health education activity or policies and regulations "intervene" in the process or flow of development and change. The purpose of intervention is to maintain, enhance, or interrupt a behavior pattern or condition of living that is linked to improved health or to increased risks for illness, injury, disability, or death (Figure 1-6). The behavior of interest is usually that of the people whose health is in question, either now or in the future. Equally important in the process of planning and developing the policies and programs are the behaviors of those who control resources or rewards, such as community leaders, parents, employers, peers, teachers, and health professionals.

Supports refer to the environmental conditions that health promotion seeks to leave in place following the intervention so that individuals, groups, or communities can continue to exercise their own control over the determinants of their health. New policies, regulatory provisions, and organizational arrangements represent environmental supports. Informed officials, committed legislators, concerned teachers, skilled parents, and understanding employers can all provide a supportive social environment, and each can be influenced by educational and political interventions. An increase in the proportion of population who hold a favorable attitude toward the behavior that some individuals wish to adopt provides a supportive environment in the form of normative enabling and reinforcing supports. For example, mass media can be used to raise the level of public awareness of the need to reduce fat in the diet. This in turn can produce a consumer demand for low-fat products in the marketplace, which in turn can cause restaurants and grocers to place more healthful products on their menus and shelves. In the end, this can make the low-fat choice easier for those who wish to change their behavior.

Health promotion programs may operate at one of three stages of prevention: primary (hygiene and health enhancement), secondary (early detection), or tertiary (therapy to prevent sequelae or recurrence). In any of these, health promotion offers interventions intended to short-circuit illness or injury, increase health, and enhance quality of life through change or development of health-related behavior (control over the determinants of health) and conditions of living (see Figure 1-6). The Precede-Proceed model takes into account the multiple factors that determine health and quality of life. It helps the planner arrive at a highly focused subset of those factors as targets for intervention. PRECEDE also generates specific objectives and criteria for evaluation. The PROCEED offers additional steps for developing policy and initiating the implementation and evaluation process (see Figure 1-7).

PRECEDE and PROCEED work in tandem, providing a continuous series of steps or phases in planning, implementation, and evaluation. The identification of priorities in one phase of PRECEDE leads to quantitative objectives that become goals and targets in the implementation phase of PROCEED. They then become the standards of acceptability or criteria of success in the evaluation phases of PROCEED. The progression within PRECEDE sets priorities in one phase that become the delimiting focus of assessment of causes at the next phase. Without the progressive narrowing of focus, the points in the causal chain where interventions would be designed would have so many predisposing, enabling and reinforcing factors listed as targets that no program could afford to cover them all or to provide much population coverage on even half of them.

As you have seen, PRECEDE is an acronym for *p*redisposing, *r*einforcing, and *e*nabling *c*onstructs in *e*ducational/ecological *d*iagnosis and *e*valuation. *Diagnosis* is defined in *A Dictionary of Epidemiology* as the process of determining health status and the factors responsible for producing it; may be applied to an individual, family, group, or community. The term is applied both to the process of determination and to its findings.[151]

We used **diagnosis** in the original model[152] and in previous editions of this book to describe each stage of the Precede planning process (e.g., social diagnosis and epidemiological diagnosis). We have replaced this term with *assessment* in this edition, mainly in response to many users who feel uncomfortable with the term *diagnosis*. Though we still consider *diagnosis* to be an appropriate denotation for the processes described in each phase, its connotation tends to associate the model with clinical procedures. It also tends to imply that all the assessments must start with or find a problem. Positive approaches to health and assets-based approaches to community assessment call for at least part of the planning process to be concentrated on aspirations and strengths, not just on needs, weaknesses, deficits, problems, and barriers.

Recall that PROCEED stands for *p*olicy, *r*egulatory and *o*rganizational *c*onstructs in *e*ducational and *e*nvironmental *d*evelopment. PRECEDE and PROCEED work in tandem, providing a continuous series of steps or phases in planning, implementation, and evaluation. The identification of priorities and the setting of objectives in the Precede phases provide the objects and criteria for policy, implementation, and evaluation in the Proceed phases.

PRECEDE-PROCEED is not the only road to quality health promotion. Other models of health behavior, health education, health planning, and health promotion predate it, and many more have emerged since its first incarnation in 1974.[153] PRECEDE-PROCEED is, however, a theoretically "robust" model that addresses a major acknowledged need in health promotion and health education: comprehensive planning. This capability has increased with the more explicit representation of ecological aspects, which were implied in earlier versions. It is also robust in the sense that it applies to health promotion in a variety of situations.[154] It has served as a successful model in the planning of several rigorously evaluated, randomized clinical and field trials and has been formally tested in some of these.[155] Local health departments have used it as a guide to developing programs adopted by several state health departments.[156] It was widely distributed as a federal guide to the planning, review, and evaluation of maternal and child health projects.[157] It has been applied as an analytical tool for health education policy on a national and international scale.[158] Adaptations of it have been published and recommended by the National Committee for Injury Prevention and Control for planning and evaluating safety programs,[159] by the American Lung Association as a *Program Planning and Evaluation Guide for Lung Associations*,[160] and by the American Cancer Society and the National Cancer Institute as the framework for a school nutrition and cancer education curriculum.[161] It has served as an organizational framework for curriculum development or training in health education for nurses,[162] pharmacists,[163] allied health professionals,[164] physicians,[165] and interdisciplinary training for behavioral scientists and health educators.[166]

Other applications and validations of the model will be mentioned or illustrated in subsequent chapters. You can visit a web site (www.ihpr.ubc.ca) for a searchable bibliography of more than 750 published applications of the model. In an interactive software version of the model, available as a training package, we illustrate its application to planning a breast cancer detection program.[167] Various manuals and field guides for application of the model make it even more accessible to practitioners.[168]

The Proceed component of the model is of more recent vintage and has had less exposure and testing. It is essentially an elaboration and extension of the administrate assessment step of PRECEDE. In a later chapter, we shall explore the Proceed framework, which has emerged with increasing detail in work on health promotion planning,[169] policy,[170] evaluation,[171] and implementation.[172]

REFERENCES

151. Last, J. M. (1995). *A dictionary of epidemiology* (3rd ed.). Oxford, England: Oxford University Press, 1995, pg. 46.

152. Green, L. W. (1974). Toward cost-benefit evaluations of health education: Some concepts, methods, and examples. *Health Education Monographs, 2*(Suppl. 1), 34-64.

153. For summaries of planning models in health promotion, see Bates & Winder, 1984; Breckon, 1982, 1997; Breckon, Harvey, & Lancaster, 1998; Dignan & Carr, 1992; Ewles & Simnett 1985, chap. 6 and 7; Gilmore & Campbell, 1996, esp. pp. 12-18; Greenberg, 1987; Longe, 1985; Manoff, 1985; Marsick, 1987; Parkinson et al., 1982; Pollock, 1987; H.S. Ross & Mico, 1980; Simons-Morton, Green & Gottlieb, 1995; Strehlow, 1983, chap. 6; Tones, 1979.

154. In the past, PRECEDE was called a framework. This was a caution against claiming too much for it as a model or a theory. A theory is "a set of

interrelated constructs (variables), definitions, and propositions that presents a systematic view of phenomena by specifying relations among variables, with the purpose of explaining natural phenomena," from Kerlinger, 1979, p. 64. The primary purpose of PRECEDE was not to explain "natural phenomena" but to organize existing theories and constructs (variables) into a cohesive, comprehensive, and systematic view of relations among those variables important to the planning and evaluation of health education. Given the extensive application and validation of the framework in practice and in research during the 1970s and 1980s, we have felt confident in calling it a model for the past decade or more. Continuing research and application of the model in the 1990s has begun to take form as a theory of health promotion. For further discussion of models and theories see Glanz, Lewis, & Rimer, 1997; Green, 1986; Green & Lewis, 1986; Kar, 1986; Lorig & Laurin, 1985; P.D. Mullen, Hersey, & Iverson, 1987; Rothman & Tropman, 1987.

155. Some of the early trials that helped validate and shape the representation of the model in the first and second editions of the book were Cantor et al., 1985; Green, 1974; Green, Fisher, Amin, & Shafiullah, 1975; Green, Levine, Wolle, & Deeds, 1979; Green, Wang, & Ephross, 1974; Hatcher, Green, Levine, & Glagle, 1986; D. M. Levine et al., 1979; Maiman, Green, Gibson, & Mackenzie, 1979; Morisky et al. 1980, 1983, 1985; Morisky, Levine, Green, & Smith, 1982; Rimer, Keintz, & Fleisher, 1986; Sayegh & Green, 1976; Wang et al. 1979. Some of the more recent clinical trials and other tests and applications of the model will be cited or described in later chapters of this edition.

156. Brink, Simons-Morton, Parcel, & Tiernan, 1988; Gielen & Radius, 1984; Health Education Center, 1977; Newman, Martin, & Weppner, 1982; PATCH, 1985.

157. Green, Wan, et al., 1978.

158. Danforth & Swaboda, 1978; Green, 1986d; Green, R. W. Wilson, & Bauer, 1983.

159. National Committee for Injury Prevention and Control, 1989. For specific applications in injury prevention and control, see also Eriksen & Gielen, 1983; Sleet, 1987.

160. Green, 1987b.

161. Light & Contento, 1989. See also the broader ACS Plan for Youth Education: Corcoran & Portnoy, 1989.

162. Ackerman & Kalmer, 1977; Berland, Whyte, & Maxwell, 1995; Shine, Silva, & Weed, 1983.

163. Fedder & Beardsley, 1979.

164. B. I. Bennet, 1977; Simpson & Pruitt, 1989.

165. Green, 1984d, 1987a; Green, Eriksen, & Schor, 1988; R. S. Lawrence, 1988; D. M. Levine & Green, 1983, 1985; Mann, 1994; Oxman, Thompason, Davis, & Haynes, 1995; Wang et al., 1979.

166. Altman & Green, 1988; L.W. Fisher, Green, McCrae, & Cochran, 1976; D.M. Levine & Green, 1981.

167. Gold, Green, & Kreuter, 1997.

168. M. W. Kreuter, Lezin, Kreuter, & Green, 1998.

169. Green, 1980b, 1987b; Iverson & Green, 1981; Kolbe et al., 1981; Kreuter, 1984; Kreuter, Christenson, & DiVencenzo, 1982; *Strategies for Promoting Health in Special Populations*, 1987.

170. Green, 1979b, 1986d, 1988c.

171. R. Bertera & Green, 1979; Bibeau et al., 1988; Cantor et al., 1985; H. Cohen, Harris, & Green, 1979; Green, 1986a, 1968e; Green & Lewis, 1986; Green, George et al., 1995; Kreuter, 1985a; Kreuter, Christenson, & Davis, 1984; Kreuter, Christianson, Freston, & Nelson, 1981.

172. Cataldo et al., 1986; deLeeuw, 1989; Green, Simons-Morton, & Potvin, 1997; Kreuter, Christenson, & DeVincenzo, 1982; C. F. Nelson, Kreuter, & Watkins, 1986; Ottoson & Green, 1987; Powell, Christenson, & Kreuter, 1984.

173. Green, 1975.

Risk Factors for Youth Violence

Source: DHHS. 2002. Excerpt from Chapter Four ("Risk Factors for Youth Violence"), in *Youth Violence: A Report of the Surgeon General.* Rockville, MD: U.S. Department of Health and Human Services.

Research has documented the magnitude of youth violence and the trends in that violence over time. But what do we know about *why* young people become involved in violence? Why do some youths get caught up in violence while others do not? There is no simple answer to these questions, but scientists have identified a number of things that put children and adolescents at risk of violent behavior and some things that seem to protect them from the effects of risk.

INTRODUCTION TO RISK AND PROTECTIVE FACTORS

The concepts of risk and protection are integral to public health. A risk factor is anything that increases the probability that a person will suffer harm. A protective factor is something that decreases the potential harmful effect of a risk factor. In the context of this report, risk factors increase the probability that a young person will become violent, while protective factors buffer the young person against those risks. The public health approach to youth violence involves identifying risk and protective factors, determining how they work, making the public aware of these findings, and designing programs to prevent or stop the violence.

Risk factors for violence are not static. Their predictive value changes depending on when they occur in a young person's development, in what social context, and under what circumstances. Risk factors may be found in the individual, the environment, or the individual's ability to respond to the demands or requirements of the environment. Some factors come into play during childhood or even earlier, whereas others do not appear until adolescence. Some involve the family, others the neighborhood, the school, or the peer group. Some become less important as a person matures, while others persist throughout the life span. To complicate the picture even further, some factors may constitute risks during one stage of development but not another. Finally, the factors that predict the onset of violence are not necessarily the same as those that predict the continuation or cessation of violence.

Violence prevention and intervention efforts hinge on identifying risk and protective factors and determining when in the course of development they emerge. To be effective, such efforts must be appropriate to a youth's stage of development. A program that is effective in childhood may be ineffective in adolescence and vice versa. Moreover, the risk and protective factors targeted by violence prevention programs may be different from those targeted by intervention programs, which are designed to prevent the reoccurrence of violence.

This report groups risk and protective factors into five domains: individual, family, peer group, school, and community, which includes both the neighborhood and the larger society (Table 7-1). Factors do not always fit neatly into these areas, however. Broken homes are classified as a family risk factor, but the presence of many such families in a community can contribute to social disorganization, an important community-level risk factor (Bursik & Grasmick, 1993; Elliott et al., 1996; Sampson & Lauritsen, 1994).

TABLE 7-1 Early and late risk factors for violence at age 15 to 18 and proposed protective factors, by domain

	Risk Factor		
Domain	**Early Onset (age 6–11)**	**Late Onset (age 12–14)**	**Protective Factor***
Individual	General offenses	General Offenses	Intolerant attitude toward deviance
	Substance use	Psychological condition	High IQ
	Being male	Restlessness	Being female
	Aggression**	Difficulty concentrating**	Positive social orientation
	Psychological condition	Risk taking	Perceived sanctions for transgressions
	Hyperactivity	Aggression**	
	Problem (antisocial) behavior	Being male	
	Exposure to television violence	Physical violence	
	Medical, physical	Antisocial attitudes, beliefs	
	Low IQ	Crimes against persons	
	Antisocial attitudes, beliefs	Problem (antisocial) behavior	
	Dishonesty**	Low IQ	
		Substance use	
Family	Low socioeconomic status/poverty	Poor parent-child relations	Warm, supportive relationships with parents or other adults
	Antisocial parents	Harsh, lax discipline; poor monitoring, supervision	Parents' positive evaluation of peers
	Poor parent-child relations	Low parental involvement	Parental monitoring
	Harsh, lax, or inconsistent discipline	Antisocial parents	
	Broken home	Broken home	
	Separation from parents	Low socioeconomic status/poverty	
	Other conditions	Abusive parents	
	Abuse parents	Other conditions	
	Neglect	Family conflict**	
School	Poor attitude, performance	Poor attitude, performance	Commitment to school
		Academic failure	Recognition for involvement in conventional activities
Peer Group	Weak social ties	Weak social ties	Friends who engage in conventional behavior
	Antisocial peers	Antisocial, delinquent peers	
		Gang membership	
Community		Neighborhood crime drugs	
		Neighborhood disorganization	

*Age of onset not known.
**Males only.
Source: DHHS. 2002. Excerpt from Chapter Four, in *Youth Violence: A Report of the Surgeon General*. Rockville, MD: U.S. Department of Health and Human Services.

Risk Factors

Risk factors are not necessarily causes. Researchers identify risk factors for youth violence by tracking the development of children and adolescents over the first two decades of life and measuring how frequently particular personal characteristics and social conditions at a given age are linked to violence at later stages of the life course. Evidence for these characteristics and social conditions must go beyond simple empirical relationships, however. To be considered risk factors, they must have both a theoretical rationale and a demonstrated ability to predict violence—essential conditions for a causal relationship (Earls, 1994; Kraemer et al., 1997; Thornberry, 1998). The reason risk factors are not considered causes is that, in most cases, scientists lack experimental evidence that changing a risk factor produces changes in the onset or rate of violence.

As used in this report, risk factors are personal characteristics or environmental conditions that *predict* the onset, continuity, or escalation of violence.

The question of causality has practical implications for prevention efforts. Prevention depends largely on risk factors being true causes of violence. In practical terms, research has amassed enough strong, consistent evidence for the risk factors discussed in this report to provide a basis for prevention programs, even though a strict cause-and-effect relationship has been established for relatively few of them.

Most of the risk factors identified do not appear to have a strong biological basis. Instead, it is theorized, they result from social learning or the combination of social learning and biological processes. This means that violent youths who have violent parents are far more likely to have modeled their behavior on their parents' behavior—to have learned violent behavior from them—than simply to have inherited it from them. Likewise, society's differing expectations of boys and girls—expecting boys to be more aggressive, for example—can result in learned behaviors that increase or decrease the risk of violence.

The bulk of the research that has been done on risk factors identifies and measures their predictive value separately, without taking into account the influence of other risk factors. More important than any individual factor, however, is the accumulation of risk factors. Risk factors usually exist in clusters, not in isolation. Children who are abused or neglected, for example, tend to be in poor families with single parents living in disadvantaged neighborhoods beset with violence, drug use, and crime. Studies of multiple risk factors have found that they have independent, additive effects—that is, the more risk factors a child is exposed to, the greater the likelihood that he or she will become violent. One study, for example, has found that a 10-year-old exposed to 6 or more risk factors is 10 times as likely to be violent by age 18 as a 10-year-old exposed to only one factor (Herrenkohl et al., 2000).

Researchers have theorized that risk factors also interact with each other, but to date they have found little evidence of interaction. What evidence does exist suggests that interactions between or among factors produce only small effects, but work in this area is continuing. To date, much more research has been done on risk factors than protective factors, but that picture, too, is changing.

Developmental Progression to Violence

Scientific theory and research take two different approaches to how youth violence develops—one that focuses on the onset of violent behavior and its frequency, patterns, and continuity over the life course and one that focuses on the emergence of risk factors at different stages of the life course. Chapter 3 describes two developmental trajectories for the onset of violent behavior—one in which violence begins in childhood (before puberty) and continues into adolescence, and one in which violence begins in adolescence.

In contrast, this chapter considers the timing of risk factors. It identifies the individual characteristics, experiences, and environmental conditions in childhood or adolescence that predict involvement in violent behavior in late adolescence—that is, age 15 to 18, the peak years of offending. Research shows that different risk factors may emerge in these two developmental periods and that the same risk factors may have different effect sizes, or predictive power, in these periods.

The timing of risk factors and the onset of violence are connected. Only risk factors that emerge in early childhood can logically account for violence that begins before puberty. However, these early risk factors may or may not be implicated in violence that begins in adolescence. In fact, studies show that many youths with late-onset violence did not encounter the childhood risk factors responsible for early-onset violence. For these youths, risk factors for violence emerged in adolescence (Huizinga et al., 1995; Moffitt et al., 1996; Patterson & Yoerger, 1997; Simons et al., 1994).

Table 7-2 lists early and late risk factors and estimates their effect sizes for violence at age 15 to 18. It does not distinguish between youths who became violent before puberty and those who first became violent in adolescence; both groups are included among youths who were violent in late adolescence. However, the table does indicate that different risk factors emerge before puberty (age 6 to 11) and after puberty (age 12 to 14) and that the same risk factors have different effect sizes in these periods. Thus, for example, the table shows that substance use in childhood has a greater effect on violence at age 15 to 18 than parental abuse or neglect does and that substance use in childhood has a greater effect on violence than substance use in early adolescence. (The table is discussed at greater length below, in A Note on Sources.)

The distinction between early and late risk factors is important. To be effective, prevention programs must address the risk factors that appear at a particular stage of development. The observed clustering of risk factors in childhood and in adolescence provides clear targets for intervention during these stages of the life course.

Limitations of Risk Factors

Risk factors are powerful tools for identifying and locating populations and individuals with a high potential for becoming

TABLE 7-2 Effect sizes of early and late risk factors for violence* at age 15 to 18

Early Risk Factors (age 6–11)	Effect Size (r =)	Late Risk Factors (age 12–14)	Effect size (r =)
		Large Effect Size (r > = .30)	
General offenses	*.38*	Weak social ties	*.39*
Substance use	*.30*	Antisocial, delinquent peers	*.37*
		Gang membership	.31
		Moderate Effect Size (r = .20 − .29)	
Being male	*.26*	General offenses	*.26*
Low family socioeconomic status/poverty	*.24*		
Antisocial parents	*.23*		
Aggression**	*.21*		
		Small Effect Size (r < .20)	
Psychological condition	*.15*	Psychological condition	*.19*
Hyperactivity	*.13*	Restlessness	.20
Poor parent-child relations	*.15*	Difficulty concentrating**	.18
Harsh, tax, or inconsistent discipline	.13	Risk taking	.09
Weak social ties	*.15*	Poor parent-child relations	*.19*
Problem (antisocial) behavior	*.13*	Harsh, tax discipline; poor monitoring, supervision	.08
Exposure to television violence	*.13*	Low parental involvement	.11
Poor attitude toward performance in school	*.13*	Aggression**	*.19*
Medical, physical	*.13*	Being male	*.19*
Low IQ	*.12*	Poor attitude toward performance in school	*.19*
Other family conditions	*.12*	Academic failure	.14
Broken home	*.09*	Physical violence	*.18*
Separation from parents	.09	Neighborhood crime, drugs[†]	.17
Antisocial attitudes, beliefs		Neighborhood disorganization[†]	.17
Dishonesty**	.12	Antisocial parents	*.16*
Abusive parents	*.07*	Antisocial attitudes, beliefs	.16
Neglect	*.07*	Crimes against persons	.14
Antisocial peers	*.04*	Problem (antisocial) behavior	*.12*
		Low IQ	*.11*
		Broken home	*.10*
		Low family socioeconomic status/poverty	*.10*
		Abusive parents	*.09*
		Other family conditions	*.08*
		Family conflict**	.13
		Substance use	*.06*

*The risk factors identified by Lipsey and Derzon are predictors of involvement in felonies and could thus be predicting serious, but nonviolent offending. However, the vast majority of serious offenders are also violent offenders (see Chapter 3). The risk factors from Hawkins et al. are predictors of serious violence only.

**Males only.

[†]Individual risk factor. As a neighborhood-level risk factor (rate of violent offending), the effect is substantially greater (r = .45). See Sampson & Groves, 1989; Simcha-Fagan & Schwartz, 1986; Sampson et al., 1997; Elliott et al. 1996.

Adapted from Hawkins et al. (1998c) and Lipsey and Derzon (1998).

Sources: Adapted from Hawkins et al. (1998c) and Lipsey and Derzon (1998). Specific risk factors are listed under general categories of risk if there is sufficient evidence to warrant it. Effect sizes in italics are from the meta-analysis by Hawkins et al. (1998c), Lipsey and Derzon (1998), or Paik and Comstock (1994). Other effect sizes are based on two or more longitudinal studies of general population samples.

violent, and they provide valuable targets for programs aimed at preventing or reducing violence. But there are important limitations to our knowledge about and use of risk factors. The following cautions are worth bearing in mind:

- No single risk factor or set of risk factors is powerful enough to predict with certainty that youths will become violent. Poor performance in school is a risk factor, for example, but by no means will all young people who perform poorly in school become violent. Similarly, many youths are exposed to multiple risks yet avoid becoming involved in violence (Garmezy, 1985; Rutter, 1985; Werner & Smith, 1982, 1992).

- Because public health research is based on observations and statistical probabilities in large populations, risk factors can be used to predict violence in groups with particular characteristics or environmental conditions but not in individuals.

- Given these two limitations, assessments designed to target individual youths for intervention programs must be used with great care. Most individual youths identified by existing risk factors for violence, even youths facing accumulated risks, never become violent (Farrington, 1997; Huizinga et al., 1995; Lipsey & Derzon, 1998).

- Some risk factors are not amenable to change and therefore are not good targets for intervention (Earls, 1994; Hawkins et al., 1998a). Being born male is an example.

- Of the risk factors that are amenable to change, some are not realistic targets of preventive efforts. Eliminating poverty is not a realistic short-term goal, for example, but programs that counter some of the effects of poverty are. (Eliminating or reducing poverty should be a high-priority long-term goal, however.)

- Some situations and conditions that influence the likelihood of violence or the form it takes may not be identified by longitudinal studies as risk factors (predictors) for violence. Situational factors such as bullying, taunting, and demeaning interactions can serve as catalysts for unplanned violence. The social context can influence the seriousness or form of violence—for example, the presence of a gun or a gathering crowd of peers that makes a youth feel he (or she) needs to protect his (or her) reputation. These may not be primary causes of violence, yet they are contributing factors and are important to understanding how a violent exchange unfolds. Such influences, although important, may not be identified in this report because of the way risk factors are defined.

- Many studies of risk factors, particularly earlier ones, drew their samples from white boys and young men. The limited focus of these studies calls into question their predictive power for girls and women and for other racial or ethnic groups. Differences among cultures and their socialization and expectations of girls and boys may modify the influences of some risk factors in these groups.

Nonetheless, most of the risk factors identified in this report do apply broadly to all young people. All children go through the same basic stages of human development—and prevention of youth violence is based on understanding when and how risk factors come into play at various stages of development. Moreover, there is some evidence that most risk factors are equally valid predictors of delinquency and violence regardless of sex, race, or ethnicity (Rosay et al., 2000; Williams et al., 1999). Sophisticated studies that identify how cultural differences affect the interplay of the individual and his or her surroundings will make possible more effective prevention efforts.

Protective Factors

There is some disagreement about exactly what protective factors are. They have been viewed both as the absence of risk and as something conceptually distinct from risk (Guerra, 1998; Jessor et al., 1995; Reiss & Roth, 1993; Wasserman & Miller, 1998). The former view typically places risk and protective factors on the opposite ends of a continuum. For example, good parent-child relations might be considered a protective factor because it is the opposite of poor parent-child relations, a known risk factor. But a simple linear relationship of this sort (where the risk of violence decreases as parent-child relations improve) blurs the distinction between risk and protection, making them essentially the same thing.[1]

The view that protection is conceptually distinct from risk (the view used in this report) defines protective factors as characteristics or conditions that interact with risk factors to reduce their influence on violent behavior (Garmezy, 1985; Rutter, 1985; Stattin & Magnusson, 1996). For example, low family socioeconomic status is a risk factor for violence, and a warm, supportive relationship with a parent may be a protective factor. The warm relationship does not improve the child's economic status, but it does buffer the child from some of the adverse effects of poverty. Protective factors may or may not have a direct effect on violence (compare Jessor et al., 1995 and Stattin & Magnusson, 1996).

Interest in protective factors emerged from research in the field of developmental psychopathology. Investigators observed that children with exposure to multiple risk factors often es-

---

1. If the relationship to violence is nonlinear, risk and protection may take on a different meaning. However, the conditions and characteristics identified as protective factors by those using the absence-of-risk conceptualization rarely, if ever, involve a nonlinear relationship to violence.

caped their impact. This led to a search for the characteristics or conditions that might confer resilience—that is, factors that moderate or buffer the effects of risk (Davis, 1999; Garmezy, 1985; Rutter, 1987; Werner, 1989). Protective factors offer an explanation for why children and adolescents who face the same degree of risk may be affected differently.

The concept of protective factors is familiar in public health. Wearing seat belts, for example, reduces the risk of serious injury or death in a car crash. Identifying and measuring the effects of protective factors is a new area of violence research, and information about these factors is limited. Because they buffer the effect of risk factors, protective factors are an important tool in violence prevention.

Like risk factors, proposed protective factors are grouped into individual, family, school, peer group, and community categories. They may differ at various stages of development, they may interact, and they may exert cumulative effects (Catalano et al., 1998; Furstenberg et al., 1999; Garmezy, 1985; Jessor et al., 1995; Rutter, 1979; Sameroff et al., 1993; Thornberry et al., 1995). Just as risk factors do not necessarily cause an individual child or young person to become violent, protective factors do not guarantee that an individual child or young person will not become violent. They reduce the probability that groups of young people facing a risk factor or factors will become involved in violence.

A Note on Sources

This chapter draws heavily on four important studies: Lipsey & Derzon's meta-analysis of 34 longitudinal studies on risk factors for violence (1998); Hawkins et al.'s study of malleable risk and protective factors drawn from 30 longitudinal studies, including some not included in the Lipsey & Derzon meta-analysis (Hawkins et al., 1998c); Paik and Comstock's meta-analysis of 217 studies of exposure to media violence and its effects on aggression and violence (1994); and the National Institute of Mental Health's *Taking Stock* report (Hann & Borek, in press), an extensive review of research on risk factors for aggression and other behavior problems.

Table 7-2 is adapted from the tables presented in the Lipsey and Derzon and Hawkins et al. meta-analyses. The risk factors in Table 7-2 predict felonies—that is, violent and property crimes—at ages 15 to 18, the peak years of involvement.[2] Entries in bold are effect sizes from the meta-analyses by Lipsey

and Derzon, Hawkins et al., and Paik and Comstock for various classes of risk factors; other entries are effect sizes reported in two or more longitudinal studies. (Risk classes are described in Appendix 4–A and later sections of this chapter.) Some of the risk classes in Table 7-2 include several separate risk factors. For example, psychological condition includes hyperactivity, daring, and attention problems.

Additional risk factors and classes of risk factors have been added from other sources. For example, there is adequate evidence to establish harsh, lax, or inconsistent discipline as a separate risk factor, although Lipsey and Derzon include it in the poor parent-child relations class. Academic failure, family conflict, and belonging to a gang are additional examples of risk factors not included in any of the meta-analyses.

The measure of effect size used in these tables is a bivariate correlation (r), or simple correlation between two variables. All estimates of effect size are statistically significant and are based on multiple studies, with those for risk classes typically involving more studies than those for separate risk factors. The studies reviewed in Lipsey and Derzon, Paik and Comstock, and Hawkins et al. are not cited here; however, other studies that were used to establish a risk factor or that are included in estimates of effect size are cited.[3]

There is a rich and extensive body of research on risks for antisocial behavior, externalizing behavior, conduct disorder, and aggression (Hann & Borek, in press). Each of these terms defines a pattern or set of behaviors that includes aggressive or violent behavior, but most of the behaviors included are either nonphysical, nonviolent acts or relatively minor forms of physical aggression. Risk factors for antisocial behavior may be quite different from those that predict violent behavior (robbery, aggravated assault, rape, and homicide). Since antisocial behavior does not present the potential for serious injury or death that violence does, this report relies on studies that identify risk factors for serious offenses generally and violent behavior specifically, bearing in mind that the vast majority of serious offenders report having been involved in violent offenses.

Summary

Risk and protective factors can be found in every area of a child or adolescent's life, they exert different effects at different stages of development, and they gain strength in numbers. The public health approach to the problem of youth violence seeks to identify risk and protective factors, determine when in the life course they typically occur and how they operate, and enable

---

2. As noted in Chapter 3, most violent offenders commit many serious property offenses (such as burglary, auto theft, and larceny), and most youths involved in serious property offenses (FBI index offenses) are also involved in violent offenses. The risk factors described here are based on longitudinal studies that use self-reports to predict violent offenses. Several of the studies also include official arrest data and thus predict self-reported offenses, arrests for serious or violent offenses, or both.

---

3. Effect sizes for risk factors not included in the meta-analyses reported by Lipsey and Derzon (1988), Hawkins et al. (1998c), and Parik and Comstock (1994) are weighted (by sample size) mean correlations. The effect sizes in Parik and Comstock are unweighted mean correlations.

researchers to design preventive programs to be put in place at just the right time to be most effective.

This chapter describes what is known about individual, family, school, peer group, and community risk and protective factors that exert their effects in childhood and adolescence. It describes the power of early risk factors, which come into play before puberty, and late risk factors, which exert their influence after puberty, to predict the likelihood of youth violence.

REFERENCES

Bursik, R. J. Jr., & Grasmick, H. G. (1993). *Neighborhoods and crime: The dimensions of effective community control.* New York: Lexington Books.

Catalano, R. F., Arthur, M. W., Hawkins, J. D., Bergland, L., & Olson, J. J. (1998). Comprehensive community- and school-based interventions to prevent antisocial behavior. In R. Loeber & D. P. Farrington (Eds.), *Serious and violent juvenile offenders: Risk factors and successful interventions* (pp. 248–283). Thousand Oaks, CA: Sage Publications.

Davis, N. J. (1999). *Resilience: Status of the research and research-based programs.* Rockville, MD: Substance Abuse and Mental Health Services Administration, Center for Mental Health Services, Division of Program Development, Special Populations and Projects, Special Programs Development Branch.

Earls, F. J. (1994). Violence and today's youth. *Critical Health Issues for Children and Youth,* 4, 4–23.

Elliott, D. S., & Menard, S. (1996). Delinquent friends and delinquent behavior: Temporal and developmental patterns. In J. D. Hawkins (Ed.), *Delinquency and crime: Current theories* (pp. 28–67). Cambridge, United Kingdom: Cambridge University Press.

Farrington, D. P. (1997). Early prediction of violent and non-violent youthful offending. *European Journal on Criminal Policy and Research,* 5, 51–66.

Furstenberg, F. F., Elder, G. H., Cook, T. D., Eccles, J., & Sameroff, A. (1999). *Managing to make it: Urban families and adolescent success.* Chicago: University of Chicago Press.

Garmezy, N. (1985). Stress-resistant children: The search for protective factors. In J. E. Stevenson (Ed.), *Recent research in developmental psychopathology* (pp. 213–233). New York: Elsevier Science.

Guerra, N. G. (1998). Serious and violent juvenile offenders: Gaps in knowledge and research priorities. In R. Loeber & D. P. Farrington (Eds.), *Serious and violent juvenile offenders: Risk factors and successful interventions* (pp. 389–404). Thousand Oaks, CA: Sage Publications.

Hann, D. M., & Borek, N. T. (Eds.). (in press). *NIMH taking stock of risk factors for child/youth externalizing behavior problems.* Washington, DC: U.S. Government Printing Office.

Hawkins, J. D., Laub, J. H., & Lauritsen, J. L. (1998a). Race, ethnicity, and serious juvenile offending. In R. Loeber & D. P. Farrington (Eds.), *Serious and violent juvenile offenders: Risk factors and successful interventions* (pp. 30–46). Thousand Oaks, CA: Sage Publications.

Hawkins, J. D., Herrenkohl, T. L., Farrington, D. P., Brewer, D., Catalano, R. F., & Harachi, T. W. (1998c). A review of predictors of youth violence. In R. Loeber & D. P. Farrington (Eds.), *Serious and violent juvenile offenders: Risk factors and successful interventions* (pp. 106–146). Thousand Oaks, CA: Sage Publications.

Herrenkohl, T. L., Maguin, E., Hill, K. G., Hawkins, J. D., Abbott, R. D., & Catalano, R. F. (2000). Developmental risk factors for youth violence. *Journal of Adolescent Health,* 26, 176–186.

Huizinga, D., Loeber, R., & Thornberry, T. P. (1995). *Recent findings from the program of research on the causes and correlates of delinquency* (U.S. Department of Justice, Office of Justice Programs, Office of Juvenile Justice and Delinquency Prevention, NCJ 159042). Washington, DC: U.S. Government Printing Office.

Jessor, R. J., van den Bos, J., Vanderryn, J., Costa, F. M., & Turbin, M. S. (1995). Protective factors in adolescent problem behavior: Moderator effects and developmental change. *Developmental Psychology,* 31, 923–933.

Kraemer, H. C., Kazdin, A. E., Offord, D. R., Kessler, R. C., Jensen, P. S., & Kupfer, D. J. (1997). Coming to terms with the terms of risk. *Archives of General Psychiatry,* 54, 337–343.

Lipsey, M. W., & Derzon, J. H. (1998). Predictors of violent and serious delinquency in adolescence and early adulthood: A synthesis of longitudinal research. In R. Loeber & D. P. Farrington (Eds.), *Serious and violent juvenile offenders: Risk factors and successful interventions* (pp. 86–105). Thousand Oaks, CA: Sage Publications.

Moffitt, T., Caspi, A., Dickson, N., Silva, P., & Stanton, W. (1996). Childhood-onset versus adolescents-onset antisocial conduct problems in males: Natural history from ages 3 to 18 years. *Development and Psychopathology,* 8, 399–424.

Patterson, G. R., & Yoerger, K. (1997). A developmental model for late-onset delinquency. *Nebraska Symposium on Motivation,* 44, 119–177.

Reiss, A. J. Jr., & Roth, J. A. (1993). *Understanding and preventing violence.* Washington, DC: National Academy Press.

Rosay, A. B., Gottfredson, D. C., Armstrong, T. A., & Harmon, M. A. (2000). Invariance of measures of prevention program effectiveness. *Journal of Quantitative Criminology,* 16, 341–367.

Rutter, M. (1985). Resilience in the face of adversity: Protective factors and resistance to psychiatric disorder. *British Journal of Psychiatry,* 147, 598–611.

Rutter, M. (1979). Protective factors in children's responses to stress and disadvantage. In M. W. Kent & J. E. Rolf (Eds.), *Primary prevention of psychopathology. Social competence in children* (Vol. 3, pp. 49–74). Hanover, NH: University Press of New England.

Sameroff, A. J., Seifer, R., & Baldwin, C. (1993). Stability of intelligence from pre-school to adolescence: The influence of social and family risk factors. *Child Development,* 64, 80–97.

Sampson, R. J., & Lauritsen, J. L. (1994). Violent victimization and offending: Individual-, situational-, and community-level risk factors. In A. J. Reiss, Jr. & J. A. Roth (Eds.), *Understanding and preventing violence. Social influences* (Vol. 3, pp. 1–114). Washington, DC: National Academy Press.

Simons, R. L., Wu, C. I., Conger, R. D., & Lorenz, F. O. (1994). Two routes to delinquency differences between early and late starters in the impact of parenting and deviant peers. *Criminology,* 32, 247–275.

Stattin, H., & Magnusson, D. (1996). Antisocial development: A holistic approach. *Development and Psychopathology,* 8, 617–645.

Thornberry, T. P. (1998). Membership in youth gangs and involvement in serious, violent offending. In R. Loeber & D. P. Farrington (Eds.), *Serious and violent juvenile offenders: Risk factors and successful interventions* (pp. 147–166). Thousand Oaks, CA: Sage Publications.

Thornberry, T. P., Huizinga, D., & Loeber, R. (1995). The prevention of serious delinquency and violence: Implications from the program of research on the causes and correlates of delinquency. In J. C. Howell, B. Krisberg, J. D. Hawkins, & J. J. Wilson (Eds.), *A sourcebook: Serious, violent and chronic juvenile offenders* (pp. 213–237). Thousand Oaks, CA: Sage Publications.

Wasserman, G. A., & Miller, L. S. (1998). The prevention of serious and violent juvenile offending. In R. Loeber & D. P. Farrington (Eds.), *Serious and violent juvenile offenders: Risk factors and successful interventions* (pp. 197–247). Thousand Oaks, CA: Sage Publications.

Werner, E. E. (1989). High-risk children in young adulthood: A longitudinal study from birth to 32 years. *American Journal of Orthopsychiatry,* 59, 72–81.

Werner, E. E., & Smith, R. S. (1992). *Overcoming the odds: High risk children from birth to adulthood.* Ithaca, NY: Cornell University Press.

Werner, E. E., & Smith, R. S. (1982). *Vulnerable but invincible: A longitudinal study of resilient children and youth.* New York: McGraw-Hill.

Williams, J. H., Ayers, C. D., Abbott, R. D., Hawkins, J. D., & Catalano, R. F. (1999). Racial differences in risk factors for delinquency and substance use among adolescents. *Social Work Research,* 23, 241–256.

PART 8

Communities and Populations as Focus for Health Promotion Programs

Identifying or developing health promotion interventions for specific populations and communities requires an understanding about the nature of these social entities and the kinds of factors and issues that need to be taken into account. Readings in this part profile approaches to *community interventions* and *interventions in a community* (as defined in the reading text). The first selection (Corby & Wolitski, 1997) outlines an HIV/AIDS prevention intervention that targets high-risk drug users and their sexual partners in Long Beach, California, including a description of that community. It is an example of a targeted *intervention in the community* and was one of several AIDS community demonstration projects funded by the Centers for Disease Control and Prevention and implemented at specific sites across the country. Following this reading are two selections that review well-known *community intervention* models: Brownson et al. (1996) on the Bootheel Heart Health Project and a US Department of Health and Human Services description of the Planned Approach to Community Health (PATCH)—one of several widely disseminated community intervention formats.

Community HIV Prevention: The Long Beach AIDS Community Demonstration Project

Source: Excerpt from Corby NH, and Wolitski RJ (Eds). 1997. *Community HIV Prevention: The Long Beach AIDS Community Demonstration Project.* Long Beach, CA: The University Press.

- ACDP: AIDS Community Demonstration Projects
- CDC: Centers for Disease Control and Prevention
- IDU: Injection drug user

THE AIDS COMMUNITY DEMONSTRATION PROJECTS: 1989–1994

Funding of the Projects. Based on the recommendations from the Unicoi Conference[1] and a review of the most recent epidemiologic data, a request for proposals (RFP) was generated for the second funding period of the ACDPs. The RFP requested applicants to design, implement, and evaluate community-level interventions with the following "high-risk and hard-to-reach" populations: IDUs not in treatment; men who have sex with men but do not self-identify as gay (MSM); women who are or may be the sex partners of men in these two groups (female sex partners or FSPs); persons who exchange sex for money, drugs, or other things (sex traders); and high-risk adolescents. Five projects were funded by the CDC through the cooperative agreement mechanism: the Dallas County Health Department (TX); the Department of Public Health, Denver Health and

Hospitals (CO); the Long Beach Department of Health and Human Services (CA); the New York State Department of Health; and the Seattle-King Department of Public Health (WA). Each project, except Dallas, developed interventions for one, two, or three of the five designated high-risk groups. The Dallas project intervened in two separate census tracts with high rates of sexually transmitted diseases (STDs) and large numbers of IDUs. Two projects sub-contracted their projects to local agencies with strong access to the target populations. In New York, the National Development and Research Institute conducted the study for the state, and in Long Beach, the Center for Behavioral Research and Services at California State University, Long Beach, conducted the study for the city.

YEAR 1: THE SHAPING OF THE ACDPS

Throughout the life of the ACDPs (1989 to 1994), representatives of each funded site met on a regular basis, first to establish the research protocol and later to assess progress and resolve problems. During the first meeting of the principal investigators, consultants, and CDC staff, it was decided by consensus that all sites would work under a common protocol to be based upon the recommendations of the participants of the Unicoi Conference. The reasons for using a common protocol were that using a common template for the content and delivery of the intervention would allow the method to be tested across diverse populations and ultimately provide prevention program managers with a general framework for a successful HIV prevention program. Furthermore, the use of common evaluation instruments and methods would enable data to be pooled across the sites and would increase the statistical

1. A strategy conference held at the Unicoi Conference Center in Georgia in 1988.

strength of analyses, allowing firmer conclusions to be drawn about the outcome of the study. The common protocol agreed upon by the participants of the ACDPs included the use of the following components: (a) formative research in the project communities before implementing the intervention, (b) behavior-change theories as a framework for the intervention, (c) small media materials with role-model stories of community individuals who are changing or had changed their risk behaviors, (d) networks of community members to distribute these materials and reinforce behavior change among at-risk community members, and (e) a joint evaluation protocol across project sites (CDC, 1996; O'Reilly & Higgins, 1991). To accomplish this strategy, in the year following the first Principal Investigators' meeting (1989–1990) the project staff were trained to conduct formative research using qualitative methods including in-depth interviews, focus groups, and direct observations; the design of the intervention was initiated; and the outcome instrument was developed.

Formative Research. As suggested by the consultants at the Unicoi Conference, all project staff sought to carefully define their target groups and come to know members of that community. To aid in this process, individual consultants with expertise in different formative research techniques were employed to train the project staff (many of whom had mainly conducted HIV-prevention interventions within clinic settings) in these techniques. These methods are described in Higgins et al. (1996), Tashima et al. (1996), and, with regard to the Long Beach project specifically, in CHAPTER 6 of this volume.

This formative research period was critical since it laid the foundation of the community-level intervention and its evaluation. During this time the first contacts were made with members of the target populations and the process of building trust with community members began. This period of formative research was completed by the end of the first year of funding. The abundant amount of information gathered was distilled using a systematic method for reducing and managing the data (Higgins et al., 1996; Tashima et al., 1996) to help each site locate the target populations in their communities, define the subgroups of the target populations, delineate comparable communities for purposes of a quasi-experimental research design, understand the meanings of HIV/AIDS and related risk behaviors among members of the target populations, and establish connections among community members who would later assist in intervention delivery. The intervention target groups also changed as a result of the information gathered in this process; for example, the female sex partners of MSMs were dropped as one of the focus populations due to the extreme difficulty in identifying and reaching this group.

Intervention Protocol Development. Intervention development also began in the first year. During the discussions surrounding the form and delivery of a community-level intervention, the project staff relied heavily upon the experience of Alfred McAlister, a key researcher on the North Karelia study (Puska et al., 1985), a community-level intervention for cardiovascular health in Sweden and the principal investigator of a large-scale community-level intervention to reduce cancer-related risk behaviors among Mexican Americans in south Texas (McAlister et al., 1992). As a former student of Albert Bandura, the creator of social learning theory, Dr. McAlister brought a social-learning perspective to the discussions. To help establish the key elements in the content of the intervention methods, assistance was sought from Martin Fishbein, a behavioral scientist at the University of Illinois. Dr. Fishbein had used his theory of reasoned action (Fishbein & Azjen, 1975) to fine-tune both health promotion messages and commercial marketing messages.

During this time, it was established that the intervention would have two key components: intervention messages and materials, and distribution of materials through networks of community members or with individuals interacting with community members. The community-level intervention was appealing for many reasons: (a) it would reach more persons in the target community than a one-on-one clinic intervention; (b) it would involve community members; (c) it would be delivered in the community where the risk behaviors were occurring; (d) it had the potential to support existing or create community norms related to a prevention behavior, thus sustaining behavior change in the community; and (e) specific populations could receive explicit prevention messages (CDC, 1996).

Evaluation Protocol Development. Each project site also worked closely to establish a joint evaluation protocol that included evaluation methods and instruments. The outcome instrument grew, in part, from information collected in the formative research process concerning beliefs and attitudes toward HIV prevention behaviors, which are key components of the theory of reasoned action (Fishbein & Azjen, 1975). It also was heavily influenced by the work of James Prochaska of the University of Rhode Island. During this period, Dr. Prochaska worked with the ACDP staff in adapting his stages of change model to HIV prevention both for the intervention and the evaluation of the ACDPs. The stages of change model (based on research in smoking cessation, diet, and psychotherapy) states that individuals pass through several stages in the process of adopting or discontinuing a behavior (Prochaska & DiClemente, 1983, 1984). These stages, termed "precontemplation," "contemplation," "preparation," "action," and "maintenance," provided the ACDPs with a model to measure behavior change among groups of individuals as they moved toward consistently performing the HIV prevention behavior. This was an important improvement over the way that public health researchers had been evaluating behavior change following an intervention.

For example, respondents had been asked in many studies "the last time you had sex, did you use a condom?" as a measure of adoption of a risk-reduction behavior. The dichotomous reply "yes" and "no" did not permit the capture of important information from a respondent who may have previously not thought of condom use but now was considering starting the prevention behavior. After working with Dr. Prochaska and his group, the ACDP researchers devised an instrument using measures based on the stages of change model to record movement toward the maintenance of the behavior goals over time.

Another measurement issue concerned the impact that attitudes, beliefs, and norms may have on different types of sex with different partners. Dr. Fishbein had advised us to define our target behaviors as narrowly as possible to understand and influence the underlying cognitive factors which contribute to specific behavior. For example, did different attitudes, beliefs, and norms influence consistent condom use during vaginal intercourse with a main partner compared to anal intercourse with a non-main partner? A preliminary elicitation study was conducted to examine this question, which determined that different cognitive factors influenced different sexual behaviors with different partner types.

The formative study was conducted in each community setting, and in each city matched treatment and comparison areas were identified for each relevant target group. Within these geographically defined areas, interviewers randomly selected and screened persons for eligibility for the interview (i.e., to determine if they fit the criteria for one of that site's target groups) and interviewed eligible individuals about their behaviors. Independent cross-sections of individuals from the target communities were sampled during a pilot wave, then ten formal waves of data collection providing periodic snapshots of the HIV-related beliefs, attitudes and behaviors of these communities were conducted over a four-year period.

YEAR 2: ESTABLISHING THE BASELINE AND GEARING-UP FOR INTERVENING

Formative Research. In the second year of the ACDPs, the information collected during the formative research process was used to establish the microsites for data collection in the intervention and comparison communities and to begin building networks of volunteers to assist in delivering the interventions.

The Intervention. Based on recommendations from the Unicoi Conference, epidemiological data, and information gathered from the formative research process, the ACDPs' research staff determined that the behavioral goals of the intervention would be consistent with condom use for intercourse (anal and vaginal) with main and "other" (non-main) partners, and consistent use of bleach for cleaning shared injection equipment among IDUs.

As noted earlier, ACDP researchers believed that the intervention should be based on established models and theories of behavior change. However, no single theory adequately described the complexity of sexual and drug-related risk behavior change among groups of individuals affected by HIV. Therefore, the intervention was built on several theories and models, some of which had overlapping elements: the health belief model, the theory of reasoned action, the transtheoretical model of behavior change (also commonly referred to as the stages of change model), social learning theory, and diffusion of innovations theory. The approach that emerged assumed that an individual's behavior was influenced by six factors related to these theories. These factors were: (a) individual's perception of risk; (b) the anticipated results of a recommended behavior change—both positive and negative outcome evaluations; (c) the perception that others in the community are also changing, and that those with whom the individual interacts most closely support the behavior change; (d) the perception by the individual that he/she is capable of making the recommended behavior change; (e) the intention to change the behavior and a commitment to make change; and (f) the acquisition of the social and physical skills necessary to carry out the new behavior (CDC, 1992, 1996). Subsequently, these elements were endorsed by key behavioral science in HIV prevention (Fishbein et al., 1992). These key psychosocial elements were reflected in the intervention messages as well as in the way the interventions were delivered in the community. To further facilitate the adoption of prevention behaviors, prevention materials such as condoms and bleach kits were distributed with the prevention messages.

In the summer of 1991, each site began implementing the intervention. The intervention process continued in each site until the summer of 1994. The components of the intervention are described in more detail below.

Intervention Messages and Materials. The behavioral intervention materials were in the form of small media materials such as brochures, pamphlets, flyers, and trading cards. These materials were chosen because they are relatively inexpensive to produce, especially when compared to the cost of mass media (television and radio commercials) or the cost of providing individual counseling sessions. Additionally, the materials were easy to distribute and, if produced with sufficient input from the target group, were attractive to that population. Initially (and later periodically), the design and the content of the media materials were tested with the target audience using focus groups and community surveys. Input from these groups reinforced the notion that small, easy-to-carry materials would be most likely to be accepted.

The materials contained role-model stories that were developed from interviews with members of the target populations and communities (Corby, Enguídanos, & Kay, 1996). A role-model story is an authentic story about an actual person from the target community. Each story is told in the person's own language and describes his or her reasons for thinking about or starting a behavior change, the type of change begun, how barriers to change were overcome, and the reinforcing consequences of the change. Each site produced unique media materials with role-model stories for each of its intervention populations.

In addition to being based on real stories of local community members, these role-model stories were written to highlight specific stages of change and theoretical factors and beliefs based on local project data. The selection of messages to be emphasized in role-model stories was guided by data collected from the study populations at each site. First, these data were used to determine the relative mix of role-model stories to be distributed in a community. For example, if survey data indicated that at one site most community members were in the precontemplation stage for adopting a certain behavior (e.g., consistent condom use), most of the site's stories concerning behavior would highlight a role model making a change from the precontemplation to the contemplation stage (e.g., from having no intention of using condoms consistently to thinking about using condoms consistently in the next six months).

Second, specific theoretical factors or beliefs were highlighted in subsequent role-model stories if site-specific data indicated that those factors were correlated with intentions to change or with a stage of change for the target behavior. For example, if people who were in the contemplative stage for consistent condom use tended to believe that condom use reduces intimacy while people in the preparation stage did not hold this belief, role-model stories would address intimacy issues. Over time, the type of stories produced in any given site changed; for example, more stories highlighted the preparation or the action stages as data from a site indicated that the target population was moving along the stages-of-change continuum. During the three years that the interventions were being implemented, more than 500 role-model stories were produced across all sites.

In addition to the role-model stories, printed materials also contained basic AIDS information, instructions on the use of condoms or of bleach to clean needles, biographies of community members participating in the project, notices of community events, or information on other health and social services, such as locations of homeless shelters or needle exchanges, schedules for free meals, mammogram screening, or drug and alcohol treatment services. In some sites, community members who were artists or writers were encouraged to contribute to the newsletter.

Intervention Delivery Through Community Networks. The printed materials, along with condoms and bleach kits, were individually delivered to people in the target community by a network of peer volunteers (e.g., IDUs, sex workers) recruited from the local community. In all sites except New York, a second tier network was also identified. This network consisted of business people, community leaders, and other persons who were not considered true peers but who were trusted by the target groups (according to data from the formative research period) and who interacted with the target groups on a regular basis. These network members were known as "interactors." In Dallas, Denver, and Seattle, peer and interactor networks were developed to distribute materials to each of the sites' multiple intervention populations separately. In Long Beach, interactors and one network of peers from all three target populations distributed materials to all three of the site's intervention populations (sex traders, IDUs and FSPs). New York maintained a peer network that distributed materials to a single population (FSPs).

All network members distributed role-model stories along with condoms and/or bleach. In one site, a group of peer network members met and distributed materials at set times throughout the day. In other sites, the peer network members distributed materials at their convenience day and night. Volunteers focused the attention of the recipients on the role-model stories and praised any mention of behavior-change attempts. The use of role-model stories was a key component of the intervention; moreover, peer network members who had attempted to or succeeded in changing their own risk behaviors were encouraged to share their personal stories and experiences with other community members. Network members were recruited through contact with a project outreach worker, referral from another service organization, or referral from current or former network members (Guenther-Grey, Noroian, Fonseka, & ACDP, 1996).

Typically, if the person was a member of the target population or had regular contact with members of the target population, he or she was eligible to become a peer network member. Having personally adopted the behavioral goal was not required for eligibility.

Each site conducted training sessions with new recruits. These sessions introduced the network members to the project, provided basic education about HIV and AIDS, explained the role-model stories, discussed different methods of approaching people on the street and getting them interested in the role-model stories, and included role-playing interactions between the network members to practice distributing the materials to the recipients. Network members received a small incentive and/or certificate after completing the training. Peer network members distributed materials alone, in pairs, or accompanied by a project outreach worker.

Four of the five projects maintained storefront offices either within or near the intervention neighborhoods (Dallas, Denver, Long Beach, and New York). These convenient locations served as a focal point for project activities such as parties for assembling intervention materials, support group meetings for peer network members or for HIV infected individuals, health screening services (HIV counseling and testing, sickle cell anemia testing), and community events such as a commemoration of World AIDS Day or participation in a Martin Luther King, Jr. parade.

The Evaluation. Early in the second year, a common protocol for data collection was established and data collection staff was hired and trained at all sites. The data collection staff remained separate from the intervention staff and from peer network members. The outcome evaluation was linked to the behavioral theories underlying the intervention and included three basic features at each site: (a) the intervention was implemented in one geographic area, while another area served as a comparison; (b) the data collection instrument measured a common set of behavioral and cognitive variables across all communities and survey periods; and (c) the data collection schedule included several waves of cross-sectional data collected in both intervention and comparison areas before the intervention began as well as during its three years of implementation. The primary data collection instrument, known as the "Brief Street Intercept" (BSI), was pilot tested and refined for use. Two waves of data were collected using the instrument, forming the baseline to which future "waves" (or cross-sections) of data would be compared. Common instruments were also created to evaluate the intervention delivery process. All sites collected the same process data concerning the intervention such as the content of role-model stories, the number of volunteers, daily outreach activities, and interviews with key observers about the changes they saw in the community or among individuals in the target population.

YEARS 3–5: INTERVENING AND EVALUATING

Formative Research. Although the primary formative research to identify the target groups had ended in year one, the formative research was ongoing. For instance, using the formative research methods, sites were able to find pockets of the target community which had been missed previously either through oversight or circumstance (e.g., had been forced out of their usual hang-outs by the police and moved to different areas). In the third year, several of the project sites experienced difficulties retaining their peer networks. To maximize retention, all sites convened focus groups with current and former members of their peer networks. The changes recommended by the peer network members were tested by the sites and resulted in several methods for maintaining the network. These included: (a) offering material incentives such as small amounts of cash, food or movie coupons, and T-shirts or buttons with the project logo; (b) providing opportunities for recognition of the network members' achievements through awards or certificates of participation; and (c) maintaining frequent contact between outreach workers (professional staff) and the network members to provide encouragement and reinforcement for their role (CDC, 1996; Guenther-Grey et al., 1996).

The Intervention. The intervention continued at all sites with ongoing refinement of the process. New stories for the media materials were produced approximately once a month; the recruitment and retention of volunteers was continual. Over time, each site sharpened its skills in these methods, resulting in fine-tuning of the community-level interventions in most of the ACDP intervention communities. Overall, 1,144 individuals from these historically under-served communities were recruited and trained to assist the ACDPs in delivering HIV prevention messages to their peers, and 585,000 role-model publications were distributed with condoms and bleach kits.

The Evaluation. During the last three years of the project, eight more waves of BSI data were collected from each target group at each site, resulting in a total of 10 cross-sectional waves of BSI data collection. Additionally, another instrument which gathered more detailed information about respondents' beliefs and attitudes concerning risk-reduction activities was developed, pilot-tested, and administered to those who were questioned with the Brief Street Intercept during three data collection waves. This instrument has provided valuable information regarding factors that motivate behavior change (e.g., Corby, Jamner, & Wolitski, 1996; Jamner, Corby, & Wolitski, 1996).

Post-ACDP Observations. Almost all of the recommendations made at the Unicoi Conference were carried out by the

ACDPs. The intervention and evaluation were thoroughly grounded in behavior-change theories, thus enabling the development of interventions aimed at changing key beliefs and factors that would be most likely to promote risk reduction in the selected target groups and communities. This theoretical foundation enabled the development of more sensitive measures of behavior change with which to evaluate the success of the interventions. By having a clearly specified behavior-change model and by carefully evaluating intervention components, both the effectiveness of the intervention and the key factors influencing behavior change in specific communities and target groups could be assessed.

Formative research enabled the clear definition of target populations, facilitated the trust of community members, and provided an understanding of the meaning of HIV prevention within the context of the lives of members of the target populations. The use of formative research throughout the project ensured that the interventions were appropriately tailored during the three-year intervention period.

Community members delivered the intervention and served as models of behavior change for their peers. These community members were recruited, in part, through social networking approaches in which community members encouraged people they knew to become a part of the program. Some individuals from the target groups were also employed to coordinate the peer networks in some sites. To encourage community members to read the materials and become more aware of the importance of HIV prevention in their community, intervention materials were developed following the guidance of members of the target community. Data examining the extent to which community members were exposed to project materials indicated that depending on the target group and city, the intervention reached from 22% to 68% of the eligible respondents by the second year of the intervention (CDC, 1996). Furthermore, exposure to the intervention continued to rise in the third year of the intervention (see CHAPTER 8 and ACDP, Fishbein, & Johnson, 1996).

The outcome and process evaluations were carefully constructed, allowing us to evaluate the efficacy of the intervention. Preliminary analyses of data across all sites examining the effect of the community-level intervention on risk behaviors indicated that this intervention resulted in individuals moving along the stage-of-change continuum for the target behaviors (CDC, 1996). Full interviews were conducted with 9,991 individuals during the first eight cross-sections of data collection (baseline and first two years of the intervention). Overall, by the end of the second year of the intervention, there was significant movement on the stage-of-change continuum toward consistent condom use for vaginal intercourse with main partners ($p = 0.0353$) and with non-main partners ($p < 0.001$) and for consistent condom use for anal intercourse for non-main partners among those reporting exposure to the project intervention compared to those in the intervention area who were not exposed. Also by this time, intervention area respondents who recalled exposure to the ACDPs messages were significantly more likely to report greater progress toward consistent bleach use for cleaning injection equipment ($p < 0.001$) compared to those who were not exposed. These findings are elaborated upon in an MMWR Reports and Recommendations (CDC, 1996). Data analyses examining the effect of exposure to the intervention in the third year of intervention have been conducted (ACDP, Fishbein, & Johnson, 1996).

The success of the ACDPs' intervention motivated several of the health agencies to continue the projects with state and local funding and to adapt the program for other populations. For example, in Denver the ACDP model is in operation with IDUs and youth at high risk for infection with STDs including HIV; in Seattle, the model has been adapted for use among gay-identifying men. The model has been adapted to intervene with substance-using gay men in Long Beach and is being used to train parents in New York housing projects to talk with their children about HIV. In addition, several projects have developed training programs to assist other communities in adopting the ACDP model; this training is being provided in the CDC's STD Training Centers and through a statewide program funded by the California State Department of Health Services' Office of AIDS.

Information learned from these projects is greatly encouraging. The results of these activities indicate that a model intervention can be successfully adapted for diverse target groups in multiple sites across the country and that community-level interventions involving members of the community can be launched and maintained in socially and economically disadvantaged communities, perhaps setting the stage for broader, community-generated, HIV prevention activities in the future.

REFERENCES

AIDS Community Demonstration Projects, Fishbein, M., & Johnson, W.D. (1996, July). *The AIDS Community Demonstration Projects: A Successful Multi-Site Community Level Intervention*. Paper presented at the XI International Conference on AIDS, Vancouver, BC.

Centers for Disease Control and Prevention (1992a). Changes in sexual behavior and condom use associated with a risk-reduction program–Denver, 1988–1991. *Morbidity and Mortality Weekly Report*, 40, 792–794.

Centers for Disease Control and Prevention (1992b). Condom use among male injecting-drug users – New York, 1987–1990. *Morbidity and Mortality Weekly Report*, 41, 617–620.

Centers for Disease Control and Prevention (1992c). NCPS AIDS Community Demonstration Projects: What we have learned, 1985–1990. Atlanta, GA: US Department of Health and Human Services, Public Health Service, June 1992.

Centers for Disease Control and Prevention (1996). Community-level prevention of human immunodeficiency virus infection among high-risk populations: The AIDS Community Demonstration Projects. *MMWR Recommendations and Reports,* 10(RR-6), 1–24.

Corby, N., Enguídanos, S.M., & Kay, L.S. (1996). Development and use of role-model stories in a community-level risk-reduction intervention. *Public Health Reports,* 111 (*Suppl. 1*), 54–58.

Corby, N.H., Jamner, M.S., & Wolitski, R.J. (1996). Using the Theory of Planned Behavior to predict condom use among male and female injection drug users. *Journal of Applied Social Psychology,* 26, 52–75.

Fishbein, M., & Ajzen, I. (1975). *Belief, attitude, intention and behavior: An introduction to theory and research.* Reading MA: Addison-Wesley Publishing Company.

Fishbein, M., Bandura, A., Triandis, H.C., Kanfer, F.H., Becker, M.H. & Middlestadt, S. (1992). Factors influencing behavior and behavior change: Final report. Rockville, MD: National Institute of Health.

Guenther-Grey, C., Noroian, D., Fonseka, J., & AIDS Community Demonstration Projects. (1996). Developing community networks to deliver HIV prevention interventions: Lessons learned from the AIDS Community Demonstration Projects. *Public Health Reports,* 111 *(Suppl. 1),* 41–49.

Higgins, D., O'Reilly, K., Tashima, N., Crain, C., Beeker, C., Goldbaum, G., Elifson, C., Galavotti, C., Guenther-Grey, C., & AIDS Community Demonstration Projects. (1996). Using formative research to lay the foundation for community-level HIV prevention efforts: An example from the AIDS Community Demonstration Projects. *Public Health Reports,* 111 *(Suppl. 1),* 28–35.

Jamner, M.S., Corby, N.H., & Wolitski, R.J. (1996). Bleaching injection equipment: Influencing factors among IDUs who share. *Substance Use and Misuse,* 31, 1973–1993.

McAlister, A.L., Ramirez, A.G., Amescua, C., Pulley, L., Stern, M.P., Mercado, S. (1992). Smoking cessation in Texas-Mexico border communities: A quasi-experimental panel study. *American Journal of Health Promotion,* 6, 274–279.

O'Reilly, K., & Higgins, D.L. (1991). AIDS Community Demonstration Projects for HIV prevention among hard-to-reach groups. *Public Health Reports,* 106, 714–720.

Prochaska, J.O., & DiClemente, C.C. (1983). Stages and processes of self-change of smoking: Toward an integrative model of change. *Journal of Consulting and Clinical Psychology,* 51, 390–395.

Prochaska, J.O., & DiClemente, C.C. (1984). The transtheoretical approach: Crossing the traditional boundaries of therapy. Homewood, Illinois: Dow-Jones/Irwin.

Puska, P., Nisinen, A., Tuomilehto, J., Salonen, J.T., Koskela, K., McAlister, A., Kottke, T.E., Maccody, N., & Farquahar, J.W. (1985). The community-based strategy to prevent coronary disease: Conclusions from the ten years of the North Karelia project. *Annual Review of Public Health,* 6, 147–93.

Tashima, N., Crain, C., O'Reilly, K.R., & Sterk-Elifson, C. (1996). The community identification (CID) process: A discovery model. *Qualitative Health Research,* 6, 23–48.

Preventing Cardiovascular Disease Through Community-Based Risk Reduction

Source: Excerpt from Brownson, RC et al. (1996). Preventing cardiovascular disease through community-based risk reduction: Five-year results of the Bootheel Heart Health Project. *American Journal of Public Health* 86: 206-213.

INTRODUCTION

Despite declines over the past few decades, cardiovascular diseases remain the leading cause of death and disability in the United States.[1] In 1992, more than 861,000 Americans died from heart disease or stroke, the main forms of cardiovascular disease.[1] Cardiovascular disease risk factors can be classified as either modifiable or nonmodifiable.[2] Among modifiable factors, physical inactivity has recently been recognized as one of the four major risk factors for cardiovascular disease[3]; the other factors are cigarette smoking, high blood pressure, and elevated blood cholesterol.[3]

Healthy People 2000,[4] the publication outlining the nation's public health goals, includes chapters on heart disease and stroke and their antecedent risk factors (physical inactivity, poor nutrition, and tobacco use). As a result of large disparities between racial groups, separate objectives have been established for reducing heart disease and stroke among Blacks.[4] Significant progress has been shown for only 5 of the 12 national health objectives for physical activity.[5]

Healthy People 2000 states that community-based intervention is a critically important method for achieving health objectives for the nation.[4] Even with modest budgets, community-based coalitions have effectively changed health policies; for example, they have instituted requirements for smoke-free schools[6] and labeling of heart healthy foods.[7] Community-based programs also are beginning to address multiple risk factors[5] (e.g., heart health coalitions for controlling multiple cardiovascular disease risk factors).

Large community-based prevention projects have used combined interventions that address both individual behavior change and community-wide change.[8,9] Most of these studies have focused on cardiovascular disease prevention. They include the North Karelia Project in Finland,[10,11] the Stanford Five-City Project,[12-15] the Pawtucket Heart Health Program,[16-18] and the Minnesota Heart Health Program.[19-22] In these projects, interventions were delivered via mass media, health professionals, education professionals, community leaders, coworkers, neighbors, friends, family members, and other community members. Among the US projects, favorable results have been reported for health knowledge,[13] smoking,[15,22] blood pressure,[14] and physical activity.[21] Recently in Minnesota, however, significant progress was not observed for most risk factors against the background of strong favorable secular trends.[21] These large cardiovascular disease intervention projects had annual budgets of $1 million to $1.5 million for 10 years or more.[7] None of the large cardiovascular disease trials in the United States have involved a significant focus on isolated, rural populations.

Recently, smaller scale cardiovascular disease prevention projects have been implemented by numerous public health agencies.[23,24] However, information on the effectiveness of these projects of relatively short duration and low budget is sparse. Data from South Carolina[7,25,26] suggest that projects with only a few years of intervention exposure can show favorable health changes. Winkleby[27] recently suggested the need for smaller, more focused studies within high-risk subgroups such as minority and low literacy populations.

In 1989, in cooperation with the Centers for Disease Control and Prevention (CDC), the Missouri Department of Health began a cardiovascular disease risk reduction project in the Bootheel area of southeastern Missouri. The long-term goal of the Bootheel Heart Health Project was to reduce morbidity and mortality due to cardiovascular disease, and the shorter term project objectives focused on reducing the major modifiable risk factors for cardiovascular disease. We report on the 5-year evaluation of the prevalence of cardiovascular disease risk factors addressed by the project.

METHODS

Data-Driven Planning and Coalition Development

The intervention region was identified following analysis of mortality data. High mortality rates for coronary heart disease deaths were found for five counties (i.e., Dunklin, New Madrid, Stoddard, Mississippi, and Scott) clustered in the six-county area in southeastern Missouri known as the Bootheel. The Bootheel is bordered on the south by Arkansas and across the Mississippi River on the east by Tennessee, Kentucky, and Illinois. Except for Kansas City and St. Louis, the Bootheel has the largest Black population in Missouri. This medically underserved rural area is characterized by high rates of poverty and low educational levels.[28] Additional details on the data-driven planning conducted in this project have been presented elsewhere.[29] Several models and theories were used in developing the Bootheel Heart Health Project, which was initially based on the planned approach to community health model.[30] Additional theoretical models underlying the project were composites of social learning theory[31,32] and the stage theory of innovation.[33] Coalition development was ensured by involving local leaders and community groups in the planning process. Local leaders were identified through established agencies (e.g., local government or voluntary agencies) and through word of mouth as the project coordinator interviewed area leaders. A detailed inventory on all key contacts was maintained. After nearly 5 months of extensive effort to identify and meet with community leaders in each of the six counties, the first coalition planning meeting was held in New Madrid County in September 1990.

By late 1990, community members in the area had organized 5 "subcoalitions" within the six-county region. By the end of the study period, 17 subcoalitions were active. The local coalitions allowed for tailored interventions and helped minimize members' travel. Once a year, each coalition submitted a proposal to the Missouri Department of Health for local projects. Each of the six county coalitions received about $5000 per year to implement community-based interventions. Coalitions were allowed to select their own priorities from a list of possible cardiovascular disease-related interventions provided by project staff. Local health agencies were a key component in the coalition development process, providing assistance in many areas, including provision of blood pressure and cholesterol screenings, training, and distribution of local funds for coalition activities.

Intervention Activities

The coalitions in all six counties developed walking clubs, aerobic exercise classes, heart healthy cooking demonstrations, community blood pressure and cholesterol screenings, and cardiovascular disease education programs.[34] Examples of coalition projects included (1) annual heart healthy fitness festivals that involved exercise demonstrations, registration for exercise classes and walking clubs, and screenings for hypertension, diabetes, and cholesterol; (2) a "High Blood Pressure Sunday," where ministers included heart disease education in the sermon, the congregations were screened for hypertension, and heart healthy dinners were served in the church; (3) poster contests sponsored by local schools, the winning entries being featured in local newspapers; (4) the "Heart Healthy Corner," a weekly newspaper column on heart disease prevention written by a coalition member; and (5) environmental changes such as the construction of a walking and fitness path.

By using coalition records and the average frequency of events, we estimated the number of intervention activities over the project period. The most frequently held events were walking club functions (n = 4000) and exercise classes (1275 class hours), followed by blood pressure screenings (n = 2050), community events (n = 415), cholesterol screenings (n = 70), cooking demonstrations (n = 60), and diabetes screenings (n = 30).

Risk Factor Survey Data

Two special surveys were conducted to evaluate the project's progress. These surveys were based on the methods of the Behavioral Risk Factor Surveillance System, which was developed in 1981 by the CDC.[35,36] This flexible, state health agency-based surveillance system assists in planning, implementing, and evaluating health promotion and disease prevention programs.[35,36] Missouri began conducting statewide Behavioral Risk Factor Surveillance System surveys in 1986.

Survey methods have been discussed in detail elsewhere[35–37]; we review them briefly here. Questions were standardized on the basis of those used in the Behavioral Risk Factor Surveillance System and were identical in the 1990 and 1994 surveys.[37] The core areas related to cardiovascular risk and sociodemographics involved a total of 87 questions. In the 1994 survey, approximately 30 questions were added to the end of the survey instrument to examine related issues such as coalition exposure, arthritis, functional status, and quality of life. Risk factors were as follows: no leisure-time physical activity (report of no exercise, recreational, or physical activities [other than regular job duties] during the past month); current smoker (respondents who had ever smoked 100 cigarettes and currently smoked cigarettes); consumes five fruits and vegetables daily (report of average daily consumption of five or more servings of fruits and vegetables); overweight (body mass index [weight in kilograms divided by height in meters squared] 27.8 for men and 27.3 for women); and cholesterol checked (response of yes to question on whether blood cholesterol had been checked within the past 2 years). Since no clinical measures were taken, no data were available on blood pressure levels.

Using random-digit dialing (as in the standard Behavioral Risk Factor Surveillance System),[38] we selected cross-sectional samples of noninstitutionalized adults in the six-county region who had telephones. Based on the 1990 census,[28] an estimated 87.2% of households in the six-county region (range = 81.4% to 90.1%) had telephones. The survey was administered by trained interviewers during January through March 1990 and again in January through May 1994. Among eligible respondents (i.e., those with working phones and nonbusiness phone extensions), the response rates were 89% in 1990 and 76% in 1994. Because intervention activities were conducted largely among Blacks, we over-sampled Blacks in the 1994 survey. In the 1994 survey, the first 1000 respondents were selected from the entire six-county area; 500 additional interviews were conducted in communities in which 20% or more of the population was Black (as reported in the 1990 census[28]). The samples were generally representative of the overall Bootheel population,[28] although they slightly underrepresented younger persons, males, and those with less education. The 1994 survey was more racially representative than the 1990 survey. Among sociodemographic categories, the only significant difference in sample percentages between 1990 and 1994 involved race (P < .05).

DISCUSSION

Our project builds on the extensive work of the "first generation"[43] cardiovascular disease prevention programs funded by the National Heart, Lung and Blood Institute.[12–22] "Second generation" programs, such as the Bootheel Heart Health Project, can be implemented by public health agencies that rely on considerably smaller intervention and evaluation budgets. Even with modest resources, community-based interventions show promise in improving behaviors related to

cardiovascular disease risk within a brief period (i.e., about 3 years of intervention exposure). Such projects are ongoing throughout the United States; however, few have included long-term evaluation components that allow systematic measurement of change over time.

The recently completed Heart to Heart Project in South Carolina is similar to ours in that it demonstrated measurable improvements in dietary fat consumption[25] and cholesterol awareness and screening.[26] Community-based interventions previously have been shown to increase physical activity among adolescents[44] and adults.[21] Our results also are consistent with earlier reports[45,46] of increases in physical activity in relation to environmental changes within a community (e.g., bike paths, exercise clubs, and access to recreational facilities).

The increase in physical activity within the target population in the Bootheel may have positive health effects, as suggested by recent epidemiologic and clinical studies[3,47] in which regular, moderate physical activity, such as walking, reduced the risk for cardiovascular disease and all-cause mortality. The CDC/American College of Sports Medicine recommendation stresses the favorable health benefits of moderate, daily physical activity.[47] The Bootheel project is unusual among physical activity interventions in that it focused on a rural Black population at very high risk of cardiovascular disease as a result of physical inactivity and other factors.

The changes resulting from the Bootheel Heart Health Project were obtained at a fairly low cost. Over the project period, the annual cost of the Bootheel project was approximately $105,000.

Our findings for two other cardiovascular disease risk factors are generally consistent with state and national data showing increasing trends in the rate of overweight[48,49] and the proportion of individuals having their cholesterol checked.[50,51] In the Bootheel risk factor survey, trends toward increases in rates of cholesterol screening and overweight were observed. Our findings of decreased physical inactivity, along with a stable rate of overweight, in active coalition areas appear to support recent studies[52] showing a relation between longitudinal weight gain and low physical activity. Larger samples and better measures of intervention exposure will be needed to further clarify this potentially important relationship.

Although this paper has summarized the major quantitative evaluation of the Bootheel project, comprehensive qualitative evaluation is also being conducted. Elements of this evaluation include focus group analyses (i.e., case studies), analyses of the coalitions' level of effort, and media content analyses. Evaluation of so-called "environmental factors"[53] is important in showing community-level changes (e.g., the addition of a walking path in a low-income neighborhood) that may occur prior to changes in behavioral risk factors or mortality rates. Case studies provide information on how and why various strategies succeed or fail.[54–56] Furthermore, community-based interventions may have beneficial effects that have little direct relation to cardiovascular disease risk reduction. For example, as a result of the Bootheel project, coalition members became more active in local government, gaining election to city councils and school boards.

The limitations of our study should be noted. The study lacked a true experimental design and comparison groups; thus, in our quasi-experimental design, we relied mainly on internal comparisons with statewide rural Behavioral Risk Factor Surveillance System data. A strength of our analysis, however, involves the two a priori measures of nonmutually exclusive intervention exposure that demonstrated measurable differences in physical inactivity between "exposed" and "nonexposed" groups. As supporting evidence, physical inactivity was the risk factor most frequently and consistently addressed in coalition activities.

We cannot precisely account for the effects of national programs (e.g., the National High Blood Pressure Education Programs[57] or the National Cholesterol Education Program[58]) on changes in cardiovascular disease risk factors in local populations. Although national campaigns can influence physical activity,[59] little national attention has been directed toward physical activity until recently.[47] In addition, our analyses showed increases in physical inactivity in Bootheel areas without active coalitions and in other rural counties in Missouri.

We relied on self-reported, cross-sectional telephone survey data and had no comprehensive information on the accuracy of the Behavioral Risk Factor Surveillance System data during the study period. However, previous studies[60–62] have shown fairly high accuracy of Behavioral Risk Factor Surveillance System data on reported risk factors for cardiovascular disease and demographic characteristics. In particular, smoking status and physical activity appear to be reported with high accuracy.[60,63,64] A 1993 test-retest study of the Missouri Behavioral Risk Factor Surveillance System found high reliability for several cardiovascular disease risk factor questions.[62] Since the surveillance system relies on telephone interviews, the potential exists for response bias due to lack of phone coverage of certain sociodemographic groups.[65] A previous study from South Carolina[66] indicates that in-person interviews may be unnecessary unless a very high proportion of nontelephone households is present; we estimate that approximately 13% of households in the study area lacked telephones. Our study did not collect in-person clinical data such as blood pressure and cholesterol measurements and biochemical validation of smoking status.

In summary, the decline in physical inactivity and increase in cholesterol screening shown in the Bootheel project suggest that a community-level reduction in cardiovascular disease risk may be achievable through relatively low-cost interventions that combine educational efforts with environmental changes. However, because of limitations in our study design, further data are needed, including longer term measurements of cardiovascular disease risk factors, morbidity, and mortality, as well as replication of similar projects in other underserved areas.

REFERENCES

1. Kochanek KD, Hudson BL. Advance report of final mortality statistics, 1992. *Month Vital Stat Rep.* March 22, 1995; 43(6)(suppl).

2. Smith CA, Pratt M. Cardiovascular disease. In: Brownson RC, Remington PW, Davis JR, eds. *Chronic Disease Epidemiology and Control* Washington, DC: American Public Health Association; 1993:83–107.

3. Fletcher GF, Blair SN, Blumenthal J, et al. Statement on exercise: benefits and recommendations for physical activity programs for all Americans, a statement for health professionals by the Committee on Exercise and Cardiac Rehabilitation of the Council on Clinical Cardiology, American Heart Association. *Circulation.* 1992;86: 340–344.

4. *Healthy People 2000: National Health Promotion and Disease Prevention.* Washington, DC: US Dept of Health and Human Services; 1990. Publication 017-001-00473-1.

5. National Center for Health Statistics. *Healthy People 2000 Review, 1993.* Hyattsville, Md: US Dept of Health and Human Services; 1994. DHHS publication PHS 94-1232-1.

6. Eischen MH, Brownson RC, Davis JR, et al. Grassroots efforts to promote tobacco-free schools in rural Missouri. *Am J Public Health.* 1994;84: 1336–1337.

7. Goodman RM, Wheeler FC, Lee PR. Evaluation of the Heart to Heart Project: lessons learned from a community-based chronic disease prevention project. *Am J Health Promotion.* 1995;9:443–455.

8. Shea S, Basch CE. A review of five major community-based cardiovascular prevention programs. Part I: rationale, design, and theoretical framework. *Am J Health Promotion.* 1990;4:203–213.

9. Shea S, Basch CE. A review of five major community-based cardiovascular prevention programs. Part II: Intervention strategies, evaluation methods, and results. *Am J Health Promotion.* 1990;4:279–287.

10. Puska P. Community based prevention of cardiovascular disease: the North Karelia Project. In: Matarazzo JD, Weiss SM, Herd JA, Miller NE, Weiss SM, eds. *Behavioral Health: A Handbook of Health Enhancement and Disease Prevention.* New York, NY: John Wiley & Sons Inc; 1984.

11. Puska P, Salonen J, Nissinen A, et al. Change in risk factors for coronary heart disease during 10 years of a community intervention programme: North Karelia Project. *BMJ.* 1983;287:1840–1844.

12. Farquhar JW, Fortmann SP, Maccoby N, et al. The Stanford Five-City Project: design and methods. *Am J Epidemiol.* 1985;122:323–334.

13. Farquhar JW, Fortmann SP, Flora JA, et al. Effects of communitywide education on cardiovascular disease risk factors. The Stanford Five-City Project. *JAMA.* 1990;264: 359–365.

14. Fortmann SP, Winkleby MA, Flora JA, Haskell WL, Taylor CB. Effect of longterm community health education on blood pressure and hypertension control: the Stanford Five-City Project. *Am J Epidemiol.* 1990;132:629–646.

15. Fortmann SP, Taylor CB, Flora JA, Jatulis DE. Changes in adult cigarette smoking prevalence after 5 years of community health education: the Stanford Five-City Project. *Am J Epidemiol.* 1993;137:82–96.

16. Lasater T, Abrams D, Artz L, et al. Lay volunteer delivery of a community-based cardiovascular risk factor change program: the Pawtucket experiment.

In: Matarazzo JD, Weiss SM, Herd JA, Miller NE, Weiss SM, eds. *Behavioral Health: A Handbook of Health Enhancement and Disease Prevention.* New York, NY: John Wiley & Sons Inc; 1984:1166–1170.

17. Carleton RA, Lasater TM, Assaf AR, Lefebvre RC, McKinlay SM. The Pawtucket Heart Health Program: an experiment in population-based disease prevention. *RI Med J.* 1987;70:533–538.

18. Carleton RA, Lasater TM, Assaf AR, et al. The Pawtucket Heart Health Program: community changes in cardiovascular risk factors and projected disease risk. *Am J Public Health.* 1995;85:777–785.

19. Blackburn H, Luepker RV, Kline FG, et al. The Minnesota Heart Health Program: a research and demonstration project in cardiovascular disease prevention. In: Matarazzo JD, Weiss SM, Herd JA, Miller NE, Weiss SM, eds. *Behavioral Health: A Handbook of Health Enhancement and Disease Prevention.* New York, NY: John Wiley & Sons Inc; 1984.

20. Jacobs DR Jr, Luepker RV, Mittelmark MB, et al. Community-wide prevention strategies: evaluation design of the Minnesota Heart Health Program. *J Chronic Dis.* 1986;39:775–788.

21. Luepker RV, Murray DM, Jacobs DR Jr, et al. Community education for cardiovascular disease prevention: risk factor changes in the Minnesota Heart Health Program. *Am J Public Health.* 1994;84:1383–1393.

22. Lando HA, Pechacek TF, Pirie PL, et al. Changes in adult cigarette smoking in the Minnesota Heart Health Program. *Am J Public Health.* 1995;85:201–208.

23. Schwartz R, Smith C, Speers MA, et al. Capacity building and resource needs of state health agencies to implement community-based cardiovascular disease programs. *J Public Health Policy.* 1993;14:480–494.

24. CVD Plan Steering Committee. *Preventing Death and Disability from Cardiovascular Diseases: A State-Based Plan for Action.* Washington, DC: Association of State and Territorial Health Officials; 1994.

25. Croft JB, Temple SP, Lankenau B, et al. Community intervention and trends in dietary fat consumption among Black and White adults. *J Am Diet Assoc.* 1994;94: 1284–1290.

26. Heath GW, Fuchs R, Croft JB, Temple SP, Wheeler FC. Changes in blood cholesterol awareness: final results from the South Carolina cardiovascular prevention project. *Am J Prev Med.* In press.

27. Winkleby MA. The future of community based cardiovascular disease intervention studies. *Am J Public Health.* 1994;84:1369–1372.

28. *1990 Census of Population and Housing Short Form.* Washington, DC: US Dept of Commerce, Bureau of the Census; 1992.

29. Brownson RC, Smith CA, Jorge NE, DePrima LT, Dean CG, Cates RW. The role of data-driven planning and coalition development in preventing cardiovascular disease. *Public Health Rep.* 1992;107:32–37.

30. Planned approach to community health. Community health promotion: the agenda for the '90s. *J Health Educ.* 1992;23:129–192.

31. Bandura A. *Social Learning Theory.* Englewood Cliffs, NJ: Prentice Hall; 1977.

32. Farquhar JW. The community-based model of lifestyle intervention trials. *Am J Epidemiol.* 1978;108:103–111.

33. Goodman RM, Steckler A. Enhancing health through organizational change: theories of organizational change. In: Glanz K, Lewis FM, Rimer BK, eds. *Health Behavior and Health Education: Theory, Research, and Practice.* San Francisco, Calif: Jossey-Bass; 1990.

34. Dabney S, Dean C, Smith C, Cates RW, Brownson RC. Missouri builds heart health coalitions in the "Bootheel." *Chronic Disease Notes Rep.* 1993; 6:11–13.

35. Gentry EM, Kalsbeek WD, Hogelin GC, et al. The Behavioral Risk Factor Surveys: design, methods, and estimates from combined state data. *Am J Prev Med.* 1985;1:9–14.

36. Remington PL, Smith MY, Williamson DF, Anda RF, Gentry EM, Hogelin GC. Design, characteristics, and usefulness of state-based behavioral risk factor surveillance: 1981–1987. *Public Health Rep.* 1988;103:366–375.

37. Siegel PZ, Brackbill RM, Frazier EL, et al. Behavioral risk factor surveillance, 1986–1990. *MMWR.* 1991;40(SS-4):1–23.

38. Waksberg J. Sampling methods for random digit dialing. *J Am Stat Assoc.* 1978;73:40–46.

39. *SUDAAN User's Manual. Professional Software for Survey Data Analysis.* Research Triangle Park, NC: Research Triangle Institute; 1991.

40. Williams PT, Fortmann SP, Farquhar JW, Varady A, Mellen S. A comparison of statistical methods for evaluating risk factor changes in community-based studies: an example from the Stanford Three-Community Study. *J Chronic Dis.* 1981;34: 565–571.

41. Koepsell TD, Martin DC, Diehr PH, et al. Data analysis and sample size issues in evaluations of community-based health promotion and disease prevention programs: a mixed-model analysis of variance. *J Clin Epidemiol.* 1991;44:701–713.

42. Kish L. *Survey Sampling.* New York, NY: John Wiley & Sons Inc; 1965.

43. Mittelmark MB, Hunt MK, Heath GW, Schmid TL. Realistic outcomes: lessons learned from community-based research and demonstration programs for the prevention of cardiovascular diseases. *J Public Health Policy.* 1993;14: 437–462.

44. Kelder SH, Perry CL, Klepp K-I. Community-wide youth exercise promotion: longterm outcomes of the Minnesota Heart Health Program and the class of 1989 study. *J Sch Health.* 1994;63:218–223.

45. Linenger JM, Chesson CV, Nice S. Physical fitness gains following simple environmental change. *Am J Prev Med.* 1991;7:298–310.

46. Sallis JF, Hovell MF, Hofstetter CR, et al. Distance between homes and exercise facilities related to frequency of exercise among San Diego residents. *Public Health Rep.* 1990;105:179–185.

47. Pate RR, Pratt M, Blair SN, et al. Physical activity and public health: a recommendation from the Centers for Disease Control and Prevention and the American College of Sports Medicine. *JAMA.* 1995;273:402–407.

48. Sharp DJ, Brownson RC, Wilkerson JC, Jackson-Thompson J, Davis JR, Smith CA. Patterns of obesity in Missouri. *Mo Med.* 1993;90:119–122.

49. Kuczmarski RJ, Flegal KM, Campbell SM, Johnson CL. Increasing prevalence of overweight among US adults. *JAMA.* 1994; 272:205–211.

50. Arfken CL, Fisher EB Jr, Heins J, et al. Increased cholesterol awareness in Missouri: urban and rural areas, 1988–1991. *MMWR.* 1992;41:323–325.

51. Schucker B, Wittes JT, Santanello NC, et al. Change in cholesterol awareness and action: results from national physician and public surveys. *Arch Intern Med.* 1991;151: 661–673.

52. Williamson DF, Madans J, Anda RF, Kleinman JC, Kahn HS, Byers T. Recreational physical activity and ten-year weight change in a US national cohort. *Int J Obes.* 1993;17:279–286.

53. Cheadle A, Wagner E, Koepsell T, Kristal A, Patrick D. Environmental indicators: a tool for evaluating community-based health promotion programs. *Am J Prev Med.* 1992;8:345–350.

54. Steckler A, Goodman RM. How to institutionalize health promotion programs. *Am J Health Promotion.* 1989;3:34–44.

55. Steckler A, McLeroy KR, Goodman RM, Bird ST, McCormick L. Toward integrating qualitative and quantitative methods: an introduction. *Health Educ Q.* 1992;19: 1–8.

56. Goodman RM, Smith DW, Dawson L, Steckler A. Recruiting school districts into a dissemination study. *Health Educ Res.* 1991;6:373–385.

57. National High Blood Pressure Education Program. The fifth report of the joint national committee on detection, evaluation, and treatment of high blood pressure (JNC V). National Heart, Lung, and Blood Institute, NIH. *Arch Intern Med.* 1993;153: 154–183.

58. *Report of the Expert Panel on Population Strategies for Blood Cholesterol Reduction.* Washington, DC: US Dept of Health and Human Services; 1990. NIH publication 90-3046.

59. Booth M, Bauman A, Oldenburg B, Owen N, Magnus P. Effects of a national mass media campaign on physical activity participation. *Health Promotion Int.* 1992;7:241–247.

60. Shea S, Stein AD, Lantigua R, Basch CE. Reliability of the Behavioral Risk Factor Survey in a triethnic population. *Am J Epidemiol.* 1991;133: 489–500.

61. Jackson C, Jatulis DE, Fortmann SP. The Behavioral Risk Factor Survey and the Stanford Five-City Project Survey: a comparison of cardiovascular risk behavior estimates. *Am J Public Health.* 1992;82:412–416.

62. Brownson RC, Jackson-Thompson J, Wilkerson JC, Kiani F. Reliability of information on chronic disease risk factors collected in the Missouri Behavioral Risk Factor Surveillance System. *Epidemiology.* 1994;5:545–549.

63. Lamb KL, Brodie DA. The assessment of physical activity by leisure-time physical activity questionnaires. *Sports Med.* 1990;10:159–180.

64. Albanes D, Conway JM, Taylor PR, Moe PW, Judd J. Validation and comparison of eight physical activity questionnaires. *Epidemiology.* 1990;1:65–71.

65. *Using Chronic Disease Data: A Handbook for Public Health Practitioners.* Atlanta, Ga: Centers for Disease Control and Prevention; 1992.

66. Wheeler F, Lackland D, Mace M, Reddick A, Hogelin G, Remington P. Evaluating South Carolina's community cardiovascular disease prevention program. *Public Health Rep.* 1991;106:536–543.

Planned Approach to Community Health: Guide for the Local Coordinator

Source: U.S. Department of Health and Human Services. ND. *Planned Approach to Community Health: Guide for the Local Coordinator.* Atlanta, GA: U.S. Department of Health and Human Services, Centers for Disease Control and Prevention, National Center for Chronic Disease Prevention and Health Promotion. Available at www.cdc.gov/nccdphp/ publications.

CHAPTER 1: OVERVIEW OF PATCH

INTRODUCTION

The Planned Approach to Community Health (PATCH) is a community health planning model that was developed in the mid-1980s by the Centers for Disease Control and Prevention (CDC) in partnership with state and local health departments and community groups. This concept guide is part of a variety of materials designed to help a local coordinator facilitate the PATCH process within a community. These materials provide "how-to" information on the process and on things to consider when adapting the process for your community.

DEFINITION AND GOAL OF PATCH

PATCH is a process that many communities use to plan, conduct, and evaluate health promotion and disease prevention programs. The PATCH process helps a community establish a health promotion team, collect and use local data, set health priorities, and design and evaluate interventions. Adaptable to a variety of situations, it can be used when a community wants to identify and address priority health problems or when the health priority or special population to be addressed has al-

ready been selected. It can also be adapted and used by existing organizational and planning structures in the community.

The goal of PATCH is to increase the capacity of communities to plan, implement, and evaluate comprehensive, community-based health promotion programs targeted toward priority health problems. CDC promotes the use of PATCH in helping achieve the year 2000 national health objectives.[1] These objectives aim to reduce the prevalence of modifiable risk factors for the leading causes of preventable disease, death, disability, and injury. Although these objectives are national in scope, achieving them depends on efforts to promote health and provide prevention services at the local level.

BACKGROUND OF PATCH

PATCH was developed in the mid-1980s by the CDC in partnership with state and local health departments and community groups. The purpose was to offer a practical, community-based process that was built upon the latest health education, health promotion, and community development knowledge and theories and organized within the context of the PRECEDE (predisposing, reinforcing, and enabling constructs in educational/ environmental diagnosis and evaluation) model.

PATCH was built on the same philosophy as the World Health Organization's Health for All and the Ottawa Charter for Health Promotion,[2] which specifies that health promotion

1. U.S. Department of Health and Human Services. Healthy People 2000: National Health Promotion and Disease Prevention Objectives. Washington, D.C.: U.S. Department of Health and Human Services, Public Health Service, 1991; DHHS publication no. (PHS) 91-50212.

2. World Health Organization, Ottawa Charter for Health Promotion, International Conference on Health Promotion, November 17–21, 1986, Ottawa, Ontario, Canada.

is the process of enabling people to increase control over their health and to improve their health. To plan effective strategies, each community must go through its own process of assessing needs, setting priorities, formulating solutions, and owning programs. A key strategy in PATCH is to encourage linkages within the community and between the community and the state health department, universities, and other regional and national levels of organizations that can provide data, resources, and consultation.

In 1984–1985, PATCH was piloted in six states and communities by CDC staff, working in partnership with the state health departments and the communities. Subsequently, PATCH was revised by CDC staff, and additional tools and materials for carrying out PATCH in a community were developed. CDC staff expanded the delivery of PATCH to include 11 more states and communities. Beginning in 1988, three evaluation studies were performed by the University of North Carolina, the Research Triangle Institute, and the PATCH National Working Group to assess the effects of PATCH and to recommend refinements on future directions. Since 1991, CDC no longer delivers PATCH directly in communities. Instead, CDC provides limited training and consultation to state health departments and the public and private sectors on the application of PATCH. Currently, most state health departments have staff trained in PATCH and a state coordinator who serves as the state contact for PATCH.

PATCH is widely recognized as an effective community health planning model and is used by many states, communities, and several nations. It is used by diverse communities and populations to address many health concerns, including cardiovascular disease, HIV, injuries, teenage pregnancy, and access to health care. It is used in states with and without a local health department infrastructure. Its community development approach is largely consistent with those of many community agencies, such as the agricultural extension services, hospitals, universities, and voluntary health agencies. Many state health departments work with agencies such as these to carry out PATCH. Universities, hospitals, worksites, military communities, area agencies on aging, voluntary health organizations, and other such groups have also adopted and used the PATCH process. Although many of the references and examples in these materials may describe its use by local health departments in conjunction with their state health department, we encourage any group or organization to use PATCH.

ELEMENTS CRITICAL TO PATCH

Five elements are considered critical to the success of any community health promotion process.

- *Community members participate in the process.* Fundamental to PATCH is active participation by a wide range of community members. These people analyze community data, set priorities, plan intervention activities, and make decisions on the health priorities of their community.
- *Data guide the development of programs.* Many types of data can be used to describe a community's health status and needs. These data help community members.
- *Participants develop a comprehensive health promotion strategy.* Community members analyze the factors that contribute to an identified health problem. They review community policies, services, and resources and design an overall community health promotion strategy. Interventions, which may include educational programs, mass media campaigns, policy advocacy, and environmental measures, are conducted in various settings, such as schools, health care facilities, community sites, and the workplace. Participants are encouraged to relate intervention goals to the appropriate year 2000 national health objectives.
- *Evaluation emphasizes feedback and program improvement.* Timely feedback is essential to the people involved in the program. Evaluation can also lead to improvements in the program.
- *The community capacity for health promotion is increased.* The PATCH process can be repeated to address various health priorities. PATCH aims to increase the capacity of community members to address health issues by strengthening their community health planning and health promotion skills.

The first and last critical elements, related to community participation and capacity building, are essential to ensure community ownership. Although the local coordinator facilitates the program, the community directs the program, and the program belongs to community members. Their decisions determine how the program progresses. All participants in the PATCH process share in its success.

THE PATCH PROCESS

Although PATCH can be adapted to various health problems and communities, the phases of the process remain the same. Thus, once the mechanisms of the PATCH process are in place, only a few modifications are needed to address additional health issues. Phases can be repeated as new health priorities are identified, new target groups are selected, or new interventions are developed. The activities within phases may overlap as the process is carried out. Each of the five phases that constitute PATCH is described hereafter. The PATCH Assessment and Tracking (PAT) tool, included as Appendix 1, also summarizes each phase.

Phase I: Mobilizing the Community

Mobilizing the community is an ongoing process that starts in phase I as a community organizes to begin PATCH and continues throughout the PATCH process. In phase I, the community to be addressed is defined, participants are recruited from the community, partnerships are formed, and a demographic profile of the community is completed. By collecting this information, participants learn about the makeup of the community for which health interventions will be planned. Knowing the makeup of the community also helps ensure that the PATCH community group is representative of the community. The community group and steering committee are then organized, and working groups are created. During this phase, the community is informed about PATCH so that support is gained, particularly from community leaders.

Phase II: Collecting and Organizing Data

Phase II begins when the community members form working groups to obtain and analyze data on mortality, morbidity, community opinion, and behaviors. These data, obtained from various sources, include quantitative data (e.g., vital statistics and survey) and qualitative data (e.g., opinions of community leaders). Community members may identify other sources of local data that should be collected as well. They analyze the data and determine the leading health problems in the community. The behavioral data are used during phase III to look at effects of behavior on health problems. During phase II, PATCH participants also identify ways to share the results of data analysis with the community.

Phase III: Choosing Health Priorities

During this phase, behavioral and any additional data collected are presented to the community group. This group analyzes the behavioral, social, economic, political, and environmental factors that affect the behaviors that put people at risk for disease, death, disability, and injury. Health priorities are identified. Community objectives related to the health priorities are set. The health priorities to be addressed initially are selected.

Phase IV: Developing a Comprehensive Intervention Plan

Using information generated during phases II and III, the community group chooses, designs, and conducts interventions during phase IV. To prevent duplication and to build on existing services, the community group identifies and assesses resources, policies, environmental measures, and programs already focused on the risk behavior and to the target group. This group devises a comprehensive health promotion strategy, sets intervention objectives, and develops an intervention plan.

This intervention plan includes strategies, a timetable, and a work plan for completing such tasks as recruiting and training volunteers, publicizing and conducting activities, evaluating the activities, and informing the community about results. Throughout, members of the target groups are involved in the process of planning interventions.

Phase V: Evaluating PATCH

Evaluation is an integral part of the PATCH process. It is ongoing and serves two purposes: to monitor and assess progress during the five phases of PATCH and to evaluate interventions. The community sets criteria for determining success and identifies data to be collected. Feedback is provided to the community to encourage future participation and to planners for use in program improvement.

USING PATCH TO ADDRESS A SPECIFIC HEALTH ISSUE OR POPULATION

The phases just described outline the steps to identifying and reducing community health problems. When you use the PATCH process to address a particular health issue of high priority, modify the steps in phases I-III accordingly. For example, make it clear to the community that you are mobilizing members to address a specific health issue. Continue to recruit broad-based membership for your community group while identifying and including community members or agencies that have a special interest in the specific health issue. Modify the forms provided in the PATCH materials, and collect data for the specific health issue. Once the risk factors and target groups are selected, the PATCH process is the same for phases III-V when the health priority is not preselected. Similarly, when using PATCH to address the health needs of a specific population, such as older adults, you should modify phases I-III as needed.

HOW TO USE THE PATCH MATERIALS

This Concept Guide is part of a three-part package of materials designed for the local coordinator, the person who initiates the PATCH process within a community. This local coordinator

- will have major coursework and experience in health education and community health promotion.
- will be able to adapt the PATCH process to meet the needs of the community.
- will serve as facilitator of this community-based process by working with a broad-based community group and ensuring community ownership.
- will use expertise and resources at the community, state, and federal levels.

These PATCH Guides are an updated version of the PATCH Books, first developed in 1986–1987 and widely used today. Current PATCH users are encouraged to use these revised materials. They provide additional "how-to" information on the process and on things to consider when adapting the process for your community.

On the basis of suggestions from PATCH users and the PATCH National Working Group, we have changed the terms used to describe PATCH participants. What was called a *core group* in the original PATCH documents is now called a *steering committee*, and a *subcommittee* is now called a *working group*. *Workshop I* is now the *meeting* for phase I. The revised materials are packaged differently: the background information from previous books has been updated and combined to make up the *Concept Guide*, and the five scripts and information to help you conduct meetings for each phase of PATCH are together in the *Meeting Guide*. Each part of the package is described subsequently.

Concept Guide

This Concept Guide presents an overview of PATCH, followed by separate chapters on each phase of the PATCH process. The guide includes tools, or forms, for planning and conducting various activities. It also provides background information on topics important to managing PATCH, such as group dynamics and statistical analysis, as well as practical information and suggestions for tailoring the process to the needs of your community. We recommend that you read the material in this guide thoroughly and review the section that corresponds to each phase of PATCH before you begin the phase.

The Concept Guide has as appendixes the PAT tool, the Program Documentation, a glossary, and a bibliography. The appendixes also include a variety of one-page tipsheets, referred to as Nutshells in earlier versions, that relate to the management of PATCH and group dynamics. You are encouraged to copy and share the tipsheets with group facilitators and working group chairpersons.

Meeting Guide

The Meeting Guide is intended for use when planning and conducting meetings. It contains an introduction, followed by a separate section for each phase of the PATCH process. For each phase, it includes meeting objectives, recommends an agenda, and suggests specific activities that can be incorporated with your own ideas. The Meeting Guide is not intended to be exhaustive; rather, it helps ensure that key points are incorporated at the appropriate times, and it reduces the amount of time you need to prepare for each group meeting. The Meeting Guide is written for one meeting per phase; however, you may find that two or more short meetings per phase are more appropriate for accomplishing tasks in your community.

Visual Aids

The packet of Visual Aids includes camera-ready copy for overheads and reproducible text for handouts. These materials are used at meetings throughout the PATCH process. The Meeting Guide indicates when to use each item, and the materials are arranged in the packet in order of use. Again, these sets of materials are by no means exhaustive. You may want to alter the suggested overheads so that they are more suited to your presentation style. You may want to modify or include other materials with the handouts so that the participants receive information more directly related to their specific community. Some of these materials are intended to serve as models for overheads and handouts you will need to develop to present data and other information for your own community.

PART 9

Application of Theory: Schools and Worksites

This part focuses on two specific intervention settings: schools and workplaces. While these are, of course, different, they share some similarities in terms of health promotion intervention because they are both settings in which a significant proportion of the population spends all or most of its time on a regular, daily basis, and both settings share a common interest in health promotion. For schools, good health and education go hand in hand. For worksites, productivity, efficiency, safety, and morale are all affected by employee health. The first reading in this chapter (Lear, 2006) is an excellent summary of key issues in school health promotion. The second (Greenberg et al., 2003) describes what is presented in the main text as a comprehensive school health approach, combining broad youth development and prevention components with the more traditional health services. The third reading (Goetzel et al., 1998) reviews one of the primary arguments advanced for worksite health promotion: the savings in health care costs that such programs bring, a very important consideration given current concerns about health care coverage.

Children's Health and Children's Schools: A Collaborative Approach to Strengthening Children's Well-Being

Source: Excerpt from Lear JG. 2006. "Children's Health and Children's Schools: A Collaborative Approach to Strengthening Children's Well-Being." In JG Lear, SL Isaacs, and JR Knickman (Eds), *School Health Services and Programs (Robert Woods Johnson Series on Health Policy)*. San Francisco, CA: Jossey-Bass.

THE SCHOOL CONTEXT FOR SCHOOL-BASED HEALTH SERVICES

The Importance of Health in the School Setting

Approximately 50 million children aged 5 to 19 attend the nearly 120,000 elementary and secondary schools in the United States. These young people require clean air, a physically safe environment, and education about how to promote their own safety and health. They also require prompt, effective emergency care; need safe administration of medications during school; need protection from communicable diseases; and for younger children especially, require treatment and timely responses to the injuries common to playgrounds and school corridors.

School health programs vary greatly from school district to school district and from state to state, but nearly all communities agree with four basic propositions:

1. There is an obligation to guarantee the safety of the public, including children, when gathered in public buildings. Either the school system or the health department must ensure the safety of the school building and its grounds.

2. There is an obligation to provide emergency services and essential medical services to people in the school building.

3. Because children are in school to learn, there is broad support for the notion that schools should educate children about keeping their bodies safe and healthy. Many states and school districts believe that a good school health program includes a strong health education curriculum.

4. All communities have a legal obligation under Section 504 of the 1973 Rehabilitation Act, the Individuals with Disabilities Education Act, and the Americans with Disabilities Act to provide for such care as is necessary to enable a child with a physical or mental disability to benefit from a free, appropriate public education.

An increasing number of communities also believe that it makes sense to invest in school health programs that go beyond the basic components. These communities find several arguments to be persuasive in supporting a broader range of school-based health programs:

1. That health programs facilitate learning and may increase test scores

2. That there are gaps in the health care system, especially for low income children and adolescents, and that there are cost savings to be achieved by providing early intervention and treatment for unserved or underserved children

3. That children's parents are frequently not available to schools and that caring for sick children for at least part of the day will fall to school staff members.

The arguments in support of more effective school-based health programs—and more of them—continue to grow. And an increasing number of communities and several states have taken specific steps to expand the scope of school-based health services. What has frequently been a surprise to those who have been enthusiastic about the potential for such services is how complex the school environment is and how many factors must be considered in pursuing links between community-based health care systems and school-based activities.

The Organization of Schools

The school environment is quite different from that found in health care. Authority tends to flow from the bottom up—from school district to state education agency, and from locally elected public officials to state and federal policymakers. Notwithstanding the move toward state standards and national guidelines, education remains a locally driven enterprise with a tradition of local decision-making and engaged power brokers that must be taken into account when attempting to change existing programs.

In contrast to health care, where strong federal agencies such as the Center for Medicare and Medicaid Services set standards of care and define eligible providers, no single federal agency establishes standards for curricula, pupil support services, facilities, or staff. Program priorities are mostly determined by 15,000 local school boards and superintendencies.

Fifty state legislatures, state education agencies, and state boards of education provide a second layer of direction for school systems. At the federal level, many federally funded discretionary programs come under federal oversight. However, the most extensive federal mandates are generated by federal legislation protecting the rights of physically disabled and learning-disabled children to "free, appropriate education." Federal enforcement of the legislation has generated an extensive set of special education requirements that shape both classroom arrangements and school-based health services.

Passage of the No Child Left Behind Act of 2001, the most recent revision of the federal Elementary and Secondary Education Act, has sharpened requirements that state and local governments must meet to secure federal funding and has increased the perception of federal oversight elementary and secondary schools. While federal funding constitutes less than 10% of K-12 spending, it supports services for low-income students, purchases of instructional materials, and development of state-level education programs.[17]

During the 1999–2000 school year, there were nearly 90,000 elementary and secondary public schools in the United States, enrolling about 46.9 million students (see Table 9-1).[18] Five million students attended 27,000 private schools, of which a third were Catholic schools.[19(tab7)]

TABLE 9-1 Schools by Level and Type of Institution

	Total	Public	Private
Elementary	79,362	62,739	16,623
Secondary	24,169	21,682	2,487
Combined	11,412	3,120	8,292
Total	114,943	87,541	27,402

Source: Lear JG. 2006. "Children's Health and Children's Schools: A Collaborative Approach to Strengthening Children's Well-Being." In JG Lear, SL Isaacs, and JR Knickman (Eds), *School Health Services and Programs (Robert Woods Johnson Series on Health Policy).* San Francisco, CA: Jossey-Bass.

Student enrollment among these schools varies considerably. The smallest public elementary schools are found in South Dakota, where total enrollment averages 160 students; the largest are found in Florida, where they average 694. High schools, typically larger than elementary schools, average an enrollment of 369 in Wyoming but 1,468 in Hawaii.[19(tab5)] Urban high schools in large school districts frequently exceed 1,500 students.[20]

As indicated in Table 9-2, nearly half (7,193) of the school districts have fewer than 1,000 students each, but the 25 largest districts enroll 12% of all public school students in the United States.[18] Indeed, 5.7% of all school districts (817 school districts) enroll half of all public school students in the nation.

Policies, Funding, and School Health

At the state level, governors, legislators, and members of state boards of education all contribute to shaping school policies and school programs, including those that relate to health. A few states help fund health services directly, but most contribute indirectly through general financial support to school districts. Many states also establish mandates for specific services or require student documentation that they have received services such as immunizations. However, as Table 9-3 indicates, school district requirements tend to be more extensive than those of state governments.[21] (pp. 295–297)

One of the most useful insights concerning children's health programs is provided by Table 9-4, which describes the current availability of some basic health equipment in schools as reported by the CDC's periodic School Health Policies and Programs Study.[21(p300)] That one-third of all schools report not having a separate locked medication storage cabinet and that fewer than 60% have a refrigerator reserved for health purposes suggest the constraints that some schools face in implementing school-based health services.

TABLE 9-2 Public School Districts in the United States by Student Enrollment, 1999–2000

District Size	Districts	Percentage of Districts	Percentage of Student Enrollment
Total, United States	**14,571**	**100.0%**	**100.0%**
100,000 or more	25	0.2	12.4
25,000–99,999	213	1.5	19.7
10,000–24,999	579	4.0	18.7
5,000–9,999	1,036	7.1	15.4
1,000–4,999	5,524	37.9	27.8
1–999	7,193	49.3	6.0

Source: Lear JG. 2006. "Children's Health and Children's Schools: A Collaborative Approach to Strengthening Children's Well-Being." In JG Lear, SL Isaacs, and JR Knickman (Eds), *School Health Services and Programs (Robert Woods Johnson Series on Health Policy)*. San Francisco, CA: Jossey-Bass.

TABLE 9-3 Most Frequently Required Health Mandates: States and District Requirements by Type of Service

Health Services	Percentage of States	Percentage of Districts
Administration of medications	64.0%	93.7%
First aid	48.0	92.1
CPR	42.0	81.5
Identification of or referral for physical, sexual, or emotional abuse	64.7	75.7
Crisis intervention for personal problems	20.4	64.8
Alcohol or other drug use prevention	22.0	64.2
Immunizations		
Kindergarten or First Grade Entry		
Diphtheria	100.0	99.1
A measles-containing vaccine	100.0	99.1
A polio vaccine	100.0	98.9
Tetanus	98.0	97.7
Hepatitis B	72.6	75.6
Middle or Junior High School Entry		
A second measles-containing vaccine	68.6	81.0
Tetanus	43.8	60.6
Senior High School Entry		
A second measles-containing vaccine	44.9	66.8
Tetanus	36.8	61.4
Screenings		
Hearing	70.6	88.4
Vision	70.6	90.4
Scoliosis	45.1	68.8
Height, weight, or body mass	26.0	38.4

Source: Brener ND, Burstein GR, DuShaw ML, Vernon ME, Wheeler L, Robinson T. Health services, results from the School Health Policies and Programs Study 2000. J Sch Health. 2001;71(7):294–303. Reprinted with permission of Blackwell Publishing Ltd.

TABLE 9-4 Percentage of Schools with Facilities or Equipment for Health Services

Type of Facility or Equipment of Schools	Percentage of Schools
Portable first aid kit	92.7%
Sick room, nurse's office, or other area reserved for health services	81.1
Medical supply cabinet with lock	73.9
Vision test, eye chart, cards, or anything else to measure vision	70.6
Scale	69.8
Separate medicine cabinet with lock	65.4
Refrigerator reserved for health services	57.3
Audiometer	48.5
Peak flow meter	27.2
Examining table	24.0
Answering machine or voice mail reserved for health services staff	20.5
Glucose meter not just for a specific individual's use	17.8
Nebulizer not just for a specific individual's use	13.0

Source: Brener ND, Burstein GR, DuShaw ML, Vernon ME, Wheeler L, Robinson J. Health services, results from the School Health Policies and Programs Study 2000. J Sch Health. 2001;71(7):294–303. Reprinted with permission of Blackwell Publishing Ltd.

Current arrangements for school financing support the dominant role of state and local governments in decision making. Despite obligations of the No Child Left Behind Act, the limited funding provided by the federal government suggests that except for the unique requirements related to services for students with disabilities, the federal government is unlikely to be proscriptive about policies and programs related to school health. In fiscal year 2003–2004, of $501.3 billion spent on public elementary and secondary schools, state funding supported 46% of the cost and local support amounted to 37%. Only 8.2% of the public schooling budget came from federal agencies. The remaining 9% came from private sources and was directed primarily to private schools.[22] Federal support for education remains well below that for health. In 2002, federal health expenditures amounted to 33% of the total.[23]

School System Capacity to Address Health Issues

While the complexity of school systems and their limited financial resources may create barriers to strengthening school-based health services, greater impediments are likely to be the absence of a structure within education to address health issues and the low priority that superintendents and school boards assign to health services. In the main, neither superintendents nor school boards view health issues as worth a fight. School board members assigned to oversee school health programs are frequently the most recently elected or appointed officials. Among school system administrators, the assistant superintendents for pupil support—those who generally have

responsibility for school-based services—are frequently not part of the school district's leadership team.

The issues that currently consume school system leadership focus on students' educational achievement and mechanisms for holding principals and teachers accountable for student outcomes. Since the primary accountability mechanism in schools is testing, many schools focus on the things that affect student performance on tests. And in many districts, school health does not make that list.

REFERENCES

17. US Department of Education. No Child Left Behind Act of 2001: Overview. Available at http://www.ed.gov/nclb/overview/intro/progsum/index.html. Accessed July 25, 2004.

18. National Center for Education Statistics. *Digest of Education Statistics, 2000.* Washington, DC: US Department of Education; 2000.

19. National Center for Education Statistics. *Overview of Public Elementary and Secondary Schools and Districts: School Year 1999–2000.* Washington, DC: US Department of Education; 2001. Available at: http://nces.ed.gov/pubs2001/overview/table07.asp. Accessed January 3, 2002.

20. National Center for Education Statistics. *Statistics of State School System; Statistics of Public Elementary and Secondary School Systems; Statistics of Nonpublic Elementary and Secondary Schools; Private Schools in American Education; Common Core Data.* Washington, DC: US Department of Education; 2000. Available at http://ces.ed.gov/pubs2001/digest/dt087.html. Accessed January 3, 2002.

21. Brener ND, Burstein GR, DuShaw ML, Vernon ME. Wheeler L, Robin J. Health services: results from the School Health Policies and Programs Study 2000. *J Sch Health.* 2001; 71: 294–304.

22. US Department of Education. 10 facts about K-12 education funding. Available at: http://www.edu.gov/nclb/landing.jhtml?src=pb. Accessed July 26, 2004.

23. Levit K, Smith C, Cowan C, Sensenig A, Caitlin A, Health Accounts Team. Health spending rebound continues in 2002. *Health Aff.* 2004; 23: 147–159.

Enhancing School-Based Prevention and Youth Development Through Coordinated Social, Emotional, and Academic Learning

Source: From Greenberg MT, Weissberg RP, O'Brien MU, Zins JE, Fredericks L, Resnik H, and Elias MJ. 2003. "Enhancing School-Based Prevention and Youth Development Through Coordinated Social, Emotional and Academic Learning." *American Psychologist* 58(6/7): 466–474.

BACKGROUND

It is little wonder that there is national consensus on the need for 21st century schools to offer more than academic instruction if one is to foster success in school and life for all children. Society and the life experiences of children and youth changed considerably during the last century (U.S. Department of Health and Human Services, 2001; Weissberg, Walberg, O'Brien, & Kuster, 2003). Among the changes are increased economic and social pressures on families; weakening of community institutions that nurture children's social, emotional, and moral development; and easier access by children to media that encourage health-damaging behavior.

Today's schools are expected to do more than they have ever done in the past, often with diminishing resources. In 1900, the average public school enrolled 40 students, and the size of the average school district was 120 students; today, an average elementary school enrolls more than 400 pupils, and a typical high school enrolls more than 2,000 pupils (Learning First Alliance, 2001). In 1900, schools were more economically, racially, and ethnically homogeneous; today's schools face unprecedented challenges to educate an increasingly multicultural and multilingual student body and to address the widening social and economic disparities in U.S. society.

In every community today's schools serve a diverse array of students with varied abilities and motivations for learning. Some are academically successful, committed, and participate enthusiastically in class and extracurricular activities. Others struggle academically and are disengaged. In addition, large numbers of students with mental health problems and deficits in social-emotional competence have difficulty learning or disrupt the educational experiences of their peers (Benson, Scales, Leffert, & Roehlkepartain, 1999). Approximately 20% of young people experience mental health problems during the course of a year, yet 75% to 80% of these do not receive appropriate interventions (U.S. Department of Health and Human Services, 1999). Furthermore, 30% of 14- to 17-year-olds engage in multiple high-risk behaviors that jeopardize their potential for life success (Dryfoos, 1997). According to the 2001 Youth Risk Behavior Survey, large percentages of American high school students are involved with substance use, risky sexual behavior, violence, and mental health difficulties.

Given this context, the demands on schools to implement effective educational approaches that promote academic success, enhance health, and prevent problem behaviors have grown (DeFriese, Crossland, Pearson, & Sullivan, 1990; Kolbe, Collins, & Cortese, 1997). Unfortunately, many child advocates and researchers, despite their good intentions, have proposed fragmented initiatives to address problems without an adequate understanding of the mission, priorities, and culture of schools (Sarason, 1996). Schools have been inundated with well-intentioned prevention and promotion programs that address such diverse issues as HIV/AIDS, alcohol, careers, character, civics, conflict resolution, delinquency, dropout, family life, health, morals, multiculturalism, pregnancy, service learning, truancy, and violence.

For a number of reasons, these uncoordinated efforts often are disruptive. First, they typically are introduced as a series of short-term, fragmented initiatives. Such programs and the needs they address are not sufficiently linked to the central mission of schools or to the issues for which teachers and other school personnel are held accountable, primarily academic performance. Second, without strong leadership and support from school administrators, there is rarely adequate staff development and support for program implementation. Programs that are insufficiently coordinated, monitored, evaluated, and improved over time will have reduced impact on student behavior and are unlikely to be sustained.

Concern for the ineffective nature of so many prevention and health promotion efforts spurred a 1994 meeting hosted by the Fetzer Institute. Attendees included school-based prevention researchers, educators, and child advocates who were involved in diverse educational efforts to enhance children's positive development, including social competence promotion, emotional intelligence, drug education, violence prevention, sex education, health promotion, character education, service learning, civic education, school reform, and school-family-community partnerships. The Fetzer group first introduced the term *social and emotional learning* (SEL) as a conceptual framework to address both the needs of young people and the fragmentation that typically characterizes the response of schools to those needs (Elias et al., 1997). They believed that, unlike the many "categorical" prevention programs that targeted specific problems, SEL programming could address underlying causes of problem behavior while supporting academic achievement. A new organization, the Collaborative for Academic, Social, and Emotional Learning (CASEL), also emerged from this meeting with the goal of establishing high-quality, evidence-based SEL as an essential part of preschool through high school education (see www.CASEL.org).

Through developmentally and culturally appropriate classroom instruction and application of learning to everyday situations, SEL programming builds children's skills to recognize and manage their emotions, appreciate the perspectives of others, establish positive goals, make responsible decisions, and handle interpersonal situations effectively (Collaborative for Academic, Social, and Emotional Learning, 2003; Lemerise & Arsenio, 2000). It also enhances students' connection to school through caring, engaging classroom and school practices (McNeeley, Nonnemaker, & Blum, 2002; Osterman, 2000). Learning social and emotional skills is similar to learning other academic skills in that the effect of initial learning is enhanced over time to address the increasingly complex situations children face regarding academics, social relationships, citizenship, and health. Therefore, skills must be developed for negotiating diverse contexts and handling challenges at each developmental level (Weissberg & Greenberg, 1998). This outcome is best accomplished through effective classroom instruction; student engagement in positive activities in and out of the classroom; and broad student, parent, and community involvement in program planning, implementation, and evaluation (Collaborative for Academic, Social, and Emotional Learning, 2003; Henderson & Mapp, 2002; Pittman, Irby, Tolman, Yohalem, & Ferber, 2001). Ideally, planned, ongoing, systematic, and coordinated SEL instruction should begin in preschool and continue through high school.

EVIDENCE SUPPORTING COMPREHENSIVE, SEL-BASED PREVENTION PROGRAMMING

The SEL approach to school-based prevention incorporates health promotion, competence enhancement, and youth development frameworks that integrate strategies for reducing risk factors and enhancing protective mechanisms through coordinated programming (Mrazek & Haggerty, 1994; Perry, 1999; Weissberg & Greenberg, 1998). Problem-prevention efforts for young people are most beneficial when they are coordinated with explicit attempts to enhance their competence, connections to others, and contributions to their community (Eccles & Appleton, 2002; Pittman et al., 2001). These positive outcomes serve both as protective factors that decrease problem behaviors and as foundations for healthy development.

Numerous successful, multiyear, school-based interventions promote positive academic, social, emotional, and health behavior. Some address changes in the school environment, some are person focused, and some include multiple approaches and components. Examples of environment-focused efforts include programming that emphasizes the following: (a) coordinated, school-level organization development and planning (Cook et al., 1999; Cook, Murphy, & Hunt, 2000; D. C. Gottfredson, 1986); (b) creation of caring communities of learners and enhancement of school and classroom climate through a combination of class meetings, peer leadership, family involvement, and whole-school community building activities (Battistich, Schaps, Watson, & Solomon, 1996; Solomon, Battistich, Watson, Schaps, & Lewis, 2000); (c) strengthening teacher instructional practices and increasing family involvement (Hawkins, Catalano, Kosterman, Abbott, & Hill, 1999; Reynolds, Temple, Robertson, & Mann, 2001); and (d) establishing smaller units within schools and building trust among school staff, families, and students, thereby increasing student access, guidance, and support from school staff and other students (Bryk & Schneider, 2002; Felner et al., 1997).

There are effective classroom-based SEL instructional programs that enhance students' social–emotional competence (Elias, Gara, Schuyler, Branden-Muller, & Sayette, 1991; Greenberg & Kusché, 1998) and health (Connell, Turner, &

Mason, 1985; Errecart et al., 1991). Others target the prevention of specific problem behaviors, including substance use (Botvin, Baker, Dusenbury, Botvin, & Diaz, 1995) and violence (Grossman et al., 1997). With older students, combined classroom instruction and volunteer service have reduced risk for teen pregnancy and adolescent failure (Allen, Philliber, Herrling, & Kuperminc, 1997). And, a growing number of multiyear, multicomponent school, family, or community programs produce multiple benefits for young people (Conduct Problems Prevention Research Group, 1999; Pentz et al., 1989; Perry, 1999).

Rather than present descriptions of individual, exemplary, evidence-based programs and their evaluations, the remainder of this section summarizes representative meta-analyses and research syntheses of school-based prevention programming that targets positive youth development, mental health, drug use, antisocial behavior, and academic performance. Although reviews from these varying domains use different language to characterize the common features of effective programming, it is noteworthy that they generally emphasize the core components of SEL interventions described throughout this article.

Positive Youth Development

Catalano, Berglund, Ryan, Lonczak, and Hawkins (2002) began with a database of 161 positive youth development programs and ultimately designated 25 programs as effective. The selected programs focused on school-age children and addressed one or more of 15 youth development (or SEL) constructs: bonding; resilience; social, emotional, cognitive, behavioral, and moral competence; self-determination; spirituality; self-efficacy; clear and positive identity; belief in the future; recognition for positive behavior; opportunities for prosocial involvement; and prosocial norms or health standards for behavior. The programs were implemented in school, family, and/or community settings, with school components used in 22 of the 25 efforts.

Catalano et al. (2002) concluded their review with an optimistic assessment: "Promotion and prevention programs that address positive youth development constructs are definitely making a difference in well-evaluated studies" (p. 62). The results included improvements in interpersonal skills, quality of peer and adult relationships, and academic achievement, as well as reductions in problem behaviors such as school misbehavior and truancy, alcohol and drug use, high-risk sexual behavior, violence, and aggression. Two general strategies evident in most effective programs were skill building and environmental-organizational change. All effective programs addressed a minimum of five SEL constructs. Programs lasting nine or more months produced better outcomes than shorter interventions. The findings highlighted the importance of using structured manuals and curricula to support consistency in program delivery, and they also indicated that the field will benefit from the development and use of standardized measures applied within a comprehensive outcomes framework that assesses youth development constructs, positive behavior outcomes, and the prevention or decrease of social, health, and school problems.

Mental Health

Durlak and Wells (1997) used meta-analysis to examine 177 primary prevention programs designed to prevent behavioral and social problems in young people under the age of 18, with schools being the setting in 73% of these studies. Their findings indicated that programming had the dual benefits of enhancing competencies (e.g., assertiveness, communication skills, self-confidence, academic performance) and reducing internalizing and externalizing problems. Most programs produced outcomes similar to or greater in magnitude than many other established treatment and prevention approaches in medicine and the social sciences.

Person-centered affective education and interpersonal problem-solving training, as well as school–environment change strategies, produced mean effect sizes ranging from .24 to .93, with the strongest benefits occurring for children ages 2 to 7 (Durlak & Wells, 1997). Interventions using behavioral approaches produced larger effects than those using nonbehavioral approaches. In spite of this positive appraisal, Durlak and Wells pointed out that future research must improve efforts to specify program goals and intervention procedures, assess program implementation, identify how intervention and participant characteristics related to program outcomes, and determine the long-term impact of programming.

Greenberg, Domitrovich, and Bumbarger (2001) reviewed more than 130 universal, selected, or indicated prevention programs for school-age children ranging in age from 5 to 18. Their objective was to identify rigorously evaluated interventions that reduced psychological symptoms (e.g., aggression, depression, anxiety) or positively influenced factors associated with risk for child mental disorders. They selected 34 programs that met the following criteria: a randomized-trial design or a quasi-experimental design with an adequate comparison group; pre-, post-, and preferably follow-up assessment; a written manual specifying the program's conceptual model and intervention procedures; and specification of the target sample's social and behavioral characteristics. The 14 school-based universal programs that met Greenberg et al.'s inclusion criteria were classified into four categories: general social–emotional cognitive skill building; violence prevention; school-ecology change; and multidomain and multicomponent.

Greenberg et al. (2001) asserted that meaningful progress has been made with school and family preventive intervention research. They highlighted the following conclusions about validated programs: (a) Multiyear programs are more likely to foster enduring benefits than short-term interventions; (b) prevention programs that focus on multiple domains (e.g., individual, school, and family) are more effective than those that focus only on the child; (c) for school-age children, the school ecology and climate should be a central focus of intervention; and (d) program success is enhanced by combining emphases on changing children's behaviors, teacher and family behavior, home–school relationships, and school and neighborhood support for healthy, competent behavior.

Substance Use

Tobler et al. (2000) examined results from 207 universal prevention programs published between 1978 and 1998. They created a classification scheme composed of two clusters of eight total program types. Five were *noninteractive* approaches that include knowledge-only, affective-only, decisions/values/attitudes, knowledge-plus-affective, and DARE-type programs. The other three represented *interactive* approaches that included social influences, comprehensive life skills, and systemwide change models.

Tobler et al. (2000) indicated that noninteractive lecture-oriented programs have minimal impact, whereas interactive programs that enhance the development of interpersonal skills have greater impact. Greater benefits were also achieved by comprehensive life skills programs that included training in refusal skills, goal setting, assertiveness, communication, and coping. The strongest impact was achieved by systemwide change efforts that involved a school-based program plus community, media, and family programming or schoolwide restructuring efforts emphasizing bonding between students and the school, cooperative learning in small interactive groups, and school–family communication. Higher intensity interactive programs with 16 or more hours of lessons had greater impact than lower intensity efforts (average delivery of 6 hours). One curious finding is that programs implemented by mental health clinicians and peers had more positive effects than those provided by teachers, although all produced significant benefits. Tobler (2000) pointed out that it will require considerable training and support for teachers to implement high-quality interactive programming.

Antisocial Behavior, School Nonattendance, and Drug Use

Wilson, Gottfredson, and Najaka's (2001) meta-analysis of 165 studies of school-based prevention included seven types of in-

dividually focused interventions (e.g., counseling, mentoring, self-control, and social competency instruction) and four types of environmentally focused interventions (e.g., establishing norms or expectations for behavior and schoolwide discipline management interventions). Self-control or social competency programming that used cognitive-behavioral and behavioral instructional methods consistently was effective in reducing dropout and nonattendance, substance use, and conduct problems. These training methods involved modeling behaviors with rehearsal and feedback, behavioral goal setting, and cues to prompt competent behavior in a variety of settings over a sustained period of time.

Environmentally focused interventions were especially effective in reducing delinquent behavior and drug use. Overall, program effects on school problems were approximately three times greater than for delinquency and substance use. In addition, the evaluated programs had stronger effects with at-risk populations.

Wilson et al. (2001) suggested that a single school-based strategy implemented in isolation will not have a large effect. They contended that future research should go beyond examining "Which program works?" to more sophisticated, ecologically based questions such as, "Which combinations or sequences of strategies work best?" and "How can schools effectively design comprehensive packages of prevention strategies and implement them in a high-quality fashion?" (p. 269).

Academic Performance and Learning

Wang, Haertel, and Walberg (1997) analyzed the content of 179 handbook chapters and reviews and 91 research syntheses and surveyed 61 educational researchers in an effort to achieve some consensus regarding the most significant influences on learning. They examined 28 categories of influence. Among the top 11 categories that affected learning, 8 involved social-emotional influences: classroom management, parental support, student-teacher social interactions, social-behavioral attributes, motivational-affective attributes, the peer group, school culture, and classroom climate. Other influences, such as state, district, or school policies, organizational features such as site-based management, curriculum and instruction, and student and district demographics, had the least influence on learning. Wang et al. (1997) concluded that "direct intervention in the psychological determinants of learning promise the most effective avenues of reform" (p. 210).

Zins, Weissberg, Wang, and Walberg (in press) made a compelling conceptual and empirical case for linking SEL programming to improved school attitudes, behavior, and performance. They noted that students' social-emotional competence fosters better academic performance in a variety of ways. For example, they reported that students who become more self-aware and confident about their learning abilities try harder, and that students who motivate themselves, set goals, manage their stress, and organize their approach to work perform better. Additionally, students who make responsible decisions about studying and completing their homework and use problem-solving and relationship skills to overcome obstacles achieve more. Interpersonal, instructional, climate, and environmental supports that produce improved outcomes include the following: (a) partnering between teachers and families to encourage and reinforce learning commitment, engagement, and positive behavior; (b) safe and orderly school and classroom environments; (c) caring relationships between students and teachers that foster commitment and connection to school; (d) engaging teaching approaches such as cooperative learning and proactive classroom management; and (e) adult and peer norms that convey high expectations and support for high-quality academic performance.

On the basis of these findings, Zins et al. (in press) asserted that the research linking social, emotional, and academic factors are sufficiently strong to advance the new term *social, emotional, and academic learning* (SEAL). A central challenge for researchers, educators, and policymakers is to strengthen this connection through coordinated multiyear programming. The SEAL perspective offers an explicit framework for school-based prevention that broadly encourages efforts to promote students' health, character, and citizenship with intentional programming to improve academic performance and other school functioning.

Summary of Research Syntheses

There is a solid and growing empirical base indicating that well-designed, well-implemented school-based prevention and youth development programming can positively influence a diverse array of social, health, and academic outcomes. Although our confidence is tempered by the limited number of replication studies examining program impacts, we nevertheless believe that the consistency of findings from multiple programs with similar mechanisms of action permits lessons to be drawn from the spectrum of prevention research. Key strategies that characterize effective school-based prevention programming involve the following student-focused, relationship-oriented, and classroom- and school-level organizational changes: (a) teaching children to apply SEL skills and ethical values in daily life through interactive classroom instruction and providing frequent opportunities for student self-direction, participation, and school or community service; (b) fostering respectful, supportive relationships among students, school staff, and parents; and (c) supporting and rewarding positive social, health, and academic behavior through systematic school–family–community approaches.

In most cases short-term preventive interventions produce short-lived results. Conversely, multiyear, multicomponent programs are more likely to foster enduring benefits. When classroom instruction is combined with efforts to create environmental support and reinforcement from peers, family members, school personnel, health professionals, other concerned community members, and the media, there is an increased likelihood that students will adopt positive social and health practices (Osher et al., 2002; Weissberg & Greenberg, 1998). Finally, competence- and health-promotion programming is best begun before students are pressured to experiment with risky behaviors and should continue through adolescence. Programming that spans preschool through high school provides continuous instruction, encouragement, and reinforcement to support students' ongoing, developmentally appropriate positive behavior.

EVIDENCE-BASED MODEL PROGRAMS IN THE CONTEXT OF SCHOOLWIDE AND DISTRICTWIDE PRACTICE: CHALLENGES AND OPPORTUNITIES

The research summaries reviewed here illustrate the potential of prevention and youth development programming to contribute to the broad mission of schools. However, their full promise will not be realized until prevention researchers and practitioners more fully understand and capitalize on recent trends in research and in education practice and reform. Our closing observations summarize these trends and their implications for effective school-based prevention.

Emphasis on Research-Based Practices

The No Child Left Behind Act of 2001 places a new emphasis on scientifically based practice. This landmark legislation represents an important opportunity to bring evidence-driven progress to education in the United States (Report of the Coalition for Evidence-Based Policy, 2002). The U.S. Department of Education now specifies that instruction, not only in core academic content areas but also in prevention interventions, should be "guided by theory; rigorously evaluated so as to determine that it actually does what it set out to do; replicable; and validated or supported by researchers in the field" (National Coordinating Technical Assistance Center for Drug Prevention and School Safety Program Coordinators, 2003). Many of the programs assessed in the reviews reported here appear on "model program" lists compiled by various federal agencies (e.g., Centers for Disease Control and Prevention, Office of Juvenile Justice and Delinquency Prevention, U.S. Department of Education). These lists are intended to help schools differentiate between nationally available programs that are effective and those with no evaluation base.

Despite the availability of evidence-based programs, many schools still do not use them (Ennett et al., 2003; G. D. Gottfredson & Gottfredson, 2001; Hallfors & Godette, 2002). For example, Ennett et al. surveyed educators from a national sample of public and private schools and found that only 14% used interactive teaching strategies and effective content in delivering substance use prevention programming. Hallfors and Godette's survey results from 81 Safe and Drug-Free School district coordinators across 11 states indicated that 59% had selected a research-based curriculum for implementation, but only 19% reported their schools were implementing these programs with fidelity. This issue is of equal if not greater importance than generating new and more accurate compendia; the level of practice would be enhanced greatly if even current knowledge was implemented to a greater degree.

Accountability, Assessment Issues, and Measurement Tools

Another recent education trend involves a growing emphasis on accountability. The federal push for a strong science base for school programming is one aspect, and so too is educators' greater use of data to guide practice and keep stakeholders informed. In our own work with schools, we frequently receive requests for measurement tools to identify prevention needs, provide implementation feedback, and document program impacts. School personnel require data to address key issues such as the following: Are implementation efforts working? Is additional training, modification of materials, or more time for program delivery needed? What changes have occurred in terms of targeted outcomes? At the same time, federal, state, and district priorities often focus on limited measures of academic achievement to gauge success. However, given the stated desire of many educators and the general public that schools have a broader vision, it is essential that brief, reliable, and valid measures of the social and emotional health of students and of school environments be developed that can create both public accountability and guidance to improve the social and emotional health of children and youth. In addition, the systematic collection of these data will enable school personnel and policymakers to determine the extent to which these factors support improved academic achievement. Such work is beyond the scope of individual researchers and labs alone and requires the convening of consortia dedicated to collaborative and integrative research with the goal of informing school-based practice in a focused manner.

Comprehensive Approaches

Another major education trend, one that provides a point of great synergy with prevention trends, is a move away from piecemeal and fragmented approaches and toward comprehensiveness and greater coordination in planning and implementation. Research and practice increasingly have shown that schools will be most successful at introducing research-based instruction when systematic decisions are made about how best to identify and implement innovative practices in the context of the entire school community. Further, the dynamic nature of schools—and programs—requires active support for high-quality program implementation and ongoing assessment of the effects of innovations on students, staff, and systems. We have found schools to almost uniformly be interested in this topic.

This experience is consistent with the national trend toward viewing the whole school and its surrounding community as a unit of change, as evidenced by both the community schools movement and the comprehensive school reform (CSR) program of the federal government. For example, the goal of community schools is to make the school a place in which many sectors of a community combine forces to work in partnership to educate children (Blank, Melaville, & Shah, 2003). CSR recognizes the need for a systemic approach to implementing innovation and is designed to foster coherent schoolwide improvements that cover virtually all aspects of a school's operations rather than uncoordinated, isolated approaches to reform. CSR seeks to raise student achievement by helping schools implement effective, comprehensive reforms based on scientifically based research and effective practices (U.S. Department of Education, 2003).

One of the larger, more complicated sets of questions in prevention programming involves how all of the elements of evidence-based programs fit together in the context of an overall schoolwide or school-district effort, and how to ensure that coordinated, multiyear programs will be implemented effectively. To date, few schools have acted strategically to integrate effective approaches to children's social, emotional, and academic learning (Adelman & Taylor, 2000; Osher et al., 2002). A variety of factors have led to this state of affairs, including the absence of long-term curricular planning, inadequate district and school infrastructure to support prevention activities, limited measures of achievement, low levels of funding, and lack of teacher preparation.

The reality is that schools today are hard-pressed to meet the many demands they face, and reforming school programming and practices is exceedingly difficult (Adelman & Taylor, 2000; Berends, Bodilly, & Kirby, 2002; Hall & Hord, 2001; Sarason, 2002). Despite the progress that has been made, substantial research and practice challenges remain. Educational leaders are faced with difficult choices about priorities. Recent years have witnessed greater interest and growing pressure from policymakers and the public regarding student achievement. Currently, educational leaders are consumed by the student academic performance requirements of the No Child Left Behind Act. Following the dictum that what gets inspected gets expected, many schools have increased the time they devote to instruction in these areas while reducing time for "nonassessed programming." Thus, rather than integrating these segments and seeing the contributions of prevention programming to academic as well as social and emotional development, educators often make the false choice to emphasize academics only. One strategy to counteract the limitations of an exclusive focus on academic performance will involve designing and evaluating new programs that simultaneously improve students' health, social-emotional behavior, and achievement. A related strategy will involve modifying graduate and postdegree training for educators and psychologists to prepare more people to take on roles requiring this set of skills.

Future Directions

There are a growing number of evidence-based prevention and youth development programs, and research on these programs provides a solid foundation for beneficial school-based programming. As we approach the next few decades of research, prevention scientists need to address a variety of higher order intervention questions that educators will find informative so that practice can be advanced. For example, educational leaders who want to implement competence-enhancement programs need to have access to more contextual research to understand how prevention programs are being delivered effectively and under what conditions such practices are occurring. Because there are few preschool through high school prevention programs, clarification is needed on how several programs can be coordinated so that a continuum of instruction can be provided. They need to know what aspects of the implementation process are most important, and what adaptations can be made without harming the integrity of the intervention. Of additional interest is information about how schools are handling the move toward comprehensive prevention programming. Moreover, better ways to measure and clarify the phenomena being examined are needed, which ultimately could be used as yardsticks for growth and as means of documenting a broader range of success (Greenberg, in press).

It is critical to establish research-based training and technical assistance approaches for superintendents, principals, teachers, and parents to foster high-quality implementation of new school innovations. The concordance between SEL programs and many teacher preparation standards is clear (Fleming & Bay, in press), but training in preventive techniques has not found its way into most schools of education or district

in-service programs. Further, it is crucial to identify state-level, district-level, and school-level policies and practices that support the successful introduction and institutionalization of school-based prevention programs.

Our review indicates that whole-school approaches to prevention based on evidence-driven interventions show much promise. The next generation of prevention research will involve multiyear evaluations of coordinated schoolwide and districtwide programming that combine comprehensive person-centered and environmental packages of effective strategies (Weissberg & Elias, 1993; Wilson et al., 2001). Building on the current scientific base, the field is ready to expand beyond circumscribed model programs and packages that target a limited number of grade levels and outcomes. We also need a better understanding of how educators make decisions to combine, adapt, and assimilate evidence-based programs and how assessment information is used to improve programs.

Additional key research questions that will inform efforts to disseminate effective school-based prevention programs also must be answered. For instance, what research-based variables are most important to assure the successful replication of effective school-based interventions? Success requires clear fidelity in implementing core program features but may also include "positive" adaptations to local conditions (Greenberg, Domitrovich, Graczyk, & Zins, in press). A related issue involves the development of research-based strategies that educators can use to coordinate the introduction of a new prevention program with those already in place. How do educators make and implement responsible, informed decisions about which programs to keep in place and which ones to drop so that sensible synergy rather than inefficient fragmentation results?

These questions about replication, program coordination, professional development, and sustainability are currently underresearched. Yet in the long run, they will be most informative as schools nationwide implement coordinated prevention programs to improve the social, emotional, physical, and intellectual development of all children.

Our experience in schools across the United States, as well as in many parts of the world, has given us the opportunity to see the many benefits of prevention and youth development programming. We have also observed the consequences of not having such programs in place. The choice is clear. We have the science to foster children's social, emotional, and academic learning even as we improve our research base (Zins et al., in press). The next generation of the science and practice of school-based prevention will require researchers, educators, and policymakers to work together to design evidence-based, coordinated youth development programming and accountability and support systems to ensure their effective implementation. Through these collaborations, we can ensure that truly no child is left behind and that all young people have a chance to realize their full potential.

REFERENCES

Adelman, H. S., & Taylor, L. (2000). Moving prevention from the fringes into the fabric of school improvement. *Journal of Educational and Psychological Consultation, 11,* 7–36.

Allen, J. P., Philliber, S., Herrling, S., & Kuperminc, G. P. (1997). Preventing teen pregnancy and academic failure: Experimental evaluation of a developmentally based approach. *Child Development, 64,* 729–742.

Battistich, V., Schaps, E., Watson, M., & Solomon, D. (1996). Prevention effects of the Child Development Project: Early findings from an ongoing multi-site demonstration trial. *Journal of Adolescent Research, 11,* 12–25.

Benson, P. L., Scales, P. C., Leffert, N., & Roehlkepartain, E. G. (1999). *A fragile foundation: The state of developmental assets among American youth.* Minneapolis, MN: Search Institute.

Berends, M., Bodilly, S. J., & Kirby, S. N. (2002). *Facing the challenges of whole-school reform: New American schools after a decade.* Retrieved March 27, 2003, from http://www.rand.org/publications/MR/MR1498/

Blank, M. J., Melaville, A., & Shah, B. P. (2003). *Making the difference: Research and practice in community schools.* Washington, DC: Coalition for Community Schools, Institute for Educational Leadership.

Botvin, G. J., Baker, E., Dusenbury, L., Botvin, E. M., & Diaz, T. (1995). Long-term follow-up results of a randomized drug abuse prevention trial in a White middle-class population. *Journal of the American Medical Association, 273,* 1106–1112.

Bryk, A. S., & Schneider, B. (2002). *Trust in schools: A core resource for improvement.* New York: Russell Sage Foundation.

Catalano, R. F., Berglund, M. L., Ryan, J. A. M., Lonczak, H. S., & Hawkins, J. D. (2002). Positive youth development in the United States: Research findings on evaluations of positive youth development programs. *Prevention & Treatment, 5,* Article 15. Retrieved August, 1, 2002, from http://journals.apa.org/prevention/volume5/pre0050015a.html

Collaborative for Academic, Social, and Emotional Learning. (2003). *Safe and sound: An educational leader's guide to evidence-based social and emotional learning programs.* Retrieved October 1, 2002, from http://www.casel.org

Conduct Problems Prevention Research Group. (1999). Initial impact of the Fast Track prevention trial for conduct problems: II. Classroom effects. *Journal of Consulting and Clinical Psychology, 67,* 648–657. [Context Link]

Connell, D. B., Turner, R. R., & Mason, E. F. (1985). Summary of the findings of the School Health Education Evaluation: Health promotion effectiveness, implementation, and costs. *Journal of School Health, 55,* 316–323.

Cook, T. D., Farah-Naaz, H., Phillips, M., Stettersten, R. A., Shagle, S. C., & Degirmencioglu, S. M. (1999). Comer's School Development Program in Prince George's County, Maryland: A theory-based evaluation. *American Educational Research Journal, 36,* 543–597.

Cook, T. D., Murphy, R. F., & Hunt, H. D. (2000). Comer's School Development Program in Chicago: A theory-based evaluation. *American Educational Research Journal, 37,* 535–597.

DeFriese, G. H., Crossland, C. L., Pearson, C. E., & Sullivan, C. J. (Eds.). (1990). Comprehensive school health programs: Current status and future prospects. *Journal of School Health, 60,* 127–190.

Dryfoos, J. G. (1997). The prevalence of problem behaviors: Implications for programs. In R. P. Weissberg, T. P. Gullotta, R. L. Hampton, B. A. Ryan, & G. R. Adams (Eds.), *Healthy children 2010: Enhancing children's wellness* (pp. 17–46). Thousand Oaks, CA: Sage.

Durlak, J. A., & Wells, A. M. (1997). Primary prevention mental health programs for children and adolescents: A meta-analytic review. *American Journal of Community Psychology, 25,* 115–152.

Eccles, J., & Appleton, J. A. (Eds.). (2002). *Community programs to promote youth development.* Washington, DC: National Academy Press.

Elias, M. J., Gara, M. A., Schuyler, T. F., Branden-Muller, L. R., & Sayette, M. A. (1991). The promotion of social competence: Longitudinal study of a preventive school-based program. *American Journal of Orthopsychiatry, 61,* 409–417.

Elias, M. J., Zins, J. E., Weissberg, K. S., Greenberg, M. T., Haynes, N. M., & Kessler, R., et al. (1997). *Promoting social and emotional learning: Guidelines for educators.* Alexandria, VA: Association for Supervision and Curriculum Development.

Ennett, S. T., Ringwalt, C. L., Thorne, J., Rohrbach, L. A., Vincus, A., Simons-Rudolph, A., & Jones, S. (2003). A comparison of current practice in school-based substance use prevention programs with meta-analysis findings. *Prevention Science, 4,* 1–14.

Errecart, M. T., Walberg, H. J., Ross, J. G., Gold, R. S., Fiedler, J. L., & Kolbe, L. J. (1991). Effectiveness of teenage health teaching modules. *Journal of School Health, 61,* 26–30.

Felner, R. D., Jackson, A. W., Kasak, D., Mulhall, P., Brand, S., & Flowers, N. (1997). The impact of school reform for the middle years: Longitudinal study of a network engaged in Turning Points-based comprehensive school transformation. *Phi Delta Kappan, 78,* 528–532, 541–550.

Fleming, J. E., & Bay, M. (in press). Social and emotional learning in teacher education standards. In J. E. Zins, R. P. Weissberg, M. C. Wang, & H. J. Walberg. (Eds.), *Building school success through social and emotional learning.* New York: Teachers College Press.

Gottfredson, D. C. (1986). An empirical test of school-based environmental and individual interventions to reduce the risk of delinquent behavior. *Criminology, 24,* 705–731.

Gottfredson, G. D., & Gottfredson, D. C. (2001). What schools do to prevent problem behavior and promote safe environments. *Journal of Educational and Psychological Consultation, 12,* 313–344.

Greenberg, M. T. (in press). Current and future challenges in school-based prevention: The researcher perspective. *Prevention Science.*

Greenberg, M. T., Domitrovich, C. E., & Bumbarger, B. (2001). The prevention of mental disorders in school-aged children: Current state of the field. *Prevention & Treatment, 4,* Article 1. Retrieved March 1, 2002, from http://journals.apa.org/prevention/volume4/pre0040001a.html

Greenberg, M. T., Domitrovich, C. E., Graczyk, P. A., & Zins, J. E. (in press). *The study of implementation in school-based prevention research: Implications for theory, research, and practice.* Rockville, MD: Center for Mental Health Services, Substance Abuse and Mental Health Services Administration.

Greenberg, M. T., & Kusché, C. A. (1998). *Blueprints for violence prevention: The PATHS Project* (Vol. 10). Boulder, CO: Institute of Behavioral Science, Regents of the University of Colorado.

Grossman, D. C., Neckerman, H. J., Koepsell, T. D., Liu, P. Y., Asher, K. N., & Beland, K., et al. (1997). The effectiveness of a violence prevention curriculum among children in elementary school. *Journal of the American Medical Association, 277,* 1605–1611.

Hall, G. E., & Hord, S. M. (2001). *Implementing change: Patterns, principles, and potholes.* Needham Heights, MA: Allyn & Bacon.

Hallfors, D., & Godette, D. (2002). Will the "Principles of Effectiveness" improve prevention practice? Early findings from a diffusion study. *Health Education Review, 17,* 461–470.

Hawkins, J. D., Catalano, R. F., Kosterman, R., Abbott, R., & Hill, K. G. (1999). Preventing adolescent health-risk behaviors by strengthening protection during childhood. *Archives of Pediatric Adolescent Medicine, 153,* 226–234.

Henderson, A. T., & Mapp, K. L. (2002). *A new wave of evidence: The impact of school, family, and community connections on student achievement.* Austin, TX: Southwest Educational Development Laboratory.

Jackson, A. W., & Davis, G. A. (2000). *Turning Points 2000: Educating adolescents in the 21st century.* New York: Teachers College Press.

Kolbe, L. J., Collins, J., & Cortese, P. (1997). Building the capacity for schools to improve the health of the nation: A call for assistance from psychologists. *American Psychologist, 52,* 256–265.

Learning First Alliance. (2001). *Every child learning: Safe and supportive schools.* Washington, DC: Author. Retrieved October 5, 2002, from http://www.learningfirst.org

Lemerise, E. A., & Arsenio, W. F. (2000). An integrated model of emotion processes and cognition in social information processing. *Child Development, 71,* 107–118.

McNeeley, C. A., Nonnemaker, J. M., & Blum, R. W. (2002). Promoting school connectedness: Evidence from the National Longitudinal Study of Adolescent Health. *Journal of School Health, 72,* 138–146.

Metlife. (2002). *The Metlife Survey of the American Teacher 2002—Student life: School, home, and community.* New York: Author.

Mrazek, P. J., & Haggerty, R. J. (Eds.). (1994). *Reducing risks for mental disorders: Frontiers for preventive intervention research.* Washington, DC: National Academy Press.

National Coordinating Technical Assistance Center for Drug Prevention and School Safety Program Coordinators. (2003). *Frequently asked questions.* Retrieved April 27, 2003, from http://www.k12coordinator.org/faqs.asp

No Child Left Behind Act of 2001. Pub. L. 107–110 (H.R.1).

Osher, D., Dwyer, K., & Jackson, S. (2002). *Safe, supportive, and successful schools, step by step.* Rockville, MD: U. S. Department of Health and Human Services, Substance Abuse and Mental Health Services Administration, Center for Mental Health Services.

Osterman, K. F. (2000). Students' need for belonging in the school community. *Review of Educational Research, 70,* 323–367.

Pentz, M. A., Dwyer, J. H., MacKinnon, D. P., Flay, B. R., Hansen, W. B., Wang, E. Y. I., & Johnson, C. A. (1989). A multicommunity trial for primary prevention of adolescent drug abuse. *Journal of the American Medical Association, 261,* 3259–3266.

Perry, C. L. (1999). *Creating health behavior change: How to develop community-wide programs for youth.* Thousand Oaks, CA: Sage.

Pittman, K. J., Irby, M., Tolman, J., Yohalem, N., & Ferber, T. (2001). *Preventing problems, promoting development, encouraging engagement: Competing priorities or inseparable goals?* Retrieved March 1, 2003, from http://www.forumforyouthinvestment.org/preventproblems.pdf

Public Agenda. (1994). *First things first: What Americans expect from the public schools.* New York: Author.

Public Agenda. (1997). *Getting by: What American teenagers really think about their schools.* New York: Author.

Public Agenda. (2002). *A lot easier said than done: Parents talk about raising children in today's America.* New York: Author.

Ravitch, D. (2000). *Left behind: A century of failed school reforms.* New York: Simon & Schuster.

Report of the Coalition for Evidence-Based Policy. (2002). *Bringing evidence-driven progress to education: A recommended strategy for the U.S. Department of Education.* Retrieved January 15, 2003, from http://www.excelgov.org/usermedia/images/uploads/PDFs/coalitionFinRpt.pdf

Reynolds, A. J., Temple, J. A., Robertson, D. L., & Mann, E. A. (2001). Long-term effects of an early childhood intervention on educational achievement and juvenile arrest: A 15-year follow-up of low-income children in public schools. *Journal of the American Medical Association, 285,* 2339–2346.

Rose, L. C., & Gallup, A. M. (2000). *The 32nd Annual Phi Delta Kappa/Gallup poll of the public's attitudes towards the public schools.* Retrieved July 7, 2002, from http://www.pdkintl.org/kappan/kpol0009.htm

Sarason, S. B. (1996). *Revisiting "The culture of the school and the problem of change."* New York: Teachers College Press.

Sarason, S. B. (2002). *Educational reform: A self-scrutinizing memoir.* New York: Teachers College Press.

Solomon, D., Battistich, V., Watson, M., Schaps, E., & Lewis, C. (2000). A six-district study of educational change: Direct and mediated effects of the Child Development Project. *Social Psychology of Education, 4,* 3–51.

Tobler, N. S. (2000). Lessons learned. *Journal of Primary Prevention, 20,* 261–274.

Tobler, N. S., Roona, M. R., Ochshorn, P., Marshall, D. G., Streke, A. V., & Stackpole, K. M. (2000). School-based adolescent drug prevention programs: 1998 meta-analysis. *Journal of Primary Prevention, 20,* 275–337.

U.S. Department of Education. (2003). *About comprehensive school reform.* Retrieved March 23, 2003, from http://www.ed.gov/offices/OESE/compreform/2pager.html

U.S. Department of Health and Human Services. (1999). *Mental health: A report of the Surgeon General.* Rockville, MD: U.S. Department of Health and Human Services, Substance Abuse and Mental Health Services Administration, Center for Mental Health Services, National Institutes of Health, National Institute of Mental Health.

U.S. Department of Health and Human Services. (2001). *Trends in the well-being of America's children and youth, 2001.* Washington DC: U.S. Government Printing Office.

Wang, M. C., Haertel, G. D., & Walberg, H. J. (1997). Learning influences. In H. J. Walberg & G. D. Haertel (Eds.), *Psychology and educational practice* (pp. 199–211). Berkeley, CA: McCatchan.

Weissberg, R. P., & Elias, M. J. (1993). Enhancing young people's social competence and health behavior: An important challenge for educators, scientists, policy makers, and funders. *Applied and Preventive Psychology: Current Scientific Perspectives, 3,* 179–190.

Weissberg, R. P., & Greenberg, M. T. (1998). School and community competence-enhancement and prevention programs. In I. E. Siegel & K. A. Renninger (Vol. Eds.), *Handbook of child psychology: Vol. 4. Child psychology in practice* (5th ed., pp. 877–954). New York: Wiley.

Weissberg, R. P., Walberg, H. J., O'Brien, M. U., & Kuster, C. B. (Eds.). (2003). *Long-term trends in the well-being of children and youth.* Washington, DC: Child Welfare League of America Press.

Wilson, D. B., Gottfredson, D. C., & Najaka, S. S. (2001). School-based prevention of problem behaviors: A meta-analysis. *Journal of Quantitative Criminology, 17,* 247–272.

Zins, J. E., Weissberg, R. P., Wang, M. C., & Walberg, H. J. (Eds.). (in press). *Building school success through social and emotional learning.* New York: Teachers College Press.

Health Care Costs of Worksite Health Promotion Participants and Non-Participants

Source: Goetzel RZ, Jacobsen BH, Aldana SG, Verdell K, and Yee L. 1998. "Health Care Costs of Worksite Health Promotion Participants and Non-Participants." *Journal of Occupational Environmental Medicine* 40(4): 341–346.

BACKGROUND

The dramatic rise in health care cost has increased exponentially for the past four decades and has grown beyond the prudent financial capabilities of many businesses. Corporate expenses for employee health care are nearly $250 billion annually and account for approximately 50% of corporate after-tax profits.[1]

In contrast to traditional medicine, which has placed primary emphasis on the treatment and cure of disease,[2] increased attention has recently been directed at health promotion and disease prevention initiatives in employer and managed care settings. Motivation for implementing worksite health promotion (WHP) programs includes a commitment to optimizing employee health, job satisfaction, and productivity, as well as a desire to reduce health care costs, accidents and absenteeism.[3,4] In the most recent of his reviews of literature focused on the cost savings associated with WHP, Pelletier[5] reported that many studies provided evidence supporting the implementation of WHP, although several contained serious methodological flaws. Previous studies have shown that WHP may reduce several modifiable risk factors,[6–11] all of which are fundamentally related to health care costs.

The purpose of this study is to retrospectively compare total and lifestyle-related medical care utilization and costs between participants and non-participants in The Procter and Gamble Company's (P&G) WHP called Health Check.

METHODS

The subjects for this cross-sectional study were restricted to active P&G employees who were continuously employed between January 1990 and December 1992 and who were eligible for the company's medical benefits plan administered by Metropolitan Life. Such subject selection avoided the threat of observed changes in health care costs due to a change in employee demographics and medical benefit plan design. Participants in the P&G Health Check program ($n = 3,993$) were defined as those who voluntarily completed an optical scan Health Check health profile questionnaire (HPQ) administered by Johnson & Johnson Health Care Systems (J&JHCS) at any time during the three-year study period and who also participated in follow-up high risk interventions. Non-participants ($n = 4,341$) were employees who did not participate in any aspect of WHP during the study period. All subjects voluntarily agreed to participate in the health profiling and were guaranteed full anonymity and confidentiality.

Of the total cohort ($n = 8,334$), 53% were males and 48% were female. Participation in the program was solicited through corporate newsletter, flyers, and word of mouth. All employees were equally encouraged to participate; no coercion or pressure was applied to increase participation, and no penalty was assessed for those employees who did not wish to participate.

Employees between the ages of 25 and 54 comprised the majority of the subject pool (87%). Six percent of the participants were over 55 years of age and 7% were under the age of 25 years. Eighty-one percent of the subjects were white, 13% black, and 6% were Native American, Asian, Hispanic, or other ethnicity. Fifty-five percent had some college education, college degrees, or graduate school education; 1% were without high school degrees; and the remainder had high school degrees and/or vocational training. Clerical workers, those in sales/marketing, and professional/technical workers constituted the largest proportion of the work-force (73%) within the study population cohort (28%, 23%, and 22% respectively).

The HPQ developed by J&JHCS was written on an eighth grade reading level and designed to be completed in approximately 30 minutes. The HPQ contained 108 items, which were separated into the following categories: tobacco use, nutrition, exercise, safety, dental health, self care, preventive medical care, men's health, women's health, medical history, alcohol use, general well-being (stress), and biometrics measures. Biometrics measures included height, weight, blood pressure, body mass index, total cholesterol and high-density lipoprotein cholesterol measurements. Questionnaire completeness and conformity to processing requirements were manually inspected, and a central computer automatically performed quality checks. If responses were missing, a J&JHCS staff member called the respondent for additional information or clarification regarding the questionnaire item. The questionnaire has been used in several previously published reports and has been shown to be a valid and reliable measurement tool.[11–13] The instrument has been shown to have a Spearman-Brown split-half reliability of 0.88, a Cronbach's alpha of 0.94, and a test-retest correlation of 0.79.

After completion of the HPQ, participants received individualized reports outlining their health status in relation to specific risk areas. Individuals were then identified to be high risk if they displayed any of the following risk factors: elevated blood pressure, elevated cholesterol, cigarette smoking, poor diet, lack of activity, stress, and multiple risks. Participants in the program who were determined to be at high risk were provided one-to-one counseling and behavior change support by P&G clinical staff. Additionally, quarterly follow-ups were conducted by health professionals. Risk factors associated with heart disease or other risk categories were communicated to participants, and a health improvement action plan designed.

The one-on-one risk intervention recommendations focused on how to modify behavior in order to reduce risk levels. High-risk individuals were referred to clinicians when appropriate. The program also focused on disease prevention and the identification and reduction of health risk factors. Ancillary health support programs included fitness flex time, after-work on-site aerobics, noon aerobics, diet/weight management programs, cholesterol and blood pressure education, smoking cessation programs, brown-bag educational programs, annual mammography screening, voluntary health screening, and exercise incentives such as participation prizes.

All employees were given equal access to all facets of the program. No attempt was made to ascertain personal decisions for participation or non-participation.

Cost experience data were collected from Metropolitan Life Medical Claims computerized database for the total study population. The analysis focused on claims incurred for a continuous three-year period. Claims were aggregated and categorized as inpatient or outpatient. Claims were further classified as either potentially lifestyle-related (resulting from modifiable risk factors) and non-lifestyle-related medical care conditions. Lifestyle-related health care costs included only health care expenditures from diseases likely to be related to individuals' behaviors and lifestyles. Claims with a potential lifestyle-related diagnoses were assigned to one of the 46 Lifestyle Diagnosis Groups (LDGs).

For example, an employee with ischemic heart disease would be assigned a specific LDG number pertaining to a lifestyle-related diagnosis. Each LDG consisted of diagnoses that, according to the epidemiological literature, are potentially caused by one or more of the following modifiable health risks: tobacco use, alcohol use, elevated blood pressure, elevated serum cholesterol, inadequate motor vehicle and home safety, excess body fat, abuse of drugs other than alcohol and tobacco, inadequate exercise, excessive stress, unsafe sexual behavior, and poor dietary habits. All claims were adjusted to 1992 dollar values. Costs relating to normal delivery pregnancy claims were excluded.

Data analysis consisted of descriptive statistics of medical care costs and utilization by participants and non-participants by year. Medical care utilization was analyzed in terms of annual inpatient care, ie, hospital admissions, and hospital bed day utilization. The effects of time and participation were examined with a 2 × 3 repeated measures analysis of variance (ANOVA). Differences between participants and non-participants were estimated with a repeated measures analysis of covariance (ANCOVA) with control for age and gender. Least square means was used to calculate the age/gender adjustment.

RESULTS

Lifestyle-related medical costs, adjusted for age and gender, comprised 34.8% ($2.3 million), 33.8% ($2.5 million), and 37.7% ($3 million) of total annual medical costs for the entire study group for the first, second and third study years respectively. On average, potential lifestyle-related medical costs accounted for about 35% of P&G's three-year total medical costs.

At the conclusion of the third year of study, non-participants' age- and gender-adjusted total medical costs were 29% higher (significant at $P < 0.05$) than those of WHP participants ($1,731 vs $1,339 respectively; Figure 9-1). Age- and gender-adjusted

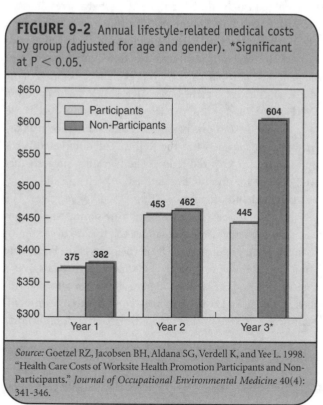

FIGURE 9-1 Total annual costs for participants and non-participants (adjusted for age and gender). *Significant at P < 0.05.

Source: Goetzel RZ, Jacobsen BH, Aldana SG, Verdell K, and Yee L. 1998. "Health Care Costs of Worksite Health Promotion Participants and Non-Participants." *Journal of Occupational Environmental Medicine* 40(4): 341-346.

non-participant annual lifestyle-related medical costs were also significantly higher (36% more expensive) than those of participants at the end of the third year ($604 vs $445) but not for the first two years of the program (Figure 9-2).

A comparison of lifestyle-related medical costs between the average of first two years and the third year indicated a 7% increase for the participants contrasted with a 43% increase for the non-participants. Similarly, in the third year, non-participants had significantly higher age and gender adjusted inpatient medical costs than participants (Figure 9-3). Although not significant, but directional, non-participants experienced 25% more lifestyle-related hospital admissions per 1,000 employees when compared with participants (22 vs 17 respectively) in the third year of participation (Figure 9-4) and 28% more lifestyle-related hospital days per 1,000 employees (106 vs 83 respectively) after adjustment for age and gender (Figure 9-5).

DISCUSSION

Employee lifestyle-related health care costs have been strongly associated with behaviors such as smoking,[14] obesity,[15] hypertension,[15] poor fitness,[10,16] and high stress,[6-8] all of which have a significant modifiable component. The results of the present study suggest a significant relationship between reduced health care utilization and costs and active participation in a WHP program. Self-selected participants in WHP experienced lower total and lifestyle related health care costs in the third year after program initiation when compared with non-participants. Careful evaluation of the current results reveals that health care cost reduction was minimal until the third year of program implementation and that the cost differential between participants and non-participants expanded from the first year to the third year of participation. This trend is consistent with other studies

FIGURE 9-2 Annual lifestyle-related medical costs by group (adjusted for age and gender). *Significant at P < 0.05.

Source: Goetzel RZ, Jacobsen BH, Aldana SG, Verdell K, and Yee L. 1998. "Health Care Costs of Worksite Health Promotion Participants and Non-Participants." *Journal of Occupational Environmental Medicine* 40(4): 341-346.

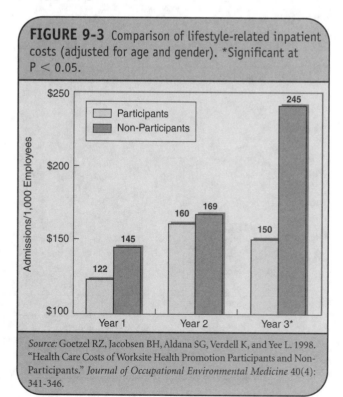

FIGURE 9-3 Comparison of lifestyle-related inpatient costs (adjusted for age and gender). *Significant at P < 0.05.

Source: Goetzel RZ, Jacobsen BH, Aldana SG, Verdell K, and Yee L. 1998. "Health Care Costs of Worksite Health Promotion Participants and Non-Participants." *Journal of Occupational Environmental Medicine* 40(4): 341-346.

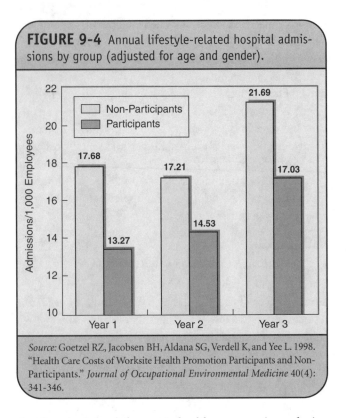

FIGURE 9-4 Annual lifestyle-related hospital admissions by group (adjusted for age and gender).

Source: Goetzel RZ, Jacobsen BH, Aldana SG, Verdell K, and Yee L. 1998. "Health Care Costs of Worksite Health Promotion Participants and Non-Participants." *Journal of Occupational Environmental Medicine* 40(4): 341-346.

that found minimal changes in health care experience during the initial stages of WHP implementation.[4,17] Since significant health care cost reductions were only evident in the third year of participation, the commitment of a WHP needs to be

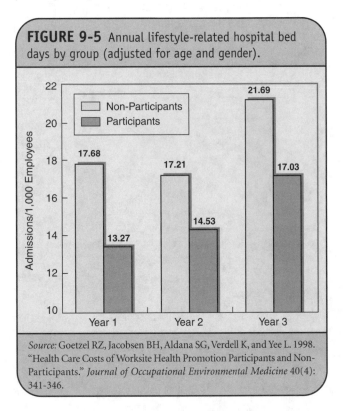

FIGURE 9-5 Annual lifestyle-related hospital bed days by group (adjusted for age and gender).

Source: Goetzel RZ, Jacobsen BH, Aldana SG, Verdell K, and Yee L. 1998. "Health Care Costs of Worksite Health Promotion Participants and Non-Participants." *Journal of Occupational Environmental Medicine* 40(4): 341-346.

made on a long-term basis in order to establish a positive benefit-to-cost ratio.

Potential lifestyle-related medical costs accounted for an average of 35% of three-year total annual medical costs, a figure congruent with previous findings.[18] This was expected since numerous health care dollars are not directly impacted by lifestyle (eg, common cold, influenza, various infections, hereditary disorders, etc). Congruous with other findings,[4,17] inpatient utilization (ie, hospital admissions, hospital bed days) was also considerably lower for WHP participants in this sample. The current study found the greatest difference in hospital admissions and bed days in the third year of the study when comparing participants and non-participants. Since many latent diseases may result from long-term unhealthy behavior, the three years examined in the present study represent a minimum time period necessary to recognize the impact that lifestyle factors have on hospital utilization and costs.

The cross-sectional design of this study does not allow for inference on causality, but the strong association between WHP participation and lower health care costs found in the present study has been noted, with some consistency, previously.[4,15,17–20] The self-selected nature of the participants further limits the inferences that can be made from this study. Participants may have been more motivated and willing to change their health risk behaviors than their non-participant counterparts. For example, did participation cause the difference in health care costs between groups, or were the groups different to begin with? If a difference existed as a result of the voluntary nature of the treatment group, one would expect obvious differences in baseline cost measures between the two groups. However, no meaningful cost differences between participants and non-participants were evident at the onset of the study. Thus it seems plausible to suggest that participation in WHP contributed to improved health status and reduced cost.

This study supports prior research that has shown a positive relationship between the well-executed, targeted WHP and health care cost reduction. The literature suggests that well-designed economic evaluations of WHP are still somewhat limited and oftentimes lack methodological rigor. The advantages of the current investigation are summarized below.

A large enough employee sample was tracked over a multi-year period. Approximately 4,000 participants in the WHP were compared with approximately 4,000 non-participants over a three-year period to establish program effects. The same individuals were tracked over time in a consistent environment. Statistical tests were feasible, given the large study population.

- Participants and non-participants began the study at about the same baseline costs (approximately $1,100 per year). Over time, costs for participants grew at a much slower pace than for those of non-participants and, in fact, costs between the two groups diverged significantly. At the outset, the two groups were about 2% apart. After three years, their total costs were 29% apart.

- Total and lifestyle-related costs were compared and contrasted over time. Whereas total costs were significantly lower for participants than non-participants, a subset of costs, those specifically linked to potential lifestyle-related diagnoses, were even lower for participants than for non-participants in year three when compared with total costs (36% difference for lifestyle-related costs vs 29% difference for total costs). The greater difference in lifestyle costs is expected since these are the disease entities most likely to be affected in the short term by intervention programs.

- The current study adjusted for demographic difference between the participant and non-participant populations when comparing costs over time. These statistical adjustments are rarely performed in health care cost evaluation studies focused on WHP.

Additional research is needed to identify which aspects of intervention contributes most to cost reductions and which categories of illness are most affected by the intervention. Furthermore, research is needed to assess if similar outcomes may be observed in other benefit areas and overall productivity—eg, absenteeism, turnover, workers' compensation, disability, and productivity—and if the costs savings can be sustained over time.

REFERENCES

1. Health Insurance Association of America and American Council of Life Insurance. *Wellness at the Worksite*. Washington, DC: Health Insurance Association of America; 1993.

2. O'Donnell MP. Definition of health promotion. *Am J Health Promot.* 1988;1:4–5.

3. Gebhardt DL, Crump C. Employee fitness and wellness programs in the workplace. *Am Physiol.* 1990;45:262–272.

4. Bly J, Jones R, Richardson J. Impact of worksite health promotion on health care costs and utilization: evaluation of Johnson & Johnson's LIVE FOR LIFE program. *JAMA.* 1986;256:3235–3240.

5. Pelletier KR. A review and analysis of the health and cost-effective outcome studies of comprehensive health promotion and disease prevention programs at the worksite: 1991–1993 update. *Am J Health Promot.* 1993;8: 50–61.

6. Donatelle RJ, Hawkins MJ. Employee stress claims: increasing implications for health promotion programming. *Am J Health Promot.* 1989;3: 19–25.

7. Cole GE, Tucker LA, Friedman GM. Absenteeism data as a measure of cost effectiveness of stress management programs. *Am J Health Promot.* 1987; 1:12–15.

8. Goodspeed RB. Stress reduction at the worksite: an evaluation of two methods. *Am J Health Promot.* 1990;4:333–337.

9. Browne DW, Russell ML, Morgan JL, Optenberg SA, Clarke AE. Reduced disability and health care costs in an industrial fitness program. *J Occup Med.* 1984;26:809–815.

10. Aldana SG, Jacobson BH, Kelly PL. Mobile work site health promotion programs can reduce selected employee health risks. *J Occup Med.* 1993;35: 922–928.

11. Goetzel RZ, Kahr TY, Aldana SG, Kenny GM. An evaluation of Duke University's LIVE FOR LIFE health promotion program and its impact on employee health. *Am J Health Promot.* 1996;10:340–342.

12. Knight KK, Goetzel RZ, Fielding JE, et al. An evaluation of Duke University's LIVE FOR LIFE health promotion program on changes in worker absenteeism. *J Occup Med.* 1994;36:533–537.

13. Fielding J, Knight K, Goetzel R, Laouri M. Utilization of preventive health services by an employed population. *J Occup Med.* 1991;33:715–717.

14. Penner M, Penner S. Excess insured health care costs from tobacco-using employees in a large group plan. *J Occup Med.* 1990;32:521–523.

15. Bertera RL. The effects of behavioral risks on absenteeism and health-care costs in the workplace. *J Occup Med.* 1991;33:1119–1124.

16. Tucker LA, Aldana SG, Friedman GM. Cardiovascular fitness and absenteeism in 8,301 employed adults. *Am J Health Promot.* 1990;5:140–145.

17. Aldana SG, Jacobson BH, Harris CJ. Influence of a mobile worksite health promotion program on health care costs. *J Prevent Med.* 1994;9:378–382.

18. Kingery PM, Ellsworth CG, Corbett BS, Bowden RG, Brizzolara JA. High-cost analysis: a closer look at the case for work-site health promotion. *J Occup Med.* 1994;36:1341–1347.

19. Warner KE, Wickizer TM, Wolfe RA, Schildroth J. Economic implications of workplace health promotion program: review of the literature. *J Occup Med.* 1988;30:106–112.

20. Hatziandreu EI, Koplan JP, Weinstein MC, Caspreson CJ, Warner KE. A cost-effectiveness analysis of exercise as a health promotion activity. *Am J Public Health.* 1988;78:1417–1421.

Application of Theory: Communications Campaigns

The Part 10 readings address a very significant field of health promotion practice and one that has, for a long time, incorporated social and behavioral theory. Communications campaigns and media advocacy together include a wide range of mass media and other options for disseminating messages and information in ways that will influence behavior. This requires careful research and planning and knowledge about the nature of the communication process. The readings in this part begin with the methods and results of a study (Farrelly et al., 2005) that examine the impact of the famous "truth campaign" on youth smoking prevalence. The second selection, from the "pink book" (DHHS, 2002) that was referred to in Part 6, covers the basics of communications programs. Finally, the strategy and practice of media advocacy is outlined in an excerpt from a manual published by the American Public Health Association.

Evidence of a Dose-Response Relationship Between "Truth" Antismoking Ads and Youth Smoking Prevalence

Source: Farrelly MC, Davis KC, Haviland ML, Messeri P, Healton CG. Evidence of a dose-response relationship between "truth" antismoking ads and youth smoking prevalence. *Am J Public Health*. 2005 Mar; 95(3):425–31.

INTRODUCTION

Mass media campaigns can be an effective public health strategy to prevent youth smoking.[1–3] Antismoking television campaigns have emphasized diverse themes to discourage smoking, including highlighting short- and long-term health consequences, deglamorizing its social appeal through humorous and unflattering portrayals, and countering misperceptions that smoking is widespread among teens. A more recent theme, first used by California in the 1990s, focuses on exposing deceptive tobacco industry marketing practices and denials of tobacco's health and addictive effects. In 1998, the Florida Department of Health launched a tobacco prevention program that featured a mass media campaign known as "truth" that countered industry influences with hard-hitting television advertisements that deglamorized smoking and portrayed youth confronting the tobacco industry. After 2 years, the prevalence of any past 30-day smoking among middle and high school students dropped by 40% and 18%, respectively.[4] In a longitudinal study, Sly et al.[5] linked exposure to the Florida "truth" campaign to declines in youth smoking prevalence.

As a result of the Master Settlement Agreement between tobacco companies and 46 states, the American Legacy Foundation (Legacy) initiated the national "truth" campaign in February 2000. From 2000 to 2002, annual funding for the campaign averaged $100 million per year. A national media purchase was employed by the campaign, as opposed to a randomized exposure design, for 2 primary reasons. First, Legacy could not ethically assign some media markets to low or zero exposure, given the documented successes of the Florida "truth" campaign. Second, a national media purchase was roughly 40% cheaper than a market-to-market purchase, which would have been necessary to randomize exposure. Although the "truth" campaign builds upon the experiences of Florida and other state campaigns, no similar large-scale national antismoking effort has occurred since the period of the Fairness Doctrine from 1967 to 1970, when TV networks were required to maintain a balance between anti- and prosmoking ads. The "truth" campaign ads are designed to avoid overt and directive messages that tell teens not to smoke and instead use graphic images depicting stark facts about death and disease caused by tobacco and exposés of manipulative marketing practices. For example, an early commercial, "Body Bags," showed youths piling 1200 body bags outside a major tobacco company's headquarters to highlight the daily death toll from tobacco use.

This is the first study to evaluate the behavioral outcomes of the campaign. Previous studies have shown that the campaign influenced campaign-related attitudes toward tobacco use and the tobacco industry and that negative attitudes about the tobacco industry are correlated with reduced risk of smoking.[6–9] The current study assessed whether there was a dose–response relationship between the level of exposure to the campaign and youth smoking prevalence during the first 2 years of the campaign.

METHODS

Study Design Overview

This study used a pre/post quasi-experimental design that related changes in youth smoking prevalence to varied exposure to the campaign over time and across media markets in the United States; secular trends in smoking prevalence and other confounding influences were controlled. The years 1997–1999 represent a precampaign study period, and although the campaign was launched nationally, the dose of campaign messages varied considerably across media markets and over time from 2000 to 2002. The primary source of variation in exposure is the presence or absence of local affiliates for 1 or more of the broadcast networks (e.g., FOX, UPN, WB) on which "truth" campaign commercials aired and variation in cable television market presence (e.g., MTV).

Study Population

Our study used data from the 1997–2002 Monitoring the Future (MTF) annual spring surveys, designed to monitor alcohol, tobacco, and illicit drug use among youths in the United States.[10] The survey, funded primarily by the National Institute on Drug Abuse and conducted by the University of Michigan's Institute for Social Research, included approximately 18,000, 17,000, and 16,000 8th-, 10th-, and 12th-grade students per year, respectively.

MTF surveys are conducted in approximately 420 public and private secondary schools per year and use a multistage random sampling design to provide nationally representative samples of students in each grade level. The sampling procedure selects geographic areas in stage 1, 1 or more schools within those geographic areas in stage 2, and classes within each school in the final stage. Schools are selected such that their probability of selection is proportionate to the size of the classes being sampled. Sample weights are applied to all respondents in the survey to adjust for school differences in probabilities of selection and school size. Up to 350 students are surveyed from each selected school. All surveys are self-administered in school classrooms during normal class periods. The average yearly student response rates for 8th-, 10th-, and 12th-grade students in the 1997–2002 MTF surveys were 89.0%, 86.2%, and 82.8%, respectively.

The primary study outcome was a dichotomous indicator for reporting any quantity of smoking in the past 30 days, based on the question "How frequently have you smoked cigarettes during the past 30 days?" Our indicator variable equaled zero for students who responded "none per day" and 1 for students who responded less than 1 cigarette, 1 to 5 cigarettes, about ½ pack, about 1 pack, about 1½ packs, and 2 packs or more per day.

Exposure

We used cumulative gross rating points (GRPs) for the "truth" campaign in each of the 210 television markets in the United States to measure each student's exposure to the campaign (note that MTF surveys do not ask about awareness of the "truth" campaign). The GRPs measure the total volume of delivery of a media campaign to a target audience. It is equal to the percentage of the target audience that is reached by the campaign times the frequency of exposure.

To illustrate the variation in potential exposure, we grouped the 210 media markets into 1 of 5 levels of exposure, on the basis of the range in total GRPs (647 to 22,389) that accumulated in each market from campaign launch in February 2000 until the second quarter of 2002 (Figure 10-1). The lowest-exposure group received an average of 3867 GRPs over this 2-year period, whereas the highest-exposure group received an average of 20367 GRPs. Market-level variation in GRPs is primarily due to the availability of television stations on which "truth" campaign advertisements aired (e.g., FOX, UPN, WB). Markets with fewer stations received lower GRPs, whereas markets with more stations received higher GRPs.

A student's exposure was defined as the cumulative number of "truth" campaign GRPs that were delivered in a school's media market from the beginning of the campaign to the time of each spring survey in 2000, 2001, and 2002. Consistent with our pre/post evaluation design, we included students surveyed from 1997 to 1999 to serve as a historical unexposed (GRP = 0) comparison group. To account for the possibility that markets that received relatively high doses of the campaign might experience diminishing returns to additional GRPs, we included a quadratic term for cumulative GRPs in our models.

Potential Confounders

Following a socioecological model[11] that recognizes multiple levels of influence on health behaviors (e.g., intrapersonal, interpersonal, community, media, policy, economic factors), we controlled for a wide array of potential confounding influences described in the following sections.

Individual Level. Our multivariable models included individual-level data from the MTF such as grade, race/ethnicity, gender, parental education, and weekly income. We created indicator variables for grade, race/ethnicity (African American, Hispanic, Asian, other race, with White as the reference), gender, and parental education for mother and father separately (high school graduate, at least some college, with less than high school diploma as the reference category). To account for missing data on race and parental education, we included indicator variables for those with unspecified race and father's and mother's edu-

FIGURE 10-1 How media markets across the country (only 48 states shown) were exposed to various levels or doses of the national "truth" campaign, 2000–2002. Ratings given are in gross rating points.

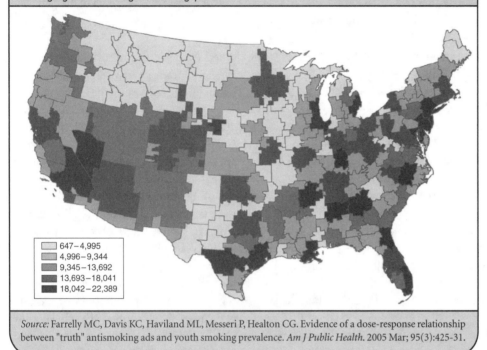

647–4,995
4,996–9,344
9,345–13,692
13,693–18,041
18,042–22,389

Source: Farrelly MC, Davis KC, Haviland ML, Messeri P, Healton CG. Evidence of a dose-response relationship between "truth" antismoking ads and youth smoking prevalence. *Am J Public Health.* 2005 Mar; 95(3):425-31.

cation in the MTF survey. We also included a measure of students' weekly income, based on 2 MTF survey questions that assess how much money students earn during an average week from a job and from other sources such as allowances. To adjust for inflation, we used the 2002 consumer price index to express our measure of income in 2002 dollars.

Media Market Level. In light of the source of variation in the media market dose of the "truth" campaign, there might be factors that determined both the dose of the "truth" campaign and the level of smoking at the media market level. For example, low-exposure markets tended to be more rural, White, and less educated and have lower incomes—all factors associated with smoking—than markets with high campaign exposure. Failing to control for these factors could lead to a spurious negative correlation between campaign exposure and smoking prevalence. We implemented 2 approaches to statistically model possible correlations between preexisting media market smoking rates and the subsequent campaign dose. We first treated each of the 210 media markets as fixed effects in a logistic regression model that included indicator variables for 209 of 210 media markets (with 1 market as a reference).[12] The fixed-effects approach was equivalent to controlling for average market-level smoking rates, effectively making each market its own control group. Our second approach included direct media

market-level measures of potential confounders—2002 data on the median household income, percentage of the population who were college graduates, and population size.

State Level. To account for potential state-level influences, we collected data on inflation-adjusted cigarette prices[13] and investments in tobacco control programs corresponding to the 1997–2002 MTF and the location of a student's school. Previous research has shown that cigarette prices and state tobacco control programs influence youth smoking prevalence.[4,14,15] Our measure of tobacco control investments is based on state per capita tobacco control program funding derived from Centers for Disease Control and Prevention State Highlight reports[16–18] and supplemented by data from state programs.

Analytic Approach

Descriptive Statistics. We began by examining the overall change in the prevalence of youth smoking from 1997 to 2002 and by grade. We also compared the annual rate of change for the period leading up to the campaign (1997–1999) and during the campaign (2000–2002) as a simple indication of whether declines in youth smoking prevalence appeared to accelerate after campaign launch.

Multivariable Logistic Regression. To more precisely isolate the association between current youth smoking prevalence and "truth" campaign exposure, we used population average logistic regression models to estimate current youth smoking prevalence as a function of individual-, media market-, and state-level influences (noted earlier). We also included a linear time variable, taking values from 0 to 6 for the MTF years from 1997 to 2002, to control for the national downward trend in the prevalence of youth smoking that began in 1997 in order to isolate the effects of the campaign from the national trend. Students from the 1997–1999 surveys served as an unexposed comparison group.

We estimated all regressions by combining the cross-sectional 1997–2002 MTF surveys to relate the odds that an individual smoked to his or her media market dose of the campaign, measured at the time of the survey. Cumulative campaign GRPs were scaled such that the estimated odds ratios indicated the odds of smoking, given an increase of 10000 GRPs. All models were estimated separately for 8th, 10th, and 12th grades and all grades combined. All analyses were estimated with sampling weights that corrected for nonresponse and sample design. Standard errors were adjusted for clustering at the school level (schools were the primary sampling unit) using Stata's (version 8.0; Stata Corp, College Station, Tex) SVYLOGIT command. We estimated 2 sets of logistic regressions: 1 with media market indicator variables and 1 with the specific market-level variables—median household income, percentage of the population who were college graduates, and average population size of telephone exchanges within each media market.

A final set of regressions examined the differential effects of the campaign in 2000, 2001, and 2002 to test the hypothesis that the campaign effects on smoking rates in spring 2001 and 2002 were substantially greater than campaign effects measured in the spring 2000 MTF survey—only a few months into the campaign.

We employed 2 methods to illustrate the relationship between youth smoking rates and campaign exposure from the logistic regressions. First, to illustrate to what extent there was evidence of diminishing campaign effects at increasing levels of exposure, we plotted the combined odds ratio for the linear (GRP) and quadratic (GRP^2) exposure variables over a range of GRPs. Second, the inclusion of a precampaign period (1997–1999) allowed us to predict the trend in youth smoking prevalence in the absence of the campaign and hence to estimate the proportion of the decline in youth smoking prevalence attributable to the "truth" campaign after 1999. To do this, we estimated the probability of smoking for each year on the basis of

the multivariable logistic regressions, setting campaign exposure to zero in each postcampaign year for all youths. The difference between the predicted and the actual smoking rates indicated how much lower smoking rates were as a result of the campaign.

RESULTS

The MTF data showed a large decline in current youth smoking prevalence overall and for each grade between 1997 and 2002 (Table 10-1). Among all grades combined, current smoking prevalence decreased by 36% from 1997 to 2002. Eighth-grade students exhibited the largest percentage decline during this period at 45%, whereas 12th-grade students showed the smallest decline at 27%. The descriptive MTF data also indicated that the decline in current smoking prevalence accelerated after the launch of the campaign between 2000 and 2002 (Table 10-1). The annual percentage decline for all grades was 3.2% before the campaign launch (1997–1999) compared with 6.8% after the campaign launch (2000–2002). T tests, based on the observed differences in ratios and a Taylor series approximation of the standard errors of these differences, showed that the post–"truth" campaign annual declines were significantly greater than the pre–"truth" campaign annual declines overall and by grade ($P < .001$). As shown later, the accelerated decline likely occurred in the latter 2 years of the campaign as a lagged effect.

Results of the logistic regression for all grades indicated that there was a statistically significant dose–response relationship between "truth" campaign exposure and current youth smoking prevalence (odds ratio [OR] = 0.78; 95% confidence interval [CI] = 0.63, 0.97; $P < .05$) (Table 10-2). The odds ratio for the quadratic GRPs provides evidence that the effect diminished at higher levels of exposure (OR = 1.11; 95% CI = 1.00, 1.25; $P < .07$). Figure 10-2 illustrates the overall relationship between youth smoking prevalence and "truth" campaign exposure between

---

TABLE 10-1 Changes in Current Smoking Prevalence Among US Students Before and After the Launch of the "Truth" Campaign in 2000: 1997–2002

Grade	Prevalence of Current Smoking, %			Average Annual Percentage Change (95% Confidence Interval)	
	1997	2002	Change	1997–1999	2000–2002
All	28.0	18.0	−35.7	−3.2 (−3.8, −2.6)	−6.8 (−7.5, −6.1)
8th	19.4	10.7	−44.8	−3.4 (−4.6, −2.1)	−9.0 (−10.4, −7.6)
10th	29.8	17.7	−40.6	−4.6 (−5.6, −3.6)	−8.7 (−9.8, −7.5)
12th	36.5	26.7	−26.8	−1.8 (−2.7, −1.0)	−5.1 (−6.1, −3.9)

Source: Farrelly MC, Davis KC, Haviland ML, Messeri P, Healton CG. Evidence of a dose-response relationship between "truth" antismoking ads and youth smoking prevalence. *Am J Public Health.* 2005 Mar; 95(3):425–31.

TABLE 10-2 Impact of "Truth" Campaign on Current Smoking Prevalence Among US Students: Monitoring the Future, 1997–2002

	All Grades, Odds Ratios (95% Confidence Intervals)				1997–2002 by Grade, Odds Ratios (95% Confidence Intervals)		
	1997–2002	1997–1999 + 2000	1997–1999 + 2001	1997–1999 + 2002	8th Grade	10th Grade	12th Grade
"truth" exposure variables							
"truth" exposure (GRP)	0.78** (0.63, 0.97)	0.90 (0.50, 1.62)	0.66** (0.45, 0.98)	0.63*** (0.45, 0.88)	0.61** (0.39, 0.94)	0.98 (0.73, 1.31)	0.79 (0.56, 1.13)
"truth" exposure squared (GRP²)	1.11* (1.00, 1.25)	0.90 (0.34, 2.38)	1.29 (0.94, 1.77)	1.25** (1.04, 1.51)	1.29** (1.01, 1.66)	0.98 (0.84, 1.14)	1.06 (0.87, 1.29)
Other explanatory variables							
Time	0.89*** (0.86, 0.94)	0.92*** (0.87, 0.98)	0.93*** (0.87, 0.98)	0.92*** (0.87, 0.97)	0.88*** (0.81, 0.96)	0.90*** (0.85, 0.95)	0.94** (0.88, 0.99)
Grade 10	1.50*** (1.40, 1.61)	1.47*** (1.34, 1.60)	1.48*** (1.36, 1.62)	1.44*** (1.33, 1.57)	…	…	…
Grade 12	1.97*** (1.84, 2.10)	1.84*** (1.71, 1.99)	1.89*** (1.76, 2.04)	1.90*** (1.77, 2.04)	…	…	…
African American	0.28*** (0.26, 0.30)	0.26*** (0.24, 0.29)	0.28*** (0.26, 0.30)	0.28*** (0.26, 0.30)	0.37*** (0.33, 0.42)	0.27*** (0.24, 0.31)	0.24*** (0.21, 0.27)
Hispanic	0.69*** (0.64, 0.74)	0.68*** (0.63, 0.74)	0.71*** (0.65, 0.77)	0.71*** (0.65, 0.76)	0.88*** (0.79, 0.98)	0.59*** (0.54, 0.67)	0.64*** (0.57, 0.71)
Asian	0.51*** (0.46, 0.56)	0.48*** (0.43, 0.54)	0.51*** (0.46, 0.57)	0.51*** (0.46, 0.57)	0.49*** (0.41, 0.59)	0.55*** (0.47, 0.65)	0.51*** (0.44, 0.58)
Other race/ethnicity	0.91*** (0.86, 0.97)	0.89*** (0.83, 0.95)	0.92*** (0.87, 0.99)	0.93** (0.87, 0.99)	0.95 (0.87, 1.04)	0.92* (0.84, 1.00)	0.86** (0.77, 0.95)
Male	0.91*** (0.88, 0.93)	0.90*** (0.87, 0.94)	0.89*** (0.86, 0.93)	0.89*** (0.86, 0.93)	0.88*** (0.83, 0.94)	0.83*** (0.79, 0.87)	0.99 (0.94, 1.04)
Weekly income	1.01*** (1.01, 1.01)	1.01*** (1.01, 1.01)	1.01*** (1.01, 1.01)	1.01*** (1.01, 1.01)	1.01*** (1.01, 1.01)	1.01*** (1.01, 1.01)	1.01*** (1.01, 1.01)
Mother is high school graduate	0.87*** (0.83, 0.91)	0.87*** (0.83, 0.91)	0.89*** (0.85, 0.94)	0.88*** (0.83, 0.92)	0.76*** (0.69, 0.82)	0.88*** (0.82, 0.94)	1.02 (0.95, 1.10)
Mother had some college	0.82*** (0.78, 0.86)	0.82*** (0.78, 0.87)	0.84*** (0.79, 0.88)	0.82*** (0.78, 0.87)	0.65*** (0.59, 0.70)	0.78*** (0.73, 0.84)	1.06 (0.99, 1.14)
Father is high school graduate	0.72*** (0.75, 0.82)	0.80*** (0.76, 0.84)	0.80*** (0.76, 0.84)	0.79*** (0.75, 0.83)	0.70*** (0.65, 0.76)	0.77*** (0.61, 0.71)	0.88*** (0.81, 0.95)
Father had some college	0.67*** (0.64, 0.70)	0.68*** (0.64, 0.72)	0.70*** (0.66, 0.74)	0.69*** (0.65, 0.73)	0.53*** (0.49, 0.58)	0.66*** (0.61, 0.71)	0.79*** (0.74, 0.86)

Note. GRP = gross rating point. All models include sampling weights, and standard errors were adjusted for school-level clustering. Control variables included media market indicator variables, inflation-adjusted state per capita tobacco control expenditures, state-level average cigarette prices, and indicator variables for missing or unspecified race and parental education data. Odds ratios for the "truth" campaign GRPs represent the odds of smoking for every increase in GRPs by 10,000.

*P < .10; **P < .05; ***P < .01.

Source: Farrelly MC, Davis KC, Haviland ML, Messeri P, Healton CG. Evidence of a dose-response relationship between "truth" antismoking ads and youth smoking prevalence. *Am J Public Health.* 2005 Mar; 95(3): 425-31.

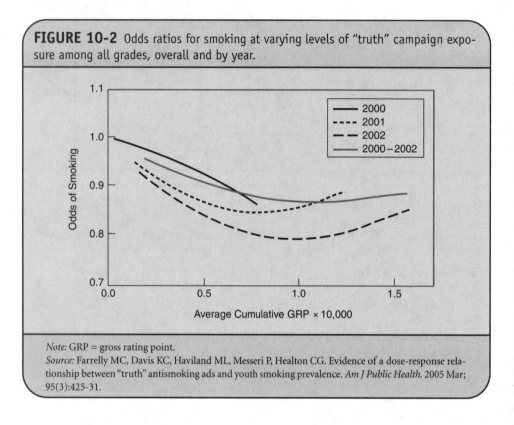

FIGURE 10-2 Odds ratios for smoking at varying levels of "truth" campaign exposure among all grades, overall and by year.

Note: GRP = gross rating point.
Source: Farrelly MC, Davis KC, Haviland ML, Messeri P, Healton CG. Evidence of a dose-response relationship between "truth" antismoking ads and youth smoking prevalence. *Am J Public Health.* 2005 Mar; 95(3):425-31.

2000 and 2002. As shown, the effect of the campaign continued to increase through 10000 GRPs and then began to attenuate as markets experienced higher average cumulative doses of the campaign but the odds ratio remained below 1. This suggested that the campaign could have a larger overall impact if it were feasible to redistribute GRPs from the highest-exposure markets to those with relatively low exposure.

Results calculated from the data presented in Table 10-2 indicate that between 1999 and 2002, the prevalence of smoking among students in all grades combined would have declined by only 5.7 percentage points to 19.6% (95% CI = 18.6%, 20.6%) instead of the actual decline of 7.3 percentage points to 18.0% had the campaign not existed. Therefore, roughly 22% (95% CI = 8.2%, 35.6%) of the total decline in youth smoking prevalence between 1999 and 2002 is attributable to the campaign.

In addition, as hypothesized, there was no statistically significant relationship between overall youth smoking prevalence and the campaign after only a few months of the campaign in 2000, but the effect was statistically significant in 2001 (OR = 0.66; 95% CI = 0.45, 0.98; $P < .05$) and 2002 (OR = 0.63; 95% CI = 0.45, 0.88; $P < .01$) (Table 10-2). To further illustrate the increasing effects of the campaign over time, we calculated the odds of smoking, based on the estimated odds ratios from Table 10-2, at varied levels of cumulative campaign exposure during each of the postlaunch cumulative periods (Figure 10-2). These results suggested that the relationship between overall youth

smoking prevalence and the campaign strengthened over time and, as expected, the campaign showed little effect in 2000.

Separate regressions by grade show the largest effects for 8th-grade students (OR = 0.61; $P < .05$), followed by statistically non-significant effects for 12th- (OR = 0.79; $P = .198$) and 10th- (OR = 0.98; $P = .884$) grade students, respectively (Table 10-2). We also estimated a set of regressions excluding the quadratic GRP term (GRP^2) (results available on request). In this set, the effect was marginally statistically significant for 12th-grade students (OR = 0.879; $P < .07$) but statistically nonsignificant overall and for 8th- and 10th-grade students.

The dose–response relationship for the "truth" campaign is robust across the alternative set of models that control for potential confounding of media market characteristics, such as median household income, percentage of the population who were college graduates, average population size of telephone exchanges within each media market, and state-specific indicator variables (results available on request).

DISCUSSION

The "truth" campaign was associated with significant declines in youth smoking prevalence; thus, its approach to appeal to youths with hard-hitting ads that show at-risk youths rejecting tobacco and that reveal deceptive tobacco industry marketing tactics appears to be effective. Previous research revealed that in its first year, the campaign reached three fourths of American youths and was associated with campaign-related attitudes toward tobacco and the tobacco industry among youths. The current results further validate these early markers of the campaign's success. These findings are consistent with previous research on the effectiveness of antismoking campaigns in general[1,2] and recent state tobacco industry manipulation campaigns.[5,19]

In addition to being consistent with previous findings, this study improves on previous research by reaching generalized conclusions about the effects of antismoking campaigns for youths across the United States and by implementing a pre/post quasi-experimental design that controlled for potential threats to validity, such as secular trends in smoking prevalence, the influence of cigarette prices, state tobacco control programs, and other factors.

Descriptive statistics show that smoking rates declined faster after the launch of the campaign. More significant, this result was confirmed in multivariable analyses that controlled for confounding influences and indicated a dose–response relationship between "truth" campaign exposure and current youth smoking prevalence. To address concerns over the environmental nature of the "truth" campaign exposure measure, we performed sensitivity analyses that showed internally consistent and intuitive results—no effect in the early months of the campaign, diminishing returns, and no statistically significant association between the campaign and drinking among youths (described later). We found that by 2002, smoking rates overall were 1.5 percentage points lower than they would have been in the absence of the campaign, which translates to roughly 300,000 fewer youth smokers based on 2002 US census population statistics. To put our findings in perspective, research indicated that youth smoking prevalence declined by about 1 percentage point per year between 1967 and 1970 during the period of the Fairness Doctrine.[20] It is important to note that these results may also reflect residual impacts from the 1964 *Smoking and Health: Report of the Advisory Committee to the Surgeon General of the Public Health Service*[21] and federal government policies requiring health warnings on all cigarette packages and in all cigarette advertising.

Our findings provide some evidence that the campaign may have the largest impact among 8th-grade students, which is consistent with evidence from Florida that indicates the Florida "truth" campaign led to declines in smoking rates and that smoking rates declined by 50% among middle school students (grades 6 through 8) and by 35% among high school students (grades 9 through 12) from 1998 to 2002.

Our analyses are not without their limitations. Our measures of youth smoking prevalence are self-reported and may be subject to social desirability bias so that youths are less likely to report smoking in areas with high exposure to the campaign than in areas with lower exposure. This would lead to an overstatement of the campaign's effects. However, previous studies have found that underreporting of smoking by youths is minimal.[22–24] Our results also rely on repeated cross-sectional surveys, not repeated measures on the same students, which weakens the strength of our causal inference. However, we included youths surveyed before 2000, so students in the 1997–1999 surveys served as an unexposed control group.

Finally, it is possible that the estimated campaign effects may have been due to other unmeasured youth-focused prevention activities (e.g., in-school substance abuse–prevention programs, the national antidrug campaign by the Office of National Drug Control Policy) that were correlated by chance with the "truth" campaign exposure. To assess this possibility, we used data from the 2000 and 2002 National Youth Tobacco Surveys to examine the correlation between the "truth" campaign exposure and exposure to tobacco use prevention education in schools. In addition, if there was a spurious correlation between "truth" campaign exposure and other prevention activities, we would also have expected to find a correlation between the "truth" campaign and other risk behaviors such as underage drinking. We addressed this potential problem by estimating a series of models identical to those presented in Table 10-2, using indicator variables for any drinking in the past 30 days and any binge drinking in the past 2 weeks as outcome variables.

Although exposure to multistrategy tobacco use prevention education programs in schools has been linked to lower smoking prevalence among middle school students,[25,26] we found no statistically significant differences in reported exposure to tobacco use prevention education programs in schools and exposure to the "truth" campaign. We tested this relationship by comparing self-reported recall of tobacco use prevention education programs in schools from the National Youth Tobacco Surveys by grouping students into the same 5 levels of "truth" campaign exposure illustrated in Figure 10-1.

In addition, we did not find any evidence of a relationship between "truth" campaign exposure and any drinking in the past 30 days (OR = 0.981; P = .848) nor any relationship between "truth" campaign exposure and any binge drinking within the past 2 weeks (OR = 0.857; P = .189), suggesting that "truth" campaign exposure is not spuriously correlated with other prevention efforts. Our results further suggest that the measured "truth" campaign effects on smoking prevalence are not the result of other efforts such as in-school tobacco use prevention education programs and prevention activities aimed at other risk behaviors such as underage drinking.

Under the Master Settlement Agreement, the tobacco industry was obligated to fund Legacy's Public Education Fund for 5 years (through 2003) and is obligated thereafter in any year in which the tobacco companies participating in the Master Settlement Agreement achieve a combined 99.05% market share of US tobacco sales. The continuation of Legacy's efforts, including the "truth" campaign, is presently in question because of these terms. Our findings are consistent with those of other studies that demonstrate that effective antismoking campaigns are critical for public health and that their elimination will likely erase gains that have been made to date in reducing youth smoking prevalence.[27–31]

ACKNOWLEDGMENTS

This study was supported by the American Legacy Foundation. We express our appreciation to Lloyd Johnson and Patrick O'Malley as the principal investigators of Monitoring the

Future (MTF) for their cooperation in providing timely access to the MTF data. We also thank Timothy Perry for his contributions to analysis of the MTF data and Susan Murchie for editorial review.

HUMAN PARTICIPANT PROTECTION

The University of Michigan institutional review board approved the MTF study and the consent information provided to the respondents. No protocol approval was needed for the analysis of the MTF data.

FOOTNOTES

Peer Reviewed

CONTRIBUTORS

M. C. Farrelly contributed to the analytic methodology and conceptual approach, directed all data analyses, and prepared the article. K. C. Davis contributed to the analytic methodology and conceptual approach, conducted all data analyses, and participated in preparing the article. M. L. Haviland participated in the final draft preparation. P. Messeri contributed to the analytic methodology and conceptual approach and participated in the data analysis and final draft preparation. C. G. Healton contributed to the analytic methodology and conceptual approach and participated in the draft and final article preparation.

Accepted for publication October 23, 2004.

REFERENCES

1. Farrelly MC, Niederdeppe J, Yarsevich J. Youth tobacco prevention mass media campaigns: past, present, and future directions. *Tob Control*. 2003; 12(suppl 1): i35–i47.

2. Siegel M. Antismoking advertising: figuring out what works. *J Health Commun*. 2002;7(2):157–162.

3. Wakefield M, Flay B, Nichter M, Giovino G. Effects of anti-smoking advertising on youth smoking: a review. *J Health Commun*. 2003;8(3):229–247.

4. Bauer UE, Johnson TM, Hopkins RS, Brooks RG. Changes in youth cigarette use and intentions following implementation of a tobacco control program: findings from the Florida Youth Tobacco Survey, 1998–2000. *JAMA*. 2000;284:723–728.

5. Sly DF, Hopkins RS, Trapido E, Ray S. Influence of a counteradvertising media campaign on initiation of smoking: the Florida "truth" campaign. *Am J Public Health*. 2001;91:233–238.

6. Farrelly MC, Healton CG, Davis KC, Messeri P, Hersey JC, Haviland ML. Getting to the "truth": evaluating national tobacco countermarketing campaigns. *Am J Public Health*. 2002;92:901–907.

7. Niederdeppe J, Farrelly MC, Haviland ML. Confirming "truth": more evidence of a successful tobacco countermarketing campaign in Florida. *Am J Public Health*. 2004:94:255–257.

8. Evans WD, Price S, Blahut S, Ray S, Hersey JC, Niederdeppe J. Social imagery, tobacco independence, and the truth® campaign. *J Health Commun*. 2004;9: 425–441.

9. Hersey JC, Niederdeppe J, Evans WD, et al. The effects of state counterindustry media campaigns on beliefs, attitudes, and smoking status among teens and young adults. *Prev Med*. 2003;37(6 pt 1):544–552.

10. Johnston LD, Bachman JG, O'Malley PM, Schulenberg J. *Monitoring the Future: A Continuing Study of American Youth (8th, 10th, and 12th Grade Surveys)*. Ann Arbor, Mich: Inter-University Consortium for Political and Social Research; 2003.

11. Glanz K, Lewis FM, Rimer BK. *Health Behavior and Health Education*. San Francisco, Calif: Jossey-Bass Publishers; 1997.

12. Heckman JJ, Hotz VJ. Choosing among alternative nonexperimental methods for estimating the impact of social programs: the case of manpower training. *J Am Stat Assoc*. 1989;84:862–880.

13. *Tax Burden on Tobacco. Historical Compilation*. Vol 37. Arlington, Va: Orzechowski & Walker; 2002.

14. *Reducing Tobacco Use: A Report of the Surgeon General*. Atlanta, Ga: National Center for Chronic Disease Prevention and Health Promotion, Office on Smoking and Health; 2000.

15. Farrelly MC, Pechacek TF, Chaloupka FJ. The impact of tobacco control program expenditures on aggregate cigarette sales: 1981–2000. *J Health Econ*. 2003; 22:843–859.

16. *State Tobacco Control Highlights 1999*. Atlanta, Ga: National Center for Chronic Disease Prevention and Health Promotion, Office on Smoking and Health; 2002.

17. *Investment in Tobacco Control: State Highlights 2001*. Atlanta, Ga: National Center for Chronic Disease Prevention and Health Promotion, Office on Smoking and Health; 2002.

18. *Tobacco Control State Highlights 2002: Impact and Opportunity*. Atlanta, Ga: National Center for Chronic Disease Prevention and Health Promotion, Office on Smoking and Health; 2002.

19. Sly DF, Trapido E, Ray S. Evidence of the dose effects of an antitobacco counteradvertising campaign. *Prev Med*. 2002;35:511–518.

20. Lewit EM, Coate D, Grossman M. The effects of government regulation on teenage smoking. *J Law Econ*. 1981;24:545–569.

21. *Smoking and Health: Report of the Advisory Committee to the Surgeon General of the Public Health Service*. Washington, DC: US Department of Health, Education and Welfare; 1964.

22. Bauman KE, Koch GG. Validity of self-reports and descriptive and analytical conclusions: the case of cigarette smoking by adolescents and their mothers. *Am J Epidemiol*. 1983;118(1):90–98.

23. Bauman KE, Koch GG, Bryan ES. Validity of self-reports of adolescent cigarette smoking. *Int J Addict*. 1982;17:1131–1136.

24. Messeri P, Haviland ML, Mowery P, Gable J, Farrelly MC. A biochemical validation study to assess effects of the "truth" campaign on truthful reporting of current smoking among high school students. Paper presented at the 130th Annual Meeting of the American Public Health Association; November 2002; Philadelphia, Pa.

25. Peterson AV Jr, Kealy KA, Mann SL, Marek PM, Srason IG. Hutchinson Smoking Prevention Project: long-term randomized trial in school-based tobacco use prevention—results on smoking. *J Natl Cancer Inst*. 2000;92: 1979–1991.

26. Wenter DL, Blackwell S, Davis KC, Farrelly MC. *Legacy First Look Report 8: Using Multiple Strategies in Tobacco Use Prevention Education*. Washington, DC: American Legacy Foundation; 2002.

27. Glantz SA. Changes in cigarette consumption, prices, and tobacco industry revenues associated with California's Proposition 99. *Tob Control*. 1993;2: 311–314.

28. Pierce JP, Gilpin EA, Emery SL, et al. Has the California tobacco control program reduced smoking? *JAMA*. 1998;280:893–899.

29. Centers for Disease Control and Prevention. Effect of ending an antitobacco youth campaign on adolescent susceptibility to cigarette smoking—Minnesota, 2002–2003. *MMWR Morb Mortal Wkly Rpt*. 2004; 53(14):301–304.

30. Fichtenberg CM, Glantz SA. Association of the California tobacco control program with declines in cigarette consumption and mortality from heart disease. *N Engl J Med*. 2000;343:1772–1777.

31. Goldman LK, Glantz SA. Evaluation of antismoking advertising campaigns. *JAMA*. 1998;279:772–777.

Overview: The Health Communication Process

Source: Department of Health and Human Services. 2002. "Overview: The Health Communication Process." In *Making Health Communication Programs Work*. Revised version. Washington, DC: National Cancer Institute, National Institutes of Health, U.S. Department of Health and Human Services.

OVERVIEW: THE HEALTH COMMUNICATION PROCESS

The Stages of the Health Communication Process

For a communication program to be successful, it must be based on an understanding of the needs and perceptions of the intended audience. In this book, we incorporate tips on how to learn about the intended audience's needs and perceptions in each of the program stages. Remember, these needs and perceptions may change as the project progresses, so be prepared to make changes to the communication program as you proceed. To help with planning and developing a health communication program, we have divided the process into four stages: Planning and Strategy Development; Developing and Pretesting Concepts, Messages, and Materials; Implementing the Program; and Assessing Effectiveness and Making Refinements. The stages constitute a circular process in which the last stage feeds back into the first as you work through a continuous loop of planning, implementation, and improvement.

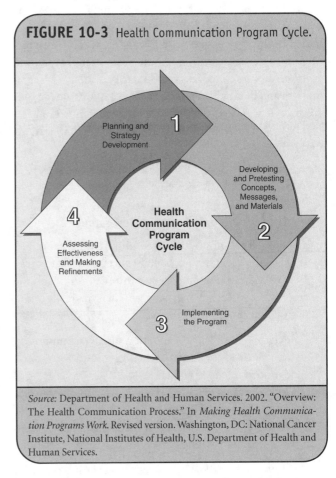

FIGURE 10-3 Health Communication Program Cycle.

Source: Department of Health and Human Services. 2002. "Overview: The Health Communication Process." In *Making Health Communication Programs Work*. Revised version. Washington, DC: National Cancer Institute, National Institutes of Health, U.S. Department of Health and Human Services.

Use this book to produce and implement a plan for a communication program. The final plan will include the following components:

- General description of the program, including intended audiences, goals, and objectives
- Market research plans
- Message and materials development and pretesting plans
- Materials production, distribution, and promotion plans
- Partnership plans
- Process evaluation plan
- Outcome evaluation plan
- Task and time table
- Budget

Because this process is not linear, do not expect to complete a stage and then move to the next, never to go back. You will be exploring opportunities, researching issues, and refining plans and approaches as your organization implements the program. This ongoing, iterative process characterizes a successful communication program.

To help work through program planning and development, we suggest many steps within each stage. You may not find all of the steps suggested in each stage feasible for your program, or even necessary. As you plan, carefully examine available resources and what you want to accomplish with the program and then apply the steps that are appropriate for you. However, if you carefully follow the steps described in each stage of the process, your work in the next phase may be more productive.

Each of the four stages is described here; they are described in more detail in the subsequent sections of this book.

Stage 1: Planning and Strategy Development

In this book, all planning is discussed within the Planning and Strategy Development section, but the concepts you learn there apply across the life cycle of a communication program. During Stage 1 you create the plan that will provide the foundation for your program. By the end of Stage 1, you will have:

- Identified how your organization can use communication effectively to address a health problem
- Identified intended audiences
- Used consumer research to craft a communication strategy and objectives
- Drafted communication plans, including activities, partnerships, and baseline surveys for outcome evaluation

Planning is crucial for the success of any health communication program, and doing careful work now will help you

avoid having to make expensive alterations when the program is under way.

Stage 2: Developing and Pretesting Concepts, Messages, and Materials

In Stage 2, you will develop message concepts and explore them with the intended audience using qualitative research methods. By the end of Stage 2, you will have:

- Developed relevant, meaningful messages
- Planned activities and drafted materials
- Pretested the messages and materials with intended-audience members

Getting feedback from intended audiences when developing messages and materials is crucial for the success of every communication program. Learning now what messages are effective with the intended audiences will help you avoid producing ineffective materials.

Stage 3: Implementing the Program

In Stage 3, you will introduce the fully developed program to the intended audience. By the end of Stage 3, you will have:

- Begun program implementation, maintaining promotion, distribution, and other activities through all channels
- Tracked intended-audience exposure and reaction to the program and determined whether adjustments were needed (process evaluation)
- Periodically reviewed all program components and made revisions when necessary

Completing process evaluations and making adjustments are integral to implementing the program and will ensure that program resources are always being used effectively.

Stage 4: Assessing Effectiveness and Making Refinements

In Stage 4, you will assess the program using the outcome evaluation methods you planned in Stage 1. By the end of Stage 4, you will have:

- Assessed your health communication program
- Identified refinements that would increase the effectiveness of future program iterations

Because program planning is a recurring process, you will likely conduct planning, management, and evaluation activities described in Stages 1–4 throughout the life of the program.

Media Advocacy Manual

Source: APHA. (No Date). *Media Advocacy Manual.* Washington, DC: American Public Health Association, www.apha.org.

ADVOCACY AND PUBLIC HEALTH

Advocacy is used to promote an issue in order to influence policy-makers and encourage social change. Advocacy in public health plays a role in educating the public, swaying public opinion or influencing policy-makers.

Media coverage is one of the best ways to gain the attention of decision-makers, from local elected officials to members of Congress. All monitor the media. Every congressional office has a staff person who monitors the news in the district or state and clips articles that mention the representative or senator by name. These articles are circulated to staff each week. Decisions to support legislative initiatives are frequently influenced by the media coverage.

Getting media coverage can be very easy. By taking a few minutes to write a letter to the editor, any APHA member or public health advocate can reach thousands of other citizens, including policy-makers and their staff. Investing just a little more time can lead to significant payoffs for public health.

You can also use the media to publicize community or state level public health events. Any meeting merits mention in the local newspaper's community calendar, and a workshop or a meeting with an outside speaker may warrant an article as well. Use each of these events to contact local reporters, editorial boards and radio and television talk show hosts. They may want to cover your event, and even if they do not, they will look to you as a resource person when they write about these issues in the future.

"Public health is what we, as a society, do collectively to assure the conditions in which people can be healthy."—The Institute of Medicine

PLANNING YOUR MESSAGE

Before you can begin your advocacy, you need to have a plan. You need to know what the message is that you are trying to get across and you need to know any actions you want to be taken by the public, by other organizations or by legislators.

First, you should establish what your overall goal is. Are you trying to motivate the community to take action on an issue? Are you advocating for a policy or law? Or are you just trying to bring attention to a certain issue? It is important that you have an overall goal before you start so that you can target your audience through the use of the media.

Here are some questions to ask yourself when developing your overall strategy.

- **What is the problem you are highlighting?**—This could be underage drinking, tobacco use, etc. But you should narrow your problem to a specific population. For example, if you start out trying to end all cigarette smoking, you will have a hard time developing a solution and gaining support. But if you narrow it down to underage smoking, you will have an easier time of coming up with a solution.
- **Is there a solution to it? If so, what is it?**—Again, try to narrow this down to a specific population. If you are trying to combat underage smoking, you could advocate for stricter laws for those who sell tobacco to minors.

- **Who can make the solution possible? Whose support do you need to gain in order to make the solution happen?**—In the example of stricter laws for those who sell to-bacco to minors, you would need to target lawmakers. You could do this on a local level or on a national level, depending upon your organization.
- **What do you need to do or say to get the attention of those who can make the solution happen?**—Do you want to use the media to get your message out by holding a news conference or briefing? Or do you want to use advertising to get the attention of the public? Remember, not all advocacy requires the use of the media. Sometimes it is easier to get your message out through marketing and advertising than through news releases and conferences.

Once you have defined your overall goal, then you can design the message that you want to get out in the public. You want your message to be simple and clear. You should point out the problem you are addressing, why your intended audience should be concerned with this problem and what should be done about the problem. Make your message powerful—persuasive and compelling. You will need to say something compelling to capture the attention of the public. Try to create a message that is new and put a human face on it. By humanizing the issue, your issues will have a greater impact on the public than if you just state statistics. Finally, make sure your message targets your intended audience. If you're targeting lawmakers, you will use different language than if you're trying to target the general community.

CONTACTING THE MEDIA

Creating a Media List

Before you begin to contact the media in your area, you should familiarize yourself with the local media. Watch the evening broadcasts and read the paper daily to get a feeling for how different stations and papers cover public health issues. This will give you an idea of who would be most likely to cover your story. Find out which reporters cover public health and track them to see how they cover the issues and if this is the type of reporter you would want to cover your story.

It is also important to think about the audience that the station/paper reaches. You want to make sure that you use the best outlet to reach your intended audience. If you want to mobilize the community, look at a local paper whose readers are mainly in the community you are trying to reach. If you are trying to get the attention of legislators, you may want to find a paper that covers politics and reaches a broader audience. If you want to send a message to your peers, you may want to try a trade magazine (i.e. Non-Profit Times, Healthcare Business Magazine).

Once you know what papers or stations you want to reach, you should create a list of media contacts. This list is perhaps the most important tool for conducting media advocacy. Developing such a list takes time, and it should continuously evolve. You need to get contact information. You will need the names of reporters, editors or producers, their address, phone numbers, fax numbers and e-mail addresses so that you will be able to send them your information in the format most appropriate for the type of story. (Also, some reporters read their e-mail—others do not. It pays to find out which type of format your key reporters prefer.) Keep all of this information for future reference.

To get this information, call the station or paper and ask. You can find out who covers a certain beat (a reporter's "beat" is the issue area he or she covers on a regular basis). If you are not sure with whom you need to talk, you can ask to speak to the news or assignment editor. This is the editor who assigns articles to the reporters and could help send you in the right direction.

Some Relevant Public Health Reporter Beats

Health	Environment	Children's Issues
Tobacco	Public Policy	Science
Medicine	AIDS	Fitness
Health Economics	Health Business	Healthcare

Phone numbers for newspapers, radio and television stations are usually listed in the phonebook. You will need the number of the news desk and once you have that, you can call and get the information you need. More information can be found in resource books such as *Bacon's Media Directories* (www.bacons.com), *Burrelle's Media Directories* (www.burelles.com), *News Media Yellow Book* (leadershipdirectories.com) and *Gale Directory of Publications and Broadcast Media* (www.gale.com). While expensive, these reference books can often be found in local libraries. Also, many stations and papers list contact information on their Web sites.

You could also ask other organizations in your area if they have a media list and share your information. Make sure the organization you are getting your list from focuses on the same type of issues as you do. If they do not, you may end up with a list of reporters who would not be interested in covering your story.

Once you have your list, keep it updated. Keep media sign-in sheets from any news events you hold and keep a log of all contacts you make with the media. Update your list with new contacts. This will keep you up-to-date on who covers which beat so that you will always have that information at your fingertips.

Finally, remember to create a good working relationship with the media. It will work to your advantage if you have a few "friends" in the media. That way, when you are contacting the media, you know that you have a few reporters you can rely on. This will make it easier than trying to contact everyone on your list. One well-placed, comprehensive story told from your organization's point-of-view, has a greater impact than a smattering of brief stories that don't adequately convey your message.

Before Making Contact with the Media

Once you have your message ready and know whom you want to contact in the media, take some time to prepare before you contact anyone. Divide up responsibility in your office, or have volunteers help out. You can divide up responsibility according to talent: designate one person to do any writing that needs to be done, have one person act as spokesperson, etc. This will make the workload lighter.

When choosing a spokesperson, make sure the person you choose is comfortable speaking with the media, answering questions, is knowledgeable on the issue and can stay calm in stressful situations. Dealing with the media can be very frustrating and fastpaced so it is important that your spokesperson be able to remain calm in these situations.

Also, designate certain people on your staff who will speak with the media. They should be the only people to communicate with the press. This way, the media will not get conflicting information from your staff, but the planned message you are trying to get across.

Remember, know the message you are trying to get across and know your information before you speak to the media. Reporters work on deadline and need to get accurate information from you in a timely manner. If a reporter makes contact with you, you do not have to speak to them right away, but may want to take a message and call them back once you are prepared to speak to them. But remember to ask when their deadline is and call back promptly. If you call back after deadline, you may have missed your chance to get your story out.

WAYS OF USING THE MEDIA

There are many different ways you can use the media in advocacy. You can hold news conferences, write letters to the editor, give interviews or arrange editorial board meetings. The method you choose should be the best one to promote your issue.

News Release

Many reporters gather information for upcoming stories from news releases. The news release tells the reporter the who, what, when, where and why of a news story. This information helps the reporter determine whether to write an article or otherwise cover your "news." But remember, reporters receive many news releases over the week, so in order to get yours noticed, your release should quickly grab the reporter or editor's attention and the rest should convince him or her of the issue's news value.

News releases generally follow a standard format. The format is designed to give the reporter or editor all the information he or she needs quickly. By following the same format, all pertinent information, such as contact information, is in the same place and easy for the reporter to find.

The following is the standard format for a news release:

- **Organization's name**. The name of your organization should run across the top of the release. The release should be run on organizational letterhead if possible.
- **Contact information**. Below the name of your organization, you need to put the name and phone/fax number and/or e-mail address of the staff person the press should contact to get more information. This is usually located on the top right-hand corner.
- **Release date**. This tells the reporter when the information in the release can be published or broadcast. The release can be for immediate release to the public, in which you can put "For immediate release" on the top. The reporters can also hold the information until a certain date. For this, you would need to put "Embargoed until (release date and/or time)." The release date is usually located on the top left-hand corner.
- **Headline**. The headline is important. It is a short phrase summing up the essence of the release. This will run under the contact information and above the body of the release.
- **Body**. This is where you will tell the reporter/editor the who, what, where, when and why of your story.

Your release should follow the inverted pyramid style of writing, in which the conclusion or most important information goes first, followed by supporting information. This style of writing is necessary for any news materials because your readers are busy and bombarded with many different pieces of news. You can't count on the reader to get through the entire page so you must give the most important information—the essentials of the story—at the start.

- **The first paragraph, the lead, should be the most powerful.** This is where you should tell the most important information of the release, in order to get the interest of the person reading it.
- **Keep your sentences and paragraphs short and use plain language.** Don't use acronyms or jargon. Also, you should try to keep your release short, one or two pages double-spaced should suffice.
- **Use quotes if possible.** This puts a human face on the news you write. The quote should substantiate the lead,

be from a significant person and add a piece of information. Try to put a quote high in the release, within the first three or four paragraphs.

- **Finish your release with a "tag."** This is usually one paragraph of "boiler plate" information to fill in information holes such as a paragraph description of APHA, your organization or the goals of the work you've highlighted in the release.
- **End.** Reporters/editors look for a symbol at the end of the release to tell them there is no more information. If your release is more than one page, at the end of the first page, type —more— to signal the release continues on the next page. At the end of the release, type —30—, END, or ###. This will be centered on the bottom of the page below the tag.

News releases can be mailed, faxed or e-mailed to reporters. You may want to call the reporter to make sure that he or she has received your release or that the right reporter has it. Remember, reporters are often busy meeting deadlines so make your call brief and to the point.

Letter to the Editor

A letter to the editor is the simplest way to communicate an opinion to the general public. The chances of having the letter printed greatly increases at smaller or less prominent newspapers or magazines. On average, many local papers publish up to 80 percent of the letters they receive. Of course, if you hope to have the letter published in *The New York Times*, then it will compete against hundreds or thousands of other letters.

The most important caveat is to write a letter no longer than what the target newspaper tends to publish. A much longer letter is more likely to be discarded, and if it is not discarded, it is the editor who will decide what information will be cut in order to fit the length requirements. Short, pithy pieces are best.

Before you begin writing your letter, look at the editorial pages of different newspapers. Often, specifications on writing letters to the editor will be on this page. If not, follow these general tips for writing your letter.

- **Be brief and concise.** Focus your letter on just one concept or idea. Limit yourself to 250–300 words.
- **Refer to other stories.** If possible, refer to other articles, editorials or letters the newspaper has recently published. This should be done as soon as possible after the article was published. This will increase its chances of being printed.
- **Include contact information.** Include your name, address and daytime and home phone number so the paper can contact you with any questions. Also, include

any titles and degrees that are relevant to help the media know you have expertise. And make sure to refer to your organization in your letter.

Op-ed

Another way of contacting the media is by writing an opinion piece to be run on a newspaper's opinion-editorial page. Writing an opinion article offers an opportunity to present an extended argument. They run on the page opposite the newspaper's editorials and are typically local and timely. Unlike editorials, op-eds are written by members of the community rather than by journalists. But like editorials, an op-ed often carries more weight than a letter to the editor; it presents a point of view with much greater detail and persuasion than a short letter allows.

Careful planning will increase your chances of placing an op-ed. In addition to submitting an article, mount a campaign to get it published. Be sure to follow up within a week after submitting an article to ensure that it was received and to answer questions the editor might have.

Before you submit your op-ed, you will want to:

- **Obtain guidelines.** Call and ask the editorial page editor or op-ed editor for the newspaper's op-ed policies, i.e., submission guidelines such as length (usually 700–800 words).
- **Talk to the editor.** Try to arrange an appointment with the editorial staff to discuss your unique qualifications for writing an op-ed and the issue's urgency. Use the meeting to sell your issue, your organization and yourself. Some newspapers will not take time to meet with you; they will make a decision based solely on the article. At the very least, the editor might have useful suggestions on how to write your article and improve its chances of being published.
- **Localize it.** Adopt a local angle in your op-ed, even on a national issue. Since you're probably competing for space with nationally syndicated columnists, a local angle can make your article more appealing.

Most papers require exclusivity; you may only submit your op-ed to their publication. If they decline to print it, you are free to submit the piece to another publication.

Editorial Board Meeting

The most powerful way to win support for your issue or reach your member of Congress or local official through the media is to gain the editorial support of your newspaper. Arranging an editorial board meeting will take more time than writing a letter to the editor, but the results are worth the effort. This will give you the chance to persuade the editor why the newspaper's readers would be interested in your story and this could increase the likelihood of more coverage by the newspaper of your issue.

Here are some tips on arranging a meeting:

- **Call the editorial page editor.** Briefly explain the issue and request a meeting. It is best if the issue is tied to a particular news event or local concern.
- **Prepare for the meeting.** Study the issue, write down key facts and list your main points. Think through the local angle. Why should your community or the newspaper's readers—and the editor—care about the issue? It might also help to familiarize yourself with the kinds of editorials and columns that appear in the paper. This will give you insight into the paper's position on certain issues.
- **Present your issue.** You might meet with one editor, or perhaps several editorial writers and reporters will decide to join your meeting. You will have five or 10 minutes to state your case as persuasively as possible, after which you will be asked questions. If you do not know the answers, offer to find out and get back to the editor later.
- **Follow up.** Leave behind some printed material reinforcing the points you have made. After the meeting, send a note of thanks to the editor. If you do not see an editorial within a few days, make a follow-up phone call to the editor. If the editor has decided not to write on your issue, ask if the paper would print an op-ed or at least a letter to the editor submitted by you. Whatever you achieve, you have established yourself and APHA as a source of information on public health issues in your community.

Interview

Another way of working with the media is to give interviews. There are more than 10,000 television and radio stations nationwide, each with producers constantly on the lookout for story ideas and guests to have on their shows. Local talk shows have also become a significant force in national politics. As a member of APHA, you know more about public health issues than most people in your community and can credibly share your concern and knowledge on a local talk show.

Following are some tips to help you arrange and prepare for an interview.

- **Arrange an appearance.** Call or write the talk show host or producer. Explain your interest and experience in a particular aspect of public health, and outline why people in your community should care. Again, it is best to have an upcoming event or a local angle as a "news peg" to make your pitch more attractive.

- **Familiarize yourself with the program.** Learn the name of the host, the show, the station and names of other guests appearing on your program. Find out whether the interview will be live or taped, if there will be call-in questions and the length of the interview. Listen to the program to become familiar with the style and positions of the host and the format of the show.
- **Prepare for the interview.** Write out the most important points you hope to make, including anecdotes and personal stories you want to share, questions you might anticipate and answers to those questions. Role-play answering those questions with a partner. Also, you may want to think out some counter-arguments to your issue and prepare responses to them. Remember that the media usually presents both sides of a story so you want to be able to counter your opponents' viewpoints.

When being interviewed, there are several things to keep in mind to help make the interview go smoothly.

- **Speak in a natural, audible tone.** Remember to remain calm during the interview, even during stressful moments. Do not get defensive or angry. Keep in mind that the reporter decides what goes in the story or what doesn't, so *you don't want to say anything that you would not want to see on the evening news.*
- **Avoid jargon and acronyms.** Remember, not everyone is an expert on your issue. You should use language that will be easily understood by someone outside of your field of expertise.
- **State your message.** Answer interview questions by stating your main message first, followed by supporting points. Use the questions as springboards into developing your message. Present your arguments as concisely as possible while showing enthusiasm for your subject. If you don't know the answer to a question, say so. Also, don't be afraid to speak up if the reporter misstates something or has a wrong fact.
- **Be concise.** It is important to keep your answers short, especially in broadcast interviews. Soundbites in broadcast interviews usually run around eight seconds long, so you want to get your message out quickly. Print reporters also look for concise quotes for their stories. Say what you have to say then wait for the next question. Don't feel compelled to fill "dead air" while waiting for the next question. Some reporters may wait a beat before asking another question, hoping you will jump in and fill the silence. This often results in remarks being made that you wouldn't normally want on the record.

- **Tape yourself.** You may want to bring along a tape recorder to make your own record of what was said in the interview. This way, if there is an error or misquote in the story, you will have your own record of what was actually said. Make sure that everyone involved in the interview knows you are taping it.

When being interviewed for television, there are several additional things to remember.

- **Clothing.** Avoid solid white or black clothing and anything with tight stripes. Solid designs in gray, blue and brown look best. Avoid large, flashy jewelry. Large jewelry will create a reflection off the TV lights. Dress professionally. If you wear a uniform to work (lab coat, military, etc.) consider wearing that for your interview.
- **Look at the interviewer.** Unless otherwise instructed, look directly at the host. Do not look at the camera. Relax and avoid nervous gestures or mannerisms. Use, but do not overuse, your smile and hand gestures.
- **Sit straight.** You want to sit up straight, but not stiff, and lean slightly forward in your chair. Do not lean into the microphone. Avoid swiveling in your chair. If standing, stand up straight. Do not place feet side to side, but plant more weight on one foot. This will keep you from swaying.
- **You're always "on."** Remember, even if you are not speaking, you may still be on camera. And any comments you make prior to or after the formal interview may be caught on camera or tape, so mind your actions.

After the interview, follow up with a note of thanks to the reporter, host or producer of the program. You can often request a taped copy or written transcript of the program for your files. If you provide a videocassette or audiocassette prior to the program, they may make a tape for you. Listen and learn for your next on-air experience. If there is an error in the story, contact the reporter and point out the error and ask for a correction. But remember to remain calm. Also, try to go directly to the reporter to fix the error instead of going over his or her head to the editor or producer. Doing this should only be done if there is a major mistake and the reporter will not acknowledge it. By going over the reporter's head, you may ruin any working relationship you had developed, so this step should only be done in extreme circumstances.

Media Event

In some cases, you may want to consider holding a media event to disseminate your information. The two most common media events are the press briefing and news conference.

A press briefing is held to provide journalists with background information on an issue. A briefing is a good way to provide journalists with an update of key developments and issues, as well as your organization's work and policy, on a certain topic. These meetings can be informal and are a good way to make contacts with the media.

A news conference is held to announce a major story—such as the release of a report, a new policy that has been developed or your organization is taking a new major initiative on an issue.

Press briefings and news conferences are major undertakings and require a lot of work and preparation. But they can be very valuable when you have important information to release, a critical situation has developed, an important speaker has become available or you have a dramatic point of presentation to make on an important issue. Most often, contacting reporters individually or holding a briefing for a small group is a better use of time and resources. But on occasion, you may need to hold a news conference to draw attention to a particular public health issue.

While such an event takes preparation and a lot of legwork, one committed person or a small group sharing the work can undertake it. Consider dividing up the work among your staff to make it easier. Following are a few suggestions for planning and holding a media event.

- **Location.** You will want to find a well-known location that is convenient for journalists to get to. Make sure the room is not too large. This way there won't be a lot of empty seats, giving the impression that few journalists showed up. Also, make sure there is a podium and a table long enough for all of the speakers to sit at. There should also be adequate open space for television cameras, lights and microphones. Usually, television cameras will be placed in the back of the room so there should be plenty of open space in the back. The room should also have plenty of electrical outlets. Popular sites for media events include hotels, local press clubs or public buildings near media offices. Also appropriate is using a location that highlights public health as a backdrop for your issue, i.e., a local health department, a children's hospital, a school or a community park.
- **Timing.** Journalists have very busy schedules so timing is important. The best time to hold an event is around 10 a.m. or 11 a.m. on a Tuesday, Wednesday or Thursday. Plan around competing events, holidays or other activities that may impede journalists from attending your event.
- **Contacting the media.** Send a media advisory several days to a week in advance if you have the luxury of time.

If not, e-mail and fax the advisory. Include in the media advisory the location, time and date of the event, with brief directions if necessary, the names of speakers and an eye-catching summary of the presentation. Follow up with phone calls to the journalists several days later. Call a day or two before the news conference to draw their attention to the release and ask if they or someone from their office plan to attend. This is critical. Newsrooms are swamped with releases, faxes and invitations to events. A follow-up phone call will ensure that your contacts know about the event and remember to put it on their calendars.

- **Materials.** You will want to have material at your press event to give out to the media. The easiest way to hand out material is to put together a press kit. A press kit usually contains news releases, fact sheets and biographies of speakers as well as copies of any reports, case studies, etc., that are being released at the event. Make sure you have plenty of copies of all material with you in case more people attend than planned for. Also, have a sign-in sheet for any journalists attending. Remember to use this sheet to add to and update your media contact list.

- **Prepare.** Set up the room for the number of people that you invited. Don't be disappointed if fewer people showed up than expected. Attendance is hard to predict. Your event may be competing against another news event. Select a moderator for the event. Determine beforehand who will make opening remarks, introduce each speaker and direct questions following the presentation.

- **Resource people.** Have extra people from your staff available to assist at the event. You will need someone to assist journalists before and during the conference. Have some help in handing out media kits, managing the sign-in sheet, directing journalists to phones or handle any other last minute details.

- **Presenting.** Make your formal statement as brief as possible—15 or 20 minutes—while still getting in all the pertinent information and allow time for questions. A general rule of thumb is to limit the number of speakers to no more than five and limit each speaker to three to five minutes. Remember, a news conference is for the media to ask questions, not attend a lecture. Also, start your event on time. Journalists work on deadlines and will need plenty of time to get your story in before deadline.

- **Interviews.** Allow time at the conclusion of the event to take personal interviews, arrange photos or answer more detailed questions.

- **Follow up.** After the event, thank reporters for attending and ask if they need any further information. You may also want to fax or e-mail material to those journalists who were unable to attend. Also, make sure your staff knows who to direct phone calls to from journalists calling for follow-up.

- **Feedback.** Respond in writing to any news stories your event or media outreach garners. Reporters pay attention to response letters—both positive and negative—and will often integrate the comments into future stories.

END NOTES

Cultivating good relationships with reporters will benefit your organization and the public health issues that you work to further. Showing reporters that you value their work—by following the news, finding the appropriate reporter to pitch, expressing your news concisely and giving reporters feedback—will help them value yours.

Some sources for information on media advocacy:

- *News for a Change: An Advocate's Guide to Working with the Media;* by Lawrence Wallack, Iris Diaz, Lori Dorfman, and Katie Woodruff; Sage Publications, Inc., 1999.

- *Media Advocacy and Public Health: Power for Prevention;* by Lawrence Wallack, Lori Dorfman and Makani Themba, Sage Publications, Inc., 1993.

Application of Theory: Global Health

The Part 11 readings center on the complex application of theory-based health promotion programs in a global context that includes multiple levels of government and organization, cross-cultural issues, poverty, globalization, natural crises, domestic politics juxtaposed against those at the global level, and much more. The first selection is an excerpt from an important early formulation of the idea of the *epidemiological transition* (Omran, 1971) that concerns the link between disease/illness patterns and economic development. Second is an excerpt from an article in *Foreign Affairs* magazine (Garrett, 2007) in which the author outlines the overall problem for global health created, among other things, by public and private giving that is narrow and focused on specific diseases, as opposed to broader problems. Finally, the third reading is an excerpt from an excellent discussion of health behavior theory as applied in a global context (Murphy, 2005).

The Epidemiological Transition: A Theory of the Epidemiology of Population Change

Source: Omran AR. 1971. "The Epidemiological Transition: A Theory of the Epidemiology of Population Change." *Milbank Memorial Fund Quarterly* 49: 509–538.

SHIFTS IN MORTALITY AND DISEASE PATTERNS

Proposition Two. During the transition, a long-term shift occurs in mortality and disease patterns whereby pandemics of infection are gradually displaced by degenerative and man-made diseases as the chief form of morbidity and primary cause of death.

Typically, mortality patterns distinguish three major successive stages of the epidemiologic transition:

1. *The Age of Pestilence and Famine* when mortality is high and fluctuating, thus precluding sustained population growth. In this stage the average life expectancy at birth is low and variable, vacillating between 20 and 40 years.
2. *The Age of Receding Pandemics* when mortality declines progressively; and the rate of decline accelerates as epidemic peaks become less frequent or disappear. The average life expectancy at birth increases steadily from about 30 to about 50 years. Population growth is sustained and begins to describe an exponential curve.
3. *The Age of Degenerative and Man-Made Diseases* when mortality continues to decline and eventually approaches stability at a relatively low level. The average life expectancy at birth rises gradually until it exceeds 50 years. It is during this stage that fertility becomes the crucial factor in population growth.

The Age of Pestilence and Famine represents for all practical purposes an extension of the pre-modern pattern of health and disease. In this stage the major determinants of death are the Malthusian "positive checks," namely, epidemics, famines and wars. Graunt's study of London's Bills of Mortality (Graunt 1939) in the mid-seventeenth century shows, for example, that nearly three-fourths of all deaths were attributed to infectious diseases, malnutrition and maternity complications; cardiovascular disease and cancer were responsible for less than six per cent. United Nations compilations, which were used to calculate the cumulative cause-of-death ratios for successive life expectancy levels, show that disease patterns change markedly as life expectancy rises (Department of Economic and Social Affairs 1962). Two sets of data are given according to the preponderant age structure, whether "young" or "old." The trends in the cause-of-death ratio for both population structures are given in Figure Q [not included] and indicate the progressive decline in infectious diseases and concomitant increase in degenerative diseases (as indicated by the cardiovascular and cancer categories) as life expectancy improves. Similar trends are described by the cause-of-death statistics for a number of individual countries, as shown in Figure R [not included]. The gradual shift in disease patterns characteristic of the classical transition can be seen in the steady decline of infectious diseases (including tuberculosis and diarrhea) and the moderate increase in cancer and cardiovascular diseases in England and Wales up to 1920. After World War I, the decline of infectious and rise of degenerative diseases is more distinct, and since 1945 the increase in cardiovascular deaths is particularly striking. The shift from infectious to degenerative disease predominance is more readily apparent for Japan, which has experienced an accelerated transition in only a few decades. Among currently developing nations, the transition from infectious to degenerative disease predominance has started but has not yet been completed, as shown by the graphs for Chile and Ceylon in Figure S [not included]. The recession of infectious diseases that began in Chile in the 1920's has been gradual but discernible. In Ceylon this shift was delayed even further until the late 1940's. The determinants of the transition from infectious to degenerative disease predominance are by no means simple. Their detailed treatment is beyond the scope of this paper; however, it may be useful to mention three major categories of disease determinants.

1. Ecobiologic determinants of mortality indicate the complex balance between disease agents, the level of hostility in the environment and the resistance of the host. More often than not, however, even these determinants cannot be categorically specified. One outstanding example is the recession of plague in most of Europe toward the end of the seventeenth century. The reasons for this recession are not fully understood, although the mysterious disappearance of the black rat may have been a contributing factor. Nonetheless, it is relatively certain that with the possible exception of smallpox, the recession of plague and many other pandemics in Europe was in no way related to the progress of medical science (McKeown and Brown 1955).

2. Socioeconomic, political and cultural determinants include standards of living, health habits and hygiene and nutrition. Hygiene and nutrition are included here, rather than under medical determinants because their improvement in western countries was a byproduct of social change rather than a result of medical design.

3. Medical and public health determinants are specific preventive and curative measures used to combat disease; they include improved public sanitation, immunization and the development of decisive therapies. Medical and public health factors came into play late in the western transition, but have an influence early in the accelerated and contemporary transitions.

The reduction of mortality in Europe and most western countries during the nineteenth century, as described by the classical model of epidemiologic transition, was determined primarily by ecobiologic and socioeconomic factors. The influence of medical factors was largely inadvertent until the twentieth century, by which time pandemics of infection had already receded significantly. The mortality decline in currently developing countries has been more recent and the effect of medical factors has been more direct and more salient, as shown by the contemporary or delayed transition model. In the Afro-Asian countries in particular, the tremendous impact of imported medical technologies on mortality has been magnified by massive public health programs. Although it would

be naive to attempt precise identification of the complex determinants in each case, it does seem apparent that the transition in the now developed countries was predominantly socially determined, whereas the transition in the "third world" is being significantly influenced by medical technology.

REFERENCES

Angel and Pearson. 1953. Cited in W.S. Woytinsky and E.S. Woytinsky, *World Population and Production: Trends and Outlook*. New York: Twentieth Century Fund.

Chambers, J. D. Three Essays on the Population and Economy of the Midlands. In *Glass and Eversley, op. cit.*, 308–53. Department of Economic and Social Affairs. 1962. *Population Bulletin of the United Nations*, No. 6, New York: United Nations, pp. 110–12. 756 *Abdel R. Omran*

Deprez, P. The Demographic Development of Flanders in the Eighteenth Century. In *Glass and Eversley, op. cit.*, 608–30.

Drake, M. 1969. *Population and Society in Norway, 1735–1865*. Cambridge, England: Cambridge University Press.

El-Badry, M. A. December, 1969. Higher Female than Male Mortality in Some Countries of South Asia: A Digest. *Journal of the American Statistical Association* 64:1234–44.

Eversley, D. E. C. 1957. A Survey of Population in an Area of Worcestershire from 1660 to 1850 on the Basis of Parish Registers. *Population Studies* 10:253–79.

Graunt, J. 1939. *Natural and Political Observations Made upon the Bills of Mortality*. Baltimore: The Johns Hopkins Press; this book was originally published in London in 1662.

Hassan, S. 1966. *Influence of Child Mortality on Population Growth*. Ann Arbor, Michigan: University Microfilms.

Heer, D. M. April, 1966. Births Necessary to Assure Desired Survivorship of Sons under Differing Mortality Conditions. Paper presented at the Annual Meeting of the Population Association of America, New York City.

Landis, P. H., and P. K. Hatt. 1954. *Population Problems: A Cultural Interpretation*. New York: American Book Company.

Mayer, K. Autumn, 1962. Developments in the Study of Population. *Social Research* 29:292–320.

McKeown, T., and R. G. Brown. 1955. Medical Evidence Related to English Population Change in the Eighteenth Century. *Population Studies* 9:119–41.

Micklin, M. April, 1968. Urban Life and Differential Fertility: A Specification of the Theory of the Demographic Transition. Presented at the annual meetings of the Population Association of America, Boston.

Reinhard, M., A. Armengaud, and J. Dupaquier. 1968. *Histoire Generale De La Population Mondiale*. Paris: Editions Montchrestien.

Ridley, J. C., et al. January, 1967. The Effects of Changing Mortality on Natality: Some Estimates from a Simulation Model. *Milbank Memorial Fund Quarterly* 45:77–97.

Rostow, W. W. 1960. *Stages of Economic Growth: An Anti-Communist Manifesto*. New York: Cambridge University Press.

Russell, J. C. June, 1958. Late Ancient and Medieval Population. *Transactions of the American Philosophical Society* 48, part 3.

Sauvy, A. 1969. *General Theory of Population*. New York: Basic Books, Inc., Publishers.

United Nations Department of Social Affairs. 1955. Population Branch, Age and Sex Patterns of Mortality: Model Life Tables for *The Epidemiologic Transition* 757 Under-Developed Countries. *Population Studies*, No. 22, New York: United Nations.

Utterstrom, G. 1965. Two Essays on Population in Eighteenth Century Scandinavia. In *Population in History*, edited by D.V. Glass and D.E.C. Eversley, pp. 523–48. Chicago: Aldine Publishing Company.

Van Nort, L., and B. P. Karon. October, 1955. Demographic Transition Reexamined. *American Sociological Review* 20:523–27.

Vielrose, E. 1965. *Elements of the Natural Movement of Populations*. Oxford: Pergamon Press, Inc.

The Challenge of Global Health

Source: Reprinted by permission of *Foreign Affairs*. Garrett L. 2007. "The Challenge of Global Health." *Foreign Affairs*, January/February 2007. Copyright 2007 by the Council on Foreign Relations, Inc. www.ForeignAffairs.org.

BEWARE WHAT YOU WISH FOR

Less than a decade ago, the biggest problem in global health seemed to be the lack of resources available to combat the multiple scourges ravaging the world's poor and sick. Today, thanks to a recent extraordinary and unprecedented rise in public and private giving, more money is being directed toward pressing health challenges than ever before. But because the efforts this money is paying for are largely uncoordinated and directed mostly at specific high-profile diseases—rather than at public health in general—there is a grave danger that the current age of generosity could not only fall short of expectations but actually make things worse on the ground.

This danger exists despite the fact that today, for the first time in history, the world is poised to spend enormous resources to conquer the diseases of the poor. Tackling the developing world's diseases has become a key feature of many nations' foreign policies over the last five years, for a variety of reasons. Some see stopping the spread of HIV, tuberculosis (TB), malaria, avian influenza, and other major killers as a moral duty. Some see it as a form of public diplomacy. And some see it as an investment in self-protection, given that microbes know no borders. Governments have been joined by a long list of private donors, topped by Bill and Melinda Gates and Warren Buffett, whose contributions to today's war on disease are mind-boggling.

Thanks to their efforts, there are now billions of dollars being made available for health spending—and thousands of nongovernmental organizations (NGOs) and humanitarian groups vying to spend it. But much more than money is required. It takes states, health-care systems, and at least passable local infrastructure to improve public health in the developing world. And because decades of neglect there have rendered local hospitals, clinics, laboratories, medical schools, and health talent dangerously deficient, much of the cash now flooding the field is leaking away without result.

Moreover, in all too many cases, aid is tied to short-term numerical targets such as increasing the number of people receiving specific drugs, decreasing the number of pregnant women diagnosed with HIV (the virus that causes AIDS), or increasing the quantity of bed nets handed out to children to block disease-carrying mosquitoes. Few donors seem to understand that it will take at least a full generation (if not two or three) to substantially improve public health—and that efforts should focus less on particular diseases than on broad measures that affect populations' general well-being.

The fact that the world is now short well over four million health-care workers, moreover, is all too often ignored. As the populations of the developed countries are aging and coming to require ever more medical attention, they are sucking away local health talent from developing countries. Already, one out of five practicing physicians in the United States is foreign-trained, and a study recently published in JAMA: The Journal of the American Medical Association estimated that if current trends continue, by 2020 the United States could face a shortage of up to 800,000 nurses and 200,000 doctors. Unless it and other wealthy nations radically increase salaries and domestic training programs for physicians and nurses, it is likely that within 15 years the majority of workers staffing their hospitals will have been born and trained in poor and middle-income countries. As such workers flood to the West, the developing world will grow even more desperate.

Yet the visionary leadership required to tackle such problems is sadly lacking. Over the last year, every major leadership position on the global health landscape has turned over, creating an unprecedented moment of strategic uncertainty. The untimely death last May of Dr. Lee Jong-wook, director general of the World Health Organization (WHO), forced a novel election process for his successor, prompting health advocates worldwide to ask critical, long-ignored questions, such as, Who should lead the fight against disease? Who should pay for it? And what are the best strategies and tactics to adopt?

The answers have not been easy to come by. In November, China's Dr. Margaret Chan was elected as Lee's successor. As Hong Kong's health director, Chan had led her territory's responses to SARS and bird flu; later she took the helm of the WHO's communicable diseases division. But in statements following her election, Chan acknowledged that her organization now faces serious competition and novel challenges. And as of this writing, the Global Fund to Fight AIDS, Tuberculosis, and Malaria remained without a new leader following a months-long selection process that saw more than 300 candidates vie for the post and the organization's board get mired in squabbles over the fund's mission and future direction.

Few of the newly funded global health projects, meanwhile, have built-in methods of assessing their efficacy or sustainability. Fewer still have ever scaled up beyond initial pilot stages. And nearly all have been designed, managed, and executed by residents of the wealthy world (albeit in cooperation with local personnel and agencies). Many of the most successful programs are executed by foreign NGOs and academic groups, operating with almost no government interference inside weak or failed states. Virtually no provisions exist to allow the world's poor to say what they want, decide which projects serve their needs, or adopt local innovations. And nearly all programs lack exit strategies or safeguards against the dependency of local governments.

As a result, the health world is fast approaching a fork in the road. The years ahead could witness spectacular improvements in the health of billions of people, driven by a grand public and private effort comparable to the Marshall Plan—or they could see poor societies pushed into even deeper trouble, in yet another tale of well-intended foreign meddling gone awry. Which outcome will emerge depends on whether it is possible to expand the developing world's local talent pool of health workers, restore and improve crumbling national and global health infrastructures, and devise effective local and international systems for disease prevention and treatment.

SHOW ME THE MONEY

The recent surge in funding started as a direct consequence of the HIV/AIDS pandemic. For decades, public health experts had been confronted with the profound disparities in care that separated the developed world from the developing one. Health workers hated that inequity but tended to accept it as a fact of life, given that health concerns were nested in larger issues of poverty and development. Western AIDS activists, doctors, and scientists, however, tended to have little experience with the developing world and were thus shocked when they discovered these inequities. And they reacted with vocal outrage.

The revolution started at an international AIDS meeting in Vancouver, Canada, in 1996. Scientists presented exhilarating evidence that a combination of anti-HIV drugs (known as antiretrovirals, or ARVs) could dramatically reduce the spread of the virus inside the bodies of infected people and make it possible for them to live long lives. Practically overnight, tens of thousands of infected men and women in wealthy countries started the new treatments, and by mid-1997, the visible horrors of AIDS had almost disappeared from the United States and Europe.

But the drugs, then priced at about $14,000 per year and requiring an additional $5,000 a year for tests and medical visits, were unaffordable for most of the world's HIV-positive population. So between 1997 and 2000, a worldwide activist movement slowly developed to address this problem by putting pressure on drug companies to lower their prices or allow the generic manufacture of the new medicines. The activists demanded that the Clinton administration and its counterparts in the G-8, the group of advanced industrial nations, pony up money to buy ARVs and donate them to poor countries. And by 1999, total donations for health-related programs (including HIV/AIDS treatment) in sub-Saharan Africa hit $865 million—up more than tenfold in just three years.

In 2000, some 20,000 activists, scientists, doctors, and patients gathered in Durban, South Africa, for another international AIDS conference. There, South Africa's former president, Nelson Mandela, defined the issue of ARV access in moral terms, making it clear that the world should not permit the poor of Harare, Lagos, or Hanoi to die for lack of treatments that were keeping the rich of London, New York, and Paris alive. The World Bank economist Mead Over told the gathering that donations to developing countries for dealing with HIV/AIDS had reached $300 million in 1999—0.5 percent of all development assistance. But he characterized that sum as "pathetic," claiming that the HIV/AIDS pandemic was costing

African countries roughly $5 billion annually in direct medical care and indirect losses in labor and productivity.

In 2001, a group of 128 Harvard University faculty members led by the economist Jeffrey Sachs estimated that fewer than 40,000 sub-Saharan Africans were receiving ARVs, even though some 25 million in the region were infected with HIV and perhaps 600,000 of them needed the drugs immediately. Andrew Natsios, then director of the U.S. Agency for International Development (USAID), dismissed the idea of distributing such drugs, telling the House International Relations Committee that Africans could not take the proper combinations of drugs in the proper sequences because they did not have clocks or watches and lacked a proper concept of time. The Harvard faculty group labeled Natsios' comments racist and insisted that, as Sachs put it, all the alleged obstacles to widespread HIV/AIDS treatment in poor countries "either don't exist or can be overcome," and that three million people in Africa could be put on ARVs by the end of 2005 at "a cost of $1.1 billion per year for the first two to three years, then $3.3 billion to $5.5 billion per year by Year five."

Sachs added that the appropriate annual foreign-aid budget for malaria, TB, and pediatric respiratory and diarrheal diseases was about $11 billion; support for AIDS orphans ought to top $1 billion per year; and HIV/AIDS prevention could be tackled for $3 billion per year. In other words, for well under $20 billion a year, most of it targeting sub-Saharan Africa, the world could mount a serious global health drive.

What seemed a brazen request then has now, just five years later, actually been eclipsed. HIV/AIDS assistance has effectively spearheaded a larger global public health agenda. The Harvard group's claim that three million Africans could easily be put on ARVs by the end of 2005 proved overoptimistic: the WHO's "3 by 5 Initiative" failed to meet half of the three million target, even combining all poor and middle-income nations and not just those in Africa. Nevertheless, driven by the HIV/AIDS pandemic, a marvelous momentum for health assistance has been built and shows no signs of abating.

MORE, MORE, MORE

In recent years, the generosity of individuals, corporations, and foundations in the United States has grown by staggering proportions. As of August 2006, in its six years of existence, the Bill and Melinda Gates Foundation had given away $6.6 billion for global health programs. Of that total, nearly $2 billion had been spent on programs aimed at TB and HIV/AIDS and other sexually transmitted diseases. Between 1995 and 2005, total giving by all U.S. charitable foundations tripled, and the portion of money dedicated to international projects soared 80 percent, with global health representing more than

a third of that sum. Independent of their government, Americans donated $7.4 billion for disaster relief in 2005 and $22.4 billion for domestic and foreign health programs and research.

Meanwhile, the Bush administration increased its overseas development assistance from $11.4 billion in 2001 to $27.5 billion in 2005, with support for HIV/AIDS and other health programs representing the lion's share of support unrelated to Iraq or Afghanistan. And in his 2003 State of the Union address, President George W. Bush called for the creation of a $15 billion, five-year program to tackle HIV/AIDS, TB, and malaria. Approved by Congress that May, the President's Emergency Plan for AIDS Relief (PEPFAR) involves assistance from the United States to 16 nations, aimed primarily at providing ARVs for people infected with HIV. Roughly $8.5 billion has been spent to date. PEPFAR's goals are ambitious and include placing two million people on ARVs and ten million more in some form of care by early 2008. As of March 2006, an estimated 561,000 people were receiving ARVs through PEPFAR-funded programs.

The surge in giving has not just come from the United States, however. Overseas development assistance from every one of the nations in the Organization for Economic Cooperation and Development (OECD) skyrocketed between 2001 and 2005, with health making up the largest portion of the increase. And in 2002, a unique funding-dispersal mechanism was created, independent of both the UN system and any government: the Global Fund to Fight AIDS, Tuberculosis, and Malaria. The fund receives support from governments, philanthropies, and a variety of corporate-donation schemes. Since its birth, it has approved $6.6 billion in proposals and dispersed $2.9 billion toward them. More than a fifth of those funds have gone to four nations: China, Ethiopia, Tanzania, and Zambia. The fund estimates that it now provides 20 percent of all global support for HIV/AIDS programs and 66 percent of the funding for efforts to combat TB and malaria.

The World Bank, for its part, took little interest in health issues in its early decades, thinking that health would improve in tandem with general economic development, which it was the bank's mission to promote. Under the leadership of Robert McNamara (which ran from 1968 to 1981), however, the bank slowly increased direct investment in targeted health projects, such as the attempted elimination of river blindness in West Africa. By the end of the 1980s, many economists were beginning to recognize that disease in tropical and desperately poor countries was itself a critical impediment to development and prosperity, and in 1993 the bank formally announced its change of heart in its annual World Development Report. The bank steadily increased its health spending in the following decade, reaching $3.4 billion in 2003 before falling back to $2.1 billion in 2006, with $87 million of that spent on HIV/AIDS, TB, and malaria programs and $250 million on child and maternal health. The bank, along with the International Monetary Fund (IMF), the OECD, and the G-8, has also recently forgiven the debts of many poor nations hard-hit by AIDS and other diseases, with the proviso that the governments in question spend what would otherwise have gone for debt payments on key public services, including health, instead.

When the Asian tsunami struck in December 2004, the world witnessed a profound level of globalized generosity, with an estimated $7 billion being donated to NGOs, churches, and governments, largely by individuals. Although health programs garnered only a small percentage of that largess, many of the organizations that are key global health players were significantly bolstered by the funds.

In January 2006, as the threat of avian influenza spread, 35 nations pledged $1.9 billion toward research and control efforts in hopes of staving off a global pandemic. Since then, several G-8 nations, particularly the United States, have made additional funding available to bolster epidemiological surveillance and disease-control activities in Southeast Asia and elsewhere.

And poor nations themselves, finally, have stepped up their own health spending, partly in response to criticism that they were underallocating public funds for social services. In the 1990s, for example, sub-Saharan African countries typically spent less than 3 percent of their budgets on health. By 2003, in contrast, Tanzania spent nearly 13 percent of its national budget on health-related goods and services; the Central African Republic, Namibia, and Zambia each spent around 12 percent of their budgets on health; and in Mozambique, Swaziland, and Uganda, the figure was around 11 percent.

For most humanitarian and health-related NGOs, in turn, the surge in global health spending has been a huge boon, driving expansion in both the number of organizations and the scope and depth of their operations. By one reliable estimate, there are now more than 60,000 AIDS-related NGOs alone, and there are even more for global health more generally. In fact, ministers of health in poor countries now express frustration over their inability to track the operations of foreign organizations operating on their soil, ensure those organizations are delivering services in sync with government policies and priorities, and avoid duplication in resource-scarce areas.

PIPE DREAMS

One might think that with all this money on the table, the solutions to many global health problems would at least now be in sight. But one would be wrong. Most funds come with strings attached and must be spent according to donors' pri-

orities, politics, and values. And the largest levels of donations are propelled by mass emotional responses, such as to the Asian tsunami. Still more money is needed, on a regular basis and without restrictions on the uses to which it is put. But even if such resources were to materialize, major obstacles would still stand in the way of their doing much lasting good.

One problem is that not all the funds appropriated end up being spent effectively. In an analysis prepared for the second annual meeting of the Clinton Global Initiative, in September 2006, Dalberg Global Development Advisors concluded that much current aid spending is trapped in bureaucracies and multilateral banks. Simply stripping layers of financing bureaucracy and improving health-delivery systems, the firm argued, could effectively release an additional 15–30 percent of the capital provided for HIV/AIDS, TB, and malaria programs.

A 2006 World Bank report, meanwhile, estimated that about half of all funds donated for health efforts in sub-Saharan Africa never reach the clinics and hospitals at the end of the line. According to the bank, money leaks out in the form of payments to ghost employees, padded prices for transport and warehousing, the siphoning off of drugs to the black market, and the sale of counterfeit—often dangerous—medications. In Ghana, for example, where such corruption is particularly rampant, an amazing 80 percent of donor funds get diverted from their intended purposes.

Another problem is the lack of coordination of donor activities. Improving global health will take more funds than any single donor can provide, and oversight and guidance require the skills of the many, not the talents of a few compartmentalized in the offices of various groups and agencies. In practice, moreover, donors often function as competitors, and the only organization with the political credibility to compel cooperative thinking is the WHO. Yet, as Harvard University's Christopher Murray points out, the WGO itself is dependent on donors, who give it much more for disease-specific programs than they do for its core budget. If the WHO stopped chasing such funds, Murray argues, it could go back to concentrating on its true mission of providing objective expert advice and strategic guidance.

This points to yet another problem, which is that aid is almost always "stovepiped" down narrow channels relating to a particular program or disease. From an operational perspective, this means that a government may receive considerable funds to support, for example, an ARV-distribution program for mothers and children living in the nation's capital. But the same government may have no financial capacity to support basic maternal and infant health programs, either in the same capital or in the country as a whole. So HIV-positive mothers are given drugs to hold their infection at bay and prevent passage of the virus to their babies but still cannot obtain even the most rudimentary of obstetric and gynecological care or infant immunizations.

Stovepiping tends to reflect the interests and concerns of the donors, not the recipients. Diseases and health conditions that enjoy a temporary spotlight in rich countries garner the most attention and money. This means that advocacy, the whims of foundations, and the particular concerns of wealthy individuals and governments drive practically the entire global public health effort. Today the top three killers in most poor countries are maternal death around childbirth and pediatric respiratory and intestinal infections leading to death from pulmonary failure or uncontrolled diarrhea. But few women's rights groups put safe pregnancy near the top of their list of priorities, and there is no dysentery lobby or celebrity attention given to coughing babies.

The HIV/AIDS pandemic, meanwhile, continues to be the primary driver of global concern and action about health. At the 2006 International AIDS Conference, former U.S. President Bill Clinton suggested that HIV/AIDS programs would end up helping all other health initiatives. "If you first develop the health infrastructure throughout the whole country, particularly in Africa, to deal with AIDS," Clinton argued, "you will increase the infrastructure of dealing with maternal and child health, malaria, and TB. Then I think you have to look at nutrition, water, and sanitation. All these things, when you build it up, you'll be helping to promote economic development and alleviate poverty."

But the experience of bringing ARV treatment to Haiti argues against Clinton's analysis. The past several years have witnessed the successful provision of antiretroviral treatment to more than 5,000 needy Haitians, and between 2002 and 2006, the prevalence of HIV in the country plummeted from six percent to three percent. But during the same period, Haiti actually went backward on every other health indicator.

Part of the problem is that most of global HIV/AIDS-related funding goes to stand-alone programs: HIV testing sites, hospices and orphanages for people affected by AIDS, ARV-dispersal stations, HIV/AIDS education projects, and the like. Because of discrimination against people infected with HIV, public health systems have been reluctant to incorporate HIV/AIDS-related programs into general care. The resulting segregation has reinforced the anti-HIV stigma and helped create cadres of health-care workers who function largely independently from countries' other health-related systems. Far from lifting all boats, as Clinton claims, efforts to combat HIV/AIDS have so far managed to bring more money to the field but have not always had much beneficial impact on public health outside their own niche.

DIAMONDS IN THE ROUGH

Arguably the best example of what is possible when forces align properly can be found in the tiny African nation of Botswana. In August 2000, the Gates Foundation, the pharmaceutical companies Merck and Bristol-Myers Squibb, and the Harvard AIDS Initiative announced the launching of an HIV/AIDS treatment program in collaboration with the government of Botswana. At the time, Botswana had the highest HIV infection rate in the world, estimated to exceed 37 percent of the population between the ages of 15 and 40. The goal of the new program was to put every single one of Botswana's infected citizens in treatment and to give ARVs to all who were at an advanced stage of the disease. Merck donated its anti-HIV drugs, Bristol-Myers Squibb discounted its, Merck and the Gates Foundation subsidized the effort to the tune of $100 million, and Harvard helped the Botswanan government design its program.

When the collaboration was announced, the target looked easily attainable, thanks to its top-level political support in Botswana, the plentiful money that would come from both the donors and the country's diamond wealth, the free medicine, and the sage guidance of Merck and Harvard. Unlike most of its neighbors, Botswana had an excellent highway system, sound general infrastructure, and a growing middle class. Furthermore, Botswana's population of 1.5 million was concentrated in the capital city of Gaborone. The national unemployment rate was 24 percent—high by Western standards but the lowest in sub-Saharan Africa. The conditions looked so propitious, in fact, that some activists charged that the parties involved had picked an overly easy target and that the entire scheme was little more than a publicity stunt, concocted by the drug companies in the hopes of deflecting criticism over their global pricing policies for AIDS drugs.

But it soon became apparent that even comparatively wealthy Botswana lacked sufficient health-care workers or a sound enough medical infrastructure to implement the program. The country had no medical school: all its physicians were foreign trained or immigrants. And although Botswana did have a nursing school, it still suffered an acute nursing shortage because South Africa and the United Kingdom were actively recruiting its English-speaking graduates. By 2005, the country was losing 60 percent of its newly trained health-care workers annually to emigration. (In the most egregious case, in 2004 a British-based company set up shop in a fancy Gaborone hotel and, in a single day, recruited 50 nurses to work in the United Kingdom.)

By 2002, the once-starry-eyed foreigners and their counterparts in Botswana's government had realized that before they could start handing out ARVs, they would have to build laboratories and clinics, recruit doctors from abroad, and train other health-care personnel. President Festus Mogae asked the U.S. Peace Corps to send doctors and nurses. Late in the game, in 2004, the PEPFAR program got involved and started working to keep HIV out of local hospitals' blood supplies and to build a network of HIV testing sites.

After five years of preparation, in 2005 the rollout of HIV treatment commenced. By early 2006, the program had reached its goal of treating 55,000 people (out of an estimated HIV-positive population of 280,000) with ARVs. The program is now the largest such chronic-care operation—at least per capita—in the world. And if it works, Botswana's government will be saddled with the care of these patients for decades to come—something that might be sustainable if the soil there continues to yield diamonds and the number of people newly infected with HIV drops dramatically.

But Kwame Ampomah, a Ghana-born official for the Joint UN Program on HIV/AIDS, based in Gaborone, now frets that prevention efforts are not having much success. As of 2005, the incidence of new cases was rising eight percent annually. Many patients on ARVs may develop liver problems and fall prey to drug-resistant HIV strains. Ndwapi Ndwapi, a U.S.-trained doctor who works at Princess Marina Hospital, in Gaborone, and handles more of the government's HIV/AIDS patients than anyone else, also frets about the lack of effective prevention efforts. In slums such as Naledi, he points out, there are more bars than churches and schools combined. The community shares latrines, water pumps, alcohol—and HIV. Ndawpi says Botswana's future rests on its ability to fully integrate HIV/AIDS care into the general health-care system, so that it no longer draws away scarce doctors and nurses for HIV/AIDS-only care. If this cannot be accomplished, he warns, the country's entire health-care system could collapse.

Botswana is still clearly somewhat of a success story, but it is also a precariously balanced one and an effort that will be difficult to replicate elsewhere. Ampomah says that other countries might be able to achieve good results by following a similar model, but "it requires transparency, and a strong sense of nationalism by leaders, not tribalism. You need leaders who don't build palaces on the Riviera. You need a clear health system with equity that is not donor-driven. Everything is unique to Botswana: there is a sane leadership system in Gaborone. So in Kenya today maybe the elite can get ARVs with their illicit funds, but not the rest of the country. You need a complete package. If the government is corrupt, if everyone is stealing money, then it will not work. So there is a very limited number of African countries that could replicate the Botswana experience." And despite the country's HIV/AIDS achievements and the nation's diamond wealth, life expectancy for children born in Botswana today is still less than 34 years, according to CIA estimates.

BRAIN DRAIN

As in Haiti, even as money has poured into Ghana for HIV/AIDS and malaria programs, the country has moved backward on other health markers. Prenatal care, maternal health programs, the treatment of guinea worm, measles vaccination efforts—all have declined as the country has shifted its health-care workers to the better-funded projects and lost physicians to jobs in the wealthy world. A survey of Ghana's health-care facilities in 2002 found that 72 percent of all clinics and hospitals were unable to provide the full range of expected services due to a lack of sufficient personnel. Forty-three percent were unable to provide full child immunizations; 77 percent were unable to provide 24-hour emergency services and round-the-clock safe deliveries for women in childbirth. According to Dr. Ken Sagoe, of the Ghana Health Service, these statistics represent a severe deterioration in Ghana's health capacity. Sagoe also points out that 604 out of 871 medical officers trained in the country between 1993 and 2002 now practice overseas.

Zimbabwe, similarly, trained 1,200 doctors during the 1990s, but only 360 remain in the country today. In Kadoma, eight years ago there was one nurse for every 700 residents; today there is one for every 7,500. In 1980, the country was able to fill 90 percent of its nursing positions nationwide; today only 30 percent are filled. Guinea-Bissau has plenty of donated ARV supplies for its people, but the drugs are cooking in a hot dockside warehouse because the country lacks doctors to distribute them. In Zambia, only 50 of the 600 doctors trained over the last 40 years remain today. Mozambique's health minister says that AIDS is killing the country's health-care workers faster than they can be recruited and trained: by 2010, the country will have lost 6,000 lab technicians to the pandemic. A study by the International Labor Organization estimates that 18–41 percent of the health-care labor force in Africa is infected with HIV. If they do not receive ARV therapy, these doctors, nurses, and technicians will die, ushering in a rapid collapse of the very health systems on which HIV/AIDS programs depend.

Erik Schouten, HIV coordinator for the Malawi Ministry of Health, notes that of the country's 12 million people, 90,000 have already died from AIDS and 930,000 people are now infected with HIV. Over the last five years, the government has lost 53 percent of its health administrators, 64 percent of its nurses, and 85 percent of its physicians—mostly to foreign NGOs, largely funded by the U.S. or the British government or the Gates Foundation, which can easily outbid the ministry for the services of local health talent. Schouten is now steering a $270 million plan, supported by PEPFAR, to use financial incentives and training to bring back half of the lost health-care workers within five years; nearly all of these professionals will be put to use distributing ARVs. But nothing is being done to replace the health-care workers who once dealt with malaria, dysentery, vaccination programs, maternal health, and other issues that lack activist constituencies.

Ibrahim Mohammed, who heads an effort similar to Schouten's in Kenya, says his nation lost 15 percent of its health work force in the years between 1994 and 2001 but has only found donor support to rebuild personnel for HIV/AIDS efforts; all other disease programs in the country continue to deteriorate. Kenya's minister of health, Charity Kaluki Ngilu, says that life expectancy has dropped in her country, from a 1963 level of 63 years to a mere 47 years today for men and 43 years for women. In most of the world, male life expectancy is lower than female, but in Kenya women suffer a terrible risk of dying in childbirth, giving men an edge in survival. Although AIDS has certainly taken a toll in Kenya, Ngilu primarily blames plummeting life expectancy on former President Daniel arap Moi, who kept Kenyan spending on health down to a mere $6.50 per capita annually. Today, Kenya spends $14.20 per capita on health annually—still an appallingly low number. The country's public health and medical systems are a shambles. Over the last ten years, the country has lost 1,670 physicians and 3,900 nurses to emigration, and thousands more nurses have retired from their profession.

Data from international migration-tracking organizations show that health professionals from poor countries worldwide are increasingly abandoning their homes and their professions to take menial jobs in wealthy countries. Morale is low all over the developing world, where doctors and nurses have the knowledge to save lives but lack the tools. Where AIDS and drug-resistant TB now burn through populations like forest fires, health-care workers say that the absence of medicines and other supplies leaves them feeling more like hospice and mortuary workers than healers.

Compounding the problem are the recruitment activities of Western NGOs and OECD-supported programs inside poor countries, which poach local talent. To help comply with financial and reporting requirements imposed by the IMF, the World Bank, and other donors, these programs are also soaking up the pool of local economists, accountants, and translators. The U.S. Congress imposed a number of limitations on PEPFAR spending, including a ceiling for health-care-worker training of $1 million per country. PEPFAR is prohibited from directly topping off salaries to match government pay levels. But PEPFAR-funded programs, UN agencies, other rich-country government agencies, and NGOs routinely augment the base salaries of local staff with benefits such as housing and education subsidies, frequently bringing their employees' effective wages to a hundred times what they could earn at government-run clinics.

USAID's Kent Hill says that this trend is "a horrendous dilemma" that causes "immense pain" in poor countries. But without tough guidelines or some sort of moral consensus among UN agencies, NGOs, and donors, it is hard to see what will slow the drain of talent from already-stressed ministries of health.

GOING DUTCH?

The most commonly suggested solution to the problematic pay differential between the wages offered by local governments and those offered by international programs is to bolster the salaries of local officials. But this move would be enormously expensive (perhaps totaling $2 billion over the next five years, according to one estimate) and might not work, because of the problems that stem from injecting too much outside capital into local economies.

In a recent macroeconomic analysis, the UN Development Program (UNDP) noted that international spending on HIV/AIDS programs in poor countries doubled between 2002 and 2004. Soon it will have doubled again. For poor countries, this escalation means that by the end of 2007, HIV/AIDS spending could command up to ten percent of their GDPs. And that is before donors even begin to address the health-care-worker crisis or provide subsidies to offset NGO salaries.

There are three concerns regarding such dramatic escalations in external funding: the so-called Dutch disease, inflation and other economic problems, and the deterioration of national control. The UNDP is at great pains to dismiss the potential of Dutch disease, a term used by economists to describe situations in which the spending of externally derived funds so exceeds domestic private-sector and manufacturing investment that a country's economy is destabilized. UNDP officials argue that these risks can be controlled through careful monetary management, but not all observers are as sanguine.

Some analysts, meanwhile, insist that massive infusions of foreign cash into the public sector undermine local manufacturing and economic development. Thus, Arvind Subramanian, of the IMF, points out that all the best talent in Mozambique and Uganda is tied up in what he calls "the aid industry," and, he says, foreign-aid efforts suck all the air out of local innovation and entrepreneurship. {See Footnote 1} A more immediate concern is that raising salaries for health-care workers and managers directly involved in HIV/AIDS and other health programs will lead to salary boosts in other public sectors and spawn inflation in the countries in question. This would widen the gap

{Footnote 1} In the original version of "The Challenge of Global Health," the view that "foreign aid efforts suck all the air out of local innovation and entrepreneurship" was incorrectly attributed to Steven Radelet.

between the rich and the poor, pushing the costs of staples beyond the reach of many citizens. If not carefully managed, the influx of cash could exacerbate such conditions as malnutrition and homelessness while undermining any possibility that local industries could eventually grow and support themselves through competitive exports.

Regardless of whether these problems proliferate, it is curious that even the most ardent capitalist nations funnel few if any resources toward local industries and profit centers related to health. Ministries of health in poor countries face increasing competition from NGOs and relief agencies but almost none from their local private sectors. This should be troubling, because if no locals can profit legitimately from any aspect of health care, it is unlikely that poor countries will ever be able to escape dependency on foreign aid.

Finally, major influxes of foreign funding can raise important questions about national control and the skewing of health-care policies toward foreign rather than domestic priorities. Many governments and activists complain that the U.S. government, in particular, already exerts too much control over the design and emphasis of local HIV/AIDS programs. This objection is especially strong regarding HIV-prevention programs, with claims that the Bush administration has pushed abstinence, fidelity, and faith-based programs at the expense of locally generated condom- and needle-distribution efforts.

Donor states need to find ways not only to solve the human resource crisis inside poor countries but also to decrease their own dependency on foreign health-care workers. In 2002, stinging from the harsh criticism leveled against the recruitment practices of the NHS (the United Kingdom's National Health Service) in Africa, the United Kingdom passed the Commonwealth Code of Practice for the International Recruitment of Health Workers, designed to encourage increased domestic health-care training and eliminate recruitment in poor countries without the full approval of host governments. British officials argue that although the code has limited efficacy, it makes a contribution by setting out guidelines for best practices regarding the recruitment and migration of health-care personnel. No such code exists in the United States, in the EU more generally, or in Asia—but it should.

Unfortunately, the U.S. Congress has gone in the opposite direction, acceding to pressure from the private health-care sector and inserting immigration-control exemptions for health-care personnel into recent legislation. In 2005, Congress set aside 50,000 special immigration visas for nurses willing to work in U.S. hospitals. The set-aside was used up by early 2006, and Senator Sam Brownback (R-Kans.) then sponsored legislation eliminating all caps on the immigration of nurses. The legislation offers no compensation to the countries from which the nurses

would come—countries such as China, India, Kenya, Nigeria, the Philippines, and the English-speaking Caribbean nations.

American nursing schools reject more than 150,000 applicants every year, due less to the applicants' poor qualifications than to a lack of openings. If it fixed this problem, the United States could be entirely self-sufficient in nursing. So why is it failing to do so? Because too few people want to be nursing professors, given that the salaries for full-time nurses are higher. Yet every year Congress has refused to pass bills that would provide federal support to underfunded public nursing schools, which would augment professors' salaries and allow the colleges to accept more applicants. Similar (although more complex) forms of federal support could lead to dramatic increases in the domestic training of doctors and other health-care personnel.

Jim Leach, an outgoing Republican member of the House of Representatives from Iowa, has proposed something called the Global Health Services Corps, which would allocate roughly $250 million per year to support 500 American physicians working abroad in poor countries. And outgoing Senator Bill Frist (R-Tenn.), who volunteers his services as a cardiologist to poor countries for two weeks each year, has proposed federal support for sending American doctors to poor countries for short trips, during which they might serve as surgeons or medical consultants.

Although it is laudable that some American medical professionals are willing to volunteer their time abroad, the personnel crisis in the developing world will not be dealt with until the United States and other wealthy nations clean up their own houses. OECD nations should offer enough support for their domestic health-care training programs to ensure that their countries' future medical needs can be filled with indigenous personnel. And all donor programs in the developing world, whether from OECD governments or NGOs and foundations, should have built into their funding parameters ample money to cover the training and salaries of enough new local health-care personnel to carry out the projects in question, so that they do not drain talent from other local needs in both the public and the private sectors.

WOMEN AND CHILDREN FIRST

Instead of setting a hodgepodge of targets aimed at fighting single diseases, the world health community should focus on achieving two basic goals: increased maternal survival and increased overall life expectancy. Why? Because if these two markers rise, it means a population's other health problems are also improving. And if these two markers do not rise, improvements in disease-specific areas will ultimately mean little for a population's general health and well-being.

Dr. Francis Omaswa, leader of the Global Health Workforce Alliance—a WHO-affiliated coalition—argues that in his home country of Zambia, which has lost half of its physicians to emigration over recent years, "maternal mortality is just unspeakable." When doctors and nurses leave a health system, he notes, the first death marker to skyrocket is the number of women who die in childbirth. "Maternal death is the biggest challenge in strengthening health systems," Omaswa says. "If we can get maternal health services to perform, then we are very nearly perfecting the entire health system."

Maternal mortality data is a very sensitive surrogate for the overall status of health-care systems since pregnant women survive where safe, clean, round-the-clock surgical facilities are staffed with well-trained personnel and supplied with ample sterile equipment and antibiotics. If new mothers thrive, it means that the health-care system is working, and the opposite is also true.

Life expectancy, meanwhile, is a good surrogate for child survival and essential public health services. Where the water is safe to drink, mosquito populations are under control, immunization is routinely available and delivered with sterile syringes, and food is nutritional and affordable, children thrive. If any one of those factors is absent, large percentages of children perish before their fifth birthdays. Although adult deaths from AIDS and TB are pushing life expectancies down in some African countries, the major driver of life expectancy is child survival. And global gaps in life expectancy have widened over the last ten years. In the longest-lived society, Japan, a girl who was born in 2004 has a life expectancy of 86 years, a boy 79 years. But in Zimbabwe, that girl would have a life expectancy of 34 years, the boy 37.

The OECD and the G-8 should thus shift their targets, recognizing that vanquishing AIDS, TB, and malaria are best understood not simply as tasks in themselves but also as essential components of these two larger goals. No health program should be funded without considering whether it could, as managed, end up worsening the targeted life expectancy and maternal health goals, no matter what its impacts on the incidence or mortality rate of particular diseases.

Focusing on maternal health and life expectancy would also broaden the potential impact of foreign aid on public diplomacy. For example, seven Islamic nations (Afghanistan, Egypt, Iraq, Pakistan, Somalia, Sudan, and Yemen) lose a combined 1.4 million children under the age of five every year to entirely preventable diseases. These countries also have some of the highest maternal mortality rates in the world. The global focus on HIV/AIDS offers little to these nations, where the disease is not prevalent. By setting more encompassing goals, government agencies such as USAID and its British counterpart could both save lives in these nations and give them a legitimate reason to believe that they are welcome members of the global health movement.

Legislatures in the major donor nations should consider how the current targeting requirements they place on their funding may have adverse outcomes. For example, the U.S. Congress and its counterparts in Europe and Canada have mandated HIV/AIDS programs that set specific targets for the number of people who should receive ARVs, be placed in orphan-care centers, obtain condoms, and the like. If these targets are achievable only by robbing local health-care workers from pediatric and general health programs, they may well do more harm than good, and should be changed or eliminated.

In the philanthropic world, targeting is often even narrower, and the demand for immediate empirical evidence of success is now the norm. From the Gates Foundation on down to small family foundations and individual donors, there is an urgent need to rethink the concept of accountability. Funders have a duty to establish the efficacy of the programs they support, and that may require use of very specific data to monitor success or failure. But it is essential that philanthropic donors review the relationship between the pressure they place on recipients to achieve their narrow targets and the possible deleterious outcomes for life expectancy and maternal health due to the diversion of local health-care personnel and research talent.

SYSTEMS AND SUSTAINABILITY

Perched along the verdant hillsides of South Africa's KwaZulu-Natal Province are tin-roofed mud-and-wood houses, so minimal that they almost seem to shiver in the winter winds. An observant eye will spot bits of carved stone laying flat among the weeds a few steps from the round houses, under which lay the deceased. The stones are visible evidence of a terrifying death toll, as this Zulu region may well have the highest HIV prevalence rate in the world.

At the top of one hill in the Vulindlela area resides Chief Inkosi Zondi. A quiet man in his early 40s, Zondi shakes his head over the AIDS horror. "We can say there are 40,000 people in my 18 subdistricts," he says. "Ten thousand have died. So about 25 percent of the population has died." In this rugged area, only about ten percent of the adults have formal employment, and few young people have much hope of a reasonable future. Funerals are the most commonplace form of social gathering. Law and order are unraveling, despite Chief Zondi's best efforts, because the police and the soldiers are also dying of AIDS.

In such a setting, it seems obvious that pouring funds into local clinics and hospitals to prevent and treat HIV/AIDS should be the top priority. For what could be more important than stopping the carnage?

But HIV does not spread in a vacuum. In the very South African communities in which it flourishes, another deadly scourge has emerged: XDR-TB, a strain of TB so horribly mutated as to be resistant to all available antibiotics. Spreading most rapidly among people whose bodies are weakened by HIV, this form of TB, which is currently almost always lethal, endangers communities all over the world. In August 2006, researchers first announced the discovery of XDR-TB in KwaZulu-Natal, and since then outbreaks have been identified in nine other South African provinces and across the southern part of the continent more generally. The emergence of XDR-TB in KwaZulu-Natal was no doubt linked to the sorry state of the region's general health system, where TB treatment was so poorly handled that only a third of those treated for regular TB completed the antibiotic therapy. Failed therapy often promotes the emergence of drug-resistant strains.

There is also an intimate relationship between HIV and malaria, particularly for pregnant women: being infected with one exacerbates cases of the other. Physicians administering ARVs in West Africa have noticed a resurgence of clinical leprosy and hepatitis C, as latent infections paradoxically surge in patients whose HIV is controlled by medicine. HIV-positive children face a greater risk of dying from vaccine-preventable diseases, such as measles, polio, and typhoid fever, if they have not been immunized than do those nonimmunized children without HIV. But if financial constraints force health-care workers to reuse syringes for a mass vaccination campaign in a community with a Vulindlela-like HIV prevalence, they will almost certainly spread HIV among the patients they vaccinate. And if the surgical instruments in clinics and hospitals are inadequately sterilized or the blood-bank system lacks proper testing, HIV can easily spread to the general population (as has happened in Canada, France, Japan, Kazakhstan, Libya, Romania, and elsewhere).

As concern regarding the threat of pandemic influenza has risen worldwide over the last two years, so has spending to bolster the capacities of poor countries to control infected animal populations, spot and rapidly identify human flu cases, and isolate and treat the people infected. It has become increasingly obvious to the donor nations that these tasks are nearly impossible to perform reliably in countries that lack adequate numbers of veterinarians, public health experts, laboratory scientists, and health-care workers. Moreover, countries need the capacity to coordinate the efforts of all these players, which requires the existence of a public health infrastructure.

At a minimum, therefore, donors and UN agencies should strive to integrate their infectious-disease programs into general public health systems. Some smaller NGOs have had success with community-based models, but this needs to become the norm. Stovepiping should yield to a far more generalized effort to raise the ability of the entire world to prevent, recognize, control, and treat infectious diseases—and then move on to do the same for chronic killers such as diabetes and heart disease in the long term. Tactically, all aspects of prevention and treatment should be part of an integrated effort, drawing from countries' finite pools of health talent to tackle all monsters at once, rather than dueling separately with individual dragons.

David de Ferranti, of the Brookings Institution, reckons that meeting serious health goals—such as getting eight million more people on ARVs while bringing life expectancies in poor countries up to at least the level of middle-income nations and reducing maternal mortality by 15–20 percent—will cost about $70 billion a year, or more than triple the current spending.

Even if such funds could be raised and deployed, however, for the increased spending to be effective, the structures of global public health provision would have to undergo a transformation. As Tore Godal, who used to run the neglected-diseases program at the WHO, recently wrote in *Nature*, "There is currently no systemic approach that is designed to match essential needs with the resources that are actually available." He called for a strategic framework that could guide both donations and actions, with donors thinking from the start about how to build up the capabilities in poor countries in order to eventually transfer operations to local control—to develop exit strategies, in other words, so as to avoid either abrupt abandonment of worthwhile programs or perpetual hemorrhaging of foreign aid.

In the current framework, such as it is, improving global health means putting nations on the dole—a $20 billion annual charity program. But that must change. Donors and those working on the ground must figure out how to build not only effective local health infrastructures but also local industries, franchises, and other profit centers that can sustain and thrive from increased health-related spending. For the day will come in every country when the charity eases off and programs collapse, and unless workable local institutions have already been established, little will remain to show for all of the current frenzied activity.

DOC-IN-A-BOX

As a thought experiment, the Council on Foreign Relations' Global Health Program has conceived of Doc-in-a-Box, a prototype of a delivery system for the prevention and treatment of infectious diseases. The idea is to convert abandoned shipping containers into compact transportable clinics suitable for use throughout the developing world.

Shipping containers are durable structures manufactured according to universal standardized specifications and are able to be transported practically anywhere via ships, railroads, and trucks. Because of trade imbalances, moreover, used containers are piling up at ports worldwide, abandoned for scrap. Engineers at Rensselaer Polytechnic Institute converted a sample used container into a prototype Doc-in-a-Box for about $5,000, including shipping. It was wired for electricity and fully lit and featured a water filtration system, a corrugated tin roofing system equipped with louvers for protection during inclement weather, a newly tiled floor, and conventional doors and windows. Given economies of scale and with the conversions performed in the developing world rather than New York, it is estimated that large numbers of Doc-in-a-Boxes could be produced and delivered for about $1,500 each.

Staffed by paramedics, the boxes would be designed for the prevention, diagnosis, and treatment of all major infectious diseases. Each would be linked to a central hub via wireless communications, with its performance and inventory needs monitored by nurses and doctors.

Governments, donors, and NGOs could choose from a variety of models with customizable options, ordering paramedic training modules, supplies, and systems-management equipment as needed. Doc-in-a-Box could operate under a franchise model, with the paramedics involved realizing profits based on the volume and quality of their operations. Franchises could be located in areas now grossly underserved by health clinics and hospitals, thus extending health-care opportunities without generating competitive pressure for existing facilities.

On a global scale, with tens of thousands of Doc-in-a-Boxes in place, the system would be able to track and respond to changing needs on the ground. It would generate incentives to pull rapid diagnostics, easy-to-take medicines, new types of vaccines, and novel prevention tools out of the pipelines of biotechnology and pharmaceutical companies. Supplies could be purchased in bulk, guaranteeing low per-unit costs. And the sorts of Fortune 500 companies that now belong to the Global Business Coalition on HIV/AIDS, TB, and Malaria would be able to provide services and advice.

Over time, Doc-in-a-Box could emerge as sustainable local businesses, providing desperately needed health-care services to poor communities while generating investment and employment, like branches of Starbucks or McDonald's.

Promoting Healthy Behavior

Source: Excerpt from Murphy EM. May 2005. "Promoting Healthy Behavior." *Health Bulletin Number 2*. Washington, DC: Population Reference Bureau.

APPLYING BEHAVIOR CHANGE THEORIES AND TOOLS

Being mindful of successful programs that have used behavior-change theories and tools will help health planners design the most effective interventions[63] to address disease control priorities in developing countries or to achieve the related Millennium Development Goals. New approaches must also be tried; a wide range of interventions—both large-scale and small-scale—provide promising models.

The case histories described below use a combination of behavior-change tools and reflect the ecological behavior-change theories described earlier. Although aiming primarily to change behaviors of individuals and communities, these case histories also focus on the behavior of health system officials and policymakers, and address important contextual factors.

Case History:
Reducing Malnutrition

The first Millennium Development Goal—"Eradicate extreme poverty and hunger"—combines hunger and poverty for a good reason: both are inextricably linked in a downward spiral. Poverty predisposes people to hunger and hunger to disease. Disease in turn exacerbates poverty by draining already strained household resources and reducing or destroying the ability of

adults to work and children to attend school, further reducing actual or future earnings. A sound public health approach aims to interrupt this cycle of hunger, poverty, and disease.[64]

One important way to address malnutrition is to reduce micronutrient deficiencies, the "hidden hunger" that affects the health of billions.[65] The Canada-based nonprofit Micronutrient Initiative (MI) and its many partners around the world have done just that. Working with WHO, UNICEF, the World Bank, national governments, the private sector, and communities, MI has fostered unprecedented cooperation for widespread fortification of common foods with needed micronutrients or their distribution as food supplements. Since 1990, this remarkable partnership has brought worldwide attention to the consequences of micronutrient malnutrition and demonstrated what can be done about it. MI has worked with the Expanded Program of Immunization in countries around the world to distribute vitamin A and other micronutrient supplements during National Immunization Days, and the partnership has convinced and helped salt producers and millers of corn and wheat to fortify their products. These efforts have resulted in strong progress toward controlling widespread micronutrient malnutrition:

- As the result of a long-term MI campaign to iodize all of the world's edible salt, and with the cooperation of the salt industry, more than 70 percent of the world's population has access to iodized salt—one of the most impressive public health success stories of the latter half of the 20th century.
- In the year 2000 alone, MI met 75 percent of the world's need for vitamin A supplements. In a three-year period,

vitamin A supplements helped save the lives of more than 1 million children.

- Addressing iron deficiency is more difficult, but there are signs of progress. In Bangladesh, for example, MI and partners support government measures to protect young women from iron deficiency. Before marriage and pregnancy, adolescent girls are given iron supplements, counseling, and nutrition education to help prevent iron deficiency and anemia during pregnancy. In India, three of every four pregnant women now take at least some iron/folate tablets. In Darjeeling, a subdistrict of West Bengal, fortified flour is distributed to low-income groups through the public distribution system. Social marketing and health communications strategies have generated consumer awareness and demand for fortified flour. Mills in Iran commenced fortifying flour in 2001.

- Given the number of people who can be reached, large-scale programs are the most desirable, but are not feasible everywhere. A recent pilot study of fortification of maize with multiple micronutrients in Zambia showed that small-scale programs are also feasible and acceptable to local people and millers.

- Multiple-fortified salt—combining iodine, vitamin A, and iron—is a strong possibility for the future that MI is supporting. If all three of these micronutrient deficiencies could be addressed through a single universal mechanism, the number of lives saved would undoubtedly soar. The technology for double fortification of salt is already developed and being scaled up; research is well under way on triple-fortified salt.[66]

MI and its many partners developed an effective program model that reveals understanding of human behavior at every level: building political commitment, raising concern among community leaders and citizens, initiating and providing the tools for action, building consensus and networks, leveraging resources and transferring ownership, demonstrating success, and increasing the capacity of local entities to carry on the work. In turn, MI was itself an example of global social mobilization. Based on growing research, the scientific community first called the world's attention to micronutrient malnutrition in the late 1970s and early 1980s. The Micronutrient Initiative was born out of the pledge of the 1990 World Summit for Children to protect the world's children against malnutrition. In 2002, the UN General Assembly Special Session on Children reaffirmed the pledges to end childhood malnutrition.[67] The fact that three of the top 10 risks for the burden of disease

are micronutrient deficiencies shows that this good work must continue at an accelerated pace. The halving of hunger and poverty by 2015 as the first MDG bodes well for this possibility.

Case History: Combating HIV/AIDS

Uganda is one of the earliest AIDS success stories, having experienced first a dramatic decline in HIV incidence (new infections) and then prevalence (total infections), beginning in the early 1990s. The drop in HIV rates among pregnant women—a proxy for the general population—has been corroborated by data from the U.S. Census Bureau; the Joint United Nations Programme on HIV/AIDS (UNAIDS) and its predecessor, the WHO Global Programme on AIDS; and other research. National HIV adult prevalence in Uganda peaked at about 15 percent in 1991, fell to 5 percent by the late 1990s, and stood at just above 4 percent in 2003.[68]

What happened in Uganda? Although deaths from AIDS must be factored in, Uganda's falling HIV prevalence is most likely attributable to the nationwide diffusion of an innovation: sexual behavior change.[69] The acronym ABC stands for those primary changes in behavior the population was urged to adopt: Abstinence, or delay of sexual debut; Being faithful, or reducing one's number of partners; or using Condoms. While the relationship between the large variety of interventions to fight AIDS and the decline in HIV rates in Uganda is not completely understood, a 2002 analysis identifies these key elements:[70]

- High-level political support to address HIV led to a multisectoral response. In 1986, after 15 years of civil strife, popular Ugandan President Yoweri Museveni began addressing the population almost nonstop via the media and in face-to-face gatherings about a new enemy—the growing AIDS epidemic. Asked later about his leadership, he replied: "When a lion comes to the village, shout!"[71] He emphasized that fighting AIDS was a patriotic duty and that openness, communication, and strong leadership were needed at every level of society. By 2001, approximately 700 government agencies and NGOs were working on HIV/AIDS issues across all districts in Uganda.

- Decentralized behavior-change campaigns reached general populations and key at-risk groups. Uganda launched an aggressive public campaign against HIV that included print materials, radio, and billboards, but mostly relied on grass-roots community mobilization. Its STD/AIDS Control Programme trained thousands of community-based AIDS counselors, health educators, peer educators, and other types of specialists. Led by their leaders' examples, and because of decentralized allocation of resources, the general population in both urban and rural areas eagerly joined the fight against AIDS. HIV touched every community visibly,[72] prompting effective mobilization.

- Interventions addressed women and youth, stigma and discrimination. From the highest governmental to the grassroots levels, behavior change efforts emphasized empowerment of women and girls. Without this supportive environment, it is unlikely that women could adopt ABC behaviors.[73] Teachers and other change agents reached youth both in and out of school. Messages from leaders to fight stigma and discrimination against persons living with HIV/AIDS had an impact. Although it still exists, stigma has been reduced to a level that creates a safer climate for seeking counseling and testing and for disclosing HIV status.

- Religious leaders and faith-based organizations were mobilized to lead AIDS education and care activities. Mainstream faith-based organizations— Catholic, other Christian, Islamic, and traditional— wield enormous influence in Uganda and used this influence to fight AIDS and encourage acceptance of those infected. Mission hospitals were among the first to develop AIDS care and support programs in Uganda. One of hundreds of faith-based initiatives, the AIDS education project implemented in rural Muslim communities by the Islamic Medical Association of Uganda was selected as a "Best Practices Case Study" by UNAIDS.[74]

- Uganda initiated Africa's first confidential voluntary counseling and testing (VCT) services. In 1990, the first center for anonymous VCT opened in Kampala; within two years the services spread to centers in four major urban areas as the stigma-reduced environment encouraged large numbers of people to find out their HIV status. Rapid HIV tests gave same-day results and "Post-Test Clubs" provided long-term support for behavior change to those tested, regardless of status.

- Social marketing of condoms played an important but not a major role. In the beginning, Uganda's president and some religious leaders resisted condom promotion but, by the mid-1990s, resistance had generally faded. By that time, nearly all the decline in HIV incidence had already occurred. In more recent years, increased condom use, particularly among high-risk groups, probably has contributed to the continuing declines.

- Control and prevention programs for STIs received increased emphasis. Since 1994, after declines in HIV prevalence began to be documented, two donor-funded projects helped to improve STI diagnosis and treatment. By the end of the 1990s, drug supplies were adequate and distribution to rural health facilities had improved.

Primary behavior change—a decrease in multiple sexual partners—appears to be the single most important determinant of the reduction in HIV incidence in Uganda. For the most part, Ugandans who are sexually active now have no or significantly fewer nonregular sex partners.[75] Such behavioral changes appear related to communication of AIDS prevention information through social networks arising from nationwide grassroots mobilization. Acquiring information from trusted role models and peers is likely to have personalized risk more effectively, resulting in greater behavior change and ultimately fewer HIV infections.[76] Efforts to bring about this unprecedented decline in HIV rates were remarkably cost-effective— about $1.80 per adult per year over the 10-year period.[77]

More recently, in the Rakai district of Uganda, there has been a rise in casual sexual relationships. Although there has been an accompanying rise in reported condom use,[78] this increase in sexual networking is worrisome to some analysts.[79]

Case History:
Reducing the Toll of Malaria

According to WHO, malaria is the eighth-highest disease burden worldwide and the fifth-highest for the poorest developing countries. This mosquito-borne disease disproportionately afflicts and kills children under 5 and pregnant women. WHO's Roll Back Malaria initiative has set targets for halving the total number of deaths from malaria and ensuring that at least 60 percent of those at risk benefit from, among other things, insecticide-treated mosquito nets by the year 2010.[80] Sleeping under insecticide-treated bednets (ITNs) can reduce mortality by up to 63 percent and morbidity by at least 40 percent.[81] Because these strategies require behavior change at every level, WHO has developed a training module for health personnel managing malaria programs, Communication for Behavioural Impact to Roll Back Malaria.[82]

In one effort to help stimulate commercial investment in ITNs, the U.S. Agency for International Development (USAID) launched NetMark, an innovative consortium led by the Academy for Educational Development that has formed international partnerships with 13 major firms (representing more than 80 percent of the global capacity to produce and distribute the bednets) to develop ITN markets and expand the availability of affordable ITNs in Africa.[83] The program has helped eliminate taxes and tariffs on ITNs in Mali, Senegal, and Zambia. In 2002, the program launched ITN marketing in Ghana, Nigeria, Senegal, and Zambia, selling more than 600,000 ITNs and 500,000 insecticide re-treatments during its first five months of operation.[84]

NetMark designs and implements consumer focused marketing campaigns based on behavioral theory and research, using a full range of mass media and community-based communication tools. Commercial marketing reduces the burden on the public sector by creating demand for bednets and then supplying them to those who can afford to pay, thereby allowing the public sector to use its limited resources to focus on those who cannot afford to pay. At the same time, NetMark is working to ensure sustained equitable provision of ITNs for the poor and is supporting country efforts to access the resources of the Global Fund for AIDS, Tuberculosis and Malaria,[85] which aims to provide 40 million ITNs over a five-year period. NetMark also primes the market for commercial expansion, building the capacity and quality of local ITN production among African-based manufacturers. Given NetMark's successes in implementing its approach in several countries, this investment in a new and replicable model for a sustainable health intervention and partnership with the commercial sector bodes well for both health and economic advances in Africa.

Case History:
Helping Children Survive

As mammals, human beings are "hardwired" to protect their young. Yet each year, an estimated 10.6 million children in low- and middle-income countries die before they reach their fifth birthday.[86] Seventy percent of these deaths are due to just five preventable and treatable conditions: pneumonia, diarrhea, malaria, measles, and malnutrition. Deaths often result from a combination of these conditions.[87]

In reality, the glass is half-full as well as half-empty. When public health leaders have considered such sad statistics, they have marshaled expertise, resources, and political will to organize public health campaigns to increase child survival. These efforts have paid off. Rates of deaths to children under age 5 have dropped from 148 deaths per 1,000 children in 1955 to under 59 deaths per 1,000 children in 2000.[88] Since the 1950s, an increasingly effective public health "toolkit" has helped save children's lives. It includes vaccines to prevent major contagious diseases, antibiotics to treat infections, and oral rehydration

salts to save children suffering from extreme diarrhea—plus exclusive breastfeeding, a free and effective "technology." In addition, mass media has joined interpersonal approaches to reach millions with messages to use these lifesaving tools.

Breastfeeding is Mother Nature's way to nourish and protect young infants. Any form of breastfeeding reduces by one-half a baby's chance of dying before age 1, compared with no breastfeeding. However, doing it right—initiating breastfeeding immediately after birth, breastfeeding exclusively for the first six months, and introducing nutritious complementary feeding after six months—is an even more powerful tool for infant health. This optimal form of breastfeeding could save an estimated 1.5 million infant lives each year that otherwise would be lost to diarrhea and acute respiratory infections.[89] The USAID-funded Linkages Project is using theory-driven behavior change strategies to work with policymakers, health workers, communities, and family members to create a supportive environment for optimal breastfeeding.[90]

In each country, the Linkages Project first influences policies relevant to optimal breastfeeding by forming active partnerships with government health and nutrition leaders, NGOs, international agencies, and academic institutions. Policy analysis and stakeholder workshops have proved essential for building consensus and mobilizing resources for program interventions to support optimal breastfeeding. The Linkages Project identifies six elements common to its interventions in different countries:

- Formative research that analyzes benefits and barriers to change within each relevant segment of the population and identifies the specific and desired actions that people will be able to adopt;
- Targeted, concise, and pretested messages to promote the "do-able" actions;
- Counseling and communication skills for health and community workers;
- Consistent messages and materials across program communication channels to address critical behaviors;
- Saturation of specific audiences with messages through appropriate media (electronic, print, interpersonal, event-based, and traditional approaches such as songs and puppet shows); and
- Support of the mother and peer group interaction such as mother-to-mother support groups, women's clubs, or other existing groups at the local level.[91]

Results are impressive. The rates of timely initiation of breastfeeding almost doubled in Madagascar (from 34 percent to 60 percent) and Ghana (from 32 percent to 62 percent), and rose 25 percent in Bolivia. The rate of exclusive breastfeeding nearly doubled in Madagascar (from 46 percent to 83 percent), increased significantly in Ghana, and showed a slight rise in Bolivia. While the already high rates of timely complementary feeding did not increase in these countries, the proportion of mothers who gave better quality complementary foods to their infants went up.

Although breastfeeding helps to prevent diarrhea, oral rehydration therapy (ORT) is a lifesaver for those children who do have acute diarrheal episodes and risk of dying of dehydration. A WHO report estimates that deaths attributable to diarrhea fell from 4.6 million in 1980 to 1.5 million in 1999—a decline of two thirds—and the widespread adoption of ORT can claim much of this success. Use of ORT spread during the 1980s in several countries and eventually around the world. This diffusion occurred in spite of difficulties related to proper mixing and the limitations of oral rehydration salts (ORS) to treat only dehydration and not diarrhea itself.[92] ORT now helps save more than 1 million children's lives each year.[93]

In Egypt, deaths due to diarrhea declined by 82 percent in the 1980s. The National Control of Diarrheal Diseases Program became fully operational in 1984; by the end of the decade, ORT was being used to treat between one-third and one-half of all diarrheal episodes. To shape its approach, the ORT campaign conducted research on consumer preferences and cultural practices. Intensive behavior-change strategies were used, including the training of health professionals, pharmacists, and journalists. Education on the importance of ORT reached the general public through interpersonal channels and mass media. Evaluators consider social marketing and the mass media campaign the most important elements of success. Unlike most developing countries, television reached almost all households in the mid-1980s and thus was the primary channel that spread core messages even to poor rural households. TV spots had wide appeal and were bolstered by a popular "motherly" soap opera star as spokesperson. Billboards on roads and posters and pamphlets in pharmacies and clinics complemented the continual airing of TV spots.[94]

Community health workers provided practice sessions for mothers to mix ORS; the mothers learned quickly and most were able to mix the solution correctly. In addition, easy-to-use ORS became widely available. Mothers used ORS twice as often when diarrhea was perceived to be severe rather than mild, a specific message of the communication campaign. The campaign also urged mothers to continue feeding their babies during diarrheal episodes, in contrast to the normative practice of withholding food; there were also positive changes in this regard. Hospital admissions for severely dehydrated children dropped and deaths of infants due to diarrhea fell more rapidly than those due to other causes. The WHO evaluation concluded that the behavioral changes on the part of mothers and the health system personnel in case management accounted for most of the reduction in mortality attributable to diarrhea.[95]

Recent research shows that ORS itself can be improved: Reducing concentrations of salt and sugar in ORS and supplementing it with zinc reduces the duration and severity of diarrhea and is significantly more cost-effective than earlier formulations of ORS.[96] In addition, mothers who gave their children zinc syrup with ORS were 75 percent less likely to give them antibiotics, a common but unnecessary practice leading to antibiotic resistance.[97] New WHO/UNICEF guidelines recommend specific behaviors for mothers, health workers, and government policymakers to translate these findings into reality.[98]

No discussion of strategies to improve children's health would be complete without the joint WHO and UNICEF initiative called Integrated Management of Childhood Illness (IMCI). Its goal is to save children's lives and foster their growth and development by changing behavior at several levels. IMCI combines several effective child survival programs so that not just one but several illnesses can be averted or managed effectively at the same time. Why is this initiative necessary? Every day, many of the millions of sick children taken to hospitals, health centers, pharmacists, doctors, and traditional healers are not properly assessed or treated. Parents frequently receive either poor or no advice from health personnel and may have dangerously delayed seeking care. In poor countries, drugs, supplies, and equipment are often scarce, and diagnostic tools such as radiology and laboratory tests are minimal or nonexistent. Health workers tend to rely on history and symptoms to determine a course of treatment that makes the best use of their available resources.[99]

IMCI encourages the preventive and curative behaviors that together largely determine the health of a child. IMCI has three main components: improving case management skills of health care staff; improving overall health systems; and improving family and community health practices. While IMCI is now considered the standard in preventing and treating childhood illnesses, evaluations in Bangladesh, Brazil, Peru, Tanzania, and Uganda found that only one component was successful so far: IMCI training for health workers in first-level health facilities has led to rapid and sustained improvement in health workers' performance in managing children's illnesses. However, ministries of health and their partners in these sites have not been able to expand training beyond a few pilot districts. Evaluators conclude that scaling up IMCI will require a stronger commitment to improved management and supervision, greater funding, and reduced staff turnover. There is also a need for stepped-up outreach to communities to increase care-seeking behaviors.[100] It will be worth the effort: The synergies of this approach provide the best hope for improving child health on a grand scale.

Case History:
Improving Maternal Health

Of the 529,000 maternal deaths that occur worldwide each year,[101] 99 percent of them take place in poor countries. For every woman who dies, another 30 to 50 women suffer serious and long-term complications.[102] Consequently, pregnancy-related complications are among the leading causes of death and disability for women in developing countries. Because many people also see maternal mortality as a human rights issue,[103] interventions to influence policymakers' decisions relevant to maternal health have often included appeals to conscience. The fact that reducing maternal mortality is one of the Millennium Development Goals is itself a testimony to policy communications skills within the Safe Motherhood Initiative, a global effort to reduce deaths and illness associated with pregnancy and childbirth.

Sometimes a catchy phrase is a catalyst to awaken dormant concern. A 1985 journal article by two public health leaders made clear that maternal and child health services (MCH) were overwhelmingly oriented to child health, and neglected mothers' health. The article's subtitle—"Where is the 'M' in 'MCH'?"—became a rallying cry for advocacy.[104] Even with a few earlier, notable efforts to reduce deaths of women in childbirth, the Safe Motherhood movement did not gather steam until the mid-1980s,[105] and the widespread dissemination of "Where is the 'M' in 'MCH'?" gave it a leap forward. Health policymakers everywhere were challenged to answer the question and to provide funding. Since the obstetrical emergencies that kill women cannot be predicted, antenatal visits, vitamins, and even trained birth attendants would not be enough. Those serious about reducing maternal deaths would also have to provide emergency obstetric care (EmOC), including blood transfusions and Caesarean sections.

Sri Lanka and Malaysia were pioneers in reducing maternal mortality; well before the 1980s, committed policymakers and health planners began programs that reached key people and eventually changed health workers' and community members' behavior throughout those two countries. The programs provide well-documented lessons on how poor countries can gradually cut maternal mortality rates by one-half or more.[106] Their successes also energized the Safe Motherhood movement and provided a model to follow, thereby accelerating progress. The commitment of health policymakers reached by the Safe Motherhood Initiative has led to rapid programmatic

success in reducing maternal mortality in Bolivia, Yunan province in China, Egypt, Honduras, Indonesia, Jamaica, and Zimbabwe.[107]

In addition, successful models can be adapted and implemented on a much wider scale. The six-year, multicountry, multiagency Averting Maternal Death and Disability (AMDD) Program, supported by the Bill & Melinda Gates Foundation, provides technical assistance to improve women's access to lifesaving EmOC in more than 50 countries where health policymakers and planners have responded to the promise offered by the project.[108] Over a three-year period, AMDD Program activities covered almost 180 million people and more than 270,000 women were treated for obstetrical complications—an average increase of 144 percent. Case fatalities decreased by more than 50 percent.[109] A major element of success has been the integration of life-saving technologies with the behavior change strategies needed to make them widely available—and used.

The White Ribbon Alliance for Safe Motherhood is another large-scale initiative, a grassroots movement now in 24 countries that initiates awareness-raising campaigns and builds practical, action-oriented alliances among communities, government health workers, and NGOs to prevent needless maternal and neonatal deaths. These activities have paid off. In Indonesia, for example, 70 percent of women exposed to the campaign used a skilled provider for childbirth, compared with 44 percent who were not exposed; and 41 percent exposed to the campaign knew that bleeding during pregnancy was a danger sign, compared with 16 percent not exposed.[110] Women's health experts are pleased by such successes but are keenly aware that in addition to substantial funding, further progress in improving maternal health will require outspoken and determined champions from within the health system and among decision-makers and politicians.[111]

Case History:
Making Family Planning a Norm

Being able to control one's fertility through means other than unsafe abortions is a step forward on the long journey to women's empowerment.[112] Because unplanned and poorly timed pregnancies pose serious health risks to women and infants,[113] the adoption of modern family planning methods by millions of women in the developing world is an advance in public health and illustrates well the widespread diffusion of an innovation.[114] As of 2004, an estimated 60 percent of married women of reproductive age in developing countries were using some means of family planning, compared with 15 percent in 1960; in 2004, 54 percent were using modern contraceptives.[115] Over the same period, fertility in these countries also dropped from over six children per women to just over three; while overall development played a larger part, more than 40 percent of this change is attributable to family planning program efforts.[116]

While the history of individual efforts to regulate fertility is ancient, the first large-scale organized family planning program began in the 1950s in India. Beginning in the 1960s, as rapid population growth increasingly was perceived as a major factor in environmental deterioration and poverty, research findings and high-level political advocacy groups convinced foreign assistance agencies, foundations, and eventually government programs around the world to promote and fund family planning services. In 1965, USAID received congressional authorization to include population and family planning programs in its aid to poor nations. Eventually, USAID became the single largest population donor among a large number of bilateral donors and private foundations. Although successful in the long run, family planning programs have always generated controversy.[117]

However, "organized family planning programs" were indeed organized and worked tirelessly to overcome resistance. Governments and NGOs designed and launched networks of freestanding family planning clinics, or, in some regions of the world such as sub-Saharan Africa, integrated family planning services into maternal and child health services. China and India undertook their own programs early on and vigorously implemented. Bilateral and multilateral donors, foundations, and the International Planned Parenthood Federation provided significant funding and technical assistance to other countries, including Bangladesh, Thailand, Indonesia, Egypt, Morocco, Kenya, and Zimbabwe. These countries undertook a massive number of workshops to train doctors, nurses, and other health workers to offer modern methods of contraception and to counsel clients in their use. Counselors offered pamphlets on available methods of family planning—even if clients could not read. At the same time, significant resources were invested in developing new methods of contraception and eventually the variety of modern methods available in clinics grew to meet clients' similarly varied needs and preferences.

Some organizations focused on promoting family planning. Community events, puppet shows, dancers, singers, and other face-to-face approaches publicized the existence of family planning services, reassured potential clients of their harmlessness, and encouraged local women—and, far more rarely, men—to utilize them. While newspapers, magazines, and television reached the elite opinion leaders with messages about the negative effects of population growth, other forms of mass media—radio, posters, comic books, and billboards—reached millions of poor and often illiterate or low-literate audiences. Soap operas with family planning themes were broadcast during prime time on radio; as radio coverage grew rapidly, these soap operas reached most of the population.[118] In rural villages and poor city neighborhoods, community leaders supported group talks and films (using portable generators) on family planning. Promoters also used folk entertainment to transmit messages about the desirability of family planning while amusing the audience. Actors frequently portrayed poor mothers and fathers beleaguered by many children, while in the next scene other actors portrayed a stylish and well-off couple who chose to have only two children.[119] While this approach may not have prompted immediate contraceptive adoption, ongoing messages of this type probably contributed to smaller family size norms. Door-to-door promotion and distribution of nonclinical contraceptives was a response to cultural constraints in countries where women could not travel to clinics. This approach worked so well in increasing the number of women in rural Bangladesh who used these contraceptives that "community-based distribution" earned fame, its own acronym—CBD—and was scaled up nationally in Bangladesh and replicated elsewhere.

CBD programs, with local modifications, became a frequent adjunct to clinic-based services in many parts of the world. Also in Bangladesh, a program based on social networks used community inquiry centers called Jiggashas to help move family planning from an individual to a social norm; in these communities, family health workers became group discussion facilitators and not just transmitters of information and supplies.[120]

Social marketing soon joined other approaches to publicize, promote, and distribute contraceptive pills and condoms through pharmacies and other retailers at low subsidized prices. Social marketing used mass media, particularly radio, posters, and billboards, to encourage those with sufficient means to purchase their contraceptives in retail outlets.[121] Eventually, with perseverance in disseminating persuasive messages, expansion of available and affordable contraceptives and services, and the spread of successful models to other countries, family planning was transformed from a controversial innovation into a global norm.[122]

TOWARD EFFECTIVE HEALTH PROMOTION PROGRAMS

Lessons learned from many years of designing and implementing behavior-change interventions can be applied and adapted effectively in health promotion programs:[123]

- Identify the specific health problem to be addressed and the corresponding behaviors that, if changed, will ameliorate the problem. Identify the key actors at every relevant level, from the individual to the policymaker.

- Know and use sound behavioral theories in designing health promotion programs.
- Review and conduct thorough research about and with key actors; understand underlying behavioral reasons for the health problem, including biologic, environmental, cultural and other contextual factors, and likely motivations and constraints to change. Pay particular attention to barriers to change and vulnerabilities due to social and structural inequities.
- Include the participation of relevant stakeholders as true partners in the design, implementation, and evaluation of the intervention, using participatory assessment and learning tools.
- Do not neglect the practical necessities: careful planning and budgeting to ensure the right timing, the appropriate duration of activities to show results and undertake evaluation, identification of the right partners, and selection of the best people to work on the project. Monitor the occurrence, quality, and coverage of activities and make needed corrections.
- Ask key stakeholders to identify role models and peers who exhibit "positive deviance"—healthy behaviors different from the social norm—that the program can enlist to support its objectives. Role models who appeal to program managers may not appeal to youth or other beneficiaries.
- Work to create an enabling environment through policy dialogue, advocacy, and capacity building. Based on the likelihood that nonhealth sectors represent important contextual factors for health-related behavior, be prepared to involve and coordinate other sectoral efforts.
- Organize a multifaceted intervention that addresses both specific behaviors and contextual factors and reaches policymakers, gatekeepers, and direct beneficiaries. To reach key audiences, use communication channels identified through research such as mass media, face-to-face community activities, training of health workers, and policy-influencing conferences, with coordinated, mutually reinforcing messages and opportunities for community discussion.
- Work to ensure sustainability. Identify mechanisms and local assets for reinforcement of positive behavior on the individual level, institutionalization at the organizational level, and sound policies and resource mobilization at the policy level. Build on cultural values and traditions that foster mutual help and social cohesion.

- Build in evaluation from the beginning. Ideally, design an evaluation with experimental and control groups and gather baseline data; evaluate at the end of the project, six months later, one year later, and, if possible, up to five years later. Include qualitative and participatory methods to ensure stakeholder perspectives are represented. Disseminate findings widely in user-friendly reports and meetings.
- Form partnerships to scale up and/or adapt the most successful interventions for implementation in other settings.

CONCLUSION

Although idealistic public health officials in the late 1970s pledged to attain "health for all" by the dawn of the 21st century, recent health statistics reveal a different reality. Despite progress, good health still eludes billions of people, and serious health challenges remain everywhere. Analysis of risk factors for the major burdens of disease—deaths and disabilities caused by illness and injuries—reveals the central role of human behavior as both causes of and solutions to health problems.

Both the Millennium Development Goals and the identification of disease control priorities reflect a remarkable consensus of world leaders: to eradicate or dramatically reduce our most serious health and related development problems. Achievement will depend on behavior change at every level—individuals, families, communities, organizations, and policymaking bodies. Fortunately, evidence-based behavioral theories and successful behavior-change case histories point the way. Bolstered by political will and adequate resources, adaptations of successful programs and new approaches will go a long way toward ensuring health for all. We do not have to wait for the next millennium.

REFERENCES

63. Donald Nutbeam and Elizabeth Harris, *Theory in a Nutshell: A Guide to Health Promotion Theory* (New York: McGraw-Hill, 1999).

64. John Walley et al., *Public Health: An Action Guide to Improving Health in Developing Countries* (New York: Oxford University Press, 2001): 168.

65. World Bank, "Nutrition," *At-a-Glance* (Washington, DC: The World Bank, 2003): 1.

66. The Micronutrient Initiative, *A Decade of Progress, A Lifetime of Hope*, accessed online at www.micronutrient.org, on Nov. 28, 2004.

67. UN, *A World Fit for Children*, report of the 2002 UN General Assembly Special Session on Children, accessed online at www.unicef.org, on Dec. 2, 2004.

68. UNAIDS, *2004 Report on the Global AIDS Epidemic*, accessed online at www.unaids.org, on Dec. 2, 2004.

69. Edward C. Green, *Rethinking AIDS Prevention: Learning from Successes in Developing Countries* (Westport, CT: Praeger Publishers, 2003).

70. Janice A. Hogle, ed., *What Happened in Uganda?* (Washington, DC: U.S. Agency for International Development (USAID), 2002).

71. Arvind Singhal and Everett M. Rogers, *Combating AIDS: Communication Strategies in Action* (Thousand Oaks, CA: Sage Publications, 2002): 376.

72. Joan Haffey, personal communication, Feb. 21, 2005.

73. Elaine M. Murphy and Margaret Greene, "Defending the ABCs: A Feminist Perspective" (2005, submitted for publication).

74. UNAIDS, "The IMAU AIDS Education Project in Uganda," *UNAIDS Best Practices*, accessed online at www.unaids.org, on Nov. 13, 2004.

75. Rand Stoneburner and Daniel Low-Beer. "Population-Level HIV Declines and Behavioral Risk Avoidance in Uganda," *Science* 302, no. 30 (2004): 714–18.

76. Rand Stoneburner et al., "Enhancing HIV Prevention in Africa: Investigating the Role of Social Cohesion on Knowledge Diffusion and Behavior Change in Uganda," presentation at U.S. Agency for International Development, Washington, DC, 2000.

77. Hogle, *What Happened in Uganda?*

78. CNN.com, "Study: Condoms keep AIDS in check in Uganda," accessed online at www.cnn.com, on March 9, 2005.

79. James D. Shelton, "Partner Reduction Remains the Dominant Explanation," letter to the editor of *British Medical Journal* online, accessed online at http://bmj.bmjjournals.com, on March 9, 2005.

80. WHO, "Roll Back Malaria," accessed online at http://mosquito.who.int, on Nov. 14, 2004.

81. USAID, "Our Work: Malaria," accessed online at www.usaid.gov, on Nov. 13, 2004.

82. WHO, *Communication for Behavioural Impact to Roll Back Malaria* (Geneva: WHO, 2002): i.

83. Academy for Educational Development (AED), "NetMark," accessed online at www.netmarkafrica.org, on Nov. 14, 2004.

84. USAID, "Our Work: Malaria."

85. The Global Fund for AIDS, Tuberculosis and Malaria, accessed online at www.theglobalfund.org, on Nov. 14, 2004.

86. UNICEF, *State of the World's Children 2005*, accessed online at www.unicef.org, on Jan. 23, 2005.

87. World Bank, *Child Health at-a-Glance* 1 (2002), accessed online at www.worldbank.org, on Nov. 21, 2004.

88. Levine et al., *Millions Saved: Proven Successes in Global Health*: 1.

89. UNICEF, *Facts for Life*, 3d ed. (New York: UNICEF, 2002), as cited in *Experience Linkages* (Washington, DC: AED, 2003).

90. AED, "Linkages Project," accessed online at www.linkagesproject.org, on Nov. 22, 2004.

91. AED, *Experience Linkages*.

92. Cesar G. Victora et al., "Reducing Deaths from Diarrhoea through Oral Rehydration Therapy," *Bulletin of the World Health Organization* 78, no. 10 (2000): 1246–55.

93. Rehydration Project, accessed online at http://rehydrate.org, on Feb. 21, 2005.

94. Ruth Levine et al., "Preventing Diarrheal Deaths in Egypt," in *Millions Saved: Proven Successes in Global Health*," ed. Ruth Levine et al. (Washington, DC: Center for Global Development, 2004).

95. Victora et al., "Reducing Deaths from Diarrhoea through Oral Rehydration Therapy."

96. Bjarne Robberstad et al., "Cost-Effectiveness of Zinc as Adjunct Therapy for Acute Childhood Diarrhoea in Developing Countries," *Bulletin of the World Health Organization* 82, no. 7 (2004): 523–31.

97. Abdullah H. Baqui et al., "Zinc Therapy for Diarrhoea Increased the Use of Oral Rehydration Therapy and Reduced the Use of Antibiotics in Bangladeshi Children," *Journal of Health, Population and Nutrition* 22, no. 4 (2004): 440–42.

98. WHO and UNICEF, *WHO/UNICEF Joint Statement on Clinical Management of Acute Diarrhoea* (May 2004), accessed online at www.who.int, on March 4, 2005.

99. WHO Integrated Management of Childhood Illness website, accessed online at www.who.int, on March 4, 2005.

100. Jennifer Bryce et al., "The Multi-Country Evaluation of the Integrated Management of Childhood Illness Strategy: Lessons for the Evaluation of Public Health Interventions," *American Journal of Public Health* 94, no. 3 (2004): 406–15.

101. WHO, *Maternal Mortality in 2000: Estimates Developed by WHO, UNICEF and UNFPA* (Geneva: WHO, 2004): 2.

102. Robert M. Hecht, "Foreword," in *Investing in Maternal Health: Learning from Malaysia and Sri Lanka*, ed. Alexander Preker (Washington, DC: The World Bank, 2003): xi-xiii.

103. Jerker Liljestrand and Kristina Gryboski, "Women Who Die Needlessly: Maternal Mortality as a Human Rights Issue," in *Reproductive Health and Rights: Reaching the Hardly Reached*, ed. Elaine M. Murphy (Washington, DC: PATH, 2002): 121–28.

104. Allen Rosenfield and Deborah Maine, "Maternal Mortality—A Neglected Tragedy: Where is the M in MCH?" *The Lancet* 2, (1985): 83–85.

105. Carla AbouZahr, "Safe Motherhood: a Brief History of the Global Movement 1947–2002," *British Medical Bulletin* 67 (2003): 13–25.

106. Indra Pathmanathan et al., *Investing in Maternal Health: Learning from Malaysia and Sri Lanka* (Washington, DC: The World Bank, 2003).

107. Marjorie A. Koblinsky and Oona Campbell, "Factors Affecting the Reduction of Maternal Mortality," in *Reducing Maternal Mortality: Learning from Bolivia, China, Egypt, Honduras, Indonesia, Jamaica, and Zimbabwe*, ed. Marjorie A. Koblinsky (Washington, DC: The World Bank, 2003): 5–37.

108. Averting Maternal Death and Disability Network, accessed at http://cpmcnet.columbia.edu, on Nov. 15, 2004.

109. Therese McGinn, "Toward MDG 6: Reducing Maternal Mortality Globally," abstract submitted in October 2004 to the Global Health Council for presentation at the Global Health Council conference, May 31–June 3, 2005.

110. Kristina Gryboski, "Case Study: Indonesia's White Ribbon Alliance: Expanding Civil Society and Government Partnerships at Multiple Levels to Advocate for Maternal and Neonatal Health," report of Maternal and Neonatal Health Project (Baltimore: Johns Hopkins University, 2004).

111. AbouZahr, "Safe Motherhood: a Brief History of the Global Movement 1947–2002."

112. Family Health International, *Women's Voices, Women's Lives: The Impact of Family Planning* (Arlington, VA: Family Health International, 2000).

113. Elaine M. Murphy, "Being Born Female is Dangerous to Your Health," *American Psychologist* 58, no. 3 (2003): 205–10; and Barbara Shane, *Family Planning Saves Lives*, 3d ed. (Washington, DC: Population Reference Bureau, 1997).

114. Elaine M. Murphy, "Diffusion of Innovations: Family Planning in Developing Countries," *Journal of Health Communication* 9, Supplement 1 (2004): 123–29.

115. Carl Haub, *World Population Data Sheet 2004* (Washington DC: Population Reference Bureau, 2004).

116. John Bongaarts, "The Role of Family Planning Programs in Fertility Decline," *Population Briefs* 2, no. 3 (1996).

117. Judith R. Seltzer, *The Origins and Evolution of Family Planning Programs in Developing Countries* (Santa Monica, CA: RAND, 2002): 1–44.

118. Everett M. Rogers et al., "A Radio Soap Opera's Effects on Family Planning Behavior in Tanzania," *Studies in Family Planning* 30, no. 3 (1999): 193–211.

119. Phyllis T. Piotrow and Esta de Fossrd, "Entertainment-Education as a Public Health Intervention," in *Entertainment-Education and Social Change*, ed. Arvind Singhal et al. (Mahwah, NJ: Lawrence Erlbaum Associates Publishers, 2004): 39–60.

120. D. Lawrence Kincaid, "From Innovation to Social Norm: Bounded Normative Influence," *Journal of Health Communication: International Perspectives* 9, Supplement 1 (2004): 37–57.

121. Seltzer, *The Origins and Evolution of Family Planning Programs in Developing Countries*: 33–34.

122. John Cleland, "Potatoes and Pills: An Overview of Innovation-Diffusion Contributions to Explanations of Fertility Decline," in *Diffusion Processes and Fertility Transition*, ed. John B. Casterline (Washington, DC: National Academies Press, 2001): 39–65.

123. See for example, Andrea C. Gielen and Eileen M. McDonald, "The Precede-Proceed Planning Model," in *Health Behavior and Health Education: Theory, Research, and Practice*, 2d ed., ed. Karen Glanz et al. (San Francisco: Jossey-Bass, Inc., 1997): 359–83.

Application of Theory: High Risk and Special Populations

Part 12 reviews what is meant (and potentially obscured) by the term "high-risk population" and examines the relevance of current theoretical and program approaches for addressing these populations with health promotion interventions. The idea that health risk may be viewed differently among groups at risk is discussed, and approaches such as the Health Belief Model and the Risk and Protective Factors model are assessed with respect to their appropriateness. Alternative models, including the Harm Reduction model and Generative approach are presented. The first two readings (UNAIDS, 2000; DesJarlais et al., 1993) summarize the rationale and review the utility of Harm Reduction in addressing HIV/AIDS, particularly among high-risk substance abusing groups. The second of those two articles is a seminal statement and argument for the approach by three leading researchers. The third selection (Edberg, 2001) describes one way in which a context of significant poverty influences attitudes about risk behaviors, such as violence, by focusing on the ways in which a popular song genre (in Mexico) often portrays narcotraffickers as heroic, Robin Hood-like characters.

Preventing the Transmission of HIV Among Drug Abusers: A Position Paper of the United Nations System

Source: UNAIDS. 2000. *Preventing the Transmission of HIV Among Drug Abusers: A Position Paper of the United Nations System*. Geneva: UNAIDS.

BACKGROUND

1. The aim of this paper is to present a United Nations (UN) system wide position on policy and strategies to prevent the transmission of HIV among drug abusers. Drug abuse and HIV/AIDS issues cut across much of the work of the United Nations family. Both are directly and indirectly associated with many complex public health and social problems. They affect the workplace, undermine social and economic development, and affect the lives and well being of children.

2. This paper is based on the experiences of various UN agencies and programmes in their work to prevent and treat drug abuse and HIV infection as well as on relevant policy principles guiding the work of the United Nations. It draws on research findings to recommend evidence-based practice, to provide general guidance, and to indicate some programming principles for the prevention of drug abuse and HIV/AIDS.

3. Sharing or use of contaminated needles is a very efficient way of spreading HIV. Since injecting drug abusers are often linked in tight networks and commonly share injecting equipment, HIV can spread very rapidly in these populations. Currently, 114 countries have reported HIV infection among drug injectors. Injecting drug abuse is the main or a major mode for transmission of HIV infection in many countries of Asia, Latin America, Europe, and North America.

4. In 1998, 136 countries reported the existence of injecting drug abuse. This is a significant increase as compared to 1992, when 80 countries reported injecting. This illustrates a worrying trend for diffusion of injecting into an increasing number of developing countries and countries in economic transition, where previously the behaviour was often virtually unknown.

5. Numerous studies have also found drug injectors to be disproportionately likely to be involved in the sex industry or to engage in high-risk sexual activities. Drug injecting may also contribute to an increased incidence of HIV infection through HIV transmission to the children of drug injecting mothers, and through sexual contacts between drug injectors and non-injectors.

6. HIV risk among drug abusers does not arise only from injecting. Many types of psychoactive substances, whether injected or not, including alcohol, are risky to the extent that they affect the individual's ability to make decisions about safe sexual behaviour. Studies have associated crack-cocaine use with elevated levels of high-risk sexual behaviours, for example in the United States, where crack-cocaine abusers account for an increasing proportion of AIDS cases.

7. Deciding on the implementation of the intervention strategies to prevent HIV in injecting drug abusers is one of the most urgent questions facing policy makers.

Studies have demonstrated that HIV transmission among injecting drug abusers can be prevented and that the epidemic already has been slowed and even reversed in some cases. HIV prevention activities which have shown impact on HIV prevalence and risk behaviour include AIDS education, access to condoms and clean injecting equipment, counselling and drug abuse treatment.

8. Drug abuse treatment is one approach that may have an impact on preventing HIV infection. Many large-magnitude studies have shown that patients participating in drug substitution treatment such as methadone maintenance, therapeutic communities, and outpatient drug-free programmes decrease their drug consumption significantly. Several longitudinal studies examining changes in HIV risk behaviours for patients currently in treatment have found that longer retention in treatment, as well as completion of treatment, are correlated with reduction in HIV risk behaviours or an increase in protective behaviours. However, studies have found more effectiveness for changing illicit drug use than changing sexual risk behaviour.

9. Drug abuse treatment is not chosen by all drug abusers at risk from HIV infection, or may not be attractive to drug abusers early in their injecting habits. In addition, recovery from drug addiction can be a long-term process and frequently requires multiple episodes of treatment. Relapses to drug abuse and risk behaviour can occur during or after successful treatment episodes. Various outreach activities have been designed to access, motivate and support drug abusers who are not in treatment to change their behaviour. Findings from research indicate that outreach activities that take place outside the conventional health and social care environments reach out-of-treatment drug injectors, increase drug treatment referrals, and may reduce illicit drug use risk behaviours and sexual risk behaviours as well as HIV incidence.

10. Several reviews of the effectiveness of syringe and needle exchange programmes have shown reductions in needle risk behaviours and HIV transmission and no evidence of increase into injecting drug use or other public health dangers in the communities served. Furthermore, such programmes have shown to serve as points of contact between drug abusers and service providers, including drug abuse treatment programmes. The benefits of such programmes increase considerably, if they go beyond syringe exchange alone to include AIDS education, counselling and referral to a variety of treatment options.

UNITED NATIONS SYSTEM POLICY

11. Several UN documents provide the framework/foundation for the formulation of strategic approaches to preventing the transmission of HIV among injecting drug abusers.

UN DRUG CONTROL CONVENTIONS AND THE DECLARATION ON THE GUIDING PRINCIPLES OF DRUG DEMAND REDUCTION

12. The policy of permitting the use of narcotic drugs for medical and scientific needs, while preventing their use for non-medical purposes, goes back to the late nineteenth and early twentieth centuries. At that time there was an increasing awareness of the dangers associated with the narcotic drugs that had previously been widely used for pain relief, especially opium-based preparations. Hence, many countries began to restrict the distribution of such drugs, while permitting their use for medical and scientific purposes.

13. This policy is articulated in the preamble to the 1961 Single Convention on Narcotic Drugs, which reads as follows: "Recognizing that the medical use of narcotic drugs continues to be indispensable for the relief of pain and suffering and that adequate provision must be made to ensure the availability of narcotic drugs for such purposes, Recognizing that addiction to narcotic drugs . . . is fraught with social and economic danger to mankind . . ., Desiring to conclude a generally acceptable international convention replacing existing treaties on narcotic drugs, limiting such drugs to medical and scientific purposes . . ." The Convention further specifies that the "parties shall give special attention to the provision of facilities for the medical treatment, care and rehabilitation of drug addicts" (Article 38).

14. Also the 1971 Convention on Psychotropic Substances in its Article 20, paragraph 1 states that parties to the convention shall take all appropriate measures for the prevention of abuse of psychotropic substances and for the early identification, treatment, education, after-care, and rehabilitation and social reintegration of the persons involved.

15. The 1988 UN Convention against Illicit Traffic in Narcotic Drugs and Psychotropic Substances in its Article 14, paragraph 4 indicates that parties to the convention shall adopt appropriate measures aimed at eliminating or reducing illicit demand for narcotic drugs and narcotic substances, with a view to reducing human suffering.

16. In 1998, the UN General Assembly adopted the Declaration on the Guiding Principles of Drug Demand Reduction, the first international instrument to deal exclusively with the problem of drug abuse. The Declaration emphasises that demand reduction programmes should cover all areas of prevention, from discouraging initial use to reducing the negative health and social consequences of drug abuse for the individual and society as a whole.

UN HUMAN RIGHTS DOCUMENTS

17. The Universal Declaration of Human Rights, which was adopted fifty years ago as a common standard of achievement for all peoples and all nations, states: "Everyone, as a member of society, has the right to social security and is entitled to realization . . . of the economic, social and cultural rights indispensable for his dignity and the free development of his personality" (Article 22). "Everyone has the right to a standard of living adequate for the health and well-being of himself and of his family, including food, clothing, housing and medical care and necessary social services . . ." (Article 25).

18. In 1999, the Commission on Human Rights passed a resolution (1999/49) which invited States, United Nations bodies as well as international and non-governmental organizations "to take all necessary steps to ensure the respect, protection and fulfilment of HIV-related rights . . ."

19. In May 2000, the Committee on Economic, Social and Cultural Rights, which is the United Nations human rights monitoring body, adopted a General Comment on the right to health. The Comment proscribes "any discrimination in access to health care and the underlying determinants of health, as well as to means and entitlements for their procurement, on the grounds of race, colour, sex, language, religion, political or other opinion, national or social origin, property, birth, physical or mental disability, health status (including HIV/AIDS), sexual orientation, civil, political, social or other status, which has the intention or effect of nullifying or impairing the equal enjoyment or exercise of the right to health" (paragraph 18).

UN HEALTH PROMOTION POLICY DOCUMENTS

20. Respect for human rights and the achievement of public health goals are complementary. Health, as defined in the Constitution of WHO (1946), is "a state of complete physical, mental and social well-being and not merely the absence of disease or infirmity." The Constitution proclaims that "the enjoyment of the highest attainable standard of health" is one of the fundamental human rights of every human being without distinction for race, religion, political belief, economic or social condition.

21. The concept and vision of Health for All, which was adopted in 1977 by the Thirtieth World Health Assembly, sets the main social target of governments and WHO as "the attainment by all the citizens of the world by the year 2000 of a level of health that will permit them to lead a socially and economically productive life."

22. The Ottawa Charter on Health Promotion (1986) outlines five areas for action: building public health policy, creating supportive environments, strengthening community action, developing personal skills, and reorienting health services. These areas are all relevant to drug abuse issues and HIV/AIDS.

23. During its session in May 1998, the World Health Assembly endorsed the new World Health Declaration and the new global health policy Health for All in the 21st Century. Health for All in the 21st Century guides action and policy for health at all levels and identifies global priorities and targets for the first two decades of the 21st century. Key values such as human rights, equity, ethics and gender sensitivity should underpin and be incorporated in all aspects of health policy. A key feature is the strengthening of the participation of people and communities in decision-making and actions for health.

24. Important global "health for all" targets by 2020 include: ". . . the worldwide burden of disease will be substantially decreased. This will be achieved by implementation of sound disease-control programmes aimed at reversing the current trend of increased incidence and disability caused by tuberculosis, HIV/AIDS, . . . all countries will have introduced, and be actively managing and monitoring, strategies that strengthen health-enhancing lifestyles and weaken health-damaging ones, through a combination of regulatory, economic, educational, organizational and community-based programmes."

PRINCIPLES AND STRATEGIC APPROACH

25. Protection of human rights is critical for the success of prevention of HIV/AIDS. People are more vulnerable to infection when their economic, health, social or cultural rights are not respected. Where civil rights are not respected, it is difficult to respond effectively to the epidemic.

26. HIV prevention should start as early as possible. Once HIV has been introduced into a local community of injecting drug abusers, there is the possibility of extremely rapid spread. On the other hand, experience has shown that injecting drug abusers can change their behaviour if they are appropriately supported.

27. Interventions should be based on a regular assessment of the nature and magnitude of drug abuse as well as trends and patterns of HIV infection. Interventions need to build on knowledge and expertise acquired from research, including empirical knowledge about the social milieu around which drug taking revolves as well as lessons learned from the implementation of previous projects and interventions.

28. Comprehensive coverage of the entire targeted populations is essential. For prevention measures to be effective in changing the course of the epidemic in a country, it is essential that as many individuals in the at-risk populations as possible are reached.

29. Drug demand reduction and HIV prevention programmes should be integrated into broader social welfare and health promotion policies and preventive education programmes. Specific interventions for reducing the demand for drugs and preventing HIV should be sustained by a supportive environment in which healthy lifestyles are attractive and accessible, including poverty reduction and opportunities for education and employment. It is desirable to include multidisciplinary activities and provide appropriate training and support to facilitate joint working.

30. Drug abuse problems cannot be solved simply by criminal justice initiatives. A punitive approach may drive people most in need of prevention and care services underground. Where appropriate, drug abuse treatment should be offered, either as an alternative or in addition to punishment. HIV prevention and drug abuse treatment programmes within criminal justice institutions are also important components in preventing the transmission of HIV.

31. The ability to halt the epidemic requires a three part strategy: (i) preventing drug abuse, especially among young people; (ii) facilitating entry into drug abuse treatment; and (iii) establishing effective outreach to engage drug abusers in HIV prevention strategies that protect them and their partners and families from exposure to HIV, and encourage the uptake of substance abuse treatment and medical care.

32. Treatment services need to be readily available and flexible. Treatment applicants can be lost if treatment is not immediately available or readily accessible. Treatment systems need to offer a range of treatment alternatives, including substitution treatment, to respond to the different needs of drug abusers. They also need to provide ongoing assessments of patient's needs, which may change during the course of treatment. Longer retention in treatment, as well as completion of treatment, are correlated with reduction in HIV risk behaviours or an increase in protective behaviours.

33. Developing effective responses to the problem of HIV among drug abusers is likely to be facilitated by considering the views of drug abusers and the communities they live in. Programmes need to be reality based and meaningful to the people they are designed to reach. The development of such responses is likely to be facilitated by assuring the active participation of the target group in all phases of programme development and implementation.

34. Drug abuse treatment programmes should provide assessment for HIV/AIDS and other infectious diseases, and counselling to help patients change behaviours that place them or others at risk of infection. Attention should be paid to drug abusers' medical care needs, including on-site primary medical care services and organized referrals to medical care institutions.

35. HIV prevention programmes should also focus on sexual risk behaviours among people who inject drugs or use other substances. Epidemiological research findings indicate the increasing significance of sexual HIV transmission among injecting drug abusers as well as among crack-cocaine abusers. Drug abusers perceive sexual risk in the context of a range of other risks and dangers, such as risks associated with overdose or needle sharing, which may be perceived to be more immediate and more important. The sexual transmission of HIV among drug abusers may often be over-looked.

Harm Reduction: A Public Health Response to the AIDS Epidemic Among Injecting Drug Users

Source: Excerpts from Des Jarlais DC, Friedman SR and Ward TP. 1993. "Harm Reduction: A Public Health Response to the AIDS Epidemic Among Injecting Drug Users." *Annual Review of Public Health* 14: 413–450.

INTRODUCTION

Human use of psychoactive drugs precedes recorded history, and human misuse of such drugs is probably almost as old. Within the last century, laboratory techniques for strengthening drug preparations and the invention of injection equipment as a method of administration have greatly increased the potential for harmful consequences of psychoactive drugs. The intense effects from intravenous administration of highly refined drugs creates a higher likelihood of developing both tolerance and dependence—and of overdosing, if the quantity of drug is greater than the amount usually taken. Nonsterile injections may also lead to abscesses and diseases, such as endocarditis. Furthermore, multiperson use of drug injection equipment has spread such infections as hepatitis B.

The HIV/AIDS epidemic, however, has created an adverse consequence that is qualitatively different from the previously experienced problems associated with the injection of psychoactive drugs. In many countries, this difference has led to a conceptual reevaluation of how to approach the problems associated with psychoactive drug use. There are several components of the difference between AIDS and other adverse consequences of drug use. First (given the currently available medical treatments), HIV infection almost uniformly fatal.[1] HIV infection thus has the potential to negate the very possibility of other life goals for the individual, such as abstinence from illicit drugs, raising children, or social and vocational rehabilitation. Second, AIDS/HIV infection is a particularly unpleasant way to die, typically involving a long period of pain, physical debilitation, and sometimes mental deterioration. It is also an expensive way to die, consuming considerable portions of the finite medical resources that an ethical society would provide to persons in ill health. Third, because HIV can be transmitted both sexually and perinatally, not only the drug injectors themselves are at risk, but also their sexual partners and potential children. Hence, HIV infection is an adverse consequence of drug use that is not limited to the drug users themselves, but can spread from drug users to become a threat to the health of the entire community. Fourth, the transmission of HIV among drug injectors occurs through multiperson use of the injection equipment, rather than through the drugs themselves. Thus, at both an individual and a societal level, prevention of HIV transmission without necessarily having to cease drug use or even drug injection is possible.

Because of this urgent need to prevent HIV infection among injecting drug users (IDUs), many different prevention

---

[1]Intensive research is being conducted to develop treatments for both HIV infection and the opportunistic infections that occur in the presence of HIV-related immunosuppression. Given the nature of HIV infection, potentially successful treatments would probably require maintenance treatment, which in turn requires multiple expensive drugs with substantial toxicities. Thus, even though HIV infection would no longer be fatal, there still would be a great public health need to prevent HIV infections.

programs have been developed. A conceptual perspective, most commonly called "harm reduction," which unifies and guides many (though certainly not all) of these different prevention programs, has also emerged. Elements of the harm-reduction perspective existed before the AIDS epidemic among IDUs (5), but the epidemic has served as the catalyst for a fuller intellectual elaboration of the perspective and has been the primary reason why previously unresponsive political leaders have implemented harm-reduction programs (3, 33).

Harm-reduction programs, unlike other current approaches to the problem of drug abuse, consider reducing adverse consequences of drug use without necessarily reducing the drug use itself to be not only possible, but desirable. The prevention of HIV infection among persons who continue to inject illicit drugs is thus an especially instructive instance of harm reduction as praxis. We will discuss in detail the harm-reduction perspective, which has led to implementation and elaboration of numerous harm-reduction-based programs, after a discussion of the HIV epidemic among IDUs.

SUMMARY OF EPIDEMIOLOGY

Much has been learned about the epidemiology of HIV infection among IDUs since the discovery of the first cases of AIDS among this population ten years ago. The problem of HIV infection among IDUs is already a world-wide problem. Moreover, there is every reason to expect further spread of injecting drug use to additional countries, with HIV infection among the IDUs likely to follow. Once HIV has entered a local population of IDUs, extremely rapid spread of the virus is possible, with up to half of the group becoming infected within several years. In addition, once drug injectors are infected with HIV, they are not only subject to developing the opportunistic infections and neoplasms that constitute the surveillance definition of AIDS, but are also more likely to develop a wide variety of other potentially fatal illnesses, such as bacterial pneumonia and tuberculosis.

All of the epidemiology in the field to date thus points to an urgent need for the prevention of HIV infection among IDUs wherever groups of IDUs are found.

THE HARM REDUCTION PERSPECTIVE ON PREVENTION OF HIV INFECTION AMONG IDUs

Programs to prevent HIV infection among IDUs have by now been implemented in most of the countries where illicit drug injecting is known to occur. These programs vary greatly in their content, intensity, and coverage of the drug-injecting population. The urgent need to prevent HIV infection and the great diversity in the programs themselves have created a need for a framework to organize the programs conceptually. The

most common framework is called the "harm reduction" or "harm minimization" approach to the problems of drug use.

Harm reduction is in an ongoing process of development as a perspective on the problems of psychoactive drug use. The concept has received the most consideration and development in Holland, the United Kingdom, and Australia (8–11, 38, 93, 109). However, specialists in the field are still trying to formulate a brief but inclusive definition of what constitutes harm reduction (9, 95), and it may be premature even to attempt a formal definition at this time. Yet, despite the difficulties in trying to provide a concise and permanent definition of a field that is still undergoing rapid growth, some fundamental tenets of the approach, particularly with respect to preventing HIV infection, can be listed.

The basic premise of the harm-reduction perspective concerns the sense in which psychoactive drug use should be considered a problem. In some perspectives, the basic problem is simply the use of the illicit psychoactive drugs as such; thus, all efforts need to be concentrated upon reducing current use of the drugs and preventing new persons from ever starting to use them. The harm-reduction perspective, in contrast, sees the problem not so much as the drug use itself, but rather as the harmful consequences of some types of drug use. Harm reduction simply calls for reducing the harmful effects of drug use. If reducing the drug use is the only way in which harmful consequences can be reduced, then reduction is necessary. For many types of drug-related harm, however, it is possible to reduce at least a substantial part of the harm without necessarily eliminating (or even reducing) the drug use itself. HIV infection among IDUs is a readily comprehensible example of this type of harm. Because the multiperson use of injection equipment is the actual mode of HIV transmission, it is certainly possible to have many types of illicit drug use that do not involve HIV transmission. Within the harm-reduction perspective, therefore, reduction of the drug use itself becomes not the fundamental public goal, but merely one possible means to a multitude of public goals.

In addition to the shift from defining reduction of drug use as the fundamental goal to perceiving it as merely one possible means to other goals, harm reduction is, above all, a pragmatic approach to psychoactive drug use. Emphasis is on attainable short-term results over utopian long-term goals. The ideal method for reducing the harm associated with illicit psychoactive drug use would simply be to prevent any further use. Obviously, no one would be sharing injection equipment if heroin, cocaine, amphetamines, and other injectable drugs were not being illicitly used. However, because complete elimination of illicit drug use is extremely unlikely to occur in the foreseeable future, a harm-reduction approach focuses instead upon what can be done to reduce HIV transmission through the sharing of injection equipment.

The answer to this pragmatic question leads us to another characteristic of the harm-reduction perspective; namely, that it is based on multiple, complementary solutions operating simultaneously, rather than some single best solution. That is, there are usually many things that can be done simultaneously to reduce the specific harm, even if some of these activities might appear at first to be in conflict with each other. With respect to the prevention of HIV transmission among IDUs, for example, drug abuse treatment programs can be established to reduce the use of psychoactive drugs, while IDUs are being encouraged to use drugs either without injection or by practicing safer injection. At the same time, sterile injection equipment can be provided at no cost (or sold cheaply), so that sharing of equipment is not necessary. And, disinfectants, such as bleach, can be provided so that, whenever sharing does occur, the equipment can be disinfected before multiperson use.

Although harm-reduction offers several approaches simultaneously, no individual drug user will be involved in all of these programs at the same time. This apparent inconsistency can create troublesome complications for some political leaders, who have tended to see illicit drug users as one homogenous group that should be encouraged (or coerced) to change its behavior in a single way. Harm-reduction practitioners, on the other hand, have no difficulty in recommending a relative hierarchy of choices to individual drug users, usually in the same order of preference in which the different activities are presented above. Individual drug users are thus enabled to make informed choices as to which type of harm reduction they will follow, with the understanding that their specific choices may change over time.

Indeed, the very idea that an illicit drug user is capable of a rational, informed choice—and will exercise that choice to reduce harm both to the individual and to society as a whole—distinguishes the harm-reduction perspective from other perspectives in the drug abuse field. Other perspectives tend to emphasize the limitations on rational choice that occur when a person is physically or psychologically dependent upon psychoactive drugs. (Another common assumption is that, because illicit drug users by definition have chosen to break the laws regarding drug use, they cannot be trusted to make any decisions that will benefit society as a whole.)

The final characteristic of the harm-reduction perspective that needs to be discussed here is its concern with overcoming the marginalization of illicit drug users by the dominant society. A substantial amount of the harm incurred by illicit drug users results not so much from the use of illicit drugs themselves, but from the associated social marginaliza-

tion and stigmatization. With respect to HIV prevention, harm-reduction programs need to address the compounded stigmatization associated with both illicit drug injection and AIDS itself. This double stigmatization has created multiple new problems, as well as exacerbating numerous older problems. For instance, especially earlier in the AIDS epidemic, it has impeded community action against AIDS among some ethnic minority communities in the United States (48, 81). It has also increased the distrust between IDUs and public health authorities, thus making implementation of prevention programs that much more difficult (14). Finally, the fear of stigmatization has led some IDUs to deny their risk of transmitting AIDS to their sexual partners (A. Abdul-Quader 1991, personal communication). The harm-reduction framework responds to such stigmatization by insisting that IDUs are recognized as full members of the community, that safeguarding the public health of the entire community requires providing adequate health services to all of its members, and that IDUs should be encouraged to participate actively in AIDS prevention projects. Moreover, because HIV is transmitted from IDUs to their sexual partners and their children, the framework further emphasizes the linkage between the health of drug users and the health of the community as a whole.

HIV PREVENTION PROGRAMS FOR IDUs

The harm-reduction perspective has emerged as a unifying theoretical expression of a multitude of different HIV prevention programs that have been practiced in many different countries. In keeping with the perspective, different prevention programs have usually been implemented simultaneously to provide for the specific needs of different subsets of IDUs.

However, in those instances in which many different prevention programs have become operational at approximately the same time in the same place, evaluation of the distinct effects of each individual prevention program has been extremely difficult. Moreover, this has been only one of the methodological problems in drawing conclusions about the effectiveness of AIDS prevention programs for IDUs. Program evaluations have also tended to use different units of measurement for the relevant AIDS risk behaviors, thus making it all the more difficult to compare different programs. Similarly, the demographic and behavioral characteristics of the IDUs who participate in the different programs have usually been only briefly described in the evaluation reports, so that it has not been possible to control statistically for the differences among the participants in different programs. Finally, most evaluations have relied upon simple pre-post experimental designs, even though a large percentage of IDUs, once aware of AIDS, will already have changed their behavior in the absence of formal prevention programs (34). (Attempting to use a control group that was "protected" from learning about AIDS would, of course, be a highly unethical research procedure.)

Nonetheless, despite these numerous methodological difficulties, the present state of evaluation research on AIDS prevention programs for IDUs does permit some generalizations about the actual and potential effectiveness of the different programs. Table 4 [not included] presents results from several studies for each of the major types of AIDS prevention programs for IDUs. This table is not meant to be comprehensive; rather, studies were selected to illustrate the variety of programs in different geographical locations and in different time periods.

The syringe exchange is perhaps the prototypical harm-reduction method for preventing HIV infection among IDUs. In a syringe-exchange program, IDUs can, at no cost, exchange their used needles and syringes for new, sterile injection equipment (10, 33, 55, 56, 66, 76). In addition, by collecting the used injection equipment, syringe exchanges also provide for safe disposal of potentially HIV-contaminated equipment. Because the exchange is conducted on a face-to-face basis, syringe exchanges also provide an opportunity for delivery of other services to IDUs. Syringe exchanges typically provide AIDS education and counseling, distribute condoms (to prevent sexual transmission of HIV), and make referrals to drug abuse treatment or other medical and social services that may be desired by the participants. Many also distribute alcohol swabs (to reduce the likelihood of developing abscesses and other infections) and bleach for disinfecting injection equipment in the event it is used by more than one person. Some even do on-site testing for tuberculosis and sexually transmitted diseases.

In addition to differences in the number and kind of extra services that are offered on-site or by referral, exchanges also vary in their locations (fixed versus "roving" sites), hours of operation, the variety of needles and syringes distributed, and most notably the allowed number of syringes to be exchanged. That is, some organizations exchange only a limited number of syringes at one time, whereas others exchange without any limit. Persons exchanging large numbers at a single time—up to several hundred syringes, in some cases—are clearly exchanging for others. Some exchange workers believe that such large-volume exchangers defeat some of the secondary purposes, because there is no personal contact possible between the staff and the anonymous persons who are indirectly served through the large-volume exchangers. Limiting the number of syringes exchanged at one time, however, reduces the availability of sterile injection equipment among the local IDU population and the number of AIDS workers among the IDU population. In one study of an exchange (with a limit of five

on the number of syringes that could be exchanged), IDUs persisted in passing on used equipment to others (63). At other programs, however, the large-volume exchangers are considered to be "satellite" workers, who increase the overall coverage of the exchange among the local population of IDUs. A few exchanges have even begun training these satellite workers to provide AIDS education and referrals (52).

Syringe exchanges have not led to an increase in illicit drug use, as many opponents had feared (70). Indeed, all evaluations to date have shown that illicit drug use does not increase among participants in the exchanges and there is no detectable increase in the number of new drug injectors in any given locality where syringe exchanges have been implemented. In some American cities, such as Portland (78), Tacoma (53), and New Haven (76), the syringe exchanges have also proven to be major referral sources for helping persons into drug abuse treatment programs.

However, the precise extent to which syringe exchanges have reduced HIV transmission among IDUs is difficult to determine. The methodological concerns noted above also apply to almost all syringe-exchange studies. All evaluations have shown some reduction in AIDS risk behavior, particularly in multiperson use of injection equipment, but these have often been of a modest magnitude, and no study to date has shown complete elimination of multiperson use. On a more positive note, however, implementation or large-scale expansion of syringe exchanges has been followed by stabilization of HIV seroprevalence among IDUs in several cities (see discussion below)—and by actual reductions in hepatitis B transmission among IDUs in Amsterdam (11), San Francisco (98), and Tacoma (54)—which suggests a substantial impact on reducing the transmission of blood-borne viruses among IDUs.

Although syringe-exchange programs have so far received the most public attention as a harm-reduction strategy for preventing HIV infection, over-the-counter sale of sterile injection equipment probably can reach a very high percentage of IDUs. Before the AIDS epidemic, there was great variation in the laws regulating the sale and possession of injection equipment. In the United States, almost all states criminalized the possession of equipment for injecting illicit drugs, and the states with large numbers of IDUs also tended to require prescriptions for the sale of injection equipment. In Europe, most countries did not have laws criminalizing possession or requiring prescriptions, but many pharmacists unofficially chose not to sell injection equipment to suspected IDUs. In fact, in Amsterdam, the decision of one central-city pharmacist to stop selling injection equipment to suspected IDUs that led to organized demands from IDUs for the establishment of the world's first syringe-exchange program in 1984—even before concern about AIDS among IDUs in that city. In Edinburgh, police persuaded pharmacists not to sell injection equipment in 1982, at about the time that HIV was being introduced into the local community of IDUs (83). HIV then spread rapidly among the group—reaching 50% seroprevalence within approximately two years—an experience that served as a powerful example of the dangers of restricting legal access to sterile injection equipment.

In Innsbruck, Austria, before concern about AIDS, pharmacists would sell needles and syringes only in lots of at least 100 (50). This requirement for large-volume minimum purchase was meant to, and indeed did, discourage IDUs from purchasing injection equipment in the pharmacies. As the AIDS threat became evident, however, public health officials convinced the pharmacists to sell needles and syringes to IDUs and educated the IDUs about the need to use sterile equipment. HIV seroprevalence among drug injectors in that city has subsequently stabilized. Similarly, in Glasgow, Scotland, pharmacists were persuaded to sell injection equipment to IDUs, and an evaluation study has since shown a decrease in multiperson use of injection equipment among the IDUs (51). Before the AIDS epidemic, France required prescriptions for the sale of injection equipment. Because of concern about AIDS, the law was changed, and a national program was established to train pharmacists in how to sell injection equipment to IDUs while providing information on how to use the equipment safely. Several evaluation studies showed that, after the change in the law and the training of the pharmacists, multiperson use of injection equipment by IDUs in France declined substantially (41, 60). In yet another scenario, preexisting pharmacy availability syringes made it possible for AIDS education and counseling for IDUs to lead to rapid behavior change. This happened in Bangkok after HIV had already spread rapidly within the group. The education program was followed by rapid behavior change; indeed, studies indicate that the majority of IDUs stopped sharing injection equipment, with 80% of them now obtaining sterile injection equipment from pharmacies. This large-scale behavior change was then followed by reduced seroconversion and stabilization of HIV seroprevalence among IDUs in Bangkok (20).

Rather than thinking of these two approaches as competitive, we should emphasize that most places that have implemented syringe-exchange programs have simultaneously implemented over-the-counter sales of injection equipment to IDUs (if they did not already have legal sales). As noted above, this is consistent with the harm-reduction approach of providing multiple means toward the same specific goal. It does, however, present formidable problems for evaluation research (as also noted above). Many IDUs who are not using syringe exchanges, and who thus might have served as a comparison group for IDUs, are obtaining their injection equipment from pharmacies. Because both the exchanges and the pharmacies are providing sterile injection equipment, there is obviously no strong rationale for expecting differences in AIDS risk behavior between participants in one program or the other.

In the United States, laws enacted before AIDS—and continuing political opposition to providing legal access to injection equipment for IDUs—have combined to limit greatly both syringe exchange and over-the-counter sales as AIDS prevention activities. Despite these impediments, there are a number of legal and underground exchanges currently operating (3, 33, 53, 76, 78), and there has been a marked increase in both legal and underground exchanges over the last several years. Still, in the absence of a national system of legal syringe-exchange programs, AIDS prevention for IDUs in the US has instead emphasized drug abuse treatment (discussed below) and outreach/bleach-distribution programs. The outreach programs typically (although not exclusively) use trained ex-addicts who go into high-drug-use areas and conduct face-to-face AIDS education, as well as provide referrals to other services, such as drug abuse treatment and HIV counseling and testing. The outreach workers also typically distribute small bottles of bleach for disinfecting used injection equipment, along with condoms to reduce sexual transmission of HIV. Evaluations of the outreach/bleach-distribution programs to date have shown large pre-post reductions in drug-injection risk behavior (16, 64, 75, 106), although not complete risk elimination. Moreover, stabilization of HIV seroprevalence has been noted in several cities after the implementation of outreach/bleach-distribution programs (106). Nonetheless, although proper use of bleach clearly can kill HIV, it is still not clear whether using bleach has a protective effect under field conditions. Indeed, the self-reported use of bleach was not associated with reduced HIV seroconversions in a Baltimore study (104).

Providing increased drug abuse treatment has been advocated not only in countries that have adopted a harm-reduction perspective (e.g. Australia and the Netherlands), but also in countries that have not adopted the perspective (e.g. the United States). Studies of methadone maintenance treatment have shown that if IDUs enter high-dosage treatment before an epidemic of HIV in the local community—and remain in treatment during the epidemic they are substantially less likely to be infected with HIV (1, 6, 88). These results are hardly surprising, given the previously well-documented ability of drug abuse treatment to reduce (though not eliminate) illicit drug use as such for many persons (23, 59). Nevertheless, there are still important areas of disagreement regarding drug abuse treatment as a method of preventing HIV infection among IDUs.

With a few exceptions, HIV counseling and testing has not been adopted as a major AIDS prevention measure, whether or not the country in question has adopted an overall harm-reduction perspective. Several studies have shown that HIV testing and counseling lead to reduced AIDS risk behavior (13, 84, 87, 101), but the amount of research on this topic has been relatively small, considering the number of IDUs who have by now been counseled and tested in research projects alone. Part of the difficulty with using this approach as an AIDS prevention measure has been the need to keep the counseling and testing truly confidential and voluntary. Loss of confidentiality or anonymity can lead to severe discrimination against HIV-positive persons, and coercive testing would violate the principle of "public health officials working with IDUs to prevent AIDS," which has always been a major component of harm reduction.

Sweden has utilized HIV counseling and testing among IDUs as a prevention strategy to the greatest extent. The results from Sweden would suggest that counseling and testing generally have had a positive effect—or at least not a discernible negative one (7, 77). Particularly now that it possible to provide some effective treatment for HIV infection, as well as prophylaxis for opportunistic infections, the possibility of using HIV counseling and testing as one part of larger integrated systems for HIV prevention among IDUs increases.

Another approach to HIV prevention is the encouragement of drug users' organizations that promote risk-reducing changes in drug-injector subcultures. This approach is congruent with harm-reduction perspectives in that it is based on respect for users' ability and willingness to take responsibility for issues of public health. It is also based on the finding that peer influence and peer norms are related to risk reduction (2, 29, 45, 58, 67, 73).

The first users' organizations formed in the Netherlands in the early 1980s, where the drug users' unions (*junkiebonden*) developed mechanisms to protect users from "bad dope" being sold on the streets and where their pressure led to reforms in the way some drug treatment programs treated clients, as well as bringing about the establishment of the first syringe exchange (to prevent hepatitis B). Later, when drug users became convinced that AIDS was a threat to them, the *junkiebonden* became involved in a wide range of educational and peer-influence projects that served to delegitimate the sharing of potentially infected syringes (25, 43, 44). Drug users' organizations have been major component in Australian AIDS policy where, in addition to contributing ideas and in-

fluence in program development, they are actively involved in risk-reduction efforts. Many European countries, including Germany, the United Kingdom, Italy, and Spain, also have users' organizations. These organizations have sent representatives and held meetings of their own at both the Second (Barcelona, 1991) and Third (Melbourne, 1992) International Conferences on the Reduction of Drug-Related Harm.

In the United States, the high level of hostility toward drug users, the Federal requirements for drug-free workplaces, and the extreme levels of impoverishment in which many users live have prevented any widespread establishment of drug users' organizations. *Street Voice*, a newsletter published by IDUs in Baltimore, is a major exception, although it also has faced many problems because of the destitution of many of its members. In two of the National AIDS Demonstration Research projects, efforts have been made to organize drug injectors against AIDS in Minneapolis-St. Paul (12) and in Brooklyn. The Brooklyn project has reported widespread risk reduction among its participants, including greater use of bleach and condoms than in a comparison outreach project (47, 49, 62, 97).

HOW MUCH PREVENTION IS NEEDED FOR SUCCESS?

An almost universal finding in the studies of AIDS prevention programs for IDUs has been an outcome of substantial risk reduction, but never of complete risk elimination. Regardless of the type of program, or even the combination of programs in a given area, there still appears to be a substantial residual level of persistent risk behavior among the IDUs as a group. This residual risk behavior raises the question of whether prevention programs for IDUs will ever completely succeed. However, there are at least two localities where prevention programs for IDUs appear to be succeeding in preventing community-level HIV epidemics. The Skane province in southern Sweden has an estimated 3000 IDUs, of whom at least 90% have been tested for HIV (66). In addition to the widespread HIV counseling and testing, drug abuse treatment is also widely available (although methadone maintenance is limited). Moreover, there is a syringe-exchange program, and sterile injection equipment can be obtained from pharmacies in nearby Copenhagen. The HIV seroprevalence rate is approximately 2% and has remained stable over the last five years. Only 20% of the known HIV seropositives were infected locally (the others were infected outside of the province, and/or moved into the area after being infected).

Similarly, Australia has a wide variety of AIDS prevention programs for IDUs. There are numerous syringe exchanges, which also distribute bleach, and injection equipment is also sold over-the-counter. Treatment is sufficiently available to constitute a true treatment-on-demand situation. User groups have been supported by the government to implement prevention programs and provide policy advice. There are specialized prevention programs targeted at subgroups of IDUs, e.g. youth, gays, prisoners. As a result of all this, the HIV seroprevalence rate varies somewhat from city to city, but overall is less than 2%. And, the rate has been stable for the last several years in all of Australia's major cities (24).

These two examples suggest that it may be possible to prevent an epidemic of HIV among IDUs with currently available prevention programs. One critical factor appears to be starting prevention programs early enough. In both Skane and Australia, the prevention programs were begun before there was any rapid spread of HIV among IDUs. A second critical factor appears to be providing a variety of means for behavior change simultaneously, as soon as the IDUs themselves have recognized the threat of HIV and AIDS. Consistent with the harm-reduction perspective, different IDUs will avail themselves of different programs, and the same IDUs may utilize different programs at different times.

Much more research is clearly needed to determine precisely how much prevention and how much risk reduction is needed to prevent epidemics of HIV among IDUs. The current evidence indicates, however, that prevention of HIV epidemics should be considered a realistic, attainable goal.

LITERATURE CITED

1. Abdul-Quader, A. S., Friedman, S. R., Des Jarlais, D. C., Marmor, M., Maslansky, R., Bartelme, S. 1987. Methadone maintenance and behavior by intravenous drug users that can transmit HIV. *Contemp. Drug Prob.* 14:425–34

2. Abdul-Quader, A. S., Tross, S., Friedman, S. R., Kouzi, A. C., Des Jarlais, D. S. 1990. Street-recruited intravenous drug users and sexual risk reduction in New York City. *AIDS* 4:1075–79

3. Anderson, W. 1991. The New York needle trial: the politics of public health in the age of AIDS. *Am. J. Public Health* 81:1506–17

5. Berridge, V. 1992. *Harm reduction: An historical perspective.* Presented at 3rd Int. Conf. on Reduct. of Drug-Relat. Harm, Melbourne

6. Blix, O., Gronbladh, L. 1988. *AIDS and IV heroin addicts: the preventive effect of methadone maintenance in Sweden.* Presented at 4th Int. AIDS Conf., Stockholm (abstr. #8548)

7. Bottiger, M., Forsgren, M., Grillner, L., Biberfeld, G., Eriksson, G., Janzon, R. 1988. *Monitoring of HIV infection among IV drug users in Stockholm.* Presented at 4th Int. AIDS Conf., Stockholm (abstr. #4709)

8. Bowtell, B. 1992. *Development of policy relating to the prevention of HIV among injecting drug users.* Presented at 3rd Int. Conf. on Reduct. of Drug-Relat. Harm, Melbourne

9. Brettle, R. P. 1991. HIV and harm reduction in injection drug users. *AIDS* 5:125–36

10. Buning, E. C. 1989. *The role of the needle exchange project in preventing HIV infection among drug users in Amsterdam.* Presented at What Works Conf: An Int. Perspect. on Drug Abuse Treat. and Prev. Res., New York

11. Buning, E. C., van Brussel, G. H. A., van Santen, G. 1988. Amsterdam's drug policy and its implications for controlling needle sharing. In *Needle Sharing Among Intravenous Drug Abusers: National and International Drug Perspectives,* ed. R. J. Battjes, R. W. Pickens, pp. 59–74, Res. Monogr. 80. Rockville, Md: Natl. Inst. on Drug Abuse

12. Carlson, G., Needle, R. 1989. *Sponsoring addict self-organization (Addicts Against AIDS): A case study.* Presented at 1st Annu. Natl. AIDS Demonstr. Res. Conf., Rockville, Md.

13. Casadonte, P. P., Des Jarlais, D. C., Friedman, S. R., Rotrosen, J. P. 1990. Psychological and behavioral impact among intravenous drug users of learning HIV test results. *Int. J. Addict* 25:409–26

14. Casriel, C., Des Jarlais, D. C., Rodriguez, R., Friedman, S. R., Stepherson, B., Khuri, E. 1990. Working with heroin sniffers: clinical issues in preventing drug injection. *J. Subst. Abuse Treat.* 7:1–10

16. Cent. Dis. Control. 1990. Update: reducing HIV transmission in intravenous drug users not in drug treatment—United States. *Morbid. Mortal. Wkly. Rep.* 39:529, 535–38

20. Choopanya, K., Vanichseni, S., Plangsringarm, K., Sonchai, W., Carballo, M., et al. 1991. Risk factors and HIV seropositivity among injecting drug users in Bangkok. *AIDS* 5:1509–13

23. Cooper, J. R. 1989. Methadone treatment and acquired immunodeficiency syndrome. *J. Am. Med. Assoc.* 262:1664–68

24. Crofts, N., Stevenson, E. 1992. *The epidemiology of HIV infection among injecting drug users in Australia.* Presented at 3rd Int. Conf. on Reduct. of Drug-Related Harm, Melbourne

25. de Jong, W. M. 1986. *De sociale beweging van opiatengebruikers in Nederland.* Doctoraal-scriiptie sociol., Erasmus Univ., Rotterdam

29. Des Jarlais, D. C., Casriel, C., Friedman, S. R., Rosenblum, A. 1992. AIDS and the transition to illicit drug injection: results of a randomized trial prevention program. *Br. J. Addict.* 87:493–98

33. Des Jarlais, D. C., Friedman, S. R. 1992. The AIDS epidemic and legal access to sterile equipment for injecting illicit drugs. *Ann. Am. Acad. Polit. Soc. Sci.* 521:42–65

34. Des Jarlais, D. C., Friedman, S. R., Hopkins, W. 1985. Risk reduction for the acquired immunodeficiency syndrome among intravenous drug users. *Ann. Intern. Med.* 103:755–59

38. Des Jarlais, D. C., Sotheran, J. L. 1990. The public health paradigm for AIDS and drug use: shifting the time frame. *Br. J. Addict.* 85:348–49

41. Espinoza, P., Bouchard, I., Ballian, P., Polo DeVoto, J. 1988. *Has the open sale of syringes modified the syringe exchanging habits of drug addicts.* Presented at 4th Int. AIDS Conf., Stockholm (abstr. #8522)

43. Friedman, S. R., de Jong, W. M., Des Jarlais, D. C. 1988. Problems and dynamics of organizing intravenous drug users for AIDS prevention. *Health Educ. Res.* 3:49–57

44. Friedman, S. R., de Jong, W. M., Des Jarlais, D. C., Kaplan, C., Goldsmith, D. S. 1987. *Drug users' organizations and AIDS prevention: Differences in structure and strategy.* Presented at 3rd Int. AIDS Conf., Washington, DC

45. Friedman, S. R., Des Jarlais, D. C., Sotheran, J. L., Garber, J., Cohen, H., Smith, D. 1987. AIDS and self-organization among intravenous drug users. *Int. J. Addict.* 22:201–19

47. Friedman, S. R., Neaigus, A., Jose, B., Sufian, M., Stepherson, B., et al. 1990. *Behavioral outcomes of organizing drug injectors against AIDS.* Presented at 2nd Annu. Natl. AIDS Demonstr. Res. Conf., Rockville, Md.

48. Friedman, S. R., Sotheran, J. L., Abdul-Quader, A., Primm, B. J., Des Jarlais, D. C., et al. 1987. The AIDS epidemic among Blacks and Hispanics. *Milbank Q.* 65(Suppl. 2):455–99

49. Friedman, S. R., Sufian, M., Curtis, R., Neaigus, A., Des Jarlais, D. C. 1992. Organizing drug users against AIDS. In *The Social Context of AIDS*, ed. J. Huber, B. E. Schneider, pp. 115–30. Newbury Park, Calif: Sage

50. Fuchs, D., Unterweger, B., Hausen, A., Reibnegger, G., Werner, E. R., et al. 1988. Anti-HIV-1 antibodies, anti-HTLV-1 antibodies and neopterin levels in parenteral drug addicts in the Austrian Tyrol. *J. AIDS* 1:65–66

51. Goldberg, D., Watson, H., Stuart, F., Miller, M., Gruer, L., Follett, E. 1988. *Pharmacy supply of needles and syringes-the effect on spread of HIV among intravenous drug misusers.* Presented at 4th Int. AIDS Conf., Stockholm (abstr. #8521)

52. Guilfoile, A. 1991. *Boulder, Colorado needle exchange program.* Presented at ll9th Annu. Meet. of Am. Public Health Assoc., Atlanta, Nov. 10–14 (session #2170)

53. Hagan, H., Des Jarlais, D. C., Purchase, D., Reid, T., Friedman, S. R. 1991. The Tacoma syringe exchange. *J. Addict. Dis.* 10:81–88

54. Hagan, H., Des Jarlais, D. C., Purchase, D., Reid, T., Friedman, S. R., Bell, T. A. 1991. The incidence of HBV infection and syringe exchange programs (letter). *J. Am. Med. Assoc.* 266:1646–47

55. Hart, G. J., Carvell, A. L. M., Woodward, N., Johnson, A. M., Williams, P., Parry, J. 1989. Evaluation of needle exchange in central London: behaviour change and anti-HIV status over one year. *AIDS* 3:261–65

56. Hartgers, C., Buning, E. C., Coutinho, R. A. 1989. *Evaluation of the needle exchange program in Amsterdam.* Presented at 5th Int. AIDS Conf., Montreal

58. Huang, K. H. C., Watters, J., Case, P. 1989. *Compliance with AIDS prevention measures among intravenous drug users: health beliefs or social-environmental factors?* Presented at 5th Int. AIDS Conf., Montreal (abstr. #M.D.O.5)

59. Hubbard, R. L., Marsden, M. E., Rachal, J. V., Harwood, H. J., Cavanaugh, E. R., Ginzburg, H. M. 1989. *Drug Abuse Treatment: A National Study of Effectiveness.* Chapel Hill/London: Univ. North Carolina Press

60. Ingold, F. R., Ingold, S. 1989. The effects of the liberalization of syringe sales on the behaviour of intravenous drug users in France. *Bull. Narc.* 41:67–81

62. Jose, B., Friedman, S. R., Neaigus, A., Sufian, M. 1990. *Condom use among drug injectors in an organizing project neighborhood.* Presented at 2nd Annu. Natl. AIDS Demonstr. Res. Conf., Rockville, Md.

63. Klee, H., Faugier, J., Hayes, C., Morris, J. 1991. Risk reduction among injecting drug users: changes in the sharing of injection equipment and in condom use. *AIDS Care* 3:63–73

64. Liebman, J., Sepulveda-Irene, B. 1989. *Effectiveness of street outreach as an AIDS-prevention strategy for IV drug users, their sexual partners, and prostitutes in Philadelphia.* Presented at 1st Annu. Natl. AIDS Demonstr. Res. Conf., Bethesda, Md.

66. Ljungberg, B., Christensson, B., Tunving, K., Andersson, B., Landvall, B., et al. 1991. HIV prevention among injecting drug users: three years of experience from a syringe exchange program in Sweden. *J. AIDS* 4:890–95

67. Magura, S., Grossman, J. I., Lipton, D. S., Siddiqi, Q., Shapiro, J., 1989. Determinants of needle sharing among intravenous drug users. *Am. J. Public Health* 79:459–62

70. Miller, H. G., Turner, C. F., Moses, L. E., eds. 1990. *AIDS: The Second Decade.* Washington, DC: Natl. Acad. Press

73. Neaigus, A., Friedman, S. R., Curtis, R., Des Jarlais, D. C., Furst, R. T., et al. 1993. *HIV Risk Networks and Social Networks Among Drug Injectors,* NIDA Rev. Monogr. Rockville, Md: Natl. Inst. of Drug Abuse. In press

75. Neaigus, A., Sufian, M., Friedman, S. R., Goldsmith, D., Stepherson, B., et al. 1990. Effects of outreach intervention on risk reduction among intravenous drug users. *AIDS Educ. Prev.* 2:253–71

76. O'Keefe, E., Kaplan, E., Khoshnood, K. 1991. *Preliminary Report: City of New Haven Needle Exchange Program.* New Haven, Conn: Off. of Mayor Daniels

77. Olin, R., Käill, K. 1989. *HIV status and changes in risk behavior among arrested and detained intravenous drug abusers in Stockholm 1987-1988.* Presented at 5th Int. AIDS Conf., Montreal (abstr. #W.D.P. 76)

78. Oliver, K. J., Maynard, H., Des Jarlais, D. C. 1991. *Portland, Oregon needle exchange program.* Presented at l19th Annu. Meet. of Am. Public Health Assoc., Atlanta, Nov. 10–14 (session #2170)

81. Quimby, E., Friedman, S. R. 1989. Dynamics of Black mobilization against AIDS in New York City. *Soc. Prob.* 36:403–15

83. Robertson, J. R., Bucknall, A. B. V., Welsby, P. D., Roberts, J. J. K., Inglis, J. M., et al. 1986. Epidemic of AIDS related virus (HTLV-III/LAV) infection among intravenous drug users. *Br. Med. J.* 292:527–29

84. Roggenburg, L., Sibthorpe, B., Tesselaar, H. 1990. *IDUs' perception of the effect of HIV counseling and testing on behavior.* Presented at 2nd Annu. NADR Natl. Meet., Bethesda, Md., Nov. 28–30

87. Rugg, D. L., MacGowan, R. J. 1990. *Assessing the effectiveness of HIV counseling and testing: A practical guide.* Backgr. paper for WHO Global Programme on AIDS (GPA), Geneva, Nov. 13–16

88. Schoenbaum, E. E., Hartel, D., Selwyn, P. A., Klein, R. S., Davenny, K., et al. 1989. Risk factors for human immunodeficiency virus infection in intravenous drug users. *N. Engl. J. Med.* 321:874–79

93. Stimson, G. V. 1990. *The prevention of HIV infection in injecting drug users: recent advances and remaining obstacles.* Presented at 6th Int. AIDS Conf., San Francisco

95. Strang, J. 1992. *Harm reduction: responding to the challenge.* Presented at 3rd Int. Conf. on Reduct. of Drug Relat. Harm, Melbourne

97. Sufian, M., Friedman, S. R., Neaigus, A., Stepherson, B., Rivera-Beckman, J., Des Jarlais, D. C. 1990. The impact of AIDS on Puerto Rican intravenous drug users. *Hisp. J. Behav. Sci.* 12:122–34

98. Taylor, F. 1991. Decline in hepatitis B cases. *Am. J. Public Health* 81:221–22

101. Vanichseni, S., Choopanya, K., Des Jarlais, D. C., Plangsringarm, K., Sonchai, W., et al. 1992. HIV testing and sexual behavior among drug injectors in Bangkok, Thailand. *J. AIDS* 5:1119–23

104. Vlahov, D., Celentano, D. D., Munoz, A., Cohn, S., Anthony, J. C., Nelson, K. E. 1991. *Bleach disinfection of needles by intravenous drug users: association with HIV seroconversion.* Presented at 7th Int. AIDS Conf., Florence (abstr. #M.C.49)

106. Watters, J. K., Cheng, Y., Segal, M., Lorvick, J. Case, P., Carlson, J. 1990. *Epidemiology and prevention of HIV in intravenous drug users in San Francisco, 1986-1989.* Presented at 6th Int. AIDS Conf., San Francisco (abstr. #F.C. 106)

109. Wodak, A. 1992. *Implementation of policy into programs.* Presented at 3rd Int. Conf. on Reduct. of Drug Relat. Harm, Melbourne

Drug Traffickers as Social Bandits: Culture and Drug Trafficking in Northern Mexico and the Border Region

Source: Excerpts from Edberg M. August 2001. "Drug Traffickers as Social Bandits: Culture and Drug Trafficking in Northern Mexico and the Border Region." *Journal of Contemporary Criminology* 17(3): 259–277.

INTRODUCTION

This article reviews selected aspects of ethnographic research recently conducted by the author in the U.S.-Mexico border region concerning the way in which narco-traffickers, and by extension the drug war, are portrayed via a culturally specific and popular media genre. Specifically, the research investigated the ways in which the narco-trafficker, as a persona, is *in part* constructed, disseminated and connected with day-to-day practice through the medium of the *narcocorrido*, a recently emergent variation of a traditional border song form called the corrido. Narcocorridos have become very popular in the U.S.-Mexico border region (as well as elsewhere), and they feature narratives about drug traffickers, who are often represented as models, admired persons, or *social bandits* (as described in Hobsbawm 1969, pp. 14–16) for those living in poverty. Key to the role of these narratives in constructing the narco-trafficker persona is the fact that, as songs, they are largely understood to be corridos — border ballads with a long history of recounting epic themes of heroes who resisted the Texas Rangers, American authorities, or in some cases even central Mexican authorities (Paredes 1993; 1958; Herrera-Sobek 1993). These new corridos have situated their protagonists in the current border context, and have gained a substantial amount of popularity among a wide range of Mexican, Mexican-American, and other Hispanic audiences.

BASIC RESULTS

To investigate these questions, the author conducted participant-observation, 55 interviews (youth and adults), and several focus groups on both sides of the border in El Paso, Texas/Juarez, Mexico as well as in other border locations and in Los Angeles, California (where a number of small studios are located that record and produce narcocorridos).

Interpretation. I found multiple interpretations of these songs, depending not only on class or social position but also on situation: In one situation the same corrido would be taken as serious; in another, as fun, almost as humor in the same vein as other Mexican and border styles of joking (e.g., *relajo*). Some of the ways these songs were interpreted are discussed below.

Interpreting narcocorridos as reality: Although they are not strict accounts of facts or events, corridos are typically grounded in real events and contexts that are understood by the listening community. Based on data collected for this study, narcocorridos follow this pattern and are interpreted as a reflection of reality by many (although not all) of the listening community. These realities were many.

In the rural, mountainous Sierra region south of Juarez, for example, growing drug-related plants (opium poppies, marijuana) has for a long time been closely integrated into the life of many rural villages. One interview respondent in El Paso, a man in his 60s, recalled that, even in the late 1940s, in his small village in Sinaloa (western Sierra), there was a man who grew opium poppies in between the rows of maize. The man would pay him and his friends a peso (a significant payment at the time) to take a razor blade and slice all the poppy bulbs so that the "milk" would run. Apparently, the milk granulates after a day or two, and the man would later come by and collect the granulated poppy milk. Three adult prisoners in the central Juarez jail (the *cereso*) with whom I talked also spoke of the drug industry and trade as a matter-of-fact, normal occurrence, a central part of the economy of their pueblos in south Chihuahua, Michoacan, and Sinaloa. The narco-traffickers are big men, as the term is often used, providing wealth and jobs to the community.

In addition, there is simply the multigenerational reality of smuggling, whether what is smuggled is drugs, tequila, or something more benign like wax. Smuggling often occurs across generations, and a set of cultural understandings go with it (famed drug kingpin Pablo Acosta of Ojinaga, Mexico, came from a long family line of smugglers, as described in Poppa, 1990).

Even the weapons used by traffickers have cultural nicknames: The AK-47, for example, is popularly known as a *cuerno de chivo* (horn of the goat) after its long, curved clip. Most respondents were familiar with the term.

Another related factor is the degree to which narcotraffickers are an integral part of the tapestry of community. A *norteño* music group I interviewed, whom I will call *Plata Norte*, was tapped to write a corrido about a local trafficker they knew, who they viewed as a "humble man, with a good heart, loved by the community," despite his involvement in trafficking. His life and his death were significant in the community. A corrido was, therefore, warranted by virtue of community esteem.

Youth interviewed on the U.S. side and on the Mexican side, who live in *barrios* or *colonias* where there is a high prevalence of drug trade activity, gangs, and so on, viewed narcocorridos as a reflection of "how it is" on the streets. This response is virtually identical to the oft-heard comment about gangsta rap. Narcocorridos are viewed as how it is not only because of the exact circumstances of the narratives, which often refer to the drug trade in and from Mexico, but also because of the attitudes, character types, and environment of risk that is presented. For these listeners, narcocorridos thus reflect an "atmospheric of the street." The music is even called hardcore, according to narcocorrido performers and producers interviewed during extended fieldwork in Los Angeles. (At least one Web site devoted to narcocorridos that reports listener reaction in the same manner.)

On the other hand, I was fascinated and even surprised by another aspect of narcocorridos-as-reality, given the current mass-media hype surrounding the genre. The Arizona-based norteño band Plata Norte explained that, at almost every one of their shows (they perform all along the border in Mexico and the United States), someone will come from the audience and give them handwritten lyrics, or a home-recorded tape, for a cor-

rido about something that happened in their town or area. These offerings are requests that the band make a corrido out of the material given to them. The events recounted may be a local tragedy (e.g., a woman whose sister was killed came to the band and asked them to do a corrido about her sister), or in some cases, a drug trafficking situation, which is an everyday fact of life in some border areas and northern Mexican communities.

Interpreting narcocorridos as political statements: Political undertones and overtones were present in a number of the corridos I reviewed, but, as noted below, these elements were not necessarily inherent in the character of the narcotrafficker himself (the term is gendered male here because most narcotraffickers, at this time, are male). This differs from the political aspect of traditional corridos, where it is the hero and subject of the corrido that either makes the political statement or whose actions constitute a political statement. Often, where the political content existed in the narcocorridos I reviewed, the content involved a statement by the *corridistas*, the singers. For example, note the following stanzas in "The General" (Tigres del Norte), referred to earlier:

> Different countries are certified by the gringo (American) government,
>
> And that government says it doesn't want drugs to exist
>
> The gringo government says drugs are dangerous
>
> But tell me, who certifies
>
> The United States?
>
> Mexico has tried honestly and hard
>
> To apprehend the narcotraffickers
>
> It is the gringos who buy the cocaine
>
> They'll pay for it any price
>
> They say they don't want drugs to exist
>
> But when it comes to certification
>
> They give themselves a big break

In some interviews, admiration for the narcotraffickers sung about in narcocorridos had to do specifically with narratives in which the narcotrafficker "defeated" or managed to transport drugs past the police, Border Patrol, or other authorities. On one Web site devoted to narcocorridos, the music is described as "defeating" the preference of "authorities" that these realities (the realities of drugs and their related context) be "buried" by telenovelas and the passing of time. Instead, the narcocorridos "impede forgetting, immortalize people and situations, and defeat the conventional interpretations about what is happening."

Interpreting narcocorridos as heroic tales or allegories:
This is a key element in understanding the role and place of the narcotrafficker persona. First, as can be seen from a sample of lyrics, there is a mixed message in the narcocorridos with respect to the glorification of drug trafficking. The portrayal is one of power and daring but also treachery, betrayal and tragedy. Young people in particular talk about narcotraffickers as powerful and fearsome, as "players" with money, women and an aura of excitement . . . as *valientes* (valiant, "men with balls"), *or vatos*. The narcotraffickers are just one kind of character who can be viewed as "crazy," as willing to take serious risks so as to be the subject (said a former gang member and now gang prevention project director) of comments such as, "That fool *did it!*"

Second, whether narcotraffickers were viewed as heroes—and whether narcocorridos were viewed as songs about heroes in the manner of Pancho Villa or Gregorio Cortez[1]—varied greatly. In Juarez and El Paso, not many people viewed narcotraffickers as heroes (I only heard about a few narco-traffickers who remained in and were said to contribute to their communities). This was in part because Juarez is the "dirty end of the business" where narcotraffickers try to get drugs across the border, dump (for cheap) those they can't, and shoot it out amongst each other. In other locations, particularly as one moves south into the Sierra, this picture changes. There, narcotraffickers may be seen more as "big men" in the sense that they are the ones (especially in rural areas south of Juarez) who often provided employment and various services to the community. As noted above, they are also seen as political foils or tricksters, vicariously confronting, undercutting, critiquing, and escaping both Mexican and American authorities, but not always as social bandits, at least in the sense described by Hobsbawm. The line, however, is a thin one.

Still, even in Juarez (more than in El Paso, based on discussions/interview responses thus far, the image of narcotraffickers referred to above coexists with a number of commonly cited folktales and gossip items about narcotraffickers, who have near mythical status (throughout Mexico). One of these is the story of Caro Quintero (famous in the 1980s, he is perhaps the prototype of the recent crop of mega-narcotraffickers in Mexico), who made a famous declaration from jail that he could pay off Mexico's massive external debt with his wealth. Another is the story (told in many versions) of former Juarez cartel head Amado Carillo Fuentes, called "lord of the skies," who attained a near mythical reputation for his fleet of airplanes and his ability to appear in one place, then another, at will. Some people still think that Amado Carillo is not dead, that he staged his 1997 death in order to live life as he wanted, free from the constant danger and precariousness of his position as cartel head.

There is also another dimension related to the mythic aspect of the drug trade. I heard various stories (see Astorga 1997; and Kaplan 1998) about *El Narcosanto* a narcotrafficker-saint[2], who is honored at a popular shrine in Culiacán in the state of Sinaloa. The narco-saint is named Jesus Malverde, who, depending upon the source, is said to be a Sinaloan *bandido generoso* who robbed the rich and gave to the poor during the rule of Porfirio Díaz (Astorga 1997) or a bandit of some sort who died (or was killed) in the 1970s, or other things. His exact connection to the drug trade is not clear; nevertheless, his shrine is commonly viewed as a "poor people's shrine," and people who visit the shrine often leave mementos or flowers.

Hearing about El Narcosanto, however, and experiencing it are different matters. In the Juarez prison, which is on the outskirts of the city, next to dry, dusty and poverty-ridden Colonia Revolución, I interviewed three men who were convicted of drug trafficking. These three men, coincidentally, had formed a corrido group, either before they were arrested or while in prison. In any case, the prison director let them keep their instruments—bass violin, accordion, and guitar—and allowed them to come up (with their instruments) to the small staff kitchen and do a show. Although the kitchen staff acted as if they had seen the group perform before, this seemed unusual to me, certainly not something one would see in an American prison, especially with inmates locked up for a comparable offense. These corridistas wore street clothes: hats, boots, belts, jeans, Western shirts. No prison garb. They were quite good, as good as anyone I heard on CDs or the radio. They sang several narcocorridos as well as corridos they wrote about life in prison. As I listened, I saw that the lead singer wore a large pendant bearing a photo or picture. I asked him who it was. "El Narcosanto," he said in a matter-of-fact manner. Then he spoke briefly about his faith in El Narcosanto—as I interpreted it, not faith in a formal religious sense as much as an instrumental faith in the protective powers of the saint, as something that would keep him from harm.

By contrast, adult and older respondents who were not recent immigrants or who had more formal education in their background than most (recent) immigrants tended to shake their heads and, with some gravity, deplore the way in which the corrido tradition has been "cheapened" by the narcocorridos, saying that these are nothing like the old corridos

---

[1]Protagonist of a well known and prototypical corrido of the late 19th century, who fought against and confounded the Texas Rangers.

[2]Not, of course, an official canonized saint. A people's saint, as it were.

about revolutionary heroes or figures like Pancho Villa. The primary value underlying narcocorridos, it was said, is money. At the same time, several of these respondents acknowledged that "poor people" view narcotraffickers and the money they are able to distribute as a "dream," particularly because most narcotraffickers also come from a background of poverty.

One of the early narcocorrido stars, Chalino Sanchez, is a clear example of popular appeal among those in poverty. He is widely revered today as a folk hero. Reputed to be a trafficker himself, he was also a narcocorrido singer who made money, and made it big. Yet, he was from a poor rural background, sang with a rough, untrained voice, and, it is said, never separated himself from his people. Like rapper Tupac Shakur, he was shot and killed in the early 1990s.

Interpreting narcocorridos as inevitable tragedy: It is important to note that the corridor, and by extension those represented in its narratives, is a "marked genre" to start with because the corrido form itself, at least this genre of corrido, focuses on misfortunes and/or death as part of the narrative structure through which the protagonist is represented and interpreted as a hero. This is a very interesting ontological element of corridos that may have some ties, I believe, to ontological elements of other music/aesthetic genres that grow out of situations of concentrated or recurring poverty, where the life or the character of the protagonist (in this case the narcotrafficker) is created, or at least defined, by his/her death. As such, death is part of the developmental process, and the life of the protagonist achieves a kind of completeness after death, as an ongoing iteration of a moral type.

The connection between corridos (and narcocorridos) and death is clearly a strong undercurrent. Members of one norteño group told me that because a corrido is a memorial, a corrido should never be written about someone who is alive—or if it is done, at least no name should be mentioned. In fact, as discussed earlier, a man they knew who was a well-liked community figure and a narcotrafficker had a corrido written about him while he was alive. Sure enough, said the group members, he was shot a few months later. They were then called on to write and perform the corrido written about him post mortem. However, the corrido-death connection is not necessarily the rule, since there are in fact many narcocorridos written about those who are living.

Interpreting narcocorridos as moral lessons: To the outsider, this may seem unlikely, given the subject matter. But (as noted earlier), it is not uncommon for narcocorridos to contain a warning about the consequences of involvement in trafficking. In addition, members of Plata Norte said that some of the lyrics address moral issues that have meaning beyond their drug context. For example, there is a corrido about a man who was so involved in the drug business—a kind of workaholic—that he forgot to feed his children, and the corrido describes his children in the back of his truck eating cocaine because they were starving due to his neglect. It is not only a narcocorrido but also a statement about being a responsible parent in this interpretation.

Interpreting narcocorridos as jests: Another way in which narcocorridos, and thus the narcotrafficker character, are sometimes interpreted is as a form of "intercultural jest" (Paredes, 1993). Such jests are called *tallas*, according to Paredes (1993). One form documented by Paredes was the *curandero* belief tale, stories told about situations in which sick people were cured by a curandero after the American doctor could not cure them. In these tales, the doctors are "shown up" by the curandero because, after the doctors pronounce the patient as incurable, the curandero is easily able to cure him or her by a simple remedy of herbs, specific rituals, washing in a certain well or spring, and so on. When the doctors approach the curandero to find out how he did it, the curandero tells them nothing, other than a pious "God cured him, not I." The doctors then leave, mystified. Another kind of joking tradition that narcocorridos may draw from is known as *relajo*, described by Barriga (1997) as "a joking relationship that involves a suspension of seriousness that undercuts normative values" (p. 50; quoting Portilla, 1966, p. 25), often involving themes of class or social stratification.

With this in mind, a number of narcocorridos can be viewed as making a jest about tricking, evading, or otherwise showing up the *migra* (Border Patrol), Mexican or U.S. police and other officials. For example, the corrido "Las Tres Monjitas" (Exterminador) tells the story of narcotraffickers who dressed up as nuns to transport their drugs across the border (They were eventually discovered, but then pulled their *cuernos* (AK-47s) out of their habits and engaged in a gunfight.) This is a popular topic for song in general. I also heard, for example, about a song by Vicente Fernandez in which he jokes about dying his hair blond to get past the migra.

Several of the youth I interviewed, in fact, said that they look at narcocorrido lyrics as fun, or as funny, in the manner of cartoon action or professional wrestling. The narcotrafficker character here is not interpreted as real but as a fantasy and entertainment, although one that draws on resonant themes. Norteño musicians in Plata Norte said that they themselves listen to narcocorridos along with other norteño music, in part because "we get a kick out of the lyrics," according to one member. And when I attended a large concert by well-known norteño group Los Tigres del Norte, the crowd responded with great enthusiasm when they played a set of narcocorridos. On stage, there was an exaggerated display of simulated gunshots and sound. In one sense, there was clearly a sense of play involved in the performance. Yet, a substantial number of the audience were dressed the way narcotraffickers often dress, with boots, hats, silk shirts, and cellphones (a look labeled *chero* by many interview respondents). In the same vein, narcocorrido lyrics often employ rural themes as humorous double entendres to communicate drug-related messages: for example, the use of animal names to signify drugs (e.g. parakeet for cocaine) or phrases such as "cow's tail with no ticks" (to mean marijuana with no seeds).

Interpreting narcocorridos as an image enhancer and source of power: Many sources described narcocorridos as *canciones fuertas* (strong or powerful songs). Even more, it was said that playing narcocorridos helps in the self-creation of an image that is more powerful than the person "doing the creating" may actually be. Narcocorridos, said sources from Plata Norte, "portray you as an image either that you want others to believe or that you want to believe." By having them around, and playing them, "other people will give you credit for being stronger than you are, more powerful than you are." Thus, it is said that narcocorridos "make you braver, make you stronger." In this way, they function like an intoxicant, an intoxicant of power. A gathering of men, listening to narcocorridos and drinking alcohol, will get "pumped up."

In a sense, this aspect of narcocorridos is similar to the effect that corridos had as songs of the Mexican revolution, and, for that matter, as songs of the Chicano movement in the United States. One source told me, for example, that when he was in prison, Latino inmates would sing corridos from the Chicano movement as a source of group solidarity and strength.

Interpreting narcocorridos as "country music" and/or lower class music: For many respondents, corridos were clearly a regional signifier, an urban-rural signifier, and a class signifier. This refers on the one hand to their appeal as music that reminds rural-based listeners of their home setting. The obverse of the positive rural signification for listeners in this category, though, is the negative connotation attached by others to the same signification. Echoing an opinion heard from a number of adults, a middle-aged woman and mother of several children, who ran a small restaurant in downtown Juarez, said that narcocorridos and corridos in general are music that appeals to people with lower levels of education, or to maquiladora (border industrial) workers. She said that she loved the beautiful norteño romantic ballads, but as for corridos, "They [corrido singers] sing like they are squeezing their necks." Moreover, executives I interviewed who manage a group of radio stations in Juarez delineated each station's audience by class. Not surpris-

ingly, the station that played corridos/narcocorridos was unapologetically categorized as lower class.

An additional and important class issue is certainly the connection made between common northern Mexican images and portrayals of rural men from the hills or the Sierra who can survive, who can take it, who refuse to give way to anyone. That image in itself is intermingled with portrayals of narcotraffickers. There is, in some narcocorrido lyrics, a great love expressed for this tough land, and at times a pride in the marijuana-growing business, as a business that is of the hills, and that has helped people survive and prosper (even if they are not members of the elite).

Narcocorridos as marketing tool: It is also important to note that narcocorridos are now big business, and the narcotrafficker persona is a hot commodity in itself. Interviews with small and large studios/producers showed that corridos and other norteño music, once rejected by radio stations as "poor people's music," have attracted their attention—and thereby that of the media producers—because of the underground popularity of narcocorridos and the play that is made of the narcotrafficker persona (now increasingly both male and female). Thus, and this is important, the persona is further constructed and amplified by the music producing industry because it sells CDs and tapes. The narcotrafficker persona is used, I would argue, in its most shallow and sensationalized form on ads, CD covers, and so on, and the focus is primarily on the "in your face" or outrageous element of the persona, though there is sometimes the social bandit element is involved. In this way, there are many parallels to gangsta rap, and, in fact, the further construction of the persona via the music industry draws (by their own admission) from the marketing and construction of the gangsta rap image.

Along with this is another related and important phenomenon. Narcotraffickers themselves, seeing the power of their caricature as a marketing tool in the media, often commission norteño groups to write corridos about them as a kind of advertisement, and as a creation of self through the commodified narcotrafficker persona (which, as noted, includes social bandit and other socially positive components).

CULTURAL "PERSONAS" AND SOCIAL STRATIFICATION

If cultural "personas" [*such as the narcotrafficker*] have this kind of representational function (as I argue more extensively elsewhere), then, as noted, it makes perfect sense that personas would be created over time that represent values/understandings associated with social divisions and different social segments, whether of class, subculture, or other origin. It also makes sense that at least some of the personas originating with or popular among subaltern/subordinate strata would represent a conglomeration of contesting meanings vis-à-vis the dominant social groups. There are clear elements of this in the narco-trafficker persona, and these elements are quite similar to aspects of other personas that I have encountered as characteristic of high-poverty urban settings, for example, the dealer or hustler persona.

With the urban dealer persona, the emphasis again is on performance, on establishing a reputation and carrying out a daily performance that validates the performer as a dealer and deserving of his reputation as one who makes things happen. The reputation must include a willingness to be ruthless when necessary (e.g., when territory or reputation is challenged, when double crossed), a show of wealth as a demonstration of efficacy and ability (and as a not-so-subtle rejection of the dominant society's rules for how properly to achieve success), and, in the most enduring examples, at least the pretense of attachment to community in the form of services, help and money provided to community members. Maintaining this kind of reputation is a richly coded task. I used to hear, for example, that the way to hold a gun during a shooting was horizontally, with arm extended out to the side as opposed to in front. This was a stylized way of demonstrating power and insouciance vis-à-vis the victim.

Although the details are different, this is very close to some of the basic elements of the narco-trafficker persona. Moreover, there is a striking similarity in the way that both personas (narco-trafficker and hustler), as symbols, appear to simultaneously contest and accept dominant group meanings with respect to the criteria for establishing oneself as a significant or admired person. Like Warner's (1959) classic parable of the disfavored but socially mobile outsider Biggy Muldoon, there is both a tendency to 'want in' via demonstrations of the material trappings of success and a rejection of the dominant rules for how to get there, the accepted 'cultural performance of success.' Because having status or being notable is such a symbolically laden task, an individual who rejects participation in that performance may be precluded from ever really being there. (Yet, on the other hand, such a person may end up as the progenitor of a new model of acceptable cultural performance for success or status, or even gender role.) This, in fact, is one of the subtle ways in which racism and other forms of discrimination work even when the overt or de jure constraints are gone. Moreover, if people do attempt the cultural performance along with the material performance, the dilemma so often lies in the consequent rejection of themselves, and therefore of their original reference group, as described in another classic work, by Whyte (1943/1993) with respect to Chick Morelli, the former 'corner boy' who became a success in the

mainstream world. Thus, one of the comments I heard repeatedly during this research about Chalino Sanchez, who was both narco-corrido singer and a (reputed) narco-trafficker himself, and who made a substantial amount of money from his music, was that he 'valued his people' over the money and status he gained, and that he 'never left his people.'

A third and important parallel (noted earlier) is in the way that death seems to complete the persona; death is not the ending but the 'launching' of an individual into a timeless existence as an iteration of the persona, whose life will float in the popular imagination, reputation cemented and memorialized forever, free from the barriers that prevented attainment of full status in this world. As noted, there are cultural roots in Mexico for this with respect to the narco-trafficker persona, but because this is a characteristic of personas that exist in other settings, it is not just a cultural idiosyncrasy. Something else is involved. It is possible that, in a situation of poverty where options for being a significant person are limited (at least in this world), a notable death, in fact, becomes one way of living, one way of having made a dent in the cosmos, so to speak. This may be a sentiment that exists across cultures in situations of social stratification and poverty, and one that becomes embodied in culturally specific ways through the invention of personas like those described here. In this society, at least, poverty among other things is facelessness; yet, people yearn to be known, to have had an existence that produced at least some trace.[3] Moreover, it is not a great leap to say that, in a global context of stratification by nation-state, by center-periphery, by West/non-West or other such divisions, these general sentiments are akin to the ethic of martyrdom which is so common among those who are called terrorists.

With the narco-trafficker persona, however, there is less clarity with respect to who are represented as dominant versus subordinate groups. The element of racial polarization that is part of the urban U.S. hustler persona is not so clearly part of the narco-trafficker persona. In El Paso/Juarez, and other locations on the border, socioeconomic disparities cannot always be linked a priori with racial or ethnic categories, because populations on both sides of the border are predominantly Mexican in ethnic origin (see Martinez 1988, 1994), and the dominant subgroups (in socioeconomic terms) include either (a) Anglo, Mexican, and other foreign nationals who own or manage maquiladoras and their related businesses or (b) drug lords. In Juarez, I saw a number of walled neighborhoods and compounds where the elite or top families live. These are

---

[3] In another context, see Liebow (1993) on this sentiment among homeless women.

largely Mexican families. And some narco-corrido lyrics focus on the Mexican police, just some focus on the U.S. Border Patrol and the Immigration and naturalization Service. In a way, the lack of clarity allows for more exploitation of the persona, because the ambiguity can be glossed over or presented in ways that are more suggestive than clear.

Let us assume, without trying to be overly glib, that on the U.S.-Mexico border, the narco-trafficker persona draws some part of its meaning from (a) conditions of poverty set against the domination (perceived and real, in different measures) of global industry (via the maquiladora factories), the United States, and the still-salient class/race structure in Mexico; (b) the long tradition of border conflict between the United States and Mexico and the underlying antagonism that flows from the conflict;[4] (c) a Mexican tradition of individuals as centers of power and agency, the tradition of *personalismo* (Suchlicki 1996); and (d) long-held images of a Northern Mexican man, clever, brave, and tough. The narco-trafficker then represents a certain, culturally shaped, individual route to power for those who feel powerless, a challenge to the customary rules for how to achieve status and influence, and a route to status for those usually shut out. Thus, it is not just the modeling effect (e.g., Bandura, 1986) that is key. When constructing themselves as an iteration of the narco-trafficker persona, people take on the stance that this persona represents. Particular behaviors, including violence and drug use, are not simply mechanical imitations of a model; they are pursued to the extent that they are part of the expression of that stance.

In the context of the border, this kind of representation is powerful. Moreover, I would argue that identical or similar representations are just as salient in other situations of poverty, disaffection and alienation, whether that is in the inner city, a rural area, or somewhere else. Fleisher (1998) has documented, for example, how youth gang leaders are mythologized, again, not just as models, but as representations of a stance. Bourgois (1989, 1996) has noted the connection between crack selling and respect in New York City. Anderson (1992) has described a young man's involvement in drugs as a redress of the humiliation experienced in the mainstream world. In my own research and program work, I have encountered a number of similar examples (see Edberg, 1998).

Consequently, actions that are often spoken of as risk behaviors need to be viewed as more than behaviors. They are also expressions. This is, of course, not the only factor involved, and it may be more or less important in different cases. But the discourse of behavior tends to push aside these considerations in establishing causality and in developing social/health prevention and intervention modalities. As elaborated more fully in a forthcoming book (Edberg, forthcoming), a prevention/intervention approach that views behavior also as expression, I would argue, must address that which is being expressed through the specific behaviors at issue and seek to resolve or change what lies behind the expressive stance, or to find other ways through which it can be channeled.

REFERENCES

Anderson, E. 1992. "The Story of John Turner." In *Drugs, Crime and Social Isolation.* A.V. Harrell and G.E. Peterson (Eds). Washington, DC: Urban Institute Press.

Aramoni, A. 1965. *Psicoanalisis de la Dinamica de un Pueblo.* Mexico, D.F.: B. Costa-Amic.

Astorga, L. 1997. "Los Corridos de Traficantes de Drogas en México y Columbia." *Revista Mexicana de Sociologia* 59(4): 245–261.

Bandura, A. 1986. *Social Foundations of Thought and Action: A Social-Cognitive View.* Englewood Cliffs, NJ: Prentice–Hall.

Barriga, M.D. 1997. "The Culture of Poverty as Relajo." *Aztlan* 22(2): 43–65.

Barthes, R. 1972. *Mythologies.* Translated by Annette Lavers. New York: Hill & Wang.

Bourgois, Phillipe. 1996. *In Search of Respect: Selling Crack in El Barrio.* Cambridge: Cambridge University Press.

Bourgois, Phillipe. 1989. "In Search of Horatio Alger: Culture and Ideology in the Crack Economy." *Contemporary Drug Problems* 16(4): 619–650.

Edberg, M. 1998. "Street Cuts: Splices from Project Notebooks and Other Indelible Impressions." *Anthropology and Humanism* Spring 1998.

Edberg, M. Forthcoming. *Making a Dent in the Cosmos: Narcocorridos and the Narcotrafficker Persona on the U.S.-Mexico Border.* Manuscript under review by University of Texas Press.

Fleisher, M.S. 1998. *Dead End Kids: Gang Girls and the Boys They Know.* Madison, WI: University of Wisconsin Press.

Goldwert, M. 1985. "Mexican Machismo: The Flight from Femininity." *The Psychoanalytic Review* 72: 161–169.

Hernandez, G. 1992. "El Corrido Ayer y Hoy: Nuevas Notas Para su Estudio." In J.M. Valenzuela Arce (Ed), *Entre la Magia y la Historia: Tradiciones, Mitos y Leyendas de la Frontera.* Tijuana: El Colegio de la Frontera Norte.

Herrera-Sobek, M. 1993. *Northward Bound: The Mexican Immigrant Experience in Ballad and Song.* Bloomington: Indiana University Press.

Hobsbawm, E. 1969. *Bandits.* New York: Delacorte Press.

Kaplan, R.D. 1998. "Travels into America's Future: Mexico and the Southwest." *Atlantic Monthly* July 1998: 47–68.

Katz, F. 1998. *The Life and Times of Pancho Villa.* Stanford: Stanford University Press.

Kun J. 1997. "Narcocorridistas." *Village Voice*, December 2, P. 67.

Liebow, E. 1993. *Tell Them Who I Am: The Lives of Homeless Women.* New York: Free Press.

Martinez, O.J. 1994. *Border People: Life and Society in the U.S. Mexico Borderlands.* Tucson: University of Arizona Press.

Martinez, O.J. 1988. *Troublesome Border.* Tucson: University of Arizona Press.

Mirande, A. 1997. *Hombres y Machos: Masculinity and Latino Culture.* Boulder, CO: Westview Press.

Nicolopulos, J. 1997. "The Heroic Corrido: A Premature Obituary?" *Aztlan* 22(1): 114–138.

---

[4] I might note, for example, that in Mexico, on Good Friday (before Easter Sunday), figures of Judas Iscariot are sometimes burned, along with other figures representing popular or moral enemies, antagonists, or persons subject to popular opprobrium. A perennial favorite for burning is Uncle Sam.

Paredes, A. 1993. "The Mexican Corrido: Its Rise and Fall." In R. Bauman (Ed), *Folklore and Culture on the Texas-Mexican Border*. Austin, TX: Center for Mexican-American Studies.

Paredes, A. 1958. *"With a Pistol in His Hand": A Border Ballad and Its Hero*. Austin, TX: University of Texas Press.

Paz, O. 1985. *The Labyrinth of Solitude and Other Writings*. New York: Grove Press.

Poppa, T. E. 1990. *Drug Lord: The Life and Death of a Mexican Kingpin*. New York: Pharos Books.

Portilla, J. 1966. *La Fenomenologia del Relajo*. Mexico: Fondo de Cultura Economica.

Suchlicki, J. 1996. *Mexico: From Montezuma to NAFTA, Chiapas, and Beyond*. Washington: Brassey's, Inc.

Warner, W.L. 1959. *The Living and the Dead: A Study of the Symbolic Life of Americans*. Yankee City Series Volume 5. New Haven: Yale University Press.

Whyte, William Foote. 1993 (1943). *Street Corner Society: The Social Structure of an Italian Slum (Fourth Edition)*. Chicago: University of Chicago Press.

Evaluation: What Is It? Why Is It Needed? How Does It Relate to Theory?

In Part 13, the importance of evaluation and its relevance to the current health promotion program environment is discussed. Because there is an increased demand for theory-driven and evidence-based programs, building evaluation into a health promotion program is no longer an option. This part briefly summarizes the basic types of evaluation—process, impact, and outcome—along with the technique of using a "logic model" to tie the components of a program to the planning and assessment process, theory, and evaluation. Basic evaluation designs are also described. The first two selections in this part include a set of principles and a rationale for evaluation developed by the World Health Organization (WHO, 1980) and an overview of evaluation types and terminologies from a well-known evaluation text (Windsor et al., 2004). The third selection provides an example of, and a guide to, evaluation as applied to health communications programs from the well-known "pink book" (DHHS, 2002), available from the National Cancer Institute.

Health Program Evaluation: Guiding Principles for Application of the Managerial Process for National Health Development

Source: WHO. 1980. Excerpt from *Health Program Evaluation: Guiding Principles for Application of the Managerial Process for National Health Development.* Geneva: World Health Organization.

I. INTRODUCTION

1. In 1978, at the request of Member States, WHO prepared provisional guidelines for health programme evaluation for use both by countries for their programmes and activities, and by WHO for its collaborative programmes. These general guidelines, which were endorsed by the Thirty-first World Health Assembly, have been adapted in the text that follows with a view to integrating evaluation into the overall managerial process for national health development.

2. Evaluation, in the context of that managerial process, should be a continuing process aimed mainly at correcting and improving actions in order to render health activities more relevant, more efficient and more effective. In this perspective evaluation calls for an open mind capable of constructive criticism. It further requires willingness to communicate freely with professional peers and other persons or groups concerned at various policy and operational levels of health systems as well as other related social and economic systems, whether national or international.

3. Evaluation implies judgement based on careful assessment and critical appraisal of given situations, which should lead to drawing sensible conclusions and making useful proposals for future action. It should not be seen as "pronouncing a sentence" in a judicial sense. The judgement has to be based on valid, relevant and sensitive information that is readily and easily available and that is provided to all those who need it.

4. The process outlined in these guiding principles should therefore be regarded as a model to provide a systematic basis for evaluation. The use of such a model should help to free the mind to concentrate on the judgement required.

5. It should be noted that the guiding principles are—as the words imply—intended for flexible use, and should not be considered as a formal manual. The process of evaluation requires adaptation of these guiding principles to each specific situation and would suffer in its usefulness if too rigid a system were proposed. It should also be noted that the guiding principles that follow are a first step towards better integration of the evaluation process into the overall managerial process.

II. GENERAL PRINCIPLES

6. Evaluation is a systematic way of learning from experience and using the lessons learned to improve current activities and promote better planning by careful selection of alternatives for future action. This involves a critical analysis of different aspects of the development and implementation of a programme and the activities that constitute the programme, its relevance, its formulation, its efficiency and effectiveness, its costs and its acceptance by all parties involved.

7. Thus, the purpose of evaluation in health development is to improve health programmes and the services for delivering them, and to guide the allocation of human and financial resources in current and future programmes and services. It should be used constructively and not for the justification of past actions or merely to identify their inadequacies. It is essential to perceive evaluation as a decision-oriented tool, and to link the evaluation process closely with decision-making, whether at the operational or the policy level. The very process of carrying out an evaluation can be just as important as the conclusions drawn, since involvement in the process itself often induces a better understanding of the activities being evaluated, and a more constructive approach to their implementation and to any future action required.

8. Evaluation, difficult in any field, presents particular problems in health work owing to the very nature of the activities, which often do not lend themselves easily to the measurement of what has been attained against predetermined, quantified objectives. It is therefore often unavoidable to apply qualitative judgement, supported, wherever possible, by reliable, quantified information. Account has to be taken of the intricate interrelationships between the health and other social and economic sectors. Changes in a health situation are often brought about by elements outside the health sector, making evaluation, particularly of effectiveness and impact, even more difficult. This accentuates the need to define reliable and sensitive indicators for identifying changes in health status or in the improvement of health care delivery. The problems related to the collection of information for these indicators have repercussions on the feasibility of their use.

9. Another constraint that is often encountered is a certain in-built resistance in principle to accepting evaluation and its results as a valid management tool. Self-defence often leads to rejection; it is not difficult to prove that an evaluation process was not "scientific" enough to provide a "sound" basis for making programme decisions, or to discredit the evaluation results by challenging the validity of certain criteria used.

10. The purpose of the managerial process for national health development is to build up the health system in a rational and systematic way. Health programme evaluation is part of the managerial process for national health development, as described in the volume already mentioned. The diagram opposite (see Fig. 1 [not shown]) illustrates the place of evaluation in the overall managerial process.

11. In order to carry out evaluation as part of the managerial process, it has to be planned for when working out that process in each country; for example, evaluation of broad programming has to be taken into account before detailed programming is initiated.

12. There is a great variety of national health systems. Thus, national health policies vary according to political, economic and social systems. Most countries have plans to develop their health systems, some more formal than others. Some countries have health programmes with well-defined objectives and targets. All have various types of health services and institutions as well as different types of professional and other health workers.

13. Governments are taking an increased interest in health development. In some countries the government provides all health care. In others, various types of social security and health insurance schemes exist, sometimes alongside government health care and sometimes with their own health institutions. In addition, in some countries health care is provided by voluntary agencies and by the private sector.

14. The process suggested in these guidelines for evaluation as part of the managerial process is general in nature and has to be adapted for use within the large variety of national health systems. A model of one such system has been used for convenience.

15. Such a model of a government-directed health system of a medium-sized country would include local, district and central levels. At the local level some or all of the essential elements of primary health care would be provided. At district level there would be a district health office to manage all the health affairs of the district, a district hospital with an outpatient dispensary, a public health laboratory, and schools for nurses and auxiliaries. Sometimes the environmental health services would be managed from the district health office; sometimes they would be managed by other sectors. At central level there would be a ministry of health or equivalent body dealing with health planning, the management of the government health services and institutions and certain environmental services, large general and specialized hospitals, medical schools, as well as schools for nurses and other professional health workers, and central public health laboratories.

16. Health systems are undergoing profound change in many countries. Numerous countries have introduced the managerial process for national health development or an equivalent process, and this will no doubt

facilitate evaluation once programmes have been well defined. Other countries will have to define in other ways programmes and their component parts that are to be evaluated. The establishment and management of health services and institutions for programme implementation are often of particular importance, calling for specific kinds of evaluation.

17. As for the responsibility for evaluation, the principle whereby evaluation should be conducted as an integral part of the various steps of the overall managerial process implies that individuals and groups responsible for the development and application of that process at the various policy and operational levels also carry responsibility for its evaluation.

18. Thus, to revert to the model outlined above, responsibility will lie at the local level with those in charge of primary health care. Communities themselves will also carry responsibility for evaluating the appropriateness of the services they receive and the satisfaction of community members with the health care available to them. At district level, responsibility will be with directors of district hospitals, public health laboratories, environmental health services, training schools and, finally, the district health officer; at central level, it will be with the directors of the various hospitals, deans of medical and nursing schools, central public health laboratories, programme directors in the ministry of health, the director-general of health services in the ministry of health, the minister of health, and, possibly, the state controller, the minister of finance, the parliament or other governmental institutions, as appropriate in each country.

19. An important part of the responsibility at each level is to ensure that other individuals and groups concerned at the same level or at other levels, whether more centrally or more peripherally located, are in a position to contribute to the evaluation, are kept informed of its results, and are requested to take appropriate action. This is essential in order to initiate or maintain the dialogues required among these persons.

20. As some of the evaluation issues might be of a sensitive or controversial nature, the evaluation activity as well as its findings should be shared at regular intervals by all involved in the process. To facilitate this task a current record should be maintained of the important decisions and options, of the reasons for selecting one of several courses of action, and of the actual events and intermediate results as they occur.

21. The following are the main features of the components of the evaluation process:

(1) Relevance relates to the rationale for adopting health policies in terms of their response to social and economic policy; and to having programmes, activities, services or institutions, in terms of their response to essential human needs and social and health policies and priorities.

(2) Adequacy implies that sufficient attention has been paid to certain previously determined courses of action, such as the various issues to be considered during broad programming.

(3) Progress is concerned with the comparison of actual with scheduled activities, the identification of reasons for achievements or shortcomings, and indications for remedies for any shortcomings. The purpose of a progress review is to facilitate the monitoring and operational control of ongoing activities. In this context monitoring is the day-to-day follow-up of an activity during its implementation to ensure that operations are proceeding as planned and are on schedule. It keeps track of ongoing activities, milestones achieved, personnel matters, supplies and equipment, and money spent in relation to budgets allocated.

(4) Efficiency is an expression of the relationships between the results obtained from a health programme or activity and the efforts expended in terms of human, financial and other resources, health processes and technology, and time. The assessment of efficiency is aimed at improving implementation, and adds to the review of progress by taking account of the results of monitoring. Under this heading, a check is also made on such matters as the appropriateness of existing plans of operations, work schedules, methods applied, manpower used, and the adequacy and use of financial resources, with a view to improving them, if necessary, at the least cost.

(5) Effectiveness is an expression of the desired effect of a programme, service, institution or support activity in reducing a health problem or improving an unsatisfactory health situation. Thus, effectiveness measures the degree of attainment of the predetermined objectives and targets of the programme, service or institution. The assessment of effectiveness is aimed at improving programme formulation or the functions and structure of health services and institutions through analysis of the extent of attainment of their objectives. Where feasible, the extent of attainment should be quantified. Where this is not feasible, a qualitative

analysis of the relevance and usefulness of the achievement has to be performed, however subjective and impressionistic such an analysis may be, until a more precise way of measuring is developed. The evaluation of effectiveness should also include an assessment of the satisfaction or dissatisfaction expressed by the community concerned regarding the effects of the programme, service or institution. If possible, cost-effectiveness should be assessed and a cost-benefit analysis made.

(6) Impact is an expression of the overall effect of a programme, service or institution on health and related socioeconomic development. The assessment of impact is thus aimed at identifying any necessary change in the direction of health programmes so as to increase their contribution to overall health and socioeconomic development.

22. The description of these components of evaluation would be incomplete without reference to the frequency with which they can be considered. While evaluation is a continuing process, its results have to be summarized and reported on at given times or specified intervals. It will no doubt be found easier to summarize the assessment of progress and efficiency, say, once a year than to assess effectiveness, for which a longer time-span might be required. This results from the need to identify significant changes in the specific health situation that are indicative of a programme's effectiveness. An even longer time-span is likely to be required in relation to the assessment of impact; at least five years from the inception of a programme may be required.

23. Indicators and criteria are used as aids throughout the evaluation process. They can also be used as aids for planning and programming.

24. Indicators are variables that help to measure changes. They are evaluation tools which can measure change directly or indirectly. For example, if the objective of a programme is to train a certain number of auxiliary health personnel annually, a direct indicator for evaluation could be the number of such personnel actually trained each year. If the subject of evaluation is the result of a programme aimed at improving the level of health of a child population, it may be necessary to assess any improvement by using several indicators that could indirectly measure a change in this level. Such indicators could be the nutritional status as illustrated by weight in relation to height, the rate of immunization, learning capacity, age-specific mortality rates, disease specific morbidity rates, and disability rates of a child population.

25. When selecting indicators, full account has to be taken of the extent to which they are valid, reliable, sensitive, and specific.

26. Validity implies that the indicator actually measures what it is supposed to measure. Reliability implies that even if the indicator is used by different people at different times and under different circumstances, the results will be the same. Sensitivity means that the indicator should be sensitive to changes in the situation or phenomenon concerned. However, indicators could be sensitive to more than one situation or phenomenon. Specificity means that the indicator reflects changes only in the situation or phenomenon concerned. For example, the infant mortality rate is a sensitive, although very crude, indicator of the level of health of a child population. It is a direct measure of death and only an indirect measure of health, but within this limitation it is both a valid and a reliable indicator. It is not specific, however, in relation to any particular health action, since its reduction can result from a large number of factors related to social and economic development, including health development, and can rarely be attributed to any one health action.

27. Health and health-related indicators, often considered in various combinations, are used in particular to assess effectiveness and impact. A vast number of indicators exists. They can be placed in groups relating to health policy, socioeconomic conditions, provision of health care, and health status. While indicators of health policy and of the provision of health care are useful mainly for assessing effectiveness, social and economic indicators and indicators of health status have to be used in the final analysis to assess impact. The following are examples of such indicators:

(1) HEALTH POLICY INDICATORS
— High-level political commitment to health for all
— Allocation of adequate resources for primary health care
— Degree of equity of distribution of resources
— Level of community involvement in attaining health for all
— Establishment of a suitable organizational and managerial framework for the national strategy for health for all

— Practical manifestations of international political commitment to health for all

(2) SOCIAL AND ECONOMIC INDICATORS
— Rate of population increase
— Gross national product (GNP) or gross domestic product (GDP)
— Income distribution
— Work availability
— Adult literacy rate
— Adequacy of housing expressed as number of persons per room
— Per capita energy availability

(3) INDICATORS OF THE PROVISION OF HEALTH CARE
— Availability
— Physical accessibility
— Economic and cultural accessibility
— Utilization of services
— Indicators for assessing quality of care

(4) INDICATORS OF COVERAGE BY PRIMARY HEALTH CARE
— Level of "health literacy"
— Availability of safe water in the home or within short walking distance
— Adequate sanitary facilities in the home or immediate vicinity
— Access of mothers and children to local health care
— Birth attendance by trained personnel
— Percentage of children at risk immunized against the major infectious diseases of childhood
— Availability of essential drugs throughout the year
— Accessibility of referral institutions
— Ratio of population to different kinds of health worker in primary health care and at referral levels

(5) HEALTH STATUS INDICATORS
— Percentage of newborn infants with birth weight of a least 2500 g
— Percentage of children that have a weight for age that corresponds to specified norms
— Indicators of the psychosocial development of children
— Infant mortality rate
— Child mortality rate
— Under-5-year mortality rate
— Life expectancy at a given age
— Maternal mortality rate
— Disease-specific mortality rates
— Disease-specific morbidity rates
— Disability rates
— Indicators of social and mental pathology, such as rates of suicide, drug addiction, crime, juvenile delinquency, alcoholism, excessive smoking, obesity and consumption of tranquillizers

28. Criteria are standards by which actions are measured. Criteria may be technical or social, technical criteria being normally highly specific to programmes. For example, a technical criterion for the guarantee of the safety of drinking-water would have to be a certain technical standard for the purity of water. A social criterion for the guarantee of the continuation of the water supply could be the existence of a community organization for the maintenance of the supply.

29. The main purpose of criteria is to provoke thought leading to judgement. Such judgement can rarely be arrived at only through adding up numerical values resulting from certain quantified evaluation criteria.

30. Nevertheless, criteria for the evaluation of health programmes should be quantified wherever possible, although in practice this will not always be possible, particularly where social criteria are concerned. It is therefore often necessary to resort to an evaluation based on qualitative rather than quantitative assessment.

31. Another very important attribute of both indicators and criteria is the availability of the information required: that is, it should be possible to obtain the data required without undue difficulty. Indicators and criteria should be included in the programme at the planning stage, so that the information requirements can be determined early on.

32. It has to be realized that there will be health activities for the evaluation of which no suitable indicators and criteria may be available. In these cases, pertinent questions should be asked concerning the activity to be evaluated. Answers to these questions will help to guide evaluation and will, in turn, help to define and refine indicators and criteria. For example, the following illustrative questions could be asked:

(1) Has "health for all" received endorsement as policy at the highest official level?

(2) Have mechanisms been formed or strengthened for involving people in the national strategy for health for all?

(3) How much of the GNP is spent on health, and how much of this is spent on various population groups or geographical areas, such as urban and rural areas?

(4) How much of the health budget is spent on local health care?

(5) What percentage of health expenditure in developed countries is transferred to support strategies for health for all in developing countries?

(6) Is safe water available in the home, or how far away is it available in terms of walking distance?

(7) Are there adequate sanitary facilities in the home or immediate vicinity?

(8) What proportion of children is immunized against the major infectious diseases of children?

(9) What walking or travel time is required to obtain local health care?

(10) Is childbirth attended by trained personnel?

(11) Is the nutritional status of children adequate?

(12) Do large numbers of children die during their first year of life?

(13) Is there a high proportion of elderly people?

(14) Can most adults read and write, and is there a great difference between women and men in this respect?

(15) What is the GNP per head?

33. Evaluation has to be based on valid, relevant and sensitive information. There is often an excess of only marginally relevant and sensitive information. Often the most needed information is not available and its collection can be extremely costly. For the above reasons an approach of high selectivity should be adopted and only that information should be collected which has been identified as being really crucial for the issue being evaluated.

34. The types of information required may include political, social, cultural, economic, environmental and administrative factors influencing the health situation as well as mortality and morbidity statistics. Any of this information may form the basis of indicators and criteria for use in the various steps of the evaluation process. The information required may also concern health and related socioeconomic policies, plans and programmes, as well as the extent, scope and use of health systems, services and institutions. Thus, the information sought may be historical, social, political, economic, scientific, technological, demographic, epidemiological, organizational, legislative, or related to inventories of resources.

35. Information collection is least costly when the information emanates from the operation of the programmes or services of a health system. The required flow of information will vary by countries, e.g., from the periphery through various administrative levels to the ministry of health, with subsequent feedback from the centre to local health units. It may be necessary to have specific information collected in the absence of well developed health information support to the managerial process. This in itself could help to strengthen such information support, including a well organized reporting system.

Evaluation of Health Promotion, Health Education, and Disease Prevention Programs

Source: Excerpt from Windsor R, Clark N, Boyd NR, and Goodman RM. 2004. *Evaluation of Health Promotion, Health Education and Disease Prevention Programs (Third Edition).* Boston, MA: McGraw Hill.

EVALUATION PHASES FOR HP-DP PROGRAMS

Planning an evaluation requires a comprehensive synthesis of the quality of the HP-DP intervention literature: a meta-evaluation (ME) or meta-analysis (MA). As noted in the definition of terms later in this chapter, an ME is an evaluation of completed evaluation studies, a qualitative assessment of the internal validity of HP methods. An evaluation team needs to know what is known about how to intervene with specific groups, problems, and settings, and what to measure. The meta-evaluation tells us what the successful and unsuccessful interventions for a population at risk are. If a sufficient number of evaluation studies of high quality exist to confirm internal validity, a meta-analysis is performed to document external validity.

MA and ME define the quality, strengths, and weaknesses of the science base for specific HP intervention methods. They define the evaluation phase for an intervention program for a specific population at risk, problem, and setting. [Table 1.4] [not included] identifies four evaluation phases to consider in reviewing the science, practice, and policy bases for a specific HP program. As noted in Table 1.4, qualitative, process, and cost evaluations are foundation (core) methods to be applied in all four evaluation phases. The arrows reflect the continuous refinement, by empirical study, of the HP science-policy-practice base.

Phases 1 and 2 are developmental evaluation phases that can be described as evaluation research. They are designed to determine intervention feasibility, acceptability, efficacy, and cost for a defined population at risk. In Phase 1 and 2 evaluations, specialized HP intervention and assessment staff, typically under the supervision of faculty/senior scientists at academic research centers, implement studies to answer specific questions about the value of a new "best practice" program. An experimental (E) group vs. usual care control (C) group comparison is made.

Phases 1 and 2 should be theory-based evaluations (TBE). A specific model, such as social cognitive theory or the theory of reasoned action and related literature, is used to create multiple HP program intervention procedures and measurement methods. An excellent first reference for a description of the major behavioral science theories commonly used to develop health promotion interventions is Glanz and Rimer, "Theory at a Glance: A Guide for Health Promotion Practice" (1997).

The primary objective of Phase 1 and 2 evaluations is to document the internal validity of an HP intervention. If very few or no rigorous evaluations have been conducted, a Phase 1 formative evaluation should be planned to document efficacy. If several rigorous formative evaluations have been conducted and internal validity is confirmed for a specific population at risk, a larger, Phase 2 efficacy evaluation, with more sites and participants, is planned. The behavioral impact (effect size) and the feasibility of a new program is documented under "ideal" practice conditions in Phase 1 and 2 evaluations.

In Phase 1 and 2 evaluations, critical questions to be answered are: Can the new, untested program be delivered by staff (process evaluation) under optimal circumstances to the target population? Was the intervention used by the target group (qualitative evaluation)? Did the intervention produce a significant change in behavior (impact evaluation)? What resources were expended and saved (cost evaluation)? How valid was the model used by the TBE? Approximately 90% of all HP published intervention studies are Phase 1 and 2 evaluation research.

Phases 3 and 4, program evaluations, in theory should not be conducted unless the evidence from Phases 1 and 2 is positive, consistent, and conclusive. Was the efficacy—internal validity—of an HP intervention based on a sufficiently large number of studies among multiple samples and sites of the population at risk? Phase 3 and 4 evaluations should include large samples of participants, e.g., 500 to 1,000 or more per study, and involve multiple sites, e.g., 4 to 50. Phase 3 and 4 program evaluations ideally should use representative cohorts of participants from a defined population for specific health problems for which behavioral and population-attributable risk factors (PAR) are established. A significant, direct association exists between improvements in the behavior of the target population and improvements in a health outcome rate. The epidemiological evidence (PAR) should be confirmed for all phases. Phase 3 and 4 program evaluations, because they are evaluations of effectiveness, should be designed to answer questions about both internal and external validity.

In its ideal application, a Phase 4 study is an evaluation of an ongoing HP program for a defined population. Quality, efficacy, and cost have been documented. Almost without exception, Phase 1, 2, and 3 evaluations should apply randomized experimental designs. Typically, the objective of a Phase 4 impact-dissemination evaluation is to confirm the behavioral impact of routine delivery of evidence-based methods for an existing program for a defined delivery system and staff. It is an evaluation of the dissemination and routine application of "best practice" methods by regular staff. An experimental or quasi-experimental design is typically selected. Although a randomized experimental design is preferred, a nonequivalent comparison group design or a single or multiple time series design may be strong alternative evaluation designs for a Phase 4 impact-dissemination evaluation.

Phase 3 and 4 program evaluations should answer four questions:

1. Are the HP intervention methods feasible and effective when delivered with fidelity by regular staff to the target population under normal practice conditions?
2. Are the numbers of evaluation participants and sites of sufficient size to meet statistical power and impact analysis assumptions?
3. Is the evaluation sample and number of study sites sufficiently large and representative to provide new, additional evidence to support the external validity

(generalizability) of these methods and results to a defined population at risk?
4. Were the costs, cost-effectiveness, and, if appropriate, cost-benefits associated with the existing vs. new program documented?

Rigorous reviews of evaluation studies will provide insights to help a program define and plan the next phase of HP intervention development for a specific public health problem and setting. Only from a comprehensive review of valid evidence can an HP program define the scientific horizon and decide what to evaluate next and how. Once the phase has been defined from a rigorous review and synthesis of the literature (ME or MA), the next evaluation phase should be designed to answer specific new questions about quality, process, impact, and cost. The evidence base will define the evaluation phase and define the measurement and intervention methods of each new evaluation.

An insightful discussion of how to improve the evidence base for health education and health promotion interventions is presented by Rimer, Glanz, and Rasband in *Health Education and Behavior* (2001). They and their colleagues noted in their review of methodological issues that the science base could be derived only from well-designed evaluation studies. The maturation of the science-evidence base for all health promotion programs is a continuous process. It needs to be grounded in evaluation methods that produce strong qualitative and quantitative empirical results. The major challenge for the next decade in health promotion is to significantly expand the quality and quantity of evaluation research and program evaluation for all phases. In future evaluations, we need to complement the strong science base in changing the individual behavior of populations at high risk with a broader focus on changes in environment settings—clinics, schools, school systems, families, and communities—and changes in public health policy for large at-risk populations.

EVALUATION TERMS

Good communication by an evaluation team using accurate technical language is essential. Although there may be some variation in these definitions, we present a set of common terms frequently used in this text. These definitions will help you to synthesize, comprehend, and discuss the evaluation literature, and to actively contribute to planning an evaluation.

- HP Intervention (Program): A planned and systematically implemented combination of standardized, replicable methods designed to produce changes in cognitive, affective, skill, behavior, or health status objectives for a defined population at risk at specified sites and during a defined period of time.

- Efficacy: An evaluation of the extent to which a new (untested) intervention produced significant changes in a behavioral impact or a health outcome rate: Did the intervention produce significant changes among a sample of the population at risk under optimal program-practice conditions?

- Internal Validity: The degree to which an observed significant change in a behavioral impact or health status outcome rate (A) among a sample of a population at risk (B) can be attributed to an intervention (C): "Did C cause A to change among B?"

- Effectiveness: An evaluation of the extent to which an existing (tested) intervention with documented internal validity produced a significant change in a behavioral impact or health outcome rate: Did the intervention produce a significant change among a large, representative sample of a well-defined population at risk under normal program-practice conditions?

- External Validity: The degree to which an observed significant change in an impact (behavior) or outcome (health status) rate attributable to an HP intervention can be generalized from a representative sample to a large, well-defined population at risk.

- Process Evaluation (Feasibility Study): An evaluation designed to document the degree to which replicable program procedures were implemented with fidelity by trained staff according to a written plan: How well and how much of the assessment and intervention procedures were provided, to whom, when, and by whom?

- Qualitative Evaluation: An evaluation designed to explain why a program succeeded or failed, using a systematic process of in-depth, open-ended interviews, indirect and direct observations, and written reports to inductively assess and to describe the perceived value of HP intervention procedures by program staff, participants, and the community.

- Formative Evaluation: An evaluation designed to produce qualitative and quantitative data and insight during the early developmental phase of an intervention, including an assessment of (1) the feasibility of program implementation; (2) the appropriateness of content, methods, materials, media, and instruments; and (3) the immediate (e.g., 1 hour to 1 week) or short-term (e.g., 1 week to 6 months) cognitive, psychosocial, psychomotor (skill), and/or behavioral impact of an intervention for a well-defined population at risk.

- Evaluation Research (ER): An evaluation using an experimental or quasi-experimental design designed to establish the feasibility, efficacy, and cost-effectiveness or cost-benefit of a new intervention for a specific behavioral impact or health outcome rate during a defined period of time among a well-defined population at risk.

- Program Evaluation (Summative Evaluation): An evaluation using an experimental or quasi-experimental design to assess the feasibility, effectiveness, and cost-effectiveness or cost-benefit of a tested intervention in producing long-term (e.g., 1 to 5 years) cognitive, psychosocial, skill, and/or behavioral impact during a defined period of time among a well-defined population at risk.

- Health Outcome Evaluation: An evaluation using an experimental or quasi-experimental design to document intervention feasibility, efficacy or effectiveness, and cost-effectiveness or cost-benefit in producing long-term changes (e.g., 1 to 10 years) in the incidence or prevalence of a morbidity or mortality rate or other health status indicator for a clinically diagnosed medical condition among a well-defined population at high risk.

- Cost-Effectiveness Analysis (CEA): An evaluation designed to document the relationship between intervention program costs (input) and an impact rate (output); a ratio of cost per unit to percent impact.

- Cost-Benefit Analysis (CBA): An evaluation designed to document the relationship between intervention program costs (inputs) and a health outcome rate, expressed as a monetary benefit-consequence (outputs) or a ratio of costs per unit of economic benefit and net economic benefit (savings).

- Meta-Evaluation: An evaluation of the methodological quality of impact or outcome evaluation studies, using standardized rating criteria in six areas, to document internal validity: (1) evaluation design; (2) sample size and sample representativeness; (3) population characteristics; (4) measurement validity and reliability; (5) appropriateness and replicability of intervention methods; and (6) process evaluation.

- Meta-Analysis: An evaluation using quantitative analysis and standardized procedures to review completed experimental evaluation research with high internal validity for a well-defined population at risk to estimate the degrees of external validity of a health promotion intervention.

REFERENCES

Glanz K, and Rimer BK. 1997. *Theory at a Glance: A Guide for Health Promotion Practice.* NIH Publication 97-3896. Bethesda, MD: National Cancer Institute.

Rimer BK, Glanz DK, and Rasband G. 2001. "Searching for Evidence About Health Education and Health Behavior Interventions." *Health Education and Behavior* 2 (April 28): 231-248.

Assessing Effectiveness and Making Refinements

Source: Department of Health and Human Services. 2002. "Stage 4: Assessing Effectiveness and Making Refinements." In *Making Health Communication Programs Work.* Revised version. Washington, DC: National Cancer Institute, National Institutes of Health, U.S. Department of Health and Human Services. (Also known as the "pink book")

STAGE 4: ASSESSING EFFECTIVENESS AND MAKING REFINEMENTS

Questions to Ask and Answer

- How can we use outcome evaluation to assess the effectiveness of our program?
- How do we decide what outcome evaluation methods to use?
- How should we use our evaluation results?
- How can we determine to what degree we have achieved our communication objectives?
- How can we make our communication program more effective?

In Stage 3, you decided how to use process evaluation to monitor and adjust your communication activities to meet objectives. In Stage 4, you will use the outcome evaluation plan developed in Stage 1 to identify what changes (e.g., in knowledge, attitudes, or behavior) did or did not occur as a result of the program. Together, the progress and outcome evaluations will tell you how the program is functioning and why. (If you combine information from the two types of evaluation, be sure that you focus on the same aspects of the program, even though you look at them from different perspectives.) This section will help you revise your plans and conduct outcome evaluation. You should begin planning assessment activities either before or soon after you launch the program.

Why Outcome Evaluation Is Important

Outcome evaluation is important because it shows how well the program has met its communication objectives and what you might change or improve to make it more effective. Learning how well the program has met its communication objectives is vital for:

- Justifying the program to management
- Providing evidence of success or the need for additional resources
- Increasing organizational understanding of and support for health communication
- Encouraging ongoing cooperative ventures with other organizations

Revising the Outcome Evaluation Plan

During Stage 1, you identified evaluation methods and drafted an outcome evaluation plan. At that time, you should have collected any necessary baseline data. The first step in Stage 4 is to review that plan to ensure it still fits your program. A number of factors will influence how your communication program's outcomes should be evaluated, including the type of communication program, the communication objectives, budget, and timing. The outcome evaluation needs to capture intermediate outcomes and to measure the outcomes specified in the communication objectives. Doing so can allow you to show progress toward the objectives even if the objectives are not met.

Exhibit 13-1

Examples of Effectiveness Measures for Health Communication Programs

Knowledge

A public survey conducted before and after NCI's 5 A Day campaign found that knowledge of the message (a person should eat 5 or more servings of fruits and vegetables each day for good health) increased by 27 percentage points.

Attitude

In 1988, the U.S. Surgeon General sent a pamphlet designed to influence attitudes on AIDS to every U.S. household. An evaluation conducted in Connecticut showed no change in attitude between residents who read the pamphlet and those who did not.

Behavior

The Pawtucket Heart Health Program evaluated a weight-loss awareness program conducted at worksites. More than 600 people enrolled, and they lost an average of 3.5 pounds each compared with their preprogram weight.

Source: Department of Health and Human Services. 2002. "Stage 4: Assessing Effectiveness and Making Refinements." In *Making Health Communication Programs Work.* Revised version. Washington, DC: National Cancer Institute, National Institutes of Health, U.S. Department of Health and Human Services.

Consider the following questions to assess the Stage 1 outcome evaluation plan and to be sure the evaluation will give you the information you need:

- *What are the communication objectives?*
  What should the members of the intended audience think, feel, or do as a result of the health communication plan in contrast to what they thought, felt, or did before? How can these changes be measured?
- *How do you expect change to occur?*
  Will it be slow or rapid? What measurable intermediate outcomes (steps toward the desired behavior) are likely to take place before the behavior change can occur? The behavior change map you created in Stage 1 should provide the answers to these questions.
- *How long will the program last?*
  What kinds of changes can we expect in that time period (e.g., attitudinal, awareness, behavior, policy changes)? Sometimes, programs will not be in place long enough for objectives to be met when outcomes are measured (e.g., outcomes measured yearly over a 5-year program).

To help ensure that you identify important indicators of change, decide which changes could reasonably occur from year to year.

- *Which outcome evaluation methods can capture the scope of the change that is likely to occur?*
  Many outcome evaluation measures are relatively crude, which means that a large percentage of the intended audience (sometimes an unrealistically large percentage) must make a change before it can be measured. If this is the case, the evaluation is said to "lack statistical power." For example, a public survey of 1,000 people has a margin of error of about 3 percent. In other words, if 50 percent of the survey respondents said they engage in a particular behavior, in all likelihood somewhere between 47 percent and 53 percent of the population represented by the respondents actually engages in the behavior. Therefore, you can conclude that a statistically significant change has occurred only if there is a change of 5 or more percentage points. It may be unreasonable to expect such a large change, and budgetary constraints may force you to measure outcomes by surveying the general population when your intended audience is only a small proportion of the population.
- *Which aspects of the outcome evaluation plan best fit with your organization's priorities?*
  Only rarely does a communication program have adequate resources to evaluate all activities. You may have to illustrate your program's contribution to organizational priorities to ensure continued funding. If this is the case, it may be wise to evaluate those aspects most likely to contribute to the organization's mission (assuming that those are also the ones most likely to result in measurable changes).

Exhibit 13-2

Quantitative Versus Qualitative Evaluation

Quantitative research is used to gather objective information by asking a large number of people a set of identical questions. Results are expressed in numerical terms (e.g., 35 percent are aware of X and 65 percent are not). If the respondents are a representative random sample, quantitative data can be used to draw conclusions about an intended audience as a whole. Quantitative research is useful for measuring the extent to which a knowledge set, attitude, or behavior is prevalent in an intended audience.

Qualitative research is used to gather reactions and impressions from small numbers of intended audience members, usually by engaging them in discussion. Results are subjective and are not described numerically or used to make generalizations about the intended audience. Qualitative research is useful for understanding why people react the way they do and for understanding additional ideas, issues, and concerns.

Quantitative research methods are usually used for outcome evaluation because they provide the numerical data necessary to assess progress toward objectives. When evaluating outcomes, qualitative research methods are used to help interpret quantitative data and shed light on why particular outcomes were (or were not) achieved. See the Communication Research Methods section for detailed explanations of quantitative and qualitative research methods and the circumstances under which you should use each.

Source: Department of Health and Human Services. 2002. "Stage 4: Assessing Effectiveness and Making Refinements." In *Making Health Communication Programs Work.* Revised version. Washington, DC: National Cancer Institute, National Institutes of Health, U.S. Department of Health and Human Services.

Conducting Outcome Evaluation

Conduct outcome evaluation by following these steps:

1. Determine what information the evaluation must provide.
2. Define the data to collect.
3. Decide on data collection methods.
4. Develop and pretest data collection instruments.
5. Collect data.
6. Process data.
7. Analyze data to answer the evaluation questions.
8. Write an evaluation report.
9. Disseminate the evaluation report.

Exhibit 13-3

Evaluation Constraints

Every program planner faces limitations when conducting an outcome evaluation. You may need to adjust your evaluation to accommodate constraints such as the following:

- Limited funds
- Limited staff time or expertise
- Length of time allotted to the program and its evaluation
- Organizational restrictions on hiring consultants or contractors
- Policies that limit your ability to collect information from the public

- Difficulty in defining the program's objectives or in establishing consensus on them
- Difficulty in isolating program effects from other influences on the intended audience in "real world" situations
- Management perceptions of the evaluation's value

These constraints may make the ideal evaluation impossible. If you must compromise your evaluation's design, data collection, or analysis to fit limitations, decide whether the compromises will make the evaluation results invalid. If your program faces severe constraints, do a small-scale evaluation well rather than a large-scale evaluation poorly. Realize that it is not sensible to conduct an evaluation if it is not powerful enough to detect a statistically significant change.

Source: Department of Health and Human Services. 2002. "Stage 4: Assessing Effectiveness and Making Refinements." In *Making Health Communication Programs Work.* Revised version. Washington, DC: National Cancer Institute, National Institutes of Health, U.S. Department of Health and Human Services. (Also known as the "pink book")

See a description of each step below.

1. **Determine What Information the Evaluation Must Provide**

   An easy way to do this is to think about the decisions you will make based on the evaluation report. What questions do you need to answer to make those decisions?

2. **Define the Data You Need to Collect**

   Determine what you can and should measure to assess progress on meeting objectives. Use the following questions as a guide:

   - Did knowledge of the issue increase among the intended audience (e.g., understanding how to choose foods low in fat or high in fiber, knowing reasons not to smoke)?
   - Did behavioral intentions of the intended audience change (e.g., intending to use a peer pressure resistance skill, intending to buy more vegetables)?
   - Did intended audience members take steps leading to the behavior change (e.g., purchasing a sunscreen, calling for health information, signing up for an exercise class)?
   - Did awareness of the campaign message, name, or logo increase among intended audience members?
   - Were policies initiated or other institutional actions taken (e.g., putting healthy snacks in vending machines, improving school nutrition curricula)?

3. **Decide on Data Collection Methods**

    The sidebar Outcome Evaluation Designs describes some common outcome evaluation designs, the situations in which they are appropriate, and their major limitations. (See the Communication Research Methods section for more information.) Complex, multifaceted programs often employ a range of methods so that each activity is evaluated appropriately. For example, a program that includes a mass media component to reach parents and a school-based component to reach students might use independent cross-sectional studies to evaluate the mass media component and a randomized or quasi-experimental design to evaluate the school-based component.

    The following limitations can make evaluation of your communication program difficult:

    -   *Lack of measurement precision* (e.g., available data collection mechanisms cannot adequately capture change or cannot capture small changes).

        Population surveys may not be able to identify the small number of people making a change. Self-reported measures of behavior change may not be accurate.

    -   *Inability to conclusively establish that the communication activity caused the observed effect.*

Experimental designs, in which people are randomly assigned to either receive an intervention or not, allow you to assume that your program causes the only differences observed between the group exposed to the program and the control group. Outcome evaluations with experimental designs that run more than a few weeks, however, often wind up with contaminated control groups, either because people in the group receiving the intervention move to the control group, or because people in the control group receive messages from another source that are the same as or similar to those from your program.

The more complex your evaluation design is, the more you will need expert assistance to conduct your evaluation and interpret your results. The expert can also help you write questions that produce objective results. (It's easy to develop questions that inadvertently produce overly positive results.) If you do not have an evaluator on staff, seek help to decide what type of evaluation will best serve your program. Sources include university faculty and graduate students (for data collection and analysis), local businesses (for staff and computer time), state and local health agencies, and consultants and organizations with evaluation expertise.

Exhibit 13-4

Outcome Evaluation Designs Appropriate for Specific Communication Programs

Programs Not Delivered to the Entire Population of the Intended Audience

Evaluation Design

Randomized experiment. Members of the intended audience are randomly assigned to either be exposed to the program (intervention group) or not (control group). Usually, the same series of questions is asked pre- and postintervention (a pretest and posttest); posttest differences between the two groups show change the program has caused.

Major Limitations

-   Not appropriate for programs that will evolve during the study period.
-   Not likely to be generalizable or have external validity because of tight controls on program delivery and participant selection. Delivery during the evaluation may differ significantly from delivery when the program is widely implemented (e.g., more technical assistance and training may be available to ensure implementation is proceeding as planned).
-   For programs delivered over time, it is difficult to maintain integrity of intervention and control groups; group members may leave the groups at different rates of attrition.
-   Often costly and time-consuming.
-   May deprive the control group of positive benefits of the program.

Quasi-experiment. Members of the intended audience are split into control and intervention groups based simply upon who is exposed to the program and who is not.

Before-and-after studies. Information is collected before and after intervention from the same members of the intended audience to identify change from one time to another.

Independent cross-sectional studies. Information is collected before and after intervention, but it is collected from different intended audience members each time.

Panel studies. Information is collected at multiple times from the same members of the intended audience. When intended audience members are differentially exposed to the program, this design helps evaluators sort out the effects of different aspects of the program or different levels of exposure.

Time series analysis. Pre- and postintervention measures are collected multiple times from members of the intended audience. Evaluators use the preintervention data points to project what would have happened without the intervention and then compare the projection to what did happen using the postintervention data points.

- Same as randomized experiments.
- Difficult to conclude that the program caused the observed effects because other differences between the two groups may exist.
- Difficult to say with certainty that the program (rather than some unmeasured variable) caused the observed change.

- Cannot say with certainty that the program caused any observed change.

- Generalizability may be compromised over time. As participants age, leave, or respond to repeated questions on the same subject, they may no longer closely represent the intended audience.
- Can be difficult to say with certainty that the program caused the observed change.

- Large number of pre- and postintervention data points are needed to model pre- and postintervention trends.
- Normally restricted to situations in which governmental or other groups routinely collect and publish statistics that can be used as the pre- and postintervention observations.

Source: Department of Health and Human Services. 2002. "Stage 4: Assessing Effectiveness and Making Refinements." In *Making Health Communication Programs Work*. Revised version. Washington, DC: National Cancer Institute, National Institutes of Health, U.S. Department of Health and Human Services. (Also known as the "pink book")

Exhibit 13-5

Examples of Outcome Evaluation for Communication Programs

The Right Turns Only Program

Right Turns Only is a video-based drug education series produced by the Prince George's County, Maryland, school system. The effects of this series (including collateral print material) on student knowledge, attitudes, and behavioral intentions were tested among approximately 1,000 seventh grade students.

Twelve schools were assigned to one of four groups: three intervention groups and one control group. One intervention group received only the video-based education, a second received both the video-based and a traditional drug education curriculum, a third received only the traditional curriculum, and the control group received no drug abuse prevention education. All interventions were completed within a 3-week period.

The six outcomes measured included: 1) knowledge of substance abuse terminology, 2) ability to assess advertisements critically, 3) perception of family, 4) conflict resolution, 5) self-efficacy in peer relationships, and 6) behavioral intentions related to substance use/abuse prevention.

Changes were measured using data from questionnaires completed by students before and after the interventions. The data were analyzed to identify differences based on gender, race, grades (self-reported), and teacher. Groups that received drug education scored higher than the control group on all posttest measures except self-efficacy. On two of the six measures, the group receiving the combination of the video series and traditional curriculum scored significantly higher than other groups.

The evaluation demonstrated that instructional videos (particularly when used in conjunction with print materials and teacher guidance) could be an effective tool for delivering drug education in the classroom.

Note. Adapted from *Evaluating the Results of Communication Programs* (Technical Assistance Bulletin), by Center for Substance Abuse Prevention, August 1998, Washington, DC: U.S. Government Printing Office. In the public domain.

NIDDK's "Feet Can Last a Lifetime" Program

In 1995 the National Institute of Diabetes and Digestive and Kidney Diseases (NIDDK) developed a feedback mechanism for the promotion of its kit, "Feet Can Last a Lifetime," that was designed to reduce the number of lower extremity amputations in people with diabetes. The first printing of the kit included a feedback form for health care providers to comment on the materials. Based on the feedback, NIDDK revised the kit in 1997. The new kit's contents were then pretested extensively with practitioners for technical accuracy, usefulness, and clarity. The original kit was developed primarily for providers; based upon evaluation results, the revised kit also includes materials for patients. These include an easy-to-read brochure; a fact sheet with "foot care tips" and a "to do" list that contains steps for patients to follow to take care of their feet; and camera-ready, laminated tip sheets for providers to reproduce and give to patients.

Source: Department of Health and Human Services. 2002. "Stage 4: Assessing Effectiveness and Making Refinements." In *Making Health Communication Programs Work.* Revised version. Washington, DC: National Cancer Institute, National Institutes of Health, U.S. Department of Health and Human Services. (Also known as the "pink book")

4. **Develop and Pretest Data Collection Instruments**

Most outcome evaluation methods involve collecting data about participants through observation, a questionnaire, or another method. Instruments may include tally sheets for counting public inquiries, survey questionnaires, interview guides. Select a method that allows you to best answer your evaluation questions based upon your access to your intended audience and your resources. To develop your data collection instruments—or to select and adapt existing ones—ask yourself the following questions:

WHICH DATA?

The data you collect should be directly related to your evaluation questions. Although this seems obvious, it is important to check your data collection instruments against the questions your evaluation must answer. These checks will keep you focused on the information you need to know and ensure that you include the right measures. For example, if members of your intended audience must know more about a topic before behavior change can take place, make sure you ask knowledge-related questions in your evaluation.

FROM WHOM?

You will need to decide how many members of each group you need data from in order to have a sufficiently powerful evaluation to assess change. Make sure you have adequate resources to collect information from that many people. Realize that you may also need a variety of data collection instruments and methods for the different groups from whom you need information.

HOW?

Before you decide how to collect your data, you must assess your resources. Do you have access to, or can you train, skilled interviewers? Must you rely on self-reports from participants?

Also consider how comfortable the participants will be with the methods you choose to collect data. Will they be willing and able to fill out forms? Will they be willing to provide personal information to interviewers? Will the interviews and responses need to be translated?

Exhibit 13-6

Conducting Culturally Competent Evaluation

When you evaluate communication programs, you form a set of assumptions about what should happen, to whom, and with what results. Recognize that these assumptions and expectations may vary, depending on the cultural norms and values of your intended audiences.

You may need to vary your methods of gathering information and interpreting results. Depending on the culture from which you are gathering information, people may react in different ways:

- They may think it is inappropriate to speak out in a group, such as a focus group, or to provide negative answers. (This does not mean that you should not use focus groups within these cultures; observance of nonverbal cues may be more revealing than oral communication.)
- They may be reluctant to provide information to a person from a different culture or over the telephone.
- They may lack familiarity with printed questionnaires or have a limited ability to read English.

Remember that the culture of the evaluator your program uses can inadvertently affect the objectivity of your evaluation. When possible, try to use culturally competent evaluators when you examine program activities. If your program cuts across cultures and you adapt your evaluation methods to fit different groups, you may find it difficult to compare results across groups. This type of evaluation is more complicated, and if you plan to conduct one, enroll the help of an expert evaluator.

5. **Collect Data**

   Collect postprogram data. You should have collected baseline data during planning in Stage 1, before your program began, to use for comparison with postprogram data.

6. **Process Data**

   Put the data into usable form for analysis. This may mean organizing the data to give to professional evaluators or entering the data into an evaluation software package.

7. **Analyze the Data to Answer the Evaluation Questions**

   Use statistical techniques as appropriate to discover significant relationships. Your program might consider involving university-based evaluators, providing them with an opportunity for publication and your program with expertise.

8. **Write an Evaluation Report**

   A report outlining what you did and why you did it, as well as what worked and what should be altered in the future, provides a solid base from which to plan future evaluations. Your program evaluation report explains how your program was effective in achieving its communication objectives and serves as a record of what you learned from both your program's achievements and shortcomings. Be sure to include any questionnaires or other instruments in the report so that you can find them later.

   See Appendix A [not included] for a sample evaluation report. As you prepare your report, you will need someone with appropriate statistical expertise to analyze the outcome evaluation data. Also be sure to work closely with your evaluators to interpret the data and develop recommendations based on them.

WHY?

Writing an evaluation report will bring your organization the following additional benefits:

- *You will be able to apply what you've learned to future projects.* Frequently, other programs are getting under way when evaluation of an earlier effort concludes, and program planners don't have time to digest what has been learned and incorporate it into future projects. A program evaluation report helps to ensure that what has been learned will get careful consideration.

- *You will show your accountability to employers, partners, and funding agencies.* Your program's evaluation report showcases the program's accomplishments. Even if some aspects of the program need to be modified based on evaluation results, identifying problems and addressing them shows partners and funding

agencies that you are focused on results and intend to get the most benefit from their time and money.

- *You will be able to give evidence of your program and methods' effectiveness.* If you want other organizations to use your materials or program, you need to demonstrate their value. An evaluation report offers proof that the materials and your program were carefully developed and tested. This evidence will help you explain why your materials or program may be better than others, or what benefits an organization could gain from using its time and resources to implement your program.

- *You will provide a formal record that will help others.* A comprehensive evaluation report captures the institutional memory of what was tried in the past and why, which partners had strong skills or experience in specific areas, and what problems were encountered. Everything you learned when evaluating your program will be helpful to you or others planning programs in the future.

Exhibit 13-7

Evaluation Report Helps CIS Promote Program Areas, Strengths

NCI's CIS used an evaluation report, "Making a Difference," to show its partners, the research community, NCI/CIS leadership, and the media that its programs are effective. The document both quantified CIS results (e.g., making 100,000 referrals a year to research studies, providing information on breast cancer to 76,000 callers in 1996, providing information that increased fruit and vegetable consumption among callers) and put a human face on the calling public. Quotations from callers and leaders in the cancer community illustrated the personal impact of the service on people's lives and health.

The report was written in lay language and used pull-outs and simple charts to explain statistics. Ideas for using the report with regional partners, the media, and community leaders were included with the copies sent to each CIS office. To maximize opportunities for using the report, CIS has also made it available on computer disk and as a PowerPoint® slide presentation.

Source: Department of Health and Human Services. 2002. "Stage 4: Assessing Effectiveness and Making Refinements." In *Making Health Communication Programs Work.* Revised version. Washington, DC: National Cancer Institute, National Institutes of Health, U.S. Department of Health and Human Services. (Also known as the "pink book")

HOW?

Consider the Users

Before you write your evaluation, consider who will read or use it. Write your report for that audience. As you did when planning your program components in Stage 1, analyze your audiences for your report before you begin to compose. To analyze your audience, ask yourself the following questions:

- Who are the audiences for this evaluation report?
  - Public health program administrators
  - Evaluators, epidemiologists, researchers
  - Funding agencies
  - Policymakers
  - Partner organizations
  - Project staff
  - The public
  - The media
- How much information will your audience want?
  - The complete report
  - An executive summary
  - Selected sections of the report
- How will your audience use the information in your report?
  - To refine a program or policy
  - To evaluate your program's performance
  - To inform others
  - To support advocacy efforts
  - To plan future programs

Consider the Format

Decide the most appropriate way to present information in the report to your audience. Consider the following formats:

- Concise, including hard-hitting findings and recommendations
- General, including an overview written for the public at the ninth-grade level
- Scientific, including a methodology section, detailed discussion, and references
- Visual, including more charts and graphics than words
- Case studies, including other storytelling methods

Selected Elements to Include

Depending on your chosen audience and format, include the following sections:

- Program results/findings
- Evaluation methods
- Program chronology/history
- Theoretical basis for program
- Implications
- Recommendations
- Barriers, reasons for unmet objectives

9. **Disseminate the Evaluation Report**

   Ask selected stakeholders and key individuals to review the evaluation report before it is released so that they can identify concerns that might compromise its impact. When the report is ready for release, consider developing a dissemination strategy for the report, just as you did for your program products, so the intended audiences you've chosen will read it. Don't go to the hard work of writing the report only to file it away.

   Letting others know about the program results and continuing needs may prompt them to share similar experiences, lessons, new ideas, or potential resources that you could use to refine the program. In fact, feedback from those who have read the evaluation report or learned about your findings through conference presentations or journal coverage can be valuable for refining the program and developing new programs. You may want to develop a formal mechanism for obtaining feedback from peer or partner audiences. If you use university-based evaluators, the mechanism may be their publication of findings.

   If appropriate, use the evaluation report to get recognition of the program's accomplishments. Health communication programs can enhance their credibility with employers, funding agencies, partners, and the community by receiving awards from groups that recognize health programs, such as the American Medical Writers Association, the Society for Technical Communication, the American Public Health Association, and the National Association of Government Communicators. A variety of other opportunities exist, such as topic–specific awards (e.g., awards for consumer information on medications from the U.S. Food and Drug Administration) and awards for specific types of products (e.g., the International Communication Association's awards for the top three papers of the year). Another way to get recognition is to publish articles about the program in professional journals or give a presentation or workshop at an organization meeting or conference.

PART 14

Culture, Diversity, and Health Disparities: Are Current Theories Relevant?

Part 14 addresses a major issue in the field of health promotion—the existence of significant disparities in health status and treatment between racial/ethnic minority populations and the majority population in the United States. The extent and nature of these health disparities is reviewed, along with key causal and contributing factors. The question is asked: Is current theory relevant? A sample of the theoretical approaches discussed in the book are linked to their potential application in addressing some of the key contributing factors. The first reading (DHHS, 1985) is a short introductory excerpt from the seminal report that placed health disparities front and center as an issue of national importance. The second selection investigates the complex but important tie between socioeconomic inequality and health disparities (Ashford et al., 2006). The third reading (Brach & Fraser, 2000) presents a model for understanding the role of cultural competency in the provision of health care, and the fourth selection is one example of a comprehensive approach at the state level (in California) for identifying the contributing factors and eliminating racial/ethnic health disparities (Prevention Institute, 2003).

The Task Force on Black and Minority Health

Source: Brief introductory excerpt from DHHS 1985. *Report of the U.S. Department of Health and Human Services Secretary's Task Force on Black and Minority Health, Volume I, Executive Summary.* Washington, DC: DHHS.

INTRODUCTION AND OVERVIEW OF THE TASK FORCE ON BLACK AND MINORITY HEALTH

Perspective of the Task Force Study

Despite the unprecedented explosion in scientific knowledge and the phenomenal capacity of medicine to diagnose, treat, and cure disease, Blacks, Hispanics, Native Americans, and those of Asian/Pacific Islander heritage have not benefited fully or equitably from the fruits of science or from those systems responsible for translating and using health sciences technology. With full cognizance of this tragic dilemma in the United States, the Secretary of Health and Human Services, Margaret Heckler, established the Task Force on Black and Minority Health.

Since the turn of the century, the overall health status of all Americans has improved greatly. In 1900, the life expectancy for the United States population at birth was 47.3 years; for Blacks it was much lower—33 years. In little more than three generations, remarkable changes have occurred in health care and biomedical research. As pointed out by the Surgeon General in the 1979 report, Healthy People, the leading causes of death in 1900 were influenza, pneumonia, diphtheria, tuberculosis, and gastrointestinal infections. In the first half of the century, improved sanitation, better nutrition, and immunizations brought a drastic decline in infectious diseases. Today, these diseases cause a relatively small percentage of deaths compared to 1900.

Knowledge about life processes in health and disease is being acquired at an incredible pace. Because of one spectacular achievement after another, it is predicted that many of the diseases not now curable, will be controlled by the year 2000. This "biological revolution" has placed into the hands of health professionals effective medications, new and complex diagnostic instruments and treatment modalities not dreamed of in 1900.

Since 1960, the United States population has experienced a steady decline in the overall death rate from all causes. Remarkable progress in understanding the causes and risks for developing diseases such as heart disease and cancer have important implications for the health of all Americans. The decline in cardiovascular disease mortality from 1968 to 1978 alone improved overall life expectancy by 1.6 years. Advances in the long-term management of chronic diseases mean that conditions such as hypertension and diabetes no longer necessarily lead to premature death and disability.

Concomitantly, advances in social and behavioral sciences research and methodology have elucidated relationships among biological, behavioral, and social factors that affect health and illness. The link among these factors is critical to understanding the behavioral underpinnings of health, identifying effective strategies for disease prevention, maintaining treatment regimens, and suggesting ways to change behavior for more healthful living habits.

Although tremendous strides have been made in improving the health and longevity of the American people, statistical trends show a persistent, distressing disparity in key health indicators among certain subgroups of the population. In 1983, life expectancy reached a new high of 75.2 years for Whites and 69.6 years for Blacks, a gap of 5.6 years. Nevertheless, Blacks today have a life expectancy already reached by Whites in the early 1950s, or a lag of about 30 years. Infant mortality rates have fallen steadily for several decades for both Blacks and Whites. In 1960, Blacks suffered 44.3 infant deaths for every 1,000 live births, roughly twice the rate for Whites, 22.9. Moreover, in 1981, Blacks suffered 20 infant deaths per 1,000 live births, still twice the White level of 10.5, but similar to the White rate of 1960.

The Task Force on Black and Minority Health was thus conceived in response to a national paradox of phenomenal scientific achievement and steady improvement in overall health status, while at the same time, persistent, significant health inequities exist for minority Americans. As the Task Force came into being in April 1984, it was evident that to bring the health of minorities to the level of all Americans, efforts of monumental proportions were needed.

Designing Health and Population Programs to Reach the Poor

Source: Excerpt from Ashford LS, Gwatkin, DR, Yazbeck AS 2006. "Designing Health and Population Programs to Reach the Poor." Population Reference Bureau. Available at: http://www.prb.org/pdf06/ DesigningPrograms.pdf.

THE RICH–POOR GAP IN HEALTH

The Poor Are Less Healthy Than the Rich

Throughout the world, inequalities in health status between the rich and poor are pervasive. The disparities are particularly noticeable in many of the poorest countries, where millions of people suffer from preventable illnesses, such as infectious diseases, malnutrition, and complications of childbirth, simply because they are poor. These wide differences in health status are considered unfair, or *inequitable*, because they correspond to different constraints and opportunities rather than individual choices.[1]

Numerous studies from developing countries show that the poor are more likely to suffer health problems and less likely to use health services than the better-off. ("Better-off," "wealthy," "rich," or "least poor" refer here to the highest economic groups in a country, even if the country is poor by world standards.)

One of the most extensive of these studies, commissioned by the World Bank, uses data from Demographic and Health Surveys (DHS) in 56 countries in Africa, Asia, and Latin America.[2] DHS surveys interview women of reproductive age on issues related to fertility and maternal and child health. The surveys measure socioeconomic status by asking respondents about household characteristics. These include assets owned, such as a refrigerator, television, or motor vehicle, and the household dwelling's construction, plumbing, and electricity. Using these data, the researchers have constructed a household asset (or wealth) index and divided the population in each country into five groups of equal size, or quintiles, based on individuals' relative standing on the household wealth index in the country.

The results show that the poorest quintiles fare worse than the wealthiest quintiles on a range of health outcomes, including childhood mortality and nutritional status. Figure J [not included] shows childhood mortality levels by wealth quintile in Bolivia, Egypt, and Vietnam, which reflect this relationship. Among all of the countries included in the analysis, a child from the poorest wealth quintile is twice as likely on average as a child in the richest quintile to die before age 5. The disparity is similar in maternal nutrition, with women in the poorest quintile about twice as likely as those in the wealthiest to be malnourished.[3]

Similar patterns exist across more than 100 indicators of health status and health care drawn from the DHS, though the magnitude of the disparity differs among indicators and across regions and countries. The rich are consistently healthier and better cared for than the poor, even where the explicitly stated intent of programs and public health goals is to improve the health of the poor.[4]

Inequalities in health exist not only by wealth but also by other socioeconomic measures, such as sex, race, ethnic group, language, educational level, occupation, and residence. For example, in parts of India and China, infant girls are more likely to die than infant boys, because cultural preferences for sons put daughters at a disadvantage for nutrition and health care early in life. Many initiatives to improve equity in health try to address these and other social disadvantages.

The analysis and case studies in this report focus on program efforts to reduce inequalities among economic groups in the use of health services. Until recently, researchers have encountered problems measuring the economic status of health services users. But these problems have been greatly reduced with an asset approach to measurement used in the case studies in Part 3 and described further in Part 4. Readers should be aware that economic poverty is not the only type of poverty that matters, and that it is often intertwined with social, geographic, and other disadvantages. Individuals at the bottom of the economic scale often suffer from multiple disadvantages.

Public Health Spending Favors the Better-off

Government expenditures on health are often designed to give everyone equal access to health care. Yet, in practice, equal access is usually elusive. Most research conducted in developing countries in the last 20 years has confirmed that publicly financed health care benefits the well-off more than the poor. The World Bank's *World Development Report 2004* summarized the available evidence on the extent to which publicly financed health and educational services reach different economic groups. In 21 country studies, on average, the wealthiest 20 percent of the population received about 25 percent of government health spending, while the poorest 20 percent received only around 15 percent.[5] In 15 of the 21 cases, spending patterns favored the highest income groups, and in only four (Argentina, Colombia, Costa Rica, and Honduras) did a greater share of spending benefit the poor. Even the health programs that address illnesses afflicting the poor, such as infectious diseases, childhood diarrhea, and complications of childbirth, and that explicitly give high priority to serving the poor, tend to benefit the rich more than the poor. Evidence from the DHS analysis in 56 countries found that gaps in the use of services are closely related to economic status. The lower a group's economic status, the less it uses health services, including basic services such as immunization, maternity care, and family planning. On average, across countries, children in the wealthiest quintile are more than twice as likely as those in the poorest quintile to have received all of the basic childhood vaccinations.[6]

The use of modern contraceptives and professional health care during delivery also varies considerably according to wealth. On average, married women in the wealthiest quintile are more than four times more likely than those in the poorest quintile to use contraception.[7] Births to women in the richest quintile are nearly five times more likely, on average, to be attended by a trained professional such as a doctor, nurse, or midwife. These data confirm the "inverse care law," a term coined more than 30 years ago, which states that the availability of good medical care is inversely related to the need for it in the population served.[8]

Why Do the Poor Receive Less Health Care?

As noted in the World Bank's *World Development Report 2006: Equity and Development*, the distribution of wealth in a country is closely related to social distinctions that stratify people and communities into groups with relative amounts of power.[9] Inequities occur when certain groups of people have less say and fewer opportunities to shape the world around them. Social, cultural, and political differences between people create biases and rules in institutions that favor more powerful and privileged groups. The persistent differences in power and status between groups can become internalized into behaviors, aspirations, and preferences that also perpetuate inequalities.

In the case of health, an individual's lack of power and status often translates into a lower likelihood of taking preventive health measures and seeking and using health care. The striking differences in health status among different economic groups reflect inequalities in access to information, to facilities that provide decent standards of care, and to the means to pay for good care.

Specific barriers to quality health care can be categorized as follows:[10]

- **Lack of information and knowledge.** Nearly everywhere, the poor are less educated than the rich and lack knowledge about hygiene, nutrition, good health practices, and where to go for specific services. Lack of knowledge can keep people from seeking care even when they need it and the free care is available.
- **Lack of "voice" or empowerment.** Poorer members of a community often have less voice, or say, in whether to seek care, than wealthier members, and this can affect the level of resources used in their interest. Similarly, within a family, women and children may have less voice than men and older family members. For example, a woman's lack of power relative to her husband can delay a decision to seek emergency care to address a serious complication during pregnancy or delivery.
- **Inaccessible and poor quality services.** City dwellers usually live closer to health services, while rural residents face greater costs in terms of transportation and travel time to reach services. Aside from distance, health facilities can vary tremendously in quality: Some facilities are badly run down, lack essential drugs and sup-

plies, and are run by poorly trained or unmotivated staff. The people who are most economically disadvantaged are precisely those most likely to struggle with dysfunctional health services.

- **Unresponsive service providers.** Health systems are challenged to entice urban-educated doctors to work in poor areas. Poor areas are more likely to have lower paid health providers who may miss work often or have little motivation or incentive to provide good care. In addition, some health providers openly discriminate against individuals from certain economic classes or ethnic groups. The "social distance" between service providers and their clients can be large, leaving clients feeling looked down upon or neglected.[11]

- **Prohibitive cost of some services.** In developing countries, primary health care is often available for free through the public health sector, but treatments for major illnesses and injuries can be prohibitively expensive for poor families. In principle, services may often be free of charge, but that doesn't mean they are cost-free to the user. The actual cost of treatment may become too expensive when informal payments are needed to ensure receipt of certain drugs and services or when transportation costs or time away from work are unaffordable.

REFERENCES

1. Adam Wagstaff, "Poverty and Health Sector Inequalities," *Bulletin of the World Health Organization* 80, no. 2 (2002): 97.

2. Davidson Gwatkin et al., *Socioeconomic Differences in Health, Nutrition, and Population, Round II Country Reports* (Washington, DC: World Bank, 2004).

3. PRB analysis of Davidson Gwatkin et al., *Initial Country-Level Information About Socio-Economic Differences in Health, Nutrition, and Population,* Vols. I and II (Washington, DC: World Bank, 2003).

4. Further information about analysis of DHS studies, including all of the data produced, is available in the "Country Data" section of the World Bank Poverty and Health Website at www.worldbank.org/povertyandhealth.

5. Deon Filmer, "The Incidence of Public Expenditures on Health and Education," *Background Note for World Development Report 2004* (Washington, DC: World Bank, 2003).

6. PRB analysis of Gwatkin et al., *Socioeconomic Differences in Health, Nutrition, and Population.*

7. PRB analysis of Gwatkin et al., *Socioeconomic Differences in Health, Nutrition, and Population.*

8. Julian Tudor Hart, "The Inverse Care Law," *Lancet* 1, no. 7696 (1971): 405–12.

9. World Bank, *World Development Report 2006: Equity and Development* (Washington, DC: World Bank, 2005): 5.

10. Adapted from World Bank, *World Development Report 2006:* 142–143.

11. World Bank, *World Development Report 2004: Making Services Work for Poor People* (Washington, DC: World Bank, 2003): 25.

Can Cultural Competency Reduce Racial and Ethnic Health Disparities? A Review and Conceptual Model

Source: Brach C, and Fraserirector I. 2000. "Can Cultural Competency Reduce Racial and Ethnic Health Disparities? A Review and Conceptual Model." *Medical Care Research and Review* 57 (Supplement 1): 181–217.

With minority Americans expected to comprise more than 40 percent of the U.S. population by 2035 and 47 percent by 2050 (U.S. Bureau of the Census 1996), addressing their health needs has become an increasingly visible public policy goal (Agency for Health Care Policy and Research 1999; U.S. Department of Health and Human Services [DHHS] Office for Civil Rights 1998; U.S. DHHS 1999; U.S. DHHS Office of the Secretary 1999). Making sure that the health care provided to this diverse population takes account of their linguistic and cultural needs constitutes a major challenge for health systems and policy makers.

Arthur Kleinman's seminal *Annals of Internal Medicine* article (Kleinman, Eisenberg, and Good 1978) articulated the importance of culture in health care. Culture, defined as the "integrated pattern of human behavior that includes thoughts, communications, actions, customs, beliefs, values and institutions of a racial, ethnic, religious or social group" (Cross et al. 1989) is relevant to everyone's health care. However, its importance is heightened for minority patients who receive health care from systems that are largely organized by and staffed with majority group members. Examples of negative health consequences that could result from ignoring culture include missed opportunities for screening because of lack of familiarity with the prevalence of conditions among certain minority groups; failure to take into account differing responses to medication; lack of knowledge about traditional remedies, leading to harmful drug interactions; and diagnostic errors resulting from miscommunication (Lavizzo-Mourey and Mackenzie 1996; Lawson 1996; Moffic and Kinzie 1996). A growing body of federal and state laws, regulations, and standards seeks to guarantee that health systems respond to these diverse linguistic and cultural needs by becoming "culturally competent" (Sec. 601, *Civil Rights Act of 1964*; 78 Stat. 252; 42 U.S.C. 2000d; Chang and Fortier 1998; Fortier and Shaw-Taylor 1999; Kennedy, Stubblefield-Tave, and Smith 1999; Perkins et al. 1998; Perkins and Vera 1998; 63 Fed. Reg, 52021 et seq. 29 September 1998; U.S. DHHS Office of the Secretary 1999; Woloshin et al. 1995). Every organization and author define cultural competency somewhat differently (e.g., Adams 1995; Association of Asian Pacific Community Health Organizations 1996; Association of State and Territorial Hospital Officials 1994; Orlandi 1995; Tirado 1996; U.S. DHHS Goal 6 Work Group 1998). However, most definitions are variants of one developed by mental health researchers more than a decade ago, who defined cultural competence as "a set of congruent behaviors, attitudes, and policies that come together in a system, agency or amongst professionals and enables that system, agency or those professionals to work effectively in cross-cultural situations" (Cross et al. 1989).

Because this article considers cultural competency in the context of reducing racial and ethnic health disparities, we limit our use of the term to racial and ethnic minority groups, although the term *cultural competency* has been used to include other groups (such as women, the elderly, gays and lesbians, people with disabilities, and religious minorities). We do, however, include linguistic competence when we speak of cultural competency. Predicated on theories that language and culture affect health care beliefs, choices, and treatment (Ashing-Giwa 1999; Flores and Vega 1998; Gordon 1995; Gropper 1998; Kleinman, Eisenberg, and Good 1978; Lipton et al. 1998; Pachter 1994; Torres 1998), the idea of cultural competency is an explicit statement that one-size-fits-all health care cannot meet the needs of an increasingly diverse American population. Cultural competency goes beyond cultural awareness or sensitivity. It includes not only possession of cultural knowledge and respect for different cultural perspectives but also having skills and being able to use them effectively in cross-cultural situations (Cross et al. 1989; Orlandi 1995; Tirado 1996). Taken one step further, the term *cultural competency* has been used to refer to an ongoing commitment or institutionalization of appropriate practice and policies for diverse populations (Denboba et al. 1998; Tervalon and Murray-Garcia 1998). The concept of cultural competency is also presented as a continuum, in recognition that individuals and institutions can vary in the effectiveness of their responses to cultural diversity (Andrulis, Delbanco, and Shaw-Taylor 1999; Cross et al. 1989).

Some advocate for cultural competency as a matter of social justice. According to this perspective, the high value we as a society place on informed consent, choice of providers, and equity creates an entitlement to cultural competency regardless of its impact on outcomes (Kennedy, Stubblefield-Tave, and Smith 1999; Richardson 1999). Cultural competency is therefore a mechanism to ensure the observance of consumer rights, such as the right to respect and nondiscrimination enunciated in the Consumer Bill of Rights and Responsibilities (President's Advisory Commission on Consumer Protection and Quality in the Health Care Industry 1997).

Cultural competency, however, could also be a mechanism to change the health outcomes of minority Americans. A large body of literature has documented significant racial and ethnic disparities in health care and health outcomes, with minority Americans generally receiving less health care and suffering worse health (Baquet and Commiskey 1999; Collins, Hall, and Neuhaus 1999; Ferguson et al. 1998; Gaston et al. 1993; Mayberry et al. 1999; Sheifer, Escarce, and Schulman 2000; U.S. DHHS 1999). The question addressed in this article is as follows: Could cultural competency reduce racial and ethnic health disparities?

NEW CONTRIBUTION

We conducted a review of both the cultural competency and disparity literature using Medline and HealthStar, concentrating on articles published within the past 10 years. More than 40 search terms (e.g., cultural competency, disparity, minority, race, ethnicity, language barriers, access) were used in various combinations. In addition, we reviewed bibliographies that

had been compiled by various sources, such as a workgroup of the DHHS Secretary's Quality Initiative and the DHHS Office of Minority Health Resource Center. Finally, we contacted knowledgeable sources in this field and uncovered unpublished or nonindexed literature as well. We discovered that the literature on cultural competency has, by and large, not linked cultural competency activities with the outcomes that could be expected to follow from them. We also found the literature on racial and ethnic disparities weak on identifying the sources of disparities, and almost no attention has been paid to techniques for reducing them. Researchers have generally focused on rigorously documenting disparities and offered only speculative explanations for their findings.

This article brings together the two bodies of literature to explore whether cultural competency has the potential to reduce disparities. It begins by identifying the major cultural competency techniques described in the literature. Then it draws on the literature on cultural competency and health care disparities to provide a conceptual model and evidence of ways in which cultural competency techniques could affect the processes—and, therefore, outcomes—of care for racial and ethnic minorities.

CULTURAL COMPETENCY TECHNIQUES

The need for cultural competency is frequently discussed on the level of the patient-clinician interaction. (The term *clinician* as used in this article encompasses physicians, nurses, and other health professionals.) However, most health care is now delivered by clinicians who are part of groups or systems. These clinicians will become culturally competent only with the support and/or encouragement of the health systems in which they participate. Furthermore, cultural competency must be addressed by health systems if it is to become institutionalized. Much of the cultural competency literature discusses the importance of cultural awareness, knowledge, attitudes, and skills but does not describe how a health system is supposed to become culturally competent. While the literature overall identifies a wide array of cultural competency techniques, most articles discuss only a single approach, making it difficult for health systems to possess an overview of the options available to them. We have therefore described the techniques most frequently discussed in the cultural competency literature, clustering them into nine categories.

1. **Interpreter services.** Providing foreign language or American Sign Language interpreter services is one obvious and common way to improve communication among persons who speak different languages and come from different cultures. There are numerous

approaches to interpretation, including on-site professional interpreters; ad hoc interpreters (e.g., staff pulled away from other duties to interpret, friends and family members, strangers from the waiting room); and simultaneous remote interpretations, using earphones and microphones with off-site professional interpreters (Hornberger et al. 1996; Riddick 1998). Professional interpreters can be part-time or full-time employees, acquired through an agency, or hired on a freelance basis (Riddick 1998).

2. **Recruitment and retention.** Minority staff, because of their shared cultural beliefs and common language, may improve communication, create a more welcoming environment, and structure health systems to better reflect the needs of minority communities (Cooper-Patrick et al. 1999; Nickens 1992). Techniques for recruiting and retaining minority group members in health systems include (1) setting up minority residency or fellowship programs, (2) hiring minority search firms, (3) adapting personnel policy to create a comfortable and welcoming work place for minority group members, (4) mentoring of minority employees by senior executives, (5) subcontracting with minority health providers, (6) tying executive compensation to steps taken to match hiring to community needs, (7) expanding on traditional affirmative action programs aimed at attracting employees who match the race and ethnicity of the patient populations, (8) establishing a set of principles for respectful treatment of all people, (9) reviewing fairness of human resource practices and compensation of all staff, and (10) tracking staff satisfaction by racial and ethnic groups (Chang and Fortier 1998; B. R. Williams 1997).

3. **Training.** Cultural competency training programs aim to increase cultural awareness, knowledge, and skills, leading to changes in staff (both clinical and administrative) behavior and patient-staff interactions. Training provides a way to ameliorate problems stemming from the cultural mismatches that result whenever patient and staff do not share a common subculture and mutual understanding of each other's health beliefs. Persons may be culturally competent in serving members similar to themselves but not serving others. The diversity even within racial or ethnic groups and the complexity of associated subcultures make cultural competency training appropriate for all health system staff, including members of minority groups. Training can be part of undergraduate or graduate medical or other professional school education, an

orientation process for new staff or network members, or part of in-service training programs. Cultural competency training can be a separate activity, either a regularly occurring activity or a discrete one-time occurrence. Cultural competency training also can be achieved by infusion, integrating a multicultural perspective throughout a curriculum or training activities. Training can be targeted to increasing knowledge about specific minority groups and/or can focus on the process of interacting with minority group members. Training also can be focused on a specific task, such as working with interpreters. In lieu of or in addition to in-person training, handbooks and other educational materials can be distributed.

4. **Coordinating with traditional healers.** Many minority Americans use traditional healers while they are seeking biomedical care (Elder, Gillcrist, and Minz 1997; Kim and Kwok 1998; Ma 1999; Marbella et al. 1998; Skaer et al. 1996; Pang 1989). Clinicians need to coordinate with these healers as they would with any other care provider whom a patient is seeing to ensure continuity of care and avoid complications due to incompatible therapies. In addition, presenting patient education and treatment regimens in a conceptual framework concordant with cultural beliefs and traditional health practices may increase the chances that patients will concur with and adhere to behavioral and treatment recommendations.

5. **Use of community health workers.** Internationally and across the United States, members of minority communities are used to reach out to other community members as well as to provide direct services such as health education and primary care (e.g., E. A. Baker et al. 1997; Earp and Flax 1999; Jackson and Parks 1997; Rodney et al. 1998; Sherer 1994). Because they are known and respected by the community, these liaisons reportedly serve as guides to the health system. They bring in individuals who had not previously sought care, provide cultural linkages, overcome distrust, and contribute to clinician-patient communication, increasing the likelihood of patient follow-up and providing cost-effective health services to isolated communities that have traditionally lacked access (Goicoechea-Balbona 1997; Riddick 1998; Witmer et al. 1995; Zablocki 1998).

6. **Culturally competent health promotion.** Health promotion seeks to encourage good health through healthy behaviors and risk reduction, early detection and treatment, and proper care of chronic or acute

diseases (Kok, van den Borne, and Mullen 1997). Health promotion can take several forms. Clinicians can use screening tools and conduct brief interventions. Public information campaigns can be conducted by health systems or in the community. In an attempt to make health-promotion efforts more culturally competent, culture-specific attitudes and values have been incorporated into messages and materials.

7. **Including family and/or community members.** While patient autonomy has become a core principle of health care in the United States, some minority groups believe that family members should be involved in health care decision making. For example, one study found that Korean and Mexican Americans were more likely than European or African Americans to hold a family-centered model, preferring that family members—not patients—be told about terminal conditions and make treatment decisions (Blackhall et al. 1995). Involving families—and, in hierarchical societies, even community leaders—may be crucial in obtaining consent for and adherence to treatment (Fadiman 1997).

8. **Immersion into another culture.** Members of one cultural group have been reported to develop sensitivity and skills working with another culture by immersing themselves in that culture (Kavanagh et al. 1999; St. Clair and McKenry 1999). It is reported that immersion enables participants to overcome their ethnocentrism, increase their cultural awareness, and integrate cultural beliefs into health care practices (St. Clair and McKenry 1999).

9. **Administrative and organizational accommodations.** A variety of administrative and organizational decisions related to clinic locations, hours of operation, network membership, physical environments, and written materials also can affect access to and utilization of health care. Health systems can make sure that providers are located near enrollees, especially if public transportation is not readily available. Health systems may even decide to go on the road to reach their population (Lane 1998). They can also make sure they are not consigning minority patients to a restricted pool of clinicians and, in particular, that minority patients are provided equal access to high-quality clinicians whose expertise is in great demand. Systems can also alter physical environments to make them more welcoming to minority group members. They can make sure that linguistic competency extends beyond the clinical encounter to the appointment desk, advice lines, and membership and other written materials.

Many of these techniques have been combined in sites targeting specific minority populations (e.g., Chinese or Hispanic health centers).

CULTURAL COMPETENCY AND HEALTH DISPARITIES

Health systems might wish to adopt one or more of the cultural competency techniques described above for several reasons. They might want to increase their market share of growing minority populations (Torres 1998) and certainly will want to comply with growing federal and state regulations calling for culturally competent care. One important reason to adopt them, however, could be as a way to reduce racial and ethnic health disparities. The literature reveals a consistent gap between majority and minority populations in terms of outcomes of health care. Black women are more likely than white women to die from breast cancer, despite having a lower incidence of the disease (Collins, Hall, and Neuhaus 1999). Infant mortality rates are 2.5 times greater for African Americans and 1.5 times greater for Native Americans than for white Americans (U.S. DHHS 1998a). Influenza death rates are higher for African Americans and American Indians/Native Alaskans than they are for white Americans (Grantmakers in Health 1998). Mortality for colorectal cancer is highest for African Americans, followed by Native Alaskans, and then Hawaiians (Baquet and Commiskey 1999). Might cultural competency techniques make some inroad to reduce these disparities? Racial and ethnic disparities have many diverse causes. Low socioeconomic status (SES) is certainly a major cause. Minority Americans are disproportionately represented among the poor, the unemployed, and the undereducated, and low SES is correlated with poorer access to health care services and poorer health outcomes (Lillie-Blanton and Laveist 1996). But even minority Americans who are not socioeconomically disadvantaged have systematically different health experiences from nonminority Americans (Ford and Cooper 1995; Gornick et al. 1996; Mayberry et al. 1999; Kington and Smith 1997; D. R. Williams 1999; Nickens 1995).

Furthermore, minority Americans have different experiences in the health care system, even when they have similar medical conditions and insurance coverage. For example, disparities have been documented within health systems that provide equal financial benefits to all covered individuals—such as the Veterans Health Administration, Medicare, and single health plans (Ayanian et al. 1993; Carlisle, Leake, and Shapiro 1997; Conigliaro et al. 2000; Goldberg et al. 1992; Oddone et al. 1999; Peterson et al. 1994; Robbins, Whittemore, and Van Den Eeden 1998). Since financial barriers should not be a factor in these cases, researchers have concluded that the health

FIGURE 14-1 Conceptual model of how interpreter services could reduce health disparities

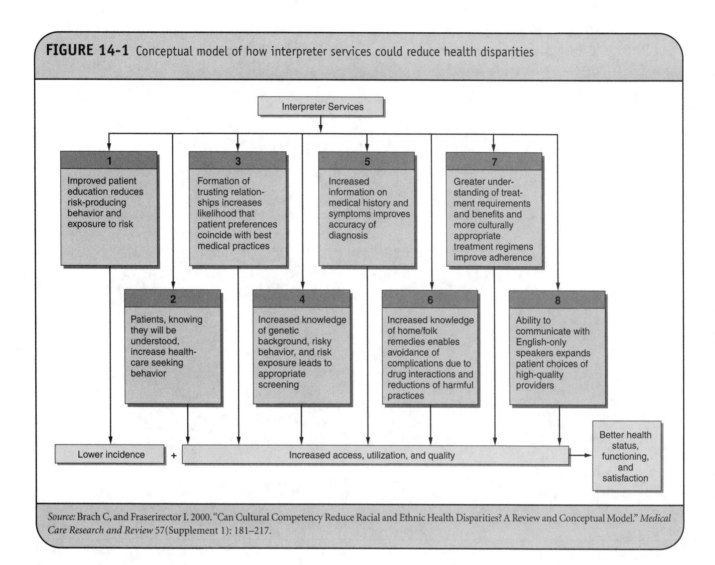

Source: Brach C, and Fraserirector I. 2000. "Can Cultural Competency Reduce Racial and Ethnic Health Disparities? A Review and Conceptual Model." *Medical Care Research and Review* 57(Supplement 1): 181–217.

care delivery system, for whatever reasons, must be doing an inferior job in meeting the needs of racial and ethnic minorities than in meeting the needs of the nonminority population. In the next section, we explore how one cultural competency technique—interpreter services—might theoretically reduce these disparities in care and outcomes. We also review the research evidence that lays the foundation for the model and informs assessments of its validity.

BROADENING THE MODEL

This conceptual model of how interpreter services could reduce disparities can be broadened to include any of the eight other cultural competency techniques. Figure 14-2 illustrates this expansion of the model. Cultural competency techniques potentially could change both clinician and patient behavior by improving communication, increasing trust, creating a greater knowledge of the differences among racial and ethnic groups

in epidemiology and treatment efficacy, and expanding understanding of patients' cultural behaviors and environment. The behavioral changes, in turn, could lead to the provision of more appropriate services: prevention and screening activities undertaken with full knowledge of risk factors, better informed diagnoses, treatment options formulated and presented in cultural contexts, and patient education on treatment regimens culturally tailored to improve the likelihood of adherence.

When appropriate services are provided, good outcomes—such as higher levels of health status, increased functioning, and improved satisfaction—could then follow. The following sections draw on the evidence to suggest how five of the other cultural competency techniques shown in Figure 14-2 could reduce disparities: recruitment and retention of minority staff, training, coordinating with traditional healers, use of community health workers, and culturally competent health promotion. The analysis of these five techniques, along with the interpreter services

FIGURE 14-2 Conceptual model of how nine cultural competency techniques could reduce health disparities

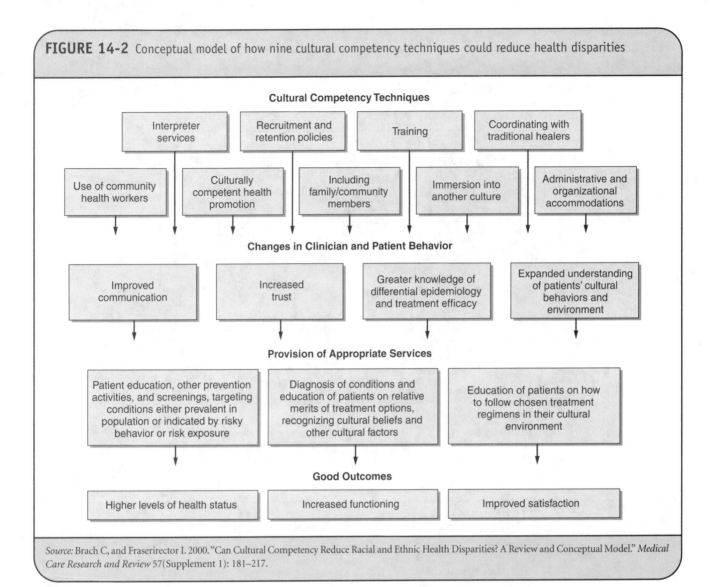

Source: Brach C, and Fraserirector I. 2000. "Can Cultural Competency Reduce Racial and Ethnic Health Disparities? A Review and Conceptual Model." *Medical Care Research and Review* 57(Supplement 1): 181–217.

technique discussed above, demonstrates how the theoretical promise of the three remaining techniques—techniques discussed less frequently in the literature—would be appraised.

CONCLUSION

The pervasive presence of major racial and ethnic disparities in health presents a serious public policy problem requiring multiple approaches. While improvements in economic and social conditions and the physical environment would in all likelihood make substantial contributions to reducing health disparities, health services interventions can also reduce inequalities (Arblaster et al. 1996; Schur, Albers, and Berk 1995). Our review of the literature on disparities and cultural competency provides strong reason to believe that careful and appropriate implementation of sound cultural competency

techniques in delivering health services could go a long way toward reducing disparities, as shown in Figure 14-3. Unfortunately, at this point there is little by way of rigorous research evaluating the impact of particular cultural competency techniques on any outcomes, including the reduction of racial and ethnic disparities. The only exception is that subset of techniques related to overcoming language barriers. Most linkages among cultural competency techniques, the processes of health care service delivery, and patient outcomes have yet to be empirically tested. Comparisons of culturally competent interventions with interventions uninformed by patients' language and culture are particularly critical, given that the research literature has not been able to firmly rule out the confounders of education, literacy, and class as causes for racial and ethnic disparities.

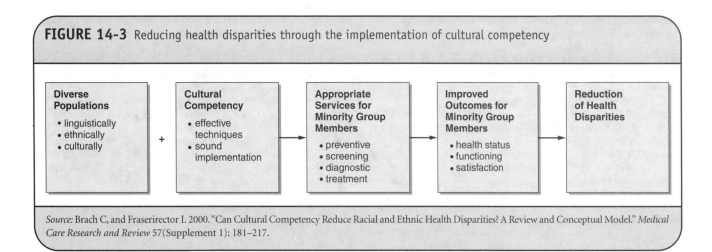

FIGURE 14-3 Reducing health disparities through the implementation of cultural competency

Source: Brach C, and Fraserirector I. 2000. "Can Cultural Competency Reduce Racial and Ethnic Health Disparities? A Review and Conceptual Model." *Medical Care Research and Review* 57(Supplement 1): 181–217.

Amassing this evidence is an essential step if cultural competency is to be widely adopted by health systems. Health systems are struggling to improve their services to minority populations. They are being held more accountable for their patient outcomes and therefore want proof that cultural competency "works" (Coye and Alvarez 1999; Lavizzo-Mourey and Mackenzie 1996). Although there is substantial research to suggest that cultural competency should work, health systems have little evidence about which cultural competency techniques are in fact effective and less evidence on how to implement them properly. Like anything else, cultural competency techniques can be sound or unsound, done well or not well. Rigorous research on cultural competency would both enable the testing of cultural competency's theoretical premises and provide health systems with constructive information about which techniques are most successful and under what circumstances.

REFERENCES

Adams, D. L., ed. 1995. *Health Issues for Women of Color: A Cultural Diversity Perspective.* Thousand Oaks, CA: Sage.

Agency for Health Care Policy and Research. 1999. *Understanding and Eliminating Minority Health Disparities* (RFA: HS-00-003). Rockville, MD: Agency for Health Care Policy and Research.

Andrulis, D. P., T. L. Delbanco, and Y. Shaw-Taylor. 1999. *Cross Cultural Competence in Health Care Survey.* Washington, DC: National Public Health and Hospital Institute.

Arblaster, L., M. Lambert, V. Entwistle, M. Forster, D. Fullerton, T. Sheldon, and I. Watt. 1996. Asystematic Review of the Effectiveness of Health Service Interventions Aimed at Reducing Inequalities in Health. *Journal of Health Services Research & Policy* 1 (2): 93–103.

Ashing-Giwa, K. 1999. Health Behavior Change Models and Their Socio-Cultural Relevance for Breast Cancer Screening in African American Women. *Women and Health* 28 (4): 53–71.

Association of Asian Pacific Community Health Organizations. 1996. *State Medicaid Managed Care: Requirements for Linguistically Appropriate Health Care.* Oakland, CA: Association of Asian Pacific Community Health Organizations.

Association of State and Territorial Health Officials. 1994. Multicultural Public Health Capacity Building Pilot Projects: Final Report. U.S. Department of Health and Human Services, Office of Minority Health.

Ayanian, J. Z., S. Udvarhelyi, C. A. Gatsonis, C. L. Pashos, and A. M. Epstein. 1993. Racial Differences in the Use of Revascularization Procedures after Coronary Angiography. *Journal of the American Medical Association* 269 (20): 2642–46.

Baker, D.W., R. M. Parker, M.V. Williams, W. C. Coates, and K. Pitkin. 1996. Use and Effectiveness of Interpreters in an Emergency Department. *Journal of the American Medical Association* 275 (10): 783–8.

Baker, E. A., N. Bouldin, M. Durham, M. E. Lowell, M. Gonzalez, N. Jodaitis, L. N. Cruz, I. Torres, M. Torres, and S. T. Adams. 1997. The Latino Health Advocacy Program: A Collaborative Lay Health Advisor Approach. *Health Education & Behavior* 24 (4): 495–509.

Baquet, C. R., and P. Commiskey. 1999. Colorectal Cancer Epidemiology in Minorities: A Review. *Journal of the Association of Academic Minority Physicians* 10 (3): 51–8.

Blackhall, L. J., S. T. Murphy, G. Frank, V. Michel, and S. Azen. 1995. Ethnicity and Attitudes toward Patient Autonomy. *Journal of the American Medical Association* 274 (10): 820–5.

Carlisle, D. M., B. D. Leake, and M. F. Shapiro. 1997. Racial and Ethnic Disparities in the Use of Cardiovascular Procedures: Associations with Type of Health Insurance. *American Journal of Public Health* 87 (2): 263–7.

Chang, P. H., and J. P. Fortier. 1998. Language Barriers to Health Care: An Overview. *Journal of Health Care for the Poor and Underserved* 9 (Supplement): S5–19.

Collins, K. S., A. Hall, and C. Neuhaus. 1999. *U.S. Minority Health: A Chartbook.* New York: Commonwealth Fund.

Commonwealth Fund. 1995. *National Comparative Survey of Minority Health Care.* New York: Commonwealth Fund.

Conigliario, J., J. Whittle, C. B. Good, B. H. Hanusa, L. J. Passman, R. P. Lofgren, R. Allman, P. A. Ubel, M. O'Connor, and D. S. Macpherson. 2000. Understanding Racial Variation in the Use of Coronary Revascularization Procedures: The Role of Clinical Factors. *Archives of Internal Medicine* 160 (9): 1329–35.

Cooper-Patrick, L., J. J. Gallo, J. J. Gonzales, H. T. Vu, N. R. Powe, C. Nelson, and D. E. Coye, M., and D. Alvarez. 1999. *Medicaid Managed Care and Cultural Diversity in California.* New York: Commonwealth Fund.

Cross, T. L., B. J. Bazron, K.W. Dennis, and M. R. Isaacs. 1989. *Towards a Culturally Competent System of Care: A Monograph on Effective Services for Minority Children Who Are Severely Emotionally Disturbed.* Washington, DC: CASSP Technical Assistance Center, Georgetown University Child Development Center.

Denboba, D. L., J. L. Bragdon, L. G. Epstein, K. Garthright, and T. M. Goldman. 1998. Reducing Health Disparities through Cultural Competence. *Journal of Health Education* 29 (5, suppl.): S47–53.

Earp, J. A., and V. L. Flax. 1999. What Lay Health Advisors Do: An Evaluation of Advisors' Activities. *Cancer Practice* 7 (1): 16–21.

Elder, N. C., A. Gillcrist, and R. Minz. 1997. Use of Alternative Health Care by Family Practice Patients. *Archives of Family Medicine* 6 (2): 181–4.

Fadiman, A. 1997. *The Spirit Catches You and You Fall Down: A Hmong Child, Her American Doctors, and the Collision of Two Cultures*. New York: Farrar, Straus & Giroux.

Ferguson, J. A., M. Weinberger, G. R. Westmoreland, L. A. Mamlin, D. S. Segar, J. Y. Greene, D. K. Martin, and W. M. Tierney. 1998. Racial Disparity in Cardiac Decision Making. *Archives of Internal Medicine* 158 (13): 1450–3.

Flores, G., and L. R. Vega. 1998. Barriers to Health Care Access for Latino Children: A Review. *Family Medicine* 30 (3): 196–205.

Ford, E. S., and R. S. Cooper. 1995. Implications of Race/Ethnicity for Health and Health Care Use. *Health Services Research* 30 (1): 237–52.

Fortier, J. P., and Y. Shaw-Taylor. 1999. *Cultural and Linguistic Competence Standards and Research Agenda Project: Part One. Recommendations for National Standards*. Silver Spring, MD: Resources for Cross Cultural Health Care.

Gaston, R. S., I. Ayres, L. G. Dooley, and A. G. Diethelm. 1993. Racial Equity in Renal Transplantation. The Disparate Impact of Hla-Based Allocation. *Journal of the American Medical Association* 270 (11): 1352–6.

Goicoechea-Balbona, A. 1997. Culturally Specific Health Care Model for Ensuring Health Care Use by Rural, Ethnically Diverse Families Affected by HIV/AIDS. *Health and Social Work* 22 (3): 172–80.

Goldberg, K. C., A. J. Hartz, S. J. Jacobsen, H. Krakauer, and A. A. Rimm. 1992. Racial and Community Factors Influencing Coronary Artery Bypass Graft Surgery Rates for All 1986 Medicare Patients. *Journal of the American Medical Association* 267 (11): 1473–7.

Gordon, A. K. 1995. Deterrents to Access and Service for Blacks and Hispanics: The Medicare Hospice Benefit, Healthcare Utilization, and Cultural Barriers. *The Hospice Journal* 10 (2): 65–83.

Gornick, M. E., P.W. Eggers, T.W. Reilly, R. M. Mentnech, L. K. Fitterman, L. E. Kucken, and B. C. Vladeck. 1996. Effects of Race and Income on Mortality and Use of Services among Medicare Beneficiaries. *New England Journal of Medicine* 335 (11): 791–9.

Grantmakers in Health. 1998. Chartbook: Eliminating Racial and Ethnic Disparities in Health. Paper read at Grantmakers in Health, 11 September 1998, Potomac, MD.

Gropper, R. C. 1998. Cultural Basics and Chronic Illness. *Advances in Renal Replacement Therapy* 5 (2): 128–33.

Hornberger, J. C., C. D. Gibson, W. Wood, C. Dequeldre, I. Corso, B. Palla, and D. A. Bloch. 1996. Eliminating Language Barriers for Non-English-Speaking Patients. *Medical Care* 34 (8): 845–56.

Jackson, E. J., and C. P. Parks. 1997. Recruitment and Training Issues from Selected Lay Health Advisor Programs among African Americans: A 20-year Perspective. *Health Education & Behavior* 24 (4): 418–31.

Kavanagh, K., K. Absalom, J.W. Beil, and L. Schliessmann. 1999. Connecting and Becoming Culturally Competent: A Lakota Example. *Advances in Nursing Science* 21 (3): 9–31.

Kennedy, S., B. Stubblefield-Tave, and C. Smith. 1999. *Report on Recommendations for Measures of Cultural Competence for the Quality Improvement System for Managed Care*. Cambridge, MA: Abt Associates.

Kim, C., and Y. S. Kwok. 1998. Navajo Use of Native Healers. *Archives of Internal Medicine* 158 (20): 2245–9.

Kington, R. S., and J. P. Smith. 1997. Socioeconomic Status and Racial and Ethnic Differences in Functional Status Associated with Chronic Diseases. *American Journal of Public Health* 87 (5): 805–10.

Kleinman, A., L. Eisenberg, and B. Good. 1978. Culture, Illness, and Care: Clinical Lessons from Anthropologic and Cross-Cultural Research. *Annals of Internal Medicine* 88 (2): 251–8.

Kok, G., B. van den Borne, and P. D. Mullen. 1997. Effectiveness of Health Education and Health Promotion: Meta-Analyses of Effect Studies and Determinants of Effectiveness. *Patient Education and Counseling* 30 (1): 19–27.

Lane, J. 1998. An Enduring Partnership: Kaiser Permanente and Su Salud. *The Permanente Journal* 2 (3). Available: http://www.kaiserpermanente.org/medicine/permjournal/permjournal.html

Lavizzo-Mourey, R., and E. R. Mackenzie. 1996. Cultural Competence: Essential Measurements of Quality for Managed Care Organizations. *Annals of Internal Medicine* 124 (10): 919–20.

Lawson, W. B. 1996. The Art and Science of the Psychopharmacotherapy of African Americans. *Mount Sinai Journal of Medicine* 63 (5–6): 301–5.

Lillie-Blanton, M., and T. Laveist. 1996. Race/Ethnicity, the Social Environment, and Health. *Social Science and Medicine* 43 (1): 83–91.

Ma, G. X. 1999. Between Two Worlds: The Use of Traditional and Western Health Services by Chinese immigrants. *Journal of Community Health* 24 (6): 421–37.

Marbella, A. M., M. C. Harris, S. Diehr, G. Ignace, and G. Ignace. 1998. Use of Native American Healers among Native American Patients in an Urban Native American Health Center. *Archives of Family Medicine* 7 (2): 182–5.

Mayberry, R. M., F. Mili, I.G.M. Vaid, A. Samadi, E. Ofili, M. S. McNeal, P. A. Griffith, and G. LaBrie. 1999. *Racial and Ethnic Differences in Access to Medical Care: A Synthesis of the Literature*. Menlo Park, CA: The Henry J. Kaiser Family Foundation.

Moffic, H. S., and J. D. Kinzie. 1996. The History and Future of Cross-Cultural Psychiatric Services. *Community Mental Health Journal* 32 (6): 581–92.

Nickens, H. W. 1990. Health Promotion and Disease Prevention among Minorities. *Health Affairs (Millwood)* 9 (2): 133–43.

Oddone, E. Z., R. D. Horner, R. Sloane, L. McIntyre, A. Ward, J. Whittle, L. J. Passman, L. Kroupa, R. Heaney, S. Diem, and D. Matchar. 1999. Race, Presenting Signs and Symptoms, Use of Carotid Artery Imaging, and Appropriateness of Carotid Endarterectomy. *Stroke* 30 (7): 1350–6.

Orlandi, M. A., ed. 1995. *Cultural Competence for Evaluators: A Guide for Alcohol and Other Drug Abuse Prevention Practitioners Working with Ethnic/Racial Communities*. 2d ed. Vol. 1. OSAP Cultural Competence Series. Rockville, MD: U.S. Department of Health and Human Services.

Pachter, L. M. 1994. Culture and Clinical Care: Folk Illness Beliefs and Behaviors and Their Implications for Health Care Delivery. *Journal of the American Medical Association* 271 (9): 690–4.

Pang, K. Y. 1989. The Practice of Traditional Korean Medicine in Washington, D.C. *Social Science and Medicine* 28 (8): 875–84.

Perkins, J., H. Simon, F. Cheng, K. Olson, and Y. Vera. 1998. *Ensuring Linguistic Access in Health Care Settings: Legal Rights and Responsibilities*. Los Angeles: National Health Law Program.

Perkins, J., and Y. Vera. 1998. Legal Protections to Ensure Linguistically Appropriate Health Care. *Journal of Health Care for the Poor and Underserved* 9 (Suppl.): S62–80.

Peterson, E. D., S. M. Wright, J. Daley, and G. E. Thibault. 1994. Racial Variation in Cardiac Procedure Use and Survival Following Acute Myocardial Infarction in the Department of Veterans Affairs. *Journal of the American Medical Association* 271 (15): 1175–80.

President's Advisory Commission on Consumer Protection and Quality in the Health Care Industry. 1997. *Consumer Bill of Rights and Responsibilities*. Washington, DC: Advisory Commission on Consumer Protection and Quality in the Health Care Industry.

Richardson, L. D. 1999. Patients' Rights and Professional Responsibilities: The Moral Case for Cultural Competence. *Mt. Sinai Journal of Medicine* 66 (4): 267–70.

Riddick, S. 1998. Improving Access for Limited English-Speaking Consumers: A Review of Strategies in Health Care Settings. *Journal of Health Care for the Poor and Underserved* 9 (Suppl.): S40–61.

Robbins, A. S., A. S. Whittemore, and S. K. Van Den Eeden. 1998. Race, Prostate Cancer Survival, and Membership in a Large Health Maintenance Organization. *Journal of the National Cancer Institute* 90 (13): 986–90.

Rodney, M., C. Clasen, G. Goldman, R. Markert, and D. Deane. 1998. Three Evaluation Methods of a Community Health Advocate Program. *Journal of Community Health* 23 (5): 371–81.

Schur, C. L., L. A. Albers, and M. L. Berk. 1995. Health Care Use by Hispanic Adults: Financial vs. Non-Financial Determinants. *Health Care Financing Review* 17 (2): 71–88.

Sheifer, S. E., J. J. Escarce, and K. A. Schulman. 2000. Race and Sex Differences in the Management of Coronary Artery Disease. *American Heart Journal* 139 (5): 848–57.

Sherer, J. L. 1994. Neighbor to Neighbor: Community Health Workers Educate Their Own. *Hospitals* 68 (20): 52–6.

Skaer, T. L., L. M. Robison, D. A. Sclar, and G. H. Harding. 1996. Utilization of Curanderos among Foreign Born Mexican-American Women Attending Migrant Health Clinics. *Journal of Cultural Diversity* 3 (2): 29–34.

St. Clair, A., and L. McKenry. 1999. Preparing Culturally Competent Practitioners. *Journal of Nursing Education* 38 (5): 228–34.

Tervalon, M., and J. Murray-Garcia. 1998. Cultural Humility versus Cultural Competence: A Critical Distinction in Defining Physician Training Outcomes in Multicultural Education. *Journal of Health Care for the Poor and Underserved* 9 (2): 117–25.

Tirado, M. D. 1996. *Tools for Monitoring Cultural Competence in Health Care.* San Francisco: Latino Coalition for a Healthy California.

Torres, R. E. 1998. The Pervading Role of Language on Health. *Journal of Health Care for the Poor and Underserved* 9 (Suppl.): S21–5.

U.S. Bureau of the Census. 1996. *Current Population Reports, Series P25-1130: Population Projections of the United States by Sex, Race, and Hispanic Origin, 1995 to 2050.* Washington, DC: U.S. Bureau of the Census.

U.S. Department of Health and Human Services. 1998a. *The President's Initiative on Race, Health Care Rx: Access for All. Barriers to Health Care for Racial and Ethnic Minorities: Access, Workforce Diversity, and Cultural Competence.* Washington, DC: U.S. Department of Health and Human Services.

———.1999. *Eliminating Racial and Ethnic Disparities in Health.* Washington, DC: U.S. Department of Health and Human Services.

U.S. Department of Health and Human Services Goal 6 Workgroup. 1998. *Cultural and Linguistic Competency as a Consumer Protection Issue in DHHS.* Washington, DC: U.S. Department of Health and Human Services.

U.S. Department of Health and Human Services Office for Civil Rights. 1998. *Title VI Prohibition against National Origin Discrimination—Persons with Limited-English Proficiency.* Washington, DC: U.S. Department of Health and Human Services.

U.S. Department of Health and Human Services Office of the Secretary. 1999. Call for Comments on Draft Standards on Culturally and Linguistically Appropriate Health Care and Announcement of Regional Informational Meetings on Draft Standards. *Federal Register, 15 December 1999, 64* (240): 70042–4.

Williams, B. R. 1997. HPHC's Diversity Journey. In *Harvard Pilgrim Care Diversity Journal*, edited by B. Stern. Brookline, MA: Harvard Pilgrim Health Care.

Williams, D. R. 1999. Race, Socioeconomic Status, and Health: The Added Effects of Racism and Discrimination. *Annals of the New York Academy of Sciences* 896:173–88.

Witmer, A., S. D. Seifer, L. Finocchio, J. Leslie, and E. H. O' Neil. 1995. Community Health Workers: Integral Members of the Health Care Work Force. *American Journal of Public Health* 85 (8): 1055–8.

Woloshin, S., L. M. Schwartz, S. J. Katz, and H. G. Welch. 1997. Is Language a Barrier to the Use of Preventive Services? *Journal of General Internal Medicine* 12 (8): 472–7.

Zablocki, E. 1998. Health Plans Strive for Diversity. *Healthplan* 39 (2): 21–4.

Executive Summary, California Campaign to Eliminate Racial and Ethnic Disparities in Health, 2003

Source: Excerpt from *Executive Summary, California Campaign to Eliminate Racial and Ethnic Disparities in Health. 2003. Health for All: California's Strategic Approach to Eliminating Racial and Ethnic Health Disparities.* Washington, DC: American Public Health Association. Oakland, CA: The Prevention Institute. Sacramento, CA: The California Health and Human Services Agency.

INTRODUCTION: PROMOTING HEALTH FOR ALL IN A DIVERSE STATE

California has long been a leader in health—and has developed tremendous capacity in health research, treatment, and prevention. The stage is set for California to play an even greater leadership role in improving health for all and, in particular, for those most at risk for poor health outcomes. Far too frequently, Californians become unnecessarily ill or injured from preventable conditions. Without effective medical treatment, these health problems are then exacerbated and cause greater suffering, disability, and premature death. People of color in California consistently face higher rates of morbidity and mortality than whites. These higher rates are experienced not just for one or two diseases, but across a very broad spectrum of illnesses and injuries. Further, health disparities are not the result of specific populations experiencing a *different* set of illnesses than those affecting the general population. Generally the diseases and injuries that affect the population as a whole, affect low-income, minority populations *more*, with people experiencing multiple negative health conditions.

The *California Campaign to Eliminate Racial and Ethnic Disparities in Health* was initiated to address this inequity.

Formed through a partnership between the American Public Health Association and the California Health and Human Services Agency, the Campaign is a statewide coalition of leaders from the public and private arenas of policy, health care, public health, and philanthropy. Its approach is three-fold:

1. to better understand the roots and pathways to health disparities,
2. to determine what can be done, and
3. to set a process in motion to reduce and eliminate health disparities in California.

Addressing health disparities requires a multi-faceted strategy because the underlying factors producing health disparities are complex. Disparate health outcomes are not primarily due to one microbe or one genetic factor. Rather, a broad range of social, economic, and community conditions interplay with individual factors to exacerbate susceptibility and provide less protection. These conditions, such as deteriorated housing, poor education, limited employment opportunities and role models, limited household resources, and ready availability of cheap high-fat foods, are particularly exacerbated in low-income neighborhoods where people of color are more likely to live. Research has now shown that after adjusting for individual risk factors, there are neighborhood differences in health outcomes.[i] Many neighborhood conditions are related to a history of bias directed against people of color.

Therefore, it is not surprising that there are disparities in health. In fact, it is the relationship of place, ethnicity, and poverty that can lead to the greatest disparities. There is a risk that prevalence of disparities may increase in California as the population becomes even more multicultural. By the year 2040, it is expected that two out of three Californians will be people of color. As the state becomes increasingly diverse, the reality of a healthy and productive California will increasingly rely on the ability to keep all Californians healthy and eliminate racial and ethnic disparities by improving the health of communities of color. Healthcare is among the most expensive commitments of government, businesses, and individuals. Illness and injury also generate tremendous social costs in the form of lost productivity and expenditures for disability, workers' compensation, and public benefit programs. Eliminating racial and ethnic health disparities is imperative both as a matter of fairness and economic common sense. This tremendous challenge can—and must—be met with a focused commitment of will, resources, and cooperation to institute change.

The California Strategic Approach delineates how the resources of diverse governmental and private institutions can be marshaled to work with communities to make significant progress towards eliminating health disparities in California. It illuminates the critical pathways that affect health and the key points for intervention to ensure health for all. The California Campaign identified nine Priority Medical Issues which cause significant morbidity and/or mortality among people of color and are associated with the achievable objectives outlined in Healthy People 2010.

DEVELOPING A STRATEGIC APPROACH: UNDERSTANDING THE CRITICAL PATHWAYS TO HEALTH

The frequency and severity of injury and illness is not inevitable. An analysis of the underlying causes of medical conditions reveals a trajectory by which health outcomes develop and worsen. By analyzing the pathways from root factors to illness and injury experienced by people of color, the necessary actions to prevent these medical conditions are illuminated. Nearly 50% of annual deaths—and the impaired quality of life that frequently precedes them—are preventable[ii] because they are attributable to external environmental and behavioral factors. The following diagram delineates the pathways by which root factors such as oppression and discrimination increase the frequency and severity of injury and illness.

An analysis of the underlying causes of the nine Priority Medical Issues reveals three stages in the trajectory to poor health outcomes. First, people of color are born into a society that discriminates against them and are disproportionately subject to living in impoverished communities. Second, these fundamental conditions shape behaviors and the social and physical environment which people encounter. Third, lack of access to medical care and lower quality diagnosis and treatment for people of color leads to higher rates of sickness, dis-

ability, and mortality. Understanding these pathways in greater detail clarifies what action is needed to eliminate health disparities. A further value of focusing on the critical pathways is that it illuminates the roots of not just one but multiple medical conditions. Based on this trajectory, two primary goals emerged from the findings of the Campaign: 1. Prevent the development of illness and injury by fostering healthy behaviors, healthy community environments, and institutional support of good health outcomes and 2. Reduce the severity of illness and injury by providing high-quality medical care to all. Strengthening community environments and improving access and quality of health care are not only necessary elements in the strategy to reduce health disparities but are mutually supportive. High quality, accessible health care contributes to improving community environments. Positive behaviors and environments equally improve the success of treatment and disease management.

Goal 1:

Prevent the development of illness and injury by fostering healthy behaviors, healthy community environments, and institutional support of good health outcomes.

Health can be enhanced and disparities reduced through greater attention to prevention.

Improving health-related behaviors and fostering health-supporting community environments is fundamental for effective prevention. The California Campaign identified several key behaviors along the pathways to the Priority Medical Issues: tobacco use, poor nutrition and lack of physical activity, unsafe sex, and drug and alcohol use. Each of these behaviors is associated with more than one health problem. Altering these behavioral pathways requires action at several levels. While education plays a valuable role in influencing individual behavioral choices, it is important not to 'blame the victim' by focusing strictly on lifestyle choices; "Getting people to behave . . . encompasses only a small fraction of the routes to risk reduction and does not stand alone without significant support from major societal mechanisms."[iii] Addressing the social and physical environment that influences behavioral choices is an essential element of a strategy to change behavioral patterns throughout a population. Far more than air, water, and soil, the environment refers to the broad social and community context in which everyday life takes place.

In addition to shaping behavior, the environment also has direct influences on health. The quality of air, water, and soil tends to be worse in areas in which the population is either low-income or primarily people of color. Beyond specific toxins, other physical and social neighborhood conditions can directly affect health by producing higher stress levels which can contribute to poorer mental health and health outcomes. The

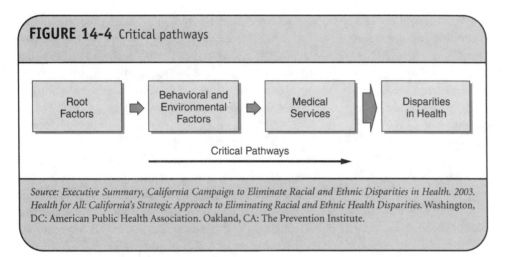

FIGURE 14-4 Critical pathways

Root Factors → Behavioral and Environmental Factors → Medical Services → Disparities in Health

Critical Pathways

Source: Executive Summary, California Campaign to Eliminate Racial and Ethnic Disparities in Health. 2003. Health for All: California's Strategic Approach to Eliminating Racial and Ethnic Health Disparities. Washington, DC: American Public Health Association. Oakland, CA: The Prevention Institute.

impact of social, economic and political exclusion results in a 'weathering' whereby health reflects cumulative experience rather than chronological or developmental age.[iv] Stressors such as discrimination, inadequate incomes, unsafe neighborhoods, lack of neighborhood services, and multiple health problems all contribute to a wearing down of the body and subsequent poor health.

Given the influence of the environment on health and health behaviors, it is critical to specifically identify those factors that have the greatest impact on the development of health disparities. These factors comprise the pathways through which root factors play out on the community level and, if ameliorated, can help to reduce and eliminate disparities. Twenty key factors 'cluster' into four areas: built environment factors, social capital factors, services and institutions, and structural factors.[v] The built environment is the man-made infrastructure of a community such as street design, public transportation, and permitted uses of buildings. Social capital includes the "connections among individual-social networks and the norms of reciprocity and trustworthiness that arise from them."[vi] The availability of and access to high quality, culturally competent, and appropriately coordinated public and private services and institutions is a critical element for good health. Structural factors are overarching in nature, and rooted in broader systems or structures that have an impact on people and communities everywhere. Examples include employment and economic opportunities and marketing and advertising practices.

Goal 2:

Reduce the severity of illness and injury by providing high-quality medical care to all.

Once injuries and diseases do occur, their impact can be reduced through accessible, high quality care. In addition, many conditions can be prevented by quality medical services.

The California Campaign identified two critical pathways for medical care: 1) late diagnosis (in part due to lack of access) and 2) improper treatment (including unequal care). These pathways can by altered by improving a) access to care, b) quality of care, and c) culturally and linguistically appropriate services.

Overcoming barriers to accessing care is vital. An important element of this is increasing health insurance rates. In 1999, 6.8 million Californians were uninsured, with people of color having the highest uninsurance rates.[vii, viii, ix] It is also important to minimize the fear of stigma and discrimination that immigrant families face—even legal immigrants—when seeking health care.

In addition to minimizing barriers to accessing health care, it is critical that people receive quality care after they have accessed it. There is considerable evidence that people of color experience discrepancies in care compared to that received by whites. "Evidence of racial and ethnic disparities in healthcare is, with few exceptions, remarkably consistent across a range of illnesses and healthcare services."[x] These differences in diagnosis, quality of care, and treatment methods lead to consistently poorer health outcomes among people of color,[xi] and these differences must be addressed. Part of improving the quality of care requires ensuring culturally and linguistically appropriate

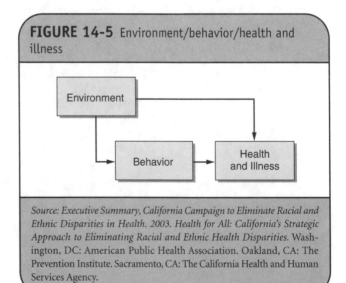

FIGURE 14-5 Environment/behavior/health and illness

Environment → Health and Illness

Environment → Behavior → Health and Illness

Source: Executive Summary, California Campaign to Eliminate Racial and Ethnic Disparities in Health. 2003. Health for All: California's Strategic Approach to Eliminating Racial and Ethnic Health Disparities. Washington, DC: American Public Health Association. Oakland, CA: The Prevention Institute. Sacramento, CA: The California Health and Human Services Agency.

care. This promotes improved communication with patients and enables providers to address health concerns within the cultural context of the patient. An element of culturally appropriate care is a diverse workforce. The vast majority of medical professionals, including physicians, registered nurses, and mid-level providers such as nurse practitioners and physician assistants are white, exceeding the percentage of whites in the general population.[xii] There is a need to promote a more diverse healthcare workforce.

TOWARD A HEALTHY & PRODUCTIVE CALIFORNIA: ENGAGING STAKEHOLDERS & MOVING FORWARD

Achieving health for all Californians is both a moral imperative and a matter of good economics. The cost of poor health is far greater than the cost of preventing it. Illness and injury is not only a concern for doctors and patients; it has far reaching implications for on well-being, productivity, and the quality of life for everyone. The health of the state depends, literally, on the health of all its residents. Eliminating racial and ethnic health disparities and improving health outcomes requires participation from key public and private institutions working in partnership with communities. Institutions, including banks, businesses, government, schools, health care, and community service groups, have a major influence on community environments. The decisions they make—such as whether to accommodate pedestrian and bicycle travel on city streets, where to locate supermarkets or alcohol outlets, or what efforts to take to reduce hazardous emissions—influence health behaviors and health outcomes. Engaging all communities in shaping solutions and taking action for change is critical. Communities need to be involved in identifying the health problems of greatest concern, examining the critical pathways to illness and injury, and working to alter these pathways. In many cases, these decisions are made without awareness of their relationships to health outcomes. When communities and institutions make decisions more explicitly, they can improve health and reduce disparities.

The *California Campaign* points the way towards interventions California and Californians must take. Action is needed to strengthen community environments and shift behaviors to prevent disease and injury. Action is needed to ensure health services are high quality, accessible, and culturally competent. Efforts must build on community strengths—their healthy traditions, their resilience, their diversity, and their committed institutions.

TABLE 14-1 Sources of Health Disparities

Housing
- Sub-prime loans (loans with excessive mortgage fees, interest rates, and penalties) are five times more likely in African American neighborhoods than in white neighborhoods. Fully 39% of homeowners in upper-income African American neighborhoods have sub-prime loans compared to only 18% of homeowners in low-income white neighborhoods.[7]
- Minorities tend to be segregated in neighborhoods characterized by lower-quality schools and public services, limited access to quality healthcare, and greater exposure to environmental-based health hazards.[8]

Education
- Schools serving large concentrations of low-income students—African Americans, Latinos, and Native Americans—often have many teachers with emergency teaching permits who lack the expertise to teach. These teachers often teach at sites in poor states of maintenance and that lack proper instructional support materials. High professional staff turnover is also common.[9]
- Nearly four of ten Hispanics (39%) have less than a high school education, compared with one of ten whites (11%).[10] In California, the 2001–2002 dropout rates for American Indians (14.4%), Pacific Islanders (11.0%), Hispanics (14.8%), and African Americans (18.9%) exceeded dropouts for all races combined (10.9%).[11]

Labor
- Of senior-level male managers in Fortune 1000 industrial and Fortune 500 service industries in 1995, almost 97% were white, 0.6% were African American, 0.3% were Asian, and 0.4% were Hispanic.[12]
- In California the August 2003 unemployment rate among whites was 6.1 compared to 8.9 among non-whites, 11.7 among African Americans, and 7.7 among Hispanics.[13]

Economics
- In 1997, 41% of Hispanics, 35% of African American, and 45% of Native American non-elderly lived in a family experiencing food problems (i.e., skipping meals for lack of money to buy food), compared to 23% for all races.[14]

TABLE 14-1 Sources of Health Disparities (continued)

- While 26% of whites and 29% of Asians are low-income, the rate is 49% for African Americans, 54% for Native Americans, and 61% for Hispanics.[15]

Technology

- White (46%) and Asian American (57%) households continue to have internet access at levels more than double those of African American (24%) and Hispanic (24%) households.[16]
- Most U.S. colleges have access to T-3 internet lines, while only 1 of 32 American Indian tribal colleges has this access.[17]

Criminal Justice

- In 1997 African Americans, Hispanics, Asian Americans, and American Indians constituted about one-third of juveniles in the U.S. yet represented two-thirds of detained and committed youth in juvenile facilities.[18]
- While the prevalence of both crack and powder cocaine use is higher among whites than African Americans, almost 97% of all crack cocaine defendants are African American or Latino.[19]
- In the 1990's, the chance an African American U.S. born male would be imprisoned for a felony sometime in his life approached 30%, while the chance for a white male was 4.4%.[20]

Transportation

- California commuter systems requiring equipment to serve largely wealthier, suburban populations receive funding while urban bus transit systems requiring funding for repair, maintenance and operations experience cutbacks.[21]

Environmental

- People of color suffer environmental burdens more than whites[22]; they experience 27% more exposure to toxic chemicals and 32% more cancer risk from hazardous air pollutants.
- Nearly twice as many toxic waste superfund sites per square mile are in neighborhoods of color, along with more than twice as many facilities emitting air pollutants.[23]

---

7. U.S. Department of Housing and Urban Development. Unequal burden: Income and Racial Disparities in Subprime Lending in America. Available at: http://www.hud.gov/library/bookshelf18/pressrel/subprime.html. Accessed on 9/18/02.

8. Smedley B, Stith A, Nelson A eds., *Unequal Treatment: Confronting Racial and Ethnic Disparities in Health Care.* Washington, D.C.: The National Academies Press; 2003: 96, 100.

9. Joint Committee to Develop a Master Plan for Education—Kindergarten through University. Master Plan for Education in California, May 2002 Draft. Available at: http://www.ucop.edu/acadinit/mastplan/020507FinalDraftOneThePlan.doc. Accessed 10/22/03.

10. Collins, KS, Hughes, D, et al. Diverse communities, common concerns: assessing health care quality for minority Americans: findings from The Commonwealth Fund 2001 Health Care Quality Survey. New York, NY: The Commonwealth Fund; 2002.

11. California Department of Education. Available at: http://data1.cde.ca.gov/dataquest/DrpGrdEthState.asp?cYear=2001-02&cChoice=GradeEth&Level=State. Accessed 10/9/03.

12. Federal Glass Ceiling Commission. Good for business: making full use of the nation's human capital, the environmental scan. Washington, DC: US Department of Labor; 1995.

13. California Employment Development Department. Available at: http://www.calmis.ca.gov/file/lfother/fig8.htm. Accessed 10/9/03.

14. Staveteig, S, Wigton, A. Racial and ethnic disparities: key findings from the National Survey of America's Families. Washington, DC: The Urban Institute; 2000.

15. Staveteig, S, Wigton, A. Racial and ethnic disparities: key findings from the National Survey of America's Families. Washington, DC: The Urban Institute; 2000.

16. Digital Divide Network. Digital Divide Basics Factsheet. Available at: www.digitaldividenetwork.org/content/stories/index.cfm?key=168. Accessed 10/27/02.

17. American Indian College Fund. Available at: http://www.collegefund.org/news/news00/techneeds.shtml. Accessed 10/13/03.

18. Smedley B, Stith A, Nelson A eds. *Unequal Treatment: Confronting Racial and Ethnic Disparities in Health Care.* Washington,D.C.: The National Academies Press; 2003: p.100–101.

19. National Association for the Advancement of Colored People. Action Alert: Racial Disparities in Cocaine Sentencing. Available at: http://www.naacp.org/work/washington_bureau/CocaineSent080703.shtml. Accessed 10/22/03.

20. RAND Policy Brief. America Becoming: The Growing Complexity of America's Racial Mosaic. Available at: www.rand.org/publications/RB/RB5050. Accessed 9/18/02.

21. Surface Transportation Policy Project. Public Transit Finance. Available at: http://www.transact.org/ca/public_transport7.htm. Accessed. 10/22/03.

22. Environmental Defense. Scorecard: Distribution of Environmental Burdens in California by Race/Ethnicity. Available at: http://www.scorecard.org/community/ej-summary.tcl?fips_state_code=06&backlink=tri-st#dist. Accessed 10/22/03.

23. Environmental Defense. Scorecard: Distribution of Environmental Burdens in California by Race/Ethnicity. Available at: http://www.scorecard.org/community/ej-summary.tcl?fips_state_code=06&backlink=tri-st#dist. Accessed 10/22/03.

The vision of a healthy, productive California must be translated into commitment. There is a critical job for the health sector to improve the availability and quality of medical care for all California's ethnic and racial groups. It is also vital that every public and private institution step forward to improve the environments that beget good health. The next step is to coordinate action by institutions and in communities across the state. Now that the pathways to health for all have been described, taking action to alter them is essential.

ENDNOTES:

i. PolicyLink. *Reducing health disparities through a focus on communities.* A PolicyLink Report. Oakland, CA: 2002.

ii. McGinnis JM, Foege WH. Actual causes of death in the United States. *Journal of the American Medical Association.* 1993;270:2207–2213.

iii. Blum HL. Social perspective on risk reduction. *Family and Community Health.* 1981;3(1):41–50.

iv. Geronimus A. Understanding and eliminating racial inequalities in women's health in the United States: the role of the weathering conceptual framework. *Journal of the American Medical Women's Association.* 2001; 56(4):133–136.

v. Davis R, Cohen L. Strengthening Communities: A Prevention Framework for Eliminating Health Disparities. Oakland, CA: Prevention Institute; 2003.

vi. Putnam, Robert. Bowling Alone: The Collapse and Revival of American Community. New York, NY: Simon & Schuster, 2000.

vii. Brown E R, Ponce N, Rice T, Lavarreda SA. The state of health insurance in California: findings from the 2001 California Health Interview Survey. Los Angeles, CA: UCLA Center for Health Policy Research; 2002.

viii. Wyn R, Ojeda V. Data brief: health insurance coverage of women ages 18–64 in California, 1998. Berkeley, CA: California Alliance for Women's Health Leadership; 2002.

ix. National Center for Health Statistics. *Health United States, 2002.* Atlanta, GA: U.S. Department of Health and Human Services, Centers for Disease Control and Prevention; 2002.

x. Smedley B, Stith A, Nelson A eds., *Unequal Treatment: Confronting Racial and Ethnic Disparities in Health Care.* Washington, D.C.: The National Academies Press; 2003: 5.

xi. Smedley B, Stith A, Nelson A eds., *Unequal Treatment: Confronting Racial and Ethnic Disparities in Health Care.* Washington, D.C.: The National Academies Press; 2003: 5.

xii. American Medical Association, Physician Characteristics and Distribution in the US 2001–2002. Chicago, IL.

Index